Springer Series on Cultural Computing

Founding Editor

Ernest Edmonds

Series Editor

Craig Vear, De Montfort University, Leicester, UK

More information about this series at https://link.springer.com/bookseries/10481

Eugene Ch'ng · Henry Chapman ·
Vincent Gaffney · Andrew S. Wilson
Editors

Visual Heritage: Digital Approaches in Heritage Science

 Springer

Editors
Eugene Ch'ng
NVIDIA Joint-Lab on Mixed Reality,
NVIDIA Technology Centre
University of Nottingham Ningbo China
Ningbo, China

Henry Chapman
Department of Classics, Ancient History
and Archaeology
University of Birmingham
Birmingham, UK

Vincent Gaffney
School of Archaeological and Forensic
Sciences
University of Bradford
Bradford, UK

Andrew S. Wilson
School of Archaeological and Forensic
Sciences
University of Bradford
Bradford, UK

ISSN 2195-9056   ISSN 2195-9064   (electronic)
Springer Series on Cultural Computing
ISBN 978-3-030-77030-3   ISBN 978-3-030-77028-0   (eBook)
https://doi.org/10.1007/978-3-030-77028-0

This Springer imprint is published by the registered company Springer Nature Switzerland AG
The registered company address is: Gewerbestrasse 11, 6330 Cham, Switzerland

Foreword

I am the specter who returns

Unto some desolate world in ruin borne afar

On the black flowing of Lethean skies:

Ever I search, in cryptic galleries,

The void sarcophagi, the broken urns

Of many a vanished avatar:

Or haunt the gloom of grumbling pylons vast

In temples that enshrine the shadowy past.

Viewless, impalpable and fleet,

I roam stupendous avenues, and greet

Familiar sphinxes carved from everlasting stone,

Or the fair, brittle gods of long ago,

Decayed and fallen low.

And there I mark the tall clepsammiae

That time has overthrown

Revenant (1934)

Clark Ashton Smith

Viewless, impalpable and fleet, the returning spectre, the revenant, laments the passage of time that has overthrown any sense of the past. The poem was published in *The Fantasy Fan* magazine in the 1930s, now online thanks to Project Gutenberg. The revenants in *Visual Heritage: Digital Approaches in Heritage Science* are the sense-extending tools deployed in diverse digitisation, visualisation and virtual/augmented reality projects explored in this impressive and accessible volume.

Several lines from *Revenant* are reproduced in the introduction to *Citadels of Mystery: Unsolved Puzzles of Archaeology* by L. Sprague de Camp and Catherine C. de Camp. My 1970s Fontana edition, one the first archaeology books I acquired, remains in my collection. Growing up in rural Suffolk, the nearest museum was over 10 miles away. My interest in the past was supplemented by occasional day trips to London, once joining many others queuing to glimpse objects from the tomb of Tutankhamun in the 1972 exhibition at the British Museum. Forty-four years later I had the privilege of joining the Museum to lead its scientific research programme.

More than 30 of the intervening 44 years was spent at the University of Bradford, the academic home of two of the editors of this volume. As an undergraduate student in Archaeological Sciences in the early 1980s, computers were largely used to store, retrieve and visualise data and to speed up data analysis via statistical methods. Bradford's pioneering research in geophysical survey techniques in numerous archaeological settings, together with chemical analysis of archaeological objects, provided an impetus to draw on computer applications to visualise datasets. The growing availability of personal 'microcomputers' in the late 1970s and early 1980s stimulated interest in quantitative methods of data analysis. A computer scientist, Sue Laflin, convened the first meeting of the Computer Applications in Archaeology group at the University of Birmingham in 1973, where three of the editors, building on these early developments, later developed large-scale pioneering applications in data science, visualisation and landscape archaeology.

Three of the editors of the current volume collaborated to produce the first volume in the series published in 2013. Re-reading the excellent introduction to *Visual Heritage in the Digital Age* by Ch'ng and Gaffney reinforces the contribution that visualisation has made to heritage research. It also signals the rapid pace of change in technology in less than a decade to the collection presented here. Yet heritage science is much more than a record of innovations in technology and new applications, important though these are. There are many important themes in *Visual Heritage: Digital Approaches in Heritage Science* and the editors have made important interconnections in the introduction between the individual contributions to the book. The reach in chronological terms and scope in terms of subjects and objects is testimony to the diverse impact of digital technologies across disciplines. Increasing attention is focussing on the people who create, own and use the resources. The subjects of digital programmes are also coming into greater focus and are being explored by evaluating ethical issues and tackling barriers to engagement.

Several contributions to *Visual Heritage: Digital Approaches in Heritage Science* remind us that other factors, not simply the passage of time, represent enormous threats to cultural heritage. The denudation of cultural resources has myriad causes and require urgent and concerted action. Digital approaches can help to highlight the severity of accelerated anthropogenic change, directly at the site of the impact or remotely through web-scraped capture and crowd-sourced imagery. *Visual Heritage: Digital Approaches in Heritage Science* draws on the latest digital technologies to document tangible and intangible heritage across a wide sweep of time and context and to enrich understanding of the past.

Carl Heron

Carl Heron is Director of Scientific Research at the British Museum. He studied Archaeological Sciences at the University of Bradford before undertaking a Ph.D. at University College, Cardiff, and postdoctoral research at the University of Liverpool. He returned to the University of Bradford in 1990, before joining the British Museum in 2016. His research interests span molecular and isotopic applications of archaeological materials, with a focus on the origins and adoption of pottery container technology and the history of interactions between the sciences and the study of the human past.

Contents

About the Editors

Professor Eugene Ch'ng graduated with a best PhD from the Electronics, Electrical and Computer Engineering Department at the University of Birmingham in 2007. He has 20 years of interdisciplinary research experience, with formal training in art and design, design for the built environment, computational sciences, and humanities and social sciences research. He is founding director for both the NVIDIA Joint-Lab on Mixed Reality and the Digital Heritage Centre, both at the University of Nottingham's China campus. Professor Ch'ng's research focuses on VR and Mixed Reality. He is editor in chief for PRESENCE: Virtual and Augmented Reality MIT Press, the longest established journal on VR research. He has authored over 120 publications and has led international grant-funded research which establishes cross-cultural and interdisciplinary collaboration, pioneering the development and adoption of digital technologies across all areas and activities within the cultural heritage domain.

Professor Henry Chapman FSA is Chair of Archaeology at the University of Birmingha. Following an undergraduate degree in Archaeology at the University of Exeter, he moved to the Royal Commission on Historical Monuments of England. Based within their Exeter office, he worked as an archaeological landscape investigator before moving to the University of Hull as a member of the English Heritage funded Humber Wetlands Project, and undertaking a PhD focusing on the application of GIS in landscape archaeology at the same time. Henry subsequently worked on various other wetland archaeology projects at the University of Hull, before moving to Birmingham, initially as part of "Visual and Spatial Technology Centre" (Vista). He was a founding director of the Digital Humanities Hub, before becoming a lecturer. With a primary focus on later prehistory and wetland archaeology, and applied digital technologies, his research centres on the use of GIS, technical survey, and other digital technologies for the study of the past.

Professor Vincent Gaffney MBE, FSA Professor Vincent Gaffney is Anniversary Chair in Landscape Archaeology at the Department of Archaeological Sciences at the University of Bradford. His undergraduate degree was taken at the University of Reading, and, following fieldwork at Stonehenge and on the Berkshire Downs, he spent a number of years in museums. Deciding to study for a PhD at Reading he moved to former Yugoslavia, was based in Ljubljana (Slovenia), but worked on the island of Hvar in Croatia. On returning to Britain, he worked at the University of Birmingham before moving to the University of Bradford. His research has included studies of Roman urbanisation at Wroxeter, survey of Diocletian's Mausoleum, the wetland landscape of the river Cetina (Croatia), fieldwork in Italy and historic landscape characterisation at Fort Hood (Texas). An early adopter of GIS in archaeology, and an advocate of digital applications in heritage research, he founded the "Visual and Spatial Technology Centre" (Vista) at Birmingham, and is now part of the "Visualising Heritage" team at Bradford. He leads the UK team within the UK/LBI_ArchPro "Stonehenge Hidden Landscapes" project, and is Principal Investigator on the ERC Advanced Grant project 'Europe's Lost Frontiers'. In 2022, Professor Gaffney was part of the University of Bradford team awarded a Queen's Anniversary Prize for Higher and Further Education.

Professor Andrew S. Wilson, MCIfA, FHEA is an Archaeologist and Heritage Scientist with wide-ranging research interests in Digital Heritage, Human Bioarchaeology, Conservation, Taphonomy, and Forensic Archaeology. He is based in the School of Archaeological & Forensic Sciences at the University of Bradford. He trained in Conservation at UCL Institute of Archaeology and in Human Bioarchaeology at Sheffield and Bradford. He has worked for the Smithsonian Institution, Wiltshire County Council Conservation Service and in commercial archaeology. Awards include Museums & Galleries Commission National Conservation Award (1999); World's Archaeological Research Awards (2017); ALT Learning Technologist of the Year Research Award (2020 - Highly Commended); Queen's Anniversary Prize (2022). His research has featured in major interdisciplinary publications including Nature, Science, PNAS, Current Biology, Nature Scientific Reports, PLoSONE. He is Member of the Editorial Board for the Journal of World Prehistory and a member of the Forensic Archaeology Expert Panel for CIfA. He Co-Directs Visualising Heritage with varied imaging and visualisation capabilities at the University of Bradford and has led landmark Digital Heritage projects with research and capital infrastructure funding from sources including AHRC, Jisc, GCRF, British Academy, HEIF, The Wellcome Trust, Research England, Historic Environment Scotland, Shetland Amenity Trust, HS2 and City of Bradford Metropolitan District Council.

Chapter 1
Introduction

Eugene Ch'ng, Henry Chapman, Vincent Gaffney, and Andrew S. Wilson

Heritage Science is an emerging domain, which is inherently interdisciplinary, reaching from the arts and humanities to encompass practice from the sciences and engineering. Increasingly trends in digital technologies have influenced, and indeed transformed many aspects of the process and activities that are core to cultural heritage. The visual quality of this contribution is manifest both in the imaging methods used for capture and in the value of the visual outputs—ranging from digitised 3D models of cultural heritage to transformative visualisations that communicate meanings via embedded memories and narratives.

Although the term Heritage Science emerged in the early 2000s, the domain, in general, has seen massive, parallel developments across key related disciplines, in collaboration with the sciences and engineering. However, as Heritage Science emerges as a fully fledged discipline in its own right, exemplary methods and technologies that may originate within science and engineering have frequently derived from opportunities to work with heritage data. Increasingly there is, therefore, a symbiotic relationship between these domains that are led by research questions that are inherently embedded within heritage disciplines. *Visual Heritage in the Digital Age*, the first volume in the series looked at cultural heritage from the perspective of

E. Ch'ng (✉)
University of Nottingham Ningbo China, Ningbo, China
e-mail: eugene.chng@nottingham.edu.cn

H. Chapman
University of Birmingham, Birmingham, UK
e-mail: h.chapman@bham.ac.uk

V. Gaffney · A. S. Wilson
University of Bradford, Bradford, UK
e-mail: v.gaffney@bradford.ac.uk

A. S. Wilson
e-mail: a.s.wilson2@bradford.ac.uk

© Springer Nature Switzerland AG 2022
E. Ch'ng et al. (eds.), *Visual Heritage: Digital Approaches in Heritage Science*,
Springer Series on Cultural Computing,
https://doi.org/10.1007/978-3-030-77028-0_1

how digital approaches, and especially visualisation, have contributed to processes of heritage research, as well as its value in communication and participatory practices (Ch'ng et al. 2013). This earlier publication revealed the formative relationship between heritage and science and the emerging link through the application of cutting-edge technologies, especially our ability to process and visualise large amounts of data. The current book demonstrates how the domain has progressed, led by major digital advancement, and a more mature approach to how science and heritage researchers interact, and how heritage issues have shaped technological development rather than being passive consumers of technology for either research or dissemination. The book as a whole presents a wealth of international experience in digital heritage science. The chapters within the volume demonstrate the purpose and value of digital applications for both tangible and intangible heritage research (Bortolotto 2007; Vecco 2010) and span two million years of history recorded via natural and cultural processes, applied to sites and objects of which are distributed across the world (Fig. 1.1).

Heritage and technology are fundamentally global issues requiring a research community comprising both individual research groups and a larger theoretical coherence (Ippolito 2017). Researchers may work within their own community in tackling issues that are highly specific to one's opportunity and on cultural heritage that is of value to that locality. On the other hand, there is a critical need to work together in cohesion as a community possessing a global vision, for this is our shared heritage, and addressing universal value is of fundamental importance. Working at a community scale brings to the fore the importance of participatory approaches to co-design, co-production and sustainability, seeing the critical need to ensure that local community groups are involved from the outset wherever possible. The mandate to work in cohesion warrants the need for a continual, global dialogue that focuses on the use of digital sciences in the heritage domain.

Whilst progress is often attributed to any technology that has produced impacts leading to a paradigm shift in research culture, the same technology may also lead to issues that are unforeseen and even unwelcome. Appropriation and misrepresentation of heritage through technology is a real issue with potentially major consequences and demands consideration in how such technologies are governed professionally and ethically.

The present volume gathers contributions from across the world, with exciting themes and chapters reflecting the value of the interdisciplinary methods which lie at the heart of this discipline. Following the success of the first volume, the editors have chosen to present a broad range of heritage research including archaeology, conservation, museology, memory studies, forensic science and heritage management, as well as studies in metrology and applied technologies including object and terrestrial laser scanning, structured light scanning, multi-spectral imaging, visualisation, GIS, agent-based modelling, mobile technologies, 3D printing, and virtual and augmented reality. In doing so, the volume presents theoretical, methodological and technical contributions from across the whole of Heritage Science and draws from related areas including building information modelling and use of mixed reality (Bolognesi and

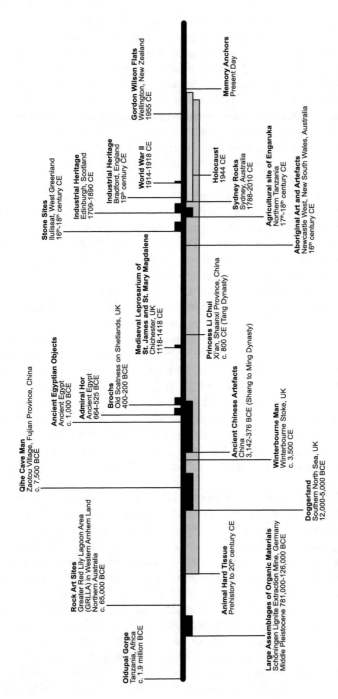

Fig. 1.1 Digital applications for both tangible and intangible heritage demonstrated in two million years of history recorded via natural and cultural processes, applied to sites and objects which are distributed across the world (E. Ch'ng)

Villa 2021). The involvement of visual heritage as a key component within several artistic works again highlights the interdisciplinarity of this domain.

Within this large body of work, a number of themes emerge. There is a common understanding that the physical properties of objects at a variety of scales are often susceptible to change, and that materiality is temporal. Change, therefore, is inevitable and there is a shared urgency to preserve, conserve and document with digital tools designed as a 'pragmatic approach that anticipates change to cultural heritage'. 3D recording, documentation and management of cultural heritage are key considerations (Stylianidis and Remondino 2016). Physical threats to cultural heritage include factors such as development, neglect, disasters, conflict and vandalism, and this frequently results in situations where direct recording of heritage objects may not be possible.

The ability to digitally reconstruct heritage sites to a level of detail from web-scraped and crowd-sourced imagery reveals the synergy that can be created at the intersection of the ubiquity of consumer-grade imaging devices and the accessibility of close-range photogrammetry software. This intersection of technology includes a pipeline of affordable tools for processing and visualising 3D data that can be applied in territories peripheral to heritage disciplines. No single method of capture is suited to all applications, meaning that the pros and cons of digital techniques for documenting cultural heritage need to be evaluated (Bentkowska-Kafel and MacDonald 2017; Ch'ng 2019a, b). Appropriate selection of methods for acquisition, curation and dissemination of spatial cultural heritage data remains key to this approach (Vincent et al. 2017). Heritage data that can be ethically shared via 3D model publishing platforms and that can be embedded in social media can create awareness beyond that of physical museums, which may directly lead to visits to the museums hosting these objects and an enhanced interpretation and understanding of their meaning and significance. Digital surrogates do not replace the need to conserve heritage sites, rather they can inform the management of these monuments, sites and landscapes as with challenges posed by heritage tourism (Garrod and Fyall 2000), and contribute to enhancing access, education, interpretation and even well-being and societal cohesion.

The use of digital technologies has also provided a means of documenting heritage at scale that is by nature participatory, and that involves communities via crowd-sourcing in an otherwise resource-sparse environment and institutions that are keen, but do not yet have digital readiness as evident in the Global South (White and Ch'ng 2019) but also in other regions (Price and James 2018). Involving participants in crowdsourcing activities not only creates awareness, but also fosters civic pride and community engagement with the need to care for heritage. Indeed, digital tools are revolutionising the cultural heritage landscape through copies, and these are shared and made accessible to new audiences globally, inspiring creativity, enabling learning and aiding preservation (Cormier 2018). Crowdsourcing can certainly help to build a more open, connected and smart cultural heritage (Oomen and Aroyo 2011), and present digital technologies can do more to facilitate such activities, including activities that promote the mass photogrammetry of cultural heritage objects (Ch'ng et al. 2019).

As we progress deeper into a world where digitality is pervading every aspect of our society, and as our value system shifts towards the functionality, and perhaps even the intrinsic value of born-digital objects and digital copies of cultural constructs (Ch'ng 2019a, b), we may begin to marvel at how adaptable contemporary society is in a new reality that daily processes, manipulates, and consumes digital information expressed via media in all aspects of our lives, and how cultural heritage is finding new pathways within our digital culture.

Our present ability to digitally document a copy of heritage using accessible technology is the first step towards digitalisation—the use of digital cultural heritage for digital transformation beyond that of curatorial and conservation practice towards the communicative prospects of engaging audiences in the experience and learning of heritage. The goal of digital heritage goes far beyond the investigative roles of research institutions, and certainly far beyond the need for permanent records for preservation purposes. Digital heritage is important as the functional roles of digital technologies can enrich traditional modes of viewing objects by providing the 'ability to privilege the role of interpretation itself' (Witcomb 2007), democratised and shifting away from object-centredness towards a new discourse where objects and meanings can be fluid and polysemic, and that allows for interpretations that are contingent towards different individuals, groups and contexts (Hooper-Greenhill 2000), all through the visual nature of digitally facilitated visualisation of heritage information (Ch'ng et al. 2013, 2014). It is this transformational step that allows intangible cultural heritage to be woven into the fabric of digital content—drawing from visual heritage to contextualise narratives, enhance meaning and enrich experiences. Furthermore, the use of extended reality and gaming technologies are drawn into the realm of storytelling using cultural heritage anchors (Liarokapis et al. 2020).

Within these contexts, this book presents case studies and ideas that highlight a breadth of digital heritage approaches and applications, and the ways in which these are used to engage with and co-create with the wider public. Using five themes, this book explores—(i) Global perspectives in heritage science and technology; (ii) Modelling, interpreting and reconstructing the past; (iii) Digital and virtual heritage research and applications; (iv) Cultural connections and creative industries' and add (v) Intangible and hidden narratives.

The first section of the book presents a series of chapters that highlight the global perspectives in heritage science and technology, exploring how digital approaches can be applied to specific heritage challenges at a variety of different scales, extending across built heritage, landscapes and objects and intangible cultural heritage using a range of different technologies:

In the chapter *Open World, Open Minds: Keeping a Global Dialogue, Reflections on the ReACH Initiative (Reproduction of Art and Cultural Heritage)*, Anaïs Aguerre, the founder and managing director of Culture Connect Ltd. probes the question of what truly lies behind the immense promise that digital technologies have to offer to the field of heritage conservation, historic preservation and the construction of tomorrow's heritage, and in reflecting on her experience as ReACH project director, expounds the critical need for global dialogue and transformative open access to data and ideas.

In *Developing an Ethical Framework for the Digital Documentation of Heritage Sites*, we benefit from the work of Mario Santana Quintero, Michelle Duong and Laurie Smith, who have provided a critical insight into the potential applications and threats of technology, and how the issue of ethics plays an essential role in governing the professional activity of recording heritage sites.

Physical threats to cultural heritage include factors such as development, neglect, disasters, conflict and vandalism, often meaning that emergency recording is simply not possible. In the *Curious Travellers* project, the chapter by Andrew S. Wilson, Vince Gaffney, Chris Gaffney, Eugene Ch'ng, Richard Bates, Elgidius, B. Ichumbaki, Gareth Sears, Tom Sparrow, Andrew Murgatroyd, Eddy Faber, Adrian Evans and Robin Coningham, focuses on the use of web-scraped and crowd-sourced imagery for the digital documentation of heritage sites using Structure-from-Motion technologies that can be fused with mobile mapping data. The chapter details the numerous advantages of these approaches, and some of the challenges in implementation in such extreme environments. In doing so the provisional results encourage some optimism in our ability to record heritage sites and landscapes at a distance even when damage has already occurred, and in the case of Tanzania and the 1.9 mya site Olduvai Gorge, presenting the need for baseline information of heritage assets.

The second section of the volume extends to Modelling, Interpreting and Reconstructing the Past:

In '*Visualising Deep Time History in Context Using Accessible and Emergent Technologies: The GLAM Sector Experience*', the authors Ann Hardy, Gaute Rasmussen and Gionni di Gravio discuss the collaborative process that facilitates a diversity of 'voices' and values around Indigenous artefacts from the digital, IT, and GLAM perspective in the use of innovative technologies.

The use of Structure-from-Motion (SfM) photogrammetry as a valuable research tool in archaeology that allows spatially accurate representation of rock art sites and landscapes is explored by Jarrad Kowlessar, Ian Moffat, Daryl Wesley, Tristen Jones, Max Aubert, Mark Willis, Alfred Nayinggul and the Njanjma Aboriginal Corporation. This methodology allows the creation of immersive representations of important cultural-heritage sites using widely available, inexpensive equipment and software which produce data that can be readily used by Indigenous custodians to manage, record and monitor rock art sites and enhance site access and visitor experiences.

The impact of climate change on the archaeology of Greenland is in evidence within this chapter by Chiara Villa, Marie Louise Jørkov, Christian Koch Madsen and Jens Fog Jensen. The advantages and disadvantages of both Structure-from-Motion (SfM) photogrammetry and Computed Tomography (CT) scanning were assessed in this study used to document and interpret isolated stone graves and associated human remains, which were excavated in Greenland during the summers of 2018 and 2019.

Guohua Geng, Mingquan Zhou, Wen Yang, Tao Ruan Wan, Wen Tang review the issues of digital craniofacial reconstruction. They also describe novel approaches to recreation using archaeological evidence also statistical data from contemporary populations. The results, represented by reconstructions of the faces of a Tang Dynasty Princess Li Chui, an ancient Qihe skull and a Qin female skull demonstrates the potential use of such tools in VR reconstructions' and also within the fields of anthropology and forensic sciences.

'*Resurrecting Hor*' by Carl G. Elkins contrasts the cultural metaphors of imagery through the intentionality of creation and fragmentation of images in the past, exemplified through the (re)creation of the admiral Hor statue and the ritual structures of Egyptian society. The fetishisation of digital imagery and the comparative processes at work are highlighted here allowing us to question what digital images mean to contemporary society.

In the final chapter in the Modelling, interpreting and reconstructing the past section, the focus moves to the use of digital approaches for the characterisation of animal hard tissues. Using both 2D and 3D methods, authors Sonia O'Connor, Tom Sparrow, Andrew D. Holland, Rachel Kershaw, Emma Brown, Rob Janaway, Hassan Ugail and Andrew S. Wilson document methods that have extensive implications for the identification of materials that impacts on the understandings of cultural choice in the selection of materials. These methods have resulted in an accessible resource to assist others not only with interpretation, but also supporting conservation and supporting the mitigation against illegal hunting and trafficking of globally endangered species.

The third section of the book covers Digital and Virtual Heritage Research and Applications:

The chapter by Kit Devine examines the '*Virtual Sydney Rocks*' through time, with users able to explore the built environment of the Sydney Rocks area from 1788 to 2010. Each building is linked to an individual webpage with detailed information that can be accessed by clicking on the building. Additional discussion explores the potential for drawing upon further public involvement through the crowd-sourcing and co-creation of virtual heritage resources.

Public dissemination of the relationships between environmental change and past human activity can be challenging. A solution to this challenge is provided in the chapter by Philip Murgatroyd, Micheál Butler and Vincent Gaffney. Here they present the use of augmented reality simulation using an interactive sandbox. Using a combination of technologies, including Xbox Kinect and projection, the simulation provides a method for understanding the interactions between environment, climate, flora, fauna and humans. In addition to providing detail regarding the workflow, this chapter also considers public reception of the AR sandbox, including both its advantages and limitations.

Hannah Rushton and Marc Aurel Schnabel examine the *Gordon Wilson Flats*, a Modernist apartment building in Wellington, New Zealand, to understand how the historical significance of a building can be translated into the virtual realm. This discussion considers the role of multimedia and GLAMs in the construction of meaning and communication of authenticity for architectural heritage to educate members of the public about the building and its history using virtual reality.

The chapter by Li Sou, Julie Bond, Stephen Dockrill, James Hepher, Al Rawlinson, Tom Sparrow, Val Turner, Lyn Wilson, Andrew S. Wilson addresses the challenging theme of retrospective photogrammetry using archive imagery. It focuses on the broch site of Old Scatness on Shetland, exploring the potential of both analogue and digital archive photography originally captured for condition monitoring of stone-built structures. The authors present the entire workflow, demonstrating which datasets worked well and, importantly, highlighting which datasets turned out to be less valuable for retrospective 3D modelling using Structure-from-Motion photogrammetry. This presents valuable lessons for any studies using archive imagery, in addition to helpful advice for how standard excavation photography can be undertaken to maximise its potential for future 3D modelling.

The chapter by Andrew D Holland, Jarod M Hutson, Aritza Villaluenga, Tom Sparrow, Andrew Murgatroyd, Alejandro García-Moreno, Elaine Turner, Adrian Evans, Sabine Gaudzinski-Windheuser and Andrew S. Wilson on digital refit analysis presents a contemporary approach to a classic archaeological question. How representative is the fragmentary archaeological record and what can we say about the past using such data. The unique find of a group of anthropologically fragmented animal bones of Palaeolithic date is explored through the process of digital refitting and in doing so reveal significant clues regarding human behaviour in the deep past.

The chapter by Lyn Wilson, Alastair Rawlinson, Adam Frost, James Mitchell, Damian Liptrot and Dominic Liptrot shares experiences in a range of case studies that apply a rich variety of data capture techniques on a diverse range of industrial heritage sites. Drawing on details from six case studies, the authors explore themes of monument inspection and analysis, reverse engineering, and the ways in which digital data can be used in the restoration of monuments. The range of case studies also provides examples of data visualisation, and considers the ways in which this can facilitate learning and public engagement to a wide range of audiences.

In the following chapter, the focus shifts to novel applications of aerial imagery and the use of Structure-from-Motion (SfM) techniques. Here, Tabitha Kabora and Katie Campbell focus on local heritage management, presenting the case study of Engaruka in Tanzania. They demonstrate how archive aerial photography can be used to generate digital orthostatic maps and Digital Elevation Models (DEMs), and show how these can be used alongside new survey data from Unmanned Aerial Vehicles (UAVs), using similar SfM techniques for processing. The chapter usefully presents the workflows used, highlighting both the benefits and challenges of these approaches in relation to understanding archaeological landscapes as well as their importance for local heritage management.

Techniques for the rapid recording and documentation of built heritage assets are of key importance, particularly in the contexts of threats to their continued survival, which might range from direct action such as vandalism, to decay wrought through weathering and non-occupancy. In the chapter by Joe Moore, Chris Gaffney, Tom Sparrow, Henry Irving, Saira Ali, Richard Middleton, Sheena Campbell, Jon Ackroyd, Adrian Walker, Sydney Simpson, Joe Ritchings, Andrew S. Wilson, an application of Mobile Mapping Systems for the rapid capture of an area of the internationally important industrial heritage relating to the textile industry in the city of Bradford, UK. The chapter explores the significant benefits of the approach, which centre on the speed of data capture and processing, as well as some of the limitations.

The fourth section of the book covers the relevance of visual heritage for Cultural Connections and the Creative Industries:

Large classical statues figure frequently in the public's imagination of the past, but they are often broken and fragmentary, and it may be imagined that the job of a curator/conservator is simply to piece them together. Artist and sculptor Kate Johnson brings together a multidisciplinary team with Adrian Evans, Tom Sparrow, Leon Black, Rob Harman, Dongmin Yang and Andrew S. Wilson to provide an alternative view to the sculptural past in the present through a performative art piece in 'Project code-named Humpty'. As part of a project investigating fragmented heritage, Johnson and colleagues explore the creation of a sculpture and how to break it prior to reconstruction, and how this relates to our understanding of such objects.

Textile artist Karina Thompson explores the development of artworks inspired by digital data derived from human skeletal remains that were scanned and radiographed as part of the landmark *Digitised Diseases*, and *From Cemetery to Clinic* digital bioarchaeology projects. Together with colleagues Keith Manchester, Jo Buckberry, Tom Sparrow, Andrew D. Holland, Andrew S. Wilson from the Biological Anthropology Research Centre and Visualising Heritage, the combined team examine how this collaboration has collectively drawn attention to the need to humanise the documentation of disease through time.

In *Fad Touch: Creative Economy Engagement*, the authors Daniel Pett, Catriona Cooper, Abi L. Glen, Melanie Pitkin and Jennifer Wexler discuss the outcomes of the Fitzwilliam museum's practice-driven, development programme and knowledge transfer activity in collaboration with educational technology start-ups using 3D scanning and printing of the Museum's collection that demonstrated value for the museum's audience engagement activities.

Stonehenge may be the most famous archaeological site in the world, but it is frequently difficult to imagine the people who actually lived in the landscape containing the famous stones. Oscar Nilsson, Tom Sparrow, Andrew D. Holland and Andrew S. Wilson provide one remarkable example of a reconstruction of a skull recovered during the nineteenth century from a tomb predating Stonehenge. Using digital scanning and 3D printing, they explain the challenges of recreating the face of our ancestors and how the final artefact was used in the presentation of a humanised past within the new Stonehenge visitor centre.

In the chapter by Yue Li and Eugene Ch'ng, the focus is on user engagement and interaction with virtual objects and, specifically, how an approach that combines both virtual and augmented reality can enable users to engage from different levels of digital immersion can interact, engage and communicate. The intentions behind the design of the hybrid system are made clear and are informed by theories relating to how people learn. In addition to outlining the theoretical context and design of the hybrid system, the chapter usefully provides the details from an extensive user study which provides some fascinating insights into adherence with social norms that might be associated with museum visits, treating virtual objects in similar ways compared with physical objects.

In the final thematic section, the book picks up on the importance of Intangible and Hidden Narratives.

Ross Wilson re-assesses one of the most prominent examples of crowdsourcing and co-creation connected to the commemoration of the First World War during the recent centenary. '*Lives of the First World War*' was a platform created by the Imperial War Museum to serve as a public repository of images, as a memorial and as a future research tool. By examining the platform as a mode of representation, composed of genres, discourses and styles, the structures of knowledge presented in this resource are assessed as reinforcing the role of the institution and challenging the wider processes of social memory.

Author Gabriele Neher provides a case study that focuses on storytelling as a narrative device in audience engagement. The chapter '*Telling difficult stories: VR, storytelling and active audience engagement in heritage sites and museums*' provides new strategies in rethinking storytelling in museums in view of the interpretations and experiences of the audience.

The chapter by Eugene Ch'ng on '*Virtual Environments as Memory Anchors*' challenges how we interact with the digital past at a very personal level and in contrast to the institutional role of guardian of the great and good. This goes beyond the question of who's history is it, and asks how that can be recorded digitally and, most importantly, how will present and future users interact with virtual pasts. We conclude the book with an afterword.

Summary

In summary, the wealth of knowledge contained within this book illustrates how digital approaches in Heritage Science continue to drive forward innovations at a scale that contribute highly visual and arresting contents, delivering new findings that transform our understanding of the past and ultimately make it more accessible to varied audiences.

This book is aimed at a very broad academic and practice-led readership, which extends across many disciplines and will be of considerable value to students at all levels working across heritage and computer science. The content will be appreciated by a generalist audience as well as those wishing to explore the vast range of potential, technical applications. The case studies presented here are international and have a global reach across a range of diverse topics. Examining digital technologies with a goal to preserve cultural and natural heritage at a global level and in the face of previously unimaginable threats from climate change, through fake news to catastrophic insurrection.

References

Bentkowska-Kafel A, MacDonald L (eds) (2017) Digital techniques for documenting and preserving cultural heritage. ARC Humanities Press

Bolognesi C, Villa D (2021) From building information modelling to mixed reality. Springer tracts in civil engineering

Bortolotto C (2007) From objects to processes: UNESCO's 'Intangible Cultural Heritage.' J Mus Ethnogr 19:21–33

Ch'ng E (2019a) The first original copy and the role of blockchain in the reproduction of cultural heritage. PRESENCE 27(1):151–162

Ch'ng E (2019b) Asking the right questions when digitising cultural heritage. In: International conference on digital heritage: 'convergence of digital humanities', Gyeongju, Republic of Korea, 20 September 2019, pp 58–67

Ch'ng E, Gaffney V, Chapman H (eds) (2013) Visual heritage in the digital age. Springer, London

Ch'ng E, Gaffney VL, Chapman HP (2014) From product to process: new directions in digital heritage. Digital heritage and culture: strategy and implementation, pp 219–243

Ch'ng E, Cai S, Zhang T, Leow FT (2019) Crowdsourcing 3D cultural heritage: best practice for mass photogrammetry. J Cult Herit Manag Sustain Dev 9(1):24–42

Cormier B (2018) Copy culture: sharing in the age of digital reproduction. V&A Publishing, London

Garrod B, Fyall A (2000) Managing heritage tourism. Ann Tour Res 27(3):682–708

Hooper-Greenhill E (2000) Museums and the interpretation of visual culture (Museum meanings). Routledge, London

Ippolito A (2017) Handbook of research on emerging technologies for architectural and archaeological heritage. IGI Global, Hershey

Liarokapis F, Voulodimos A, Doulamis N, Doulamis A (2020) Visual computing for cultural heritage. Springer series for cultural computing

Oomen J, Aroyo L (2011) Crowdsourcing in the cultural heritage domain: opportunities and challenges. In: Proceedings of the 5th international conference on communities and technologies, pp 138–149

Price K, James D (2018) Structuring for digital success: a global survey of how museums and other cultural organisations resource, fund, and structure their digital teams and activity. In: Proceedings of museums and the web

Stylianidis E, Remondino F (eds) (2016) 3D recording, documentation and management of cultural heritage. Whittles Publishing, Dunbeath

Vecco M (2010) A definition of cultural heritage: from the tangible to the intangible. J Cult Herit 11:321–324

Vincent M, Lopez-Menchero Bendicho V, Ioannides M, Levy TE (eds) (2017) Heritage and archaeology in the digital age. Springer quantitative methods in the humanities and social sciences

White A, Ch'ng E (2019) China Museum's digital heritage profile: an evaluation of digital technology adoption in cultural heritage institutions. In: Lewi H, Smith W, Cooke S, vom Lehn D (eds) The Routledge international handbook of new digital practices in galleries, libraries, archives, museums and heritage sites

Witcomb A (2007) The materiality of virtual technologies: a new approach to thinking about the impact of multimedia in museums. In: Cameron F, Kenderdine S (eds) Theorizing digital cultural heritage: a critical discourse. The MIT Press, Cambridge, pp 19–34

Part I
Global Perspectives in Heritage Science and Technology

Chapter 2
Open World, Open Minds: Keeping a Global Dialogue. Reflections on the ReACH Initiative

Anaïs Aguerre

Abstract In the twenty-first century, the development and democratization of technologies such as 3D scanning and photogrammetry are radically changing the way cultural heritage is recorded. As a result, and as noted by Brendan Cormier in *Copy Culture: Sharing in the Age of Digital Reproduction*, "a parallel world of digitized monuments [...]" and artefacts "[...] exists on stand-by (Cormier 2018)." What does that really mean for the museum and heritage sector charged with the study, preservation and sharing of our cultural heritage and its 'transmission' to future generations? What truly lies behind the immense promise that digital technologies offer to the field of historic preservation and more broadly to the building of tomorrow's heritage? Why does this transmission in a connected and digital world require global dialogue and open access? Reflecting on her experience as ReACH project director, Anaïs Aguerre analyzes in this article the context in which the ReACH initiative was born, its ambitions, achievements and some of the ethical questions it raises in our digital and connected world.

Keywords ReACH · Reproduction · Collective intelligence · Digital reproduction · Global dialogue · Digital heritage · Museums · Digital reproductions

---

ReACH stands for Reproduction of Art and Culture Heritage. It is the name given to a global initiative spearheaded by the Victoria and Albert Museum which explores how we can collectively re-think our approach to the reproduction, storage and sharing of works of art and cultural heritage in the twenty-first century.

A. Aguerre (✉)
Culture Connect Ltd., London, UK
e-mail: anais.aguerre@culture-connect.net

© Springer Nature Switzerland AG 2022   15
E. Ch'ng et al. (eds.), *Visual Heritage: Digital Approaches in Heritage Science*,
Springer Series on Cultural Computing,
https://doi.org/10.1007/978-3-030-77028-0_2

2.1 Introduction

"Through advances in technology and connectivity, we now have a revolutionary opportunity to enhance learning, creativity and innovation, and to reach new audiences worldwide, through the reproduction and sharing of works of art and cultural heritage ('Works'). Furthermore, digital technologies can enable us to record, document and, in some instances, recreate Works that are threatened by environmental hazards, conflicts, terrorism, rapid economic development, mass tourism, thefts and other natural and human-made disasters [...] or that have been lost. For cultural institutions that hold collections for the benefit of the public, the opportunity to provide open access now or in the future to Works in digital format is an exciting new frontier in their mission to preserve and transmit knowledge, culture and history for present and future generations [...]" states the ReACH Declaration launched at the Victoria and Albert Museum (V&A) in December 2017, 150 years after the V&A founding director Sir Henry Cole's *Convention for Promoting Universally Reproduction of Works of Art for the Benefit of Museums of All Countries* (Henry Cole Convention).

In the twenty-first century, the development and democratization of technologies such as 3D scanning and photogrammetry are indeed radically changing the way cultural heritage is recorded. As a result, and as noted by Brendan Cormier in *Copy Culture: Sharing in the Age of Digital Reproduction*, "a parallel world of digitized monuments [...]" and artefacts "[...] exists on stand-by (Cormier 2018)." What does that really mean for the museum and heritage sector charged with the study, preservation and sharing of our cultural heritage and its 'transmission' to future generations? What truly lies behind the immense promise that digital technologies offer to the field of historic preservation and more broadly to the building of tomorrow's heritage? Why does this transmission in a connected and digital world require global dialogue and open access?

On the occasion of the 150th anniversary of the Henry Cole Convention, I had the privilege of coordinating and leading an unprecedented global consultation spearheaded by the Victoria and Albert Museum (V&A), which gathered experts from across the world tasked with the mission to explore, and co-author, a twenty-first-century version of Henry Cole's convention. Beyond the ReACH Declaration and subsequent technical guidelines produced by the initiative, I would like to share here some reflections on the importance of harnessing collective intelligence and keeping a global dialogue open when it comes to building these new 'digital cast courts[1]' and highlight some ethical questions raised by the process of collectively building tomorrow's heritage in our digital age.

---

[1] The notion of 'Digital Cast Courts' is derived from the 'Cast Courts' of the Victoria and Albert Museum in London, which comprises two large galleries and house the Museum's collection of plaster copies of outstanding national monuments and notable sculptures.

2.2 A Brave New World? Digital 'Disruption' and the New Museum Landscape

To a large extent, disruption and chaos have been defining trends of the first two decades of the twenty-first century. In his book *Everyday Chaos: Technology, Complexity and How We're Thriving in a New World of Possibility* (D. Weinberger, Boston, 2019), the American technologist and philosopher David Weinberger explains that artificial intelligence, big data, modern science, and the Internet are all revealing that the world is vastly more complex and unpredictable than we have, so far, allowed ourselves to see. He concludes: "This future isn't going to settle down, resolve itself, or yield to simple rules and expectations. Feeling overwhelmed, confused, surprised, and uncertain is our new baseline stance toward the world (Weinberger 2019)." Similarly, when the Founder and Executive Chairman of the World Economic Forum, Klaus Schwab, introduced in 2015 the notion of 'Fourth Industrial Revolution' in his seminal article "The Fourth Industrial Revolution: What It Means and How to Respond" published in *Foreign Affairs* (Schwab 2015), complexity and uncertainty were also clearly part of this new world radically transformed by the digital revolution. Schwab explains:

> "We stand" on the brink of a technological revolution that will fundamentally alter the way we live, work, relate to one another. In its scale, scope, and complexity, the transformation will be unlike anything humankind has experienced before. We do not yet know just how it will unfold, but one thing is clear: the response to it must be integrated and comprehensive, involving all stakeholders of the global polity, from the public and private sectors to academia and civil society. The First Industrial Revolution used water and steam power to mechanize production. The Second used electric power to create mass production. The Third used electronics and information technology to automate production. Now a Fourth Industrial Revolution is building on the Third, the digital revolution that has been occurring since the middle of the last century. It is characterized by a fusion of technologies that is blurring the lines between the physical, digital and biological spheres (Schwab 2015).

As Schwab stressed, this new revolution is impacting all aspects of our lives, in an unprecedented manner. Disruption has become the norm. It is not surprising therefore that the rapid development of digital technologies is challenging and transforming the museum landscape as well, in ways that are still difficult to fully grasp. The fast pace of technological developments today makes harnessing the possibilities of these new technologies even more complex for a sector that is often positioned as the 'guardian of the long-time,' conceived as the institutional link between the past, the present and the future against the contemporary buzz of the short term. But despite some pockets of resistance, a new museum landscape has emerged in the past fifteen years in which sharing digital reproduction (2D and increasingly 3D) is transforming the way we study, preserve and share cultural heritage.

One of the first major game-changers was Google Arts & Culture (formerly Google Art Project). Started in 2009 as one of the company's '20 percent time' policy, by which employees are encouraged to spend 20% of their time working on an innovative project of their own interest, the platform was officially launched in 2011. The ambition was to build 'a museum of museums on the web'[2] as Amid Sood, director of Google Culture Institute describes when he explains how he initiated and developed the Art Project. Today, Google Arts & Culture provides an online platform through which the public can access high-resolution images of arts from world-class museum collections housed by their museum partners (The British Museum; The J. Paul Getty Museum; The Met; MoMA, Musée d'Orsay; The National Gallery, London; the National Gallery of Washington D.C; Rijksmuseum; The State Hermitage Museum; Tate Britain; Uffizi Gallery; Van Gogh Museum to name a few). The promise is "for the culturally curious" to "discover artworks, collections and stories from all around the world in a new way,"[3] enabling, in principle, the 4.2 billion citizens now online (55% of the world's population) (World Economic Forum 2019) to "explore cultural treasures in extraordinary detail and easily share with (their) friends."[4] For cultural institutions, the draw—according to the Google Arts & Culture's website—is the provision of powerful technologies that can amplify the long-standing mission of cultural institutions: the collection and safeguarding of our history and heritage, all while preserving these artefacts for a worldwide audience today and tomorrow."[5]

The spread of 3D reproductions is more recent but is nonetheless rapidly transforming the way works of arts and cultural heritage are recorded, stored, shared and used. From Sketchfab to Iconem or the more controversial "#NefertitiHack" of Nora Al Badri and Nikolai Nelles, 3D digital reproductions of works of arts and cultural heritage are indeed increasingly shaping a new (alternative?) museum and cultural heritage landscape. With a membership of over 2 million users and over 3 million uploaded models,[6] Sketchfab, launched in 2012, has successfully been working to popularize the 3D format by providing an online platform to upload, share and view digital 3D content on a website compatible with all browsers and VR headsets. Although the platform is not dedicated to museums, there are more and more cultural artefacts on the platform and major cultural institutions such as the British Museum, the Kunsthistorisches Museum Wien or the RMN-Grand-Palais have joined and used the site to host their collection of 3D objects. Iconem offers another example of how 3D models have entered the museum and cultural heritage landscape. Founded in Paris in 2013, Iconem is a start-up specialised in the digitisation in 3D of endangered cultural heritage sites using drone technology and associated scanning tools to design site-specific architectural 3D models. In 2016, Iconem collaborated with The Louvre and the Rmn-Grand Palais on to launch the exhibition project, "Eternal Sites: From Bamiyan to Palmira, A journey to the heart of universal heritage." The exhibition displayed at the Grand Palais in Paris from 14 December 2016 to 9 January 2017 offered an exploration of major archaeological sites which had become inaccessible. The exhibition was a resounding success beyond the organisers' expectations. After its record-breaking attendance in Paris, it went on tour to

---

[2] https://www.ted.com/talks/amit_sood_building_a_museum_of_museums_on_the_web/.

[3] https://www.google.com/culturalinstitute/about (accessed December 2019).

[4] https://www.google.com/culturalinstitute/about (accessed December 2019).

[5] https://www.google.com/culturalinstitute/about (accessed December 2019).

[6] https://sketchfab.com/about (accessed December 2019).

Morocco. Since then, Iconem has collaborated with other museums, such as the Institut du Monde Arabe (IMA) in Paris with the 2018 exhibition "Cités millénaires. Voyage virtuels de Palmyre à Mossoul" created in partnership with UNESCO. Other collaborations include those with the Cité de l'architecture et du patrimoine on the exhibition, "Le Crac des chevaliers. Chroniques d'un rêve de pierre" in 2018 and with their partner Pascal Convert on the 2019 exhibition "Carte blanche à Pascal Convert: Revoir Mamiyan" at the Musée Guimet. Finally, the so-called #NefertitiHack by German artists Nora Al-Bari and Jan Nikolai Nelles represents another (although controversial) example of how 3D scanning is transforming the way museum arte-facts are shared, accessed and 'virtually owned'. In 2015, the two artists staged an artistic intervention they called 'The Other Nefertiti' whereby they claim to have secretly scanned the famous bust of Nefertiti in the Neues Museum Berlin without permission of the Museum. A digital file was then released freely under the public domain. Thousands of people downloaded it, 're-mixing' Nefertiti in various digital and 3D-printed forms. "With the data leak as part of this counter narrative," stated the artists, "we want to activate the artefact, to inspire a critical re-assessment of today's conditions and to overcome the colonial notion of possession in Germany."[7] There is a myriad of other examples I could have invoked. However, the three examples cited here provide a fair account of this new landscape, and the common character-istic shared by the initiators of these innovative endeavours, although diverse in their nature and size is their identity as neither museum nor cultural heritage organisations. It is particularly telling, for instance, in the case of the Nefertiti bust at the Neues Museum Berlin that, although the museum had created a detailed digital scan, it is an outsider who brought this new digital reality to the public, inviting a global audience to engage with this 'icon' of world heritage like never before and thus broadening its access in an unprecedented fashion. It seemed as if the Museum wasn't quite sure about what to do and how to engage with this new digital reality. As a result, letting the outside world setting the agenda: if the museums don't publish and circulate these digital copies, it is likely that others will do.

The question, therefore, is: if the initiatives are coming from 'outsiders', how can the museum and heritage sector fully harness this new world of possibilities that technological advances promise? Given the pace of transformation, it felt at the start of ReACH that there was some urgency to address this question and ensure museum and cultural heritage organisations could join the conversation and play a stronger and more proactive role in this rapid transformation and shaping of a new landscape.

2.3 ReACH: A Collective and Global Re-think

In 1867, Sir Henry Cole, founding director of the Victorian and Albert Museum, launched the *Convention for Promoting Universally Reproduction of Works of Art for the Benefit of Museums of All Countries*. Recognising the new opportunities that

---

[7] http://aksioma.org/the.other.nefertiti/ (accessed in January 2020).

technological advances of the time (namely photography, electrotype and new casting techniques) made possible, the 1867 Convention helped usher in a period in which museums actively engaged in the reproduction of great works of art and architecture produced from around the world "for the benefit of museums of all countries." As noted by Professor Mari Lending, author of *Plaster Monuments: Architecture and the Power of Reproduction*, "Cole's convention marks a key moment in the translation of national monuments into portable global patrimony (Landing 2018)." The need to collectively preserve and share a common world heritage was clearly asserted, as well as the necessity of the museums to take advantage of the new technology available to them.

150 years later, in response to not only increasing global threats (pollution, terrorism, conflicts or mass tourism) to our shared heritage but also to new technological promises, the ReACH initiative on the Reproduction of Art and Cultural Heritage was launched. One of the main objectives of ReACH was to establish what a twenty-first-century version of the 'Henry Cole Convention' should look like.

Building on Cole's legacy, our ambition was to explore collectively if, and how, the museum and cultural heritage sector could take a greater lead in this phase of transition to ensure that these new technologies could help them deliver better on their core mission of preserving, studying and sharing the collections in their care. As outlined previously, digital technologies are changing the cultural landscape, offering new ways to produce, store and share museum and heritage assets like never before. However, there was no clear methodology for how museums and heritage organisations should engage with these technologies. To complicate matters, legal protocols and procedures had not adapted to these new realities, and often acted as roadblocks to the new practice. The ambition with the ReACH initiative was, therefore, to bring clarity—by highlighting best practices, debating pressing issues and drafting a new declaration—and ultimately offer our heritage and museum community a useful roadmap for dealing with reproductions in the future.

Officially launched in Paris at UNESCO's headquarters in May 2017, the ReACH initiative has brought the global museum and heritage community together to collectively re-think how our imperilled cultural heritage can be preserved and debate at a global scale the creative opportunities that copying these works offers a global audience. With the support of key research partners—Factum Arte, The Louvre Museum, The Smithsonian Institution, The State Hermitage Museum, The Vorderasiatisches Museum, The Warburg Institute and Yale Institute for the Preservation of Cultural Heritage—the core research activity took place between May and December 2017. Through a series of five roundtable discussions—hosted in Washington with the Smithsonian Institution, in St Petersburg with The State Hermitage Museum, in Abu Dhabi with the Department of Culture and Tourism, in Beijing with The Palace Museum and in London at the V&A—we have drawn together over than 100 experts from across the world (individuals as well as institutions, start-ups as well as public organisations, scholars, lawyers, curators and digital experts) and conducted an unprecedented global consultation, to broaden our collective knowledge, and to share this with others.

This resulted in the production of the ReACH Declaration launched at the V&A in December 2017 and reproduced here. The text was signed by over twenty directors of world-class museums from across the globe as initial signatories. This twenty-first-century version of Henry Cole's Convention invites us to embrace with confidence advances in technology and connectivity to better study, share and preserve our cultural heritage.

2.4 The Need to Keep a Global Dialogue and an Open World

Beyond the Declaration, ReACH has also outlined the benefits of activating our collective intelligence when tackling issues that no individual museum or country could address alone. Since December 2017, we have kept the #ReACHDialogue open. Keeping this conversation on a global scale is critical to ensure that issues at stake won't be taken hostage by nationalist discourses or weaponised. In an online article on Slate dated from 15 November 2019, the executive director of the Engelberg Centre on Innovation Law & Policy at the NYU School of Law, Michael Weinberg, asserts that "museums do not hold our shared cultural heritage so that they can become gatekeepers. They hold our shared cultural heritage as stewards in order to make sure we have access to our collective history." Shared heritage requires shared solutions that could only be found if the conditions for a truly global dialogue are created. In her essay *Radical Museology* (Bishop. C, London, 2014), Claire Bishop goes further, affirming that "Contemporary museums have to address the question of decolonising the museum (seeing the world from the perspective of the global south and the commons (which seeks to produce new models of collective ownership)." In this context, it is only by maintaining an open and global dialogue that we can truly embrace the unprecedented opportunity offered by new technologies: the potential coexistence of multiple heritage narratives on the shared global stage, and the subsequent unlocking of a 360° view of our cultural heritage. As Hartwig Fischer, the Director of the British Museum, eloquently explains in his 2019 essay *Collections entail responsibility—Note on a global institution,* "the Museum has the ability to constitute a 'shared common ground of intelligibility,' each object in its collections has the potential to generate a dialogue." The online lives of these objects amplify this dialogue potential and, as such, the ability to redefine collective ownership and explore constructively the complex question of reclaimed histories.

Championing open access appears, therefore, as a prerequisite to fully unlock the promises of this new digital world. This equates to translating the notion of public access museums have fought for in the analogue world to an online equivalent. The challenge of open access is another ethical question that the ReACH initiative has raised. The majority of the benefits of digitization rely on the willingness of the Stewards of the collections to adopt open access policies for their digital resources.

Although a number of museums—such as the Getty, the National Gallery of Washington, the Rijksmuseum or the Metropolitan Museum of Art—had adopted such an approach before ReACH, the ReACH discourse contributed to advancing this agenda among the museum community as a whole. Merete Sanderhoff, a contributor to the ReACH consultations who has championed #OpenGlam at SMK—National Gallery of Denmark and through her role as Chair of Europeana,[8] is convinced that in our digital age, museums have to rethink their relations to their collections. Open art collections are key to reaching a worldwide audience. This is also Loic Taillon, former Chief Digital Officer at the Metropolitan Museum of Art (The Met)'s view. Loic Taillon, who also contributed to the ReACH roundtable, explains the rationale behind the Met's 2017 decision to make their images of public domain artworks freely available under a Creative Common Licence: "Success with digital is centred around content engagement and not necessarily visits to the institutional website. It is about users engaging with the collection, no matter where they encounter the collections." His view is that, given the breadth of The Met collections, there should be an "artwork in the collection that can inspire every single person on the planet."

Finally, the work on ReACH has triggered for me some interrogations in reaction to what felt like a limited reflection on the legacy of our digital work. It is rare to hear today, at the outset of a digitization project, considerations about what it may convey to future generations regarding what we valued culturally and how responsibly and sustainably (or not?) we embarked on these digital endeavours. Firstly, there is an evident risk of bias and distortion. To some degree, our digitisation work is currently limited by two factors: money and technical constraints. For instance, we know that recording reflective surfaces for 3D models is difficult with today's tools. We tend, therefore, to refrain from selecting this type of object for our projects. If 100 years from now, there is no 3D record of the silver in the Rosalinde and Arthur Gilbert Collection in the care of the V&A, what will that mean? Will our great-great-grandchildren think this was a collection we overlooked and undervalued? Likewise, a number of projects are funded thanks to the generous support of private sponsors who may have a specific agenda not necessarily in sync with the collective. What will these projects driven by individual interests say about our shared collective culture and the heritage we valued? Secondly, the environmental impact of these projects is yet to be fully assessed. As Brendon Cormier and I highlighted in the introduction of *Copy Culture: Sharing in the Age of Digital Reproduction* (Ed. B. Cormier, London, 2018) "the impulse to record should never outweigh asking the fundamental question of why and how." In the face of the urgent imperative to develop more sustainable practices in the museum and heritage sector, the ecological impact of our work should also be taken into account. Our responsibility to the past is intimately connected to our responsibility to the future. Once again this requires a collective re-think and engagement.

---

[8] Europeana is a web portal created by the European Union and launched in November 2008. It contains digitalised museum collections of more than 3,000 institutions across Europe and includes records of over 10 million cultural and scientific artefacts.

2.5 Conclusion

To conclude with we may want to reflect on the latest initiative from Tim Berners-Lee, the inventor of the Internet. In November 2019, he launched a 'Contract for the Web' that consists of a number of principles aiming to secure the future of the Internet. The Contract's preamble reads:#

> The Web was designed to bring people together and make knowledge freely available. It has changed the world for good and improved the lives of billions. Yet, many people are still unable to access its benefits and, for others, the Web comes with too many unacceptable costs. Everyone has a role to play in safeguarding the future of the Web. The Contract for the Web was created by representatives from over 80 organizations, representing governments, companies and civil society, and sets out commitments to guide digital policy agendas. To achieve the Contract's goals, governments, companies, civil society and individuals must commit to sustained policy development, advocacy, and implementation of the Contract text.

It took 30 years to set some ethical guidelines for the web. Let's, for once, work more rapidly than the tech world and, ensure that, as we push new digital frontiers, the excitement of these new horizons do not blind us on the why and how we do things nor prevent us from facing the responsibility we owe to future generations. We are all responsible for building tomorrow. 'The future starts now'.

ReACH Declaration

The ReACH Declaration
2017
Promoting Universally the Reproduction, Storage and Sharing of Works of Art and Cultural Heritage through Digital Technologies

VISION

This declaration promotes the vision that works of art and cultural heritage should be preserved and shared as widely as possible throughout the world.

Through advances in technology and connectivity, we now have a revolutionary opportunity to enhance learning, creativity and innovation, and to reach new audiences worldwide, through the reproduction and sharing of works of art and cultural heritage ('Works'). Furthermore, digital technologies can enable us to record, document and, in some instances, recreate Works threatened by environmental hazards, conflicts, terrorism, rapid economic development, mass-tourism, theft and other natural and human-caused disasters ('Endangered Works'), or Works that have already been lost.

For cultural institutions that hold collections for the benefit of the public, the opportunity to provide open access now, or in the future, to Works in a digital format is an exciting new frontier in their mission to preserve and transmit knowledge, culture and history for present and future generations. Such opportunities and possibilities also present responsibilities. Digital Records need to be responsibly created and safeguarded for the long-term, to ensure integrity as well as retrieval, and reuse by future generations. Furthermore, as the means and skills required to use and access digital technology are not distributed evenly around the world, it is incumbent on those with the capacity to do so to provide support and training.

This Declaration is intended to promote the production, sharing and preservation of digital records and reproductions ('Records') by both individuals and organisations. Owners and Stewards of Works and others involved in the process of generating these Records are encouraged to disseminate and use the ReACH Declaration as widely as possible.

The text herein is the result of an extensive global consultation on the occasion of the 150th anniversary of the 1867 H Cole Convention for Promoting Universally Reproductions of Works of Art for the Benefits of Museums of All Countries. The Convention, inspiring in its clarity, practicality and openness to the creation and sharing of reproductions, served as the basis for the establishment of this new Declaration.

The ReACH Declaration for Promoting Universally the Reproduction, Storage and Sharing of Works of Art and Cultural Heritage Through Digital Technologies was adopted at the final ReACH roundtable held at the Victoria and Albert Museum in London on 8 December 2017.

REPRODUCTION

Article 1—Stewards of Works are encouraged, for the benefit of the public of today and future generations, to take advantage of technological advances to create Records of Works entrusted to their care, for purposes of documenting and preserving all Works, but in particular Endangered Works.

Article 2—Those involved in the process of documenting and producing digital Records are encouraged to work to then-current accepted standards that support academic study and the monitoring of the condition of the original object.

Article 3—The process of documenting and producing Records should be non-invasive for the Works involved. The preservation of the Work itself remains of paramount importance. Digital Records are a tool that can support preservation, but are not a substitute for preservation.

Article 4—The process used to produce Records, as well as the intended purpose for each specific Record, should be documented, to better enable usage and interpretation of such Records today, and by future generations.

Article 5—Before making and sharing Records, the historic context of and possible cultural and national sensitivities about the Works should be considered, as well as applicable legal and ethical constraints, and the rights of donors and third parties. Transparency, and participation by communities or cultural groups with ties to the Works, should be encouraged.

STORAGE

Article 6—Digital Records should be contemporaneously archived and maintained by the Steward of the Work. Works should be recorded in a manner that renders them likely to be retrievable and reproducible even if technology changes. Enabling data migration is of paramount importance.

Article 7—The Steward of the Work should own or, at a minimum, retain unrestricted and perpetual rights to use, reproduce and share the Records, unless applicable law or a contractual agreement requires otherwise.

Article 8—Digital Records should be linked to metadata that enriches the digital asset for research, education and preservation.

Article 9—Digital and Physical Records should be marked or otherwise identified as copies using methods that are sustainable and, to the extent feasible, do not rely on technologies at risk of obsolescence. Those involved in the process of making these Records are encouraged to develop an international system to identify copies.

SHARING

Article 10—Stewards of Works are encouraged to make Records freely available to the public for personal use and enjoyment and for non-commercial research, educational, scientific and scholarly uses.

Article 11—Stewards of Works and other parties involved in the process of documenting and producing Records are encouraged to share those Records of Works as widely as possible but, in particular to reach new audiences, especially those with special needs. This includes, where possible, proactively addressing issues of equal access to digital technology on a global scale.

Article 12—Stewards of Works and other parties involved in the process of documenting and producing Records of Works are encouraged to use established and standardized licensing schemes and symbols that convey to the public the manner in which the Records of Works may be shared and reused, including open access content.

Article 13—When Records are shared and disseminated, Stewards of Works involved should provide attribution to the original author of the Works and, where practicable, provide credit to those involved in the process of documenting and producing Records of Works.

COLLABORATIONS

Article 14—Stewards of Works with resources, skills and access to digital technology are encouraged, as much as they possibly can, to provide support and training to develop the skills needed to document and produce high-quality Records to other cultural institutions in the world who lack such means.

Article 15—Stewards and other parties engaged in making Records should share digital technology, where feasible, and collaborate on strategies to make it more affordable.

Article 16—Stewards of Works and other parties engaged in making Records are encouraged to work collaboratively to develop compatible systems to enable the exchange of recorded data and metadata on a global scale. A set of specific technological standards and practical guidelines will be produced by a ReACH technical committee. These standards and guidelines will be revised as technology changes.

Article 17—In light of the major infrastructure requirements to ensure long-term preservation and transfer of digital Records, public–private partnerships should be encouraged as well as collaborations between countries.

DEFINITIONS

A.   **ReACH** stands for Reproduction of Art and Cultural Heritage.
B.   *'Work'* means a work of art or other cultural item. The term Work is intended to be broadly construed and includes, but is not limited to, works of art in all media and from all eras, for example paintings, works on paper, sculpture, murals, antiquities, monuments, architecture and architectural elements, and archaeological sites.
C.   *'Endangered Work'* means Work threatened by environmental hazards, conflicts, terrorism, mass tourism and all other natural and human-made disasters.
D.   *'Steward'* means any governmental or private entity that owns or possesses Works held for the benefit of the public. The term Steward is intended to be broadly construed and includes, but is not limited to, museums, heritage sites, monuments, libraries, repositories, archives, places of worship, whether governmental, sovereign, or private.
E.   *'Record'* means a digital recording or reproduction of a Work and the data generated in the process of faithfully capturing images and data regarding the Work so as to create a high quality digital or physical reproduction of the Work.
F.   *'High quality'* means a level of quality sufficient to constitute a representation of a Work as faithful as possible.

References

Cormier B (ed) (2018) Copy culture: sharing in the age of digital reproduction, 1st ed. V&A Publishing, p 29

Landing M (2018) Preserved in plaster. In: Cormier B (ed) Copy culture: sharing in the age of digital reproduction, 1st ed. V&A Publishing, p 41

Schwab K (2015) The fourth industrial revolution: what it means and how to respond. Foreign Affairs

Weinberger D (2019) Everyday chaos: technology, complexity and how we're thriving in a new world of possibility, 1st ed. Harvard Business Review Press, p 193

World Economic Forum (2019) This is the staggering amount of people using the internet available at https://www.weforum.org/agenda/2019/03/chart-of-the-day-more-than-half-of-the-global-population-is-now-online/. Accessed Dec 2019.

Chapter 3
Developing an Ethical Framework for the Digital Documentation of Heritage Sites

Mario Santana Quintero, Michelle Duong, and Laurie Smith

Abstract This contribution provides an overview of the potential applications and threats of technology and how the issue of ethics plays an essential role in governing the professional activity of recording heritage places. The current application of digital workflows to the understanding, promotion, and conservation of heritage sites involves many technical challenges and should be governed by strict ethical protocols. Recording involves capturing or mapping the physical character-defining elements that express the significance of heritage sites. Usually, the outcome of this work is to create the cornerstone information necessary for the conservation of the site, whether it is used directly for site maintenance, or to ensure a posterity record in case of destruction. The records produced will guide the decision-making process at different levels by property owners, site managers, public officials and conservators, as well as presenting historic knowledge and the heritage values of the site. Rigorous documentation may also serve a broader purpose: over time, it becomes the primary means by which scholars and the public apprehend a site that has since changed radically or disappeared.

Keywords Documentation · Recording · Cultural heritage · Best practice · Ethical commitment · Digital workflows

M. Santana Quintero (✉) · M. Duong · L. Smith
Carleton Immersive Media Studio, Carleton University, 1125 Colonel by Drive, Ottawa, ON K1S 5B6, Canada
e-mail: Mario.Santana@carleton.ca

M. Duong
e-mail: Michelle.Duong@carleton.ca

L. Smith
e-mail: Laurie.Smith3@carleton.ca

© Springer Nature Switzerland AG 2022   27
E. Ch'ng et al. (eds.), *Visual Heritage: Digital Approaches in Heritage Science*,
Springer Series on Cultural Computing,
https://doi.org/10.1007/978-3-030-77028-0_3

3.1 Introduction

Conserving the past is in the human DNA. Attributing significance to places and things and wanting to save them in order to pass on certain ideas is an inherent part of the human condition. Significant places are our homes and communities—they remind us of important events, people, and families in our communities and bind us together with past, present, and future generations. These places are tangible examples of education, memory, and history (Fig. 3.1).

The purpose of conserving cultural heritage is to safeguard artefacts, architecture, or historic places as they exist; to preserve their authenticity, integrity, materials, and values. By their very nature, conservators work thoughtfully, with study and testing. They work to understand the significance of these places and objects and accept that their interventions must be careful and deliberate with every possible avenue discussed, debated, and researched.

The conservation profession has gone through a logical evolution to embrace a broader perspective that is more inclusive of different approaches beyond merely physical interventions. These include the necessity for communication, interpretation, and education in relation to the values and significance of heritage sites. The profession is truly multi-disciplinary and includes not only architects and engineers but also historians, archaeologists, surveyors, and highly specialized conservators, such as those who work on wall paintings.

Fig. 3.1 Aerial image of the Paphos Theatre site, Cyprus captured using an unmanned aerial system (M. Santana Quintero) an unmanned aerial system

Alberts et al. identify the contextual challenges for the conservation of heritage places: the world today is undergoing massive changes due to global phenomena such as climate change, globalization, economic integration, human migration flows, and ongoing developments in information and communication technologies (Alberts et al. 2015). Within this framework of conditions affecting heritage places, the notion of sustainable development can be considered the most important guiding principle for the twenty-first century. Sustainability and sustainable development are increasingly shaping the worldwide discourse surrounding cultural, social, economic, and environmental issues, including those connected with heritage places.

Heritage documentation specialists, commissioned professionals, academics, and others working at for-profit or not-for-profit organizations are predominately concerned with obtaining information that can better inform the conservation of heritage sites. Impressive developments in the ability of digital technologies to record pertinent information about these sites have increased the potential information available, but also give rise to new threats that could undermine the efforts of conservation professionals to conserve and protect sites.

The application of digital techniques for recording, visualization, and fabrication (Hayes et al. 2015) of cultural heritage resources is a powerful tool. However, appropriate applications should address the conflicts and compromises involved in ensuring that these techniques will deliver adequate and reliable heritage information to support the conservation of these places as well as their dissemination. The appropriate selection and application of recording and documentation tools will be assured when the approach is based on the needs of the heritage record.

Furthermore, all records resulting from documentation activities should be kept in an accessible repository and managed as part of an integrated project dossier, using an approach that ensures longevity. For example, contributing the records to an existing digital library initiative will ensure that the information can be updated and transferred in the future and that the appropriate provenance information will be included so that future users can judge the integrity and quality of those records (e.g., date of compilation, author, accuracy, etc.).

A holistic approach is of paramount importance, centred in the relevance of the information to understand the significance, integrity, and threats to our heritage. Value continues to be a crucial concept in defining the extent and practicality of capturing and disseminating knowledge of heritage places.

This contribution will first consider the relevant background to this issue: the extent to which heritage is under threat; the concept of heritage conservation as a value-centred activity, and the Ethical Principles developed by the International Committee on Monuments and Sites (ICOMOS). The central discussion will consider the need for and recommended components of an ethical framework to address the issue. The conclusion will consider what steps might be taken next.

3.2 Background

3.2.1 Is Heritage Under Threat?

Heritage sites do not die; they are damaged, demolished, or destroyed. The effects of natural disasters, like fires, earthquakes, flooding, landslides, storms, and hurricanes, are amongst the major causes of loss and damage to physical objects and human lives. These disasters result in irreplaceable losses to the integrity of heritage sites (UNESCO 2011).

The loss of cultural heritage is also due to armed conflicts, terrorism, negligence, and abandonment (Fig. 3.2).

Although it is impossible to estimate the number of properties designated as "heritage" by federal, provincial, and local authorities in each country, this number is growing significantly. A large number of these properties require some degree of documentation to identify risk, monitor the physical condition, assess value, and understand their contribution to history, as well as to design management and conservation programs for their protection in the short, mid, and long terms.

In addition to the expanding number of properties that are considered cultural heritage, there are new issues to consider within heritage conservation files, such as the impact of adapting and mitigating the effects of climate change; meeting sustainability targets; and adapting sites to meet updated construction codes and requirements.

Heritage sites face two potential threats from the effects of climate change. Firstly, will they have the resilience to survive increased temperatures, flooding, fires, etc.?

Fig. 3.2 Carved rock face collapsed at Petra Archaeological Park, 2011 (M. Santana Quintero)

Secondly, will government pressure to reduce CO_2 emissions by making the Architecture, Engineering, and Construction Industry more energy-efficient favouring the replacement of heritage structures with new net-zero dwellings and infrastructure?

Arguably, the most energy-efficient new building cannot offset its embodied energy for many years. Rehabilitating existing structures, especially those with significant value, can contribute to the reduction of the carbon footprint and may help mitigate the acceleration of climate change.

Gelfand and Duncan argue that "the vast majority of the buildings to be occupied during the next thirty years are already constructed[;] existing buildings are the most important places to realize big changes now and in the near future" (Gelfand and Duncan 2011). As suggested by the National Trust for Historic Preservation report "The Greenest Building: Quantifying the Environmental Value of Building Reuse" (2011), "for those concerned with climate change and other environmental impacts, reusing an existing building and upgrading it to maximum efficiency is almost always the best option regardless of building type and climate, reusing existing buildings can offer an essential means of avoiding unnecessary carbon outlays and help communities achieve their carbon reduction goals in the near term." Expertise and resources on how to document the energy performance of existing buildings are needed to effect these changes.

In many instances, these issues are being addressed in the field. However, in order to develop and deploy advanced digital technologies, materials, and methods for the assessment, conservation, rehabilitation, and sustainability of existing structures and designated heritage buildings, there is a pressing and critical need for interdisciplinary training amongst heritage specialists, authorities, and community stakeholders in general. In addition, there is a growing concern about over-reliance on digital recording as a means to preserve heritage sites. For example, many organizations currently working in the field of recording cultural heritage claim that they are making digital reproductions of sites for long-term safeguarding. This is an overly simplistic approach to addressing the issue—recording the outer aspect of a heritage resource only allows us to record one layer of the many layers of meaning associated with a heritage site.

Sustainability is a crucial concept in heritage conservation. While the involvement of experts is necessary for most conservation projects, the meaningful engagement of local community organizations can ensure that projects will be sustainable and achievable in the long term. Participatory processes are fundamental and essential in achieving the protection of cultural heritage.

3.2.2 Heritage Is a Value-Centred Activity

According to the Standards and Guidelines for the Conservation of Historic Places in Canada, in the conservation field, scientists and practitioners operate in what is referred to as a 'values-based context' using a system that identifies and manages heritage places according to values attributed through an evaluation process (Parks Canada 2010).

Values attributed to monuments, places, and landscapes are at the core of decision-making in conservation and risk management plans. Studies aimed at protecting, promoting, or conserving a site are based on the identification and evaluation of its inherent values.

Understanding the significance of a site is of paramount importance; a values-based study is a preliminary step for the assessment of risk impact, the identification of priorities, and the application of mitigation strategies. The outcome of such a study, using internationally recognized value assessment systems, will provide an indication of the required level of integrity necessary to preserve an important heritage property.

3.2.3   ICOMOS Ethical Principles

The International Council on Monuments and Sites (ICOMOS), founded in Warsaw in 1965, is the largest not-for-profit organization dedicated to conserving and promoting the world's Cultural Heritage. ICOMOS is also the official advisory body on Cultural Heritage to the UNESCO World Heritage Committee, developing theoretical and practical guidance on best practices.

ICOMOS is a network of experts that benefits from the interdisciplinary exchange of its members, amongst whom are architects, historians, archaeologists, art historians, geographers, anthropologists, engineers, and town planners. Currently, ICOMOS counts over 10,000 individuals and 320 institutions amongst its members in 153 countries. Furthermore, it has established 110 National Committees and 28 International Scientific Committees in relevant thematic areas of conservation.

The members of ICOMOS contribute to improving the preservation of heritage sites by applying the standards and techniques that are appropriate for each type of cultural heritage property: buildings, historic cities, cultural landscapes, and archaeological sites.

One of the most significant contributions of ICOMOS has been to strengthen the concepts of cultural heritage authenticity and integrity, which are the basis of world-wide policies for the conservation of cultural heritage. In 2014, ICOMOS launched the ICOMOS Ethical Principles for its members; these articles allow ICOMOS to govern the roles and responsibilities of its members. They will be used in this contribution to argue the need for an ethical framework.

3.3   An Emerging Framework

In any professional association that serves the public interest, members have to abide by a number of ethical principles. This is currently missing in the heritage recording field. For this reason, in the framework of this contribution, six ethical categories have been selected from the ICOMOS Ethical Principles (ICOMOS 2014) and one supplementary category from the Canadian Association of Heritage Professionals (CAHP) Code of Professional Conduct and Ethics (CAHP 2017). These represent the most common ethical issues identified in the reviewed literature:

- related to ethical conduct;
- related to best practices;
- related to cultural heritage;
- related to the public and communities;
- related to other heritage recording specialists; and
- related to qualifications.

3.3.1   Related to Ethical Conduct

This category relates to the professional behaviour of specialists when conducting their activities: showing respect, integrity, impartiality, accountability, and maintaining open, upright, and tolerant attitudes. This also addresses issues related to conflicts of interest.

3.3.2   Related to Best Practices

This category relates to the professional advice and services that heritage recording specialists render to potential clients or community stakeholders. Also, it relates to the accessibility, retrieval, and posterity of records produced by specialists for the enjoyment of future generations.

3.3.3   Related to Cultural Heritage

This category relates to respect for the values and integrity of cultural heritage, as well as preparedness in case of deterioration or damage.

3.3.4   Related to the Public and Communities

This category relates to the acknowledgement of the role of the public and communities in the conservation of cultural heritage. It also relates to the promotion of heritage recording amongst the public and the transmission of documented information to present and future generations. Issues concerning the privacy rights of communities to share knowledge about their heritage and rights-based approaches are also considered.

3.3.5   Related to Other Heritage Recording Specialists

This category relates to the behaviour of recording specialists towards other experts in the cultural heritage field in terms of collegiality, consideration, exchanging of expertise, and mentoring of others. Recognizing and respecting differences of opinion, interdisciplinarity, and solidarity are also included.

3.3.6   Related to Qualifications

This category relates to the need for heritage recording specialists to have appropriate qualifications, such as certification or university training. In addition, it relates to the commitment of heritage recording specialists to professional development and their participation in specialist conferences in order to present their approaches and obtain valuable feedback.

3.4   Discussion

Interventions to heritage sites require experts to gather a variety of information, ranging from historical to physical. Experts should improve the communication and management of different types of acquired data; interaction amongst experts is always encouraged.

There is a vast number of digital tools available; many of them can be useful to professionals studying heritage. However, because they have been predominantly created for other purposes, the job of a heritage recording specialist is to develop an optimal workflow to offer reliable, cost-effective results for recording historic places. The quality of the workflow can be judged in terms of performance, speed, field operability restrictions, and other essential variables. This is important, as cultural heritage funding is scarce.

In recent years, a debate has emerged around the speed at which new technologies have emerged, and the complex and problematic manner in which some of these techniques have been adopted in heritage recording.

The speedy adoption of new technologies has sometimes given rise to misleading attempts to document heritage places that offer only limited perspectives on those heritage places based on minimal amounts of information. These include idealized visualizations of the state of conservation that provide only simple geometric representations of assets at the site. The best solution to avoid using incompatible or obsolete equipment is the careful study of the different technologies available and consultation with heritage recording specialists.

In this respect, the role of the heritage recording specialist is essential. In this contribution, it is argued that the development of an ethical framework can support better design, planning, implementation, and information sharing of digital workflows for heritage conservation in a number of relevant ways:

- to assist heritage recording specialists in meeting obligations that will improve the role of digital information in the decision-making process for the conservation of heritage places;
- to assist international governmental and non-governmental organizations to draft terms of reference for the design and implementation of digital workflows in the conservation of heritage places;
- to update the ICOMOS Principles for the Recording of Monuments, Groups of Buildings and Sites (1996) to address new challenges and opportunities presented by digital information in the conservation of heritage places;
- to prevent the use of digital workflows that might negatively affect the communities associated with heritage places;
- to improve the collegiality of heritage recording specialists and encourage the exchange of practice points between members, making digital workflows more effective and sustainable;
- to improve information sharing amongst stakeholders and the public in general who use digital workflows for the conservation of heritage places; and
- to provide a framework for the preservation of digital records produced by these workflows that will allow for future accessibility.

Furthermore, it is important to point out that there are a number of potential beneficiaries to the correct application of ethical principles in heritage recording:

- the heritage recording specialist. As explained extensively in the literature review outlined below, the specialist will benefit from the possibility of practising her/his work without prejudice and in a collaborative manner;
- the public in general, including communities who live on heritage sites and those who are interested in the conservation of cultural heritage; and
- cultural heritage organizations, including for-profit, not-for-profit, government, intergovernmental, academic, and funding agencies.

3.5 Professional Obligations to Meet an Ethical Commitment

A substantial literature review was conducted on the existing ethical principles and codes of professional practice available to heritage recording specialists. These included the ICOMOS Ethical Principles (ICOMOS 2014), academic literature, and the Royal Institution of Chartered Surveyors' (RICS) Global Professional and Ethical Standards (RICS 2018).

During this research period, a number of interviews were conducted with: professionals specializing in the conservation of heritage places, not-for-profit organizations working in the field of digital heritage, and contractors.

Using a relational database, quotes were extracted from the literature review revealing around 70 ethical obligations that a heritage recording specialist should meet. These obligations were then classified into one or more of the six ethical categories previously described.

In the following paragraphs, a selection of these obligations and their relation to the ethical categories are provided.

3.5.1 Obligation to Produce High-Quality Records

A clear example of obligations related to the "best practices" category is the production of "high quality" digital records. In the ReACH Declaration (V & A 2017), this concept is defined as "with a level of quality sufficient to constitute a representation…as faithful as possible."

Further, with respect to the degree of quality, it is also important to take into consideration the following methodological obligations:

- abide by principles of objectivity, reliability, and validity of scholarly claims (Munster et al. 2016);
- "appropriate scope, level, and methods of recording" should be applied and "records must clearly and accurately identify and locate the heritage places" (Letellier 2011); and
- use the best approach and justify (ICOMOS 2014).

Furthermore, this obligation can be linked to ethical conduct issues, such as "objective, rigorous and scientific" methods (ICOMOS 2014) and providing the best service, advice, and support according to the terms of agreement (RICS 2018).

To illustrate these obligations, in 2017 the GCI commissioned the Carleton Immersive Media Studio (CIMS) to record the as-found condition of historically decorated surfaces of KV 62—Tomb of Tutankhamen in order to produce a high-quality post-conservation digital record for posterity.

Following Letellier (2011) and utilizing the appropriate and suitable technology such as 3D scanning and photogrammetry, CIMS produced high-resolution ortho-corrected photographic elevations with millimeter resolution and accurate colour correction (see Figs. 3.3 and 3.4).

The production of this deliverable was explained in the project report, meeting the obligation to "be transparent" in the working procedures used so that the work is understood (RICS 2018).

Fig. 3.3 Recording the surface of the burial chamber of the Tomb of Tutankhamen using 3D scanning, for The Getty Conservation Institute (M. Santana Quintero)

Fig. 3.4 Ortho-corrected image of the as-found condition of the north facade of the burial chamber of the Tomb of Tutankhamen after conservation, for The Getty Conservation Institute (C. Ouimet and M. Santana Quintero)

3.5.2 Obligation to Raise Awareness with Digital Heritage Records: What About Conflict of Interest, Preventing Personal Gain, and Respecting Privacy?

This obligation is controversial, especially with the increasing practice of capturing images of heritage places and their communities using Remotely Piloted Aircraft Systems (RPAS) or as commonly known as drones or Unmanned Aerial Systems (UAS) (see Fig. 3.5). There are issues related to privacy but also to the ability to capture accurate information of as-found conditions, particularly in areas affected by conflict.

For example, the important work conducted by ICONEM and their exhibit at the Arab World Institute in 2018–2019 involved the extensive mapping of the devastation in Syria and the production of an impressively immersive experience.

This exhibition raised awareness of the impact of war on heritage, therefore meeting the obligation to "support the promotion of public awareness" and "community involvement in cultural heritage conservation" (ICOMOS 2014).

However, in terms of potential conflict of interest, it can be argued that the organizers have gained a lot of credibility and fame by exposing this work to the public. The CAHP Code of Professional Conduct and Ethics (2017) recommends that all information gathered should be regarded as confidential and that personal or financial gain shall not be taken. Also, these images may have been taken without the consent of the community—as suggested by ICOMOS Australia (1998), in conservation it

Fig. 3.5 Drone undertaking heritage mapping (M. Santana Quintero)

is important to accept "the cultural right of groups to withhold certain information" (ICOMOS 1988).

An alarming investigation by Thompson on the status of copyright and other intellectual property law considerations of digitization projects in Syria raises "digital colonialism" concerns, given the fact that these projects are conducted by Western experts and that in many cases Western attention has not always proven beneficial for either the historical or modern residents of Middle Eastern sites (Thompson 2017).

This illustrates the profound need to balance the obligation to raise awareness with the obligation to respect the cultural right to privacy. The potential positive and/or negative impacts of the products of these technologies on local communities require further attention.

3.5.3 Obligation to Ensure Transmission of Information to Present and Future Generations

As described by the Archaeology Data Service (ADS), and English Heritage, the two organizations have "collaboratively conducted a project that sets out a programme for investigating preservation (storage methods), reuse (usability) and dissemination (delivery mechanism) strategies for exceptionally large data files generated by archaeologists, researchers and cultural resource managers undertaking fieldwork and other research" (ADS 2007).

However, "currently there is little understanding of the implications for cost and good practice in data preservation, dissemination, reuse and access. This lack of understanding is potentially exacerbated by the proprietary nature of formats generally used by the new research technologies now being used in archaeology and cultural resource management" (ADS 2007).

The project seeks to answer immediate questions regarding cost and to develop recommendations and strategies for archaeologists, researchers, cultural resource managers, and archivists dealing with 'Big Data'. The project recognizes that computing capacity, both to create and to archive data, will continue to rise.

This project exemplifies obligations related to the best practice category, such as the obligation to ensure that "complete, durable, and accessible records" (ICOMOS 2014) are "kept in a central repository" (Letellier 2011). In this interface, the heritage records are described, stored, and retrievable, guaranteeing their longevity for posterity (Cormier 2018).

Also, in a partnership between York University and Historic England (formerly part of English Heritage), the two organizations have developed a sustainability strategy to "ensure that [digital record] processes and outcomes [are] preserved for transmission to future generations" (Denard 2009).

3.5.4 Obligation to Ensure Procedural Transparency When Producing Records

Cultural Heritage Imaging, a not-for-profit organization, is currently developing the Digital Lab Notebook (DLN), "a software pipeline made up of open source software tools and associated good practices. The DLN provides a greatly simplified, ordinary-language-based, nearly automatic method to build the digital equivalent of a scientist's lab notebook" (CHI 2018).

This DLN software will allow a heritage recording specialist "to radically simplify the scientific workflow used to digitally capture, build, archive, and reuse the digital representations that document humanity's cultural heritage" (CHI 2018).

The transparency provided by the DLN separates "scientific reliability" from "academic authority" (CHI 2018).

This initiative is an excellent example of providing procedural transparency by allowing other experts to assess the quality of the records produced and to make use of the data more easily.

3.5.5 Obligation of Sharing Technology and Collaborating to Make It More Affordable

The Arches Project "is an open-source, geospatially-enabled software platform for cultural heritage inventory and management, developed jointly by the Getty Conservation Institute (GCI) and World Monuments Fund (WMF)" (GCI 2019).

The GCI and WMF have endeavoured to tackle a number of issues in the field of heritage recording, several of which are very relevant to meeting ethical obligations. By organizing workshops and training sessions and supporting an online forum (see Fig. 3.6), Arches is promoting the further development of its system through a continuous exchange between experts, helping to develop the profession by advancing knowledge, and improving methods and technical applications. This, as stated in the ReACH declaration, "encourages sharing technology and collaborat[ing] to make them more affordable" (V&A 2017).

Furthermore, the system has been designed with "clear documentation policies" (Letellier 2011) and is transparent and customizable to the needs of specific heritage organizations.

Fig. 3.6 Arches workshop during the 26th CIPA International Symposium on Heritage Documentation, Ottawa, Canada (M. Santana Quintero)

3.5.6 Obligation to Commit to Provide Training and Capacity Building to Fellow and Emerging Experts

The Conservation and Rehabilitation Plan for the Kasbah of Taourirt project in Morocco is a project of the GCI and the Centre de Conservation et de Réhabilitation du Patrimoine Architectural des zones atlasiques et subatlasiques (CERKAS).

In this project, CIMS developed a recording and capacity-building approach to record the as-found condition of the Kasbah that would assist in the training of Moroccan experts.

The Cancino et al. (2016) report on the "CERKAS documentation resources assessment" underlines that an appropriate metric survey of Kasbah Taourirt to produce "as-found" CAD drawings (annotated floor plans, cross-sections, and elevations) was needed (see Figs. 3.7 and 3.8).

Furthermore, to achieve this as-found record, a combination of image-based surveying tools, such as photogrammetry, and architectural surveying devices, such as a total station, was used. These techniques were selected in order to transmit the skills to the CERKAS team utilizing off-the-shelf technology. This aligns with the ICOMOS Ethical Principles "need for capacity building" (ICOMOS 2014) and the Seville principles statement, "heritage recording is a discipline that requires specific training" (International Forum of Virtual Archaeology 2011).

Lastly, the records were used by an interdisciplinary team to design and implement the rehabilitation plan (see Fig. 3.9). The information produced was used to create

Fig. 3.7 CIMS team training CERKAS experts on recording techniques (The Getty Conservation Institute)

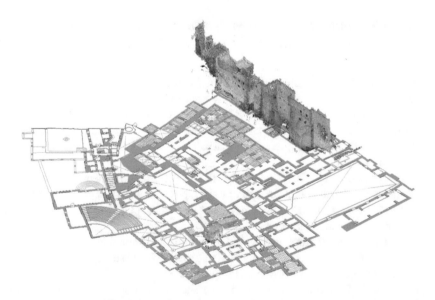

Fig. 3.8 3D point cloud from photogrammetry used for the preparation of accurate line drawings of the Kasbah of Taourirt (The Getty Conservation Institute and Carleton Immersive Media Studio)

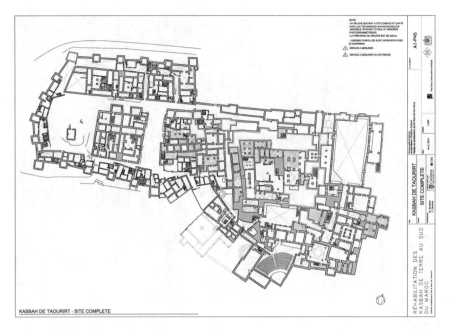

Fig. 3.9 Line drawing for the rehabilitation plan of the Kasbah of Taourirt (Prepared for The Getty Conservation Institute using various recording methods)

a posterity record, given that the Kasbah is endangered by the effects of climate change. These approaches illustrate two obligations set out in the ICOMOS Ethical Principles: to obtain "interdisciplinary reflections" in the work and, "where cultural heritage is in immediate danger or at risk, ICOMOS members offer all possible assistance that is practicable and appropriate, provided that it does not put their own health and safety or that of others in jeopardy" (ICOMOS 2014).

3.5.7 Obligation to Participate in Professional Networks to Share Experiences and Further Development of Heritage Recording Practices

The active participation of heritage recording specialists on the ICOMOS/ISPRS scientific committee on heritage documentation (CIPA) as expert members, as well as attending summer schools, biennial symposia, and other gatherings meets several important ethical obligations, such as:

- exchange with other experts, especially internationally (ICOMOS 2014);
- increased public understanding of professional practice (NCPH 2007); and

Fig. 3.10 CIPA 2017 symposium attendees, Christian Ouimet (C. Ouimet and M. Santana Quintero)

- helping to develop the profession by advancing knowledge, improving methods and technical applications (NCPH 2007).

Through its website http://cipa.icomos.org, CIPA provides not only access to an international body of experts (see Fig. 3.10), but also to a considerable amount of research and project papers on the topic of recording cultural heritage for conservation. These contributions provide an informed perspective on the types of approaches and techniques utilized in the field.

Membership in an expert group allows the heritage recording specialist to acquire credibility and become a better-informed specialist. As indicated by Letellier (2011) "heritage recording should be done primarily by professionals."

3.6 Biohazards and Lockdown Affecting Access to Heritage Places: What Is the Potential Role of Digital Technologies?

The declaration of a global pandemic and the subsequent lockdowns worldwide have generated unprecedented impacts on cultural heritage. According to Rossler, director of the UNESCO World Heritage Centre (UNESCO 2020), 90% of state parties who are signatories to the World Heritage convention have fully or partially closed sites during the quarantine.

The ongoing effects of the COVID-19 crisis point to a lack of preparedness in dealing with the potential impacts of biohazards and the need to update procedures. UNESCO's Managing Disasters for World Heritage, published in 2020, only mentions epidemics in a typology of hazards caused by infrastructure failure and deals mostly with hydrological issues caused by high rainfall (UNESCO 2010).

Government, academia, industry, and public organizations have recognized the importance of digital technologies in mitigating and adapting to the realities of the COVID-19 pandemic. For example, artificial intelligence and supercomputers have been deployed to understand the spread of the virus, develop treatments, and design strategies to return to normal conditions.

Heritage sites raise unique concerns—not only can visitors not access sites, but the absence of security staff and site custodians can lead to secondary threats such as looting, fires, earthquakes, and floods. Digital technologies are proving to be a key component in providing remote access for staff and visitors, monitoring sites, reducing risk, and eventually ensuring safe re-entry.

A growing push to strengthen networks, online platforms, connectivity, and telecommunications have allowed many people to remain at home. This digital revolution has allowed a substantial number of heritage organizations to quickly move their existing digital assets to social media and digital platforms.

One example is the platform created by Google Arts and Culture in partnership with UNESCO. It hosts digital exhibits with thousands of photographs, street views, and written narratives of heritage places, which provide access for the community at large and communicate the Outstanding Universal Values of these places.

Other examples include: using the Internet to take a semi-immersive tour of the Sydney Opera House while listening to the soprano Nicole Car and the Sydney Symphony Orchestra (Google Arts and Culture); enjoying an immersive virtual experience of the iconic elements of the Canadian Parliament buildings (Parliament of Canada), and visiting the temples of Angkor Wat with a tour guide on YouTube using 360-degree videos (VR Gorilla).

The pandemic situation has also provided evidence of the vital role played by the communities that live adjacent to heritage sites and their relationship with site managers. Site managers have prepared several video reports that have been sent to UNESCO World Heritage Centre, which are posted in an online repository. These videos provide updates about their sites during this difficult time (UNESCO World Heritage Centre).

Two of the most important roles that digital tools can play in mitigating the impacts of the pandemic and the associated requirements to quarantine and socially distance, are: providing public access using digital storytelling platforms, and potentially providing remote access to monitor sites.

Addressing the first issue of access to the public, a series of five webinars on the topic "Accessing Heritage Places from Home" was organized in the spring and summer of 2020 by the Emerging Professionals of the ICOMOS Scientific Committee on Heritage Documentation (CIPA) in collaboration with the National Trust for

Canada, the NSERC CREATE Heritage Engineering program and ICOMOS. The webinar series had over four hundred participants from places such as Canada, Italy, Jordan, Palestine, Australia, India, the Philippines, and Indonesia. The final webinar dealt with the need for a code of ethical principles that would apply to the heritage recording specialist in terms of conduct, responsibilities, and professional practice, especially when "Accessing Heritage Places from Home".

Some key points were made within these webinars about the need for inclusiveness and transparent communication, consultation, accessibility, ownership/access to/control of digital information, and including different voices within the community.

For example, consideration should be given to who is involved in the production of the record, the type of interpretation that is utilized, the format for dissemination (e.g. semi-interactive, static, immersive), and the need for adequate archiving for longevity and posterity of data.

Participants asked: who has control over gathering and using the data? What power lies in communication? To what extent should we control access through laws, policy, private agreements, etc.? How have the expectations shifted since the release of the ICOMOS Principles for the recording of monuments, groups of buildings, and sites in 1996 in terms of accessibility, ownership, and fair use?

Ethical behaviour is thinking beyond our own interests and values (person or organization) to consider those of the community and the world. When we create an ethical code of conduct, we are agreeing on a decision-making framework in which we will privilege the priorities of the group above our own.

We need to engage in honest dialogue with each other, to discover the realities of our situations and the true impacts of our actions. Because these can change over time, it is important to revisit past ethical frameworks to confirm whether they are still relevant. The practical result of the ethics webinar was the creation of a working group that will revise the ICOMOS Principles for the recording of monuments, groups of buildings, and sites (1996) with contributions from different voices and stakeholders.

3.7 Conclusions

3.7.1 Closing Remarks

The information retrieved from historic places is unique and irreplaceable; it supports the identification and classification of heritage sites so that custodians and decision-makers can develop appropriate policies for conservation and maintenance, as well as to promote and interpret those sites for cultural tourism. The records produced can also serve as posterity information for future generations.

Recording and documentation are very important components in the process of understanding and protecting a heritage site. Base data created during the recording phase allows experts to make decisions on the appropriate interventions to augment and conserve heritage sites.

Recent developments in digital technologies provide new approaches to increase the efficiency of documenting heritage places and disseminating that information. These technologies should be used wisely, meaning that they should be adapted to the needs of the process, the realities of the field of valuing and studying monuments, and with respect for the custodian communities. To achieve this, it is important to consider the condition of the fabric of the heritage place, its history, values, stakeholders, and other components.

3.7.2 What's Next

The content of this chapter focused on identifying obligations that would form a framework of ethical principles relevant to the duties of heritage recording specialists involved in the conservation of heritage places. One of the key goals of the framework is to ensure that the records produced are shared in the present and the future using sustainable strategies.

This work emphasizes the need to develop ethical benchmarks for utilizing digital workflows that will respect the cultural heritage values of sites and the communities associated with them, while allowing for the dissemination and secure storage of digital knowledge about sites.

The next steps involve formulating a platform for experts to discuss ethical principles and a code of ethics to govern the work of heritage recording specialists. Some suggested activities include:

- organizing several panels with heritage recording specialists;
- designing an online survey to collect opinions from different stakeholders;
- producing a publication with best practice examples that illustrate the fulfilment of obligations to meet ethical principles;
- developing, updating, and launching new doctrinal documents to assist heritage recording specialists with their work; and,
- developing a ranking system to assess and accredit organizations that record heritage places.

Acknowledgements The author would like to thank the Getty Conservation Institute for the support provided to conduct the scholarly work that are the basis of this chapter and for providing access to their knowledge and expertise. Further thanks to Reem Baroody, Claudia Cancino, David Carson, Martha Demas, Leslie Friedman, David Myers, Tom Roby, Reem Awad, Lorinda Wong, and other colleagues from the Getty Conservation Institute and Carleton Immersive Media Studio, who provided useful information for this contribution.

References

ADS (Archaeology Data Service), and English Heritage (2007) Preservation and management strategies for exceptionally large data formats: 'Big Data'. https://archaeologydataservice.ac.uk/resources/attach/bigdata_final_report_1.3.pdf. Accessed 27 Dec 2019

Albert M, Lawrence C, Andreyev J (2015) Perceptions of sustainability in heritage studies. De Gruyter, Berlin

CAHP (The Canadian Association of Heritage Professionals) (2017) Code of professional conduct and ethics. https://cahp-acecp.ca/wp-content/uploads/2017/07/2017-CAHP-ACECP-Code-of-Conduct-Ethics-Agreement.pdf. Accessed 8 Dec 2019

Cancino C, Marcus B, Boussalh M (2016) Conservation and rehabilitation plan for Tighermt (Kasbah) Taourirt, Southern Morocco. The Getty Conservation Institute, Los Angeles; CERKAS, Ouarzazate, Morocco. http://www.getty.edu/conservation/publications_resources/pdf_publicati ons/pdf/taourirt_plan.pdf. Accessed 7 Dec 2019

CHI (Cultural Heritage Imaging) (2018) Digital Lab Notebook (DLN). http://culturalheritageim aging.org/Technologies/Digital_Lab_Notebook/. Accessed 8 Dec 2019

Cormier B (ed) (2018) Copy culture: sharing in the age of digital reproduction. V&A Publishing, London. https://vanda-production-assets.s3.amazonaws.com/2018/06/15/11/42/57/e8582248-8878-486e-8a28-ebb8bf74ace8/Copy%20Culture.pdf. Accessed 31 Dec 2019

Denard H (d) (2009) The London Charter for the computer-based visualisation of cultural heritage. http://www.londoncharter.org/. Accessed 11 Dec 2019

GCI (The Getty Conservation Institute), and WMF (World Monuments Fund) (2019) What is arches? https://www.archesproject.org/what-is-arches/. Accessed 09 Dec 2019

Gelfand L, Duncan C (2011) Sustainable renovation: strategies for commercial building systems and envelope. Wiley, Hoboken, NJ

Google Arts and Culture (2020) Opera Australia. https://artsandculture.google.com/exhibit/opera-australia-sydney-opera-house/qAKy4JYquM0VJg?hl=en. Accessed 1 Sept 2020

Hayes J, Fai S, Kretz S, Ouimet C, White P (2015) Digitally-assisted stone carving of a relief sculpture for the parliament buildings national historic site of Canada. ISPRS Ann Photogramm Remote Sens Spat Inf Sci II-5/W3(5):97–103. https://doi.org/10.5194/isprsannals-II-5-W3-97-2015

ICOMOS (International Council of Monuments and Sites) (1996) Principles for the recording of monuments, groups of buildings and sites. https://www.icomos.org/charters/archives-e.pdf. Accessed 18 Dec 2019

ICOMOS (International Council of Monuments and Sites) Australia (1998) Code on the ethics of co-existence in conserving significant places. https://australia.icomos.org/wp-content/uploads/Code-on-the-Ethics-of-Co-existence-in-Conserving-Significant-Places-1998.pdf (8 December 2019)

ICOMOS (International Council of Monuments and Sites) (2014) Ethical principles. https://www.icomos.org/images/DOCUMENTS/Secretariat/2015/GA_2014_results/20150114-ethics-asadopted-languagecheck-finalcirc.pdf. Accessed 8 Dec 2019

International Forum of Virtual Archaeology (2011) The Seville principles: international principles of virtual archaeology. http://smartheritage.com/wp-content/uploads/2015/03/FINAL-DRAFT.pdf. Accessed 11 Dec 2019

Letellier R (2011) Recording, documentation, and information management for the conservation of heritage places: guiding principles. Donhead Publishing, Dorset

Munster S, Hegel W, Krober C (2016) A model classification for digital 3D reconstruction in the context of humanities research. In: Munster S, Pfarr-Harfst M, Kuroczynski P, Ioannides M (eds) 3D research challenges in cultural heritage II: how to manage data and knowledge related to interpretive digital 3D reconstructions of cultural heritage. Springer, Cham, pp 3–31

NCPH (National Council on Public History) (2007) Code of ethics and professional conduct. https://ncph.org/about/governance-committees/code-of-ethics-and-professional-conduct/. Accessed 7 Dec 2019

Parks Canada (2010) Standards and guidelines for the conservation of historic places in Canada a federal, provincial and territorial collaboration. https://www.historicplaces.ca/en/pages/standards-normes. Accessed 7 Dec 2019

Parliament of Canada (2020) Parliament: the virtual experience. https://learn.parl.ca/sites/Learn/default/en_CA/VR. Accessed 1 Sept 2020

Preservation Green Lab National Trust for Historic Preservation (2011) The greenest building: quantifying the environmental value of building reuse. https://living-future.org/wp-content/uploads/2016/11/The_Greenest_Building.pdf. Accessed 7 Dec2019

RICS (Royal Institution of Chartered Surveyors) (2018) Regulation: the global professional and ethical standards. https://www.rics.org/globalassets/rics-website/media/upholding-professional-standards/standards-of-conduct/the-global-professional-and-ethical-standards.pdf. Accessed 8 Dec 2019

Thompson EL (2017) Legal and ethical considerations for digital recreations of cultural heritage. Chapman Law Rev 20(1):153–176

UNESCO World Heritage Centre (2010) Managing disasters for world heritage. https://whc.unesco.org/en/managing-disaster-risks/. Accessed 15 May 2020

UNESCO World Heritage Centre (2011) Preparing world heritage nominations. http://whc.unesco.org/en/preparing-world-heritage-nominations/. Accessed 15 Dec 2019

UNESCO World Heritage Centre (2020) Site managers' report on Covid-19. https://whc.unesco.org/en/news/2101. Accessed 1 Sept 2020

V & A (Victoria and Albert Museum) (2017) ReACH declaration on reproduction of art and cultural heritage. https://vanda-production-assets.s3.amazonaws.com/2017/12/15/14/49/22/a743acd8-6522-48ce-8700-7b78e59c8bf2/ReACHDeclaration.pdf. Accessed 19 Dec 2019

VR Gorilla (2019) Angkor Wat & Siem Reap Cambodia guided tour—6K 360 VR Video. https://www.youtube.com/watch?v=66rRr3fFTLw. Accessed 1 Sept 2020

Chapter 4
Curious Travellers: Using Web-Scraped and Crowd-Sourced Imagery in Support of Heritage Under Threat

Andrew S. Wilson, Vincent Gaffney, Chris Gaffney, Eugene Ch'ng, Richard Bates, Elgidius B. Ichumbaki, Gareth Sears, Tom Sparrow, Andrew Murgatroyd, Eddy Faber, Adrian Evans, and Robin Coningham

Abstract Designed as a pragmatic approach that anticipates change to cultural heritage, this chapter discusses responses that encompass records for tangible cultural heritage (monuments, sites and landscapes) and the narratives that see the impact upon them. The Curious Travellers project provides a mechanism for digitally documenting heritage sites that have been destroyed or are under immediate threat from unsympathetic development, neglect, natural disasters, conflict and cultural vandalism. The project created and tested data-mining and crowd-sourced workflows that enable the accurate digital documentation and 3D visualisation of buildings, archaeological sites, monuments and heritage at risk. When combined with donated content, image data are used to recreate 3D models of endangered and lost monuments and heritage sites using a combination of open-source and proprietary methods. These models are queried against contextual information, helping to place and interrogate structures with relevant site and landscape data for the surrounding environment. Geospatial records such as aerial imagery and 3D mobile mapping laser scan data serve as a framework for adding new content and testing accuracy.

A. S. Wilson (✉) · V. Gaffney · C. Gaffney · T. Sparrow · A. Murgatroyd · E. Faber · A. Evans
Visualising Heritage, School of Archaeological & Forensic Sciences, University of Bradford, Bradford, UK
e-mail: a.s.wilson2@bradford.ac.uk

E. Ch'ng
NVIDIA Joint-Lab on Mixed Reality, University of Nottingham Ningbo China, Ningbo, China

R. Bates
School of Earth Sciences, University of St Andrews, St Andrews, Scotland

E. B. Ichumbaki
Department of Archaeology and Heritage Studies, University of Dar-Es-Salaam, Dar es Salaam, Tanzania

G. Sears
Department of Classics, Ancient History and Archaeology, University of Birmingham, Birmingham, UK

R. Coningham
Department of Archaeology, University of Durham, Durham, UK

© Springer Nature Switzerland AG 2022   51
E. Ch'ng et al. (eds.), *Visual Heritage: Digital Approaches in Heritage Science*,
Springer Series on Cultural Computing,
https://doi.org/10.1007/978-3-030-77028-0_4

In preserving time-event records, image metadata offers important information on visitor habits and conservation pressures, which can be used to inform measures for site management.

Keywords UNESCO · Heritage conservation · SfM photogrammetry · Multi-view stereo

4.1 Introduction

Cultural heritage is subject to immense pressures, with potential change evident whether due to policy, practice or the challenges of upkeep and change of use at the individual level. The United Kingdom, in common with many countries, has organisations in the public, private and charitable sectors that are involved with the upkeep of heritage sites. Yet, many countries do not have the benefit of unified historic environment records, and thus do not have the baseline information, let alone the mechanisms to document sites, monitor change and ensure that rich records exist to inform, connect with and support societal needs.

Cultural heritage sites face many challenges ranging from the fragile nature of construction materials used (Prieto et al. 2019); their remoteness (Hammer et al. 2018); to agricultural encroachment, largescale looting and urban/industrial sprawl (Hesse 2015), large and small-scale developments (Ichumbaki and Mjema 2018) as well as pressure from increased tourist numbers (Allen and Lennon 2018). A recent study has shown that around 60% of all UNESCO world heritage sites are at potential risk from geological hazards (Pavlova et al. 2017). Other potential risks include fire (Wilson et al. 2018) and flooding (Cigna et al. 2018; Langhammer and Vackova 2018), which points to the need for disaster risk preparedness (Coningham et al. 2019; Ravez et al. 2019). The challenge of loss with built heritage has begun to be recognised more widely—as with architectural heritage in Qatar (Fali and AlSaeed 2019), with heritage now a key consideration as part of urban regeneration in developing countries (Amado and Rodrigues 2019).

Within the past 5–10 years, a wide range of photogrammetric software tools (Aicardi et al. 2018) have seen widespread uptake for archaeology and heritage applications (Green et al. 2014; McCarthy 2014; Historic England), with combined workflows for managing cultural heritage restoration (Campanaro et al. 2016) and other monitoring tasks (Campiani et al. 2019; Quagliarini et al. 2017), in which 3D data is seen as an asset that can contribute to virtual tours, as well as documenting the conservation state of cultural heritage sites (Napolitano et al. 2018). When considered alongside other digital documentation tools such as 3D laser scanning (Historic England 2018; Frost 2018), these approaches are supportive of conservation management and buildings information management (Historic England 2019).

The use of structure-from-motion photogrammetry is not unique to heritage applications and has been applied in a wide range of different areas, ranging from agriculture to biomedical sciences (Struck et al. 2019). It has found considerable uptake within the field of physical geography (Smith et al. 2016), with applications ranging from geology (Brush et al. 2019) and geomorphological research (Fawcett et al. 2019); to the monitoring of topographic change (Cucchiaro et al. 2018); specific to the nature of the caldera of volcanoes (Thiele et al. 2017); and form of glaciers; gully erosion; monitoring of coastal morphology change (Westoby et al. 2018); ecology and environmental monitoring; forestry (Iglhaut et al. 2019); geological features; canopy heights and openings (Swinfield et al. 2019); particularly with the support of LiDAR and digital aerial photogrammetry (Agüera-Vega et al. 2018).

Data fusion has increasingly been needed as the workflows for data capture, processing and application have become more inter-disciplinary in nature (Fritsch and Klein 2018). However, diachronic perspectives have largely utilised airborne data for heritage applications (Risbol et al. 2015; Papworth et al. 2016) and have been valuable for analysing change to glacier surface elevation (Molg and Bolch 2017; Vargo et al. 2017); changes in land use management/geomorphology (Nyssen et al. 2016; Riquelme et al. 2019; Vinatier et al. (2018) and in assessing the aftermath of hurricanes (Sherwood et al. 2018).

This chapter focuses on digital approaches that provide support to documenting cultural heritage, whilst anticipating the reality that change is inevitable. Even conservation policy recognises that change can only really be slowed at best. Strategies such as the 'Preservation of archaeological remains in-situ' introduced by English Heritage in the 1990s in response to public campaigns to save the archaeological heritage, such as the Rose Theatre in London recognise that they are primarily concerned with mitigation strategies and monitoring approaches (Historic England 2016). The chapter uses the aftermath of the fire at Notre Dame to explore the use of web-scraped imagery and the challenge of capturing this within geographically constrained environments. Similarly, the chapter highlights the nature of the urban setting of built structures within Kathmandu, Nepal, and the rationale for using mobile mapping technology to anchor 3D models within the constraints of this setting. The chapter also highlights the experience of using crowd-sourced imagery for the site of Palmyra in Syria.

4.2   Heritage and Societal Need

Heritage is one of the most applied disciplines, and whilst the United Nations Sustainable Development Goals (SDGs) do not explicitly refer to it, heritage offers key opportunities to develop dialogues and approach the needs of communities in developing countries (Wilson et al. 2019), as well as supporting communities where the challenge of deprivation also exists within the developed world. Collectively these intractable challenges are often multi-dimensional and require complex approaches to address these needs. Yet heritage can also offer cross-cutting support and a new lens through which to view and assist in these efforts. Whilst much of the focus has been concerned with digital documentation, increasing attention is being paid to the wider societal benefits of 3D data as part of cultural resilience and community engagement (Tait et al. 2016).

International relief efforts are nothing new to urban environments in the aftermath of widespread destruction. When the built heritage of the port city of Arica (at the time part of Peru, now Chile's northernmost port) was decimated by the tsunami that followed the catastrophic 8.5–9 scale earthquake on 13 August 1868, the immediate relief efforts involved French, US, British and Peruvian ships and a disaster relief commission was set up. Newly elected Peruvian President José Balta sought to use the disaster as a means for economic opportunity and inducement for investment from North America and Europe, linked in particular to infrastructure in support of the international guano trade (Vizcarra 2009). Prefabricated buildings for commerce (Arica customs house—commissioned 1871) and religious worship (Cathedral of San Marcos—inaugurated 1876) were subsequently commissioned from the workshops of Gustave Eiffel (Niell and Sundt 2015).

Modern relief efforts are similarly concerned both with the immediate humanitarian efforts and longer term sustainability-based around economic opportunities and investment. The aftermath of the April 2015 Earthquake in Kathmandu has highlighted the need for renewed efforts in disaster planning and cultural heritage protection in post-disaster contexts (Coningham et al. 2019). Cultural heritage documented prior to the Syrian conflict (Andres et al. 2012) can contribute to resilience, as with communities displaced from their homelands who face the challenge of maintaining the connection to their cultural heritage, and the ability to share those connections across displaced communities and generational boundaries. This is something that the related BReaTHe project (Evans et al. 2020) is seeking to address with the use of digital content and virtual reality in support of refugees from the conflict in Syria.

4.3   Harnessing Public Interest

Visibility serves as an important hook, with media attention often grabbing public interest. The advent of citizen science has made it possible to harness this attention for particular campaigns. The advent of affordable digital cameras and the ubiquitous nature of smartphone technology with high-resolution sensors has made digital imagery ever more accessible to the wider public. Crowd-sourcing of imagery, therefore, exists as a resource that can be utilised in targeted ways. The potential for terrain modelling in the aftermath of natural disasters using crowd-sourced SfM-photogrammetry data offers potential for understanding topographic data (Ratner et al. 2019). Image calls have become commonplace in the aftermath of heritage destruction with varying degrees of success. The particular challenge exemplified by sites such as Palmyra in Syria is that tourist access has been restricted since the beginning of the Syrian Civil War in March 2011, with the high-profile destruction of the Temple of Bel in August 2015 and subsequent destruction of the Triumphal Arch at Palmyra in October 2015 drawing international condemnation (Cunliffe and Curini 2018). It would have been unethical to place individuals in-country at even greater risk whilst under the control of IS using local imaging campaigns.

In terms of digital imagery, the Syria conflict highlights a watershed time period in the democratisation of photography which has posed challenges for the development of infrastructures to support heritage that has faced serious threats. Whilst 2003 was the first year that the sale of digital cameras out-sold film cameras in the developed world (Rubenstein and Sluis 2008), it was not until the 2010s that smartphones had integrated cameras in more widespread use, and after the Syrian conflict had begun that consumer-grade digital SLR cameras included full-frame sensors, and mirror-less digital cameras were in widespread circulation. Couple this with the fact that Syria was just starting to push forward with reforms to develop its tourist industry, immediately prior to the Civil War, whilst international sanctions were still in place (Sands 2011). As a consequence, the potential pool for crowd-sourced imagery for Palmyra was limited, with much of the content focused on principal monuments such as the Triumphal Arch (Fig. 4.1) and Temple of Bel, with many who responded providing film-based images, which also reflects the fact that many image donors were also retired. This ranged from tourists from Mediterranean cruise ships to former military personnel who had been posted to Syria during and in the immediate aftermath of World War II.

The advent of the smartphone has changed the public's approach to image-taking (Gómez Cruz and Meyer 2012) and whilst photography in public places has become normalised, it is not without its constraints (Borissova 2018), particularly, when this chapter shows that it may be necessary to train individuals to rethink how they take photographs to consider the potential 'heritage value' of what they capture and thus raise awareness of the methods of image capture that best optimise this (Historic England 2017). There is a fine balance between making observations and letting

Fig. 4.1 Triumphal Arch at Palmyra, Syria

the camera do that for you without proper attention to image composition and/or standardised methods of survey photography intended for SfM-photogrammetry. The lasting benefit of tailoring crowd-sourced imaging methodologies is that contributors get the opportunity to co-create 3D content, whilst being able to 'revisit' sites and to 'look afresh' at details after the fact.

The increased potential of using crowd-sourced imagery is being recognised (Alsadik 2018) across a number of different fields, with examples including community-based environmental monitoring using smartphone technology (Andrachuk et al. 2019; Dabove et al. 2019). The challenge of working with crowd-sourced imagery is that there will be differences in accuracy using different cameras and lenses (Elkhrachy 2019). Furthermore, the performance of different SfM software has been compared showing the potential of cloud-based solutions over commercially available desktop software (Pena-Villasenin et al. 2020).

4.4   Web-Scraped Imagery

Our experience with web-scraped imagery for Syria has shown that it is possible to reconstruct heritage sites such as the Temple of Bel at Palmyra that has been destroyed. We used both web-crawling and web-scraping for acquiring images from Google and Microsoft Bing, using targeted keywords in image search. Backend server technologies and distributed database (Ch'ng 2014), with NodeJS server-side JavaScript for crawling, scraping, and processing data from links and images through querying each web page's Document Object Model (DOM). In sharing initial content (Faber et al. 2017), we have received further public donations of imagery. Furthermore, we have also realised the potential therapeutic value of these models as part of psycho-social support through Follow-on funding as part of the BReaTHe project that has been using heritage for resilience amongst displaced Syrian communities (Mercy Corps 2019).

Increased attention is being paid to evaluating the accuracy of 3D historic BIM (Anton et al. 2018; Fryskowska and Stachelek 2018). Collectively this imagery is used not only for reconstruction, but also to determine the locations from which that imagery was captured. This use of photography can be purposed towards understanding the passage of visitors through a site, which in turn can be used to inform future site management. Such viewshed analysis coupled with image heat maps for visitor photographs can inform the management of sites that have particular vulnerabilities. This includes sites in marginal environments where soil erosion, fragile ecological habitats or weak sedimentary geology can benefit from this type of data to inform visitors of the potential impact that they can have on long-term site care (Historic Environment Scotland 2016). The visitor heat map can be used both for long-term care, and also enhanced visitor experience, by redirecting them away from traditional routes towards locations of greater heritage significance.

Geography can constrain the capture of imagery. This was particularly noticeable with web-scraped imagery collated in the aftermath of the fire at the medieval

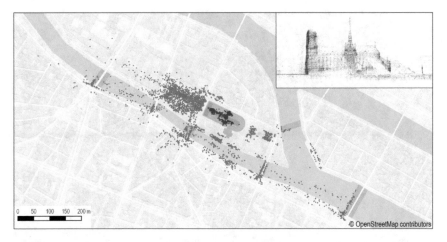

Fig. 4.2 Camera locations for imagery showing Notre Dame de Paris

cathedral of Notre Dame in Paris (Fig. 4.2). This site located on the Île de la Cité is visible from open ground to the west, south and east, including from the routes that border and bridges that cross the River Seine, as well as imagery that had clearly been taken from tourist boats that ply the River. Imagery to the North is constrained by the proximity of buildings on the Île de la Cité and the resulting point cloud is sparser.

4.5 Mobile Mapping in Support of Web-Scraped Imagery

The urban centres of the Kathmandu Valley World Heritage Site in Nepal encompass the Durbar squares, temples, palaces and public spaces of the city. These dense urban settings within the historic heart of Kathmandu, Nepal, were severely impacted by the major earthquake of April 2015. Its aftermath resulted in massive loss of life and numerous temples and structures destroyed, with major relief efforts concentrating on clearance, rather than recording. Web-scraped imagery was collected in an effort to support the restoration of temples that has begun in Nepal under the auspices of UNESCO and ICOMOS. Although frequented by tourists, meaning a wealth of target imagery, these sites are constrained by the spatial geography of their contextual setting and it is only possible to observe temples and other buildings from certain aspects.

The challenge of photographic imaging in urban settings has similarly been recognised with survey work undertaken within the historic heart of Santiago de Compostela, Span (Pena-Villasenin et al. 2017) and within historic urban centres in India (Rossato et al. 2019). The consequence of this in Nepal was that much of the web-scraped imagery is obscured at ground-level by people, animals (birds, dogs,

Fig. 4.3 Contextualised web-scraped imagery for Kathmandu Bhaktapur square

etc.) and activity (stalls, funerary practices, etc.). In order to overcome this, the web-scraped imagery was contexualised, scaled and anchored relative to ground-level and extant survey plans, through mobile mapping which was undertaken using the Zeb-Revo (GeoSLAM) hand-held 3D laser scanner—an advancement on the original Zeb-1 (GeoSLAM) scanner (Zlot et al. 2014) (Figs. 4.3 and 4.4). Work with the newer Zeb-Horizon (GeoSLAM) hand-held 3D laser scanner is discussed in the chapter by Moore et al. (this volume).

4.6 Mapping Heritage at a Country Scale

Whilst our understanding of cultural heritage is often a shared response that reflects the 'outstanding universal value' (OUV) of heritage, to use terminology in common with UNESCO, that can mean very different things to communities and individuals throughout the globe. Within Tanzania, it has been recognised that local communities often have stronger connections with the natural environment (such as individual baobab trees or the ocean) than they do with recognisable heritage sites (Ichumbaki and Mapunda 2017). Yet, both tangible and intangible heritage have a valid place with

Fig. 4.4 Kathmandu streetscape showing contextualised imagery

strategies for cultural heritage protection and in support of sustainable development in countries such as Tanzania (Ichumbaki and Lubao 2020). Whilst localised mapping of certain sites such as Olduvai Gorge (Jorayev et al. 2016) and conservation assessment of the Engare Sero footprint site (Zimmer et al. 2018) has been undertaken, much of Tanzania remains with relatively poor coverage.

At a country scale, cultural heritage sites in Tanzania have been explored using the web-scraping workflow which targets historic image uploads. Although only concentrating on one digital image repository—a comprehensive analysis of tagged imagery (using both frequency of terms based on a gazetteer of sites and EXIF metadata) available for Tanzania online (see Figs. 4.5, 4.6 and 4.7), show a sparsity of available image data for the country as a whole. Collectively this highlights the need for baseline data on cultural and natural heritage assets through the establishment of Historic Environment Records for Tanzania. Furthermore, this data support potential site management needs, as shown with the heat maps that relate to established trails at MtKilimanjaro National Park and the Ngorongoro Conservation Area. Such localised heat-map data is significant—since it informs the establishment of marked trails, the potential erosion and targeting of resources in support of the upkeep needs of these trails.

Total hits for imagery based upon keyword searches for sites listed in the gazetteer are seen in Table 4.1. When mapped these appear to concentrate largely in the national parks and at a handful of cultural heritage sites. This demonstrates a particular need to develop the infrastructure to support a wider framework for cultural heritage protection and to thereby encourage further economic development and tourism.

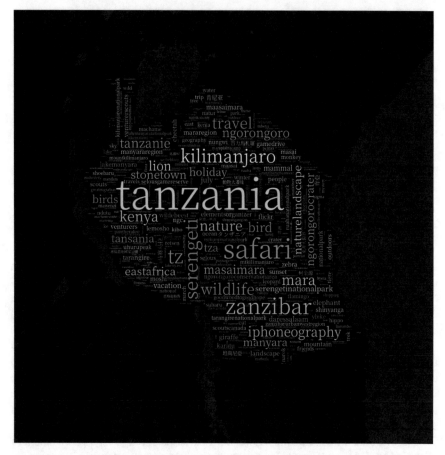

Fig. 4.5 Graphic showing the relative frequency of image tags for web-scraped imagery concerned with Tanzania. Keywords are conveyed as word clouds with their size relative to frequency/count. Mapping from Made with Natural Earth (https://www.naturalearthdata.com/about/terms-of-use/)

4.7 Conclusions

The meaning and values attached to heritage vary depending on geography and scale. Whilst heritage can have contested meaning and may pose particular challenges, the potential for heritage to offer wide-scale universal value means that it is deserving of attention. Digital-based infrastructures represented by the Curious Travellers methodology can offer key support to documenting sites, monitoring and evaluating change, and can contribute towards the presentation of meaning and support to a wide range of interpretations and potential uses for societal benefit.

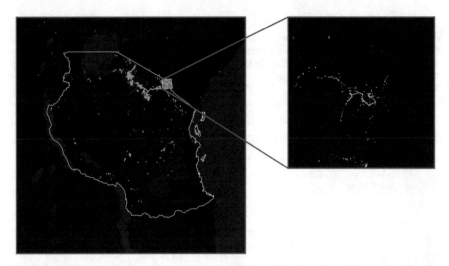

Fig. 4.6 Heat-map data shown for trails at Mt Kilimanjaro National Park. Mapping from Made with Natural Earth (https://www.naturalearthdata.com/about/terms-of-use/)

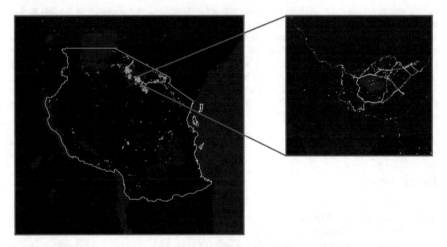

Fig. 4.7 Heat-map data shown for trails at the Ngorongoro Conservation Area. Mapping from Made with Natural Earth (https://www.naturalearthdata.com/about/terms-of-use/)

Table 4.1 shows the overwhelming focus towards Tanzania's natural heritage, in contrast to cultural heritage sites. Variance in spelling is a challenge with the choice of search terms—Olduvai, Oldupai. Olduvai Gorge and Oldupai Gorge all refer to the same location. There have been recent moves towards recognising the local name—'Oldupai Gorge'—rather than the corruption of this name 'Olduvai' that is in widespread usage

Keyword	Hits
Tanzania	568,539
Kilwa Kisiwani	343
Bagamoyo	3,111
Ngorongoro	78,686
Nogorongoro Crater	41,973
Oldupai	896
Oldupai Gorge	585
Olduvai	2,473
Olduvai Gorge	1,173
Isimila	161

Acknowledgements The Curious Travellers project was initiated as a response to the destruction of cultural heritage seen through both deliberate means and as a consequence of a natural disaster. It was funded as a component of the AHRC Digital Transformations Theme Large Grant 'Fragmented Heritage' (AH/L00688X/1). AHRC Follow-on funding has seen this approach contribute to the BReaTHe project (AH/S005951/1) which seeks to Build Resilience Through Heritage for displaced communities and with a contribution to the BA Cities and Infrastructures Scheme project, 'Reducing Disaster Risk to Life and Livelihoods by evaluating the seismic performance of retrofitted interventions within Kathmandu's UNESCO World Heritage Site during the 2015 Earthquake', with Durham University (KF1\100109).

References

Agüera-Vega F et al (2018) Reconstruction of extreme topography from UAV structure from motion photogrammetry. Measurement 121:127–138

Aicardi I et al (2018) Recent trends in cultural heritage 3D survey: the photogrammetric computer vision approach. J Cult Herit 32:257–266

Allen A, Lennon M (2018) The values and vulnerabilities of 'Star Wars Island': exploring tensions in the sustainable management of the Skellig Michael World Heritage Site. Int J Sust Dev World 25(6):483–490

Alsadik B (2018) Practicing the geometric designation of sensor networks using the Crowdsource 3D models of cultural heritage objects. J Cult Herit 31:202–207

Amado M, Rodrigues E (2019) A heritage-based method to urban regeneration in developing countries: the case study of Luanda. Sustainability 11(15)

Andrachuk M et al (2019) Smartphone technologies supporting community-based environmental monitoring and implementation: a systematic scoping review. Biol Cons 237:430–442

Andres AN et al (2012) Generation of virtual models of cultural heritage. J Cult Herit 13(1):103–106

Anton D et al (2018) Accuracy evaluation of the semi-automatic 3D modeling for historical building information models. Int J Architect Herit 12(5):790–805

Borissova V (2018) Cultural heritage digitization and related intellectual property issues. J Cult Herit 34:145–150

Brush JA et al (2019) Evaluation of field methods for 3-D mapping and 3-D visualization of complex metamorphic structure using multiview stereo terrain models from ground-based photography. Geosphere 15(1):188–221

Campanaro DM et al (2016) 3D GIS for cultural heritage restoration: a 'white box' workflow. J Cult Herit 18:321–332

Campiani A et al (2019) Spatial analysis and heritage conservation: leveraging 3-D data and GIS for monitoring earthen architecture. J Cult Herit 39:166–176

Ch'ng E (2014) The value of using big data technologies in computational social science. In: Proceedings of the 2014 international conference on big data science and computing, pp 1–4

Cigna F et al (2018) Geological hazards in the UNESCO World Heritage sites of the UK: from the global to the local scale perspective. Earth Sci Rev 176:166–194

Coningham et al (2019) Reducing disaster risk to life and livelihoods by evaluating the seismic safety of Kathmandu's historic urban infrastructure: enabling an interdisciplinary pilot. J British Acad 7(s2):45–82. https://doi.org/10.5871/jba/007s2.045

Cucchiaro S et al (2018) Monitoring topographic changes through 4D-structure-from-motion photogrammetry: application to a debris-flow channel. Environ Earth Sci 77(18)

Cunliffe E, Curini L (2018) ISIS and heritage destruction: a sentiment analysis. Antiquity 92(364):1094–1111

Dabove P et al (2019) Smartphone-based photogrammetry for the 3D modeling of a geomorphological structure. Appl Sci-Basel 9(18)

Elkhrachy I (2019) Modeling and visualization of three dimensional objects using low-cost terrestrial photogrammetry. Int J Architect Herit

Evans, A.A. et al (2020) Virtual Heritage for Resilience Building. doi:10.5281/zenodo.3950360 (accessed 10th March 2022). https://doi.org/10.5281/zenodo.3950360

Faber E et al (2017) Special report curious travellers: preserving endangered heritage across the world. Curr World Archaeol 82:11

Fadli F, AlSaeed M (2019) Digitizing vanishing architectural heritage; the design and development of Qatar historic buildings information modeling [Q-HBIM] Platform. Sustainability 11(9)

Fawcett D et al (2019) Two decades of digital photogrammetry: revisiting Chandler's 1999 paper on "Effective application of automated digital photogrammetry for geomorphological research"—a synthesis. Progress Phys Geography-Earth Environ 43(2):299–312

Fritsch D, Klein M (2018) 3D preservation of buildings—reconstructing the past. Multimedia Tools Appl 77(7):9153–9170

Frost A (2018) Applied digital documentation in the historic environment. Historic Environment Scotland, Edinburgh

Fryskowska A, Stachelek J (2018) A no-reference method of geometric content quality analysis of 3D models generated from laser scanning point clouds for hBIM. J Cult Herit 34:95–108

Gómez Cruz E, Meyer ET (2012) Creation and control in the photographic process: iPhones and the emerging fifth moment of photography. Photographies 5(2):203–221. https://doi.org/10.1080/17540763.2012.702123

Green S et al (2014) A comparative assessment of structure from motion methods for archaeological research. J Archaeol Sci 46:173–181

Hammer E et al (2018) Remote assessments of the archaeological heritage situation in Afghanistan. J Cult Herit 33:125–144

Hesse R (2015) Combining Structure-from-Motion with high and intermediate resolution satellite images to document threats to archaeological heritage in arid environments. J Cult Herit 16(2):192–201

Historic Environment Scotland (2016) The Heart of Neolithic Orkney World Heritage Site Management Plan 2014–19 https://www.historicenvironment.scot/archives-and-research/publications/publication/?publicationId=c96546cf-ff4d-409e-9f96-a5c900a4f5f2. Accessed 13 Dec 2019

Historic England (2016) Preserving archaeological remains: decision-taking for sites under development. Swindon, Historic England

Historic England (2017) Photogrammetric applications for cultural heritage. Guidance for good practice. Swindon, Historic England

Historic England (2018) (3rd edn) 3D laser scanning for heritage: advice and guidance on the use of laser scanning in archaeology and architecture. Swindon, Historic England

Historic England (2019) BIM for heritage: developing the asset information model. Swindon, Historic England

Ichumbaki EB, Mapunda BB (2017) Challenges to the retention of the integrity of World Heritage Sites in Africa: the case of Kilwa Kisiwani and Songo Mnara Tanzania, Azania. Archaeol Res Africa 52(4):518–539. https://doi.org/10.1080/0067270X.2017.1396665

Ichumbaki EB, Mjema E (2018) The impact of small-scale development projects on archaeological heritage in Africa: the Tanzanian experience. Conservat Manage Archaeol Sites 2(1):18–34

Ichumbaki EB, Lubao CB (2020) Musicalizing heritage and heritagizing music for enhancing community awareness of preserving world heritage sites in Africa. Int J Herit Stud 26(4):415–432. https://doi.org/10.1080/13527258.2019.1644527

Iglhaut J et al (2019) Structure from motion photogrammetry in forestry: a review. Curr for Rep 5(3):155–168

Jorayev G et al (2016) Imaging and photogrammetry models of Olduvai Gorge (Tanzania) by Unmanned Aerial Vehicles: a high-resolution digital database for research and conservation of Early Stone Age sites. J Archaeol Sci 75:40–56

Langhammer J, Vackova T (2018) Detection and mapping of the geomorphic effects of flooding using UAV photogrammetry. Pure Appl Geophys 175(9):3223–3245

McCarthy J (2014) Multi-image photogrammetry as a practical tool for cultural heritage survey and community engagement. J Archaeol Sci 43:175–185

Mercy Corps (2019) https://www.mercycorps.org/press-room/releases/how-virtual-reality-helps-refugees. Accessed 13 Dec 2019

Molg N, Bolch T (2017) Structure-from-motion using historical aerial images to analyse changes in glacier surface elevation. Remote Sens 9(10)

Napolitano RK et al (2018) Virtual tours and informational modeling for conservation of cultural heritage sites. J Cult Herit 29:123–129

Niell P, Sundt R (2015) Architecture of colonizers/architecture of immigrants: gothic in Latin America from the 16th to the 20th Centuries. Postmedieval 6:243. https://doi.org/10.1057/pmed. 2015.23

Nyssen J et al (2016) Recovery of the aerial photographs of Ethiopia in the 1930s. J Cult Herit 17:170–178

Papworth H et al (2016) Assessing 3D metric data of digital surface models for extracting archaeological data from archive stereo-aerial photographs. J Archaeol Sci 72:85–104

Pavlova I et al (2017) Global overview of the geological hazard exposure and disaster risk awareness at world heritage sites. J Cult Herit 28:151–157

Pena-Villasenin S et al (2017) 3-D modeling of historic facades Using SfM photogrammetry metric documentation of different building types of a historic center. Int J Architect Herit 11(6):871–890

Pena-Villasenin S et al (2020) Desktop vs cloud computing software for 3D measurement of building facades: the monastery of San Martin Pinario. Measurement 149

Prieto AJ et al (2019) Protection value and functional service life of heritage timber buildings. Build Res Inf 47(5):567–584

Quagliarini E et al (2017) Fast, low cost and safe methodology for the assessment of the state of conservation of historical buildings from 3D laser scanning: the case study of Santa Maria in Portonovo (Italy). J Cult Herit 24:175–183

Ratner JJ et al (2019) Crowd-sourcing structure-from-motion data for terrain modelling in a real-world disaster scenario: a proof of concept. Progress Phys Geography-Earth Environ 43(2):236–259

Revez MJ et al (2019) Analysing the cost-effectiveness of heritage conservation interventions: a methodological proposal within project STORM. Int J Architect Herit

Riquelme A et al (2019) Digital landform reconstruction using old and recent open access digital aerial photos. Geomorphology 329:206–223

Risbol O et al (2015) Monitoring cultural heritage by comparing DEMs derived from historical aerial photographs and airborne laser scanning. J Cult Herit 16(2):202–209

Rossato L et al (2019) Digital tools for documentation and analysis of vernacular cultural heritage in Indian City Centers. Int J Architect Herit

Rubinstein D, Sluis K (2008) A life more photographic. Photographies 1(1):9–28. https://doi.org/10.1080/17540760701785842

Sands P (2011) Syria sees tourist numbers leap 40%, The National. https://www.thenational.ae/business/travel-and-tourism/syria-sees-tourist-numbers-leap-40-1.583832. Published 25 Jan 2011. Accessed 11 Dec 2019

Sherwood CR et al (2018) Rapid, remote assessment of hurricane Matthew impacts using four-dimensional structure-from-motion photogrammetry. J Coastal Res 34(6):1303–1316

Smith MW et al (2016) Structure from motion photogrammetry in physical geography. Progress Phys Geography-Earth Environ 40(2):247–275

Struck R et al (2019) Application of photogrammetry in biomedical science. Biomed Visualisat 1(1120):121–130

Swinfield T et al (2019) Accurate measurement of tropical forest canopy heights and aboveground carbon using structure from motion. Remote Sens 11(8)

Tait E et al (2016) (Re)presenting heritage: laser scanning and 3D visualisations for cultural resilience and community engagement. J Inf Sci 42(3):420–433

Thiele ST et al (2017) Thermal photogrammetric imaging: a new technique for monitoring dome eruptions. J Volcanol Geoth Res 337:140–145

Vargo LJ et al (2017) Using structure from motion photogrammetry to measure past glacier changes from historic aerial photographs. J Glaciol 63(242):1105–1118

Vinatier F et al (2018) The use of photogrammetry to construct time series of vegetation permeability to water and seed transport in agricultural waterways. Remote Sens 10(12)

Vizcarra C (2009) Guano, credible commitments and sovereign debt repayment in nineteenth-century Peru. J Econ Hist 69(2):358–387

Westoby MJ et al (2018) Cost-effective erosion monitoring of coastal cliffs. Coast Eng 138:152–164

Wilson AS et al (2019) Curious travellers: repurposing imagery to manage and interpret threatened monuments, sites and landscapes. In: Dawson M James E, Nevell M (eds) Heritage under pressure, threats & solutions: studies of agency and soft power in the historic environment, pp 107–122

Wilson L et al (2018) 3D digital documentation for disaster management in historic buildings: applications following fire damage at the Mackintosh building, The Glasgow School of Art. J Cult Herit 31:24–32

Zimmer B et al (2018) Using differential structure-from-motion photogrammetry to quantify erosion at the Engare Sero footprint site, Tanzania. Quatern Sci Rev 198:226–241

Zlot R et al (2014) Efficiently capturing large, complex cultural heritage sites with a handheld mobile 3D laser mapping system. J Cult Herit 15(6):670–678

Part II
Modelling, Interpreting and Reconstructing the Past

Chapter 5
Visualising Deep Time History in Context Using Accessible and Emergent Technologies: The GLAM Sector Experience

Ann Hardy, Gaute Rasmussen, and Gionni di Gravio

Abstract This chapter discusses the collaborative work of the University of Newcastle's IT Services' Innovation Team (ITSIT) and the university library's Cultural Collections (UONCC) and the GLAMx Living Histories Digitisation Lab to create the heritage visualisation project Deep Time. The collaborative process facilitates a diversity of 'voices' around heritage in the digital age by taking a digital and information technology, and GLAM (Galleries Libraries Archives and Museums) perspective. The team creating the 3D model of firstly an Aboriginal archaeological site, and custom virtual reality (VR) software for the project and using new technology to enhance teaching and learning at the University. The case study relies strongly on Indigenous artefacts as archival and historical aspects to interpret cultural sources for application to digital formats such as VR. This chapter explores digitisation and digitalisation concepts and specific technical detail such as 3D modelling and texturing. The collaborative process also involved the wider community and work-integrated learning (WIL) students and volunteers in the GLAMx Lab. The wide approach (professionally and academically) demonstrates the use of innovative technologies and how the GLAM sector can add value to visualisations that comprise heritage digital reproductions and contextualisation.

Keywords GLAM · GLAM Lab · Digitisation · Digitalisation · Deep time · 3D · VR

5.1 Introduction

Since 2017, the university's IT Services' Innovation Team (ITSIT), Cultural Collections and the GLAMx Living Histories Digitisation Lab at the University of Newcastle (Australia) Auchmuty library have collaborated on digitisation projects. The visualisation project has incorporated cultural heritage themes; Deep Time

A. Hardy (✉) · G. Rasmussen · G. di Gravio
University of Newcastle, Callaghan, Australia
e-mail: ann.hardy@newcastle.edu.au

© Springer Nature Switzerland AG 2022　　　　　　　　　　　　　　　　　　69
E. Ch'ng et al. (eds.), *Visual Heritage: Digital Approaches in Heritage Science*,
Springer Series on Cultural Computing,
https://doi.org/10.1007/978-3-030-77028-0_5

project requiring 3D scanning technology to recreate a virtual archaeological dig containing Aboriginal artefacts. The digitisation coincided with the UON library embarking on a new venture to promote and augment established Work Integrated Learning (WIL) course in the BA, and to provide for placements at the GLAMx Lab (Di Gravio and Hardy 2018). The lab provides a unique opportunity in the tertiary teaching and learning sphere. Students were able to engage in practical education and learn the technical knowhow to be able to transform any physical format into a digital object, and access to the entire gamut of GLAM professions across conservation and preservation, archival science, librarianship, digitisation, metadata and data management, curatorial, 3D scanning, Virtual Reality technologies and digital heritage skills.

The aim of this chapter is twofold. Firstly, it shows the relationship between 'digitisation' and 'digitalisation' concepts and secondly, to highlight the benefits of working collaboratively with heritage professions and wider communities to create a stimulating learning environment and resources for gaining GLAM sector skills.

The ITSIT was responsible for the technical side of projects, including acquiring 3D scanning technology, cloud storage, as well as custom VR software. The ITSIT are situated in the same location at the Auchmuty Library as UONCC and the GLAMx Lab. The focus of projects at the GLAMx Lab in 2017 was Aboriginal Rock Art and Indigenous heritage and the University's archival holdings in Cultural Collections. One of these holdings were a collection of Aboriginal artefacts that would become part of the Deep Time project (University of Newcastle (UON) 2019a, b), whereby technologies were required to visualise the archaeological trench and the artefacts within it.

The Deep Time project was not funded through academic and research grants, instead it was funded within the university to demonstrate the use of technologies for teaching and learning purposes.

The Deep Time visualisation of Aboriginal stone tools in a virtual archaeological trench is unique and unlikely to be known outside Australia. The digitisation of each artefact is not the unique aspect of this project, but what were done with the assets via 'digitalisation' and creating the virtual archaeological trench. The broader significance of this project is its potential to be replicated internationally to further research and compare stone tool collections created by humankind. Archaeology is a distinctive and informative frame of inquiry to further understand Aboriginal cultural values and material culture. This chapter discusses 3D scanning and VR technologies in visualising Australian Aboriginal culture and how GLAM institutions, including university libraries can get involved.

This project has broad significance in terms of the accessibility of 3D artefacts on a digital platform and research of Aboriginal stone tools in Australia, to understand how they were made. Furthermore, by having 3D artefacts available to a global audience this makes international comparative studies more likely including other stone tools collections and how they can be documented, digitised and visualised in a similar fashion. This is particularly relevant in the Australian context to build knowledge of trade routes relating to Indigenous stone tools. The Deep Time project has gained some media coverage locally and nationally in Australia (Smith 2019;

Bevan 2017), however is relatively unknown in academic writing. The project was not steered by a specific discipline or professional body, instead it was a pilot project relating to GLAM sector studies, methodologies and processes.

The Deep Time project enables Aboriginal heritage to be experienced by making 3D artefacts available on a digital platform and accessible to students, researchers and the general public. The visualisation project was documented and shared with a global audience on the Hunter Living Histories website and the university digital platform 'Livinghistories@UON' (Hunter Living Histories (HLH), Nov 21, 2019). Further to this, the 3D scans of artefacts are then able to be viewed using a VR headset in the virtual archaeological trench. The site where the artefacts were excavated now has a fast food store, erected in 2012. To experience the VR, one needs to visit the UON, however there is also a model available in portable headsets.

The introduction of the students and volunteers assisted greatly with the digitisation of archives, objects and documentation for the Deep Time project. Digitisation of some parts of the collection and archive were undertaken by WIL students and volunteers at the GLAMx Lab. A student was employed by the Vera Deacon Regional History Fund (Bevan 2018). This fund was established in 2008 in honour of the generosity of Mrs. Vera Deacon and provides paid employment to UON students and volunteers, researching and sharing knowledge about the history of the Hunter Region with the wider global community. It also provides students the opportunity to engage with communities and individuals external to the UON. This is a good way of engaging students on visualisation projects even if they are only contributing in a small way.

5.2 Background/Literature Review

The Deep Time visualisation project discussed in this chapter has two digital processes in play and relate to the conceptual terms digitisation and digitalisation. These terms are closely related and often used interchangeably in the literature (Brennen and Kreiss 2014). There is a large body of literature on these concepts, particularly on 'digitisation' a popular concept in the computer age. This term has also become a big part of the humanities during late last century and increasingly in the twenty-first century (Warwick et al. 2012; Koche 2017). Understanding the development of the concepts is important, especially when considering how far digital knowledges have advanced in terms of VR and AR technologies. In essence 'digitalisation' is a method of using existing digitised assets to construct new ways to visualise and communicate the assets, and link with other information to create new knowledge. Defining these two concepts will make it simpler to understand how the Deep Time visualisation was created and how there is a layering of digitised and digitalised methodologies. The following describes each concept in more detail.

Digitisation is converting analog or non-digital items such as written records into a digital format (Hamill 2017). A digitised format can then be used by a computing system for a number of other possible purposes. Digitisation has also been described as the digital representation of the physical with the goal to digitise and automate processes or workflows (i-SCOOP 2016). Whereas, 'digitalisation' and 'digital transference' are a more considerable part of the literature and complex in definition, furthermore, are also having a greater influence on the contemporary world. Digitisation in the corporate sector is vast, as are the effects of digitalisation across a diversity of sectors. With 'digitisation' there is usually a focus on methods that assist to improve workflows and efficiencies, often with the aim of improving profits. The corporate world is highly invested in digital concepts because of the financial efficiencies that can be made.

Beniger (1986) suggests that digitisation has the ability to simulate or consolidate other diverse forms of information. This diversity has had extensive impacts because of the way it has influenced convergence across sectors. This amassing of huge amounts of digitised material across many sectors has brought together previously disparate sectors of social life and this is now driving wider social and technological changes (Dobson 2019).

A huge body of literature has grown relating to 'digitalisation' and the multi-layered uses of digital and analog sources to create diverse relationships. The first use of the term 'digitalisation' was in 1971 when Walchal referred to 'digitalization of society' and the social implications of computers used in humanities research (Brennen and Kreiss 2014). Much of the contemporary literature associated with 'digitalisation' relates to the business sector and mass digitisation of records (i-SCOOP 2016). However, Castells (2010), talks about a 'network society' whereby digitalisation is enabling organisations to connect.

Digitalisation and a networked society are defining characteristics of the contemporary era. Digital technologies and 'digitisation' offer new modes of experiencing the world. The immergence of technologies such as AR/VR have strengthened interactions between humans, objects and information that can be digitally redesigned and constructed using new digital approaches. The cultural sector particularly in the northern hemisphere, including Europe, the United Kingdom and Middle East are embracing virtual technologies to visualise cultural heritage (Santachiara et al. 2018; Santos et al. 2017). Many of the digital cultural platforms follow primary scientific guidelines associated with Europe and United Kingdom, such as the London Charter (Denard 2009) and the Seville Principles (2011) and documents with international obligations from ICOMOS (2017) and UNESCO (1972, 2002, 2008). These guidelines (except for those from ICOMOS and UNESCO) do not apply in Australia. Statham has undertaken an in-depth analysis of public online platforms for 3D digital heritage and reveals that many of them often fail to contextualize the items (Statham 2019). Compared to elsewhere there is limited research in the international academic literature relating to virtual heritage projects in the Australian context, and that even less refer to Australian Aboriginal culture and traditions.

Most of the literature on digital approaches and cultural heritage relate to the management of sources, or the safeguarding, and restoration of cultural heritage. Other literature explores innovative ways for visitors to experience and interact with artefacts in the museum environment (Guidi et al. 2010), and the majority of research in this space is between museum and digital technologies (Tsichritzis and Gibbs 1991;

Guidi and Remondino 2012). Luigini et al. (2019) suggest that digital technologies can be used to replicate actual artefacts and such work can be carried out either on-site or off-site remotely in locations other than the museum. This is the case for the Deep Time project whereby artefacts were digitised not at a museum but a university library for the purpose of teaching and learning and GLAM sector training.

Many contemporary digital approaches to cultural heritage and virtual technologies use archaeological knowledge and artefacts. However, Gherardini et al. (2019) advise that 3D modelling is rarely used in archaeology because of the heavy paper-based documentation and time-consuming nature of obtaining digital data from the documentation. Practical constraints in capturing stratigraphic layers and the detailed archaeological features are often a deterrent. In contrast to this, the project described in this chapter suggests otherwise where documentation was crucial in accurately relocating 3D artefacts into a virtual trench in the position they were found in the actual trench. The Deep Time project was created almost ten years after the archaeological dig took place and scanning of the stratigraphic layers was not required. Instead, the focus was on digitising artefacts so they could be relocated back into the virtual trench. This model could be simulated where a collection of artefacts exists from the same dig.

In terms of maintaining appropriate management practices. Guidi and Remondi (2012) advise that 3D scanning and access to virtual models of artefacts reduces the need for contact with the real artefact. Viewing cultural artefacts virtually reduces handling and this was particularly pertinent to the Deep Time project whereby many Aboriginal artefacts are fragile. Viewing Aboriginal artefacts virtually has other benefits too, cultural sensitivities are reduced promoting culturally safe practice for those who choose not to view or touch the Aboriginal stone tools for cultural reasons. Virtual availability diminishes cultural sensitivities to some extent.

Access to 3D cultural objects on digital platforms is nothing new. The SketchFab digital platform is the largest and most diverse 3D library and is available for cultural organisations. Creators of 3D scans and models can upload and access digital files using Sketch-Fab, and content can be publicly shared (PR Newswire, Mar 2020). In 2020, SketchFab made over 400,000 USDZ files available for download, ancient and contemporary objects can now be accessed to be reused and re-imagined (PR Newswire, Feb 2020)). This is a platform that could have been used to upload the Deep Time artefacts, however in order for the 3D scans to be viewed in VR it was necessary that they were uploaded to the university's digital platform Livinghistories@uon because the two technologies work in tandem (HLH, 2019). Technical details of how the Deep Time project was created are discussed further in this chapter.

Digitalisation in the twenty-first has diversified to use physical items combined with digital interfaces. This is opening up exciting opportunities for the GLAM sector, especially in the use of AR and VR to enhance the audience experience. Fazio and Lo Brutto (2020) suggest that many virtual technologies may not generally be applied in the context of traditional museums. The Deep Time project is an example of this, whereby the virtual archaeological trench offers another way of disseminating content and knowledge and unlike many other virtual models is not occupied with virtual museum concepts. Instead it is a library and archival resource for teaching and learning and at the centre are the Aboriginal artefacts and 3D and VR concepts. The project has been integrated in Digital Humanities courses at the UON.

The field of digital humanities is a growing discipline incorporating digital technologies to communicate facets of social and cultural life. Digital humanities first emerged in the early twenty-first century 'as an educational and institutional label for a set of disconnected approaches, objects, and strategies for addressing the growing awareness that the digital transformation of everyday life and the methods used in academic work in the past few decades have altered the protocols of humanities research' (Castells 2010). It has only been two decades that we have seen the rapid transformation in the digital humanities due to the worldwide web and this has encouraged greater networks to be formed. Van Dijk (2005) reminds us that for the first time in history there will be a single communications infrastructure that links all activities in society. Reflecting on this fast pace of digital transformation it is inevitable that fresh and innovative projects are born and continue to be born. Data and new knowledge are far more accessible, and this ease of accessibility is enabling collaborations forming across disciplines and sectors and the creation of innovative new projects.

The Deep Time project is an example of digital humanities work, communicating cultural and social knowledge by using immersive digital infrastructure. The project required primary sources to be digitised, either so that the digital files can be interpreted in order to create the VR model or for files to be directly downloaded and viewed in VR. The method of direct download was used for the Deep Time VR and is an example of both 'digitisation' and 'digitalisation'. Digitisation of the stone tool artefacts (primary source) involved creating a digital 3D file or virtual artefact that can be viewed in its virtual context, the virtual archaeological trench of the VR. This 'Digitalisation' represented in this virtual trench involving digitised artefacts that in a sense are the disparate secondary sources or copies in digital format. As briefly described here there are several layers of digital transference at play in the Deep Time project.

An ambitious digitalisation heritage project underway in Australia is using 4D concepts that include narratives and architecture associated with Australia's Afghan cameleers (Rashid and Antlej 2020). This use of 4D methodologies incorporates ideas around reconstructions, web retrieved sources and visualisation of cultural heritage (Kyriakaki et al. 2014) and use of geospatial platforms and immersive tools to promote social cohesion. The 4D component contextualises architectural-archaeological heritage both spatially and chronologically and has the capacity to rapidly disseminate heritage knowledge to a wider public including schools, community and health centres, and aged care homes by use of VR/AR portable systems. Many of the VR/AR cultural representations are from an architectural perspective and built heritage (Banfi et al. 2019; Carnevali et al. 2019; Charbonneau et al. 2018; Cuperschmid et al. 2019; Doulamis et al. 2019).

This pioneering 4D work allows the diverse and rich heritage of a single site to be visualised and interpreted. Considering the 'deep time' Australian context the

4D method is particularly pertinent in being able to visualise Aboriginal and non-Aboriginal heritage together to better understand how expansive the time periods were relating to human occupation.

The creative industries are also relevant in this space. Andrade and Dias (2020) suggest there are new opportunities for the expression and experiencing of culture, and for the creative industries because of immerging technological development. These authors also refer to disruptive innovations related to the Internet of Things (IoT), whereby there are profound and complex intertwining of online and offline experiences that can contribute to a phygital society. The concept of phygital considers virtual aspects and the real separately, and also intersecting (Turkle 1997; Baudrillard 1994), whereas Castells (2005) and Floridi (2003) put forward the idea that the physical and virtual realities are somehow simultaneously intertwined. These are important concepts when thinking about digital technologies and cultural heritage, because much of what we work within this space pertains to tangible objects, artefacts and sites.

As already mentioned the digitisation of the Deep Time artefacts was undertaken in the GLAMx Lab (Fig. 5.1). Labs offer an experimental space for the dissemination of disruptive innovations. Innovation in digitalisation methodologies has meant opportunities for a closer alliance among the disciplines, such as humanities, science and the creatives industries. New creative teams assist in visualising and communicating knowledge and data. This is very exciting especially in terms of broadening engagement in the GLAM sector.

Fig. 5.1 GLAMx Living Histories Digitisation Lab (2019), University of Newcastle (Australia). Courtesy UON

Labs are becoming innovative spaces in many institutions and the GLAMx Lab at the UON provides opportunities aimed at 'digitisation' and 'digitalisation' practices (in collaboration with UONCC and IT Services' Innovation Team (ITSIT) situated at the Auchmuty Library). Innovation labs including GLAM Labs are becoming increasingly prevalent worldwide. Papaioannou suggests that Innovation Labs are considered as the next 'big thing' for institutions embracing innovation, development, new ideas and generating opportunities (2019). The publication 'How to Open a GLAM Lab' affirms this growth of innovation Labs and how Galleries, Libraries, Archives and Museums sector are part of this new 'Lab' phenomena (Mahey et al. 2019). The UON has been at the forefront of the GLAM Lab movement at tertiary institutions in Australia. The GLAMx Lab is a sector first initiative for the UON and provides unique opportunities in the tertiary teaching and learning sphere for students (Di Gravio et al. 2017). Emerging technologies enable digital and information technologies to be used in the GLAM sector and new practices in the sector include specialists in the IT sector to carry out the technical side of projects. These new spaces (Labs) enable experimentation and the exchange of fresh ideas, as well as nurturing interactions that can culminate in dynamic projects being initiated. As Statham (2019) mentioned multidisciplinary teams are widely regarded as a necessary component of any heritage study, and this project was no exception.

Deep Time Project

The Deep Time Project is a digitisation project of Aboriginal artefacts for VR simulation (University of Newcastle, 2019). As mentioned, the project was undertaken in the GLAMx Lab with support of the ITSIT from the UON. The team created the project in 12 weeks.

Before describing this project, it is important to explain the concept 'Deep Time'. The term very much relates to Australian archaeology and historian. Griffith (2018) describes the concept in his book Deep Time Dreaming, however refers to the grandeur of the past in a global perspective. He surmises that much archaeological significance in the northern hemisphere is evident in the pyramids, pottery or gold. Griffith refers to Nicholas Jose's observation stating that Deep Time is not so much in the gems and antiquities 'but time itself'. This relates to evidence demonstrating longevity in terms of human occupation at a certain place. This is particularly relevant to the Australian context whereby evidence of human occupation has been located at many archaeological sites where deep levels of excavation have taken place. What is highly significant is the depth that evidence is found, signifying age and time itself. Not only are the type of artefacts found of importance, but also the depth in which they were found. Depth equals time, thus 'deep time'.

The excavated Aboriginal artefacts located at Newcastle West, NSW are part of the Deep Time Project and highly significant to Indigenous peoples of the area. The evidence of stone tools demonstrates that Indigenous people occupied the area for thousands of years.

The collection of Aboriginal artefacts was retrieved at a 6,500-year-old factory site, arguably one of the country's most significant heritage sites, in Newcastle West, NSW. Over 5,000 artefacts were found during the excavation in 2009, 600 of these are recorded as Aboriginal stone tools (NBN News, May 2011). The artefacts belong to four local Traditional owner groups and it is with great respect to the Aboriginal ancestors who created these objects that they are shared to gain knowledge for all people. The artefacts are in a Care and Control Agreement with the UON to house them at the University's Archives.

Traditional owner groups were informed during the process and acknowledged within the VR experience to respect cultural values. The team consulted regularly with Dr. Greg Blyton, Senior lecturer of Indigenous studies at the UON who provided valuable Indigenous knowledge. Participants were always mindful of cultural sensitivities around touching and interacting with artefacts and experiencing the project at the Lab.

Gionni di Gravio, UON archivist is a strong advocate for the protection of Indigenous heritage and raising public awareness of the cultural significance of the Indigenous artefacts located at Newcastle West. He also appealed to the wider community to comprehend the depth of history that 'lays beneath their feet' and of the importance for that history to be understood, respected and safeguarded for future generations (Di Gravio 2011). Di Gravio says

Without history, our community suffers, and like a patient with dementia we are confused and fearful. There is unfinished business here, and the sooner re-examine our shared memory, the healthier we will be.

The archaeological excavation also drew national attention that increased public awareness of the significance of the Aboriginal heritage and triggered a review into Aboriginal heritage legislation in NSW. The NSW Upper House unanimously passed a motion to review the Aboriginal heritage protection regime and consider measures to ensure that a similar tragedy does not occur in the future (NSW Parliament, 2011). This was a direct response to the loss of unique Aboriginal heritage (stone tools) at Newcastle West. The NSW Government has proposed a new system for managing and conserving Aboriginal cultural heritage and supported by a new legal framework that respects and conserves Aboriginal cultural heritage. The reform has been under review since 2010 and in 2020 legislation is drafted, however no Bill has yet been adopted by the NSW parliament (NSW Government).

It is rare to have such a deep excavation undertaken. The archaeological finds found at Newcastle West were intact in a trench containing tools and the cores that are culturally significant. Artefacts are of various sizes and types. What was excavated was a deep 'archive' of artefacts and this dig is unique because of the depth of the trench (3.5 m) and artefacts were found at the lower part of the trench. Most other collections of Aboriginal stone tools in Australia are surface finds only, often found in rural areas and collected at random, usually haphazardly found and brought together as a collection. Whereas the assemblage of artefacts excavated at Newcastle West are considered an 'archive' because of the intact context in which artefacts were found. Items in the Deep Time archive were handled/made/used by the Aboriginal people who occupied this site in Newcastle over the many thousands of years. The University Library also holds non-Aboriginal artefacts, the European layer of occupation at the same site. This is a separate report and a different methodology was used.

From the outset, there was no clear preference for one universal methodological approach and the specific needs and objectives of the project were to visualise the ancient stone tools. This culturally significant archive of Aboriginal tools provided inspiration when developing and visualising the project. The chosen methodology reflected this, and the VR project is described in the following section.

5.3 Methodology

The Deep Time project extends existing digitisation practices and introduces digitalisation processes as well as innovative and immersive technologies relevant and beneficial to users in the twenty-first century. The Deep Time was very much a collaborative process and concepts 'digitalisation' and 'digitisation' relevant because of the dual processes in creating the VR. Community engagement and outreach with Aboriginal communities and the general community was integral in the success of the project.

The ITSIT created the visualisation project and as mentioned the GLAMx Lab provided digitisation opportunities, bringing together new sectors and communities for research, learning and inspiration. The GLAMx Lab was established in 2017. There are three rooms in the GLAMx Lab, the main lab containing 10 workstations each having computers and flatbed scanners. This Lab also has a VR and Oculus Rift set up where VR and 3D projects can be viewed on a large screen. The screen is also useful for group learning and sharing and viewing visualisation projects. The Deep Time VR is able to be viewed there and are accessible to the wider community on request. The Artefact Conservation Atelier is a smaller Lab containing a 3D scanner, reflective 3D scanning light box and turntable, and laptop computer with Artec Studio software. Approximately 2.5 m of shelving is available in this Lab used to hold artefacts in the interim for accessioning, ease of access for research and illustration. The digitisation of Aboriginal Australian artefacts for VR simulation (Deep Time Project) is also done in this Lab (Fig. 5.2). The third space is the audio-visual digitisation Lab housing the NBN Television archive and has specialised digitisation equipment providing for the various (at risk) film formats (NBN News, Sept 2019).

The UONCC has been digitising cultural sources since the 1995, mostly 2D digitisation and audio digitisation projects (Hardy et al. 2018). In 2016, a state-of-the-art digital online platform was created by Recollect, New Zealand Micrographic Services. This new digital platform livinghistories@UON brought together over 20 years of digital files including 60,000 photographs on Flickr and hundreds of audio and audio-visual files, as well as thousands of PDFs (Wright and Keily 2018). In 2018, during the design phase of the Deep Time project discussions occurred with the Recollect team on how 3D digital assets could be uploaded to the new digital platform. What resulted was a new feature added to the livinghistories@UON digital platform enabling the upload of 3D digital assets and for 3D models to be viewed online. This was an important feature because it was from this platform that 3D assets could be downloaded to the virtual archaeological trench of the Deep Time project to

Fig. 5.2 Artefact Conservation Atelier is a smaller Lab containing a 3D scanner, reflective 3D scanning light box (2019), University of Newcastle (Australia). Courtesy UON

be viewed in VR. The team opted for 3D assets to go into new digital platform because it meant all types of digital formats held at the University's Cultural Collections could be accessed from one digital location. Furthermore, it was a platform whereby 3D assets could be downloaded from into the VR software. The availability of digitised sources in VR provides a platform for teaching and learning whereby users can acquire new knowledge through visualisations rather than by reading text-based sources.

Evolution of the Project

When the project first started, the agreed-on direction was to make an archaeological simulation where the user would put on a set of VR goggles, pick up virtual archaeological tools and start excavating the trench, finding 3D versions of artefacts as they went along. The team used pictures of real excavations along with the archaeological report from the dig to create a digital version of the dig site the way it looked during excavation in 2009 (Archaeological Management & Heritage Solutions (AMHS), May 2011). They then made a digital trench where users could dig into the soil and see the depth and look of the trench floor change as they dug through the layers. This trench is then populated with the digital scans of the artefacts. In parallel, they also developed a separate 'viewer' version of the trench, where users could see through the layers of the trench and see all the artefacts at the same time.

Over time, it became clear that the 'viewer' component of the project was more interesting than simulating the actual excavation process. It was more important to be able to show the context of the artefacts and how they relate to one another, than have the experience of digging them up. As a result, the excavation portion of the simulation was deprioritised. The only part of it that is still left in the final product is the main menu of the program, where users can look around at a 3D modelled version of the city block where the excavation took place.

Visualising the Trench

One of the big challenges of the project was how to visualise the trench in a way that allowed the user to see through it and see the distribution of the artefacts within. The Innovation Team used a 3D graphics-modelling program called 3D Studio Max to create a 3D model of the trench. The trench was separated into different layers based on the kinds of soils that were found during the excavation, and these layers were modelled based on the measurements found in the archaeological report.

Within the 3D Studio Max package, these layers can easily be visualised as transparent solid objects with different colours, so that the user can see through them, looking like layers of coloured glass with little objects embedded in each layer. The user can easily see through the layers to see the objects inside but can also see the different layers. This works well in a package like 3D Studio Max because the computer has all the time it wants to render the image for the user. Depending on the complexity of the model, it can take several minutes, or even several hours, to render a single image. In VR a new image needs to be rendered 60 times every second. When rendering this quickly, the transparent layers do not always look correct, with layers further away suddenly appearing to be closer to the user. This becomes jarring for the user and distracts away from interacting with the historical artefacts.

The solution was to forgo the transparency and instead make each layer of the trench out of a grid, kind of like modelling it out of chicken wire. Each layer could still have a different colour to identify it, and the user can easily see through the gaps in the 'wire'. The inside of each layer is also filled with a point cloud in the same colour, to give the layer a sense of volume. The result is a digital VR model that looks transparent to the user, but which uses only solid objects, making it much easier to render in real time (Fig. 5.3).

Some Technical Details

The ITSIT specialise in using new technology to enhance teaching and learning at the UON. The Deep Time application allows users to look at digitised three-dimensional copies of historical artefacts. The artefacts are digitised using a 3D scanner called the Artec Space Spider a process to create a realistic 3D representation.

The Artec Space Spider handheld high-speed 3D laser scanner was chosen over photogrammetry because of its metrological accuracy, and ability to capture the detail of the relatively small objects in high resolution. This specification was very important to enable the scans to be uploaded to VR. Laser scanning is also known as lidar and takes a rapid reading of a distance measurement at every direction capturing the surface shape of an object (Dassot et al. 2011).

The scanner uses 'blue light' technology to read the surface geometry of an object and releases ultra-short-pulse (USP) lasers providing maximum-precision creating

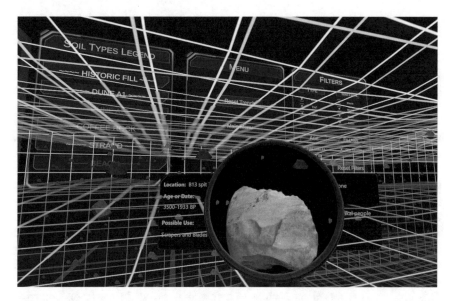

Fig. 5.3 Deep Time VR showing the virtual dig and digitised artefact, GLAMx Lab at University of Newcastle (2020). Courtesy UON

extremely detailed 3D models. This is then combined with pictures taken automatically during the scanning process to create a realistic 3D representation of the artefact. The handheld 3D scanner is able to provide high accuracy resolution and the least possible distance between any two given points within a 3D model, usually expressed by millimetres, or microns. The Innovation Team worked with a company called Thinglab to acquire the machine and provide initial support to allow the GLAMx Lab team to start scanning artefacts.

The 3D digital models require a post-processing phase to create high image quality and point cloud decimation. The Artec scanner also had a good track record and is used quite widely internationally. Other considerations when choosing equipment was the availability of software updates, the speed of processing and whether the scanner was user-friendly and easy to learn.

The 3D scans of artefacts are digitised and uploaded to a state-of-the-art digital online platform (Livinghistories@UON) and farmed out to the 3D VR, where they can be accessed and examined in the original places they were found in the archaeological dig. Recollect is usually used for two-dimensional items such as documents and images. The Innovation Team worked with the Recollect development team to get the system expanded to also be able to accept three-dimensional objects.

The digitised 3D objects can be accessed and viewed from the cloud via a webpage but are also downloaded into the custom VR application that was created for the Deep Time project. This application was created in a middleware package called Unity, which allows for easy deployment to multiple platforms. In the case of Deep Time, the application can be used on normal PCs or on HTC Vive VR headsets.

The availability of technology and expertise, as well as a new digital platform were timely in terms of having the Deep Time visualisation come to fruition. In 2018 the introduction of this new platform coincided with the establishment of the GLAMx Lab and WIL programs, and as mentioned a new feature was added to the digital platform enabling the upload of 3D digital files where 3D models could be viewed online.

The process of scanning each artefact and uploading to the digital platform is very time-consuming and can take up to one hour per artefact. The 3D scanning process involves placing the small artefact on a wooden revolving board for scanning. A similar technique is used in photogrammetry. Two separate scans are created by scanning one side of the artefact, then turning it over and scanning the other side ensuring enough overlapping features are present for alignment (Fig. 5.4). Next is the editing stage to illuminate any outliers or unnecessary geometry from the 3D scans. This involves erasing any part of the wooden base that may have been captured during the scanning process. This is done by selecting 'Base selection' and using an eraser tool so that only the scanned object is shown. The software also has a 2D tool that assists in tidying up the edges of a scan and deletes unnecessary geometry. This process is repeated on each scan before it is saved. In the 'tools' function 'fine registration' is run on each scan and then the alignment process is undertaken. Alignment can be achieved by either using the 'auto align' function or can be done manually (Fig. 5.5). When this is complete, the 'tools' application is opened to run 'global registration', 'outlier removal' and the 'sharp fusion' functions. 'Mesh simplification' is one of the final steps in the process whereby the size of the file is reduced. This is done by reducing the number of polygons to 300,000, which is an optimal size and quality for uploading and viewing in the VR because the lower the polygon count the more manageable the files. Essentially polygons are the shapes used to build the surface of a scan model. Polygons are the faces on the scan (with 3 or more edges) and in most cases in the shape of triangles, they are the building blocks of the data set that the computer must keep track of for any shape. The more polygons used the better the resolution and detail (Lee et al. 2005). There is no correct number of polygons to use when scanning, the basic rule is as many as required to describe the form of the object.

Finally, the texture is applied to the 3D scan; this adds colour to the 3D scan. Gherardini et al. (2019) emphasise a virtual model can include additional texture, such as colour to give the appearance of the real artefact, and providing the end-user with a permanent source, a true digital copy of the artefact (Fig. 5.6). The three files ('mtl', 'obj', 'jpeg') are then uploaded to the Livinghistories@UON digital platform where they can be viewed in the 3D viewer function.

As mentioned the ITSIT worked with the Recollect development team who created the Livinghistories@UON digital platform to allow the platform to display three-dimensional objects using the '3D viewer' function. Each artefact was accessioned and given a 'call number' like any item in the library's archive or collection number, and this number was recorded in an excel spreadsheet. This special call number relates to co-ordinates according to the archaeologist's report describing their location in the trench. This associated metadata (call number) is embedded in each digital scan

Fig. 5.4 3D scanning process using Artec software (2019), University of Newcastle (Australia). Courtesy UON

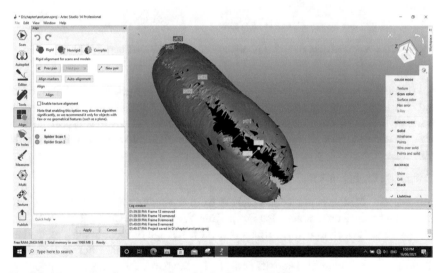

Fig. 5.5 3D scanning alignment process (2019). Courtesy UON

so they can be viewed in a virtual archaeological trench in the location in which they were found. When the 3D digital files are uploaded to Livinghistories@UON platform the digitised 3D artefacts are automatically downloaded into the custom VR application created for the Deep Time project.

As previously mentioned this project was not funded by research grants, therefore there were no restrictions in terms of a completion date. Since 2017, WIL students

Fig. 5.6 3D scanned artefact alongside Aboriginal stone tool (2019). Courtesy UON

and volunteers have worked on the project 3D scanning artefacts to propagate the VR and 68 artefacts have been digitised. The Artec Studio 3D scanning software is now available on the 10 computers in the GLAMx Lab for students to use. This allows multiple users to work on the post-processing phase to create 3D scans, which is the most time-consuming phase. And allows fast-tracking the project.

Navigating the dig in VR

Considerable feedback has been received from the many visitors, volunteers and students who have experienced the Deep Time VR at the GLAMx Lab. In 2019, the VR has been revised to include filters that show the age of the artefacts, as well as the particular 'type' of stone tool being viewed. The additional filtering functions allows the user to switch on and off fields to display particular types of stone tool. A revised VR model used in portable VR headsets has also been developed so that the project can be taken off-site and shared with the wider community. There has been particular interest from educators from local schools in the area.

5.4 Discussion

The visualisation Deep Time project discussed in this chapter relates to Aboriginal cultural heritage, archives using immersive technologies. And an example of 'digitisation' and 'digitalisation' processes to create a unique project specific to cultural heritage, history and archives. This is a shift away from innovative and immersive visualisations that relate to present day or futuristic themes that may not require digitisation, research and interpretation of archival records when conceptualising the projects. This digitisation project relied greatly on digitised artefacts. This also meant a greater level of negotiation was required in terms of arranging access and digitisation and engagement with Aboriginal communities of Newcastle. This brought unique opportunities for the team and collaborators to interrogate the collection of stone tools. The sharing of cultural knowledge was an important factor in the success of this visualisation project and provided a rare opportunity for engagement, resulting in the project having a sense of authenticity and exclusivity.

When working on immersive projects that have cultural themes there is often an expectation of accuracy in terms of the virtual modelling, design and rendering. Historical research is very important in finding 'evidence' about a building or place, and where historical evidence cannot be located then research of similar sites is essential to provide as accurate as possible renditions. The aim was to have the final visualisation as accurate as humanly possible based on the sources available. In this case, it was advantageous that the artefacts were housed at the university.

Projects that harness digitalization to offer diverse experiences can help shape the contemporary world. Digitalization of cultural material can help convey meaning and knowledge to new audiences such as marginalised and disadvantaged groups, or remote communities who may not otherwise have access to cultural knowledge. This is also suggested by Andrade and Dias (2020) Another remote use of 3D scanning technology would be to physically use the portable laser scanner in the field (with a battery pack) enabling remote sites or objects to be digitised, as suggested by Esclapés et al. (2013). The 3D scanning is portable technology and enables remote sites or objects to be digitised and is particularly applicable in the Australian context because of sensitive culture heritage sites often in remote locations.

Collaborations between Aboriginal groups and the university was fundamental to the project, as well as between academics and experts from across disciplines and sectors to promote university-community engagement. These collaborations were not only across the university, but promoted university-community engagement, something the UONCC is accustomed to (Hardy and Eklund 2014). The visualisation project has provided opportunities for UON's WIL students and volunteers at the GLAMx Lab to gain experience working with GLAM sector professions and innovation specialists. It also gave users the chance to develop GLAM sector skills and enhance their employability.

This is where the GLAM sector has a role to play in providing new experiences through accessible immersive experiences. Virtual technologies are fast becoming infrastructure of knowledge transference and connectivity, and users do not necessarily need to visit a museum or library. This is also reflected in the aims of the 4D narrative of architecture of Australia's Afghan cameleers project, referred to earlier supporting communities unable to access GLAM institutions. Instead audiences will be able to access immersive experiences remotely via outreach whereby technologies can be taken off-site and into communities. 4D methodologies have enormous potential bridging the gap between Aboriginal and non-Aboriginal cultural heritage in Australia. Archaeological heritage could be used as a tool for achieving cultural cohesion and increase cultural awareness to minimise cultural differences between Aboriginal and non-Aboriginal people in Australia. The Newcastle West site where the stone tools were located also has a rich non-Aboriginal heritage (AHMS, Aug 2011) and a future project could apply 4D methodology to visualise deep histories with non-Aboriginal to represent all human occupation on this single site. This brings together the past with the present living histories.

Interpreting archaeological or living sites provides a sense of authenticity to visualisation projects. With this comes a level of anticipated realism. When working on immersive projects that have cultural themes there is often an expectation of accuracy in terms of the virtual modelling, design and rendering and important 'evidence' about place.

5.5   Conclusion

The Deep Time study discussed in this chapter is exemplar of visualisation projects that relate to 'heritage sites' and has a deep sense of uniqueness and authenticity. Digitalisation that incorporates 'history' can extract history and cultural heritage from the bookshelves of libraries and archives and place in the virtual realm. Through immerging digitalisation methods and technologies such as VR and AR there are huge opportunities for innovation and immersive technologists to connect and work more closely with GLAM sector professionals to integrate 'history' and 'culture' into projects. It is certainly an effectual way to relay important knowledge. Further to this, Lewi and others suggest 'heritage sites' should be included in the GLAM mix, as heritage and site-specific interpretations are increasingly evident in digital practices used by those in the GLAM sector (Lewi et al. 2020). Visualisation projects that incorporate history and culture can shape the contemporary world.

An important message about this visualisation project that has a foundation in history and heritage are the virtual sources that represent copies of the actual artefact. Immersive technologies are platforms that display and convey knowledge and by no means replaces original sources. The 'real' experience comes when the user engages with the actual archival source and this usually means visiting an archive or museum. The immersive experience is only an introduction to cultural heritage, however may be the catalyst to dig deeper into archives to learn more. It is very important that original collections, archives and historical artefacts continue to be cared for. They most definitely should not be destroyed, firstly because of the cultural significance that they hold, and secondly, we do not know what advances there will be in terms of immersive technologies. There will be technologies in the future that have not even begun to be conceptualised, and where archival sources will be required to be digitised or redigitised. If we consider ways in which cultural heritage knowledge can be transferred and experienced, then the archive is 'gold' and the virtual is 'silver'. That is not to say that virtual experiences do not have value, it simply means that nothing re-places the actual authentic object or artefact. This chapter has highlighted that immersive heritage projects can be engaging and introduced new audiences to GLAM projects. And most important teach us to value the archive.

Finally, adopting multidisciplinary collaborations on any project is highly recommended. The Deep Time project is a good example of collaborations across disciplines. The benefits to this approach meant new knowledge about this important Aboriginal 'archive' could be created (Hardy and Di Gravio 2018). The Aboriginal artefacts are exceptional hand-hewn stone tools crafted by Indigenous people who occupied the area in present-day Newcastle thousands of years ago. There are many archaeological collections containing Aboriginal stone tools in institutions across Australia, however these mostly sit on shelves and are rarely studied or shared. Virtual realisation in this case enables artefacts to be shared online, fostering greater recognition and acknowledgement of Aboriginal culture. Australian Aboriginal culture is a continuous living culture, the oldest on the planet and the Deep Time project is an example of tangible and intangible heritage keeping Aboriginal culture alive. The concept of a virtual trench could be replicated using other stone tool archives, either in Australia or globally allowing artefacts to be researched to explore differences and similarities. Furthermore, in Australia other stone tool sites could be studied to look at possible trade routes, and to build new knowledge about interactions between the many Aboriginal cultures.

It is a very exciting time for libraries and archives especially in tertiary institutions to consider digitisation and digitalisation concepts and approaches of 3D digitising artefacts as discussed in this case study. Adopting a collaborative approach and intersection of disciplines augments creativity and provides new ways of conveying cultural knowledge through immersive technologies Danaher (2004) .

Lastly, the GLAM sector can provide new opportunities through employment. The GLAM sector is rapidly expanding with institutions undergoing a great deal of transformation in the twenty-first century due to the recent Covid-19 pandemic and rapid advances in immersive technologies.

Acknowledgements The Deep Time Project is conducted in memory and respectfully honours the First Australian People, the Aboriginal People of this land. We are very grateful to the Traditional owners and Aboriginal communities who supported the project. Thank you to Ben Myers (Director of 3D Scanning) ThingLab, Australia.

References

Andrade JG, Dias P (2020) A phygital approach to cultural heritage: augmented reality at Regaleira. Virt Archaeol Rev 11(22), 15–25 (2020). ISSN 1989-9947. https://doi.org/10.4995/var.2020. 11663

Archaeological Report Palais Royale Final Excavation Report for SBA Architects. August 2011 DRAFT. Archaeological & Heritage Management Solutions (AHMS)

Archaeological Management & Heritage Solutions (AMHS) (2011) Section 87/90 Aboriginal Heritage Impact Permit #1098622 Excavation Report for SBA Architects Pty Ltd. Final report, May

Banfi F, Brumana R, Stanga C (2019) Extended reality and informative models for the architectural heritage: from scan-to-BIM process to virtual and augmented reality. Virt Archaeol Rev 10(21):14–30. https://doi.org/10.4995/var.2019.11923

Baudrillard J (1994) Simulacra and simulation. University of Michigan Press, Michigan

Beniger J (1986) The control revolution. Harvard University Press, Cambridge, MA

Bevan S (2017) University of Newcastle team time travels with virtual reality. Newcastle Herald, 18 November 2017. http://www.theherald.com.au/story/5057677/virtual-digging-through-hunter-history/. Accessed 22 Sept 2019

Bevan S (2018) Breaking bread: Vera Deacon, Stockton resident, historian and author. Newcastle Herald, 16 June 2018. https://www.newcastleherald.com.au/story/5459686/vera-deacon-a-child-of-the-river-an-icon-of-newcastle/. Accessed 13 Nov 2019

Brennan S, Kriess D, Digitalization, 23 October 2016. The international encyclopedia of communication theory and philosophy, pp 1–11. Brennan S, Kriess D (2014, September 8) Digitalization and digitization. http://culturedigitally.org/2014/09/digitalization-and-digitisation/. Accessed 26 Nov 2019

Brennen S, Kreiss D (2014) Digitalization and digitisation. http://culturedigitally.org/2014/09/digitalization-and-digitisation/. Accessed 10 Aug 2020

Carnevali L, Lanfranchi F, Russo M (2019) Built information modelling for the 3D reconstruction of modern railway stations. Heritage 2(3):2298–2310. https://doi.org/10.3390/heritage2030141

Castells M (2010) The rise of the network society. Wiley Blackwell, Malden, MA

Castells M (2005) A era da informação: Economia, Sociedade e Cultura. Volume I: A sociedade em rede. Fundação Calouste Gulbenkian, Lisboa

Charbonneau N, Spiric N, Blais V, Robichaud L, Burgess J (2018) 4D modelling of built heritage: a system offering an alternative to using BIM. Digital Stud/Le champ numérique 8(1), 8. https://doi.org/10.16995/dscn.283

Danaher S (2004) The complete guide to digital 3D design. The Ilex Press Ltd., UK

Dassot M, Constant T, Fournier M (2011) The use of terrestrial LiDAR technology in forest science: application fields, benefits and challenges. Ann for Sci 68(5):959–974

Denard H (ed) (2009) The London charter for the computer-based visualisation of cultural heritage, version 2.1. King's College London, London, UK

Di Gravio G, Hardy A, Tredinnick D, Wood K (2017) Engaging tertiary students with university archival collections, ASA-ITIC 2017 Australian Society of Archivists 2017 conference, Melbourne. Session Abstracts available at https://www.archivists.org.au/learning-public ations/asa-2017-conference/session-abstracts. Accessed 10 Aug 2020. Presentation available on YouTube at, https://youtu.be/_FwUKTnZiPE

Di Gravio G (2011) Hunter Living Histories, University of Newcastle (Australia). Aboriginal archaeological report for former Palais site released. https://hunterlivinghistories.com/2011/05/20/abo riginal-archaeological-report-for-former-palais-site-released/. Accessed 10 Aug 2020

Di Gravio G, Hardy A (2018) GLAMx Lab Living Histories Digitisation Lab—engaging tertiary students with university archival collections (2018) by Taylor & Francis in Archives and Manuscripts. https://www.tandfonline.com/doi/full/10.1080/01576895.2018.1467272

Dobson E (2019) Critical digital humanities, the search for a methodology. University of Illinios

Esclapés J, Tejerina D, Esquembre MA, Bolufer J (2013) Methodological proposal to generate interactive virtual walkthrough. Virt Archaeol Rev 4(9):212–222

Fazio L, Lo Brutto M (2020) 3D survey for the archaeological study and virtual reconstruction of the "Sanctuary of Isis" in the ancient Lilybaeum (Italy). Virt Archaeol Rev 11(22):1–14 (2020). ISSN 1989-9947. https://polipapers.upv.es/index.php/var/article/view/11928. Accessed 10 Aug 2020. https://doi.org/10.4995/var.2020.11928

Floridi L (ed) (2003) The Blackwell guide to the philosophy of computing and information. Blackwell, Londres

Gherardini F, Santachiara M, Leali F (2019) Enhancing heritage fruition through 3D virtual models and augmented reality: an application to Roman artefacts. Virt Archaeol Rev 10(21):67–79 (2019). ISSN 1989-9947. https://polipapers.upv.es/index.php/var/article/view/11918. Accessed 26 Apr 2020. https://doi.org/10.4995/var.2019.11918

Griffith B (2018) Deep time dreaming. Black Inc

Guidi G, Remondino F (2012) 3D modelling from real data. In: Alexandru C (ed) Modeling and simulation in engineering, pp 69–102

Guidi G, Trocchianesi R, Pils G, Morlando G, Seassaro A (2010) A virtual museum for design: new forms of interactive fruition. In: 16th international conference on virtual systems and multimedia, VSMM 2010, pp 242–249

Hamill L (2017) Archival arrangement and description, analog to digital. Rowman & Littlefield, London

Hardy A, Eklund E (2014) Multidisciplinary approach to university-community engagement. Australasian J Univ-Comm Engage 9:77–99

Hardy A, Di Gravio G (2018) Rock art archive. Hunter Living Histories, University of Newcastle (Australia). https://hunterlivinghistories.com/2018/10/08/rock-art-archive/. Accessed 10 Aug 2020

Hardy AV, di Gravio G, Martin C, Rigby R, Davidson T (2018) Newcastle time machine a multi-disciplinary approach to digital cultural heritage, Brisbane, QLD. In: Proceedings of digital cultural heritage: FUTURE VISIONS. Digital cultural heritage: FUTURE VISIONS, State Library of Queensland, Brisbane, 19–21 April 2017. Brisbane, QLD Australia: Architecture Theory Criticism History Research Centre, School of Architecture, The University of Queensland

Heritage, Media, Parliament. NSW Upper House takes action on Aboriginal heritage Jun 23, 2011. https://davidshoebridge.org.au/2011/06/23/nsw-upper-house-takes-action-on-aboriginal-heritage/. Accessed 10 Aug 2020

Hunter Living Histories, University of Newcastle (Australia) (2011) NSW Upper House takes action for the sake of our Aboriginal Heritage. https://hunterlivinghistories.com/2011/06/23/nsw-upper-house-takes-action-for-the-sake-of-our-aboriginal-heritage/. Accessed 10 Aug 2020

Hunter Living Histories, University of Newcastle (Australia). https://hunterlivinghistories.com/. Accessed 21 Nov 2019

Hunter Living Histories, University of Newcastle (Australia) (2018) Deep time virtual reality—transforming humanities in the digital age. https://hunterlivinghistories.com/2018/05/09/deep-time-vr/. Accessed 10 Aug 2020

i-SCOOP (2016) Digitization, digitalization and digital transformation: the differences. https://www.i-scoop.eu/digitisation-digitalization-digital-transformation-disruption/. Accessed 10 Aug 2020

ICOMOS (2017) The florence declaration on heritage landscape as human values. Florence 18th ICOMOS General Assembly. https://bit.ly/2MQB1eO. Accessed 10 Aug 2020 Charter for the Interpretation and Presentation of Cultural Heritage Sites

Koche G (ed) (2017) Digitisation: theories and concepts for empirical cultural research. Routledge, New York

Kyriakaki G, Doulamis A, Doulamis N, Ioannides M, Makantasis K, Protopapadakis E, Hadjiprocopisb A, Wenzelc K, Fritschc D, Klein M, Weinlingerd G (2014) 4D reconstruction of tangible cultural heritage objects from web-retrieved images. Int J Herit Digital Era 3(2):431–451. https://doi.org/10.1260/2047-4970.3.2.431

Lee S, Byeongwook M, Daiyong K, Eun-Young C, Namho H, Soo In L, Euee SJ (2005) An adaptive quantization schee for efficient texture coordinate compression in MPEG 3DMC, p 74. In: Advances in Multimedia Information Processing - PCM 2005: 6th Pacific Rim Conference on Multimedia, Jeju Island, Korea, November 11–13, Proceedings, Part I. Germany, Springer Berlin Heidelberg

Lewi H, Smith W, vom Lehn D, Cooke S (eds) (2020) The Routledge international handbook of new digital practices in galleries, libraries, archives, museums and heritage sites. Routledge, New York

Livinghistories@UON, University of Newcastle (Australia) (2019a) Three-dimensional scanned artefacts. https://livinghistories.newcastle.edu.au/nodes/index/q:WDXM/faceadd:4e5 449443a3a338. Accessed 10 Aug 2020

Livinghistories@UON, University of Newcastle (Australia) (2019b) Three-dimensional scanned artefacts. from https://livinghistories.newcastle.edu.au/nodes/view/102273. Accessed 2 Nov 2020

Luigini A, Brusaporci S, Vattano S, Tata A (2019) 3D digital models for a widespread museum: the Renon's "Bauernhöfe". Int Arch Photogram Remote Sens Spat Inf Sci XLII-2/W9:447–453. https://doi.org/10.5194/isprs-archives-XLII-2-W9-447-2019

Mahey M, Al-Abdulla A, Ames S, Bray P, Candela G, Chambers S, Derven C, Dobreva-McPherson M, Gasser K, Karner S, Kokegei K, Laursen D, Potter A, Straube A, Wagner S-C, Wilms L, with forewords by: Al-Emadi TA, Broady-Preston J, Landry P, Papaioannou G (2019) Open a GLAM Lab. Digital Cultural Heritage Innovation Labs, Book Sprint, Doha, Qatar, 23–27 September, 2019

NBN News. 6,700-Year-Old Aboriginal Artefacts Discovered Newcastle Australia. May 24, 2011. https://youtu.be/SWZMmMTZB-E. Accessed 10 Aug 2020

NBN News. Star Hotel Riot—40 years to the day. September 19, 2019. https://www.nbnnews.com.au/2019/09/19/star-hotel-riot-40-years-to-the-day/?fbclid=IwAR1Z-6caHet_bPY1GSMWL JQkZ1_9uhPvrc7rnG-rcC_Jz9FC2Wm-tKDuUdE. Accessed 10 Aug 2020

NSW government, aboriginal cultural heritage. https://www.environment.nsw.gov.au/topics/aborig inal-cultural-heritage/legislation. Accessed 10 Aug 2020

Papaioannou G (2019) Digital cultural heritage innovation labs. In: Open a GLAM Lab. Book Sprint, Doha, Qatar, 23–27 September, 2019

PR Newswire. Sketchfab releases USDZ conversion, making millions of 3D models available in Apple's AR. New York. March 25, 2020 /PRNewswire-PRWeb/

PR Newswire. Sketchfab launches public domain dedication for cultural heritage with the Smithsonian Institution and World-class Organizations. New York. Feb. 25, 2020

Rashid Md M, Antlej K (2020) Geospatial platforms and immersive tools for social cohesion: the 4D narrative of architecture of Australia's Afghan cameleers. Virt Archaeol Rev 11(22):74–84 (2020). ISSN 1989-9947. https://polipapers.upv.es/index.php/var/article/view/12230. Accessed 10 Aug 2020. https://doi.org/10.4995/var.2020.12230

Santachiara M, Gherardini F, Leali F (2018) An augmented reality application for the visualization and the pattern. IOP Conf Ser Mater Sci Eng 364(1):012094

Santos P, Ritz M, Fuhrmann C, Fellner D (2017) 3D mass digitization: a milestone for archaeological documentation. Virt Archaeol Rev 8(16):1–11. https://doi.org/10.4995/var.2017.6321

Seville Principles (2011) http://sevilleprinciples.com. Accessed 10 Aug 2020

Statham N (2019) Scientific rigour of online platforms for 3D visualization of heritage. Virt Archaeol Rev 10(20):1–16. https://doi.org/10.4995/var.2019.9715

Tsichritzis D, Gibbs S (1991) Virtual museums and virtual realities. In: Proceedings of International Conference on Hypermedia and Interactivity in Museums, Pittsburgh, 14–16 October, pp 17–25

Turkle S (1997) A vida no ecrã: a identidade na era da internet. Relógio d´Água, Lisboa

UNESCO (1972) Convention concerning the protection of the world cultural and natural heritage. UNESCO general conference, seventeenth session. http://bit.ly/1xBRhFO. UNESCO (2002).

Convention concerning the protection of the world cultural and natural heritage: 30th anniversary (1972–2002). World Heritage Committee, Twenty-sixth session. http://bit.ly/2mamwHI. Accessed 10 Aug 2020. UNESCO (2008)

University of Newcastle (UON), Australia. Deep time explainer (2019) https://youtu.be/ydp_RD3 fKLI. Accessed 10 Aug 2020

University of Newcastle (UON), Australia. Deep time explainer (2019) https://youtu.be/ydp_RD3 fKLI. Accessed 22 Sept 2019. Hunter Living Histories, University of Newcastle (Australia) (2018) Deep time virtual reality—transforming humanities in the digital age. https://hunterlivinghistor ies.com/2018/05/09/deep-time-vr/. Accessed 21 Nov 2019

Van Dijk J (2005) The network society: social aspects of new media. Sage, London

Virtual-reality project showcases ancient Aboriginal artefacts. Douglas Smith. NITV News. 17 April 2019. Accessed April 26, 2020, https://www.sbs.com.au/nitv/article/2019/04/17/virtual-reality-project-showcases-ancient-aboriginal-artefacts. Accessed 10 Aug 2020

Warwick C, Terras M, Nyhan J (2012) Digital humanities in practice. Facet Publishing, London

Wright P, Keily L (2018) VALA 2018: libraries, technology and the future. In: VALA2018 proceedings (Melbourne 13–15 February, 2018) conference paper. https://www.vala.org.au/vala2018-pro ceedings/1238-vala2018-session-10-wright

Chapter 6
Applications of 3D Modelling of Rock Art Sites Using Ground-Based Photogrammetry: A Case Study from the Greater Red Lily Lagoon Area, Western Arnhem Land, Northern Australia

Jarrad Kowlessar, Ian Moffat, Daryl Wesley, Tristen Jones, Maxime Aubert, Mark Willis, Alfred Nayinggul, and the Njanjma Aboriginal Corporation

Abstract The creation of high-resolution 3D models using structure from motion (SfM) photogrammetry is an emerging research tool in archaeology that allows the spatially accurate representation of rock art sites and landscapes. This methodology allows the creation of immersive representations of important cultural-heritage sites using widely available, inexpensive equipment and software which produce data that can be easily managed by the appropriate Indigenous custodians. In this study, ground-based photography was used to create high-resolution, georectified three-dimensional (3D) models of five rock art sites in the Greater Red Lily Lagoon Area (GRLLA) in western Arnhem Land, Northern Australia. Located directly between the East Alligator River and the Arnhem Plateau, on the Traditional Lands of the Australian Indigenous Manilakarr Clan, the rock art and cultural-heritage sites present in the GRLLA are of national heritage significance and are immediately

---

The original version of this chapter was revised: The co-author's name "Max Aubert" has been changed as "Maxime Aubert". The correction to this chapter is available at https://doi.org/10.1007/978-3-030-77028-0_28

J. Kowlessar (✉) · I. Moffat · D. Wesley · T. Jones · M. Willis
Archaeology, College of Humanities, Arts and Social Sciences, Flinders University, Adelaide, Australia
e-mail: Jarrad.Kowlessar@flinders.edu.au

T. Jones
School of Culture, History and Language, The Australian National University, Canberra, Australia

M. Aubert
Place, Evolution and Rock Art Heritage Unit (PERAHU), Griffith University, Brisbane, Australia

M. Willis
Sacred Sites Research, Inc, Albuquerque, NM, USA

A. Nayinggul · the Njanjma Aboriginal Corporation
Njanjma Aboriginal Corporation, Gunbalanya, Australia

adjacent to World Heritage-registered Kakadu National Park. This corpus of rock art is threatened by limited land management resources, tourism and visitor pressures, and land access issues. The creation of high-resolution 3D models of rock art using SfM photogrammetry provides a cost-effective approach to assist Indigenous cultural-heritage land managers to manage, record, and monitor rock art sites and enhance site access and visitor experiences.

Keywords Rock art · Photogrammetry · Structure from motion · Cultural-heritage management tools · Rock art visitor experiences

6.1 Introduction

Red Lily Lagoon and the Greater Red Lily Lagoon Area (GRLLA) are situated on the edge of the northern coastal plains of western Arnhem Land, Australia (Fig. 6.1). This environment is at the interface between the 'stone country', consisting of an elevated sandstone plateau incised by multiple gorges, and the floodplains surrounding the East Alligator River. This landscape is argued to have been continuously occupied by humans for over 60,000 years (Clarkson et al. 2015, 2017) and in that time has seen dramatic palaeogeographic change driven by sea-level variation (Reeves et al. 2013; Woodroffe 1988; Woodroffe 1993). During this extensive human occupation, inhabitants have left significant cultural markings in the form of painted and engraved rock art on the sandstone of this province (Chaloupka 1993; David et al. 2013a, b). These sites present a unique Indigenous vision of society and environment (Gunn 2018) and have great cultural significance to the Traditional Owners of this landscape (Gunn 1992; Guse 2008; Jones and Wesley 2016; Wesley 2016). Unfortunately, these important sites are under an increasing threat from a diverse range of natural and anthropogenic taphonomic processes including weathering, road usage, site visitation, and wildfire damage (Carmichael et al. 2018; Guse 2008; Marshall 2019; Wesley 2016).

Rock art sites of the GRLLA present significant challenges for cultural-heritage management as well as archaeological research. The primary challenge is to develop a time- and cost-efficient methodology for making a detailed record of the complex natural and cultural structures of rock art sites, including both the individual rock art motifs and the site physiography. This record must be of sufficient resolution and clarity to facilitate ongoing site management and monitoring as well as providing a means of cataloguing and organising motifs. This challenge is made more difficult by significant limitations to site access caused by seasonal flooding and inaccessible terrain. This drives a need for a detailed site recording methodology that is highly time efficient and limits the use of heavy and difficult-to-transport equipment. A 3D approach to site recording and representation using ground-based photogrammetry allows these management outcomes to be achieved. The data produced by this methodology provide a means to view and experience the sites in a meaningful and immersive way from a remote location. Given the need for site conservation

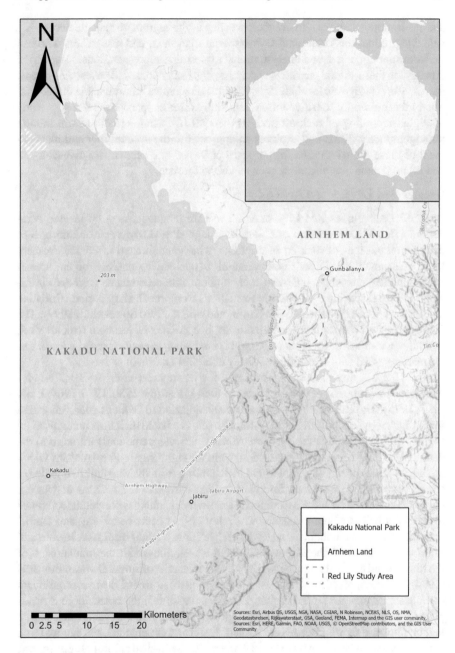

Fig. 6.1 Greater Red Lily Lagoon Area rock art study area

and the remote location of many rock art sites in the region, virtual site access is a valuable product for Traditional Owners, land managers, and researchers who can perform spatial queries and analyse directly on virtual representations. Despite the efficacy of these digital products for satisfying Indigenous and researcher needs, they may create significant challenges for the management, curation, and dissemination of this culturally sensitive virtual repository. This chapter presents a case study of digital recording of rock art sites in the GRLLA using structure from motion photogrammetry (SfM) and explores an approach to the accessibility and management of these digital records for purposes of virtual site access, site management, and future potential applications such as virtual tourism.

Greater Red Lily Lagoon Area Rock Art

The GRLLA includes Red Lily, or Wulk in Erre language, Lagoon located adjacent to a dense concentration of cultural-heritage sites (known as Minjamirndaab) depicting thousands of rock art inscriptions, which are situated where the Arnhem Land escarpment meets the floodplain and wetlands. The geology of the area is predominantly sandstone, quartzite, and conglomerate bedrock, with igneous intrusions and extensive areas of lateritic formations from the Tertiary period (Christian and Stewart 1953; Needham 1984; Senior and Smart 1976; Sweet et al. 1999). The cultural-heritage site complex, Minjamirndaab, consists of 77 known rock art sites, including a number of dreaming (*djang*) rock art sites, in particular a site known as Urrmarning (Red Lily Dreaming) (Wesley et al. 2017).

The GRLLA first came to prominence for its rock art after the 1949 Anglo-American Scientific Expedition to Arnhem Land (Mountford 1950, 1956, 1964, 1965, 1967, 1975). The area of sandstone escarpment adjacent to Wulk Lagoon was called Inagurdurwil by Mountford (1956) (although this is a name no longer recognised by Manilakarr Traditional Owners). Mountford (1956) was particularly attracted to the detailed hunting scenes and discussed in detail the significance of the rock art which included images of running figures and men hunting from the Inagurdurwil galleries (Jones et al. 2017a, b). Mountford (1964: 12) referred to the rock art of western Arnhem Land as by far the most colourful known in Australia, with specific reference to the paintings at Minjamirndaab. McCarthy (1965) described X-ray and 'spirit' paintings from rockshelters in the GRLLA. McCarthy (1965) discussed *Mormo* and *Mimi* spirits along with the purpose of Indigenous religious and ceremonial aspects of the rock art and cultural knowledge held by Manilakarr Traditional Owners. Edwards (1974: 136) recognised the GRLLA (Minjamirndaab) as one of the most significant complexes of rock art in the region. Edwards (1974: 37–38) noted the numerous painted 'scenes' of ceremony, dancing figures, and didjeridoo players whilst stating that hunting and fighting scenes are a major feature of the precinct. Further research at GRLLA was undertaken by the well-known Czech physical anthropologist Jelinek (1986) who attempted to place the rock art from the area into a generalised study of greater western Arnhem Land rock art. Rock art from Red Lily Lagoon would feature as key examples in Chaloupka's (1993) regional rock art stylistic chronology. Chaloupka (1984: 34–35) observed that the best examples of Northern Running Figures are found in these site complexes. Gunn (1992) undertook a detailed survey of GRLLA concentrating on recording rock art imagery from sacred sites including Urrmarning. This is the last known recording of Urrmarning before it was destroyed in 2006 from wildfires. The Red Lily Lagoon area has been shown to be an area of intensive rock art production during the late Holocene with a focus on depicting human figures and fish (Wesley et al. 2017). Rock art sites in this area have also contributed to significant advances in the understanding of Arnhem Land rock art chronologies (Jones et al. 2017a, b). Radiocarbon age determinations for the Northern Running Figure rock art have produced a minimum age of 9400 cal. BP and suggests production over at least 3500 years (Jones 2017b: 88).

An important consideration for understanding GRLLA rock art is to place it within the context of the occupation of Arnhem Land over the last 65,000 years (Clarkson et al. 2017; Jones 1985). Significant environmental variability occurred during this period resulting in substantial landscape alteration which all strongly influenced the geomorphological development and ecology of Arnhem Land (Wasson 1992; Woodroffe 1988). The combination of climate variation, sea-level rise, and palaeo-geographic change throughout the period of human habitation provided the impetus for considerable disruption and change to occupation and land use and to the emergence of new rock art traditions and other technologies (Bourke et al. 2007; Faulkner 2009; Hiscock 1996, 1999; Jones 2017; Taçon and Brockwell 1995). Models of rock art chronology and Indigenous occupation closely mirror these environmental changes (Chaloupka 1993; Hiscock 1999). Occupation of the GRLLA has been investigated through excavations at three rockshelter sites: Birriwilk (Shine et al. 2013), Ingaanjalwurr (May et al. 2017; Shine et al. 2016), and Minjamirndaab (MN05) (Wesley et al. 2017). These three sites all show that the highest occupation density occurred in the last 1000 years associated with a focus by Indigenous people on the nearby freshwater environment of the East Alligator wetlands that emerged in the late Holocene (Shine et al. 2013, 2016; Wesley et al. 2017). The archaeological connections to the freshwater environment correspond with *djang* (dreaming) (Shine et al. 2013: 76) and associated cultural narratives (May et al. 2017: 62) and suggest that much of the rock art production is dated to the last 750 years at these sites. The cultural-heritage sites of the GRLLA and the rock art depictions therein provide a lens through which to explore the nature and magnitude of change in Indigenous communities that have occurred over millennia and, thus. are exceptionally significant for both the Indigenous Traditional Owners and archaeological research.

The destruction of the Urrmarning dreaming rock art site by wildfire in the aftermath of Cyclone Monica in 2006 prompted senior Traditional Owners to seek professional and academic support to ensure cultural-site safety through a local management approach. The Njanjma Aboriginal Corporation (NAC) and an Indigenous ranger program were established in response to concerns by Traditional Owners regarding the ongoing management and conservation of their country. By 2015, NAC had identified the conservation of rock art and other Indigenous cultural-heritage places as a major priority for Traditional Owners (Njanjma Rangers 2015). The rock art sites of the GRLLA are managed by the Njanjma Rangers who are tasked with locating, monitoring, and conserving rock art and Indigenous cultural heritage (Njanjma Rangers 2015). Detailed records of cultural-heritage places are required for

conservation planning and management. Accurate and detailed records are important as a tool to allow Indigenous rangers to monitor conditions at the rock art sites.
A wide variety of micro and macro threats to the rock art sites have been noted in
a number of studies in the GRLLA (Guse 2008; Marshall 2019; Njanjma Rangers
2015; Wesley 2016). Primary risks to all sites include encroaching vegetation and
weeds, insects (i.e. termites and mud-wasps), dust, weathering and erosion, mineral
deposits and staining, fire, visitation, and changes to rock surfaces such as exfoliation
and cracking (Guse 2008; Marshall 2019; Wesley 2016). These risks to the rock art
of the GRLLA are not inconsequential and can result in the catastrophic loss of rock
art as seen at Urrmarning (Wesley 2016). Furthermore, there is a tangible risk to rock
art from climate change (Carmichael et al. 2018). Monitoring these impacts requires
a constant and detailed record of rock art conditions.

Aims of a Digital Approach to Rock Art

Rock art recording (summarised by Domingo Sanz 2014) is primarily aimed at
making as detailed a record of the site as possible to facilitate research, accessibility,
and cultural-heritage management. This has historically been undertaken by drawing,
photography, site plans, or surveying (Brady et al. 2019). This record can serve a
multiplicity of functions, depending on the aim of the survey, but digital technologies
now make it possible to record data of sufficient resolution to address all of these
aims (Alexander et al. 2015; Chandler et al. 2007; El-Hakim et al. 2004; Meijer
2015). As a result, SfM photogrammetry is now becoming a widely applied tool in
rock art research (Brophy 2018; Davis et al. 2017; González-Aguilera et al. 2009;
Scopingno et al. 2011).

One important goal for the recording of rock art is to document changes to the
site over time to quantify deterioration and to identify its key agents (Plets et al.
2012). For change detection, a geometric record of the site must be generated as
well as a detailed visual record of every motif present. This has traditionally been
undertaken for rock art with photography (Groom 2016) but SfM photogrammetry is
much better suited to this task (Plets et al. 2012), and data of this resolution provide
the opportunity for automated change detection (Abate 2019).

An additional goal of site recording is to facilitate remote interaction with rock
art, principally using virtual reality techniques. This goal was designed to allow
interaction for management purposes (i.e. Lee et al. 2019) as well as for providing
access to community members with limited mobility. Similar approaches are used
in a routine way for built heritage (e.g. Greenop and Landorf 2017) but have rarely
been used for rock art studies (Alexander et al. 2015; Rogerio-Candelera 2015).

In addition to providing information for cultural-heritage management and
community engagement, rock art recording aims to produce a data set detailed enough
to allow analysis for archaeological research. This requires accurate scale information
for the site and each motif depicted therein. This has traditionally been accomplished
by including a scale bar within rock art photography, but this doesn't allow accurate
measurement of individual features when used in a single photograph. Additionally,
the placement of the motifs within the geometry of the shelter and their relative
positions to one another are critical to archaeological rock art analysis. This has

traditionally been accomplished in rock art studies by drawing a baseline offset plan of the site or with a compass and tape. The placement of the site in its contextual landscape is also of critical importance so that its aspect, elevation, and relationship to other landscape features can be determined (Bradley 1991; Bradley et al. 1994).

In addition to these considerations, the chosen method of recording would require low-cost equipment as well as a rapid recording method (Westoby et al. 2012). This is important as this region has an abundance of rock art sites and access is severely limited by precipitous terrain, seasonal flooding, and pockets of thick forest. As a result, much rock art recording is undertaken using a helicopter to access the sites.

6.2 Methods

Structure from motion photogrammetry (SfM) (reviewed for archaeological applications by Sapirstein and Murray 2017) was chosen as the method of three-dimensional recording of the rock art sites. SfM generates spatial measurements from multiple digital images and ultimately can digitally reconstruct an entire area or a discrete subject in three dimensions. This method requires multiple digital images taken of the same subject from many different angles and camera positions. The SfM photogrammetry method reconstructs the camera locations by first detecting features present in multiple images and then computing the changes in the angle that account for the differences between images (Westoby et al. 2012). By reconstructing the camera position of each image, the distance between subject and camera can be calculated. This method has a two-phase workflow: data capture followed by data processing.

The SfM method has been employed numerous times in an archaeological context for Indigenous Australian rock art recording (Fritz et al. 2016; Davis et al. 2017; Jalandoni et al. 2018). In some cases where persistent site access is possible, the process of data capture has been approached iteratively. In these cases, issues with data capture that become apparent during post-processing can be easily resolved with a site revisit (Fritz et al. 2016). This approach is not applicable throughout the Njanjma management area because most sites are situated in difficult-to-reach terrain which severely limits the opportunity for revisit. Therefore, complete capture in one visit is a requirement. Iterative site visits are possible, however, on a longer time scale for the purposes of change detection.

For this case study, using SfM, data have been collected and modelled separately for comparison in 2015 and again in 2019. To achieve this, a detailed visual inspection of every surface of each recorded rock art site was conducted before SfM image capture to ensure a recorders complete capture of every motif and required site feature. To aid in the detection of faded pigments, the DStretch image enhancement software (Harmon 2009) was run on a portable Android tablet. DStretch provides a number of pre-set contrast ratios that can recolour digital images to accentuate a variety of faint pigment colours (Fig. 6.2). A number of colour space enhancements are available through the DStretch software which accentuate different pigment colours. The LYE enhancement, for example, accentuates yellow colours which are

Fig. 6.2 Panel before (top) and after (bottom) applying the DStrech LYE enhancement to accentuate yellow ochres

often very difficult to observe even with close-up visual inspection on site. Whilst every surface will be recorded and DStretch can be performed in post-processing of the SfM constituent image set, the live surface inspection was also conducted to ensure that any visible pigments are located and imaged in appropriate detail and distance during the SfM image capture (Davis et al. 2017: 5). After conventional and DStretch images demonstrated the presence of rock art motifs, we proceeded to capture images suitable for constructing SfM models.

SfM photogrammetry recording requires multiple photographs of every surface from different angles. Image capture was achieved in two major passes for each site (Fig. 6.3). The first or 'far pass' is aimed at capturing the rock geometry itself. This pass aims to capture all of the surfaces of the site and will define the extent of the recorded area but does not pay particular focus on the motifs themselves. This capture is done from a distance that allows wide-scale coverage of the site, and photographs are captured gradually moving in from the extents until satisfactory overlap has been achieved covering all of the desired areas. The resolution of the images recorded is an important consideration. Whilst the first pass will image the entire surface of the site, distance and angle of view are insufficient to provide the necessary clear and distinguishable details of the motifs. The second pass focuses on

Fig. 6.3 Camera placement relative to the rock art site showing the far pass and the close pass

the art itself. Identifying each panel and each motif is critical in achieving a detailed site record. The photographs of the second pass include close-up shots of the motifs and this is captured in a panel-by-panel approach moving left to right across the site. Image overlap is not as important for this phase as alignment is achieved based on the first pass. For larger motifs, overlapping photographs allow more pixels to be captured than a single image framed on the motif extents. For smaller motifs, framing each motif in a single photograph may provide an adequate and clear record at an acceptable resolution to clearly distinguish all the details of each motif. Similarly, as a means of recording the superimposition of the motifs, each panel should be recorded with an overlapping approach with detailed images of all of its surfaces. In this way, the resolution of the ultimate photo-merged surface can be thought of as variable and scalable to the needs of each motif. To reduce projection distortion when viewing these panels and motifs in isolation, the images are taken at as close to a 90° angle as possible.

The actual image resolution in this study varied between sites due to the use of different cameras with different technical specifications. The largest image resolution recorded by this project was 8688 pixels by 5792 pixels in a RAW image format. High-resolution images are only needed when the details that are being captured by that image require a high resolution to be clearly distinguished in the image. For this reason, the first pass aimed at capturing the overall site geometry was often recorded at a lower resolution and in a JPEG format to save memory space in the field, whereas larger formats were used for the close passes that captured motif details.

The rock art in the Wulk lagoon area has been inscribed in expansive rockshelters and surrounding open rock faces. These open outdoor environments present a number of complications to recording including issues caused by sunlight, vegetation, and the complexity of the rock geometry itself. The recording is conducted at a time when the sunlight is most evenly dispersed over the site and mottled shadows are avoided, especially in areas where motifs are visible on the rock surface. Changing lighting conditions are also a significant consideration for site recording such that any area that has been captured in one image should be captured in all subsequent images in the same lighting conditions. This, importantly, helps with both the alignment of the cameras during the post-processing phase as well as the comprehension of the model when it is viewed and interacted with.

Vegetation can have a significant impact on the model alignment and appearance. Interferences to the generation of a clear and comprehensible geometric record come from both the occlusions caused by vegetation prohibiting a record of concealed surfaces as well as the fine and dense nature of foliage. Wherever possible, obstructing foliage was cleared before image capture. Where clearing was not feasible, image capture was taken in a more intense way with a dense close-range record made of surfaces that are close to the foliage.

A final, and important, consideration is the complexity of the rock geometry itself. Rockshelters are a highly erosional area with a great deal of complexity from factors such as disconnected boulders, caverns and cracks in the rock, and deep shadow contrasting with bright light. This geometry requires individual consideration to ensure capture of all sections is achieved.

Photo targets were used as markers to aid in subsequent image alignment during post-processing and allowing rockshelter models to be aligned to drone-based landscape models using shared markers visible in both data sets. The placement of these markers was made to evenly distribute across the width of a shelter with more placement focussed on areas of complex geometry. At least three photo targets were placed in locations that will be visible in both ground-based and aerial images.

The total number of photographs used to construct the models varied between sites. Larger, more complex, sites require more photographs to capture the geometry in the large sweeping pass, and additionally, sites with a larger painted surface area require more photographs to capture at the close-range pass level. The largest number of photographs used in these recordings was 3858 images.

Model Processing

The digital model produced for each site was generated using Agisoft Metashape. The total processing time for each model varied based on the number of photographs used and the resolution of those images. The processing time for the models varied between a few hours in most cases and in the longest case more than 24 h. The processing was performed on a computer with 32 gigabytes of ram, NVIDIA Geforce GTX 1080 Graphics card, and Intel I7 Central Processing Unit. Model alignment, dense point cloud, and mesh generation were processed using the 'High' quality settings for each. The texture was generated using the 'generic' texture mapping mode. This texture mapping was chosen as it is able to evenly distribute the texture of the surface area of the rockshelter. The texture file produced has a resolution of 4096 (4 k) pixels (width and height). This texture is evenly distributed over the entire surface area of the mesh. This does not result in a detailed texture for the motifs themselves and the quality will be increasingly poor with an increased surface area. To achieve a detailed texture for the motifs, the model (Fig. 6.4a) was divided into panels (Fig. 6.4b, d) that represented discrete and relatively flat areas where motifs had been inscribed. Mesh faces that made up panel sections were extracted into separate chunks and treated as an independent model for texture generation. The panels were textured again with

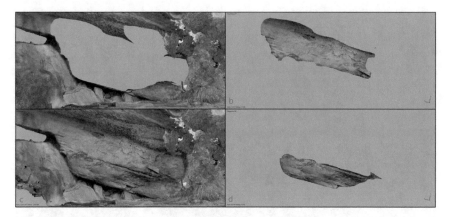

Fig. 6.4 Original model with panels individually extracted (**a**), individual panels (**b, d**), the final model with separately textured panels merged back into one mesh (**c**)

Fig. 6.5 Original photo (left). Texture fit to full geometry (middle). Texture fit to panel (right)

4 k resolution before being merged with the shelter mode (Fig. 6.4c). This way the unpainted rock surfaces and each painted panel were independently textured at 4 k resolution giving painted images enough resolution to be clearly visible in the final model (as shown in Fig. 6.5).

Because the textures are generated directly from the underlying images used to align the model, these images can be altered with the DStrech program after model generation to accentuate different ochre colours. This image can then be used to texture the underlying model as long as identical photographs were used, with no changes to their file names or their dimensions. Figure 6.6 shows the same site model textured with both original photographs and the same photographs with the DStretch LYE enhancement which accentuates the almost invisible yellow pigments on the site.

To georeference the models, the markers placed in the scene were given position and scale information. This information was derived from a total-station survey geolocated using a static GPS position recorded on the site. The GPS position was post-processed using the AUSPOS service and was provided in a geographic coordinate space using eastings and northings and elevations in the Australian Height Datum. For subsequent recordings of these sites, the models were aligned and scaled using the models generated in the first survey (2015) as a reference. This alignment

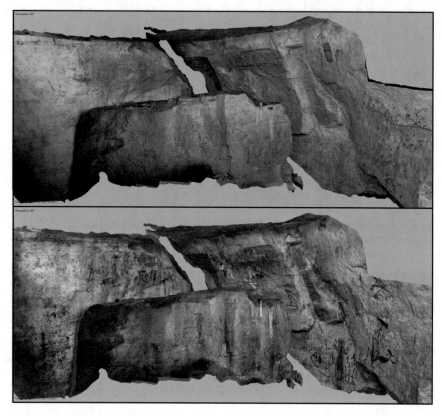

Fig. 6.6 Rock art site model textured from RGP photographs (top) and DStretch LYE enhanced Photographs (bottom)

was conducted with the 'Align Chunks' point-based alignment function within the Agisoft Metashape software. As the 2015 models were georeferenced using a total-station survey and Static GPS Positions, this quality of georeferences was made available to the subsequent models generated in 2019 using this alignment method.

To georeference the models of sites that weren't recorded in conjunction with a total-station survey, shared markers were used between the aerial photography captured with the drone and the rockshelter photogrammetry models. The aerial photography was georeferenced firstly with the onboard GPS with low accuracy and secondly fit to recognisable features in landscape satellite imagery.

By using aerial photography to georeference SfM photogrammetry models, it was possible to avoid undertaking a total-station survey for difficult-to-access locations in subsequent revisits. This is beneficial in reducing the recording time and cost of equipment used. A large-scale aerial photography survey was conducted over the landscape using a DJI Mavic 2 Pro drone and an Event 38 E384 unmanned aerial vehicle (UAV) mapping drone to provide a total coverage of $18.14 \, \text{km}^2$, which covers the entire study area. This survey recorded ground control points which were measured with an Emlid

RS + RTK GNSS or a CHC X90 + static GPS to georeference the resulting digital elevation model and orthophoto. This serves as a model to align future drone surveys and provide an accurate georeference. By placing markers that are captured by both drone survey and ground-based photogrammetry, new recordings can be conducted and effectively georeferenced without the need to bring heavy and expensive survey equipment. Figure 6.7 shows the Digital Elevation Model produced by the extensive aerial survey. This process was used for one new site recording in 2019 and will be the procedure for future site recordings within the coverage of this aerial survey.

In addition to the textured models produced from the ground-based photogrammetry, Metashape was also used to produce high-resolution orthomosaic images of each painted panel from each recorded site. Orthomosaic images (Fig. 6.8) are composite images formed from combining the original captured images that overlap a representative surface in the model. As the photo locations are known, the mosaic images can be produced with a seamless transition so long as photographic clarity and lighting are maintained as closely as possible between images. Such a photomosaic is, however, a projection of the surface as it is a two-dimensional representation of the three-dimensional surface. Photomosaics were generated for each panel by positioning a camera as close to 90° to the flattest rotation of the panel to minimise any projection distortion. Panels with a great deal of curvature are required to be projected several times to maintain an undistorted perspective in the orthomosaic images produced.

6.3 Data Hosting and Virtual Accessibility

The GRLLA sites were recorded to satisfy a variety of purposes including management, research, community access, and engagement, as is common for rock art studies (Cassidy et al. 2019). Rock art is a cultural artefact and belongs to the Traditional Owners and descendant community who live and manage the country in which it is situated. Rock art has contemporary cultural value and is impacted by a social framework and cultural protocols that manage site access and information about associated stories. This is true of physical places as well as virtual spaces that represent these places. This diversity of use means that choosing how these data are stored, curated, and accessed is challenging. To satisfy these many purposes as well as cultural protocols that govern this access, a web-based approach has been chosen using a purpose-built website (Digitalrockart.com 2020). This website was developed with the aim of both providing password-limited access to the data produced as well as explaining the methods used to capture the data. This management approach to virtual cultural spaces follows the directions visible in modern Indigenous cultural database management systems (Cohen et al. 2010; Gibson 2007; Smith et al. 2013) but with a particular focus on the nuances that come with highly immersive virtual spaces (Brown and Nicholas 2012).

Web hosting is an advantageous means of sharing these data as it provides password-protected access without the need for proprietary software or extensive

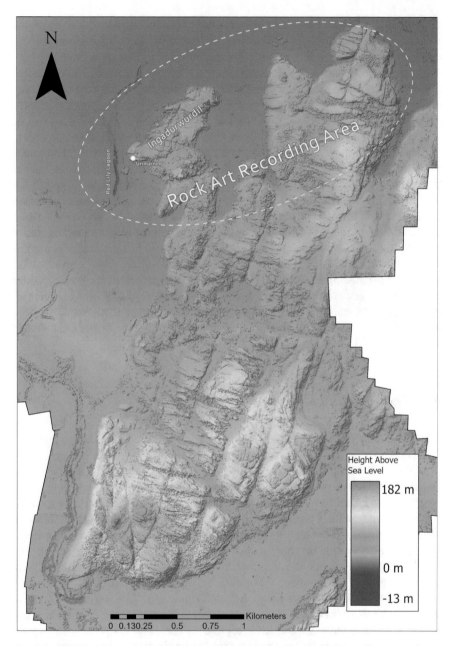

Fig. 6.7 GRLLA study area digital elevation model derived from drone-based aerial photogrammetric recording

Fig. 6.8 Orthomosaic panel showing northern running figures

computer power. Whilst the website manages the data access, Sketchfab was used to host the 3D models in a web-based platform. Sketchfab was used as it allows 3D model viewing and web-page embedding of the 3D model inspection window. Sketchfab importantly provides optional password protection to uploaded models. This allows the privacy of a model to be controlled whilst using this web-accessible platform. Sketchfab also provides support for virtual reality (VR) interaction with any uploaded 3D models. This allows any 3D model to be viewed using a smart-phone housed in a virtual reality (VR) head mount. Alternatively, a purpose-built VR system such as Oculus Rift or Vive can view the model using the embedded Sketchfab model. As part of this research, two VR smartphone head mounts were provided to the Njanjma Rangers to facilitate community interaction with the virtual spaces representing the sites recorded in 3D.

The benefits of remote site access are important when considered in the context of remote indigenous communities. The effects of colonisation have led to continued socio-economic disadvantage and health inequality for Australian Aboriginal and Torres Strait Islander communities (AIHW 2017). As chronic diseases such as asthma, diabetes, cancer, and heart disease are more prevalent in Indigenous communities, a reduction in physical activity occurs which can inhibit participation in social and cultural activities (Bailie et al. 2015). The rock art sites in the GRLLA are particularly difficult to access for people with limited mobility, and so remote virtual sites can improve accessibility and support the continuation of cultural activities in this region, with a demonstrated positive impact on wellbeing (Taçon and Baker 2019). This fits into a broader movement to use digital cultural-heritage techniques to support Indigenous Australians (Moffat et al. 2016; Wallis et al. 2008) through collaborative archaeologies (Smith et al. 2019).

Limitations and Challenges

The methodology developed for this study has faced a number of challenges in the recording and subsequent data management process that proceeds field recordings. This methodology has been developed iteratively through the process of repeated subsequent recording efforts and data management and post-processing throughout the five-year lifespan of this work. Many of the nuanced issues are discovered and addressed throughout the study and have been retroactively added to the methodology described above. These include the issues of recording around vegetation, in lower light conditions, multiple passes to capture image detail, and the geolocation of ground-based site models using drone-based models. However, there are several limitations and challenges that are still present in the described methodology.

Foremost the methods described and developed require a high level of technical expertise and in some cases considerable equipment cost. Whilst SfM photogrammetry is a relatively low-cost recording method and only requires a hand heled camera, tape measure, and printed aerial targets, the post-processing does require computer hardware that increases the overall cost of the method. Additionally, the Agisoft software and licencing prices add considerably to the overall cost of the methodology. Equipment costs may be reduced with the use of cheaper cameras or using mobile phone cameras provided they can adequately capture the details of the rock art but to undertake recordings in the fashion described would require an upfront investment of approximately A\$6,099 in equipment and A\$200 in annual costs for data hosting and visualisation.

Sketchfab adds an additional cost to this methodology as it has a subscription cost in order to expand its monthly upload limit from one model per month which is offered for the free use of the website to 30 uploads per month and the ability to add password protection to these models. Sketchfab offers unlimited model uploads for downloadable models; however, this option has not been selected so as to impose individual site access restrictions to different models. By making models view only and not downloadable, the Rangers and Traditional Owners have the option of making models temporarily available to the public or a specific group and changing this access in the future without the possibility of that model being downloaded or otherwise duplicated. A continual subscription fee is required to gain the benefits of this service. Should the account cancel this subscription private models will remain private and can be accessed again once subscription is renewed. Sketchfab also imposes a file size limit which can limit the size of individual models to 200 megabytes. This may further limit the size of models being uploaded. This can be a challenge and require the models created for this purpose to limit the number of faces and texture sizes used especially for larger sites. Another solution is to split the site record into two separate models if face count and texture size reduction are not possible.

The website used to manage user access to the different Sketchfab models and allow data to be digitally curated also adds both a technical expertise requirement for such web development to this methodology as well as requiring a server to host this website which is an additional cost over time.

Despite these limitations and costs, this web-based method of data storage and access control offers a robust, flexible, and safe way for the management of cultural-heritage materials that would otherwise require physical storage on hard drives which severely limits access possibilities.

6.4 Discussion

The methodology used for recording, curating, and displaying the rock art sites of the Wulk Lagoon area has been designed to satisfy the requirements of archaeological survey, cultural-heritage management, and community engagement and interaction. By creating products with multiple purposes, the digital 3D approach satisfies a broad range of interests in recording these important sites. This project considers a 3D approach as not ending with the creation of a 3D record but also incorporating the accessibility and management of such digital spaces.

A benefit of SfM photogrammetry is rapid site recording using low-cost and lightweight equipment. This articulates well with a broader scale survey using UAVs to provide coverage to locate additional sites in the area. This approach allows future site recording to be conducted with a hand-held camera, portable measuring tape for scale, and a drone for landscape context capture. This achieves the goal of low-cost and easy-to-transport equipment. One limitation of this approach is the requisite technical expertise in the photogrammetric recording process. This process has so far been conducted by archaeologists and spatial survey experts. However, future training and development programs are being conducted to equip the Njanjma Rangers with the expertise and equipment to continue these recording methods independently with site revisits. It is also notable that where a site revisit has occurred individual images can be aligned to the existing models and compared for changes. This reduces the need for full-site modelling to be performed with every revisit to conduct change detection and site monitoring.

The use of Sketchfab integration to a website that can be controlled by NAC and Traditional Owners to curate this digital collection is one example of the robust usability of the highly detailed 3D models produced. This work has extended the use of these 3D applications from simply a visual record into useful products for site management, virtual site access to the community, and to ongoing archaeological analysis. The use of these virtual records may extend to tourism and the integration of models with other information such as ambient sounds, and recorded audio information about the sites is possible.

6.5   Conclusion

We present a methodology for the digital recording of rock art using SfM photogrammetry that has created a high-resolution, immersive product suitable for cultural-heritage management, archaeological research, and community engagement from a number of sites in the Greater Red Lily Lagoon Area of Northern Australia. In all cases, the sites, both physically and virtually, remain in the management and care of their Traditional Owners, allowing the effective management of these important sites in new ways within a digital cultural space.

Acknowledgements Thanks to Njajma Rangers, Alfred Nayinggul, Kenneth Mangiru, Anita Nayinggul, Katie Nayinggul, Manbiyarra (Grant) Nayinggul, Tex Badari, Sebastian Nagurrgurrba, Hilton Garnarradj, Jacob (Junior) Nayinggul, Lawrence Nayinggul, James Dempsey, Ursula Badari, Timothy Djumburri, Thomas Falck, Daniel McLoney, and Shay Wrigglesworth who provided invaluable assistance in carrying out this research. This research was supported by Australian Research Council grants DE160100703 (Moffat), DE170101447 (Wesley), and FT170100025 and DE140100254 (Aubert); by George Chaloupka Fellowships to Moffat, Jones, and Wesley; by a National Geographic Grant to Wesley and Jones; and by a Flinders University Early Career Researcher Impact Seed Grant to Moffat.

References

Abate D (2019) Built-heritage multi-temporal monitoring through photogrammetry and 2D/3D change detection algorithms. Stud Conserv 64:423–434

Alexander C, Pinz A, Reinbacher C (2015) Multi-scale 3D rock-art recording. Digital Appl Archaeol Cultural Herit 2:181–195

Australian Institute of Health and Welfare (AIHW) (2017) Aborginal and Torres Strait Islander Health Performance Framework (HPF) report 2017. 2017. Australian Government. https://www.aihw.gov.au/reports/indigenous-australians/health-performance-framework/contents/overview. Accessed 01 Nov 2019

Bailie J, Schierhout G, Laycock A, Kelaher M, Percival N, O'Donoghue L, McNeair T, Bailie R (2015) Determinants of access to chronic illness care: a mixed-methods evaluation of a national multifaceted chronic disease package for Indigenous Australians. BJM Open 5(11):e008103

Bourke P, Brockwell S, Faulkner P, Meehan B (2007) Climate variability in the mid to Late Holocene Arnhem Land Region, North Australia: archaeological archives of environmental and cultural change. Archaeol Ocean 42(3):91–101

Bradley R (1991) Rock art and the perception of landscape. Camb Archaeol J 1:77–101

Bradley R, Boado FC, Valcarce RF (1994) Rock art research as landscape archaeology: a pilot study in Galicia, North-West Spain. World Archaeol 25:374–390

Brady LM, Hampson J, Sanz ID (2019) Recording rock art. In: David B, McNiven IJ (eds) The Oxford handbook of the archaeology and anthropology of rock art. Oxford University Press, Oxford. https://doi.org/10.1093/oxfordhb/9780190607357.013.37

Brophy K (2018) 'The finest set of cup and ring marks in existence': the story of the Cochno Stone, West Dunbartonshire. Scott Archaeol J 40:1–23

Brown D, Nicholas G (2012) Protecting indigenous cultural property in the age of digital democracy: institutional and communal responses to Canadian First Nations and Māori heritage concerns. J Mater Cult 17(3):307–324

Carmichael B, Wilson G, Namarnyilk I, Nadji S, Brockwell S, Webb B, Hunter F, Bird D (2018) Local and Indigenous management of climate change risks to archaeological sites. Mitig Adapt Strat Glob Change 23(2):231–255

Cassidy B, Sim G, Robinson DW, Gandy D (2019) A virtual reality platform for analyzing remote archaeological sites. Interact Comput 31:167–176

Chaloupka G (1984) From paleoart to casual paintings: the chronological sequence of Arnhem Land Plateau Rock Art. In: Northern Territory Museum of Arts and Sciences Monograph Series 1. Northern Territory Museum of Arts and Sciences, Darwin

Chaloupka G (1993) Journey in time: the 50,000 year story of the Australian rock art of Arnhem Land. Reed Books Australia, Chatswood

Chandler JH, Bryan P, Fryer JG (2007) The development and application of a simple methodology for recording rock art using consumer-grade digital cameras. Photogram Rec 22(117):10–21

Christian CS, Stewart GA (1953) General report on survey of Katherine-Darwin Region, 1946. Land Research Series No. 1. Commonwealth Scientific and Industrial Research Organization, Melbourne

Clarkson C, Smith M, Marwick B, Fullagar R, Wallis LA, Faulkner P, Manne T, Hayes E, Roberts RG, Jacobs Z, Carah X (2015) The archaeology, chronology and stratigraphy of Madjedbebe (Malakunanja II): a site in northern Australia with early occupation. J Hum Evol 83:46–64

Clarkson C, Jacobs Z, Marwick B, Fullagar R, Wallis L, Smith M, Roberts RG, Hayes E, Lowe K, Carah X, Florin SA, McNeil J, Cox D, Arnold LJ, Hua Q, Huntley J, Brand HEA, Manne T, Fairbairn A, Shulmeister J, Lyle L, Salinas M, Page M, Connell K, Park G, Norman K, Murphy T, Pardoe C (2017) Human occupation of northern Australia by 65,000 years ago. Nature 547:306–310

Cohen H, Morley R, Dallow P, Kaufmann L (2010) Database narratives: conceptualising digital heritage databases in remote aboriginal communities. In: 2010 14th international conference information visualisation. IEEE, pp 422–427

David B, Barker B, Petchey F, Delannoy J, Geneste J, Rowe C, Eccleston M, Lamb L, Whear R (2013a) A 28,000 year old excavated painted rock from Nawarla Gabarnmang, northern Australia. J Archaeol Sci 40(5):2493–2501

David B, Geneste JM, Petchey F, Delannoy JJ, Barker B, Eccleston M (2013b) How old are Australia's pictographs? A review of rock art dating. J Archaeol Sci 40(1):3–10

Davis A, Belton D, Helmholz P, Bourke P, McDonald J (2017) Pilbara rock art: laser scanning, photogrammetry and 3D photographic reconstruction as heritage management tools. Heritage Sci 5:25

Digitalrockart.com http://digitalrockart.com.au/. Accessed Aug 2020

Domingo Sanz I (2014) Rock art recording methods: from traditional to digital. In: Smith C (ed) Encyclopedia of global archaeology. Springer, pp 6351–6357

Edwards R (1974) The art of the Alligator Rivers Region. Alligator Rivers Region Environmental Fact-Finding Study, Canberra

El-Hakim S, Fryer J, Picard M, Whiting E (2004) Digital recording of Aboriginal Rock Art. In: Proceedings of the 10th international conference on virtual systems and multimedia, pp 344–353

Faulkner P (2009) Focused, intense and long-term: evidence for granular ark (*Anadara granosa*) exploitation from late Holocene shell mounds of Blue Mud Bay, northern Australia. J Archaeol Sci 36(3):821–834

Fritz C, Willis MD, Tosello G (2016) Reconstructing Paleolithic cave art: the example of Marsoulas Cave (France). J Archaeol Sci Rep 10:910–916

Gibson J (2007) People, place and community memory: creating digital heritage databases in remote aboriginal communities. In: Conference of the Australian Society of Archivists, August 22–25

González-Aguilera D, Muñoz-Nieto A, Gómez-Lahoz J, Herrero-Pascual J, Gutierrez-Alonso G (2009) 3D digital surveying and modelling of cave geometry: application to paleolithic rock art. Sensors 9:1108–1127

Greenop K, Landorf C (2017) Grave-to-cradle: a paradigm shift for heritage conservation and interpretation in the era of 3D laser scanning. Historic Environ 29:44

Groom KM (2016) The applicability of repeat photography in rock art conservation: a case study of mixed methods in the Arkansan Ozarks. Zeitschrift Für Geomorphologie, Supplementary Issues 60:11–28

Gunn RG (1992) Mikinj: rock art, myth and place. Sites of Significance to Jacob Nayinggul. Unpublished report to AIATSIS. Canberra, AIATSIS

Gunn RG (2018) Art of the ancestors: spatial and temporal patterning in the ceiling rock art of Nawarla Gabarnmang, Arnhem Land, Australia. Archaeopress Archaeology, Oxford

Guse D (2008) Urrmarning cultural heritage conservation and management plan. Unpublished report to the Northern Land Council. Earth Sea Heritage Surveys

Harmon J (2009) Image enhancement using DStretch. http://www.DStretch.com

Hiscock P (1996) Mobility and technology in the Kakadu coastal wetlands. Indo-Pacific Prehistory Assoc Bull 15:151–157

Hiscock P (1999) Holocene coastal occupation of western Arnhem Land. In: Hall J, McNiven I (eds) Australian coastal archaeology. Department of Archaeology and Natural History, Australian National University, Canberra, pp 91–103

Jalandoni A, Domingo I, Taçon PSC (2018) Testing the value of low-cost Structure-From-Motion (SfM) photogrammetry for metric and visual analysis of rock art. J Archaeol Sci Rep 17:605–616

Jelinek JJ (1986) The great art of the Early Australians: the study of the evolution and role of rock art in the Society of Australian Hunters and Gatherers. Anthropos Institute, Moravian Museum Brno, Prague

Jones R (1985) Archaeological research in Kakadu National Park. Australian National Parks and Wildlife Special Publications 13, Canberra

Jones T, Wesley D (2016) Towards multiple ontologies: creating rock art narratives in Arnhem Land. Hunter Gatherer Res 2(3):275–301

Jones T, Levchenko V, Wesley D (2017a) How old is X-ray art? Minimum age determinations for early X-ray rock art from the Red Lily' (Wulk) Lagoon rock art precinct, western Arnhem Land. In: David B, Taçon PSC, Delannoy JJ, Geneste JM (eds) The archaeology of rock art in Western Arnhem Land in Northern Australia, Terra Australis 47:129–144. ANU Press, Canberra

Jones T, Levchenko VA, King PL, Troitzsch U, Wesley D, Williams AA, Nayingull A (2017b) Radiocarbon age constraints for a Pleistocene-Holocene transition rock art style: the Northern Running Figures of the East Alligator River region, western Arnhem Land, Australia. J Archaeol Sci Rep 11:80–89

Jones T (2017) Disentangling the styles, sequences and antiquity of the early rock art of Western Arnhem Land. Unpublished doctoral thesis, ANU, Canberra

Lee J, Kim J, Ahn J, Woo W (2019) Context-aware risk management for architectural heritage using historic building information modeling and virtual reality. J Cult Herit 38:242–252

Plets G, Verhoeven G, Cheremisin D, Plets R, Bourgeois J, Stichelbaut B, Gheyle W, De Reu J (2012) The deteriorating preservation of the Altai rock art: assessing three-dimensional image-based modelling in rock art research and management. Rock Art Res 29(2):139–156

Marshall M (2019) Rock art conservation and management: 21st century perspectives from Northern Australia. Unpublished PhD School of Archaeology and Anthropology, The Australian National University

May SK, Shine D, Wright D, Denham T, Taçon PSC, Marshall M, Sanz ID, Prideaux F, Stephens SP (2017) The rock art of Ingaanjalwurr, western Arnhem Land, Australia. In: David B, Taçon PSC,

Delannoy JJ, Geneste JM (eds) The archaeology of rock art in Western Arnhem Land, Australia, Terra Australis 47:51–68. ANU Press, Canberra

McCarthy FD (1965) The Northern Territory and Central Australia: Report from the Select Committee on the Native and Historical Objects and Areas Preservation Ordinance 1955–1960, together with minutes of proceedings of the committee. Unpublished manuscript. Australian Institute of Aboriginal and Torres Strait Islander Studies

Meijer E (2015) Structure from Motion as documentation technique for Rock Art. Adoranten 66–73

Moffat I, Garnaut J, Jordan C, Vella A, Bailey M, the Gunditj Mirring Traditional Owners Corporation (2016) Ground penetrating radar investigations at the Lake Condah Cemetery: locating unmarked graves in areas with extensive subsurface disturbance. Artefact 39:8–14

Mountford CP (1950) Primitive art of Arnhem Land. South-West Pacific (24)

Mountford CP (1956) Art, myth and symbolism, vol 1. Records of the American Australian Scientific Expedition to Arnhem Land. Melbourne University Press, Melbourne

Mountford CP (1964) Aboriginal paintings from Australia. Collins, London

Mountford CP (1965) Aboriginal art. Longmans, Green and Company, Croydon

Mountford CP (1967) The cave art of Australia. In: Australian Aboriginal art: primitive traditional decorative. Newcraft, Melbourne

Mountford CP (1975) The aborigines and their country. Rigby, Adelaide

Njanjma Rangers (2015) Karribolkmurrngrayekwon: Our plan for strong, healthy Bininj (people) and Kunred (country). Unpublished report by Njanjma Rangers via Djabulukgu Association Incorporated

Needham RS (1984) Alligator Rivers, Northern Territory. 1:250,000 geological series explanatory notes. Department of National Resources, Bureau of Mineral Resources, Geology and Geophysics. Australian Government Publishing Service

Reeves JM, Barrows TT, Cohen TA, Kiem A, Bostock HC, Fitzsimmons KE, Jansen JD, Kemp J, Krause C, Petherick L, Phipps SJ, Members OZ-INTIMATE (2013) Climate variability over the last 35,000 years recorded in marine and terrestrial archives in the Australian region: an OZ-INTIMATE compilation. Quatern Sci Rev 74:21–34

Rogerio-Candelera MÁ (2015) Digital image analysis based study, recording, and protection of painted rock art. Some Iberian experiences. Digital Appl Archaeol Cultural Heritage 2:68–78

Sapirstein P, Murray S (2017) Establishing best practices for photogrammetric recording during archaeological fieldwork. J Field Archaeol 42:337–350

Scopigno R, Callieri M, Cignoni P, Corsini M, Dellepiane M, Ponchio F, Ranzuglia G (2011) 3D models for cultural heritage: beyond plain visualization. Computer 44(7):48–55

Senior, BR, Smart PG (1976) Coburg Peninsula—Melville Island, Northern Territory 1:250,000 geological series explanatory notes. Department of National Resources, Bureau of Mineral Resources, Geology and Geophysics. Australian Government Publishing Service

Shine D, Wright D, Denham T, Aplin K, Hiscock P, Parker K, Walton R (2013) Birriwilk rockshelter: a mid to late Holocene site in Manilikarr Country, southwest Arnhem Land, Northern Territory. Aust Archaeol 76:69–78

Shine D, Hiscock P, Denham T (2016) The archaeology of Ingaanjalwurr rockshelter in Manilikarr Country, western Arnhem Land. Aust Archaeol 82(1):67–75

Smith C, Burke H, Ralph J, Pollard K, Gorman A, Wilson C, Hemming S, Rigney D, Wesley D, Morrison M, McNaughton D, Domingo I, Moffat I, Roberts A, Koolmatrie J, Willika J, Pamkal B, Jackson G (2019) Pursuing social justice through collaborative archaeologies in aboriginal Australia. Archaeologies 15:1–34

Smith S, McDonald J, Blame J, MacLaren G, Paterson A (2013) Creating a paperless recording system for Pilbara Rock Art. In: Papers from the 41st conference on computer applications and quantitative methods in archaeology. Amsterdam University Press, Perth, pp 89–96

Sweet IP, Brakel AT, Carson L (1999) The Kombolgie Subgroup—a new look at an old 'formation.' AGSO Res Newslett 30:26–28

Taçon PSC, Baker S (2019) New and emerging challenges to heritage and well-being: a critical review. Heritage 2:1300–1315

Taçon PSC, Brockwell S (1995) Arnhem Land prehistory. Antiquity 69(265):676–695

Wallis LA, Moffat I, Trevorrow G, Massey T (2008) Locating places for repatriated burial: a case study from Ngarrindjeri ruwe, South Australia. Antiquity 82:750–760

Wesley D (2016) Urrmarning: Red Lily Lagoon Rock Art Project. George Chaloupka Fellowship Report 2010–2011. Unpublished report to the Museum and Art Gallery of the Northern Territory

Wesley D, Jones T, Whitau R (2017) People and fish: late Holocene rock art at Wulk Lagoon, Arnhem Land. In: David B, Taçon PSC, Delannoy JJ, Geneste JM (eds) The archaeology of rock art in Western Arnhem Land in Northern Australia, Terra Australis 47:21–50. ANU Press, Canberra

Westoby MJ, Bransington J, Glasser NF, Hambrey MJ, Reynolds JM (2012) 'Structure-from-Motion' photogrammetry: a low-cost, effective tool for geoscience applications. Geomorphology 179:300–314

Woodroffe C (1993) Late Quaternary evolution of coastal and lowland riverine plains of Southeast Asia and northern Australia: an overview. Sed Geol 83:63–175

Woodroffe C (1988) Changing Mangrove and Wetland Habitats over the Last 8000 Years, Northern Australia and Southeast Asia. In: Wade-Marshall D, Loveday P (eds) Northern Australia: progress and prospects, vol 2: floodplain research. North Australia Research Unit, Australian National University, Darwin

Wasson RJ (ed) (1992) Modern sedimentation and late quaternary evolution of the magela creek plain. Research Report 6, Supervising Scientist for the Alligator Rivers Region, AGPS, Canberra

Chapter 7
3D Documentation of Stone Sites at Ilulissat, West Greenland

Chiara Villa, Marie Louise Jørkov, Christian Koch Madsen, and Jens Fog Jensen

Abstract In this chapter, we show how Structure from Motion (SfM) photogrammetry and Computed Tomography (CT) scanning were implemented for documenting and interpreting graves and human remains, which were excavated in Greenland during the summers of 2018 and 2019. The burial sites are characterised by isolated stone graves that were built with either single or multiple chambers. Both single- and multi-individual graves were discovered. Photogrammetric documentation as well as traditional sketches of the graves were performed during each excavation phase. Here, we discuss how these two approaches correlate and complement each other, including highlighting the advantages and drawbacks of each method. We also show how 3D models of the human remains from CT scanning and 3D models of a grave obtained from SfM photogrammetry were combined and used to give an illustrative and more comprehensive view of the stone-built features, as well as to assist in the overall interpretation.

Keywords SfM photogrammetry · 3D models · CT scanning · Greenland · Stone grave

C. Villa (✉) · M. L. Jørkov
Department of Forensic Medicine, University of Copenhagen, Copenhagen, Denmark
e-mail: Chiara.villa@sund.ku.dk

C. Villa
Faculty of Life Sciences, School of Archaeological & Forensic Sciences, University of Bradford, Bradford, UK

C. K. Madsen
National Museum of Greenland, Nuuk, Greenland

J. F. Jensen
Natural History Museum of Denmark, University of Copenhagen, Copenhagen, Denmark

© Springer Nature Switzerland AG 2022
E. Ch'ng et al. (eds.), *Visual Heritage: Digital Approaches in Heritage Science*,
Springer Series on Cultural Computing,
https://doi.org/10.1007/978-3-030-77028-0_7

7.1 Introduction

Since their introduction in bioarcheology, 3D imaging techniques have been essential tools for the rigorous documentation of archaeological sites, artefacts and human remains. The resultant 3D models are important for the preservation, interpretation, analysis and dissemination of cultural heritage (Dell'Unto 2014; Faber et al. 2017; Gaffney et al. 2016; Ch'ng and Gaffney 2013).

There are diverse 3D technologies, but none can be considered optimal for all applications (Hassani 2015). Indeed, the selection of the technique and the equipment depends on the location and extension of the site, the dimension of the object of interest, the desired scale of details and, definitively, the availability of resources both in terms of available funds for equipment and expertise. Total stations, terrestrial and airborne laser scanners, structured light scanners and SfM photogrammetry are some of the techniques that can accurately capture the reality in 3D. Each technique comes with advantages and disadvantages. For more details about the techniques, the readers can refer, among others, to Agugiaro (2014), Bennet (2014), Galiatzatos (2014), Guidi (2014), Hassani (2015), Siebke et al. (2018), Themistocleous et al. (2019) and Tobiasz et al. (2019).

In particular, SfM photogrammetry has seen a considerable uptake in recent years. Its use has greatly improved the documentation of archaeological sites, artefacts and even human remains. Photogrammetry is "the art and science of determining the position and shape of objects from photographs" (Kraus 1994). It is based on triangulation principles (for more details, see Luhmann et al. 2013). SfM Photogrammetry enables the creation of high-resolution, true-to-scale 3D coloured models from 2D images, if the photographs are properly taken. It is a versatile tool that can be used to create 3D objects, ranging from large archaeological sites (Kucukkaya 2004) to tiny insects (Nguyen et al. 2014). Based on the camera positions, photogrammetry can be classified (Luhmann et al. 2013) as (1) Satellite photogrammetry: processing of satellite images; (2) Aerial photogrammetry: processing of aerial photographs acquired from plane or drones; (3) Terrestrial photogrammetry or close-range photogrammetry: processing of photograph measurements from a fixed terrestrial location.

A particular type of close-range photogrammetry especially used in bioarcheology is Structure from Motion (SfM) photogrammetry. By overlapping photographs, the photogrammetry programs can calculate 3D coordinates (x, y and z) of the subject of interest based on the position of the camera (assessed from the common features that are identified among the photographs), as it moves through 3D space (structure from motion). Any camera can be used to take photographs (e.g. compact cameras, phones and tablets), although digital single-lens reflex (DSLR) cameras should be preferred (Villa 2017). DSLR cameras have a better resolution, i.e. more points and thus more details in the photographs, and the lenses in these cameras are more rigidly assembled, leading to better picture-to-picture repeatability, i.e. the lens distortion can be more accurately calculated to improve 3D models. SfM photogrammetry is a very attractive technique because it is accurate, portable and affordable for most museums and universities: it only requires a camera and a software. It is also a very robust technique that under all weather conditions and at extremely unfavourable sites still produces reliable results (Ahrens and Borvik 2016). The products of a photogrammetric analysis are 3D models (point cloud or surface mesh), lines (sketches, maps), distances, areas and volumes. There are several commercial photogrammetry software packages available: Agisoft Metashape (www.agisoft.com/), previously known as Agisoft PhotoScan, Reality Capture (www.capturingreality.com/), PhotoModeler (www.photomodeler.com) and 3DF Zephyr (www.3dflow.net). Some free programs are also available: Visual SfM (www.ccwu.me/vsfm/) or Python Photogrammetry Toolbox (github.com/steve-vincent/photogrammetry).

Another 3D imaging technique used in bioarcheology is Computed Tomography (CT) scanning. This technique is used to document, in particular, not only human skeletal remains but also small objects, e.g. urns, amulets and wood artefacts (Beckett and Conlogue 2009; Chhem and Brothwell 2008; Eriksen et al. 2016). CT scanning is a non-invasive and non-destructive technique in common with SfM photogrammetry but with the advantage of visualising the internal structures of an object. Consequently, CT scanning is an important diagnostic tool for examining mummified and skeletal remains (Lynnerup 2007; Villa et al. 2019; Villa and Lynnerup 2012). Fossils or other archaeological materials embedded in a burial matrix can also be scanned to preserve the specimens and, for example, to guide the following micro-excavation (Limaverde et al. 2018). A CT scanner is definitively expensive equipment, not easily available and non-portable (even though mobile equipment exists). Access to such equipment can be granted through forensic departments or the nearby hospitals. Indeed, CT scanning has been introduced at several forensic medical institutes around the world in the last two decades (Poulsen and Simonsen 2007; Rutty et al. 2008). CT scanning is a radiographic technique that uses X-rays to visualise in 3D the internal structures of the object. For a full presentation of the topic, please refer to, for example, Goldman (2008), Kalender (2011), Seibert (2004) and Seibert and Boone (2005). X-rays are electromagnetic waves able to penetrate materials. Materials absorb the X-rays passing through them differently based on their density, thickness and atomic number. The X-rays that pass through the examined object have a pattern of intensity that reflects the absorption characteristics of the object of interest. This pattern is recorded to form the image, i.e. CT images. A CT scanning can produce hundreds of cross-sectional images, i.e. slices of the scanned object. These images can be singularly visualised or can be post-processed with specialised software applications, e.g. Mimics (www.materialise.com/en/medical/ software/mimics), 3D slicer (www.slicer.org), Myrian (www.intrasense.fr) and Osirix (www.osirix-viewer.com).

The creation of the 3D models is generally based on the different absorptions (i.e. attenuation) of the object's part. The differences in X-ray attenuation can be measured using the Hounsfield unit (HU) scale. The HU scale is calibrated arbitrarily according to the attenuation of water (HU 0) and air (HU 1000). The materials with a high density, such as metal, stone and compact bones, inhibit the passage of the X-rays and are visualised in white or light grey and correspond to high HU values (e.g. bones have HU over 200, metals over 3000). Less dense materials, e.g. wood, soft tissues and bandages, allow the majority of X-rays to pass through, and are visualised in black-grey and correspond to lower HU values (e.g. soft tissues have values around HU 20–100). 3D models of anything present in the CT images can be created based on its attenuation through the process of segmentation. It is possible to generate not only 3D models of the bones, internal organs and amulets but also 3D model of the air inside an object (Eriksen et al. 2016). 3D models obtained from CT scanning are scaled models, without texture, and with a resolution of around 0.5 mm (when appropriate CT scanning parameters are selected). The maximal dimension of the object that can be scanned and visualised is around 50–70 cm in diameter (it depends on the gantry size) to 200 cm in length (i.e. the length of the table).

Here, we show how 3D models obtained from SfM photogrammetry and CT scanning have been used to document and interpret burial sites that were excavated in Greenland during the summers of 2018 and 2019. Three different types of graves are considered, with each illustrating the advantages of these 3D technologies: (1) a multi-chamber grave is used to show the advantages and disadvantages of traditional sketch plans and top views from 3D models; (2) a single-individual grave is used to show how it is possible to document each excavation phase; and (3) a multi-individual grave is used to show the utility of combining 3D models generated from SfM photogrammetry and CT scanning.

7.2 Materials and Methods

7.2.1 Graves

Archaeological surveys and excavations were carried out in Ilulissat (West Greenland) during 2017–2019. They fulfilled a commissioned contract project that was carried out by the Greenland National Museum and Archives prior to a projected expansion of the airport and runway. In total, 12 graves were identified and excavated. The graves are believed to belong to the Inuit population and were likely from the sixteenth to the eighteenth centuries (radiocarbon dates were not yet available).

The following graves are presented:

- Grave A: a multi-chamber grave;
- Grave K: a grave containing the remains of an individual;
- Grave L: a grave containing the remains of multiple individuals.

7.2.2 Sketch Plans

Drawings of the graves were carried out on a 1:10 or in some cases a 1:20 scale on millimetre paper using an A3 drawing frame with a 1-mm grid. Numerous different drawings were created; primarily one set describing the grave construction, and other more focused sketches depicting the situation of bones, stones and any other relevant findings at different levels in the individual burial chambers. The distances between the objects were measured with a ruler. In addition, GNSS positions were recorded for each grave. The drawings were then digitalised and assembled in vector graphics in CorelDraw (www.coreldraw.com).

7.2.3   3D Models from SfM Photogrammetry

Photographs of the graves were taken using a Canon EOS 5DS R (8688×5792 pixels) with a fixed focal length of either 35 mm or 24 mm. During the documentation, the camera was set to the priority aperture setting, with the ISO between around 400/800. The shutter speed was 1/80 or faster, and the white balance was set in automatic mode. A variable number of photographs was taken based on the dimension of the grave. Image stabilisation and chromatic aberration were turned off. A scale and a colour check were recorded during the photographic sessions; no coded target and no tripod were used (see discussions for the explanation of these choices). Photographs were taken with an overlap area of about 80–90%. Two people (CV, MLJ) with training in SfM photogrammetry documentation took the photographs. PhotoModeler (www.photomodeler.com) was used for processing the images. The applied workflow was as follows:

(1)   The photographs were uploaded, and the software determined the position of the camera using inverse calibration (automatic calibration);
(2)   Based on the smart points (points in common among the photographs) that were used to orient the photographs, the software calculated a dense point cloud (default settings were used, with "the number of iterations" set at 5);
(3)   Based on the smart points, a surface mesh was created (default settings were used, with "mesh smoothing/sharpness" set at 5).

The 3D models have been saved as a point cloud (.pts) and a surface mesh (.obj).

7.2.4   Human Remains: Anthropological Analyses and CT Scanning

Anthropological analyses for estimating sex, age, stature and pathologies were carried out following the standard methods, among others, e.g. Alqahtani et al. (2010), Ubelaker (1989), Scheuer and Black (2000) and Waldron (2009). After the anthropological analyses of the human remains, CT scanning was performed for each individual, separately. The bones of each individual were anatomically positioned on the CT table and arranged such as they did not touch each other, thus to facilitate the subsequent 3D segmentation process. CT scanning was carried out using a Siemens Somatom AS (a medical CT scanning) using the following settings: 120 kV, 300 mAs, 0.6-mm slice thickness, 0.4 pitch, 0.4-mm slice increment and sharp/medium-sharp kernel (Br58 or Br51). 3D models of the bone were created using Mimics software (www.materialise.com/en/medical/software/mimics) and exported as .stl files. 3D models of single bones or areas (e.g. foot, hand) were generated using automatic segmentation by applying a HU range of 200–3,071.

7.2.5 Combination of the Digital Data

Alignment between the 2D sketch plans and the top views from the 3D models was performed using Gimp (www.gimp.org) using translation and rotation tools. The transparency effect was used to visualise both layers at the same time.

Alignment of the 3D models was performed using Cloud Compare (www.cloudcompare.org), and the following steps were performed to align the different models by using the default values:

(1) A manual alignment tool "Translate /rotate";
(2) A rough alignment of the two meshes using the function "aligns two clouds by picking (at least four points) equivalent point pairs";
(3) A fine alignment using the function "finely registers already (roughly) aligned entities (clouds or meshes)" with a final overlap value equal to 50%.

More details on the alignment process can be found in Villa et al. (2018).

7.3 Results

Grave A

Grave A was a multi-chamber grave, with five chambers: A1, A2, A3, A4 and A5. Five individuals were identified, with one in each chamber, including two adult women and three small children (see Table 7.1). The bones and the teeth were very frail, and only a few bones were preserved for the children. No signs of trauma or severe pathologies were observed.

Figures 7.1 and 7.2 show the sketch plan and the top view obtained from the 3D

Table 7.1 Overview of the individuals present in Grave A

Chamber	Sex	Age	State of preservation
A1	Female	50 years or older	Relatively complete skeleton
A2	–	Small child	Few remains of the skull
A3	–	Ca. 3.5 years	Few bones of both skull and postcranial
A4	Female	30 years ± 10	Relatively complete skeleton
A5	–	Ca. 3.5 years	Few remains of the skull

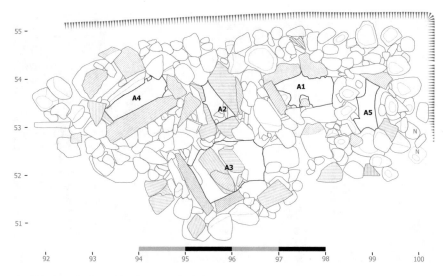

Fig. 7.1 Sketch plan of the Grave A. Scale bar: 4 m

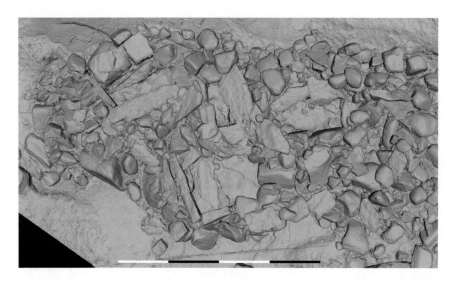

Fig. 7.2 Top view of Grave A generated from the 3D mesh surface. Scale bar: 4 m

model, respectively. They show the cleaned grave after the removal of the human remains. Figure 7.3 shows the overlap of the two techniques; the alignment was carried out using chamber A3 as a reference. The edges of the chamber A3 well align between the two techniques, while there are discrepancies (Fig. 7.3, indicated with arrows) of around 10–15 cm on the edges of the other chambers. However, the single chambers can be well aligned, when considered individually (Fig. 7.4).

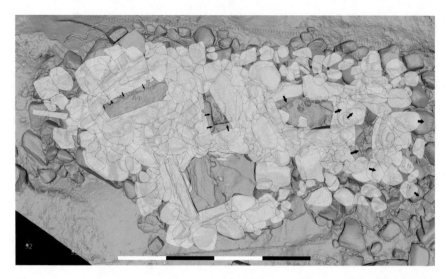

Fig. 7.3 Overlap of the sketch plan and top view. The alignment was carried out using chamber A3 as a reference. The arrows show the discrepancies between the two techniques. Scale bar: 4 m

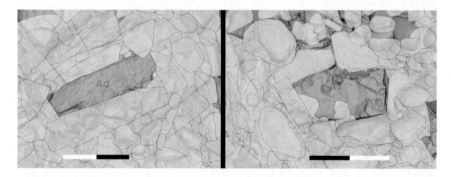

Fig. 7.4 Overlap of the sketch plan and top view for the chamber A4 and A1. The alignment was carried for each chamber individually. The edges of the chambers are well aligned between the two techniques. Scale bar: 1 m

Grave K

Grave K was a single individual grave. It contained a female, 30–40 years old at the time of her death. No signs of trauma or severe pathologies were observed.

Photographic sections were taken during the different phases of the excavation as follows:

(1)   the grave before the opening (Fig. 7.5);
(2)   the grave open, revealing the skeleton (Fig. 7.6, left);
(3)   the chamber with the exposed skeleton after a quick cleaning (Fig. 7.6, right);
(4)   the chamber after the removal of the bones and the exposition of stone pavement (Fig. 7.7).

Grave L

Grave L contained the remains of several individuals. The remains of three individuals were identified: two males around 30–40 years old and a female around 50 years old. No signs of trauma or severe pathologies were observed.

Fig. 7.5   Grave K, top view (point cloud). Scale bar: 2 m

Fig. 7.6 Grave K (point clouds): on the left, view of the grave just open; on the right, exposed skeleton. Scale bar: 2 m

Photographic sections were taken during the different phases of the excavation. Figure 7.8 shows the exposed skeletons (point cloud and the mesh surface).

3D models of the bones were obtained from CT scanning and positioned in the grave to better illustrate the position of the separated individuals (Figs. 7.9 and 7.10). The alignment of the 3D models of the bones was performed using the 3D mesh of the graves with the exposed skeletons (Fig. 7.8) as a reference. The bones were attributed to the different individuals based on the anthropological analysis. Each individual was marked with a different colour: individuals 1 and 2, the males, were identified with green and blue, respectively, while individual 3, the female, was identified with orange.

The bones of individual 3 (in orange), as shown in Fig. 7.9, were assembled at the bottom of the chamber, while the skull was moved to the upper right corner. Individual 3, as shown in Fig. 7.10, was in the lowest level of the grave, while individual 2 (in blue) was in the middle and under individual 1 (in green). The skull and the vertebrae of individuals 1 and 2 were still in an anatomical position, while the lower extremities and the pelvis of individual 2 and part of the lower leg of individual 1 were moved.

7.4 Discussion

3D technologies play a fundamental role in the accurate and precise documentation of reality in 3D. They should be implemented in the archaeological workflow, whenever possible, to document the entire site, the artefacts and the human remains. A multi-modality approach, meaning not only a combination of traditional methods (e.g.

Fig. 7.7   Grave K: close up of the chamber after the skeleton was removed (point cloud). Scale bar: 1 m

manual drawings) with 3D techniques but also integration of diverse 3D techniques (e.g. SfM photogrammetry and CT scanning), is also desirable. Indeed, each method contributes to a holistic record of cultural heritage.

In this chapter, we demonstrated that SfM photogrammetry is an extremely powerful 3D documentation tool that allows the creation of measurable 3D replicas of archaeological sites, in particular, stone graves. Photogrammetry has previously been used for documenting both traditional and forensic graves with great success for many years, especially mass graves (Baier and Rando 2016; Siebke et al. 2018). Archaeological and forensic excavations are a destructive process, and the recording process is extremely important (Dell'Unto 2014). Both 3D digital recording and sketch plans are the only data sources that are available for post-excavation interpretation, reconstruction and visualisation. They should be used in a complementary way, since both methods provide important information, with each having certain

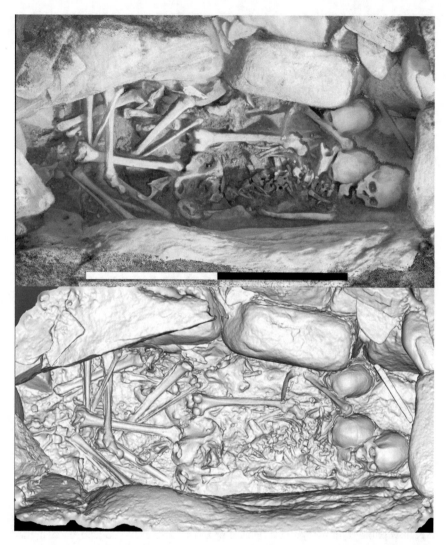

Fig. 7.8 Grave L, top view of the grave with exposed skeletons. Above, point cloud, below, mesh surface. Scale bar: 1 m

advantages and disadvantages, as we are going to illustrate. Sketch plans are a 2D representation of a 3D reality that cannot completely reproduce all the details. On the other hand, 3D models that are generated from SfM photogrammetry (if the photographs have been properly taken) are extremely precise and accurate, as shown for Grave A. In addition, a 3D model can be rotated and visualised from different points of view that are inaccessible on the field and can thus reveal new details. However, one of the advantages of sketch plans is that they do not require preparation of the site: they can be drawn independently of the weather conditions; and they

Fig. 7.9 Grave L, top view of the grave with the 3D bones obtained from CT scanning. Individual 1 in green, individual 2 in blue and individual 3 in orange. Scale bar: 1 m

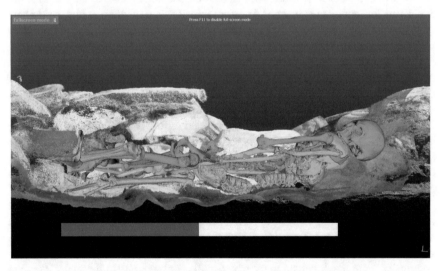

Fig. 7.10 Grave L, lateral view of the grave with the 3D bones obtained from CT scanning. Individual 1 in green, individual 2 in blue and individual 3 in orange. Scale bar: 1 m

are direct documentation on site (i.e. they can be immediately reviewed at the site). They can also be used to check the progress during excavation and allow for direct interpretations of the site's findings. By contrast, photogrammetry requires some preparation: e.g. the site needs to be "cleaned", and all the objects, such as buckets and utensils, which do not need to be recorded, have to be removed. Differently from general guidance, e.g. Historic England (2017), we did not use coded targets on the scene: based on our experience, photogrammetry software such PhotoModeler and Agisoft can well process images with or without coded targets with the same accuracy. The fundamental thing is that rulers, scales or reference measurements must be present during the photographic sessions; these are essential to properly scale the project and, consequently, the site or the object of interest. Weather conditions can influence photographs' quality: cloudy conditions are the best, while sunny days can create shadows, making the post-process difficult because of details being obscured by those shadows. As a possible solution, we conducted one photographic session in the morning and one later in the day to have different areas in the shadows. Documentation of the site in the rain is also difficult, and 3D models that are obtained under this condition can be noisy.

Different from a sketch plan, the result of SfM photogrammetry is not immediately available; 3D models take time to be created. In addition, 3D models depend on the photographs and capability of the photographer, but it is not so difficult to learn how to take good photographs for the SfM photogrammetry process. The fundamental aspect is to understand how aperture, shutter speed and ISO are related to each other and to find an appropriate balance between the different settings (please refer to the "triangle of exposure"). We had to document outdoor stone graves of the size of about 5×10 m. The camera was set on "Aperture Priority" and medium to high f-numbers (e.g. f/8 or f/16) were used. To keep the selected f-number fixed during the entire photograph session and obtain good photographs, we adjusted the other parameters, i.e. ISO and shutter speed. Even though it would argue that a tripod should always be used if possible, for maximum stability and to ensure good capture for longer exposures (higher f-values), in our situation, it was more practical to take pictures with a hand-held camera, due to the irregular and unstable conditions of the terrain. Consequently, we used a minimum shutter speed setting of 1/80 to properly capture a good image and we used an ISO around 400/800. There is no optimal condition and predefined camera settings; one needs to find a balance and compromises based on the situation. Based on our experience, general advice is to acquire as much as possible images of the same subject or area repeating the photographic sessions.

An innovative approach, shown in this chapter, is the combination of 3D models of the graves generated with SfM photogrammetry with the 3D models of the human remains obtained from CT scanning, after the anthropological analysis. In particular, we could locate the 3D bones in the grave and distinguish the individuals by colourcoding. This approach helped to clearly visualise the separate individuals. We were able to precisely locate each bone in the grave, because we assigned a number to each bone at the time of the excavation. After the analysis and the attribution of bones to each individual, the process of combination of 3D data from CT with those from SfM photogrammetry was quite easy using Cloud compare and the alignment functions. Entire bones or part of the bones were visible on the SfM photogrammetry 3D model and were used as a reference. Each bone was aligned, singularly. Undoubtedly, the process was time-consuming, but the obtained results are worthwhile and add value to the interpretation. One can argue that Fig. 7.9 can be partially reproduced by adding colours to the bones, as visualised on the sketch plans. However, the profile section (Fig. 7.10) cannot be produced on the sketch plan, and it does add important information. Indeed, the 3D visualisations made it clear that the female (individual 3, orange bones) occupied the lowest layer and that her bones were moved to give space to subsequent burials. The two males (individual 1 and individual 2) could have been buried at the same time or within a short time distance. A similar result could have been obtained combining SfM photogrammetry and 3D bones obtained from a surface scanner, instead of the CT scanning. However, the process of surface scanning all bones, singularly, would have required a huge amount of time. CT scanning of an entire skeleton requires around 5 minutes and if the bones are properly placed on the CT table, i.e. separate from each other, the process of segmentation is also fast and automatic. Furthermore, CT scanning provides internal information and could help in identifying pathologies or any sign of trauma not visibly on the surface, even though, in our case, this advantage was not demonstrated, since the individuals did not show any several pathology or trauma.

Combination of 3D data from CT scanning and SfM photogrammetry data has been used before in bioarchaeological context but they have been used as complementary tools to illustrate different aspects of the same object of interest: see, for example, the project "Digitised Diseases" (www.digitiseddiseases.org), where pathological human bones have been digitised using diverse 3D techniques. Similarly, 3D data from CT scanning and SfM photogrammetry have been used in combination to fully document the deceased (Villa et al. 2018; Villa and Jacobsen 2019): CT scanning provides the internal information of bones, and internal organs, while SfM photogrammetry records of the "colour" information and thus the information about bruises or superficial lesions not visible on CT imaging.

To sum up, 3D imaging techniques enable a permanent 3D documentation of the object of interest. Moreover, they can facilitate both the contextualisation and the interpretation of the burial sites (Dell'Unto 2014). Thus, they are important tools for preserving endangered heritage worldwide (Faber et al. 2017). In addition, the use of these tools has the potential to be of huge benefit in education, outreach and collection preservation (Gaffney et al. 2016). 3D models can also add value by delivering a more immersive visual experience to the local community and the wider public by providing a collective experience of archaeological sites (Dell'Unto 2014).

Finally, it is important to note that new visualising tools need to be found to properly present 3D models. Showing them in 2D causes a loss of significant information. A 3D pdf may be a useful format for sharing data. Alternatively, an online repository, such as 3D HOP or Sketchfab, may be used. These solutions should be easy to implement and accessible to everyone.

7.5   Conclusion

In conclusion, we demonstrated, once again, the utility of using SfM photogrammetry in the case of burial sites to document the different phases of the excavation. In addition, we also showed how 3D models of the human remains (obtained from

CT scanning) can be integrated with the 3D models of the graves (obtained from SfM photogrammetry) for a better interpretation and visualisation of the findings. 3D imaging techniques are becoming important tools in bioarchaeology and should be implemented, whenever possible, in the archaeological/anthropological workflow. Indeed, 3D models play an important role in documentation, interpretation, education and outreach of Cultural Heritage. They have a strong visualisation power, adding value by delivering a more immersive, visual experience to both the local community and the wider public by providing a collective experience of archaeological sites.

References

3D flow www.3dflow.net. Accessed 4 Aug 2020

Agisoft. www.agisoft.com/. Accessed 4 Aug 2020

Agugiaro G (2014) 2D GIS vs. 3D GIS theory. In: Remondino F, Campana S (eds) 3D recording and modelling in archaeology and cultural heritage, vol BAR international series 2598. British archaeological reports, pp 103–114

Ahrens S, Borvik R (2016) Measurement and mapping of ship finds based on 2D and close range photogrammetry techniques. In: Garhøj N, Pilati M (eds) Why 3D? Challenage and solutions with the use of 3D visualization in archaelogy. Lasertryk A/S, Denmark, pp 9–20

Alqahtani SJ, Liversidge HM, Hector MP (2010) Atlas of tooth development and eruption. Am J Phys Anthropol 54–54

Baier W, Rando C (2016) Developing the use of structure-from-motion in mass grave documentation. Forensic Sci Int 261:19–25

Beckett RG, Conlogue GJ (2009) Paleoimaging: field applications for cultural remains and artifacts. CRC Press

Bennet R (2014) Airborne laser scanning for archeological prospection. In Remondino F, Campana S (eds) 3D recording and modelling in archaeology and cultural heritage, vol BAR international series 2598. British archaeological reports, pp 27–38

Capturing Reality. www.capturingreality.com/. Accessed 4 Aug 2020

CCWU. www.ccwu.me/vsfm/. Accessed 4 Aug 2020

Ch'ng E, Gaffney V (2013) Seeing things: heritage computing, visualisation and the arts and humanities. In: Ch'ng E, Gaffney V, Chapman H (eds) Visual heritage in the digital age, vol Springer series on cultural computing. Springer, London, pp 1–14

Chhem RK, Brothwell DR (2008) Paleoradiology. Imaging mummies and fossils. Springer, Berlin

Cloud Compare. www.cloudcompare.org. Accessed 4 Aug 2020

Corel Draw. www.coreldraw.com. Accessed 4 Aug 2020

Dell'Unto N (2014) The use of 3D models for intra-site investigation in archaeology. In: 3D recording and modeling in archaeology and cultural heritage: theory and best practices—theory and best practices. BAR international series. Archaeopress, pp 151–158

Digitised Diseases. www.digitiseddiseases.org. Accessed 4 Aug 2020

Eriksen AM, Gregory DJ, Villa C, Lynnerup N, Botfeldt KB, Rasmussen AR (2016) The effects of wood anisotropy on the mode of attack by the woodborer Teredo navalis and the implications for underwater cultural heritage. Int Biodeterior Biodegradation 107:117–122. https://doi.org/10.1016/j.ibiod.2015.11.018

Faber E, Sparrow T, Murgatroyd A, Wilson AS, Gaffney V, Gaffney C (2017) Special report curious travellers: preserving endangered heritage across the world. Curr. World Archaeol. 11

Gaffney V, Bates R, Ch'ng E, Cuttler R, Gaffney C, Wilson A (2016) BradPhys to BradViz or from archaeological science to heritage science. Paper presented at the 22nd international conference on virtual system & multimedia (VSMM)

Galiatzatos N (2014) Exploring archaelogical landscapes with satellite imagery. In: Remondino F, Campana S (eds) 3D recording and modelling in archaeology and cultural heritage. Vol BAR international series 2598. British archaeological reports, pp 91–102

Gimp. www.gimp.org. Accessed 4 Aug 2020

github.com/steve-vincent/photogrammetry. Accessed 4 Aug 2020

Goldman LW (2008) Principles of CT: multislice CT. J Nucl Med Technol 36(2):57–68. quiz 75–56 (2008). https://doi.org/10.2967/jnmt.107.044826.

Guidi G (2014) Terrestrial optical active sensors—theory & applications. In: Remondino F, Campana S (eds) 3D recording and modelling in archaeology and cultural heritage, vol BAR international series 2598. British archaeological reports, pp 39–64

Hassani F (2015) Documentation of cultural heritage techniques, potentials and constraints. In: 25th international Cipa symposium 2015, 40-5(W7), pp 207–214. https://doi.org/10.5194/isprsa rchives-XL-5-W7-207-2015

Historic_England (2017) Photogrammetric applications for cultural heritage. Guidance for good practice. Historic England, Swindon

Kalender WA (2011) Computed tomography: fundamentals, system technology, image quality, applications, 3rd edn. Publicis

Kraus K (1994) Photogrammetry, vol Bonn. Verd. Dümmler Verlag, Bonn

Kucukkaya AG (2004) Photogrammetry and remote sensing in archeology. J Quant Spectrosc Radiat Transf 88(1–3):83–88. https://doi.org/10.1016/j.jqsrt.2003.12.030

Limaverde S, Pêgas RV, Damasceno R, Villa C, Oliveira G, Bonde N et al (2018) Interpreting character variation in turtles: Araripemys barretoi (Pleurodira: Pelomedusoides) from the Araripe Basin, Early Cretaceous of Northeastern Brazil. PeerJ PrePrints 6:e27262v1. https://doi.org/10.7287/peerj.preprints.27262v1

Luhmann T, Robson S, Kyle S, Boehm J (2013) Close-range photogrammetry and 3D imaging. Walter de Gruyter & Co.

Lynnerup N (2007) Mummies. Yearb Phys Anthropol 50(50):162–190. https://doi.org/10.1002/ajpa.20728

Mimics. www.materialise.com/en/medical/software/mimics. Accessed 4 Aug 2020

Myrian. www.intrasense.fr. Accessed 4 Aug 2020

Nguyen CV, Lovell DR, Adcock M, La Salle J (2014) Capturing natural-colour 3D models of insects for species discovery and diagnostics. PLoS One 9(4)

Osirix Viewer. www.osirix-viewer.com. Accessed 4 Aug 2020

Photomodeler. www.photomodeler.com Accessed 4 Aug 2020

Poulsen K, Simonsen J (2007) Computed tomography as routine in connection with medico-legal autopsies. Forensic Sci Int 171(2–3):190–197. https://doi.org/10.1016/j.forsciint.2006.05.041

Rutty GN, Morgan B, O'Donnell C, Leth PM, Thali M (2008) Forensic institutes across the world place CT or MRI scanners or both into their mortuaries. J Trauma-Inj Infect Crit Care 65(2):493–494. https://doi.org/10.1097/TA.0b013e31817de420

Scheuer L, Black SMD (2000) Developmental juvenile osteology. Academic Press, San Diego, CA

Seibert JA (2004) X-ray imaging physics for nuclear medicine technologists. Part 1: basic principles of x-ray production. J Nucl Med Technol 32(3):139–147

Seibert JA, Boone JM (2005) X-ray imaging physics for nuclear medicine technologists. Part 2: X-ray interactions and image formation. J Nucl Med Technol 33(1):3–18

Siebke I, Campana L, Ramstein M, Furtwängler A, Hafner A, Lösch S (2018) The application of different 3D-scan-systems and photogrammetry at an excavation—A Neolithic dolmen from Switzerland. Digit Appl Archaeol Cult Herit 10:e00078. https://doi.org/10.1016/j.daach.2018. e00078

Slicer. www.slicer.org. Accessed 4 Aug 2020

Themistocleous K, Mettas C, Evagorou E, Hadjimitsis D (2019) The use of UAVs and photogrammetry for the documentation of cultural heritage monuments: the case study of the churches in Cyprus. Earth Resour Environ Remote Sens Gis Appl X:11156. https://doi.org/10.1117/12.253 3056

Tobiasz A, Markiewicz J, Lapinski S, Nikel J, Kot P, Muradov M (2019) Review of methods for documentation, management, and sustainability of cultural heritage. Case study: museum of King Jan III's Palace at Wilanow. Sustainability 11(24). https://doi.org/10.3390/su11247046

Ubelaker DH (1989) Human skeletal remains: excavation, analysis, interpretation. Manuals on archeology, vol 2. Taraxacum, Washington D.C.

Villa C (2017) Forensic 3D documentation of skin injuries. Int J Legal Med 131(3):751–759. https://doi.org/10.1007/s00414-016-1499-9

Villa C, Flies MJ, Jacobsen C (2018) Forensic 3D documentation of bodies: simple and fast procedure for combining CT scanning with external photogrammetry data. J Forensic Radiol Imaging 12:e2–e7. https://doi.org/10.1016/j.jofri.2017.11.003

Villa C, Frohlich B, Lynnerup N (2019) Chapter 7 - The Role of Imaging in Paleopathology. In: Buikstra JE (ed) Ortner's identification of pathological conditions in human skeletal remains, 3rd edn. Academic Press, San Diego, pp 169–182

Villa C, Jacobsen C (2019) The application of photogrammetry for forensic 3D recording of crime scenes, evidence and people. In: Rutty G (ed) Essentials of autopsy practice. Springer, Cham

Villa C, Lynnerup N (2012) Hounsfield units ranges in CT-scans of bog bodies and mummies. Anthropol Anz 69(2):127–145. https://doi.org/10.1127/0003-5548/2012/0139

Waldron T (2009) Palaeopathology. Cambridge University Press, New York, USA

Chapter 8
The Digital Restoration of an Ancient Skull's Appearance for Palaeoanthropological Study

Guohua Geng, Mingquan Zhou, Wen Yang, Tao Ruan Wan, and Wen Tang

Abstract With the rapid development of 3D scanning, image processing and virtual reality, we have now entered the era of information technology for cultural heritage protection. Digital conservation of cultural relics has become an important subject of scientific research and the results have been widely applied in archaeology, palaeoanthropology and other fields. This study introduces applications for the digital and virtual restoration of an ancient human skull, the study of which holds considerable significance for the study of history and civilisation. The application of digital technology in palaeoanthropology is introduced, including the analysis of human evolution along with statistical analysis, racial differences, and restoration of physiognomy. The key digital technologies applied are described along with methods such as craniofacial data modelling, craniofacial restoration and realistic digital appearance processing. The examples provided are virtual restorations of the skull of a Tang Dynasty Princess Li Chui, an ancient Qihe skull and a Qin female skull in order to demonstrate the technologies for restoration and digitising ancient remains. The continuous development and innovation of computer technologies and the improvement of relevant methodologies will support researchers undertaking research in the field of palaeo-anthropology.

Keywords Ancient anthropology · Digital Technology · Virtual restoration · Craniofacial reconstruction · Realistic processing

G. Geng · W. Yang
College of Information Science and Technology, Northwest University, Xi'an, China

M. Zhou
College of Information Science and Technology, Beijing Normal University, Beijing, China

T. R. Wan (✉)
Faculty of Engineering and Informatics, University of Bradford, Bradford, UK
e-mail: T.Wan@bradford.ac.ukWhen

W. Tang
Faculty of Science and Technology, Bournemouth University, Poole, UK

© Springer Nature Switzerland AG 2022
E. Ch'ng et al. (eds.), *Visual Heritage: Digital Approaches in Heritage Science*,
Springer Series on Cultural Computing,
https://doi.org/10.1007/978-3-030-77028-0_8

8.1 Introduction

Craniofacial reconstruction is a technology used to reconstruct the face of a person from their skull. The technology can be used in many fields including forensic science, archaeology, anthropology, plastic surgery, etc. In this chapter, we discuss the application of digital craniofacial reconstruction in palaeoanthropology. The digital data relating to human skulls, and other characteristics considered here include the skull inner surface morphology, inner ear structure, microanatomical characteristics of bones and teeth and the surface morphology of various parts of the brain and are of significance to the study of human physical characteristics. The comparative analysis of such facial features between ancient and modern human, through cranio-facial reconstruction technology, may also assist when considering the physiological evolution of human faces.

In order to avoid secondary damage to the skull and support data reuse, this application utilised computer tomography, imaging processing and 3D reconstruction technologies to digitise and obtain skull models. The skulls are digitally repaired, given the impacts of natural processes and later damage. The geometry of the inner and outer surface of the skull, as well as virtual measurements of the skull itself, are statistically analysed to obtain the reconstruction rules While the traditional methods only focus on the outer surface measurements of reconstructed skulls, the application here allows us to digitally cut the skull along the coronal plane, sagittal plane, axial plane and at any position parallel to these three planes. It is also possible to slice the skull at any angle digitally, without damage to the original object, in order to visualise the morphology of the inner surface of the skull.

Traditional craniofacial reconstruction methods are often subjective, and early computer-assisted craniofacial reconstruction methods could not accurately reflect the essential relationship between the skull and facial morphology. Here, we use a new craniofacial statistical reconstruction method based on analysis on a large craniofacial dataset. The statistical model learns prior knowledge of craniofacial reconstructions and extracts the internal relationship between the skull and the facial form. It then performs facial reconstruction based on this relationship. In addition, the restored model undergoes face shape editing, texture mapping and hair modelling, making the reconstruction results more realistic. These processes were applied, with good results, to reconstructions of the skulls of the princess Li Chui of the Tang Dynasty, skulls of the ancient Qihedong man and females of the Qin Dynasty.

Although statistical modelling has become a mainstream method of craniofa-cial reconstruction, there are many issues associated with statistical methods. For example, obtaining a representative sample at a large scale to developing a statistical model with an expressive ability, as well as modelling craniofacial deformation are great challenges. The contribution to these practical issues within this chapter can be summarised as follows:

1. The method can produce high-fidelity digital skull reconstructions that can not only be reused but are appropriate for use in digital conservation.

2.   A new statistical model that is able to learn the relationship between the skull and the face, and effectively represent the complexity and diversity of craniofacial morphological changes, and can more accurately reflect the essential relationship between the skull and the face.
3.   New computer-aided, craniofacial morphological analysis, the results of which are more objective, and have a more rigorous scientific basis compared to other approaches.
4.   An exemplar study for the restoration of ancient faces, skulls and related objects.

8.2   Related Work

Craniofacial reconstruction technique was first introduced to restore the appearance of famous historical bodies or those recovered through archaeology (Grasimov 1958). Typical cases include reconstructions of mummies of Egyptian pharaohs, face reconstructions of a series of famous historical figures, such as the emperor of the Timur Empire and Oliver Cromwell (Grasimov 1958). Many techniques for craniofacial reconstruction assume that there is a relationship between the skull and the face, but none describe the relationship explicitly.

Traditional facial morphology research and applications are based on the physical skull and based on anatomical measurement determined by the thickness rule of soft tissues of the face. Such approaches are often conducted subjectively by anthropologists, artists and doctors (Wilkinson 2001; Prag and Neave 1997). In addition, earlier methods relied on an individual's experience of craniofacial features, and the results were greatly affected by subjective factors. With the development of CT technology, computer 3D visualisation technology and interdisciplinary research, new technologies and methods are now available to analyse craniofacial morphology. Computer-aided craniofacial reconstruction now attracts considerable attention across the fields of international informatics, anthropology, forensic medicine and has become a 'hot' research topic worldwide.

Computer-aided craniofacial restoration technology can be divided into two main categories: computer-simulated, manual restoration methods and statistical methods. Computer simulation and manual restoration projects have been widely reported in the media. Vanezis successfully identified many crime victims using soft tissue thickness data to support manual restoration (Vanezis et al. 1989). Vandermeulen (2006) used implicit equations to reconstruct the cranial surface in CT images. Simon (2000) used body models, Archer (1977a) used B-splines, Kolja (2003) and Zhouused, from 1996, deformation to reconstruct the cranial surface (Zhou et al. 1997). Since then a great deal of work has been undertaken on craniofacial reconstruction and interactive editing based on triangular mesh representation. Shrimpton et al. (2014) first proposed using statistical analysis of the thickness of soft tissues of dense feature points of skulls for reconstruction. Based on 156 sets of craniofacial CT data, soft tissues for approximately 7500 feature points were calculated, and the relationship between the thickness of these dense soft tissues and gender, age and BMI were analysed by a partial least-square regression method. In contrast, Deng et al. (2011a) used a method combining a thin-plate spline function TPS and radial basis functions with tight support. Gietzen et al. (2018) proposed an automatic forensic facial reconstruction method, based on dense statistics of soft tissue thickness, that could automatically solve probabilistic facial estimation. The reconstruction processes of these methods are convenient, but selected feature points are too sparse. It is difficult to represent rich details of a face based on the thickness of soft tissues at the key points and, consequently, the accuracy of this method is not great.

Two of the most influential 2D shape statistical models are the ASM (Active Shape Model) proposed by Cootes (1998) and the AAM (Active Appearance Model) which describes the texture features of edge points statistically. ASM/AAM models have achieved great success in 2D feature location, edge search, shape description and data registration. Feng et al. (2004, 2005) extended this work to a 3D model. However, it is difficult to select feature points on the surface of complex 3D organisms such as face and skull, and the limited number of samples also makes it difficult to obtain an effective point distribution model. Berar et al. (2006) used a sparse grid representation model to establish a craniofacial statistical model, whilst Zhang et al. (2010) proposed a facial reconstruction algorithm based on a Regional Statistical Craniofacial model (RSCM). Her, specifically, the shape of the craniofacial model is decomposed into segments, such as eyes, nose and mouth regions. Joint statistical models of different regions are constructed independently to address the problem of a small sample size. Facial reconstruction is formulated as a missing data problem and is processed on a region by region basis. Finally, the regions are reassembled to achieve a complete face model. Duan et al. (2014) proposed a 3D craniofacial reconstruction method based on statistical learning. In order to adequately represent the craniofacial shape variation and to adequately utilise the linkages between different regions, two tensor models are constructed for the skull and the face skin, respectively, and a multi-linear subspace analysis is used to extract the craniofacial subspace features. A partial least-squares regression (PLSR), based on mapping from skull subspace to skin subspace, is established, along with attributes such as age and BMI. For an unknown skull, the 3D face skin is reconstructed using the acquired mapping, with the help of the skin tensor model. Shui et al. (2019) used PCA to construct the statistical shape space of the skull and face within the dense corresponding vertices, analysed the correlation of PC scores based on skull and face and used linear regression to fit the craniofacial relationship to achieve cranial face reconstruction.

The craniofacial restoration method uses reference data on facial soft tissue distribution to support the restoration of tissue distribution over the skull to approximate appearance (Vanezis et al. 1989; Shui et al. 2013; Guyomarch et al. 2013; Archer 1997b). This method first calculates the average soft tissue thickness at a small number of facial feature points for people of different ages, genders and races. The method then uses these data to restore the soft tissue thickness at the corresponding feature points of the skull to be restored, so as to achieve craniofacial restoration through interpolation or skinning techniques. The process has limitations in the number of defined feature points and the lack of uniform standards. In order to overcome this problem, scholars have proposed craniofacial restoration technology based on skull registration (Deng et al. 2011b; Shui et al. 2011; Turner et al. 2005; Quatre-homme et al. 1997). This method first selects the appropriate skull and facial model from a 3D craniofacial database as the reference skull and reference face, and then uses a non-rigid deformation method to geometrically deform the reference skull to the target skull based on skull feature points, ridgelines and other information. This transformation is applied to the reference facial model to achieve craniofacial restoration. The choice of reference data will affect the result, as the thickness distribution of facial soft tissue is affected by various factors such as age, gender, nutrition, ethnicity and region (Shui et al. 2016; Dong et al. 2012). Consequently, it is more difficult to choose a suitable average soft tissue for the restoration of an ancient human skull.

Alternative statistical learning methods provide us with a powerful tool for obtaining complex object shape information from a large number of training samples. The craniofacial statistical reconstruction method learns the relationship between the skull and facial geometry from the skull model and facial model of large samples, which makes the facial reconstruction results more accurate and efficient. To do this, statistical model-based craniofacial restoration methods use a parameterised deformable template matching method and template dynamic adjustments can be achieved by changing parameters. The effective extraction of sample information can support craniofacial learning, and the parameters of a statistical model can be analysed to obtain the control parameters of craniofacial explicit attributes. However, there are still some shortcomings in that the small samples affect the results of restoration.

8.3 Methodology

8.3.1 Cranial Surface Data Modelling

The main methods of craniofacial data acquisition are traditional measurement, CT scanning, laser scanning and ultrasound. In this chapter, the craniofacial data were obtained by CT scanning. We used a multi-detector spiral CT to collect volume data. For this purpose, the voltage of the scanner data acquisition tube was 120 kV, the scanning mode was spiral with axis position. The pitch was 1.5, the thickness of the reference value was 0.75 mm, the size of each slice was 512×512 pixels, and colour depth was 16 bits. The reconstruction thickness was 0.75 mm and the reconstruction interval was 0.1 mm. The DICOM 3.0 standard was used for data description, transmission and storage. In addition, we also recorded the age, sex, height, birthplace and other information of the subjects.

In addition to the acquisition parameters, the acquisition criteria and steps also require body position and acquisition rules. The craniomaxillofacial position of the subjects cannot have metal prostheses or non-removable metal decorations. Before the collection, all participants provided personal information including age, sex,

origin, birthplace, parental and current residence, etc. All metal ornaments and pros-
thetics were removed. Participants lay in a supine position, the head close to sensor,
hands drooping naturally, feet close together, eyes forward-looking, the laser sagittal
line coinciding with the median line, the laser coronal line was parallel to the external
auditory canal, axis parallel to the eye can thus line. A three-view fast and high-
precision fixed-parameter image acquisition device was also developed to collect all
data automatically.

Our modelling method is based on modern image techniques and can obtain
both skull and facial information accurately. This starts with collecting multi-view
data located in different local coordinate systems. By looking for the corresponding
relationship between the overlapping areas of different depth images in different
coordinate systems, the data can be transformed into a unified global coordinate
system under the constraint of the minimum distance of the overlapping areas of the
depth images. The accuracy of the registration directly determines the quality of the
model reconstruction. Poor registration will cause the details of the fused model to
become blurred, and incorrect registration results will directly cause the modelling
to fail. Finally, the reconstruction is finished with all the data, using a contour and
voxel-based method.

This method has three advantages.

1.   The modelling accuracy of this method is higher than traditional image data
     modelling methods.
2.   The proposed method can collect texture information whilst also collecting
     model geometric information, enhancing the realism of the face; the device
     is easy to carry, and more suitable for modelling at the scene of criminal
     investigation and archaeological excavation.
3.   The method can also support the construction of a craniofacial database.

8.3.2   Craniofacial Morphology Analysis

The definition of characteristic points of skull and face is based on the basic theories
of anatomy and forensic anthropology. Here, we defined 78 skull feature points for
craniofacial morphology research and facial restoration. Of these, 12 feature points
are located on the midline, while the other 66 feature points are symmetrically located
on both sides of the median sagittal plane. The skull feature points defined in Fig. 8.1a
can be divided into five main appearance facial features' points (brows, eyes, ears,
nose, and mouth) and other selected facial points, which will affect the morphology
and appearance of a face. These points can fully reflect the anatomical characteristics
of the skull and the morphological characteristics of the face. The skull feature point
diagram is shown in Fig. 8.1a.

The measurement in the craniofacial database and the soft tissue thickness directly
affect the reliability of craniofacial restoration results. We define the direction of soft
tissue measurement as measured along a straight line. Along the opposite direction
of the ray, P0 is taken as the starting point and the face produces the intersection point

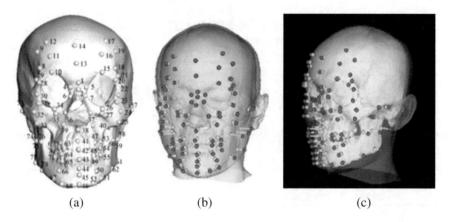

| (a) | (b) | (c) |

Fig. 8.1 Feature point and soft tissue thickness. **a** 78 feature points on the skull; **b** Front view of soft tissue thickness; **c** Side view of soft tissue thickness (National-Local Joint Engineering Research Center of Cultural Heritage Digitization, Northwest University)

P1(x1, y1, z1), which can be calculated by Formula (8.1). Euclidean distance is the thickness of soft tissue. Soft tissue thickness and its measurement direction are shown in Fig. 8.1b, c. Points in a light colour represent the apex of skull, dark coloured points represent the corresponding points of the face, line segments represent the thickness of soft tissue, and vectors run from light to dark colour points.

$$thick_i = \frac{1}{n} \sum_{i=1}^{n} \| P0 - P1 \| \tag{8.1}$$

The soft tissue thickness measurement of skull feature points cannot fully reflect the distribution of the whole facial soft tissue thickness. In practical applications, such as skull restoration and 3D face recognition, people pay more attention to information on the front and side of the head. Therefore, this section mainly focuses on the analysis of the soft tissue thickness distribution in these positions.

The intersection point between the vertex of the skull and the face model is used to calculate the thickness of soft tissue at each vertex on the skull. In order to improve the speed of intersection, a K-D tree is used to accelerate the intersection and reduce the number of triangles used.

Table 8.1 shows the mean and standard deviation of soft tissue thickness at 43 characteristic points of the skull and 10 characteristic points of the cheek region in male samples of different ages. By comparing the mean soft tissue thickness of the 43 skull facial features at different ages, it was found that the soft tissue thickness of the 20–30 age group was the thinnest, the soft tissue thickness of the 50–60 age group was second and the soft tissue thickness of the 30–40 age group was the thickest.

The soft tissue thickness is similar between the ages of 30–40 and 40–50. The mean values of the standard deviation of soft tissue thickness of the 43 skull points and the 10 skull points of the cheek region were further compared. We found that

Table 8.1 Soft tissue thickness in males of different ages/unit: mm

Age	Index	Average value of 43 facial feature points	Average value of 10 cheek feature points
20–30	Mean	10.68	16.58
	standard deviation	1.69	2.73
30–40	Mean	13.07	21.36
	standard deviation	2.38	4.26
40–50	Mean	12.67	21.31
	standard deviation	2.77	5.22
50–60	Mean	11.64	19.93
	standard deviation	2.19	4.13

the mean value of the standard deviation of the soft tissue thickness of the cheek feature points in each age group, was significantly larger than the standard deviation of the 43 skull feature points. The mean value indicates that the soft tissue thickness at these characteristic points varies greatly, which may reflect changes in the facial appearance of the craniofacial sample.

Table 8.2 shows the mean and standard deviation of soft tissue thickness of the 43 characteristic points on the skull and 10 characteristic points in the cheek region of female specimens of different ages. By comparing the mean soft tissue thickness of the 43 skull features at different ages, it was found that the mean and standard deviation of soft tissue thickness was lowest in the 20–30 years' group. The mean soft tissue thickness and the standard deviation in the 30–40 years old are the next. The mean thickness and standard deviation in the group 40–50 years old are the largest. However, the mean and standard deviation of soft tissue thickness decrease in the 50–60 age group. The mean values of the standard deviation of soft tissue thickness of the 43 skull points and the 10 skull points of the cheek region were further compared. It was found that the mean value of the standard deviation of the soft tissue thickness of the cheek region feature points, in each age group, was

Table 8.2 Soft tissue thickness in females of different ages/unit: mm

Age	Index	Average value of 43 facial feature points	Average value of 10 cheek feature points
20–30	Mean	11.07	7.59
	standard deviation	1.46	2.36
30–40	Mean	11.69	19.40
	standard deviation	1.66	2.55
40–50	Mean	12.94	21.58
	standard deviation	2.24	4.01
50–60	Mean	12.07	20.41
	standard deviation	1.97	2.89

significantly larger than the standard deviation of the 43 skull feature points. The mean value indicates that the soft tissue thickness at the above characteristic points changes greatly, which may reflect the facial appearance of the craniofacial sample.

8.3.3   Craniofacial Reconstruction Based on Statistical Model

For a complex 3D organism such as the cranium, it is difficult to obtain an accurate mathematical description of its 3D shape due to the lack of adequate, explicit data. Early computer-aided craniofacial restoration methods depended on the knowledge of average soft tissue thickness or deformation of a single craniofacial reference (Zhou et al. 1997). Using such a method it is difficult to express the complexity and diversity of craniofacial morphological changes effectively. It thus cannot accurately reflect the essential relationship between craniofacial morphology and skull. Statistical learning provides us with a powerful tool to obtain shape information on complex objects from a large number of training samples. Compared with the traditional method of craniofacial restoration based on soft tissue measurement, a statistical craniofacial restoration method (Hu 2010; He 2012; Claes et al. 2010a) attempted to learn the prior knowledge of craniofacial restoration through statistical analysis of a large number of craniofacial data. These methods extracted the internal relationship between craniofacial bone and morphology and restored the face according to this internal relationship. Statistical restoration has become a mainstream method of craniofacial restoration.

Statistical craniofacial reconstruction generally includes two stages: statistical model training and statistical recovery. In the model training stage, the training samples collected are pre-processed this includes filling holes, smoothing and data registration to ensure that each craniofacial sample has the same grid representation with the same posture, the same number of vertices and the same semantics. Following this, the data representation of skull and face is determined depending on the feature data used to build the statistical model. Finally, a skull with the same structure is established. In the statistical recovery stage, the statistical model is matched to the feature data of the target skull to support facial restoration.

Statistical, deformable models of the cranial surface are, essentially, a parameterised deformable template (Hu et al. 2013; Luo et al. 2013). Each cranial surface has a parametric representation, and each cranial surface corresponds to a point in parametric space, whereas each point in parametric space corresponds to a cranial surface. Modelling of statistical deformation model is essential to establish the point distribution model of craniofacial surface within parameter space. To establish a statistical deformation model of craniofacial surface data, this method searches for a set of orthogonal axes that can reflect the true distribution of training sample data sets. The origins of these orthogonal axes are located in the centre of the data set, representing a set of directions with the largest variance in the training data, and which can reconstruct the data with the minimum variance, thus achieving the final result effectively.

The earliest methods for restoring statistical deformational models of craniofacial surfaces were based on least-squares fitting (Berar et al. 2006). This then places a reconstructed face with missing data within a statistical deformational model and uses least-squares fitting to resolve missing data and to complete a craniofacial restoration. The method is based on the maximum posterior probability (Claes et al. 2006, 2010b), and is the classical statistical deformation model restoration method and uses Bayesian estimation to determine model parameters. In this example, 52 skull markers represented the skull, dense point clouds the face, and nasal tips were used as additional skin markers.

Following the theory of craniofacial morphology, there are potential connections between the whole and the local parts of the craniofacial, and between the local parts. Therefore, it is difficult to describe, relatively, the independent morphological changes of the craniofacial region using a single global craniofacial model. In order to construct a statistical model that can better reflect the change rules of craniofacial morphology, the researchers propose a restoration model based on the zonal statistical model (Zhang et al. 2010) and a hierarchical craniofacial statistical model (Hu et al. 2013; Feng 2010). The hierarchical statistical model divides craniofacial restoration into two levels: a global statistical model and a local statistical model. The restoration of the global statistical model was aimed at the restoration of the basic craniofacial shape and overall structure. The local statistical model is similar to the zonal statistical model, and was used to represent the changes in local morphology.

8.3.4 Realism Treatment

Research is undertaken on the post-processing of the 3D face model for skull facial reconstruction mainly focuses on two aspects: shape editing of the 3D face model and skin and hair modelling. Firstly, it is often necessary to edit and modify the face model interactively, and according to the views of anatomists and anthropologists. This involves tasks such as the fine adjustment of the shape of certain areas or replacing individual facial organs. In addition, face restoration models are usually simple 3D geometric models, and the lack of corresponding texture data, skin colour, eyebrows, hair and other important facial components, will seriously affect the authenticity and recognisability of the restoration. Therefore, realistic processing of face restoration needs to be carefully conducted under the guidance of experts.

In order to personalise, scientifically, the reconstructed face, it is often necessary to transform and edit the reconstructed face interactively. Face shape editing is a specific example of surface editing. The content of surface editing mainly includes surface clipping and pasting, surface fusion, local shape adjustment, geometric texture migration and so forth. Providing users with an intuitive and efficient tool for surface editing is an important component in the fields of solid and geometric modeling. There are four common kinds of surface editing methods: the Barr deformation method, a free deformation method and surface editing based on subdivision attributes and constrained deformation methods.

Five main features replacement refers to the selection of an appropriate five main features model from the five main features database to replace the corresponding regions in the existing face model. The problem is to ensure that the five main features model used for replacement completely coincides with the splicing boundary of the face model and provides a smooth transition after the five main features replacement. There are two main processes in the replacement of the five senses: division and integration.

Organ segmentation of the 3D face model is mainly based on 2D or 3D feature points and feature contours. According to the feature and feature contours, a region of the 3D face model is segmented, and the segmentation results should be merged to generate meaningful model regions. Five-sense segmentation of a 3D face is a specific case of a 3D mesh model segmentation. 3D mesh model segmentation refers to the decomposition of the mesh model into a set of connected sub-meshes according to the geometric characteristics and topological structure of the model (Sun and Li 2005). Based on the relationship between skull feature points and facial features along with the expert knowledge of anthropologists, a model from a facial features database can be used to replace the corresponding area in the restored facial model. Without the need to change the topological structure of the model, the given facial grids of the replacement organs are removed and automatically adapted to the geometric models of the corresponding organs. This process is adjusted by the data and user's selection from the database while ensuring complete matching and a smooth transition at the splicing boundary.

Texture mapping is a correspondence between a texture domain and a 3D surface. The dimension of the texture domain can be one, 2D or 3D, and is represented as an array, or a function, or a picture. The original image (texture) mapped to a surface in a 3D target space is called a mapping image (screen). The texture domain is denoted as (u, v) and the target space is denoted as (x, y, z).

Texture mapping, therefore, maps a 2D texture to a 3D object surface. To complete this process, the corresponding relationship is established between object space coordinates (x, y, z) and texture space coordinates (u, v). The most commonly used method of texture mapping is to parameterise the 3D mesh model, so the definition of texture coordinates of the 3D mesh model can be regarded as a parameterization of the 3D mesh model to define a 2D parameter value for each 3D vertex in the model. However, parameterization methods are complex, so simple spherical or cylindrical texture mapping technology is frequently used in practical applications (Bier and Sloan 1986).

Traditional hair modelling methods mainly include hair modelling, kinematics simulation and rendering. In computer-aided skull restoration, hair modelling does not involve the dynamic simulation of a hair model, so the related research mainly focuses on hair modelling and rendering technologies. In research on hair styling, there are mainly two kinds of hairstyling methods: interactive styling and non-interactive styling. With respect to hair rendering, the related research mainly focuses on light scattering and shadows of hair.

There are four types of interactive hair modelling methods: curve editing, mesh, physical and hybrid. At present, the research into non-interactive hair modelling methods includes image-based and sample-based methods. Non-interactive hairstyling means that users directly generate new hair styling on the target model by inputting existing 3D models, images and so on. The appearance of new hairstyling based on this method is usually determined by three factors: input, configuration parameters and appearance characteristics of the target virtual role model.

With respect to light scattering and rendering, the optical property of hair is an important basis for establishing the light scattering model of realistic hair. To study the optical properties of hair, we need to understand the biological structure of hair first. The complexity of the biological structure of hair leads to unique light scattering effects. Early researchers usually used empirical models to approximate the illumination effect of real hair. This method was characterised by its speed, but the resulting models were very different from real hair.

Another difficulty in hair rendering is the calculation of hair shadows. In theory, high-quality hair shadow can be obtained by using traditional shadow testing in offline rendering methods (Pharr and Greg 2010; Suffern 2007). In fact, because of the large number of hairs, the performance and accuracy of such an algorithm go far beyond general requirements. The greatest difference between hair rendering and shadow rendering of ordinary objects is that hair rendering processes requires very complex light transmission, because each hair will produce reflected or scattered light when lit and will not completely shield incidental light.

8.4   Case Study

8.4.1   Restoration of the Face of Princess Li Chui from the Tang Dynasty

Between November 2001 and June 2003, archaeologists excavated an important tomb site in Xi'an. According to the epitaph recovered, the tomb was that of Li Chui, the fifth granddaughter of Li Yuan, Gaozu of the Tang Dynasty. She died in Kaiyuan 24, when she was only 25 years old, and more than 1200 years ago. The coffin had decayed but the bone was preserved. Archaeologists found a complete crown on the skull. Although the crown was fragmented, pieces of gold, jade, jadeite and agate were recovered. Experts believe that this type of headdress utilised almost all the decorative materials available in the Tang Dynasty (Fig. 8.2). Li Chui's noble origins and the prominence of her burial make the discovery one of the best examples of such a crown.

A virtual restoration of Li Chui's face and a crown was attempted. The restoration of the princess's face was reconstructed based on the 3D geometric data of the skull and the appearance of modern humans. A significant study was undertaken on how the skull and face changed over time in this data and the essential relationship between the skull and face, and these were used to predict and reconstruct the unknown face

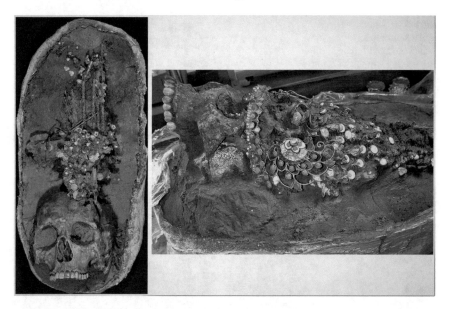

Fig. 8.2 Li Chui's skull and crown unearthed (National-Local Joint Engineering Research Center of Cultural Heritage Digitization, Northwest University)

of the skull. The validity and accuracy of the craniofacial restoration system process were also confirmed through separate tests on a living human. The knowledge and rules obtained from these studies were then used to restore Li Chui's face. The whole process followed an inductive-deductive process.

The recovery process for Li Chui's face included the following steps: (1) digitalisation of Li Li's skull; (2) virtual repair of Li Chui's skull; (3) acquisition of skull and morphological rules; (4) restoration of Li Chui's face; (5) post-processing for realistic representation.

Li Chui's skull was scanned with a multi-slice spiral CT scanner, then the CT scanned image was filtered and pre-processed filtered. A single-layer skull outline model was extracted by combining the improved Snake algorithm with a ray casting method. The 3D point cloud model of the skull was denoised and the point cloud illuminated. The final 3D mesh model of the skull was obtained by triangulation and sequential processing, as shown in Fig. 8.3.

As Li Chui's skull was incomplete and there were many missing parts, the skull was reconstructed before restoring its appearance. Initially, skull models similar to Li Chui's skull shape were selected from the database constructed from earlier research, and average models were obtained. The standard skull model was matched with Li Chui's skull model through geometric coordinate deformation using a registration algorithm. The common parts of the two models overlapped using the 3D data fusion technology. A complete skull model was obtained by repairing the missing parts of Li Chui's skull (Fig. 8.4).

Fig. 8.3 Li Chui's 3D
digital skull model
(National-Local Joint
Engineering Research Center
of Cultural Heritage
Digitization, Northwest
University)

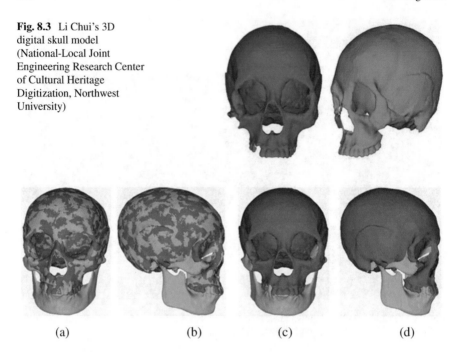

(a)   (b)   (c)   (d)

Fig. 8.4 Repair process of Li Chui's skull model. **a** Registration of Li Chui's skull with the standard skull; **b** Repaired skull model. (National-Local Joint Engineering Research Center of Cultural Heritage Digitization, Northwest University)

Based on the 3D craniofacial database established by using the techniques described in Sect. 8.3.1, a partial least-squares regression was used to analyse the relationship between skull and face. Partial least-squares regression (PLS) is a multivariate data analysis method based on principal component analysis (PCA) and canonical correlation analysis (CCA). It integrates the regression modelling of multivariate-to-multivariate and principal component analysis (PCA). After initial calculation, this simultaneously realised the prediction modelling and the comprehensive simplification of a multivariate system. N pairs of skull and face samples in the database were used for training, the skull and corresponding attributes were taken as independent variables X, and corresponding faces are taken as dependent variables Y. A regression matrix was obtained by partial least-squares regression method, which was the functional representation of Y with respect to X and is $Y = f(X)$. Because of the high accuracy and a large number of vertices of the 3D models of skull and face in the database, we used principal component analysis (PCA) to reduce the 3D models of skull and face, and provide a model representation of skull and face in low-dimensional space. We then used this model representation to carry out regression statistical analysis.

When a target skull is reconstructed, only the model representation of the skull in PCA space, the corresponding attributes and the functional expression between face and skull, obtained by regression statistics, can be used to obtain the model representation of the reconstructed skull in PCA space. Following this, the 3D model of the reconstructed skull can be obtained (Fig. 8.5).

Having obtained the PCA representation model of the skull, Li Chui's face model, the functional relationship between face and skull (including corresponding attributes) was obtained by regression according to the model and Li Chui's attribute value (Fig. 8.6). Among Li Chui's attributes, age was a known value, but whether

Fig. 8.5 Li Chui's recovery (National-Local Joint Engineering Research Center of Cultural Heritage Digitization, Northwest University)

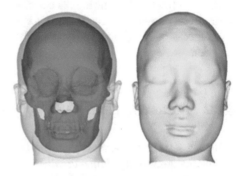

Fig. 8.6 Final recovery results (National-Local Joint Engineering Research Center of Cultural Heritage Digitization, Northwest University)

she was fat or thin was not known. According to the Tang Dynasty's known criteria for beauty, we adjusted Li Chui's characteristics as fat.

In order to provide a restoration that was more alluring, after restoring Li Chui's face we carried out realistic processing, including texture mapping and adding hair, eyebrows, etc. In addition, we also carried out the digital virtual restoration of Li Chui's crown. We also performed a digital virtual restoration of Li Zhi's crown decoration. From the final result, it can be seen that the restored Li Chi is beautiful and dignified, quiet and virtuous, and the exquisite Huaguan jade snail bun is covered with red and emerald, with blue silk and cloud temples, plus golden lotus crested head, floating emerald streamer, and princess. Even more beautiful and beautiful, especially the princess of Tang Dynasty, with golden branches and jade leaves, graceful and luxurious.

8.4.2 Restoration of the Skull of Qihedong Ancient Human

A human skull was discovered in 2011 in the Qihe Cave, Zaotou Village, Xianghu Town, Zhangping City, Fujian Province. 14C dating suggests an age of c. 9500 years ago, and this accords to the Early Neolithic period. Research shows that Qihe Cave Man was a 35-year-old male with a brain mass of 1650 ml and a large skull. The skull, characterised by a long skull, high and narrow face, low orbit and broad nose, exhibited the characteristics of both southern and northern populations from the China region as well as late Pleistocene humans.

The distinguishing morphological characteristics of Qihe Man, in contrast to modern man, based on the original computer craniofacial restoration software applied to modern exemplars, suggested a method of interactive craniofacial restoration based on least-squares regression and statistical shape model constraints should be applied. The craniofacial, morphological characteristics of contemporary populations were applied to the 3D craniofacial restoration of the Qihe Man. The modelling steps were as follows. (1) The 3D model of the skull was built using industrial CT equipment and the point cloud on the outer surface of the skull was computed by an intersection algorithm. It was then transformed into a Frankfurt coordinate system. (2) A non-rigid registration method was adopted according to the calibrated feature points for the 3D model of the skull and the face of contemporary men. The skull and face were standardised into dense point clouds. On this basis, a principal component analysis was used to represent the skull and face 3D model. A least-square regression method was used to quantitatively represent the craniofacial morphological relationship; (3) A non-rigid registration was applied to the external surface model of Qihe Cave skull. A least-squares method was applied to calculate the principal component coefficients for of each skull and the corresponding face of contemporary examples, using the coefficients and the relationship between the craniofacial morphology of living human to achieve the preliminary restoration of the 3D face. (4) A fourth step was to analyse the relationship between the principal component (PC) and the geometric shape of the face. The process allowed editing of the restored

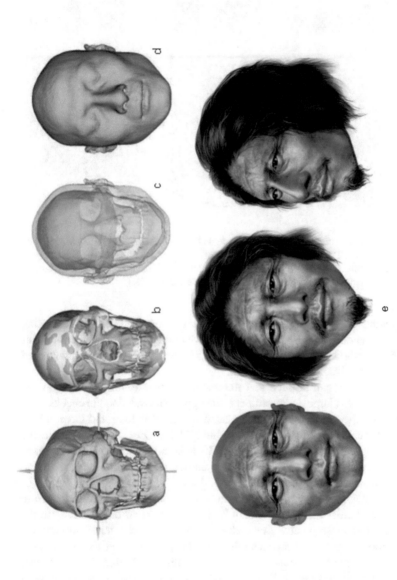

Fig. 8.7 Steps for craniofacial restoration of Qihe Man: **a** 3D model of the outer surface of Qihe Man's skull; **b** Non-rigid registration of 3D model of Qihe Man and a contemporary male skull; **c** Preliminary restoration of Qihe Man's skull and face displayed in the same coordinate system; **d** Interactive restoration of a 3D face for Qihe Man; **e** The result of realistic processing. (National-Local Joint Engineering Research Center of Cultural Heritage Digitization, Northwest University)

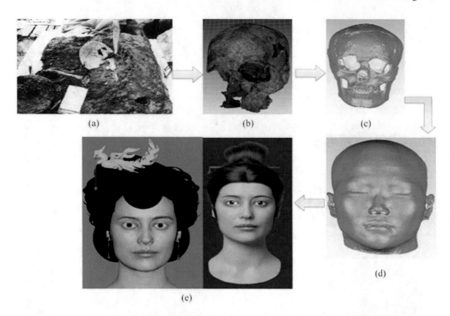

Fig. 8.8 The process of skull restoration: **a** the female skull unearthed from the Qinling Mausoleum; **b** digital skull model; **c** 3D skull model of Qin female after restoration; **d** the result of female skull restoration; **e** the result of 3D printing after realistic treatment. (National-Local Joint Engineering Research Center of Cultural Heritage Digitization, Northwest University)

face by adjusting the principal component coefficients interactively and recreating Qihe human appearance. (5) Finally, we added five main features, wrinkles and hair via a drawing method. The final modelling vividly reproduced the morphological features of an Early Neolithic man.

From the results it can be seen that the restored face was long, the zygomatic region of the face was large and prominent, the upper part was flat, the cheeks were thin and narrow, the nose was broad, the head overall was long and large. These results were basically consistent with the shape of the Qihe skull. Although the physical characteristics of Qihe Man may not be generally representative of men in that time, the reconstruction does show some unique features of a face associated with a transitional stage between Neolithic and Palaeolithic populations (Fig. 8.7).

The size, thickness and curvature of this ancient human skull were different from those of modern humans and so it cannot be completely restored according to the morphological relationship between a contemporary skull and external soft tissues. It was, therefore, necessary to design a scheme of facial restoration according to the unique anatomical characteristics of the original skull. In addition, as the original skulls were generally incomplete there was a need to spliced and repair the remains before CT scanning.

Using 3D digital techniques, it should be possible to reproduce the faces of ancient humans thousands, and perhaps even hundreds of thousands, of years ago. This approach can vividly display the process of human evolution for museum displays and other popular science projects, inspiring people to appreciate their history, satisfying human curiosity and provide results with a scientific value. Qihe man's craniofacial restoration is just the beginning of such work, and in the future, more digital reconstruction will be made available to the wider public in this manner.

8.4.3   Restoration of the Appearance of a Qin Dynasty Maid

In 2016, a female skeleton was excavated from Pit 2 of the Qinshihuang Mausoleum and attracted much attention. According to archaeologists, the skeleton was that of a concubine in the Qin Dynasty and was about 15–20 years old when buried. The skull was missing the mandible and right orbital and there were many holes of varying sizes. Although this was the most specimen recovered, the overall integrity of the skull was poor.

According to morphological characteristics, the Qin people were different from modern people. However, based on the modern human craniofacial database and computer craniofacial recovery software, it has been possible to reconstruct the face of this Qin Dynasty female. The recovery process included: (1) digitization of the skull; (2) virtual repair of the skull; (3) restoration of the face; (4) reconstructing five main features; (5) 3D printing display of the resulting reconstruction.

The method outlined in Sect. 8.3.1 was used to digitise and preprocess the Qin skulls. Because this Qin skull has a serious skull defect, the skull was repaired before the face restoration, and a complete 3D skull model was obtained. A skull model similar to the shape of the Qin people's skull was then retrieved from the modern human craniofacial database, and a point cloud correspondence between the Qin skull and a modern human 3D skull model was established to realise the normalisation of the Qin skull. A principal component coefficient for the missing region and surviving regions of the skull was used to establish the functional relationship between the two parts of the data through a regression algorithm. The missing data for the skull was calculated and the final result was obtained by a splicing and merging algorithm (Fig. 8.8).

A statistical deformation was established for the skull on the basis of the modern human 3D craniofacial database, and a regression analysis was performed in the shape parameter space. The corresponding facial skin was also computed according to the regression model, and the shape parameter was obtained from the facial statistic deformation model to obtain the estimated facial contour. To make the restoration look more realistic, the Qin man's appearance was enhanced through texture mapping and the addition of hair and eyebrows. Finally, the face was printed in 3D. It can be seen from the final results that the restored Qin face has round eyes and a high nose, and the features of the face are significantly different from those of Han Chinese.

8.5   Conclusion

For a long time, manual restoration has been the principal method for the restoration of ancient human skulls. To do this successfully, restorers required both anthropological knowledge and sculptural competence. Given this situation, and the lack of data regarding the thickness of soft tissues and muscle structure of ancient human, the process of reconstruction was both long and subjective. Computer-aided craniofacial restoration technology has the advantages of fast restoration and objective results. This chapter presents an interactive editing tool for the initial restoration of human faces. Anthropologists can quickly generate multiple 3D restorations based on experience and anthropological knowledge. They may select the most suitable face for restoration by using the tool and, combined with painting skills, the appearance of an ancient skull can be reproduced vividly.

The application of this technology within this chapter has assisted in restoring the face of the ancients in 3 case studies. Here, the application of digital and virtual restoration technologies has been carried out following the definition of feature points, the measurement of soft tissue thickness, analysis of the relationship between the top soft tissue of skull and the facial features of different genders and ages. This work provides a scientific basis for modelling and contributes to the development of digitization and virtual restoration in anthropology and archaeology. In addition, these developments may further support, important research in forensic identification and investigation, as well as medical applications.

References

Archer KM (1997a) Craniofacial Reconstruction using hierarchical B-Spline Interpolation. Master's thesis, University of British Columbia, Department of Electrical and Computer Engineering

Archer KM (1997b) Craniofacial reconstruction using hierarchical B-spline interpolation. Master Dissertation. University of British Columbia, Vancouver

Berar M, Desvignes M, Bailly G, Payan Y (2006) 3d semi-landmarks-based statistical face reconstruction. J Comput Inf Technol 14(1):31–43

Bier E, Sloan K (1986) Two-part texture mappings. IEEE Comput Graphics Appl 6(9):40–53. https://doi.org/10.1109/MCG.1986.276545

Claes P, Vandermeulen D, Greef SD, Willems G, Clement JG, Suetens P (2006) Statistically deformable face models for craniofacial reconstruction. J Comput Inf Technol 14(1):21–30

Claes P, Vandermeulen D, Greef SD, Willems G, Clement JG, Suetens P (2010a) Computerized craniofacial reconstruction: conceptual framework and review. Forensic Sci Int 201(1–3):138–145. https://doi.org/10.1016/j.forsciint.2010.03.008

Claes P, Vandermeulen D, Greef SD, Willems G, Clement JG, Suetens P (2010b) Bayesian estimation of optimal craniofacial reconstructions. Forensic Sci Int 201(1–3):146–152. https://doi.org/10.1016/j.forsciint.2010.03.009

Cootes TF, Edwards GJ, Taylor CJ (1998) Active appearance models. In: Proceedings of the 5th European conference on computer vision-volume II–Volume II. Springer, Berlin, Heidelberg. https://doi.org/10.1007/BFb0054760

Deng QQ, Zhou MQ, Shui WY, Wu ZK, Ji Y, Bai RY (2011a) A novel skull registration based on global and local deformations for craniofacial reconstruction. Forensic Sci Int 208:95–102. https://doi.org/10.1016/j.forsciint.2010.11.011

Deng QQ, Zhou MQ, Shui WY, Wu ZK, Ji Y, Bai RY (2011b) A novel skull registration based on global and local deformations for craniofacial reconstruction. Forensic Sci Int 208(1–3):95–102. https://doi.org/10.1016/j.forsciint.2010.11.011

Dong Y, Huang L, Feng ZH, Bai SH, Wu GF, Zhao YM (2012) Influence of sex and body mass index on facial soft tissue thickness measurements of the northern Chinese adult population. Forensic Sci Int 222(1–3):396.e1-396.e7. https://doi.org/10.1016/j.forsciint.2012.06.004

Duan F, Yang S, Huang DH, Hu YL, Wu ZK, Zhou MQ (2014) Craniofacial reconstruction based on multi-linear subspace analysis. Multimed Tools Appl 73(2):809–823. https://doi.org/10.1007/s11042-012-1351-2

Feng J (2010) Research on skull profile restoration technology based on hierarchical statistical deformable model. Northwest University Postdoctoral thesis

Feng J, Horace H (2005) Iterative 3D point-set registration based on hierarchical vertex signature (HVS). In: International conference on medical image computing & computer-assisted intervention. Springer, pp 279–286. https://doi.org/10.1007/11566489_35

Feng J, Horace HS, Cheng SH, Chan PK (2004) A relational-tubular (ReTu) deformable model for vasculature quantification of zebrafish embryo from microangiography image series. Comput Med Imaging Graph 28(6):333–344. https://doi.org/10.1016/j.compmedimag.2004.03.005

Gietzen T, Brylka R, Achenbach J, Hebel K, Schomer E, Botsch M, Schwanecke U, Schulze R (2018) A method for automatic forensic facial reconstruction based on dense statistics of soft tissue thickness. PLoS ONE 1–19. https://doi.org/10.1371/journal.pone.0210257

Grasimov MM (1958) The principles of facial reconstruction from skulls, 1st edn. Science Press, China

Guyomarc'h P, Santos F, Dutailly B, Coqueugniot H (2013) Facial soft tissue depths in frenchFrench adults: variability, specificity and estimation. Forensic Sci Int 231(1–3):411.e1-411.e10. https://doi.org/10.1016/j.forsciint.2013.04.007

He YY (2012) Key technologies of craniofacial statistical restoration. Xi'an: Northwest University thesis

Hu YL (2010) Research on craniofacial restoration method based on statistical deformation model. Beijing Normal University postdoctoral thesis, Beijing

Hu YL, Duan FQ, Yin BC, Zhou MQ, Sun YF, Wu ZK, Geng GH (2013) A hierarchical dense deformable model for 3D face reconstruction from skull. Multimed Tools Appl 64(2):345–364. https://doi.org/10.1007/s11042-012-1005-4

Kolja K, Jorg H, Seidel H (2003) Reanimating the dead: reconstruction of expressive faces from skull data. ACM Trans Graph 22(3):554–561. https://doi.org/10.1145/882262.882307

Luo L, Wang MY, Tian Y, Duan FQ, Wu ZK, Zhou MQ, Rozenholc Y (2013) Automatic sex determination of skulls based on a statistical shape model. Comput Math Methods Med 6. Article ID 251628. https://doi.org/10.1155/2013/251628

Pharr M, Greg H (2010) Physically based rendering: from theory to implementation (2nd edn). Elsevier, Amsterdam, pp 9–10

Prag J, Neave R (1997) making faces: using forensic and archeological evidence, 2nd edn. British Museum Press, London

Quatrehomme G, Cotin S, Subsol G, Delingette H, Garidel Y, Grevin G, Fidrich M, Bailet P, Ollier A (1997) A fully three-dimensional method for facial reconstruction based on deformable models. J Fforensic Sci 42(4):649–652

Shrimpton S, Daniels K, De Greef S, Tilotta F, Willems G, Vandermeulen D, Suetens P, Claes P (2014) A spatially-dense regression study of facial form and tissue depth: towards an interactive tool for craniofacial reconstruction. Forensic Sci Int 234:103–110. https://doi.org/10.1016/j.forsciint.2013.10.021

Shui WY, Zhou MQ, Deng QQ, Wu ZK, Ji Y, Li K, He TP, Jiang HY (2016) Densely calculated facial soft tissue thickness for craniofacial reconstruction in Chinese adults. Forensic Sci Int 266:573.e1–573.e12. https://doi.org/10.1016/j.forsciint.2016.07.017

Shui WY, Zhou MQ, Ji Y, Yin RC (2013) Facial soft tissue thickness measurement and its application in craniofacial reconstruction. Acta Anthropol Sinica 32(3):346–353

Shui WY, Zhou MQ, Steve M, He TP, Wang XC, Deng QQ (2017) A PCA-based method for determining craniofacial relationship and sexual dimorphism of facial shapes. Comput Biol Med 90:33–49. https://doi.org/10.1016/j.compbiomed.2017.08.023

Shui WY, Zhou MQ, Wu ZK, Deng QQ (2011) An approach of craniofacial reconstruction based on registration. J Comput-Aided Des Comput Graph 23(4):607–614

MMichael SD (2000) Computer aided facial reconstruction for forensic identification. In: Chen M, Kaufman AE, Yagel R (eds) Volume graphics. Springer, London

Suffern K (2007) Ray tracing from the ground up. A K Peters, Ltd., Wellesley, MA, pp 293–308

Sun XP, Li H (2005) A survey of 3D mesh model segmentation and application. J Comput-Aided Des Comput Graph 17(8):1647–1655

Turner WD, Brown REB, Kelliher TP, Tu PH, Taister MA, Miller KWP (2005) A novel method of automated skull registration for forensic facial approximation. Forensic Sci Int 154(2–3):149–158. https://doi.org/10.1016/j.forsciint.2004.10.003

Vandermeulen D, Claes P, Loeckx D, De Greef S, Willems G, Suetens P (2006) Computerized craniofacial reconstruction using CT-derived implicit surface representations. Forensic Sci Int 159:164–174. https://doi.org/10.1016/j.forsciint.2006.02.036

Vanezis P, Blowes RW, Linney AD, Tan AC, Richards R, Neave R (1989) Application of 3-D computer graphics for facial reconstruction and comparison with sculpting techniques. Forensic Sci Int 42(1–2):69–84. https://doi.org/10.1016/0379-0738(89)90200-4

Wilkinson C (2001) Forensic facial reconstruction. Cambridge University Press, Cambridge

Zhang YF, Zhou MQ, Geng GH, Feng J (2010) Face appearance reconstruction based on a regional statistical craniofacial model (RCSM). In: 20th international conference on pattern recognition, ICPR 2010, Istanbul, Turkey, IEEE. https://doi.org/10.1109/ICPR.2010.413

Zhou MQ, Geng GH, Fan JB (1997) Computer-aided forensic facial reconstruction. J Northwest Univ (natural Science Edition) 27(5):375–378

Chapter 9
Resurrecting Hor: The Philosophical Application of the Digital Tradition

Carl G. Elkins

Abstract This chapter considers the degree to which digital technology extends ontologies of the distant past by comparing modern interactions with a digital dimension to those of the ancient Egyptians with a divine dimension. Its technical foundation is provided by the methodology used to 3D scan and digitally reconstruct the fragmentary statue of the admiral Hor in the Manchester Museum (Acc. no. 3570), merging the authentic reproduction with a digitally sculpted reconstruction to grant Hor renewed presence. In Egypt, the deceased's body parts were ritually enumerated and associated with gods, transposing the individual, piece by piece, into the divine dimension. The reduction of an object to a collection of data points, and its reconstitution in digital space, would have equally been seen to be laden with magical potential, with the model transcending the original. Ancient textual sources demonstrate further parallels, such as those between the programmer's method and the priest's ritual or the inherent dangers of exposed identities in a virtual dimension. The chapter aims to recontextualise work in digital heritage by exploring how digital technology can be reinterpreted, within the context of ancient belief systems, to gain new insights into both the past and the present.

Keywords Digitality · Egyptology · Statues · Reproduction · Reconstruction

9.1 Introduction

> [I]t seemed to me that any obscurity which yet hangs over the problem of life and thought in ancient Egypt originates most probably with ourselves (Edwards 1888, p. vii).

My father began his career as a computer programmer, so I was fortunate enough to have daily access to a computer from an early age, which was by no means a given in the late 1980s. When I was 6 years old, my parents and grandparents took me to see the touring *Ramesses the Great* exhibition in Dallas, Texas. As we rounded the final

C. G. Elkins (✉)
egyptolo.gy Digital Humanities Project, Munich, Germany
e-mail: carl@egyptolo.gy

© Springer Nature Switzerland AG 2022   155
E. Ch'ng et al. (eds.), *Visual Heritage: Digital Approaches in Heritage Science*,
Springer Series on Cultural Computing,
https://doi.org/10.1007/978-3-030-77028-0_9

corner, I was stopped in my tracks as I caught sight of the king's 7.5-m colossus, which I now know had been restored from fragments only three years prior. There began my fascination with ancient Egypt. My parents bought me books and periodicals, I joined the local chapter of the American Research Center in Egypt, and I began compiling a digital record of my research illustrated with line drawings I had drawn, pixel by pixel, in Microsoft Paint. By the age of 11, I was publishing *The Egypt Connection: The Weekly Journal of Ancient Egypt*—after the first issue, it became *The Monthly Journal of Ancient Egypt*—which I printed on our dot-matrix printer, laid out using a pair of scissors and Scotch Tape and sold at school for 25 cents an issue. The digital eventually won out, and I pursued a career in graphic design and digital art. After a few years in the field of advertising, my rediscovery of an Egyptological website I had begun in my early teens rekindled my earlier passion, and I enrolled in the University of Manchester's accredited Egyptology Online programme soon thereafter.

I bother with this personal preamble, because it also serves as an analogy for the topic of this chapter. Digital technology does not merely afford us the opportunity to document and explore our past; it extends it, representing a further link in the chain of our intellectual development that has inherited the behavioural patterns of our cultural memory, of which it now finds itself guardian (e.g. Foucault and Melican 2007). I here consider these patterns by comparing our interactions with the digital dimension to those of the ancient Egyptians with a divine dimension. The parallel narrows the perceived gap between 'us' and 'them' by recalibrating our modern objectivity and helping to reveal otherwise lost experiences, while maintaining a firm foothold in the 'larger discipline' of archaeology (Perry and Taylor 2018, p. 11). Indeed, the digital 'provides an opportunity, within the framework of scientific modernity, to connect with the mystical or spiritual, or at least with the more-than-physical', and 'better aligns us with the ontologies of the assemblages we study' (Opitz 2019). The digital hardly 'represents a huge break from all previous ways of interacting with the world' (thus Jeffrey 2015, p. 145). On the contrary, the redistribution of our existence across both a physical and non-physical plane recaptures a world that had already existed, but that was previously confined to our imaginations. In this regard, to interface with the digital is to experience the past.

The heart of this study is my photogrammetric scan and digital reconstruction of the fragmentary naophorous—'shrine-bearing'—statue of the admiral Hor in the Manchester Museum (Acc. no. 3570; Fig. 9.1). Beyond his statue, Hor is not definitively attested (Price 2017, p. 369). To meet the man, we are entirely dependent upon the information it gives us. He lived during Dynasty 26 (664–525 BCE): a chapter of Egypt's Late Period (747–332 BCE) often termed the 'Saite Renaissance' in reference to the dynasty's capital at Sais in the Western Delta. He was a devotee of the goddess Bastet, within whose temple his statue was erected and whose lion-headed figure he embraces before him. He was an 'admiral of the royal fighting ships in the Mediterranean Sea' and was likely stationed where the statue was found, at Tell el-Yahudiya in the Eastern Delta along the Nile's Pelusiac branch (Price 2017, p. 374). The location was of strategic importance for its communication with both the Nile Valley and the Mediterranean. From there, he was also a 'commander of

Fig. 9.1 Scan and
reconstruction of the admiral
Hor. Polished quartzite.
Preserved height 88 cm.
Restored height 138 cm (C.
G. Elkins)

Greek mercenaries' (the Ionians and Carians of Herodotean fame: Herodotus II, 154;
cf. Price 2017, p. 373). His mother's name was Taanetenpawia.

The statue is of such extraordinary workmanship that it likely originated in a
royal atelier, though only its lower half now survives. Sometime before being put on
display in Manchester, the shrine was damaged further still, and the portion of the
inscription bearing the title of 'admiral' was lost. Fortunately, it is preserved in both
a photograph and an illustration within the excavator's original publication (Petrie
1906, Pls. XV, XX), serving as a fitting testament to the importance of documentation
and visual reproduction.

It is Hor's Egypt whence our analogies are drawn. The theological concepts and
textual sources to follow are largely taken from those contemporary with him, or of
which he would have at least been aware. Though his tomb's location is unknown, it
could be hidden among those of contemporary naval and military officials at Saqqara,
near modern Cairo (Price 2017, p. 375). Thus, we might assume that Hor's tomb and
sarcophagus were also inscribed with excerpts from funerary literature such as the Old

Kingdom (c. 2686–2160 BCE) Pyramid Texts, the Middle Kingdom (c. 2055–1650 BCE) Coffin Texts and the New Kingdom (c. 1550–1069 BCE) Book of the Dead, the latter having been revived and standardised in Dynasty 26. Other Underworld 'books' initially inscribed in the tombs of New Kingdom pharaohs, such as the Amduat and the Book of Gates, were inscribed in the tombs of Hor's southern contemporaries, such as that of the 'Chief Lector' Padiamenopet, whose title suggests that he was 'intimately familiar with the current religious thought […] of his age' (Bianchi 1982, col. 991). These texts are also made use of here.

The technical and artistic process behind the reconstruction is described in Sect. 9.3. The subsequent discussion in Sect. 9.4 builds upon the philosophical premise put forth in Sect. 9.2 to recontextualise the technology behind that process. Section 9.4.1 explores ancient Egyptian beliefs surrounding the potential of models to become the very thing they represent, thereby granting them immutability and the named individuals immortality. It investigates the parallels between ancient ritual and digitisation, looking at the technology required and culminating in Sect. 9.4.2 in the augmented ritual of Hor's rebirth in the 'temple of the muses': the museum. The remaining discussion is the software to the preceding sections' hardware. It concerns our movement between dimensions and continues the narrative of Hor's resurrection by exploring the aspects of our digital world anticipated by his beliefs: the nature of our interfaces in Sect. 9.4.3, the code we use to manipulate the digital dimension in Sect. 9.4.4 and the securities we require on our journey in Sect. 9.4.5. The digital and the divine are largely syncretised into a single 'virtual' dimension throughout the chapter; only context indicates which is meant. Translations are based upon Allen (2005) (Pyramid Texts), Faulkner (1985) (Book of the Dead) and Hornung and Abt (2014a) (Amduat) and (2014b) (Book of Gates), unless otherwise specified.

9.2   Background: Heritage, History and Digital Divinity

Any sufficiently advanced technology is indistinguishable from magic (Clarke 1973, p. 39).

My use of the term 'resurrection' is not figurative. In Egypt, to create an image was to 'give birth'. The sculptor was *sankh*, 'one who causes to live'. The image was ritually reared to ensure that it, like the natural body before it, was of sufficient maturity for its senses and faculties to serve the deceased (Roth 1992, pp. 118–122). Destroying its nose prevented it from being used to breathe, hence the patterns of damage so common to Egyptian statues. Just as human beings are reduced to an inanimate corpse, so must inanimate objects be capable of receiving life.

The restoration of monuments was, therefore, a sacred act. Postscripts to several Book of the Dead spells detail their mythical discovery during temple inspections or while undertaking restoration work. Crown Prince Khaemwaset, fourth son of the great Ramesses II (r. c. 1279–1213 BCE), was still revered as a sage and magician over a millennium after his death for his own reverence of Egypt's past and restoration of her already ancient monuments. Upon restoring a 1,200-year-old statue of a son of Khufu, the builder of the Great Pyramid, he records:

> It is the … King's Son Khaemwaset, who was glad over this statue of the King's Son Kawab, and who took it from what was cast (away) for debris(?).… Then … (he) decreed that [it be given] a place by favour of the gods, … so greatly did he love antiquity and the noble folk who were aforetime, along with the excellence (of) all that they had made… (from the throne of Kawab's restored statue; translation after Kitchen 1996, p. 566).

But a restored statue is useless without an active cult to provision it. The inscription goes on to describe Khaemwaset's restoration of the statue's cult, 'which had fallen into oblivion [in the remembrance] of men'. By restoring and providing for Kawab's statue, Khaemwaset had effectively secured his resurrection: 'that he may attain (the status of) "given life"' (Kitchen 1996, p. 566).

In Egypt, 'life' was more a cultural than a natural process, because cultural engagement—such as the social reciprocity of the mortuary cult: 'One who acts is one for whom the like will be done' (maxim from the 26th Dynasty statue of Nebnetjeru [Cairo JE 37413]; translated from the German in Jansen-Winkeln 1999, p. 58)—was the means to extending life beyond nature's limitations (Assmann 2010, p. 16). We might see culture as the first artificial intelligence: 'Like the intelligence of a machine, culture can solve problems'; it 'applies its own logic, has a memory, endures after its makers are gone, […] and can induce action' (Christakis 2015). Like culture, digital technology overcomes restrictions imposed by our biology. It too evolves, and some would say it is becoming a self-sustaining force, a 'technium' on par with nature (Kelly 2010), which in a world increasingly without gods assumes the functions of the supernatural. Indeed, it invites interactions taking the form of the religious (e.g. Lam 2001). 'Evangelists' propagate software companies' visions of the future, while the annual ritual of the product release—like the festal procession in which the cult image otherwise guarded from view and shrouded in mystery is unleashed upon the masses—results in congregations lining the streets.

In the ancient Near East, supernatural knowledge—that is, knowledge that human beings alone cannot extract from nature—was deemed divine knowledge (Assmann 2010, p. 6). In the Old Babylonian myth of the mortal Adapa, the divine king, Anu, attempts to grant Adapa eternal life in the company of the gods for the superior wisdom granted him his divine father, which is unbefitting a human being (Speiser 1978, pp. 101–103). In the Old Testament, Adam and Eve partake of fruit from the Tree of Knowledge, thus becoming enlightened and 'like God' (Gen. 3:5, New Revised Standard Version), but they are condemned to mortality for ultimately being unworthy of it. In Egypt, to possess the sun-god's knowledge of the Underworld's secrets was to be transfigured and live forever: 'He who knows these images is like the Great God himself' (Amduat, first hour).

Prior to the Third Industrial Revolution, obtaining knowledge was the purview of the human brain and thus a natural process. But the digital is capable of superhuman calculations and the execution of simultaneous processes. Big data can harvest digital identities to create complex computational models that predict human behaviour. Computational linguistics promises to surpass human translators in rendering even the rarest languages—in both written and spoken form (e.g. Asgari and Schütze

2017)—and unlock those long extinct that yet remain to be deciphered (e.g. Luo et al. 2019). Digital simulations create situations devoid of any actual consequences. We can scrub backwards through time, inhabit solid geometries, and move freely in three dimensions. In the virtual dimension, we can fly. Knowledge gained in silicon is beyond that which can be derived solely from nature and must, therefore, be classified as divine knowledge. In these ancient terms, the digital dimension is by its very nature divine, and the human beings who navigate this virtual dimension, like the transfigured dead, therefore inherit divine status.

Yet, we remain mortal. Seen from an ancient Egyptian perspective, this dichotomy would equate each of us with Pharaoh, who as the human son of the sun-god was the only mortal authorised to navigate both dimensions. Digital technology represents the ultimate democratisation: the universal right of all human beings to transcend our biological limitations while still alive. As a result, we inherit the responsibility of maintaining the king's 'struggle against the gravitational pull of the alienation of meaning' (Assmann 2001, p. 6) that accompanies progress and change. For most of us, that battle for meaning is fought in the trenches of history.

But the ancient Egyptians' sense of history was decidedly ahistorical. Progress and change were deteriorations of cosmic order: a distancing from the harmony of that mythical time when gods ruled on earth. With each king's accession, the calendar was reset to Year One. However, by Hor's Dynasty 26, Egypt had become deeply aware of her long history. Initially spearheaded nearly two centuries earlier by competing dynasts looking to bolster their legitimacy by invoking 'classical' Egypt, the period not only saw a resurgence of ancient artistic and liturgical styles but also inspired 'remixes' in which they were consciously updated or combined to make something original. The ancient Egyptian élite had always experienced an intimate connection with their past, but this level of engagement was unprecedented; this was a 'cultural revolution' (Assmann 1996, p. 377). Archives were studiously pored over for draughtsmen's original plans. Artists and their patrons scanned ancient monuments in search of elements that could be stylistically appropriated, and they applied square grids to make faithful copies. Some are so faithful, in both style and quality, that there has been debate as to whether they are originals or 26th Dynasty 'facsimiles' (e.g. Bothmer et al. 1960, pp. 42–43). The past was no longer being exploited on ideological grounds to legitimise the present but rather utilised to redefine it and give it new meaning. Parallels with the work of heritage professionals presented in this volume hardly require further comment.

9.3 Methodology

We do not wish to penalise the machine for its inability to shine in beauty competitions, nor to penalise a man for losing in a race against an aeroplane. The conditions of our game make these disabilities irrelevant (Turing 1950, p. 435).

The primary technical foundation upon which this chapter builds is provided by 3D scanning. Photogrammetric workflows such as the one used to scan Hor's statue are sufficiently documented and are not delved into here. The project began as a proof of concept for reconstructive augmented-reality (AR) applications in museums, so speed, software accessibility and cross-platform compatibility were of utmost importance. Images were taken with an Apple iPhone, and Agisoft Metashape was used for mesh and texture generation.

An exactly contemporary kneeling statue in Paris (Louvre A 94) served as the reconstruction's primary reference (for a full bibliography of references used, as well as the reconstruction's art-historical implications, see Elkins and Price 2022). Frontal- and side-view photographs were loaded into orthographic views in Blender (had the schedule permitted, the original in Paris would have been scanned instead to provide an undistorted basis), and Hor's upper body was cursorily modelled, as a separate mesh, following the Paris statue's proportions. To negate any inaccuracies caused by perspective and lens distortion, orthographic views of the reconstructed model were tested against the grid of the artistic canon of proportions: the very grid applied by 26th Dynasty copyists to ancient monuments (on using 3D models to investigate the canon's use in statuary, see Elkins and Heindl 2022). Blender's sculpting tools were then used to shape the reconstructed mesh, carve out final details and introduce imperfections, such as tool- and pockmarks, in restored recesses and crevices.

Texturing required a more specialised approach. First, it was necessary to prepare the scanned texture for transfer to the reconstruction. A physically based rendering (PBR) specular/glossiness workflow was adopted to simulate the stone's material properties. The amount of light reflected off of a given surface at a $0°$ (perpendicular) angle of incidence serves as the specular reflectance value (Fresnel zero, or F0) in PBR shaders and can be derived from a substance's real-world index of refraction (IOR) using a simple formula (see Akenine-Möller et al. 2018, p. 321 [Eq. 9.17]; cf. Lagarde 2013). The sedimentary quartzite, or orthoquartzite, of which Hor's statue is carved is a sandstone whose grains are heavily cemented with quartz (Aston et al. 2000, p. 53), of which it is up to 99% composed. Quartz's IOR is widely attested in reference tables available to 3D artists (e.g. Autodesk 2014) and falls within [1.544, 1.553], giving an F0 for Hor's statue within [0.0457, 0.0469].

Substance Painter was chosen for texturing given the need to both 'paint' the scanned texture onto reconstructed surfaces and procedurally generate lighter details in restored crevices. The high-poly mesh generated in Metashape was imported into Substance Painter, and mesh maps were baked using the mesh's geometry. I chose to manually de-light the Albedo map for increased control over overlapping shadows from the museum's lighting and to avoid the artefacts of automated tools. An inverted Ambient Occlusion (AO) map with simulated ground plane served as a mask for global levels adjustments, while localised adjustments—using colour selections generated from the World Space Normal map—equalised directional lighting and further brightened surfaces facing the dark pedestal and floor. Hard shadows were manually masked out and brightened accordingly.

While F0 can be obtained from real-world refractive indices, the greyscale Glossiness map defining surface irregularities and resultant light diffusion is more subjective. Its precise effect also depends upon the render engine (Lagarde 2011). I arrived at a base linear value of 0.6—introducing slight variation up to 0.7 using the de-lit Albedo map—to simulate the statue's polished surface in WebGL applications, which would be the reconstruction's primary deployment beyond the initial Unity-driven prototype. Using the de-lit Albedo map, it was possible to isolate the dark grains and pebbles comprising the stone's veining and the much lighter, unpolished crevices and darken them within the Glossiness map. The Albedo and Glossiness maps were then exported for later use.

With the texture maps prepared, it was necessary to retopologise and decimate the mesh, transferring high- and medium-frequency surface details to the Normal map so they could be painted onto the reconstructed areas. The scan was retopologised using Instant Meshes and reimported into Blender for final decimation and UV mapping. The low-poly mesh was then imported into Substance Painter and a new Normal map was baked from the high-poly original. The previously exported Albedo and Glossiness maps were remapped to the new mesh's UVs using Substance Designer's Transferred Texture from Mesh baker. Together, these three texture maps would serve as the material for 'painting' the reconstruction.

The high-poly scan was merged with the sculpted mesh in Blender using a simple Boolean modifier. The resultant mesh was retopologised and decimated using the same process as above, and the scan's Albedo and Glossiness maps were again transferred using Substance Designer. The merged low-poly mesh was imported into Substance Painter, where mesh maps were baked from the high-poly Boolean union. Baked seams between the scanned and reconstructed meshes were painted out of the Normal map using the Clone tool, making sure to only paint on reconstructed areas. The low-poly scan's Albedo, Glossiness and Normal maps were then loaded as channels into the Projection tool to texture the arms, torso and head. The projected material was rotated as needed to follow the contours that would have been created by the stone's 60° lateral veining. Finally, a series of procedural mask generators created lighter, unpolished details within restored crevices and imperfections using the baked Curvature and AO mesh maps (Fig. 9.2).

Fig. 9.2 Crevices in the de-lit Albedo map. **Left** Junction of left heel, buttock and back pillar (as scanned). **Right** Restored junction of left clavicle, neck and wig (procedurally generated) (C. G. Elkins)

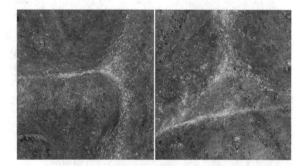

9.4 Discussion

> I etch a pattern of geometric shapes onto a stone. To the uninitiated, the shapes look myste-
> rious and complex, but I know that when arranged correctly they will give the stone a special
> power, enabling it to respond to incantations in a language no human being has ever spoken.
> I will ask the stone questions in this language, and it will answer by showing me a vision: a
> world created by my spell, a world imagined within the pattern on the stone. […] The stone
> is a wafer of silicon, and the incantations are software (Hillis 1998, p. vii).

9.4.1 Reproduction

Attempts to reproduce the materiality of real-world objects in another dimension are
in no way a recent development. Sometime around 2650 BCE, an official named
Hesyra commissioned a monumental tomb at Saqqara within which a 37-m-long,
finely plastered corridor was to be decorated with beautifully painted polychrome
diagrams of the objects he wished to take with him to the afterlife (Fig. 9.3). In earlier
tombs, provisions were included by the thousands within enormous superstructures
subdivided into dozens of storerooms. Hesyra's paintings were to circumvent not
only the massive cost of this system but also its inherent dangers of looting and
decay by essentially providing blueprints for the objects' virtual construction. For,

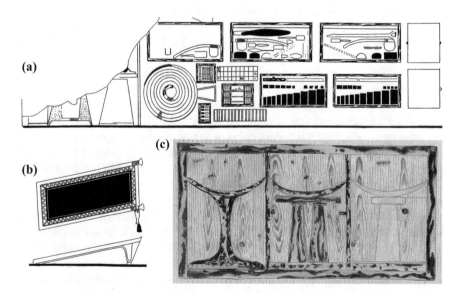

Fig. 9.3 Hesyra's schematics. **a** Line drawing of a section containing gameboards and boxes of
tools, weights and measures (after Quibell 1913, Pl. XVI). Height of the represented portion approx.
1 m. **b** Top and side views of a bed from a section depicting furnishings (after Quibell 1913, Pl.
XIX). **c** Colour facsimile of a wooden box containing headrests, also of wood (after Quibell 1913,
Pl. XIV). The box was painted just to the right of the beds (C. G. Elkins)

beyond the physical medium that contains it (and barring any further sampling: e.g. Dawson and Reilly 2019), the virtual object is free of decay (Reilly 2015, p. 229). This is not unlike our consolidation of various media and communications to a single device, and it would have undoubtedly resulted in a similar socioeconomic shift as the industries in charge of production were reorganised and the surplus redistributed. The redistributed surplus would ultimately help support a workforce large enough to build the first pyramid.

The new system's underlying magical principles were older still. Already in the more modest graves of the late Predynastic Period (c. 3500–3000 BCE), model boats and tiny model vessels such as pots and jars were provided with otherwise simpler burials. Using later parallels, we might assume that these miniatures were thought to become their full-size counterparts in the virtual dimension, while the placement of model granaries in the tomb a century or two later would support the needs of food production.

Hor's Underworld books were themselves reproductions, 'executed like this original in the secrecy of the Underworld' (Amduat, first hour). No matter how often our typed words are copied or reformatted, they would not exist but for that initial pressing of the key. This is how the model maintains its effectiveness, by directly channelling the original and creating a present reality that could 'not exist without a prior reality' (Ch'ng and Gaffney 2013, p. 3), and why the ancient Egyptians felt no need to risk the tides of history as long as repetition and proliferation maintained a channel to the purity of the original moment of creation. Indeed, in the proper context, interaction with a model can even be more effective than interaction with an 'original' (on the digitally produced facsimile's potential for superior 'authenticity', see Latour and Lowe 2011; Jones et al. [2018, esp. pp. 345–346] would here include the digital object itself).

These channelling principles applied equally to the human sphere. The prototype of successful transmutation was the god Osiris, of whom the mummy was ultimately a replica. His is the transmutational potential of new life and describes how a plant grows from 'an apparently lifeless seed' (Allen 1988, p. 35). The sun-god descends at night to become one with Osiris; thus, united with potentiality itself, he hopes of being reborn the next morning. Later stories tell of his dismemberment and the scattering of his body parts throughout Egypt. They were then gathered and reassembled by the magic of his wife, Isis, who fashioned a model of his missing phallus to conceive their son, Horus.

Like the resurrected Osiris, Hesyra's schematics were products of a visual system that reflected a worldview in which all of existence was an assemblage of disparate elements. The body could be referred to using a collective noun meaning 'body parts', Egypt was the 'Two Lands' (Upper and Lower) and the cosmos was 'sky and earth' (after Assmann 2010, p. 35). The aims of this deconstructive lens resemble those of modern data-driven approaches to reasoning:

> In a digital way of reasoning, we accept […] vast masses of non-contiguous elements, expecting the hidden connectivity to emerge as we tickle the individual pieces. Thus it is that we come to feel instinctively that the dislocation is there to be bridged, […] subject to an articulation that reveals the polarities and the resulting unity (Buccellati 2017, p. 175).

The deconstructive approach to image-making was also taken in ritual. To be transferred between the physical and virtual dimensions, objects and beings were first encoded. During the funeral ceremony, the enumerative association of the deceased's limbs with gods—a 'member apotheosis'—served as the transfer protocol by which the body was encoded, transposed and subsequently decoded in the virtual dimension:

My hair is Nun,

My face is Ra,

My eyes are Hathor,

My ears are Wepwawet,

[…] (Book of the Dead, spell 42).

The spell, variants of which are known from all major works of ancient Egyptian funerary literature, goes on to enumerate the remaining parts of the body, from the molars and incisors to the breast and spine down to the digits of the hands and feet: a literal digitisation of the individual. Should the transfer not be executed properly, and the spell (i.e. code: see Sect. 9.4.4 below) be corrupt or incomplete, the deceased would be disfigured and perish: 'I will not become corrupt, […] I do not perish, my brains are not destroyed, I am not mutilated' (Book of the Dead, spell 154; adapted after Zandee 1960, p. 147).

In another spell, the boat intended to ferry the digitised individual across the celestial river is in pieces in the dockyard of the god Aqen, and it must first be properly encoded that its transfer may be requested. Aqen asks the deceased, 'Are you complete?'; the deceased answers, 'I am complete' (Book of the Dead, spell 99). The pieces of the boat are then summoned by means of member apotheosis, but not before the deceased has proved themselves master of digitising principles by declaring, 'I know how to count my fingers'. Sixteen discrete parts are enumerated, from the mooring-post and mallet to the sail and halyards, even the ribs of the hull.

Our reduction of an object to a collection of data points, and its reconstitution in virtual space, realises these ancient processes (Fig. 9.4). The scanning of an object would have been seen to be laden with magical potential, with the digitised model, reborn into the virtual dimension, becoming immune to decay and eternal: 'Rise on your bones of bronze and on your limbs of gold, for this body of yours belongs to a god. It does not perish, it does not decompose, it does not consume' (Coffin Texts, spell 519; translated [as Pyr. Neith, 653] in Zandee 1960, p. 58). Like the gold-plated brass rods of a quantum computer, the gods' metal bones were covered in flesh 'made of gold, and thus immutable' (Allen 2005, p. 95 n. 32).

The body I am referring to is not the mummy. By virtue of its inanimation, the mummy is promoted to the status of liminal image. The ritual associated with the revived mummy was, in origin, a statue ritual (Otto 1960, pp. 1–33) or later syncretised with a statue ritual already in parallel existence (Roth 1993, pp. 74–77). The objects of this 'Opening of the Mouth' were largely those of the sculptor: chisels, adzes, even a saw. It was the woodcarving adze, held to the mummy's mouth, that ultimately revived the individual. The mummy was the seed, not the plant: a storage medium whence the encoded individual was transferred to the virtual dimension, where they were then decoded to live out a new life in an immaculate, virtual body.

(a)

(b)

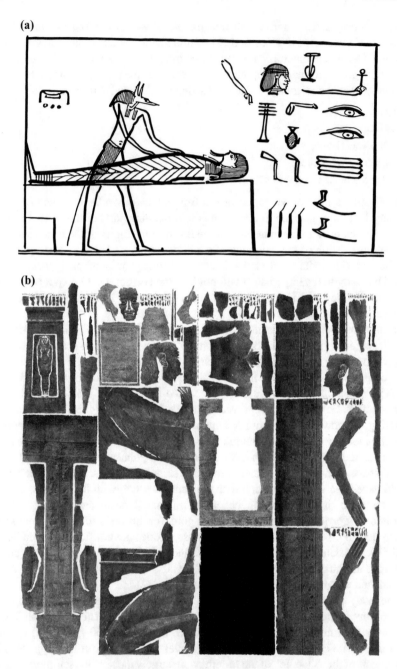

Fig. 9.4 **a** The reassembly of Osiris, with the individual members of his unwrapped body displayed to the right (after Vandier 1962, Pl. VI). From a mythical papyrus of the Graeco-Roman Period. **b** Computer-generated, UV-unwrapped mesh fragments of Hor's reconstructed statue (C. G. Elkins)

In ancient terms, this virtual body was also an 'image' of the individual. When the sun-god traversed the Underworld's waters, calling the names of the transfigured dead to induce their rebirth, *seshemu*, 'images', came forth. In a text illustrating the king's role as sun-priest, dating to the Middle Kingdom but still in use in Hor's Dynasty 26 (Assmann 1970, pp. 3, 4–5), the king 'knows the one who is in the day-barque, the great *seshemu* that is in the night-barque' (translated from the German in Assmann 1970, p. 21). During the day, the sun-god was himself, but at night, in the virtual dimension, his image occupied the solar barque. The word is the same as that for the divine cult image, which is archetypically made of gold, thus alluding to the immutability of the virtual. Then, as now, images were the extradimensional manifestations of another reality.

9.4.2 Resurrection

As the mummy was but a storage medium to be utilised between lives, compressed into a tightly wrapped shell and hidden in the cool, rejuvenating darkness of the tomb's core, the individual required more accessible images capable of receiving their digitised instantiation. By means of such an image, their name remained spoken and their needs for nourishment were satisfied, for, although we can immerse ourselves in the virtual dimension, we are ultimately in need of this-worldly sustenance. But this was not an otherworldly image like the *seshemu*; it was a this-worldly image, or *tut*: that is, a statue or relief. All of creation could be referred to as both the 'image', *tut*, of the creator and as *medu-netjer*, 'divine speech', the Egyptian term for hieroglyphs: for 'all creation is a hieroglyphic text of the creator's original concept' (Allen 1988, p. 45; cf. Assmann 1996, pp. 391–392). In a world composed of images, an image is the thing itself.

An anointing ritual performed alongside the 'Opening of the Mouth' (thus Roth 1993, pp. 67–69) has the statue 'filled' with oils: '[When I fill you] with it (oil), it will tie together your bones, join together your limbs for you, collect your flesh for you' (Pyramid Texts, spell 637). The ritual served as a transfer of power and energy to the matured statue, as indicated by the deceased's seizure of a crown at the end of it (Otto 1960, p. 124). The tying together of bones, joining of limbs and rejuvenation of flesh are qualities attributed blood in ancient Egyptian conceptions of anatomy (Bardinet 1995, pp. 128–135). Thus, the matured client-statue was equipped with a power source and brought online for the digitised individual's upload, with an artificial heart in place of a central processing unit and artificial veins in place of circuits. Indeed, it would seem that 'what matters about digitality is not so much the technical dimension of the electronic mechanism used, but the intellectual dimension which gives rise to it and nurtures it' (Buccellati 2017, pp. 204–205).

Many futurists believe that our future lies in digital brain emulation: the uploading of our consciousness to achieve 'digital immortality' (e.g. Sandberg and Bostrom 2008, p. 5). It seems the mechanics of our future ambitions promise not to differ much from those of our past. Sensors would allow us to see and hear, while an electroacoustic device would simulate our voice that we may speak: provisions for sustained integration into the social substrate that were the very objectives of the 'Opening of the Mouth'. Were our digitised self to be deleted subsequent to the death of our natural body, we would suffer what the ancient Egyptians feared most: the ultimate annihilation, a second death. 'My face is opened. My heart is in its place. My crown is with me. […] I will not die for the second time' (Book of the Dead, spell 44; translation after Zandee 1960, pp. 187–188).

I call it a substrate in the biological, life-sustaining sense. The social substrate ensured that the deceased was provided for—whether by actual offerings or the recitation of an offering formula—and their name spoken. The offering formula inscribed on monuments was ultimately 'an offering that the king gives' at the altar of a deity, and the deceased was invited to participate: a shared meal at the divine family's table. By Hor's time, a prevalent means of achieving this virtual integration was the statue's initiation into a temple. Today, the museum can be seen as that temple. As inner sancta of cultural identity, museums 'enshrine' what we hold 'to be significant and valuable' (Cameron 1971, p. 17). Like the institutional 'Houses of Life' installed in ancient Egyptian temples as record-keepers and seats of wisdom, the museum 'is, in concept, the temple of the muses where today's personal experience of life can be viewed in the context of "The Works of God […]"' (Cameron 1971, p. 17).

It was in the House of Life that the ritual knowledge required to sustain the solar cycle was preserved. As the sun occupies each of the Underworld's gated regions during this cycle—one for each of the night's 12 hours—its digitised inhabitants are temporarily granted new life: 'He breathes air at his hour' (Amduat, third hour, closing text). When we view Hor's digitally reconstructed statue within the museum, his hour has come. His image is restored and his name spoken, while the museum's steady stream of visitors maintains his cult of veneration. By placing his restored statue in a mixed-reality environment, we also bring him back into the realm of the living (the ancient Egyptian name for the Book of the Dead was the Book of Coming Forth by Day), blurring the boundaries between the physical and the virtual. But the virtual dimension bears no temporal relation to earth. In Egypt, to sleep was to temporarily experience it, and just as eight hours of sleep are traversed in the blink of an eye, so do dreams unveil mysterious worlds and permit participation in elaborate, timeless narratives. For Hor, an hour lasts a lifetime.

9.4.3 The Interface

How would Hor cope with a world in which we no longer worship the ground we walk on or the air we breathe? Beyond the deconstructive processes undertaken to restore his surrogate body, it is likely our navigation of the virtual from within the constraints of the physical that he would most recognise. As already seen with the Predynastic tomb models, the capacity for miniaturisation absent loss of effectiveness permeated the ancient Egyptian worldview. Entire monuments could be reduced to a single 'false' door that assumed all of the magical properties of its larger prototype. It was by means of this door that spirits could re-enter the physical dimension and partake of the offerings presented before it. Multiple recessed frames surrounded a central door-niche above which a semi-cylindrical drum simulated a reed mat rolled up to grant passage. Its multi-layered construction gave birth to interpretations of its containing multiple cosmic layers within a single interface: the entire tomb in microcosm (Brandt 2016, pp. 12–33).

Where they had doors, we have Windows. Our screens' frames give way to the operating system's bars within which windows layered upon windows frame access to the virtual dimension and the composite parts of our virtual existence. Complex architectures are reduced to a single device and made useable by a single interface. Like the polychrome patterns simulating colourful reed mats decorating the false door, we incorporate skeuomorphic elements, from rudimentary switches and sliders to the texture of a piece of paper and tabs of a folder. Archaising icons communicate function by essentially hieroglyphic means, in that they are symbols of things that must be unambiguous and immediately recognisable. When graphical user interfaces introduced icons, their creators 'toyed with using the word glyphs instead' (Negroponte 1995, p. 110). So, the alkaline battery becomes a symbol for all batteries to communicate charge level even on devices powered by lithium ions. We set alarms by tapping on a twin-bell alarm clock; we have trash cans, recycle bins, clipboards and notepads, and we still save 'files' via the image of a 3.5-in floppy. Some 30 years have passed since the personal computer became capable of antialiasing, yet we still use pixelated fonts to communicate a sense of the digital, the technical, indeed even the futuristic. We invoke these metaphors for the same reasons as the ancient Egyptians in their use of skeuomorphic elements in religious architecture, which invariably served as a portal between dimensions. Skeuomorphs 'disguise the monstrosity of transition between the digital and the analogue worlds. The taming of the monster is done by transferring familiar attributes onto unfamiliar territory' (Minkin 2016, p. 121). In cases both ancient and modern, past realities are engaged to communicate purpose and meaning.

9.4.4 The Code

The Underworld books are adaptations of rituals concerned with the iterative perpetuation of the first sunrise (Assmann 1970, esp. pp. 56–57). The rituals were imagined sustaining ordered existence within an infinite loop: the solar cycle. They are like a dramatic play's script (Allen 1988, pp. 27, 35, 57), with the gods acting out their roles in endless iterations. They are formulated in terms of divine actors executing cosmic functions and divine speech serving as instructions that were preprogrammed at the first sunrise. Documents written in this divine language represented knowledge, not belief. The locations and beings therein were referred to using the verb *rekh*, meaning 'to know', 'to learn', 'to experience' (consider German *Wissenschaft*, 'science', from *wissen*, 'to know', and Latin *scientia*, 'knowledge'). Holders of this knowledge were somewhat akin to Laplace's demon; to know the nature and movements of all things is to know the past and future.

These methods were invoked by the priest, whose anthropomorphising code made persistent use of the generational relationships between divine 'parent' and 'child'. We could easily call this a scripting language. Like the computer programmer, priests and magicians utilised highly specialised language and syntax to manipulate the virtual dimension. I would amend traditional analogies to physics and the natural sciences (e.g. Hornung 1975, cols. 185–186; Allen 1988, p. 56) by also seeing the ancient Egyptian *Götterwelt* as an information science, which takes us, by way of informatics, to the computer sciences.

This can be better demonstrated by examining ancient Egyptian code in its original formatting. Some 1,100 years before Hor (thus Parkinson 2009, p. 157), a collection of at least 24 separate documents—perhaps amassed over several generations by a family of professional 'magicians' (Parkinson 2009, pp. 149, 159)—was deposited in a lector priest's tomb. Most were concerned with healing and protection. Three were liturgical in nature, one of which is generally seen as the archetype of dramatic, scripted ritual (P. Ramesseum B, commonly known as the Ramesseum Dramatic Papyrus). According to a recent interpretation, it concerns a ritual for the placement of a statue of King Senusret I (r. c. 1956–1911 BCE) in a temple shrine dedicated to his mortuary cult (Geisen 2012, pp. 238–245).

Its 139 columns are divided into 48 'scenes' (Geisen 2012, pp. 31 n. 69, 37–38). We can see each scene as a function. In scene 35 (Fig. 9.5), the lector priest brings a ceremonial *qeni*-garment to the prescribed location and—assuming the role of Osiris's son, Horus, speaking to his grandfather, Geb—recites the words, 'Embrace for me this father of mine who became weary' (translation after Geisen 2012, p. 140). An embrace between father and child was a generational transfer of life force and, if shared between king and prince, dominion, while 'weariness' was a common euphemism for death. The word for 'embrace' is likewise *qeni*. Through clever use of homonymy, the *qeni*-garment serves as an object-variable, whose presence in this dimension brings about Osiris's embrace in the virtual dimension when called. It is the anchor that tethers the ritual action performed 'here' to the divine action enacted 'there' (after Assmann 2001, p. 89).

The syntax of all scenes is standardised (I follow the model put forth in Geisen 2012, pp. 32–34). A new function is defined using the phrase 'It happened that' followed by a heading describing the function to be performed, which can be considered its name. This is followed by an informal comment introduced by a copula, 'It is', which serves only to remind the priest of the function's symbolic meaning and is ignored at runtime (cf. Assmann 2001, p. 92). The body of the function follows, comprising up to four statements exchanged between two divine parties. This is the portion of the code to be executed, by means of recitation, during the ritual. Finally, a deity is associated with one or more ritual objects that carry with them, by means of their names' phonetic similarity to words describing divine actions, a hidden meaning. Translated to modern code, scene 35 reads:

Fig. 9.5 Object-oriented programming: a function of the lector's script (adapted from Sethe 1928, Pl. 20). Blue marks the function definition, grey the explanatory comment to be ignored, yellow the function's statements—one per column—and red the statements' respective object-variables. The remaining row declares the location within the temple where the function is to be called (C. G. Elkins)

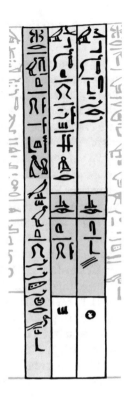

```
function lectorPriestBringsQeni () {
  /* It is Horus, who embraces his father whom he turns
     towards Geb. */

  const Osiris = { qeni: 'embrace', seneb: 'healthy' };

  Geb.listen();
  Horus.speak(Osiris.qeni +' for me this father of mine who
  became weary');
  Horus.speak('May my father indeed be '+ Osiris.seneb);
}
```

The second key in the Osiris object, *seneb*, is a type of ceremonial fringe (both the garment and fringe are articles of royal attire). It is also the word for 'healthy'.

An understanding of such frameworks and their hidden meanings constitutes the secret, divine knowledge that has so often been referenced above: 'It is efficient for a man on earth: a true remedy, (proven) a million times' (Amduat, second hour, introduction). The script was compiled with others into an extensive library, which was ultimately deposited in the lector's tomb. Not unlike his family of magicians, we use code in the diagnosis and treatment of diseases (e.g. Elenko et al. 2015; Stroud et al. 2019), and, like them, we also invoke it for our protection.

9.4.5   Security and Maintenance

The gods' names were actually epithets; one's true name was kept hidden to prevent its misuse in malicious spells. The digitised individual was one 'whose (own) mother does not know his name' (Pyramid Texts, spell 273). In a spell intended to heal the bite of a scorpion, the sun-god explains why he refuses to reveal his identity: 'I have concealed it in my belly from my children in order to prevent the use of a [...] magician's force against me' (translated in Borghouts 1978, p. 52).

We too adopt secure virtual identities and epithetical usernames to prevent the misuse of our true identities in this world (e.g. Cotoc 2017, pp. 149–186). But our reputations can nevertheless be targeted in virtual communities by malevolent entities who, by means of their anonymity, face no real consequences. Major social networks, therefore, require the use of one's true name to maintain a climate of reciprocal vulnerability in the hope of heightened security (some governments consider this an inherently dangerous requirement in violation of one's right to virtual anonymity: e.g. Cellan-Jones 2012). In ancient Egypt, a damaged reputation was as lethal as a damaged image, as both resulted in detachment from the social substrate (Assmann 1984). In a New Kingdom text known from four sources contemporary with Hor (see Black 2002, p. 266), man is prescribed good behaviour, 'So that he may be rescued from the mouths of the rabble' (Instruction of Amenemope [1, 11]; translated in Black 2002, p. 542).

Increased security demands zones of increasingly restricted access. At the threshold to the virtual was a wall of fire granting access to the worthy, while subjecting the unworthy to a fiery doom: 'Open, sky's door! You sealed door, open a path for N on the blast of heat where the gods scoop water (to extinguish the fire)' (Pyramid Texts, spell 313; gloss after Zandee 1960, p. 134). In Middle Kingdom maps of the Underworld, the labyrinthine ways of land and water are separated by a fiery lake and subdivided by gates of fire. The names later given these gates emphasise this aspect: for example, 'Red-hot' (Book of Gates, eighth gate), 'Fiery One' (Book of the Dead, spell 146, fifth gate), 'Burning of Flames' (Book of the Dead, spell 146, eighth gate). The gates themselves are secured by guardians whose names served as passwords that must be properly recited before access may be granted: 'Make a way for me, for I know you, I know your name and I know the name of the god who guards you' (Book of the Dead, spell 146).

Beyond the walls of fire, those with insufficient protection in the form of spells faced being hacked to pieces by knife-wielding demons: 'My head is not chopped off; my neck is not cut off. My name is not known among the spirits' (Coffin Texts, spell 229; translated in Zandee 1960, pp. 149–150). Thus, the documents containing the necessary code and passwords were encrypted. Like the Underworld books, the dramatic script from the lector's library was written in retrograde orientation (see Fig. 9.5), with the columns to be read counter to the direction in which the hieroglyphs were written. In some texts, cryptographic writing was employed to obscure the meaning of words (e.g. Drioton 1953, pp. 359–361).

Despite similar precautions today, we yet feel exposed, aware that we might be targeted at any moment from beyond the threshold: our virtual existence hacked, our identities stolen, our devices 'infected by disruptive, contagious bugs' (Minkin 2016, p. 122; on 'cyberphobia', see Sandywell 2006). We purchase 'spells' to detect such intrusions and infections, but we fear the use of other potentially protective measures in our surveillance and manipulation (e.g. Lupton 2015, pp. 33–38). Such is the ambivalence of the intangible. Lacking are the guarantees of the physical world. Things we own in the virtual dimension are free of decay but hardly permanent. As with the temple, tomb or statue, access is contingent upon the physical maintenance of our hardware, its compatibility with our software and our software's compatibility with our data (e.g. Richards et al. 2013). Like the priest charged with the regular maintenance of a statue's cult, we invest endless hours of 'digital labour' (Minkin 2016, p. 122) into our digital worlds, nurturing our virtual selves. Like the labour force supported by the redistributed surplus of Hesyra's day, our labour builds the 'data pyramid' (e.g. Jennex 2017) of today: 'Where once it was the physical labour of workers that produced surplus value, now the intellectual labour of the masses has monetary value, constituting a new information economy in which thought has become reified, public and commodified' (Lupton 2015, p. 22).

We perceive a great deal of liberty throughout this process. Like Hor's youthful image and idealising biography, our virtual appearance is heavily idealised, from the images we post to the information we make public. For what is the maintenance of our virtual existence but a daily ritual perpetuating idealising self-presentation, thereby maximising offerings of 'Like' on the socially prescribed understanding that they will ultimately be reciprocated (e.g. Lupton 2015, pp. 175–180).

9.5 Conclusion

On this view, anthropological analysis has little to do with trying to determine how other people think about the world. It has to do with how we must think in order to conceive a world the way they do (Henare et al. 2007, p. 15).

The epigraph with which this chapter began was employed somewhat misleadingly. Its Victorian author attributed the 'obscurity' in our understanding of the ancient world to the relative simplicity of ancient thought. However, investigations into the mechanics of ancient belief systems reveal inherently complex and elaborately reasoned approaches to understanding and interacting with the world. Digitisation is but the latest deconstructive iteration in our age-old quest to transcend nature's limitations: the pinnacle of an already ancient digital tradition.

As a virtual dimension again grows ubiquitous in every aspect of our lives, our future promises to bring us closer to our past by demanding increasingly intimate interactions with the intangible. The simultaneously transcendent and transient nature of the digital offers a level of authenticity in engaging with the past of which the physical alone is incapable. We experience not only the transcendence of a non-physical dimension but also the anxiety caused by exposure to invisible dangers, and we build virtual walls to keep the fire at bay. Recontextualising our digital world in these terms can help us better understand and indeed experience past realities. Barring considerable advances in Complex Systems Science, the nuances of ancient behaviour shall remain largely lost to us, but we can scan the landscape of commonalities to generate a model of related experiences. We can then '"listen", sympathetically, with self-awareness and self-effacement, and without imposing our own voices more than is appropriate for a dialogue' (Parkinson 2002, p. 290).

In Hor's Egypt, two- and three-dimensional images were the technology of immortality. They thrived in a world in which coded scripts granted inanimate hardware function and meaning. And, with the deconstructive and retrospective lenses worn by a cultural revolution, the answers to the future were found in the works of the past. 'People derive identity from shared remembrance—from social memory—which in turn provides them with an image of their past and a design for their future' (Alcock 2002, p. 1). Perhaps that design was the digital dimension all along: a self-fulfilling prophecy realising a dimension we could always imagine but never see.

Acknowledgements I would like to thank Dr. Nicky Nielsen of the University of Manchester for his continued encouragement and for his comments on a draft of this manuscript. I am also grateful to the editors for their consideration and helpful remarks. This is for my parents, whose relentless support from the very beginning made this journey possible.

References

Akenine-Möller T, Haines E, Hoffman N, Pesce A, Iwanicki M, Hillaire S (2018) Real-time rendering, 4th edn. CRC Press, Boca Raton, London and New York

Alcock SE (2002) Archaeologies of the Greek past: landscape, monuments, and memories. Cambridge University Press, Cambridge

Allen JP (1988) Genesis in Egypt: the philosophy of Ancient Egyptian creation accounts. Yale Egyptological Seminar, New Haven

Allen JP (2005) The Ancient Egyptian Pyramid Texts. Society of Biblical Literature, Atlanta

Asgari E, Schütze H (2017) Past, present, future: a computational investigation of the typology of tense in 1000 languages. In: Palmer M, Hwa R, Riedel S (eds) Proceedings of the 2017 conference on empirical methods in natural language processing. Association for Computational Linguistics, Copenhagen, pp 113–124. https://doi.org/10.18653/v1/d17-1011

Assmann J (1970) Der König als Sonnenpriester: Ein kosmografischer Begleittext zur kultischen Sonnenhymnik in thebanischen Tempeln und Gräbern. JJ Augustin, Glückstadt

Assmann J (1984) Reden und Schweigen. In: Helck W, Westendorf W (eds) Lexikon der Ägyptologie, vol 5, cols 195–201. Otto Harrassowitz, Wiesbaden

Assmann J (1996) Ägypten: Eine Sinngeschichte. Carl Hanser, Munich and Vienna

Assmann J (2001) The search for god in Ancient Egypt. Cornell University Press, Ithaca and London

Assmann J (2010) Tod und Jenseits im alten Ägypten, rev paperback edn. CH Beck, Munich (Original work published 2003)

Aston BG, Harrell JA, Shaw I (2000) Stone. In: Nicholson PT, Shaw I (eds) Ancient Egyptian materials and technology. Cambridge University Press, Cambridge, pp 5–77

Autodesk (2014) Refraction map. 3ds Max. Autodesk knowledge network. https://knowledge.autodesk.com/support/3ds-max/learn-explore/caas/CloudHelp/cloudhelp/2015/ENU/3DSMax/files/GUID-CCD9B76C-9AC6-46E6-8B9C-E367CFC0FDAF-htm.html. Accessed 16 July 2020

Bardinet T (1995) Les papyrus médicaux de l'Egypte pharaonique. Traduction intégrale et commentaire. Librairie Arthème Fayard, Paris

Bianchi RS (1982) Petamenophis. In: Helck W, Westendorf W (eds) Lexikon der Ägyptologie, vol 4, cols 991–992. Otto Harrassowitz, Wiesbaden

Black JR (2002) The Instruction of Amenemope: a critical edition and commentary, prolegomenon and prologue. Unpublished PhD dissertation. University of Wisconsin–Madison, Madison, WI

Borghouts JF (1978) Ancient Egyptian magical texts. EJ Brill, Leiden

Bothmer BV, De Meulenaere H, Müller HW (1960) Egyptian sculpture of the Late Period: 700 BC to AD 100. The Brooklyn Museum, Brooklyn

Brandt K-E (2016) Die Scheintüren und Entablaturen in den thebanischen Beamtengräbern des Neuen Reiches. PhD dissertation. Ruprecht-Karls-Universität, Heidelberg. heiDOK. https://doi.org/10.11588/heidok.00020243

Buccellati G (2017) A critique of archaeological reason: structural, digital, and philosophical aspects of the excavated record. Cambridge University Press, Cambridge. https://doi.org/10.1017/9781107110298

Cameron DF (1971) The museum, a temple or the forum. Curator 14(1):11–24. https://doi.org/10.1111/j.2151-6952.1971.tb00416.x

Cellan-Jones R (2012) Germany orders changes to Facebook real name policy. BBC News. https://www.bbc.com/news/technology-20766682. Accessed 17 Sept 2019

Ch'ng E, Gaffney VL (2013) Seeing things: heritage computing, visualisation and the arts and humanities. In: Ch'ng E, Gaffney V, Chapman H (eds) Visual heritage in the digital age. Springer, London, pp 1–11. https://doi.org/10.1007/978-1-4471-5535-5_1

Christakis NA (2015) Human culture as the first artificial intelligence. In: Brockman J (ed) 2015: what do you think about machines that think? https://www.edge.org/response-detail/26147. Accessed 20 July 2019

Clarke AC (1973) Profiles of the future: an inquiry into the limits of the possible, 2nd edn. Pan Books, London

Cotoc A (2017) Language and identity in cyberspace: a multidisciplinary approach. Presa Universitară Clujeană, Cluj-Napoca

Dawson I, Reilly P (2019) Messy assemblages, residuality and recursion within a phygital nexus. Epoiesen. https://doi.org/10.22215/epoiesen/2019.4

Drioton É (1953) Les principes de la cryptographie égyptienne. Comptes Rendus Des Séances De L'académie Des Inscriptions Et Belles-Lettres 97(3):355–364. https://doi.org/10.3406/crai.1953.10159

Edwards AB (1888) A thousand miles up the Nile, 2nd edn. AL Burt, New York

Elenko E, Underwood L, Zohar D (2015) Defining digital medicine. Nat Biotechnol 33(5):456–461. https://doi.org/10.1038/nbt.3222

Elkins CG, Heindl P (2022) Ancient techniques, modern technologies: using 3D models to reveal the sculptor's vision. Manuscript in preparation

Elkins CG, Price C (2022) Revisiting the 'admiral' Hor's naophorous statue. Manuscript in preparation

Faulkner RO (1985) The Ancient Egyptian Book of the Dead, rev edn. British Museum Publications, London

Foucault B, Melican J (2007) The digital and the divine: taking a ritual view of communication and ICT interaction. In: Aykin N (ed) Usability and internationalization. HCI and culture. UI-HCII 2007. Proceedings, part 1. Springer, Berlin and Heidelberg, pp 74–82. https://doi.org/10.1007/978-3-540-73287-7_10

Geisen C (2012) The Ramesseum Dramatic Papyrus: a new edition, translation, and interpretation. PhD dissertation. University of Toronto, Toronto. TSpace. http://hdl.handle.net/1807/65472. Accessed 30 Aug 2019

Henare A, Holbraad M, Wastell S (eds) (2007) Thinking through things: theorising artefacts ethnographically. Routledge, London and New York

Hillis WD (1998) The pattern on the stone: the simple ideas that make computers work. Basic Books, New York

Hornung E (1975) Amduat. In: Helck W, Otto E (eds) Lexikon der Ägyptologie, vol 1, cols 184–188. Otto Harrassowitz, Wiesbaden

Hornung E, Abt T (2014a) The Egyptian Amduat: the Book of the Hidden Chamber, 2nd edn. Living Human Heritage Publications, Zurich

Hornung E, Abt T (2014b) The Egyptian Book of Gates. Living Human Heritage Publications, Zurich

Jansen-Winkeln K (1999) Sentenzen und Maximen in den Privatinschriften der ägyptischen Spätzeit. Achet, Berlin

Jeffrey S (2015) Challenging heritage visualisation: beauty, aura and democratisation. Open Archaeol 1(1):144–152. https://doi.org/10.1515/opar-2015-0008

Jennex ME (2017) Big data, the internet of things, and the revised knowledge pyramid. Data Base Adv Inf Syst 48(4):69–79. https://doi.org/10.1145/3158421.3158427

Jones S, Jeffrey S, Maxwell M, Hale A, Jones C (2018) 3D heritage visualisation and the negotiation of authenticity: the ACCORD project. Int J Herit Stud 24(4):333–353. https://doi.org/10.1080/13527258.2017.1378905

Kelly K (2010) What technology wants. Viking Press, New York

Kitchen KA (1996) Ramesside inscriptions, translated & annotated. Translations, II: Ramesses II, royal inscriptions. Blackwell Publishers, Oxford

Lagarde S (2011) Feeding a physically based shading model. Sébastien Lagarde. https://seblagarde.wordpress.com/2011/08/17/feeding-a-physical-based-lighting-mode. Accessed 13 July 2020

Lagarde S (2013) Memo on Fresnel equations. Sébastien Lagarde. https://seblagarde.wordpress.com/2013/04/29/memo-on-fresnel-equations. Accessed 12 July 2020

Lam P-Y (2001) May the force of the operating system be with you: Macintosh devotion as implicit religion. Sociol Relig 62(2):243–262. https://doi.org/10.2307/3712458

Latour B, Lowe A (2011) The migration of the aura, or how to explore the original through its facsimiles. In: Bartscherer T, Coover R (eds) Switching codes: thinking through digital technology in the humanities and the arts. University of Chicago Press, Chicago, pp 275–298

Luo J, Cao Y, Barzilay R (2019) Neural decipherment via minimum-cost flow: from Ugaritic to Linear B. arXiv:1906.06718 [cs]. http://arxiv.org/abs/1906.06718. Accessed 26 Mar 2020

Lupton D (2015) Digital sociology. Routledge, London and New York

Minkin L (2016) Out of our skins. J Visual Art Pract 15(2–3):116–126. https://doi.org/10.1080/14702029.2016.1228820

Negroponte N (1995) Being digital. Alfred A Knopf, New York

Opitz R (2019) Messy assemblages, residuality and recursion within a phygital nexus: first response. Epoiesen. https://doi.org/10.22215/epoiesen/2019.7

Otto E (1960) Das ägyptische Mundöffnungsritual, II: Kommentar. Otto Harrassowitz, Wiesbaden

Parkinson RB (2002) Poetry and culture in Middle Kingdom Egypt: a dark side to perfection. Continuum, London and New York

Parkinson RB (2009) Reading Ancient Egyptian poetry, among other histories. Wiley-Blackwell, Oxford

Perry S, Taylor JS (2018) Theorising the digital: a call to action for the archaeological community. In: Matsumoto M, Uleberg E (eds) Oceans of data: proceedings of the 44th conference on computer applications and quantitative methods in archaeology. Archaeopress, Oxford, pp 11–22

Petrie WMF (1906) Hyksos and Israelite cities. Office of School of Archaeology, London

Price C (2017) The 'admiral' Hor and his naophorous statue (Manchester Museum acc. no. 3570). In: Jurman C, Aston D, Bader B (eds) A true scribe of Abydos: essays on first millennium BC Egypt in honour of Anthony M Leahy. Peeters, Leuven, Paris and Bristol, CT, pp 369–383

Quibell JE (1913) Excavations at Saqqara (1911–12): the tomb of Hesy. Imprimerie de l'Institut français d'archéologie orientale, Cairo

Reilly P (2015) Additive archaeology: an alternative framework for recontextualising archaeological entities. Open Archaeol 1(1):225–235. https://doi.org/10.1515/opar-2015-0013

Richards JD, Niven K, Jeffrey S (2013) Preserving our digital heritage: information systems for data management and preservation. In: Ch'ng E, Gaffney V, Chapman H (eds) Visual heritage in the digital age. Springer, London, pp 311–326. https://doi.org/10.1007/978-1-4471-5535-5_16

Roth AM (1992) The *psš-kf* and the 'Opening of the Mouth' ceremony: a ritual of birth and rebirth. J Egypt Archaeol 78:113–147. https://doi.org/10.2307/3822068

Roth AM (1993) Fingers, stars, and the 'Opening of the Mouth': the nature and function of the *ntrwj*-blades. J Egypt Archaeol 79:57–79. https://doi.org/10.2307/3822158

Sandberg A, Bostrom N (2008) Whole brain emulation: a roadmap. Technical Report No. 2008-3. Future of Humanity Institute, Oxford University. http://fhi.ox.ac.uk/reports/2008-3.pdf. Accessed 18 Aug 2019

Sandywell B (2006) Monsters in cyberspace: cyberphobia and cultural panic in the information age. Inf Commun Soc 9(1):39–61. https://doi.org/10.1080/13691180500519407

Sethe K (1928) Dramatische Texte zu altägyptischen Mysterienspielen. JC Hinrichs, Leipzig

Speiser EA (1978) Akkadian myths and epics. In: Pritchard JB (ed) Ancient Near Eastern texts relating to the Old Testament, 3rd edn. Princeton University Press, Princeton, pp 60–119 (Original work published 1969)

Stroud C, Onnela J-P, Manji H (2019) Harnessing digital technology to predict, diagnose, monitor, and develop treatments for brain disorders. npj Digit Med 2(44):1–4. https://doi.org/10.1038/s41746-019-0123-z

Turing AM (1950) I.—computing machinery and intelligence. Mind Q Rev Psychol Philos 59(236):433–460. https://doi.org/10.1093/mind/LIX.236.433

Vandier J (1962) Le papyrus Jumilhac. Centre national de la recherche scientifique, Paris

Zandee J (1960) Death as an enemy according to Ancient Egyptian conceptions. EJ Brill, Leiden. https://doi.org/10.1163/9789004377967

Chapter 10
Visualising Animal Hard Tissues

Sonia O'Connor, Tom Sparrow, Andrew D. Holland, Rachael Kershaw,
Emma Brown, Rob Janaway, Hassan Ugail, and Andrew S. Wilson

Abstract This chapter summarises AHRC/EPSRC Science and Heritage
Programme-funded research to develop a digital resource to disseminate knowledge of the identification of osseous and keratinous animal hard tissues. The choice
of materials in the manufacture of individual artefacts or classes of objects can make
a major contribution to understanding their cultural significance and questions of
provenance or authenticity. This resource builds on understanding gained through
a Fellowship to O'Connor in developing, evaluating and validating identification
criteria for these materials in raw, worked and decayed states. The resource concen-
trates on the non-destructive visual methods of particular relevance to the examination
of artworks, historic and archaeological artefacts. The chapter highlights the potential of various visualisation methods and digital technologies to capture and combine
2D images and 3D models and guide the viewer through the multi-scalar visual cues
of each material to a reliable identification. By accessing a range of collections, the
project has produced a comprehensive and accessible resource, disseminating these
findings more widely than could be achieved by a physical reference collection.
This resource supports the identification of cultural heritage objects for conservation
scientists and heritage professionals and informs the fight against the illegal hunting
and trafficking of rare and endangered species.

Keywords Raw material selection · Identification · Osseous · Keratinous ·
Cultural significance · CITES

S. O'Connor (✉) · T. Sparrow · A. D. Holland · R. Kershaw · E. Brown · R. Janaway ·
A. S. Wilson
Visualising Heritage/School of Archaeological & Forensic Sciences, University of Bradford,
Bradford, UK
e-mail: s.oconnor@bradford.ac.uk

H. Ugail
Faculty of Engineering & Informatics, Centre for Visual Computing , University of Bradford,
Bradford, UK

© Springer Nature Switzerland AG 2022
E. Ch'ng et al. (eds.), *Visual Heritage: Digital Approaches in Heritage Science*,
Springer Series on Cultural Computing,
https://doi.org/10.1007/978-3-030-77028-0_10

10.1 Introduction

This chapter reports on valuable insights drawn together as part of a visual workflow that was developed as a means of supporting the identification of objects worked in animal hard tissues. The Visualising Animal Hard Tissues (VAHT) project has far-reaching implications for object and artefact studies (in craft traditions, cultural histories, ethnography, natural history, art, archaeology, conservation, curation and collections management) and both the legal sale of cultural objects (auction houses, private sales of antiques, conservation-restoration) and illicit trade and trafficking of endangered species (anti-poaching activities, wildlife management, policing of CITES, customs and border control, wildlife forensics), all of which rely on the correct and well-authenticated identification of material.

Animal hard tissues have been exploited as a source of raw materials for tools, weapons and works of art, across every geographical zone and from the earliest human habitation to the present day. These hard tissues fall into two groups: the highly mineralised osseous tissues (e.g. bone, antler, ivories and other tooth structures) and more plastic keratinous tissues (e.g. horn, hoof, baleen and tortoiseshell). Some of these materials, such as bone, were always readily available and their use is common to all cultures. Selection of these materials for a specific practical application was largely predicated by their physical properties, but for less obviously functional objects other considerations could come into play. The use of certain materials for specific types of object may have had as much to do with cultural or social traditions as with practicality. Selection for or against certain materials or species could be influenced by belief systems: even individual skeletal elements could be endowed with magical or medicinal properties or associated with particular deities (Lemonnier 1993). Together these preferences could form part of the expression of 'otherness', that identified a person as one of 'us' and not one of 'them' (Choyke and O'Connor 2013). In addition, an individual might wish to indicate their status or wealth through the acquisition and display of decorative objects in materials with very limited availability or might be drawn to use a material purely because they found it sensually pleasing.

It is essential that these materials are correctly identified in order for historical and archaeological research to attempt to unravel and understand these complex influences on selection, to recognise changes in society, to detect indicators of long distance trade in exotic materials and to recognise the cultural significance of individual objects. Knowing what materials have been used is also necessary to ensure their preservation through the application of suitable conservation treatments and the provision of appropriate conditions for storage and display. The identification of unworked raw materials through the study of their gross morphology is the prerogative of zoologists and archaeozoologists but the overall size, shape and diagnostic details are quickly lost as these materials are processed via the *chaîne operatoire* towards the desired end product. The finished objects and working waste will consist largely of worked surfaces, cut, sawn, fractured or polished that leave little clue to the original form of the raw material, and identification has now to be based more on the details of the material's internal structure or chemistry.

10.2 Background/Literature Review

An AHRC-EPSRC Fellowship to O'Connor via the Science and Heritage Programme built upon specialist experience in the identification of worked animal hard tissues accrued over many years whilst practising as an archaeological conservator (O'Connor 1987). The project, entitled *Cultural Materials Worked in Skeletal Hard Tissues* (COWISHT), was aimed at improving the reliability and accuracy of identifications with an emphasis on the use of non-destructive techniques (O'Connor 2016). Collaboration with project partners, the Hawley Collection, Sheffield, the Horniman Museum, London, the Hull Maritime Museum, Leeds Museums, the Yorkshire Museum, York Archaeological Trust and with several other museums and private collections allowed access to thousands of objects dating from prehistoric times to the twentieth century. These natural history, archaeological, ethnographic, social history and fine art collections provided objects in a wide range of hard tissues, worked in diverse ways and in very different states of preservation. Collaborators at the Henry Moseley X-ray Imaging Facility at the University of Manchester, BioArCh at the University of York and with the School of Chemistry and Biosciences at the University of Bradford provided facilities and expertise to help in the evaluation and validation of identification techniques including vibrational spectroscopy and proteomics.

Through this work, it became evident that all the chemical and analytical techniques explored had limitations and shortcomings and were unreliable when applied to historical and, in particular, to archaeological material due to issues of contamination and deterioration (O'Connor et al. 2011; Edwards and O'Connor 2012). Only proteomic analysis of the structural collagen (Collins et al. 2010) or keratin (O'Connor et al. 2014), and DNA analysis provided reliable identification of taxa (the latter to the level of species) of material in which these biomolecules were preserved. Unfortunately, both techniques required the removal of a sample, although this is minimal for proteomics since the adoption of erasure sampling originally developed for identifying the taxon of historic parchment (Fiddyment et al. 2015), and neither technique could identify the tissue type, i.e. they do not differentiate elephant bone from ivory, or cattle horn from hoof.

To determine the tissue type requires examination of the structural arrangement of the tissue to determine how it was formed. For instance, cattle horn has a finely layered structure whilst that of the hoof is largely of closely stacked tubules. Moreover, the detail of the meso- and macro-structure of these tissue types can vary markedly between taxa and can even enable the determination of species, so providing a sound basis for the visual identification of the material (O'Connor 2016). Using this structural evidence it is possible, for instance, to distinguish an object worked in elephant ivory from one in hippopotamus ivory (Fig. 10.1). Visual identification also has the advantages of being a non-destructive process and requiring no specialist equipment, beyond a good light source, a low power, binocular microscope and a mid-range camera to help record the evidence (Fig. 10.2). The reliability of the identifications is unaffected by chemical contamination, and physical deterioration can even enhance

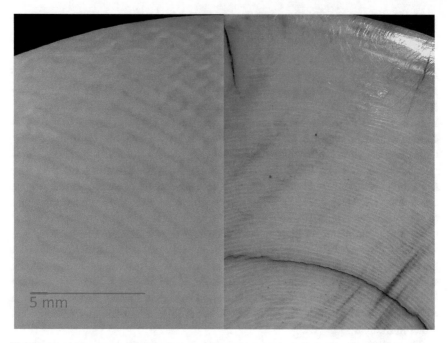

Fig. 10.1 Elephant (left) and hippopotamus (right) ivories seen in transverse section by reflected light. The intersecting arcs (Schreger pattern) are characteristic of elephant whilst the fine concentric banding is typical of hippopotamus (S. O'Connor)

the visibility of diagnostic features (O'Connor 2018). As a consequence, visual identification is the most accessible, portable and versatile of the available identification techniques, and should be undertaken before considering the application of more invasive or destructive techniques.

However, animal hard tissues have complex, anisotropic structures that vary in appearance on a 3D object depending on the orientation of the surfaces in relation to the structure. These features can also look very different depending on the way the material has been worked and its state of preservation. Even the lighting conditions under which it is viewed can hide or reveal diagnostic evidence. Correct visual identification, then, takes experience and depends on acquiring a detailed understanding of the physical properties of these tissues, their histological organisation and how these materials change when they are worked, aged and degraded. Unfortunately, the literature on visual identification has, over time, accumulated a lot of received wisdom and misconceptions; so, during the COWISHT project each identification criterion had to be explored and tested across a wide range of objects and specimens of the raw materials and validated against the findings from other analytical techniques, particularly Raman spectroscopy and proteomic analysis. Each visual criterion also had to be understood in terms of the latest research into the formation, histology, chemistry and physical properties of these tissues to help understand when their apparent presence or absence might be significant. As a result of the COWISHT

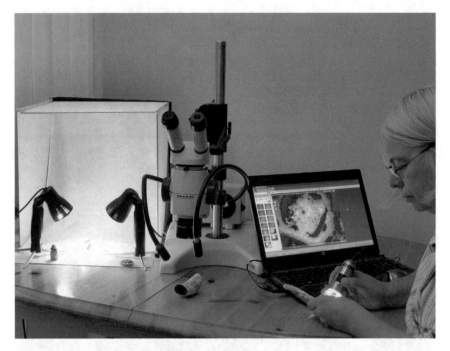

Fig. 10.2 Low cost, portable equipment for the visual identification of animal hard tissues including a Wild Heerbrugg M8 stereomicroscope, a Meiji Techno FT190/240 fibre optic lamp, a Panasonic Lumix DMC TZ6 16 megapixel compact camera, a small folding photographic booth with two table-top LED lights; and a Dino-Lite AM-7013MZT, 5 megapixel digital microscope with polariser (S. O'Connor)

project, the visual identification process was refined and developed to improve the range of osseous and keratinous materials that could be distinguished and the reliability and accuracy of identifications (O'Connor 2015, 2013; O'Connor et al. 2014; Cameron et al. 2013).

The need for a digital resource that could contribute to the visual identification of raw materials, worked and degraded objects was identified through the delivery of a series of intensive short courses for professionals working both in the heritage sector and in the detection of illegally trafficked materials. These courses, delivered by O'Connor both within the UK and overseas (Fig. 10.3) allowed participants to develop confidence in the basic skills of visual identification, combining lectures and practical sessions using a teaching collection of both raw and worked materials. Experience gained through developing and teaching this course highlighted common problems that many participants have in understanding the relative scale of features and in visualising and interpreting three-dimensional structures from their appearance on two-dimensional surfaces that are often far from flat. The potential transformative nature of digital technologies to convey some of this understanding has been explored in this study.

Fig. 10.3 Key to teaching the identification course is access to a wide range of specimens worked and unworked, ancient and modern (S. O'Connor)

Examining specimens of known materials helps to overcome these issues by allowing direct comparison with recognisable features on a variety of worked and unworked surfaces. Correctly orienting an object relative to the presumed raw material is also essential to the identification process as this helps to show whether the features seen in each surface actually matches those expected, or if an object is the wrong shape to have been cut complete from the raw material. The experience has been that outside of these bespoke courses very few have access to suitable reference collections. In addition, available identification guides vary in their scope, accuracy and usefulness. Most are centred on distinguishing elephant ivory from bone and other materials, with little or no mention of the keratinous tissues, and are illustrated in the main with photographs of polished or stained tissue sections (Penniman 1952; Espinosa and Mann 1992; Locke 2008, 2013). Only a few attempt to describe how these features appear in the round (Campbell Pederson 2004, 2015; Hornbeck 2016) or how they are affected by ageing or deposition in different archaeological environments (Krzyszkowska 1990; O'Connor 1987; Rijkelijkhuizen 2008). The development of an interactive 3D web-based resource *Visualising Animal Hard Tissues* (VAHT) was proposed to overcome these issues and to support the dissemination of visual identification skills to a wider audience.

The main objective of VAHT was to use digital documentation techniques including 3D laser scanning, CT scanning (computed tomography), high resolution focus-stack photography and photo-microscopy to acquire images that together would characterise the identification criteria of each of the materials in their raw state, when worked in different ways and in different states of preservation. A pilot web resource was developed that provided a synthetic narrative that linked the collection of 3D data and high-resolution micrographs together with explanatory text and diagrams for at least two of the materials.

10.3 Materials and Methods

The COWISHT project provided many 2D images and a shortlist of objects for VAHT. In the event, some 120 objects were selected for further imaging to develop a comprehensive archive of identification features for this web resource. Approximately, 75% of these objects were in osseous materials, including bone and antler of different species, sperm whale tooth, narwhal tusk, elephant, hippopotamus and walrus ivory. The remainder were mostly keratinous tissues such as cattle, sheep and goat horn, hoof, baleen of various whales, tortoiseshell and rhino horn. A few were plastic objects made in imitation of ivory or tortoiseshell. The study material included natural history specimens and historical and archaeological objects dating from the Roman period to the present day. A few came from private collections, but the great majority originated either from O'Connor's teaching collection or were loaned by the Leeds Museums, Hull Maritime Museum and The York Archaeological Trust, specifically for the VAHT project.

The data capture and visualisation approaches that were selected coupled with the functionality of the VAHT web resource evolved from skillsets that were developed as part of the JISC-funded open-access web resource *Digitised Diseases* (http://www. digitiseddiseases.org). This resource featured digitised specimens of human skeletal elements that had been affected by chronic pathological conditions, where accurate representation of form and subtle changes in bone texture were essential. However, image requirements for VAHT highlighted an additional range of challenges that had to be overcome through flexible approaches and experimentation. In particular, the objects varied considerably in size and shape from a few tens of millimetres in size to a 2.6 m narwhal tusk, but with the same key requirement that high resolution detail was necessary for characterisation. Furthermore, these objects varied in surface texture and optical properties. Some of the worked materials were translucent and the finely worked edges of horn combs could be so thin that they were almost transparent, whilst the highly polished surfaces of ivory and metal components of the worked objects were subject to specular reflectance, unlike anything encountered on the human bone specimens. This chapter focuses on the digital documentation techniques used, some of the problems encountered and summarises how they were overcome.

In order to maximise the information available from these visual resources, the online zoomable image interface Zoomify (Zoomify, Santa Cruz, California) was used. The focus-stack images in particular are very large and would be very slow to download in full. Zoomify works across all platforms including smart phones and keeps the image sizes small whilst allowing the user to zoom in and pan across the images revealing all the high-resolution detail.

10.3.1 Focus Stacking (Z-Stacking)

All photographic images have a depth of field, the range over which the image is in focus, and this range reduces as the camera to object distance is decreased or the focal length of the lens and size of the aperture are increased. Shallow depth of field is particularly an issue at high magnification producing images where, perhaps, only a small proportion of the detail is in focus. Focus-stacking (Z-stacking) is a technique developed to overcome these issues, particularly for the photo-microscopy of small, highly detailed 3D objects. A series of images is taken of the object from the same viewpoint but focussed at different planes, from the front to the back of the object or through the depth of a region of interest. These images are then digitally combined, the final image being formed only from the sharp pixels of each of the component images, so producing a greatly enhanced depth of field and, therefore, presenting a greater amount of intelligible information in a single image. For the software to work with accuracy, the incremental changes between exposures need to be the same size and in the same direction and small enough that the depth of field just overlaps from one image to the next. Moving the focal plane can be achieved in two different ways, either by changing the focal distance of the lens or by changing the distance between the camera and the subject. Each approach has its pros and cons, producing slight distortions in the resultant stacked image but these can be minimised through careful management of factors such as lens selection and minimum camera to object distance. The latter technique, moving the camera between exposures, was used to great effect to capture the meso- and macro-structure of the materials, the detail of fracture surfaces and the texture and form of entire small objects featured in VAHT.

The individual images were captured with a Nikon D600 camera and an AF-S micro Nikkor 105 mm lens mounted on a Cognisys Stackshot, macro rail, capable of incremental movements as small as 4 μm (Fig. 10.4). The controller for the macro rail also triggered the camera and the whole process was operated from a laptop using Helicon Remote software. This software gave a live view from the camera and enabled all the important parameters to be adjusted and set remotely, including the exposure settings of the camera, the start and stop points for the sequence and the optimum shot interval for the level of magnification, and the start of the shooting. Once captured, the images were compiled using Helicon Focus software and the resulting image examined before the next view or object was selected. It was not uncommon for the resulting image to be compiled from 40 to 90 individual images (Fig. 10.5).

Fig. 10.4 Equipment for focus-stacking photography. Details in text (S.O'Connor)

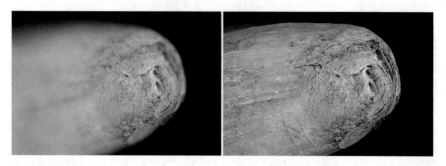

Fig. 10.5 A single macro image of the tip of a cow horn (**L**) and the compiled focus-stack of the horn tip (**R**) with a greatly enhanced depth of field (S.O'Connor)

10.3.2   Laser Scanning and Texture Photography

The 3D surface morphology of the raw materials and worked objects was captured using an arm-based laser scanner; the FARO Quantum Arm with a V3 Laser Line Probe (FARO, Lake Mary, FL, USA). The surface colour information (the 'texture') was collected separately using conventional photography and then combined with the 3D models from the laser scanner to produce high fidelity models of the objects.

The FARO arm, originally developed as a coordinate measuring machine for engineering, is articulated to provide seven degrees of freedom in a sphere of measurement 2.4 m in diameter around the origin point at its base. This allowed the laser probe at the end of the arm to be moved around the object being digitised rather than having the object moved past the laser scanner, which could have been problematic for material vulnerable to movement. The high degree of articulation also made it easier to digitise complex surface morphology, allowing access to hollows or areas of undercut, and minimising the possibility of surface contact, a particularly important consideration when working with degraded and fragile material. To eliminate errors caused by the relative movement on the micron scale between the laser scanner and the subject being scanned, the FARO arm and probe was mounted on a custom-designed steel-topped metrology instrument bench. The objects were supported in a number of different ways to prevent them from rocking and in order to lift them clear of the table to allow scanning to reach down to and around the lower edges. The most useful and versatile supports proved to be the ones fabricated from pencil erasers mounted on magnetic board pins. The eraser provided a soft point of contact with the object and the magnetic pin base remained firmly in whichever position it was placed on the steel surface of the table (Fig. 10.6).

The V3 laser probe projects a line of red laser light and then detects its return signal, reflected from the surface being scanned. Each line has 640 points so at 30 frames per second, this scanner measures 19,200 points per second. The scans were recorded in the IMAlign module of the Polyworks 2014 software suite (InnovMetric, Québec, Canada) with the FARO Laser Line Probe plugin, using 'high accuracy mode' which reduces the spacing of the points along the laser line, increasing the resolution of the line and reducing noise. As the laser line is projected onto the surface of an object, it

Fig. 10.6 Laser scanning an elephant ivory Roman clasp knife handle (York Archaeological Trust finds number 1984.32.2157). Equipment details in text (S.O'Connor)

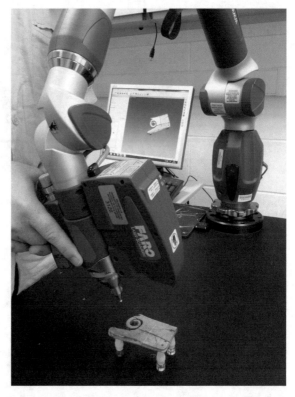

returns the 3D position of each point along the line. These points are then interpolated by grouping data returns into domains of a user defined (interpolation step) size. This results in a point cloud with a pseudo-regular grid interpolation for each scan pass. Polyworks IMAlign meshes the point cloud as the scan pass is being captured and this per scan interpolation aids scan speed and visualisation of the scan progress to the user. The interpolation step used in this research was set at either 0.05 mm or 0.1 mm depending on the level of detail of the surface. The surface colour of the object has a strong influence on the quality of the laser return and the scans were therefore optimised to the average surface colour of each sample prior to scanning, using the exposure and noise filtering threshold level functions within the FARO Laser Line Probe plugin. Multiple scan passes were made over each sample to ensure capture of the full surface. To minimise the alignment error between the point clouds of individual scan passes, a best fit alignment algorithm was applied using an iterative least squares method until a user selected convergence between each point cloud of 0.000001 was achieved. The resultant point cloud for each sample was rendered out to a 3D meshed surface model in the IMMerge module of the Polyworks 2014 software suite, using a 0.1 mm surface sampling step and a low smoothing pass. The IMMerge meshing algorithm sub-samples the combined point cloud and averages the points within each 0.1 mm domain and the point cloud is then meshed using a Delaunay triangulation method to produce the 3D surface model in .OBJ format.

Fig. 10.7 Rhino horn 3D model. From left to right, mesh, textured model, mesh with texture seams highlighted and UV texture map

Because the FARO laser scanner utilises a red laser, it is unable to capture the colour of the object's surface. To provide the surface colour information for the final 3D model, conventional photography is used. For VAHT, a Nikon D300s or a Nikon D600 were used with a range of lenses of different focal length, depending on the scale of the object, providing multiple overlapping high-quality images and complete surface coverage of the object. The lighting conditions were strictly controlled and diffused to reduce specular highlights and strong shadows that would otherwise appear on the surface of the final 3D object. All the photography was colour corrected using a colour card to provide accurate colour reproduction. These texture images then had to be applied to the 3D mesh to form the final 3D image of the original object. This is a highly skilled process, called UV mapping and texturing, with several stages that involve unwrapping the 3D mesh, creating the coloured texture map and applying the texture so that every polygon in the 3D mesh is assigned a triangle of colour information from the texture map. First a blank texture image was created for each .OBJ 3D model and UV mapping was carried out in Maya (Autodesk, San Rafael, California, United States). The 3D data and each digital photograph were then manually aligned in Mudbox (Autodesk, San Rafael, California, United States) and the colour information was transferred from the digital photograph to the 3D model's mapped texture file by 'painting' the photograph onto the 3D model's corresponding areas with a brush tool (Fig. 10.7).

10.3.3 Object Movies

As discussed below, it was not always possible to acquire 3D laser scan images of particular objects, especially those that were transparent to some extent or incorporated highly reflective elements and in such instances object movies were used to provide interactivity online. These allow the user to move and rotate an object around but the underlaying data are 2D. The amount of movement is dictated by the number of images taken, and the user does not have full control over the movement, which a true 3D dataset would allow.

The subject of the object movie was placed at the centre of a circular, rotatable glass table top. This was marked on its periphery into divisions allowing the table to be rotated by 10° between successive exposures. Three cameras (Nikon D300s) were suspended in an arc vertically above the edge of the table and triggered synchronously by wired remote before the next rotation of the table. The lighting was provided by soft boxes; lights in which the lamp is enclosed in a reflective chamber and the light is released through one or more layers of a translucent fabric which diffuses the light, producing a very even, soft illumination (Fig. 10.8). A total of 324 (3 (levels) × 36 × 3 (bracketed) exposures) high-resolution images were collected over a 360° rotation

Fig. 10.8 Equipment and set-up for taking an object movie. Object: Leeds Museums (S.O'Connor)

of the table. The images were processed using Object2VR Garden Gnome software to produce the object movies.

10.3.4 CT Scanning

A selection of raw materials and objects were imaged using the medical CT facility at Pinderfields Hospital, Mid-Yorkshire NHS Trust near Wakefield outside of the normal work schedule. Using a medical CT scanner had the advantage that being designed to image any part or all of a human, it was possible to image a whole range of specimens from a few tens of centimetres in length to the size of a sperm whale jaw (Fig. 10.9). As in conventional radiography, the X-ray image is a record of the variation in absorption of the X-ray beam as it passes through an object. The thicker and denser the material and the higher its atomic number, the more of the beam will be absorbed. In a medical CT scanner, the patient lies on a table that passes slowly through a gantry, which houses both the X-ray source and the digital detectors. As the X-ray beam and detector rotate within the gantry, the area of interest is imaged from every direction in a spiral fashion as the patient moves along. Once captured, the X-ray image is processed to provide slices through the patient which can be reconstructed to form sections in any direction or to model the surfaces of distinct structures or voids. The basis of the selection of the VAHT objects for CT scanning was material that had complex internal organisation that would not be apparent from the exterior views. Cetacean bones, for instance, may appear to present large pieces of compact tissue for working into sizable, robust objects but in reality, the compact tissue in most of whale skeletal elements is only a thin envelope over a very spongy bone core. The scanner was a Siemens Definition AS 128 slice scanner and the images were captured using the following scan parameters: 120 kV 100 mAs with a pitch of 0.8 and a slice width of 0.6 mm reconstructed every 0.4 mm using an algorithm of B80S which was the sharpest they had. The images generated by the scanner were exported on a series of DVDs and these data were processed at by the Visualising Heritage Team at the University of Bradford using the following software solutions—Avizo Fire (FEI) and Mimics (Materialise) to produce 3D images of the external and internal morphology, or specific sections revealing changes in the structure of the tissue, e.g. the distribution of compact and spongy tissue in bone and antler.

Micro-CT can be used to image internal structures down to a few microns in diameter, but to achieve this the object itself must only be a few mm in diameter as the resolution of the image is adversely affected by the increasing thickness of the material through which it passes. This limits the use of micro-CT as a tool for the identification of historical and archaeological materials, but for VAHT it was possible to image small samples of the raw materials and some fragments of worked, aged materials to explore their structure and the effects of deterioration. In micro-CT, the X-ray beam and detector are static and the object is rotated in the beam, being moved perhaps a degree at a time between exposures before the object is raised a small distance vertically and the process is repeated. High resolution scans of objects as small as a comb tooth a couple of centimetres in length can take hours to capture and then process to produce slices through the object. The micro-CT scanner used for

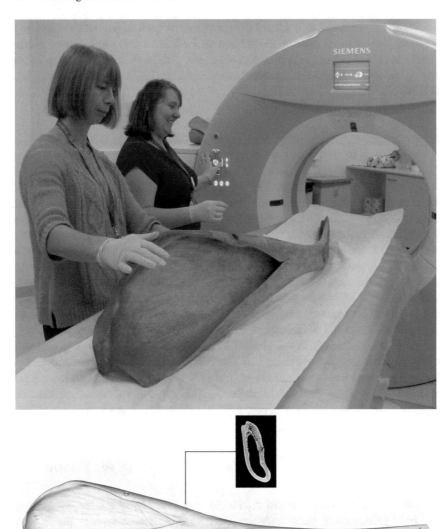

Fig. 10.9   Top, CT scanning half a sperm whale jaw at Pinderfields Hospital (Hull Museums accession number KINCM: 2013.182). Permission of Ruth Clarke and Emily Lewis (S.O'Connor). **Below,** a slice through the jaw and the reconstructed data

the VAHT material was a SkyScan1173 (software: Version 1. 6/build 7) at Smith + Nephew, York. This is a desktop cabinet unit, with a Hamamatsu 130/300 source, a flat panel sensor and camera with 50.0 μm pixel size. The individual image slices were copied to hard drive and reconstructed into sections and 3D surface reconstructions at Bradford.

10.4 Results and Discussions

The imaging for VAHT has provided a wealth of high-quality visual information for each of the materials, illustrating the appearance and form of the raw material, its structure, how it fractures or deteriorates over time and how its appearance can change when worked in different ways. Together with the linking text, all these images have the potential to provide an unrivalled, accessible resource for the confident and correct identification of these materials. Almost all the raw materials (tusks, antlers, horns, etc.) are reproduced as 3D laser scan models, the worked objects are a mixture of these and object movies whilst some of the smaller and flatter objects are presented as high-resolution, focus-stacked images or photomicrographs where this is sufficient to convey the important details. CT and micro-CT imaging helped to provide 3D imagery of the interior sculpturing of many of the raw materials ably recording the location, size and shape of natural voids, such as the pulp cavity in tusks, the medullary cavity in long bones and the distribution of compact and spongy bone. When combined with the external morphology, this information reveals the limitations of each raw material that determine the shapes and maximum dimensions of the workable material that can be cut from it for object production.

10.4.1 Problems Encountered in Imaging and Ways Forward

Initially, it had been intended to create 3D visualisations of all the objects that had been selected, but various challenges were encountered such as the interaction between the laser scanner and the optical properties of some worked surfaces, and the development of the object movies was done in response to these problems. Whilst the laser-scanned 3D visualisations are fully rotatable, typically the object movies only allow the viewer to rotate the object in the horizontal plane, with limited movement in the vertical axis. However, these object movies still give a much better impression of the characteristics of the materials, for instance, sheen, translucency and the orthogonal variation of worked surfaces, than can be gained from static, 2D images alone.

The optical properties (surface colour, specularity, opacity, etc.) of animal hard tissues are not uniform but rather are a result of a range of factors including their structural constituents, natural pigmentation, histological structure, the way they have been worked or used and their degradation over time. The surface optical properties of these materials are therefore highly variable from material to material and object to object, and as most 3D scanners rely on optical devices (usually cameras), this poses a range of challenges to both 3D digitisation and photographic recording. Separating texture capture from 3D surface capture, as described above, simplified, but did not eliminate the complexity of these challenges, especially where multiple optical properties introduced competing problems.

The most significant challenge to the production of high quality and accurate 3D models was variations in surface opacity. Whilst fully opaque objects reflect light at their surfaces, materials that are not fully opaque allow some light to penetrate and scatter sub-surface. Where the intensity of the light is high enough or the material has sufficient transparency, sub-surface reflected, refracted and scattered light can penetrate back out of the material and be returned to the instrument sensor (Coşarcă et al. 2009). When this occurs, the instrument cannot distinguish between the first good return from the surface and reflections from deeper within the material producing for each point on the surface multiple returned points at different depths. This results in poor meshing and a high degree of dimensional inaccuracy.

Long wavelength, high intensity light sources, such as the 650 nm red laser of the FARO V3 Laser Line Probe, penetrate deeper into the surface than shorter wavelength light, further exacerbating this effect. This made it impossible to gain usable 3D visualisations of some materials such as worked tortoiseshell, which has a mottled appearance formed by opaque, darkly pigmented patches dispersed in a lighter, more translucent matrix. Additionally, light paths within the material can be reflected laterally through the material, especially in animal hard tissues where the interfaces between histological structures act as internal reflective surfaces, such as the varying opacity of the criss-cross Schreger pattern in elephant and mammoth ivory. This also has the effect of dispersing the recorded points from their true values, reducing the positional accuracy of the resultant model and interfering with the alignment between scan passes. Since this project, scanners have been developed that use a lower intensity and shorter wavelength blue light source that can limit the impact of differing levels of opacity on scan quality.

Surface colour and specularity were also significant factors in 3D scanning quality. Darker coloured surfaces in general gave a poorer laser return and increased noise levels or image 'speckle'. For objects with very dark surfaces, the laser could be optimised with a slower exposure and greater noise filtering to successfully compensate for the poorer laser return. Variation in surface colour was seen in most objects but normally this fell within a range that the scanner's detector could be optimised to cover. If the variation in the brightness response of the reflected light was so large that the instrument's exposure and brightness settings could not cover the full range of responses, these areas would be missing from the scan. In such cases, it was necessary to rescan these areas after adjusting the exposure settings.

Where object surfaces exhibited a combination of both very dark and highly specular surfaces, achieving an acceptable 3D laser scan result was very challenging. In highly specular (reflective) surfaces, most of the laser light from the instrument is lost through direct reflection and not returned to the laser probe. The limited amount of light that does return was insufficient for high positional accuracy, or even to produce a point cloud at all, resulting in unreliable or missing data in the final mesh. This was particularly a problem on highly polished, darkly pigmented material but on lighter coloured surfaces multiple passes with the scanner at slightly varying angles could be used to fill the holes caused by the specularity, providing a contiguous mesh surface, albeit one with lower positional accuracy.

The worked horn object in Fig. 10.10 offered the most complex challenge for digitisation, presenting large variations in colour, highly specular surfaces and differing opacity levels. The combined effect of these optical properties produced surfaces with large areas of missing data, high levels of noise and inaccurately reconstructed surfaces.

Specular highlights are also a problem for the texturing of these 3D models, i.e. the application of the colour images to the surfaces of the model. During texture photography, specular highlights were commonly recorded on worked bone, ivory and horn and on the metal components of these objects. These specular highlights become a component of the colour information but as the 3D model is manipulated the highlight may no longer be appropriate to the current view. Whilst strictly controlling the texture photography lighting minimised the specular highlights, for highly polished objects they could not be entirely eliminated. Surface dusting with a fine powder could have removed the highlights completely but this was rejected on the grounds that it was not ethically acceptable to do this to museum objects and it would also have misrepresented the colour and light-reflective characteristics of the material, which are important physical features for identification.

To combat the highlights, it was proposed to edit the affected images to remove the bright specular highlight and replace it with the data from the same area in another image where the specular highlight was reduced due to the slight rotation of the object. This was tested with both the captured images and the resultant texture

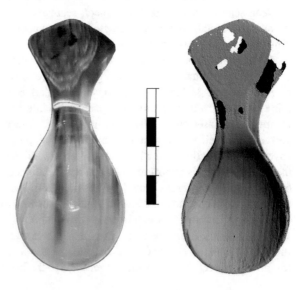

Fig. 10.10 A highly polished horn spoon (left) with its 3D scan (right) showing the problems caused by specular reflection and variations in colour and translucency. (After Holland 2017, pg 117)

image. This technique did not completely remove the highlight: the shiny appearance of the material was retained but the appearance of the misplaced highlight was muted in respect of the correctly located highlight as the model of the object was rotated in the viewer. The use of polarising filters on the camera might also have reduced this problem but cross-polarisation could be predicted to have unexpected effects with the imaging of the complex organisation of materials such as the matrix of ivories.

Today, structured light scanning might seem a more obvious choice for the capture of 3D imagery, both in terms of speed and because the specular highlights would not become mispositioned as the object view changes. Using this system, the scanner and its machine vision cameras are static and the object is rotated to the next scan position on an automated turntable after each scan pass. However, affordable high resolution structured light scanners were only just becoming widespread towards the latter stages of the project. Structured light systems are available as either blue light (greyscale), or white light scanners. White light structured light scanners enable good surface recording and some can capture the colour information using the same machine vision cameras. At the time of this project, most structured light scanners were monochrome or the software did not output colour information, but laser scanning, with photorealistic texturing had a proven record in recording similar material (Wilson 2014; Wilson et al. 2017a, b).

For the web resource, the CT data have been used to reconstruct 3D views of objects. Animations developed from the 3D views were produced using in-house code written in Python, which reads the medical image standard DICOM files and produces data volumes that can be resliced to produce the videos. In each animation, a red line passes through the 3D image, and the CT slice corresponding to that red line's location is displayed. The red line can be halted at any point in the animation to allow the information revealed in the individual slice to be examined. For each scanned object, there is one or more animation. The use of medical CT scanners poses a problem in that there are limits to the resolution of the exported data imposed by a maximum image size. This restriction was overcome to some extent by exporting the data in sections and recombining.

It had been hoped that the micro-CT images would capture the internal microstructure of the material samples in sufficient detail to allow, for instance, the comparison of long bone and antler compact tissue or of cattle and sheep horn and, perhaps, the organisation of the dentine in different species of ivory. This was successful to some extent but it did not prove possible to radiographically image all the structures that were clearly visible in light under low magnification. Features that formed voids in these materials, such as the different blood vessel systems in the bone and antler, cracks between the layers of dentine in degraded elephant ivory and the commissure (central anomaly) in ivory from a hippopotamus canine were all recorded in detail. What was missing from these images were features in the matrix around these voids, such as the boundaries of osteon structures in bone or the Schreger pattern of elephant ivory. This may have been partly because although these features are formed by differences in the organisation of the tissue matrix, they do not necessarily represent significant differences in the radiodensity of the material. In the event, it was easier to show the tissue structure and its appearance in worked and damaged surfaces by using photomicrographs linked to annotated diagrams, although the micro-CT images did prove useful in the preparation of some of these drawings.

10.4.2 Development of the Web Resource

The pilot web resource is designed to allow the user to access the information about a particular material both through the use of descriptive text and through direct interrogation of the 3D visualisations of each raw material, using 'hot-spots' to explore the characteristic features in an intuitive fashion. Each animal hard tissue has been organised around a series of story boards that start with an annotated diagram showing the location of the material in relation to the soft tissues and skeleton of the animal from which it originates and conveying basic information about its form and cross-sections. The main text covers the characterisation of the raw material, describing how it is formed, the features that should be visible when worked and how these alter with age and decay. For each description, highlighted words, such as 'bioapatite', 'cornified' and 'dentinal tubule' link directly to a glossary of terms and image thumbnails serve as visual cues that link directly to the appropriate high-resolution 2D images, 3D visualisations and CT imagery. The scaled digital imagery illustrates the structural features of different aspects at increasingly higher magnification. Other images show how the worked objects fit within the raw material explaining the orientation of the observed structures and how natural voids, such as the pulp cavity in tusks, have been avoided or exploited in the design of the finished piece. A 'search all' function also makes it possible to review all the images related to each material, when searching for a match for the features seen within a particular object. It is envisioned that further developments to this resource will make it possible to move between images of similar materials to enable comparison between analogous views or features of each.

Example pages for elephant ivory and rhino horn offer fully rotatable, 3D visualisations of the raw materials that provide a realistic impression of form, size, colour and texture. 'Hot-spots' on the 3D visualisations link to text, diagrams and other imagery to explain the formation and structure of the tissue, or link to images related to a particular characteristic of the raw material (Fig. 10.11). For instance, on the side of the rhino horn, a 'hot-spot' links to detailed images of worked surfaces showing the characteristics of the underlying protein matrix, with its longitudinally tubular structure. Similarly, 'hot-spots' on the base link to images relating to the transverse cross-section of these tubules and their appearance in a range of worked objects. Other links from these pages allow the user to examine in detail examples of historical and archaeological objects through a mixture of 2D images, 3D visualisations or object movies.

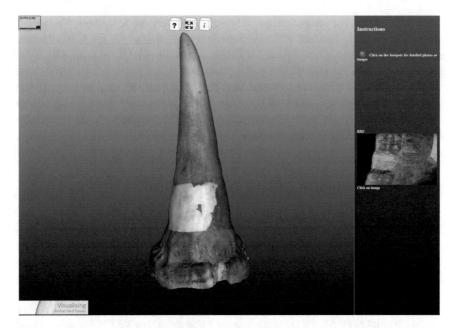

Fig. 10.11 A screen grab from the VAHT web resource of the fully rotatable 3D visualisation of a rhino horn with 'hot-spots' (marked with red spots) that link to related detailed images, diagrams and text

10.5 Conclusions

The project explored the use of digital tools to convey knowledge and understanding on material identifications, cultural significance and trends in material selection. By drawing on a synthetic narrative for each material type, it has been possible to bring together a comprehensive range of surface characteristics seen in objects fashioned from animal hard tissues—ranging from highly worked and finished objects to degraded archaeological finds. Whilst a web resource cannot replace the tactile experiences that convey density, feel (greasiness, smoothness, dryness), thermal conductivity or smell, many of these properties are hard to assess in any case when museum policies generally require the wearing of gloves to handle objects. What VAHT has provided is a resource built upon firmly identified materials, well-lit and clearly demonstrating the detail, scale and relationships of the characteristic features that enable the visual identification of the different animal hard tissues.

The development of an open-access resource with Creative Commons Licensing (CC BY-NC-ND) was used to ensure that the main resource is available for educational use, with clear attribution. This approach ensures that the copyright owner is explicit and that whilst any form of commercial use is forbidden, it does allow them to be used for personal and educational purposes, with appropriate acknowledgment. Most of the 2D and 3D images are of objects that can be identified to specific museums through their accession or collection numbers enabling users to access more information, for instance, from online collections databases, about their acquisition, provenance, date and the cultures they represent. Exceptions to this include the objects originating from private collections and those in rhino horn where this information has been withheld for security reasons. Initial responses to VAHT have been very positive from conservation and curatorial professionals in the museum sector and art world, to CITES and customs, and it is intended that funding will be acquired to develop this pilot web-site and cover the identification features of all the materials in the VAHT image archive.

10.6 Tribute to Rachael Kershaw

Rachael Kershaw was a talented young researcher, archaeologist and illustrator who embraced digital innovations in her practice. As part of the Visualising Heritage team in the School of Archaeological and Forensic Sciences at the University of Bradford, she left her mark on a vast number of visual heritage projects. These included diverse contributions to the Visualising Animal Hard Tissues (VAHT) chapter and other projects mentioned within this book, including Fragmented Heritage, Bradford Visualisation, ENTRANS, Covesea Caves and Wetwang. For VAHT, Rachael helped

Fig. 10.12 Rachael training heritage professionals from the Jordan National Museum and Jordanian Antiquities Department the practice of 3D laser scanning. Image taken as part of the AHRC/ GCRF 'Augmenting Jordanian Heritage' project (AH/P00945X/1) linked to the 'Fragmented Heritage' Digital Transformations Theme Large Grant (AH/L00688X/1).

bring uniformity to the digital images from many disparate sources and in her hands complex annotated rough sketches of tissue structures became clear, consistent and highly informative diagrams (Fig. 10.12).

More recently, she worked for CFA Archaeology on HS2 and other projects. Rachael was an outstanding colleague, always ready to offer help and encouragement, who mastered a bewildering range of hard- and softwares and always went the extra mile. Her sudden death was a terrible shock to us all, and she is sorely missed.

Acknowledgements VAHT was funded through an AHRC-EPSRC Science and Heritage Programme Research Development Award (AH/K006169/1) that developed directly from Sonia O'Connor's AHRC/EPSRC Science & Heritage Programme Fellowship (AH/H032150/1)— *Cultural Materials Worked in Skeletal Hard Tissues* (COWISHT). The project was a collaboration between Visualising Heritage, within the School of Archaeological & Forensic Sciences and the Centre for Visual Computing in the Faculty of Engineering and Informatics at the University of Bradford. The project PI was Andrew Wilson, with Co Is: Sonia O'Connor, Rob Janaway and Hassan Ugail. The COWISHT project and its partner institutions provided many of the 2D images for VAHT and the shortlist of objects for further imaging, which were loaned by the Leeds Museums, Hull Maritime Museum and York Archaeological Trust. We thank Ruth Clarke, Consultant Radiographer and her team for the CT scanning undertaken at Pinderfields Hospital, Mid-Yorks NHS Trust and David Farrar and Kerry Butcher (Smith and Nephew) for the micro-CT imaging.

References

Campbell Pederson M (2004) Gem and ornamental materials of organic origin. Elsevier Butterworth-Heinemann, Oxford

Campbell Pederson M (2015) Ivory. Robert Hale Ltd., London

Cameron E, Greaves P, Northover P, O'Connor S (2013) Royal Forteviot: the recovery, conservation strategy and analysis of a bronze age dagger from a high status cist burial. In: Hyslop E, Gonzalez V, Troalen L, Wilson L (eds) Metal, conference proceedings of the interim meeting of the ICOM-CC metal working group, pp 21–28. Historic Scotland, Edinburgh

Choyke A, O'Connor S (eds) (2013) From these bare bones: raw materials and the study of worked osseous materials. In: Proceedings of the raw materials session at the 11th ICAZ conference, Paris. Oxford, Oxbow

Collins M, Buckley M, Thomas-Oates J, Wilson J, Van Doorn N (2010) ZooMS: the collagen barcode and fingerprints. Spectrosc Eur 22(2):11–13

Coşarcă C, Jocea A, Savu A (2009) Analysis of error sources in terrestrial laser scanning. J Geodesy Cadastre 9(1):115–124

Edwards HGM, O'Connor S (2012) Archaeological ivories: a challenge for analytical Raman spectroscopy. In: Edwards H, Vandenabeele P (eds) Anal Archaeom: Select Top. RSC Publishing, Cambridge, pp 449–467

Espinoza EO, Mann M-J (1992) Identification guide for ivory and ivory substitutes, 2nd edn. World Wildlife Fund and Conservation Foundation, Washington, DC

Fiddyment S, Holsinger B, Ruzzier C, Devine A, Binois A, Albarella U et al (2015) Animal origin of 13th-century uterine vellum revealed using noninvasive peptide fingerprinting. PNAS 112(49):15066–15071. https://doi.org/10.1073/pnas.1512264112

Holland A (2017) Examining the taphonomic challenges to the 3D digitisation of fragmented bone. PhD thesis. University of Bradford

Hornbeck S (2016) Ivory: Identification and regulation of a precious material. https://www.conser
    vation-wiki.com/w/images/5/5a/HornbeckivoryidregarticleR2016.pdf. Accessed 20 June 2020
Krzyszkowska O (1990) Ivory and related materials: an illustrated guide. (Classical Handbook 3,
    Bulletin Supplement 59). Institute of Classical Studies, London
Lemonnier P (1993) Technological choices: transformation in material cultures since the Neolithic.
    Routledge, London and New York
Locke M (2008) Structure of ivory. J Morphol 269:423–450
Locke M (2013) Bone, ivory, and horn: identifying natural materials. Schiffer Publishing, Atglen
O'Connor S (1987) The identification of osseous and keratinaceous materials at York. In: Starling
    K, Watkinson D (eds) Archaeological bone, antler and ivory (Occasional Paper no. 5), pp 9–21.
    United Kingdom Institute for Conservation, London
O'Connor S (2013) Exotic materials used in the construction of Iron Age sword handles from South
    Cave, UK. In: Choyke A, O'Connor S (eds) From these bare bones: raw materials and the study of
    worked osseous objects. Proceedings of the raw materials session at the 11th ICAZ conference,
    Paris, 2010, pp 188–200. Oxbow Books, Oxford
O'Connor S (2015) Discussion on cetacean bone and Appendix IV Identification of Bronze Age
    pommels and other osseous objects. In: Woodward A, Hunter J (eds) Ritual in early Bronze Age
    grave goods (p 53 and Appendix on CD). Oxbow Books, Oxford
O'Connor S (2016) Material identifications: the key to understanding the cultural significance and
    global patterns in raw material selection. In: Proceedings of the raw materials session at the 12th
    ICAZ conference, San Rafael, Argentina, 2014. Cuadernos del Instituto Nacional de Antropología
    y Pensamiento Latinoamericano - Series Especiales 3(2):4–22
O'Connor S (2018) Conservation of bone, horn and ivory. In: López Varela SL (ed) The encyclopedia
    of archaeological sciences. John Wiley and Sons, Inc. https://doi.org/10.1002/9781119188230.
    saseas0115.
O'Connor S, Edwards HGM, Ali E (2011). An interim investigation of the potential of vibrational
    spectroscopy for the dating of cultural objects in ivory. Archaeo Sci 35:159–165. http://journals.
    openedition.org/archeosciences/3091. https://doi.org/10.4000/archeosciences.3091
O'Connor S, Solazzo C, Collins M (2014) Advances in identifying archaeological traces of horn
    and other keratinous hard tissues. Stud Conserv 60(6):393–417. https://doi.org/10.1179/204705
    8414y.0000000134
Penniman TK (1952) Pictures of ivory and other animal teeth, bone and antler (Pitt Rivers Museum
    Occasional Papers on Technology 5). University of Oxford, Oxford
Rijkelijkhuizen M (2008) Handleiding voor de Determinatie van Harde Dierlijke Materialen.
    Amsterdam University Press, Amsterdam
Wilson AS (2014) Digitised diseases: preserving precious remains. Br Archaeol 136:36–41
Wilson AS, Holland AD, Sparrow T (2017a) Chapter 9—Laser scanning of skeletal pathological
    conditions. In: Thompson T, Errickson D (eds) Human remains: another dimension: the applica-
    tion of imaging to the study of human remains, pp 123–134. Academic Press, Cambridge, Mass.
    https://doi.org/10.1016/B978-0-12-804602-9.00010-2
Wilson AS, Manchester K, Buckberry J, Storm R, Croucher KT (2017b) Digitised diseases: seeing
    beyond the specimen to understand disease and disability in the past. In: Tilley L, Schrenk AA
    (eds) New developments in the bioarchaeology of care: further case studies and expanded theory,
    pp 301–315. Springer Nature, Basel

Part III
Digital and Virtual Heritage Research and Applications

Chapter 11
Exploring 222 years in Space and Time: The User Experience of the Virtual Sydney Rocks

Kit Devine

Abstract This chapter examines the Virtual Sydney Rocks (VSR) as a proof of concept and case study of a time-based pedagogical virtual heritage city-world. The VSR consists of an interactive digital model of the historic Sydney Rocks district and an associated website. Users are able to travel freely in space and time to explore the built environment of the Sydney Rocks from 1788 to 2010. Each building is linked to an individual webpage with detailed information and accessed by clicking on the building. Users can also change the speed of time and switch to an overhead view to see a time-lapse. The design, creation and testing of the VSR are described and the findings discussed. The chapter concludes by examining opportunities for deepening public engagement with heritage by crowd-sourcing the co-creation of virtual heritage resources.

Keywords Digital heritage · Virtual heritage · Gaming technology · Virtual worlds

11.1 Introduction

A city can be likened to a living organism with a lifespan of hundreds, sometimes thousands, of years. The ordinary dynamic activities of a city's flora, fauna and human inhabitants are determined by daily, seasonal and cultural rhythms occasionally broken or over-ridden by crises caused by natural disaster, pestilence, famine or war (Devine 2018). The physical geography of each city is unique, determining or at least influencing, the placement of roads, harbours, strongpoints, religious sites and so shaping the human geography of the city (Montefiore 2011). Over time a city develops multiple interwoven layers of history which form intricate and tangled webs of tangible and intangible heritage connecting the architecture of homes, businesses, places of worship, civic buildings, streets, parks and public spaces (Tuan 1977). For a particular inhabitant, or visitor, this rich tapestry is the backdrop that infuses and informs their own particular and individual experience of the city.

K. Devine (✉)
Australian National University, Canberra, Australia
e-mail: kit.devine@anu.edu.au

© Springer Nature Switzerland AG 2022
E. Ch'ng et al. (eds.), *Visual Heritage: Digital Approaches in Heritage Science*,
Springer Series on Cultural Computing,
https://doi.org/10.1007/978-3-030-77028-0_11

Human culture is dynamic and its expression in all its forms, tangible and intangible, is equally dynamic. The built fabric of a city evolves with the conversion or demolition of old buildings and the construction of new ones. The clothing, hairstyles, customs, languages, music, religions and other cultural expressions and behaviours likewise change over time. A city is experienced not simply as a place but as a place in time (Devine 2017). London during the Blitz in 1940 was different from the 'Swinging London' of the 1960s. Even when deserted, the built fabric of a city is subject to the ravages of time and weather and, as was the case with Troy, once a city recedes from living memory the cultural memories of it can be found woven into fable and myth. The temporal nature of cities was recognised by the Scottish sociologist, geographer and pioneering town planner Sir Patrick Geddes when he wrote that a city is 'more than a place in space, it is a drama in time' (Geddes 1905).

While the direct human experience of a city is restricted to a single life-time, the popularity with both locals and visitors of museums such as the Edo-Tokyo Museum in Tokyo, the Musée Carnavalet in Paris, the Museum of the City of New York and the Museum of Sydney reveals a universal, deep and abiding interest in the histories of cities among the general public. These museums use illustrations, dioramas, animations, photographs, film/video and, increasingly, 3D computer graphics to help tell the story of their city. Time is an inherent capability of the various software used to create, animate and deliver interactive 3D computer graphics. It is therefore technically easy to give users control of time and, critically, over the speed of time. The phrase 'a river of ice' is one way to describe a glacier but it can be hard to visualise. However, the term comes vividly to life when you watch a time-lapse of a glacier (Major Glacier Calving Captured In Time-lapse Video 2013). The main difficulty with modelling a city over time is in the amount of research that needs to be done, the inevitable incompleteness of the resulting data, the size of the resulting model and the time it takes to build it. By way of comparison, the city depicted in the commercial game *Grand Theft Auto V* (*GTA 5*) is best described as an expansive world in which numerous stories play out. It is a living city with numerous characters on the pavements and vehicles on the streets, the attention to detail and amount of content is incredible. Game reviewer Hollander Cooper describes GTA 5, as 'absolutely, brutally, amazingly massive, and features so much content you could play for months without seeing it all' (Cooper 2013). It was created over 4 years by a team of 250 people with the production costs put as high as $US265 million (Farnham 2013), and all this was for a single time period. More recently, the game Red Dead Redemption 2 (2018) made with the same attention to detail by Rockstar Games (the games studio that made GTA5), is estimated to have been made by 200 employees over 8.5 years at a rough cost of $US170 million in wages alone (Takehashi 2019).

Heritage is described by Laurajane Smith as a cultural and social process carried out at individual, group and societal levels as a way of creating, representing, and negotiating identity (Smith 2006). Heritage visualisations are products of the 'Cultural Imaginary,' a term used to describe the production, identification, and reproduction of culture. Given the fragmentary nature of the archaeological record, and the equally fragmentary and sometime contradictory nature of the archival record, heritage visualisations will never be able to show the past exactly as it was (Devine

2019). Additionally, they are firmly rooted in, and shaped by, the time and circumstance of their creation. However, despite these caveats, they help the public to connect to the past by showing them a 'best-guess-given-what-we-know-now' idea of what it might have been like which is presented in ways intended to capture the imagination.

An individual's experience of a real heritage place is the gestalt of the primary sensory impression of the place itself, the cultural associations of the place and the individual's unique personal history and perspective (Tuan 1977). 3D environments, while unable to fully replicate the sensory experience of place, are well-known for being able to evoke a sense of 'presence' in users (Lombard and Ditton 1997). The term 'presence' refers to the sense of 'being there' where 'there' is inside the virtual world depicted on the screen and it has become a field of research in its own right. Interactive heritage visualisations therefore have the potential to be powerful vehicles for creating affect in heritage users by giving them a feeling of being inside the world on the screen and so fostering the creation of meaningful connections with heritage content.

11.2   Background

Sydney, being less than 250 years old, is comparatively young when compared with most major world cities. Additionally, and again unlike most capital cities, Sydney's beginning is extremely well documented (Karskens 2009). Any government project will generate paperwork and the establishment of a penal colony is no exception. As well as the 11 surviving first-hand accounts by members of the First Fleet (Cobley 1987; Irvine 1988) and copious archival text-based records, there are the not insignificant number of maps, drawings and paintings created in the early years of the colony (Di Tommaso 2012). Beginning with the First Fleet which arrived in Sydney Cove on the 26th January 1788, the transportation of British convicts to Sydney continued until 1840 by which time the population of Sydney was made of a mixture of convicts, emancipated convicts, free settlers and their descendants. In 1851, the announcement of the discovery of gold in New South Wales sparked a huge influx of people and the population of Sydney nearly doubled in 10 years, growing from 54,000 in 1851 to 96,000 in 1861 (Turnbull 1999). There have been many waves of emigration since and Sydney is now home to a multi-ethnic population approaching 5 million. Sydney Cove is no longer a sheltered cove with a small sandy beach and stream providing a safe harbour and fresh water for a small penal colony but a busy transport hub for ferries and trains flanked by the iconic Sydney Opera House and Sydney Harbour Bridge. The development of photography in the mid-1850s, cinema in the 1890s and digital cameras in the 1980s has resulted in the creation of numerous still and moving images which collectively visually document the ever-changing built environment of Sydney, and the evolving fashions and habits of its inhabitants.

In 1994, an archaeological excavation in the historic Sydney Rocks district of Sydney, uncovered the foundations of over 30 homes and shops dating back to 1795 and over 750,000 artefacts. The dig, known as the Big Dig, was a 20-week-long excavation of a site between Gloucester Street and Cumberland Street that had for many years been used by the Sydney Cove Authority for storage and as a car park (Fig. 11.1). The dig was carried out by a team of 20 archaeologists, assisted by over 400 volunteers, and a parallel investigation of archival records was undertaken by a team of historians. It proved possible to identify individual people and connect them with particular buildings, and in some cases particular items, uncovered during the dig (Karskens 1999). Given the wealth of data, both archaeological and archival, associated with the Big Dig project, the importance of the site to the history of Sydney and the relatively short time period of less than 230 years, it was an ideal subject to use for a proof of concept time-based heritage resource which would enable users to explore a part of a city at specific times of their choosing and also, by using time-lapses, to see the changes in a city over time.

Fig. 11.1 The Big Dig site in the Sydney Rocks (marked in red); *source* Microsoft Bing Maps

11.3 The Virtual Big Dig

While lacking the resources to create a city as richly detailed as the ones in current state-of-the-art computer games it was possible, using the archaeological and archival data uncovered during the Big Dig project, to build detailed models of most of the buildings for the Big Dig site and create a supporting website which would allow users to explore the Big Dig site in space and time, and easily access additional information about buildings by clicking on them. Many of the buildings on the site had been demolished in the early 1900s as part of a slum clearance program by the New South Wales State government but, prior to demolition, they were photographed and detailed plans were made by the State Architect's office (Figs. 11.2 and 11.3). In total there were architectural plans and photographs for 20 of the 30 homes and shops on the Big Dig site. These buildings were re-created in high resolution and texture mapped, with opening and closing doors and internal walls and staircases (Figs. 11.4, 11.5, 11.6 and 11.7).

The buildings were modelled and textured using Autodesk Maya software (an industry standard 3D modelling and animation program) and then exported to

Fig. 11.2 The Whaler's Arms 1901 courtesy of the NSW state archives and records (Digital Id: 4481_a026_000033)

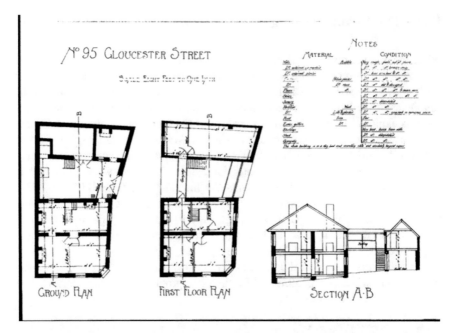

Fig. 11.3 Plan and side elevations for the Whaler's Arms NSW government architect 'plans and photographs of buildings demolished 1902–1907' courtesy of the Mitchell Library

Fig. 11.4 VSR 1: The Whalers Arms

Fig. 11.5 VSR 2: Gloucester Street 1851

Fig. 11.6 VSR 2: The King House and The Bird in Hand pub, Gloucester Street 1851

Dassault Systèmes Virtools game engine where various scripts were added to control when each building was displayed, and interactions such as the opening and closing of doors. An interface was written that allowed users to set the time, date and speed of time. The position and direction of the sunlight was controlled by the date and time, creating the correct seasonal variations for Sydney. There was a background

Fig. 11.7 VSR2: Rear view of the butcher's shop and the Bird in Hand pub 1822

audio track which played a different audio track for different historical periods. Users were able to explore at will in a first perspective fashion familiar to players of First-Person-Shooter (FPS) games. Users could also switch views to a fixed overhead camera which gave a bird's eye view of the entire model and which was recommended when viewing a time-lapse.

The 11 ships of the First Fleet and several others from later historical periods were very roughly modelled, positioned in Sydney Cove and made visible for their relevant time periods. Clicking on a building or ship opened a webpage for the relevant building or ship which provided a short summary of information about it and, where relevant, links to further information on reputable websites such as the Dictionary of Sydney. Pages were also created for particular people, such as George Cribb, who were connected to buildings on the Big Dig site.

11.4   The Virtual Sydney Rocks

While researching and modelling the buildings on the Big Dig site the author discovered that, regardless of the orientation of the streets, all of the early houses faced the harbour. While a harbour view is undeniably a thing of beauty, it must also be remembered that, until the rise in air travel from the 1950s onwards and the widespread adoption of shipping containers in the 1960s and 1970s, the harbour played a pivotal role in the economic, cultural and social life of Sydney with each ship bringing news, people, goods for sale and opportunities for work and trade. Sydney Cove and the harbour beyond were clearly visible from the Big Dig site for the first hundred years

Fig. 11.8   Extent of the Virtual Sydney Rocks. *Source* Microsoft Bing Maps

and even today glimpses can be caught between buildings and over rooftops. The central importance of the Harbour to life in the Rocks demanded its inclusion in an interactive visualisation that sought to evoke a sense of presence in users by giving them a feeling of what the Rocks might have been like at a particular time. The author decided that the area being modelled would have to be expanded to include a view of Sydney Cove. Figure 11.8 shows the Big Dig site in red and the extent of the Virtual Sydney Rocks, bounded to the North by Sydney Cove, to the South by Bridge Street and to East and West by the two ridges that run South-North down to the Harbour and end in the points on either side of Sydney Cove, one with the southern end of the Sydney Harbour Bridge and the other the site of the Sydney Opera House. This expansion involved the creation of over 200 additional buildings, more than 50% of which date back to the 1850s and are heritage listed, and the creation of an individual webpage for each one with links to more detailed related information on reputable sites such as the Heritage and Conservation Register, the Dictionary of Sydney, the New South Wales Office of Environment and Heritage and the Australian Dictionary of Biography. While the models of the Big Dig buildings were built with internal walls, doors and stairways and texture mapped, it was impossible for the author to research and model the surrounding area to the same level of detail. The additional

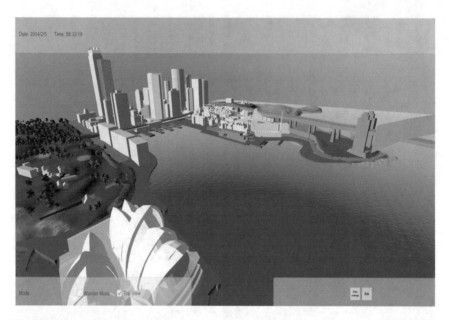

Fig. 11.9 Virtual Sydney Rocks 2.0

buildings were simply modelled to the correct external shape and size with no internal detail or external texture mapping (Fig. 11.9).

Weather can be a major contributor to the experience of place so five different weather environments were developed. These were delivered sequentially so that the first day of the month was sunny with blue skies, the second day was sunny with clouds, the third day was overcast, the fourth day was overcast with light rain and the fifth day was overcast with heavy rain, on the sixth day it was sunny with blue skies, on the seventh day sunny with clouds and so on.

11.4.1 Design Considerations

Visitors to real heritage places usually have a range of different ways to experience them including guided tours, free roaming and cultural activities such as music, dance and food related events. The author decided to support three different user interactions modes consisting of a tour, a game and free exploration in time and space. Story-telling is a long established way of connecting people in the present to life in the past, so the tour and the game both focussed on the story of George Cribb who came to Sydney as a convict and had a rags-to-riches-to-rags story with added spices of bigamy and crime (Karskens 1999). Cribb, a butcher by trade, arrived in Sydney as a convict aboard the *Admiral Gambier* in 1808, having been sentenced to 14 years transportation for being found in possession of forged banknotes. He began buying land and by 1813, he owned about half of the Big Dig site, made up of a row of property on Gloucester Street including a butcher's shop and a two-storey hotel, and the land behind which he used for a stockyard and slaughterhouse. He also kept racehorses, owned land on the Cumberland plain in the Minto district and supplied provisions such as meat, wheat, vegetables to ships and to the government stores. In 1811, he married fellow convict Fanny Barnet and they lived in a new two-storey house on the corner of what is now Gloucester Street and Cribb's Lane. However, in 1814, his first wife Martha (also known as Mary and still married to him), heard that he was doing well and left England to come to Sydney to join him. George paid Fanny three hundred pounds (about ten times the annual salary of a skilled housekeeper) to leave Sydney and return to England. In 1818 Martha died and he married again, this time to Sophia Lett, a widow with five children. Sophia left him in 1823, for his nephew.

George had continual brushes with the law in Australia. In 1812, he was arrested on charges of attempting to smuggle rum. The charges were unproven but the rum, his cart and his horse were all confiscated. He was fined for illegally selling meat in 1819. He was accused of stealing cattle and bribing a witness in 1823, and again in 1827 when he was raided, but he managed to avoid conviction. However, in 1821, he lost a number of civil suits and had to re-mortgage his properties. By 1824, he had lost them all except for the corner house to creditors. George sold the house in the same year and the last record of him was a court appearance for cattle theft in Parramatta in 1830. A trace of him remains as Cribb's Lane, a small laneway running off Gloucester Street. Some of the artefacts recovered from a filled-in well at the back of George Cribb's house during the Big Dig excavation have been linked directly to George Cribb's occupancy. These include a boning knife from the period when the slaughterhouse was in operation, some broken china bowls and an alcohol still, also dated to the Cribb's occupancy.

The game was a treasure-hunt game where players had to travel in time and space to find the boning knife, the china bowls and the alcohol still in different parts of the Cribb's property, at different periods of his occupancy. When they found each object, they were told related details about George's life. The bowls could be found on top of a dresser in the Cribb's house between 1813 and 1814. Players would then be told about George's private life. Given the nearly intact nature of the bowls when excavated, it has been speculated that Fanny may have thrown the 'good china' away so that Martha/Mary could not use it. The still could be found hidden in one of the stables that existed at the back of the house from 1810 to 1825. After finding it players would find out about George's various brushes with the law. The boning knife could be found on a chopping board in the backyard of the butcher's shop between 1817 and 1825. After finding it players would be told about George's background as a butcher and about the stockyard and butcher's shop he established on the site. The Tour consisted of a pre-recorded video that described the life of George Cribb while showing his house and properties and it concluded by showing a time-lapsed aerial view of the Sydney Rocks from 1788 to 2010.

Testing was carried out in 2013 at the Rocks Discovery Museum, a small museum dedicated to local history located in a heritage-listed building in the Rocks. The museum attracts a wide range of visitors of all ages and nationalities, including international, interstate and local tourists, school parties as well as individuals with a specific interest in the Rocks. The VSR was set up in the same room as a glass cabinet that contained items recovered from the Cribb's well including the china bowls, the alcohol still and the butcher's knife that featured in the George Cribb game. Over the course of a week museum visitors were invited to try out the VSR with the author acting as docent. After testing the objects were pointed out to testers to connect the virtual content of the VSR with real tangible objects that were physically present. Testers were then asked to fill in a questionnaire. Video and keystroke recording would not give the qualitative feedback that the author wanted and, as over three-quarters of the visitors to the Rocks Discovery Museum are from interstate or overseas, follow-up in-depth interviews were impossible (SHFA 2011).

The author used a mixed methods single questionnaire as this would yield both quantitative data and qualitative data (Driscoll et al. 2007). A key concern was not to impose too great a time burden on testers. Research into museum visitors indicates that 30–40 min is an average time for them to engage with museum content (Hein 1998). The Tour ran for 4 minutes, the Game took between 3 and 5 minutes to play and the author assumed that people would spend at least 3–5 minutes in self-directed exploring. This meant that a tester who tried all three would already have spent at least 15 minutes engaged with the VSR. The questionnaire was designed so that someone could answer the multiple-choice questions in less than 5 minutes but there was ample space for respondents to elaborate on their responses in depth if they wished to. This resulted in a rough estimate of about 25 min in total for testers who used all three modes and who also gave answers to the open response qualitative questions as well as to the multiple-choice quantitative questions.

The questionnaire began with demographic questions about age, sex and occupation followed by three questions about computer and computer game usage. These were followed by 21 numbered questions specifically to do with the VSR and the supporting website. There were six questions related to the interaction modes of Tour, Game and Explore asking testers which modes they had tried, which mode was best and would they recommend doing them in a particular order. There were 12 questions to do with Place, Presence, History and Culture. These examined the temporal, spatial and cultural immersion experienced by users in the different interaction modes and the opportunities for insight and understanding afforded by time-lapses. Finally, testers were asked to nominate their most-liked and least-liked features and suggest improvements. For all these questions testers had the opportunity to elaborate on their answers. The results are summarised below, for the complete report and analysis the author directs interested readers to Chap. 5 of her doctoral thesis (Devine 2016).

11.5 Results

Fifty-six questionnaires were returned, one of which contained data for three individuals, giving a total of 58 individuals. The respondents represented a wide range of ages (see Fig. 11.10), and professions, and an almost even number of each sex. The museum audience in general is equally wide-ranging in size and background (Falk and Dierking 2000) so the author argues that the sample size, though on the small side, is representative. The respondents were overwhelmingly familiar with computers and nearly two-thirds were currently, though to differing degrees, players of electronic games. Thirty-one of the 58 respondents reported trying all three of the interaction modes of Game, Tour and Explore and, for the other 17 respondents, the least tried mode was the Game (see Fig. 11.11).

Testers were asked to write down the two things they liked most about the Virtual Sydney Rocks and the following recurring themes were identified in the responses: navigable time (including time-lapse), navigable space and interactivity, content quality and quantity, game, connection of the game items with the real items in the

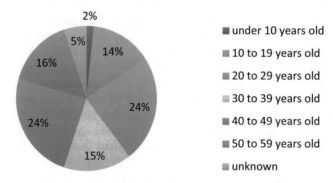

Fig. 11.10 Participant age

Fig. 11.11 Interaction modes tried—all 58 respondents

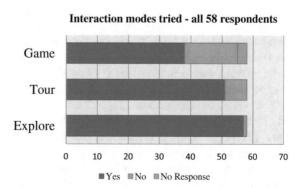

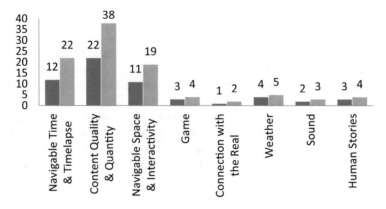

Fig. 11.12 Write down the two things you liked most about the Virtual Sydney Rocks

museum, interactivity, weather, soundtrack and human stories. Figure 11.12 shows that content quantity and quality was the most-liked feature of the VSR. The second and third most-liked features were the affordances of navigable time and navigable space. Some of the individual responses are examined in detail below.

For all respondents, the most popular feature was the quantity and quality of the data that they had access to. The VSR can be likened to an iceberg where the visible part is just the tip and the data accessed via the webpages is the much larger bulk hidden below the surface. Many respondents commented upon the depth and authority of the information they could access, and which had informed the creation of the digital model. Comments include 'Depth of Information' (Respondent 1), 'The accuracy of the history' (Respondent 17), 'Access to information, images etc.' (Respondent 23), 'Information about the history is great!'(Respondent 30), 'The info given when clicking on things' (Respondent 33), 'The information available through the program' (Respondent 34), 'Accuracy of model' (Respondent 43), 'Comprehensiveness and detail' (Respondent 44), 'Links to websites' (Respondent 46) and 'The ability to zoom around & easily link to snippets/background of history' (Respondent 38).

Navigable time and navigable space were the second and third most popular things nominated by respondents. Navigable time was mentioned by 12 respondents and navigable space by 11. Comments included 'The time shifting' (Respondent 4), 'The build up from start to end in speed 7' (Respondent 14), 'Being able to travel in time' (Respondent 15), 'I loved seeing the developments of the city's landscape by year—time travel YES!' (Respondent 26), 'Control of timing functionality' (Respondent 31), 'Seeing change over time' (Respondent 39) and 'Watching how it developed over time' (Respondent 46). The comments relating to navigable space included 'Sense of movement' (Respondent 19), 'I like the interactivity - being able to open doors, walk up steps etc.' (Respondent 20), 'Being able to navigate around and go inside buildings' (Respondent 24), 'Exploring the laneways in the game' (Respondent 36),

Which way of interacting was most effective at showing you how the Sydney Rocks has changed over time?

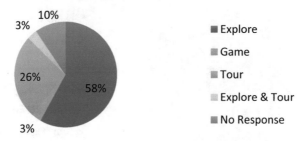

Fig. 11.13 Which way of interacting was most effective at showing you how the Sydney Rocks has changed over time? (from respondents who tried all 3 modes)

'Entering the house of G. Cribb' (Respondent 36) and 'Exploring areas' (Respondent 39). Two Respondents conflated the two and simply said 'Being able to move around in space and time' (Respondent 17) and 'Go to anywhere at any time' (Respondent 37).

For users who tried all three modes, the Explore mode (58%) was the clear favourite for showing change over time (Fig. 11.13). This may be because in the Explore mode, unlike the Tour mode, the time-lapse is under the user's control. The Tour mode still managed to be nominated as the most effective by just over a quarter of users. It is unsurprising that the Game attracted such little attention as the time travel in the Game is over a relatively short time-span during which there are few obvious changes beyond the building of some stables on the Big Dig site. A different game that features time travel to more widely separated times might produce quite different results.

However, when asked which mode was best with regard to learning the history of the Rocks, user preference was more evenly split between the Tour (32%) and Explore (37%) modes (see Fig. 11.14). Whichever mode was preferred, respondents gave considered reasons for their preferences. One person preferred the Explore mode because it 'Covers more of the area from first person perspective and gives more information about each specific part of the Rocks. Also lets me play with different time periods and observe the changes.' Another preferred the Game because 'it was fun and interactive and informative' and a third person preferred the Tour because she 'Enjoyed the guidance and the added information about Mr Cribb—Made it more personal and engaging.' These responses reveal that museum visitors have strong individual preferences for different interaction modes when they engage with virtual heritage and that there is no single interaction mode that works best for a majority of users.

Respondents were asked to indicate which mode of interaction they liked the most and why. The Explore mode was the most-liked with just under four in ten respondents

Which way of interacting helped you learn most about the history of the Sydney Rocks?

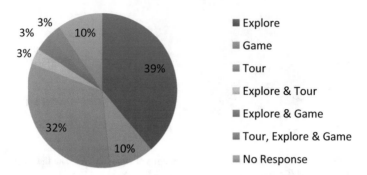

Fig. 11.14 Which way of interacting was most effective at showing you how the Sydney Rocks has changed over time?

(39%) nominating it. The Game mode was the second most-liked mode with three in ten respondents (32%) choosing it and the Tour mode was the third most-liked mode with just over two in ten respondents (23%) choosing it. One respondent indicated that they preferred all three and another that they preferred the Game and Explore modes best. Figure 11.15 shows that while there was a preference for the Explore mode, there was no mode which was preferred by a majority of all users.

Nearly one in four users (14 out of 58) chose not to play the game but tried both the tour and explore options and completed the questionnaire. Of these respondents, two were in their 30s, five in their 40s, two in their 50s, and one supplied no age data (Fig. 11.16). Nine were female, five were male and all of them reported using computers daily. Seven played games at least once a month and seven did not play

Most Liked Interaction Mode by the 31 respondents who tried all three modes

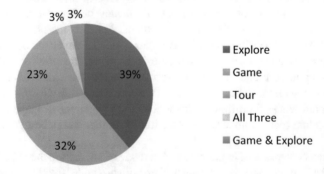

Fig. 11.15 Most-Liked Interaction Mode by the 31 respondents who tried all three modes

Age of participants who did not play the Game

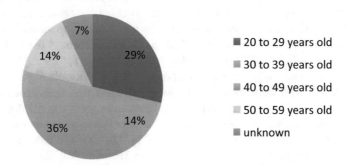

Fig. 11.16 Age of participants who did not play the Game

any games. Given the current enthusiasm for gamification in teaching and learning, the lack of interest in the game option in these users is an interesting finding and indicates that game-focussed virtual heritage may not appeal to a large minority of museum audiences. However, given the small sample size, and the positive feedback from respondents who did play the Game, further research is clearly indicated.

11.6 Discussion

As noted earlier, museums have a long history of using illustrations and dioramas to help audiences engage more deeply with heritage and foster historical understanding, insight and learning. Virtual heritage is part of this pedagogical tradition and, while virtual heritage places can match neither the physical and cultural immersion, nor the phenomenological and cultural affect, of real heritage places they can engender connection, insight and understanding in museum audiences. The ability of virtual environments to engender a sense of 'being there' makes them particularly well suited to heritage pertaining to place.

Additionally, all aspects of human culture, both tangible and intangible, are dynamic, as is the natural world. Time-based virtual heritage is able to capture this dynamism in both the phenomenological and cultural aspects of virtual place. It supports the inclusion of time-specific content that contributes to the sense of an experience of a place at a particular time for example birds singing a dawn chorus, calls to prayer by muezzin or church bell, rush hour traffic or cherry blossom. Additionally, time-lapsed virtual heritage, by showing changes in the built environment over timescales outside of normal human experience, allows heritage audiences to gain insight and understanding of historical processes, opening up a dialogic engagement with heritage itself.

A perennial problem with any digital project is obsolescence. The author began creating the VSR in 2008 while based at the iCinema Centre for Interactive Research. She chose 3DVIA Virtools software for the development environment because it was being used by the iCinema team. As she was a part-time student, the project proceeded slowly and towards the final stages of development of the VSR, Virtools was discontinued. The VSR was quickly finished enough for testing but after that there was no point to any further development using the Virtools platform.

The VSR was ported to Unity in 2016 by Wanqi Zhao, a computer science student at ANU, and used as a game world for an interactive game she developed for her Honours research project which explored the effect of fantasy elements on the acquisition of historical knowledge (Zhao et al. 2019). The time and date set by the user were used to set the relevant parameters of the Tenkoku Dynamic Sky System (a plugin for Unity) which controlled the positions of the sun, moon, planets and starfields. A script was used to set the various weather variables for cloud cover and rain so that the weather varied from day to day in a similar fashion to the Virtools version (Fig. 11.17).

In 2018, the website was re-built by the author and all the links checked and updated where necessary and new ones were researched and added. (The dynamic nature of the web means that a resource like the supporting website for the VSR, which acts as an aggregator of information, needs regular maintenance.) At the same time, the old polygon terrain was replaced with Unity terrain which enabled the easy addition of ground textures and trees and other vegetation, additional buildings were added, and individual webpages created. Unity builds of this version, VSR 2.0, only support the Explore mode, and is freely available on application to the author.

Fig. 11.17 Gloucester Street 1839, Virtual Sydney Rocks 2.0

11.7 Conclusion

The author continues to develop the VSR and there will be periodic updates. Using the weather records kept during 1788 by the fledgling colony, she has created a spreadsheet which will be used to recreate the weather for 1788. She has begun to explore a crowd-sourcing approach to the creation of additional content. There are over 30 other buildings in the Rocks for which, prior to their demolition, the NSW Government Architect's Office drew up detailed plans along with descriptions and photographs in a similar fashion as was done for the Whalers Arms and many of the other buildings on the Big Dig site (see images 2 and 3). She is reaching out to students in disciplines such as architecture, digital humanities, 3D modelling and animation, as well as interested members of the public, and asking them to create 3D models for the VSR, for which they will be fully credited. The author will also be pitching further development of the VSR as a project to students taking part in the Australian National University's Techlauncher program. This is an initiative which enables students to work on a project that develops the research and professional skills required to use technology to bring great ideas to life and have a positive impact on society. The students work closely with outside partners to complete projects addressing complex problems in a variety of disciplines and industries, or to create their own start-up enterprises. The author is very interested to see how the crowdsourcing and the Techlauncher initiatives will develop over time, and how the co-creation of heritage assets might affect the public's engagement with heritage.

GTA5 and, to a lesser extent, the Assassin's Creed series of games, show what is technically possible when using computer gaming technologies to create richly detailed, expansive, populated and interactive virtual worlds. However, for game developers their first commitment is to gameplay, not to historical accuracy (From the Garden into the City Blog 2012). For heritage visualisers with small to non-existent budgets, the VSR is an example of a sandbox project which supports ongoing development (in the form of additional content such as people and animals, ferries, trains, trams, cars and bicycles, of specific events such as the burning down of the Garden Palace in 1882 and the stories of specific individuals) and related research opportunities, which can be developed as and when resources become available. It is a project that gives insight not only into the particular heritage of the Sydney Rocks but also into heritage as cultural practice.

References

Cobley J (1987) Sydney cove 1788. Angus & Robinson, Sydney

Cooper H (2013) Grand theft auto V review. http://www.gamesradar.com/gta-5-review/. Accessed 13 Dec 2013

Devine K (2016) Testing times: virtual heritage, 'time travel' and the user experience of museum visitors: a case study of an enriched time-based virtual heritage world. Australian National University, Canberra

Devine K (2017) Sense of place: the phenomenology of virtual heritage place. In: Paper presented at the iv2017: 21st international conference information visualisation, London, UK, 11–14 July 2017

Devine K (2018) A drama in time: the life of a city. In: Gago da Câmara A, Bottaini C, Alves D, Murteira H, Barreira H, Botelho ML et al (eds) Lost and transformed cities: a digital perspective, pp 173–184. CITCEM, Porto

Devine K (2019) Grey area: the interpretive nature of heritage visualisation. In: Paper presented at the IV2019: 23rd international conference information visualisation., Paris, France, 2–5 July

Di Tommaso L (2012) The art of the first fleet. Hardie Grant Books, Richmond, Victoria

Driscoll D, Appiah-Yeboah A, Salib P, Rupert DJ (2007) Merging qualitative and quantitative data in mixed methods research: how to and why not. Ecol Environ Anthropol 3(1)

Falk JH, Dierking LD (2000) Learning from Museums: visitor experiences and the making of meaning (American Association for State and Local History Series). Altamira Press, Walnit Creek

Farnham A (2013). Grand theft auto V making shareholders, creators rich. http://abcnews.go.com/Business/grand-theft-auto-videogame-making-people-rich/story?id=20308009. Accessed 15 July 2020

From the Garden into the City Blog (2012) Early Ottoman constantinople: preliminary thoughts on the 'assassin's creed revelations' rendition. https://fromthegardenintothecity.wordpress.com/about/. Accessed 15th July 2020

Geddes P (1905) Civics: as applied sociology. In: Sociological papers, vol II. Macmillan & Co, London

Hein GE (1998) Learning in the Museum (2005 ed.). Routledge

Irvine N (ed) (1988) The Sirius letters: the complete letters of Newton Fowell, midshipman and lieutenant aboard the Sirius flagship of the first fleet on its voyage to New South Wales. Fairfax Library, Sydney

Karskens G (1999) Inside the rocks: the archaeology of a neighbourhood. Hale & Iremonger, Sydney

Karskens G (2009) The colony: a history of early Sydney. Allen & Unwin, Sydney

Lombard M, Theresa D (1997) At the heart of it all: the concept of presence. J Comput-Med Commun 3(2):0

James T (2013) Major glacier calving captured in time-lapse video https://www.youtube.com/watch?v=ovMhspvwpmw. Accessed 15th July 2020

Montefiore SS (2011) Jerusalem: the biography. Weidenfeld & Nicolson, London

SHFA (2011) Rocks discovery museum postcode trial 10 Oct 2011–10 Dec 2011

Smith L (2006) Uses of heritage. Routledge, Oxford

Takehashi D (2019) Red dead redemption 2 sells massive 23 million copies, but Take-Two stock still falls 13%. VentureBeat.com https://venturebeat.com/2019/02/06/red-dead-redemption-2-gallops-to-23-million-copies-in-a-quarter-stock-falls-13/. Accessed 15th July 2020

Tuan Y-F (1977) Space and place: the perspective of experience. Universtiy of Minnesota, Minneapolis

Turnbull LH (1999) Sydney: biography of a city. Historic Houses Trust of New South Wales, Sydney

Zhao W, Devine K, Gardner H (2019) Fantasy gaming and virtual heritage. In: Paper presented at the 2019 IEEE conference on virtual reality and 3D user interfaces (VR), Osaka, Japan

Chapter 12
The Europe's Lost Frontiers Augmented Reality Sandbox: Explaining a 2.5 Million Euro Project Using Play Sand

Philip Murgatroyd, Micheál Butler, and Vincent Gaffney

Abstract The subject area of the Europe's Lost Frontiers project, the submerged landscape of Doggerland, is inaccessible and the data by which we can understand it is complex and hard for the non-specialist to understand. To be able to present the project at public events, an Augmented Reality sandbox was constructed, which records the shape of sand in a box, interprets it as a landscape inhabited by humans, animals and plants, and projects this simulated land back on to the sand. Different software packages can be used to highlight the effects of climate change or provide examples of the different types of evidence available to archaeologists researching submerged landscapes. The end result is an interactive, accessible display which attracts all ages and can be used as a starting point to conversation regarding the project's archaeological, scientific and technological aspects.

Keywords Augmented reality · Doggerland · Agent-based modelling · Submerged landscapes · Climate change

12.1 Introduction

Europe's Lost Frontiers (ELF) is a five-year (2015–2020), multi-disciplinary project to investigate the Holocene landscapes of the southern North Sea, funded by a €2,500,000 ERC Advanced Grant. It uses data from seismic geophysics and core samples taken from the seabed in order to study the environmental changes that occurred within the inundating landscape and the possible effects these might have on the human population. As the project data consists of seismic geophysics and core samples (Fig. 12.1), presenting the project to the public involves overcoming some significant obstacles. The seismic data involves very large data sets and is often difficult to interpret. The core samples are visually unimpressive, hard to transport and are required to be in controlled conditions to preserve the integrity of samples taken from then for analysis.

P. Murgatroyd (✉) · M. Butler · V. Gaffney
University of Bradford, Bradford, UK
e-mail: P.Murgatroyd@Bradford.ac.uk

E. Ch'ng et al. (eds.), *Visual Heritage: Digital Approaches in Heritage Science*,
Springer Series on Cultural Computing,
https://doi.org/10.1007/978-3-030-77028-0_12

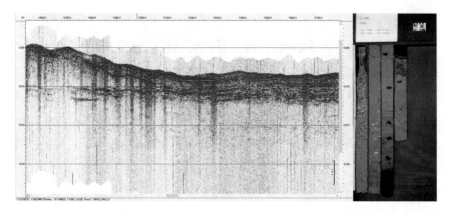

Fig. 12.1 2D seismic data and a photo showing a cross section of core ELF002 (Europe's Lost Frontiers Project)

The project also contains a computer simulation component, where models are made to test hypotheses regarding the inundated Holocene landscape of the southern North Sea, an area known as Doggerland, and its effects on the human population. Computer simulation provides a way to bridge the gap between the large-scale seismic data and the small, but data-rich, points obtained from coring. These computer models allow the incorporation of relevant data collected from other periods and areas to provide a testing ground for our hypotheses. We can put together a model of a landscape and its environment and subject it to the effects of different models of climate change to assess the differences in the effects of each one. We can then look for signals in the seismic and core data that may indicate how the environment of Doggerland may have changed through time.

These models, however, are built with specific purposes in mind and are often not meant to be interacted with in real time. They also do not need to be visually interesting or accessible to non-specialists. Their primary aim is to answer scientific questions, not look good or be fun. This means that, between the simulations, the cores and the seismic data, the project has no obviously engaging way of presenting our research to the public beyond traditional methods such as illustrated talks.

In 2015, some members of the Europe's Lost Frontiers team were working as part of the Stonehenge Hidden Landscapes Project and presented a display as part of the Royal Society Summer Science Exhibition. As part of this display, an Augmented Reality (AR) sandbox was used to illustrate the effects of different types of geophysics. This proved very popular with a whole range of visitors, from school children to pensioners and from scientists to those with no previous knowledge of geophysics.

This success prompted the creation of another AR sandbox (Fig. 12.2) for the Europe's Lost Frontiers project to enable our participation in public events and to act as a starting point for discussion about a range of different aspects of the project. We wanted to be able to use the visual appeal of the AR sandbox across all ages

Fig. 12.2 The AR sandbox running the ELF dynamic system (Europe's Lost Frontiers Project)

that had previously been noticed at the Royal Society Summer Science Exhibition to communicate the role of computer simulation within the wider Europe's Lost Frontiers project. The addition of a visually interesting, interactive exhibit was intended to allow us to take part in public events we might otherwise have little to contribute to.

12.2 Background

AR differs from Virtual Reality (VR) in that it contains a physical component, coupled with the virtual. These can either be directly combined, as in the projection of data onto the sand of the sandbox, or virtual objects can be mixed with video footage of the real world, as in mobile applications such as Pokemon Go. Although considered a relatively new technology dating to the 1990s (Berryman 2012), as a concept it has been around since at least the 1940s, with the first recognised augmented reality system being developed in 1968 by Ivan Sutherland (Sutherland 1968).

An early example of such an approach, although using clay instead of sand, is the 'Illuminating Clay' interface, where the manipulation of the clay allows for the change in the depth projection (Piper et al. 2002). The clay model is placed on a platform in the centre of the projection space, with the remaining outer areas being used to project cross sections, and landscape analysis tools which also update as the clay is manipulated. Landscape analysis functions include slope, view-shed, least cost path, water flow and erosion.

The AR sandbox was first developed by the University of California-Davis, to simulate water flow across landscapes (Kreylos et al. 2016). In teaching and learning, the use of AR sandboxes have also been applied to soil science, for example, at the University of Wyoming, as part of introductory soil science labs. This use as a teaching aid in the geosciences is a popular use of AR sandboxes, as they enable students to understand the links between 3D objects, and their 2D counterparts, acting as an interface between what is viewed on a computer screen and physical models (Woods et al. 2016). Although uses thus far are limited, and are mostly used for demonstrating hydraulic action across a landscape (Reed et al. 2014), their uses and applications are expanding. It has been suggested that present numbers exceed 150 globally, which is perhaps a conservative estimate (Kundu et al. 2017). AR sandboxes are also being developed for entertainment and therapeutic purposes (Roo et al. 2017).

From an archaeological perspective, the use of AR generally is becoming more commonplace, especially in the cultural heritage sector, with an early example being *Archeoguide* (Vlahakis et al. 2002), tested at Olympia, allowing the users to view 3D reconstructions of the archaeology which include audio narration, and virtual avatar animations. However, there are only a few instances of AR sandboxes with specifically archaeological content. The *Archaeological Sandbox* is one example which was developed to be used as an interactive user interface to investigate the contexts where artefacts have been recovered on sites supplementary to museum exhibits. A map of the archaeological site is projected onto the sand, with locations marked as hints. Digging at these will reveal information on that location and artefacts recovered (Biefang et al. 2017).

12.3   Methodology

12.3.1   Hardware

The design of the sandbox hardware follows the blueprint set out by the UC Davis AR Sandbox (Reed et al. n.d.). The equipment consists of a Microsoft Xbox Kinect v1 controller, a Benq short-throw LCD projector, a PC, a box containing play sand and aluminium framing that allows the Kinect and projector to be suspended over the sand (Fig. 12.3).

The Kinect is attached to the aluminium framing by a bespoke 3D printed part produced by the University of Bradford's Visualising Heritage team. The projector is attached via a standard projector ceiling mount and is positioned by two wooden spacers to take some of the strain from the mount (Fig. 12.4).

The equipment is mounted on a sturdy trolley for easy transportation. The aluminium struts holding the Kinect and projector can be easily removed from the

Fig. 12.3 The AR sandbox on its trolley (Europe's Lost Frontiers Project)

Fig. 12.4 The mountings for the projector and Kinect (Europe's Lost Frontiers Project)

box to facilitate transport as the whole apparatus is too tall to fit through regular office doors otherwise. Two large bags of play sand were used to provide enough depth in the box to enable interesting landscapes to be produced. The UC Davis team added a small amount of water to their sand to facilitate modelling but we found that dry sand worked well for our purposes as the softer slopes of dry sand created land surfaces which were smoother and presented fewer registration problems between the image and the sand. We also avoided having to seal the wooden elements of the box to prevent mould growth. The lack of necessity for a registration setup procedure, as is present in the UC Davis sandbox software, simplifies the software and shortens the setup time. There are areas in which the image does not perfectly line up with the sand, but these seem to go largely unnoticed by users.

The sand can be emptied in around 10 min using a scoop into heavy-duty plastic bags, but these are heavy and awkward to transport and this is only done when transporting the sandbox offsite. The whole equipment fits easily into a small van.

12.3.2 Software

The software running on the PC consists of several different elements. Our PC is a HP desktop with 8 Gb RAM, a 230 Gb HDD and an Intel Core i5 650 processor running at 3.2 GHz. It runs Windows 7 as an operating system and contains the following software packages:

Java SE SDK v8u161
The J4K Java library (Barmpoutis 2013)
Eclipse SDE
The ELF Sandbox software.

The ELF Sandbox software is available via a publicly available Github repository (https://github.com/ELFdev001/ARSandbox), and is written in the Java programming language and requires the J4K library to communicate with the Kinect sensor. There are two versions of the ELF Sandbox software detailed below but they both share a similar base. The Kinect provides a range of depth values that are treated as a Digital Terrain Model. This is a two-dimensional array of heights that is treated the same as any other terrain dataset. This provides the shape of a landscape that the ELF Sandbox software uses to create a simulated environment.

12.3.2.1   ELF Dynamic System

The ELF Dynamic System (Fig. 12.5) comprises all the main elements of the project's computer simulations, albeit in a much-simplified form. These are:

Environment
Climate
Flora
Fauna
Humans.

Environment
The terrain is split into three areas, depending on height. All areas above a set level are interpreted as above the snow line. No plants will grow here although humans and animals may cross. All areas below a set level are interpreted as underwater. Humans and animals may cross water but only humans may harvest marine resources, animals may not feed on water. The levels of the snow line and the water line are determined by the temperature.

Climate
The climate is represented by a simple temperature which varies based on keyboard input. The temperature is static unless manually increased or decreased by the operator. The temperature affects the growth of plants and the height of the water line and snow line. Lower temperatures will increase snow cover and affect the growing areas of plants (Fig. 12.6). As the temperature increases, so do the levels of the water line and snow line (Fig. 12.7).

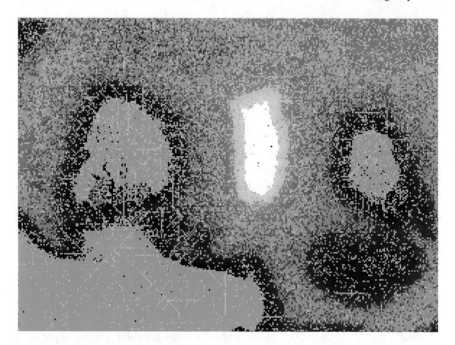

Fig. 12.5 ELF Dynamic System. Large areas of bright green, reddish pink and dark grey represent the predominant plant type in a cell. Areas of white represent snowy areas with no plant growth. Individual dots of red, yellow or dark blue represent humans. Individual dots of pale blue represent deer. Individual dots of black represent the remains of deceased deer or humans (Europe's Lost Frontiers Project)

Flora

There are three types of plants in the simulation that each occupy their own niches in the environment. Each plant type has its own height range within which it will grow. These are relative to the water line and so change as the climate does. Plant #1 is edible to humans, plant #2 is edible to animals and plant #3 is edible to both. Plants have a certain percentage chance to grow on each tick of the simulation.

Fauna

There is one species of animal in the simulation. This is named 'deer' in the code, but its behaviour is that of any medium-sized herbivorous species that is prey to human hunting. The deer will select a random location on the landscape that is neither snow nor water. It will then move to that spot and, once it reaches it, it will select another random location. Along the way, it will eat plants if it is not already satiated and there are plants of either type 2 or 3 in its current location. This increases the animal's food level by the amount of that plant in the location, up to a maximum. Each movement will expend energy, which in this simulation just decreases an animal's food level. Each animal has a highly abstract food value of 0–255 and if an animal reaches 0 food level it dies, leaving a black dot to indicate its decomposing corpse.

Fig. 12.6 ELF Dynamic System with lower temperatures. Note the larger areas of snow and different plant growth despite this being the same landscape as Fig. 12.5 (Europe's Lost Frontiers Project)

Humans

Within the simulation, humans behave a bit like deer in that they select random points in the landscape to move to, eating along the way if required and food is available. Humans can either eat plants of type 1 or 2, harvest marine resources if in a water location or will attempt to kill a 'deer' if they are in the same location. Humans start with a poor chance of killing a 'deer' but each success will increase this chance. Like animals, each movement will expend energy, and also like animals, they have a maximum food level of 255 and will die if their food level reaches 0. The humans are coloured depending on which food they have recently eaten most of, yellow for plants, red for animals and blue for marine resources. This provides an easy indication of changing human behaviours.

In Use

When the ELF Dynamic System is running, it commonly starts out as a stable system that the user can play with by rearranging the sand to create different patterns of plant growth. Initially, there is no water and little snow at the highest areas of the landscape. This allows users to become familiar with the system before introducing climate change to show how this effect the system as a whole. Once the operator increases and decreases the temperature, the users can see that the plant distribution changes which then affects the humans and animals. The system is a complex system of feedbacks

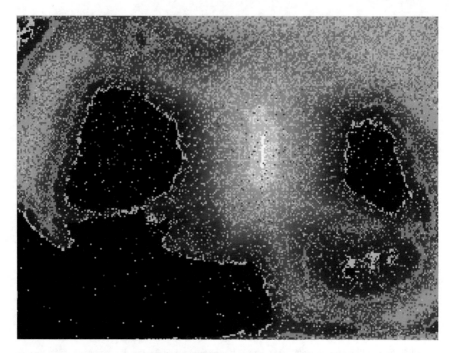

Fig. 12.7 ELF Dynamic System with higher temperatures. Very dark blue areas represent areas under water (Europe's Lost Frontiers Project)

in which changing one thing affects the others, thus providing an opportunity to observe complex interactions between agents and a changing environment.

12.3.2.2 ELF Activity Traces

The second simulation, named ELF Activity Traces, is intended to demonstrate the different techniques required to investigate a submerged landscape of hunter-gatherers and to show how different proxies can give radically different impressions. This, like ELF dynamic system, is a highly simplified simulation designed as a starting point for discussion. It comprises of three subsystems:

Biomes
Humans
Investigation techniques.

Biomes
ELF Activity Traces splits the landscape up into different biomes based on set level boundaries in the code. Like ELF Dynamic System, the temperature can be changed by the operator which increases or decreases the height boundaries for each biome

Fig. 12.8 ELF Activity Traces. Different biomes are represented by blue (water), white (snow), and yellow, bright green and dark green (abstract terrestrial biomes). Red dots represent humans and black squares represent settlements (Europe's Lost Frontiers Project)

evenly across all biomes. The biomes can be seen in Fig. 12.8 as different colours, with snow as white and water as blue, as in the previous simulation. Aside from snow and water, which can be traversed but not settled or used to find food, the biomes are there to indicate different environments but do not specifically relate to specific, real world, environment types.

Humans

Humans can be seen in red in Fig. 12.8. A set number are generated and they then find an appropriate settlement to live in, shown as black outlined squares in Fig. 12.7. A settlement is associated with the biome that it occupies and humans living in that settlement can only support themselves from that particular biome. Thus, when the climate changes and the area around the settlement changes biome, the people can no longer support themselves where they are and move to a more suitable settlement. If a settlement has no inhabitants, it disappears, being replaced by a randomly generated settlement elsewhere on the map. If there is demand for a settlement of this type, humans will move to it and it will flourish, otherwise it too will disappear and be replaced.

This pattern of biomes, humans and settlements is merely present to generate a landscape that has activity and that changes over time depending on the climate. This activity results in traces being left in the environment that can then be examined by several investigation techniques.

Investigation Techniques

There are three investigation techniques in ELF Activity Traces:

Soil geochemistry
Pollen
Magnetometer survey.

It should be stressed that these work in a very simplified way compared to their real-life counterparts and their primary purpose is to illustrate how different the data from Doggerland can be and how fragmentary its nature is.

Soil Geochemistry

The Europe's Lost Frontiers project's environmental analysis segment includes the analysis of the geochemical components of the deposits contained within the core samples. This has the capability to detect certain markers of human, animal or plant activity. Within this simulation, it stands as a representative of any technique that can detect traces left behind by any kind of activity. When displayed, it shows an activity heatmap for the landscape (Fig. 12.9), showing which areas are likely to preserve evidence of activity. As can be seen, the areas around settlements have the highest density of activity but certain pathways between settlements are also used by humans travelling between settlements in the process of changing their home base.

Pollen

Pollen data preserves best in wetland environments. To reflect this, the pollen view shows the areas that have been inundated at some point with a representative sample of the biomes in the area during the period that the area was under water (Fig. 12.10). This preserves some data about the environment but no data regarding the human activity, unlike real pollen data which may contain markers indicating the nature of human changes in the landscape.

Magnetometer Survey

Magnetometry is a form of geophysics that detects changes in the magnetic properties of the ground. This is commonly used in archaeology to detect buried features such as brick walls and hearths which have a high degree of contrast with the underlying geology. For this reason, the magnetometer survey view shows the settlement sites standing out against a background related to the terrain (Fig. 12.11).

In Use

This simulation offers a rare opportunity to see simulated human activity and switch between that and the results of three different types of archaeological landscape survey. It also highlights some deficiencies in survey techniques. The settlements visible in the magnetometer survey give no indication of whether they are populous and long-lived or transient. This information is more apparent in the soil geochemistry

Fig. 12.9 ELF Activity Traces, soil geochemistry data. Lighter areas represent areas of higher human activity (Europe's Lost Frontiers Project)

view, but the more transient settlements do not show up well at all in this view. The natural environment is much more visible in the pollen view but although this is a good record of the presence of wetlands, it is quite hard to reconstruct a full environment from this data.

These different types of survey are obviously drastic oversimplifications of much more complex techniques, but the basic message is that the more proxies that are available, the more of a complete picture we get of the landscape. The drawbacks in one technique may be mitigated by the strengths of others. Nevertheless, all these techniques put together are insufficient for anything other than a blurry reflection of the original system.

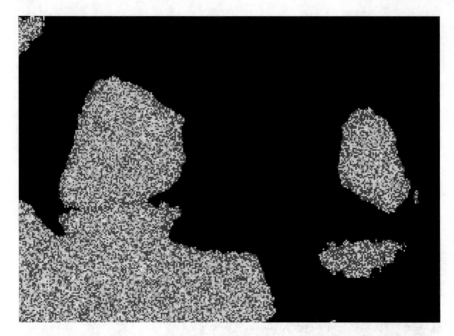

Fig. 12.10 ELF activity traces, pollen data. Black areas have no surviving pollen data. Coloured areas represent the biomes represented in the pollen in that particular cell (Europe's Lost Frontiers Project)

12.4 Discussion

12.4.1 Dissemination to Experts and the General Public. The Problem of Forcing 4D Data into a 2D Format

The ELF AR Sandbox occupies an unusual position related to the challenges of dealing with 4D data in an academic landscape that is still more focussed on producing, disseminating and rewarding 2D outputs. The outputs of the Europe's Lost Frontiers project will include monographs, along with articles in academic journals. These formats are two-dimensional, consisting of static words and images on paper, and increasingly, on computer screens in very traditional formats. The 4D data and processes used within the project's computer simulations are difficult to convey in the 2D environment of traditional academic publications.

Yet, these 2D traditional academic publications are the most valuable output for gaining credit for research, whether from universities, peers or funding bodies. Journal impact factors are important but instant impact on the general public that fosters the understanding of research is so far untracked.

4D environments like the sandbox provide a 4D method of explaining 4D data. Using narrative and diagrams to describe the interactions of a system that involves

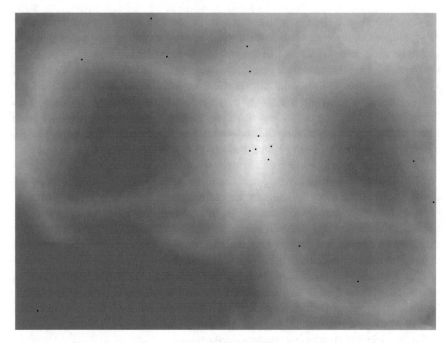

Fig. 12.11 ELF activity traces, magnetometer data. Black dots represent the locations of all settlements, former or current. The background is a greyscale representation of the landscape (Europe's Lost Frontiers Project)

plants, animals, humans, terrain and climate can lead to results that are verbose, difficult to understand and, to put it bluntly, boring for many audiences. The sandbox creates a low-friction interface into a 4D world that requires no instructions and little explanation. As of yet, plenty of people have failed to understand how the sandbox was created or the specific data values used in the simulation, but no one has failed to understand the basics of how it works. They put their hands in, move the sand, see the changes and they almost automatically know how to change the simulated world in front of them.

12.4.2 Reception

The sandbox has been used at a variety of different public events, including:

EU STEAM Researchers night
Edinburgh Science Festival
British Science Museum Lates at the Bradford Museum
Various University of Bradford Open Days.

There has always been great interest in the sandbox, with few opportunities for a rest for those manning the sandbox during public events. Children so young they have had to be dangled over the edge of the box by their parents have loved playing with the coloured sand. More mature participants are interested but usually want to know why we are presenting the sandbox at a particular event. This leads to a brief overview of the project and why we use computer simulation to examine Doggerland. This then allows participants to proceed in whichever direction they are most interested in. Some focus on Doggerland while some are more interested in the sandbox itself. Teenagers often recognise the Kinect and claim to have one themselves.

The sandbox initially had a mechanism by which the software stopped after 15 min and had to be restarted. This was quickly rendered redundant from a software development point of view but was kept in the version taken to public events as children, especially those around 8–12 years of age, had a tendency to play with the sandbox seemingly endlessly, and the stopping of the software provided a natural break for them to turn their attention elsewhere. It also enabled the simulated world to be reset, avoiding it heading off in any non-typical directions.

Media interest has resulted in photos of the sandbox on the Royal Society's social media accounts, an appearance on the Naked Scientists podcast and an article in Bradford's local paper, the Telegraph and Argus. The sandbox is used in both undergraduate and postgraduate teaching as part of lectures and seminars on archaeogaming and treating landscapes as four-dimensional objects.

Our main aim for constructing the sandbox was to use the sandbox to explain the computer simulation aspects of the project but it has actually proved to be a useful starting point for discussing all aspects of the project. As it contains technology, visualisation, an archaeological context, a changing landscape and an inundating world, it has aspects relevant to all work packages within the project. This was to a certain extent unintended, but it has been a welcome outcome of the AR sandbox programme. It engages more visitors as it allows an introduction to speak to the sandbox operators about any aspect that they find interesting. Although the sandbox was designed with a specific purpose in mind, members of the general public feel free to use it as a springboard to talk about issues that they are personally interested in. As computer simulation becomes a more common component of a variety of disciplines, this has wider implications for science communications. The fact that publicly accessible simulations can allow an element of flexibility in how users engage with them, developers of those simulations may find that the aspects which they find of most interest are not those in which the public is most interested. This has advantages and drawbacks that would require a separate study to fully explore.

12.5 Conclusion

For a cost of around £600, the sandbox has proved to be a popular way of engaging with the general public and talking about the project. With a project that touches so many areas including environmental archaeology, the Mesolithic, climate change, computer science and data visualisation, the ability to present a visually interesting exhibit which allows conversation to digress into any of these areas has proved very successful. It has enabled the project to be present at public events that we otherwise would have nothing to show at. It has enabled us to have short discussions about topics whose direction is to a great extent determined by the interests of the user. These discussions have taken place with hundreds of members of the general public and counting, and have allowed us to present the work of the project, the university and the ERC in ways that are user-led and easily digestible.

Acknowledgements The development of the Europe's Lost Frontiers Augmented Reality Sandbox was funded by the ERC Horizon 2020 Advanced Grant 670518—Europe's Lost Frontiers. The development of the original Augmented Reality Sandbox exhibited at the Royal Society Summer Science Exhibition 2015 was part of the GG-TOP project, funded by EPSRC Grant EP/I036877/1.

References

Barmpoutis A (2013) Tensor body: Real-time reconstruction of the human body and avatar synthesis from RGB-D. IEEE Trans Cybern 43(5):1347–1356

Berryman DR (2012) Augmented reality: a review. Med Ref Serv Q 31(2):212–218

Biefang K, Kunkel J, Loepp B, Ziegler J (2017) Eine Sandbox zur physisch-virtuellen Exploration von Ausgrabungsstätten. Mensch Und Computer 2017-Workshopband

Kreylos O, Kellogg LH, Reed S, Hsi S, Yikilmaz MB, Schladow G, Segale H, Chan L (2016) The AR sandbox: augmented reality in geoscience education. AGU Fall Meet Abs

Kundu SN, Muhammad N, Sattar F (2017) Using the augmented reality sandbox for advanced learning in geoscience education. In: 2017 IEEE 6th international conference on teaching, assessment, and learning for engineering (TALE), pp 13–17

Piper B, Ratti C, Ishii H (2002) Illuminating clay: a 3-D tangible interface for landscape analysis. In: Proceedings of the SIGCHI conference on human factors in computing systems, pp 355–362

Reed SE, Kreylos O, Hsi S, Kellogg LH, Schladow G, Yikilmaz MB, Segale H, Silverman J, Yalowitz S, Sato E (2014) Shaping watersheds exhibit: an interactive, augmented reality sandbox for advancing earth science education. AGU Fall Meet Abs

Reed S, Hsi S, Kreylos O, Yikilmaz MB, Kellogg LH, Schladow G, Segale H, Chan L (n.d.) Augmented reality turns a sandbox into a geoscience lesson. Eos. Accessed 18 October 2019. https://eos.org/science-updates/augmented-reality-turns-a-sandbox-into-a-geoscience-lesson

Roo JS, Gervais R, Frey J, Hachet M (2017) Inner garden: connecting inner states to a mixed reality sandbox for mindfulness. In: Proceedings of the 2017 CHI conference on human factors in computing systems, pp 1459–1470

Sutherland IE (1968) A head-mounted three dimensional display. In: Proceedings of the fall joint computer conference, Part I, pp 757–764

Vlahakis V, Ioannidis M, Karigiannis J, Tsotros M, Gounaris M, Stricker D, Gleue T, Daehne P, Almeida L (2002) Archeoguide: An augmented reality guide for archaeological sites. IEEE Comput Graphics Appl 22(5):52–60

Woods TL, Reed S, Hsi S, Woods JA, Woods MR (2016) Pilot study using the augmented reality sandbox to teach topographic maps and surficial processes in introductory geology labs. J Geosci Educ 64(3):199–214

Chapter 13
Immersive Architectural Legacies: The Construction of Meaning in Virtual Realities

Hannah Rushton and Marc Aurel Schnabel

Abstract This chapter investigates how new realities alter the experience of the tangible and intangible in Virtual Environments and how meaning can be constructed to compensate for this. In order to understand how these experiences can be digitally reconstructed to preserve their aura, this chapter examines the methodology and techniques of Digital Heritage. The *Gordon Wilson Flats*, a Modernist apartment building in Wellington, New Zealand, is presented as a case study to understand how the historical significance of a building can be translated into virtual realms. The research method utilised a range of digital technologies that documented, represented and disseminated an experience of the Gordon Wilson Flats to educate members of the public about the building and its history and look beyond the decaying facade only observed from behind barriers. The outcome of this project is exammined through the results of the exhibition *Immersive Legacies: 320 The Terrace,* which presented the virtual experiences of the Gordon Wilson Flats to the public. This discussion considers the role of multimedia and GLAMS in the construction of meaning and communication of authenticity for architectural heritage in virtual realities.

Keywords Tangible and intangible heritage · Architectural heritage · Authenticity · Multimediale virtual reality · Digital Heritage

13.1 Introduction

In one way or another, humans have always sought to capture reality. Historically, illusionistic painting rendered an interpretation of a scene onto a canvas and produced a window into another world. Then, the invention of photography brought a new era of possibility; reality could be captured with a sense of perceived realism and objectivity.

H. Rushton · M. A. Schnabel (✉)
Wellington School of Architecture, Victoria University of Wellington, Wellington, New Zealand
e-mail: MarcAurel.Schnabel@vuw.ac.nz

H. Rushton
e-mail: rushtohann@myvuw.ac.nz

© Springer Nature Switzerland AG 2022
E. Ch'ng et al. (eds.), *Visual Heritage: Digital Approaches in Heritage Science,*
Springer Series on Cultural Computing,
https://doi.org/10.1007/978-3-030-77028-0_13

Although photography was the result of technological advancement, it was two-dimensional medium, just like painting. Now, with technology that is available today, virtual worlds can be constructed to enrich the representation of reality.

In the past, reality was constructed on flat surfaces; in the digital age, it can be reconstructed in cyberspace—a window into another world that can be entered and explored. Virtual Reality offers new possibilities for the representation and communication of reality. As a result, this chapter asks: in this new era, when objects are no longer material, how can technology be used to represent the world in a meaningful way rather than simply replicating it? In light of this lineage, the question posed is not new. At the beginning of each technological era, commentators challenge advancement; observations on technological innovation seem to forget the evolving nature of technology and its capacity to capture reality. Following the invention of photography in 1839, the response of many contemporary critics can be described as 'apocalyptic' (Kemper 1998). Photography posed a threat to the standard of realistic depictions set by illusionistic painting, offering greater insight into the reality, and perceived realism, of a specific moment (Sontag 1978). Following the step from painting to photography, Walter Benjamin's 1935 essay, *The Work of Art in the Age of Mechanical Reproduction* discusses the implications of a mechanical age, and how it could change the meaning embedded in representations of reality. He argues that when mechanically reproduced, objects lose their aura (Benjamin 1969). In this context, Benjamin defines aura as a "presence in time and space" (pp. 220). Where apparitions of an intangible origin entwine with a tangible thing, the aura communicates meaning through the experience of a place. Photography of this era was a material mechanism and produced a material object—the photographs' materiality led to thoughtful capturing of one's reality (Richin 2009). Aura signifies the level of authenticity that is present within the experience of a heritage site; however, when an image only represents a single moment within a complete spatial experience, its authenticity is lost.

The digital age further changed the representation of reality; a new cultural divides for a new era of representation (Murray 1997). Just like the transition from painting to photography, the move from digital to analogue brings new possibilities. Not only does digital imagery capture a single moment, but technology allows for its manipulation. In both two-dimensional and three-dimensional realism, these technologies present new ways of constructing reality (Batchen 2001). New worlds can be entered and experienced through digitally constructed, three-dimensional representations that simulate reality. However, unlike mediums of the past, these are not material representations. Virtual Reality introduces new worlds that exist outside of our own, and within these spaces, reality can be reconstructed from recordings within the world or fabricated. This evolving technology allows for the digital translation of tangible heritage (Affleck and Kvan 2005), which embeds intangible information about the architecture within it.

This chapter follows the creation of digital heritage in order to present methods and techniques that create meaningful experiences of historical architecture in Virtual Realities. This chapter aims to distinguish between the real, virtual and in between, to discuss how the experience of new realities changes the construction and inter-pretation of meaning. In order to examine how aura is experienced when objects are no longer material, a methodology will be presented that discuses how meaning is constructed in Digital Heritage. To do this, this chapter will present the case of 'The Gordon Wilson Flats' to examine how aura is experienced when objects are no longer material. This project's methology will be discussed to illustrate how the way virtual realities change the perception of material objects and their associated aura can be overcome to generate meaning in digital heritage and authentic experiences in immersive virtual realities.

13.2 Background

Following events that damage or destroy built heritage, there are many courses of action that can be considered. The result of paths of preservation—for example, reconstruction or renovation—create questions surronding the value or aura that remains. To some, this may compare or be identical to the original; however, to others, it may no longer hold any meaning. Therefore, the ambiguity that is embedded within heritage practice raises many questions surrounding authenticity (Bold 2017; Schnabel and Aydin, 2015).

When considering authenticity, the connection of a building's tangible and intan-gible qualities create meaning as they communicate heritage significance and authen-ticity (Bouchenaki 2003). This research defines the *tangible* as the phenomenon of touching a physical object, experienced as the sensation of touch or an interaction governed by mass and collision (Seichter 2005). Tangibility can be differentiated from an object's *intangible* qualities, which communicate the social, cultural and historical significance and is created through the use of a building during a specific time or over the full lifetime (van Zanten 2004; Vecco 2010). Together, the tangible and intangible make an encounter within heritage architecture meaningful. They are connected to time and place; aura—or meaning—is not experienced without these.

In the case of tangible heritage, immersive technologies serve as a medium to trans-port a user to a site that is inaccessible to them in reality (Schnabel and Aydin 2015). In order to digitally build a heritage site, considerations must be made concerning how this task is completed. Re-creation is a popular approach that describes the heritage site's reproduction to present a window into another world (Affleck and Kvan 2008). The resulting virtual experience is a single site and time period, which disseminates information in a linear sequence. This set progression leads the viewer to understand the single narrative as fact (Uzzell 1994; Affleck and Kvan 2005).

To classify modes of dissemination within Digital Heritage, the chapter uses Miligram's Reality-Virtuality Continuum (Milgram et al. 1995) as a framework to illustrate the different realities that can disseminate digital heritage; realities that either combine with or replace the physical world (Martin et al. 2014). Figure 13.1 illustrates each of these realities that translates real objects into a digital realm. Such techniques remove a physical building from its context, consequently changing

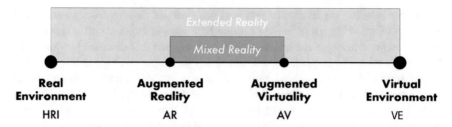

Fig. 13.1 Reality-virtuality continuum 1994 adapted from Milgram et al. (1995)

the experience of aura. This section examines the connection between the tangible and intangible and how these can be translated into Virtuality and still affect the interpretation and experience of heritage significance.

13.2.1 Real Environment (RE)

The first territory along the Reality-Virtuality Continuum is reality itself. Traditional heritage practice works within reality—within a physical, tangible, realm (Schnabel et al. 2007; Schnabel 2009). Practice within real environments does not only rely upon the building but its connection to the place it resides upon and the spaces within it. This experience within the tangible place contributes to the understanding of a cultural heritage site's significance, through the intangible value—and thus, the complete aura that is generated.

Many people desire to experience these sites first-hand; however, a site cannot be visited if it is inaccessible or has been destroyed. In many cases, they can only be viewed through two-dimensional recorded documents such as photographs or drawings, or from behind fences that prevent access (Champion 2008; Schnabel and Aydin 2015). Two-dimensional representations and recordings of architecture can be challenging to understand. These different forms of visual media may give small insights into how the building was used from a social history perspective, but this is dependent on records kept at the time. Furthermore, architectural drawings—which give many details about the tangible nature of the building—can only be understood by those with an architectural background, and this makes it difficult for a broad audience to engage with architectural history and heritage (Centofanti et al. 2014). Therefore, in the case of abandoned and decaying buildings, it is a challenge to communicate the experience of intangible heritage if the building and site cannot be visited. As a result, an argument for Digital Heritage arises—in that, the need for a building's virtual preservation is required for its legacy to be remembered.

13.2.2   Augmented Reality (AR)

Augmented Reality is a mode within mixed reality. In mixed reality, the real world and digital, computer-generated content, collide (Schnabel et al. 2007; Schnabel 2009). As illustrated in Fig. 13.1, Augmented Reality leans towards the real, adding virtual elements to a real environment. Users interact with virtual objects in a real-world environment, supported by virtual objects (Schnabel et al. 2007).

13.2.3   Augmented Virtualities (AV)

Also, within mixed reality, augmented virtualities refer to the merging of real-world objects into Virtual Environments (Schnabel et al. 2007; Schnabel 2009). In augmented Virtuality, but also Augmented Reality, virtual objects are usually digital models and recordings, which, in the case of digital architectural heritage, are three-dimensional reconstructions of the tangible built environment. Once again, this can present problems in the communication of meaning because the virtual representation of the tangible architecture usually forgets about the intangible—as they aim to recreate the site in a realistic way precisely.

In contrast to Augmented Reality, Augmented Virtuality sits closer to the virtual. The user becomes immersed within a digital realm, although they are not entirely removed from reality. In augmented Virtuality, users are within real spaces that become virtual ones through mediums such as projections. As a result, they are placed within a primarily Virtual Environment, populated by real objects and bodies.

13.2.4   Virtual Environments (VE)

As a complete digital representation and reconstruction of a Real Environment, Virtual Environments sit furthest along the Reality-Virtuality Continuum. This mode of dissemination in digital heritage completely immerses a user within a virtual simulation of heritage architecture (Schnabel et al. 2007; Schnabel 2009). Virtual environment experiences can 'realistically' recreate real environments (Rogers et al. 2018), as most approaches usually aim to replicate the tangible conditions of the building.

13.2.5 Experiencing the Tangible and Intangible in Virtual Realities

Through defining virtual realms along the Reality-Virtuality Continuum, it is clear that digital re-creations of heritage, disseminated within Virtual environments, lack intangible elements. Without an intangible connection to virtual representations of tangible architecture, the meaning associated with the physical object is lost. Re-creation can be distinguished from reconstruction, as an approach that aims to enrich rather than reproduce. Heritage can be virtually reconstructed using digital tools, which produces an array of architectural representations. Instead of being presented as truth, digitally generated information is presented in a way that relates to the past and the present. The environment is open for the viewer's interpretation and encourages the formation of their own, individual understanding. This approach acknowledges that as each visitor will bring their unique interests and experience, there will not be a consistent response across the audience. (Affleck and Kvan 2008). With this approach, there general public has agency, which reduces the distance of GLAMs.

When Virtual Environments are generated, the laws of physics and spatiality can be completely removed or altered; these characteristics can even be changed to certain extents in Augmented Reality and Virtuality. It means that the tangible interactions with objects and environments, including mass, collision and gravity, can be replaced or replicated. In some cases, these rules can be redefined or forgotten to create new worlds with new spatial experiences and interactions (Rogers et al. 2019). When users are immersed within Virtual Environments that have defined tangible interactions, the result can be described as *virtual tangibility* (Schnabel et al. 2007; Rushton et al. 2018b). Subject to both the designer and where the mode of dissemination is placed along Milgram's Reality-Virtuality Continuum, the nature of these interactions can change. When virtual tangibility is introduced to Virtuality, materiality becomes defined and perceived, and the virtual can be touched (Milekic 2007). This materiality is immaterial as it does not exist in the real world, but it can also be described as 'digital materiality:' the concept that immateriality has materiality (Lillemose 2006). The digital age, therefore, redefines materiality and establishes a material experience that is no longer connected to place or time. The theory behind the reconstruction, rather than a re-creation of heritage, supports the transcendence of time and space. Both the tangible nature and intangible characteristics of a building and the objects within it change over time (Uzzell 1998). As a result, meaning is dynamic in nature, so the public's agency is also supported—for now but also to function in the future.

In many cases, it has been found that the results of digital technologies can enrich Virtual Environments with intangible value—which present opportunities to preserve and access heritage in meaningful ways. The experience of authenticity in a digital context is different from reality as digital heritage is created with the freedom either provided or limited by the digital medium (Schnabel and Aydin 2015). Meaning can be constructed when these reconstructions of heritage sites are not necessarily concerned with photorealism. Digital depictions are more effective when the purpose of the representation is to connect tangible and intangible significance, not create a copy of the tangible architecture in Virtual Reality (Rushton et al. 2018b). Photorealistic worlds follow the approach of re-creation; in that these are usually static worlds that leave little opportunity for interpretation and education (Roussou and Drettakis 2003). Ultimately, an abstract approach may support the construction of intangibility through its call for interpretation from users (Aydin and Schnabel 2017; Jones et al. 2018). The objective of this is to construct a representation that looks beyond space and time, just as the impressionists defied the conventions of photorealistic representation in the 19th-century (Roussou and Drettakis 2003).

It is, therefore, the result of forming interpretation, not the method of which, that contributes to the level of authenticity within the virtual experiences of the heritage architecture. Public agency leads to a user's participation in public discussion, where they can discuss experiences and values after they have formed an opinion based on the building over time. Placing the Gordon Wilson Flats digitisation within a new theoretical context, this chapter proposes that without striving for photorealism and, instead, embracing available technologies, interpretation is widened because layers of information, communicate a sense of aura and authenticity through the user's transendence of time and space.

13.3   Case Study: The Gordon Wilson Flats

This chapter introduces the case study of the Gordon Wilson Flats (Fig. 13.2), a modernist, heritage-listed building in Wellington, New Zealand. This chapter follows the processes and outcomes throughout a digital heritage methodology, to illustrate how this methodology allows the virtual building to transcend time and space, and communicate meaning within these environments.

Fig. 13.2 Photographs of the Gordon Wilson Flats from the 1950s (left), and photographs of the building currently (right)

The building's construction began in 1955 and was completed in 1959 with the function of social housing. In the final year of construction, the architect, Gordon Wilson, passed away and the flats were named in his honour. Over more than 50 years of inhabitation, few changes were made to the building. The layout, scale and Modernist form have remained (Gordon Wilson Flats, 314 The Terrace 2015). However, the colour of the paint has changed from its original scheme. In 2011, engineering assessment discovered that the facade posed risks; there were severe doubts about the building's structural integrity and safety, so the decision was made to evacuate residents in May of 2012 (Gordon Wilson Flats, 314 The Terrace 2015). Now due to poor maintenance, the Gordon Wilson Flats are currently deteriorating into a state of disrepair. Due to continuing earthquake risks posed by the building's decaying exterior, the Gordon Wilson Flats are inaccessible to the public, and its legacy disregarded. Furthermore, as a result of the current situation, the heritage status of the building has been subject to debate in Wellington.

The debate surrounding this case study originates from the context of Modernist architectural heritage. A period of architectural design that is often forgotten, the public observes the decaying state of such buildings unaware of their history (Guillet 2007; Lewi 2013). Instead, this architecture is not perceived to have heritage significance (Guillet 2007). In a previous publication, the Gordon Wilson Flats experience was presented as a 'Virtual Living Museum' (Rushton et al. 2018a). In reality, a Living Museum preserves architectural heritage as it was lived in during a specific time (Cabral 2001). However, this time period shows a particular moment within the building's inhabitation, which makes the authenticity and perceived value subjective—restricting the interpretation to one thing. The preserved version of the building is decided by curators or heritage conservators, who limit a visitor's interpretation and understanding of the building's history. Furthermore, the preservation of a building in question is restricted by the heritage conventions and regulations present in reality (Schnabel and Aydin 2015).

In contrast, a virtual living museum can be digitally reconstructed in any form and presented in multiple iterations within the same or different experiences. The result of this means that the building can be visited to offer an insight into how people used or lived within it over time. Moreover, in a Virtual Living Museum, there are no barriers or limitations to where visitors can go or what they can interact with—creating more significant changes for engagement and interpretation.

This research aimed to translate the Gordon Wilson Flats into a virtual reconstruction. As the building has been inaccessible for many years, an essential part of the project was to embed intangible value and historical information into the virtual representations. The methodology of this research illustrates how meaning has been constructed in order to disseminate authentic virtual experiences of the Gordon Wilson Flats. Following the establishment and execution of this methodology, the work was presented in a public exhibition—which was an opportunity to bring digital heritage to a broad audience and further enrich interpretation. Following a discussion of this project's methodology, this chapter will consider this exhibtion and its outcome and significance as a communication tool for the communication of meaning within architectural heritage. In 2020, building consent has been requested to demolish the building (George and Te 2020).

13.4 Methodology

In each stage of this methodology, different phases compile layers of information that construct meaning. Therefore, over consecutive stages, the opportunity for value to be communicated becomes greater. Digital heritage methodology follows the stages of documentation, representation and dissemination (Rahaman et al. 2011). The methodology of this research (Fig. 13.3) illustrates how authenticity is constructed, not only through digital techniques but also within the disseminated experiences.

13.4.1 Documentation

The documentation stage collected tangible and intangible aspects of the Gordon Wilson Flats, each of which could be used and represented in different ways. This section outlines the methods that were undertaken to gather information to be tailored to different types of realities. A range of sources contributed to this stage, which formed a body of information that spanned the lifetime of the building; from the design and construction of the building, until today.

13.4.1.1 Tangible Documentation

Tangible documentation describes the information that was collected and analysed in order to generate representations of the tangible building. Different methods were used and in turn, produced different digital versions of the Gordon Wilson Flats.

To begin, the original plans and specifications from the 1950s (Fig. 13.4) were examined to make 2D versions of the technical plans in *AutoCAD*. The digital replication of these gave insight into the configuration and construction of the building. Photographs, both archival and contemporary, were examined as they depicted construction details and other indications of the tangible condition of the building. One challenge brought by archival photographs was that they are black and white, so the original colour of the building needed deeper research. In an archival journal article from the New Zealand Institute of Architects, the colour of the building was described as being light grey end walls, structural walls and slabs; dark grey precast posts and balcony surrounds; pale green horizontal walls; alternating blue and red balconies (Flat A); dark brown balconies (Flat B); white window trim; light grey fence on the roof (The Gordon Wilson Flats, Wellington: The Work of the Architectural Division, Ministry of Works 1961). This colour scheme is very different from

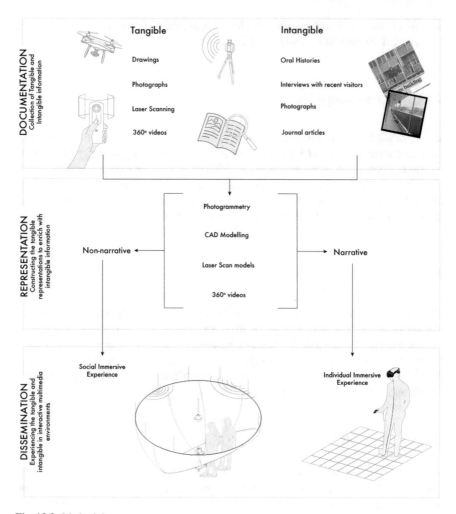

Fig. 13.3 Methodology

the gradient of blue paint that is seen today, so this journal article's description made it a surprising discovery and exciting aspect to recreate in the representation phase.

Another method to record the tangible building was laser scanning. Laser scanning captured the data from the building's interiors. The laser scanner utilises *LiDAR* technology; light measures and maps the room, to form a textured three-dimensional digital model. During the stage of collecting raw data within the building, photogrammetry was also used. Unlike laser scanning which was used to record the building's interiors, photogrammetry created digital models of the exterior and was achieved using a camera and a drone. This process began by taking multiple photos of a single subject. Similar to laser scanning, photogrammetry calculates measurements from images in order to generate a 3D model. A camera captured images of smaller

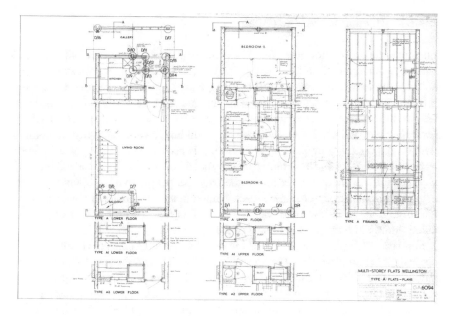

Fig. 13.4 An Example of tangible documentation—construction plans

areas on the ground-floor flats. These parts of the building were accessible to those taking photographs. Drone flights captured the whole building in approximately 1000 photos, which were then used to make a 3D model of the entire exterior of the building. These techniques document the building as it is today; however, as different methods, they produce different results—this difference will be discussed in the next section.

Finally, a 360° camera was used to capture videos with three-hundred-and-sixty-degree views of the building (Fig. 13.5). It was recorded in the first-person perspective, walking around and through the building in its current condition.

Fig. 13.5 360° videos

13.4.1.2 Intangible Documentation

Intangible documentation was classed as data that could give social and historical context to the tangible building (Fig. 13.6). Over the building's lifetime as social housing, the experience within the building and the attitude towards it changed. Initially, following construction, the building was celebrated in the 1961 February issue of the Journal of the New Zealand Institute of Architects (Kernohan 1996). Recently, many articles have condemned the building, an argument resting nothing more on the popular opinion that the building is an 'eyesore.' Changes in attitude towards the building and generally towards social housing in New Zealand indicate why the building changed over time—the way that people lived in it and the inter-actions that took place in it. There were many articles written about the building—both from today, and since the opening of the Gordon Wilson Flats—that give an understanding of intangible attributes of the building over time.

Similarly to the documentation of the tangible, photographs also contributed to the intangible narrative of the Gordon Wilson Flats. They indicate not only what the building looked like but also who lived in it and how the condition changed.

Oral histories—completed as part of a project of the flats—were included in collected documentation. Previous tenants were interviewed about their time living in the flats, which ranged from when the building opened to its evacuation and closure. As a result, these personal stories describe the experience of living in the flats; and when listened to together, present a narrative of the building over its lifetime. Finally, further interviews were conducted with those who had visited the building following its closure. Those interviewed offered an insight into the experience of being inside the building today. The current tangible condition is recorded with photogrammetry, laser scanning and 360° videos; however, these aural conversations describe how it feels to be inside the building.

News Articles

Old Photographs

Oral Histories

Fig. 13.6 Modes of intangible documentation

13.4.2   Representation

The representation stage prepares the documented data to produce meaningful environments, models and interactions. A range of computer software is used during this phase in order to analyse and make use of the data from the documentation stage to represent it within Virtual Reality. It is completed in two stages: the first stage prepares the data and digital models; the second stage places it into a game engine to generate the experience.

In the first stage, raw tangible data is imported into computer software to prepare them for the second stage. Photogrammetry models are generated in a process that combines photographs to create a detailed three-dimensional model. It gives an impression of the exterior of the flats as they are today. Several separate models were made and then stitched together in three-dimensional modelling software to make an overall impression of the building. The process of photogrammetry and optimisation in the representation stage creates a model that is not accurate in its geometry. However, this allows users to form meaning from these unconventional photogrammetric depictions. Therefore, these somewhat abstracted depictions then become topics of discussion and generate further interpretation (Schnabel et al. 2016).

The same is done for laser scanning, ensuring that the model can be placed into three-dimensional modelling software to combine models, if necessary, to form representations of the building in its current state. Like photogrammetry, the models generated by the laser scanner are not entirely accurate as the process begins to abstract the tangible nature of the building. The imperfections of both processes lead to representations of the flats that emphasise their state of decay (Silcock et al. 2018).

The laser scan and photogrammetry models directly contrast with the CAD representation of the building, which represents the building in a pristine state, as it would have been immediately following construction (Fig. 13.7). Then to import these into Rhinoceros3D, extruding these drawings and adding further details. When analysing the plans and specifications, the design of the building was noted. An interesting characteristic is the building's concrete superstructure, in which a single timber-framed maisonette flat is placed within. Three different flat layouts were included throughout the structural grid; they were named flat A, B and C. There are 70 apartments that are classified as 'Flat A'.

Along with a kitchen and lounge on the first floor, there are two double bedrooms and a bathroom on the second floor. There are five apartments with 'Flat B' layouts. Each has one double and one single bedroom, a bathroom on the second floor, and a lounge and kitchen on the lower floor. On the ground floor, there are 12 bedsit flats. These are composed of a single room with a separate kitchen and bathroom. This design is very characteristic of Modernism, as it indicates the rising influence of the International Style of Europe in New Zealand during the 1950s. Housing shortages in Europe had led to the embrace of Modern architecture as it could efficiently produce high quality, high-density architecture (Gatley 2000). In the mid-1930s, it became clear that there was a housing shortage in New Zealand (The Gordon Wilson Flats, Wellington: The Work of the Architectural Division, Ministry of Works 1961).

Fig. 13.7 Comparison of different generated representations: photogrammetry, Laser Scan, CAD model (left to right)

The Labour Government was elected in 1935 and used Europe's new architecture as a model to solve New Zealand's housing problems. The Government Housing Construction Department was formed a year later (Gatley 2000). This Government agency was most closely aligned with the social programme of European Modernism (Gordon Wilson Flats 314 The Terrace 2015). The Gordon Wilson Flats came towards the end of this influence of Modernism on state housing, and as a result it is considered by some as one of the best examples of Modern and high-density state housing in New Zealand. In reconstructing the flats, therefore, these became essential features to distinguish, so that this characteristic, and ultimately the characteristics of the architectural style and social context, could be communicated in later stages of the project.

During the second stage, the prepared representations of the tangible are combined with the intangible data. These methods of representation are dependent on the available different types of dissemination. In this case study, these are Individual Immersion and Social Immersion.

13.4.2.1 Narrative

Enriching the tangible, a game engine combines the tangible and the intangible to add meaning and context to the virtual models. A game engine allows for different scenes or environments to be made. When experienced in Virtual Reality, these scenes can be presented in an order or as a constructed narrative. These consecutive scenes can develop upon passing the time, which communicates the deterioration of the buildings

Fig. 13.8 Interactions within construction museum

(Rushton et al. 2018a). For this type of representation, three scenes select and combine different types of documentation to illustrate how the building has changed and the reasons for its current decay. This narrative takes the documentation and places it within the timeline of the evolution of the building to contextualise the building's decay and thus encourage users to understand the significance of the building—based both on the socio-cultural history contributing to the building's decay and tangible architectural value (Bouchenaki 2003).

The first of these recreate the construction site of the building during the late 1950s. The construction site features models of the building that sequence the construction process, from the beginnings of the structural form to the complete apartments. This scene aimed to engage users with the architectural design and construction processes of the building. There are two ways that this historical significance is presented. A construction office, reconstructed from photographs taken throughout the building's construction, becomes a museum—or a virtual living museum (Fig. 13.8). In that, its interior includes architectural models, technical drawings, photographs, specification and correspondence. Secondly, immersed users can switch between the different stages of construction, watching the construction phases of the building at 1:1 scale (Fig. 13.9). These are all things that signify a working construction office from the period, however making this setting in a game engine allows for all these items to be scripted, so the environment is interactive and in the dissemination phase, users are immersed within this environment.

Following the construction scene, the completed interiors of the building are shown. These include the interior models of the building—laser scans and CAD representations (Fig. 13.10). These are placed into the game engine at one-to-one scale and scripted to switch on and off. It means that in the dissemination stage, a

Fig. 13.9 User switch between different construction phases

Fig. 13.10 Different interior conditions

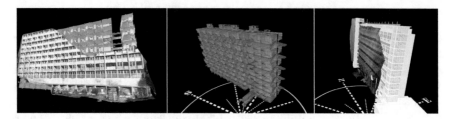

Fig. 13.11 Different exterior representations of the building's current condition

user can be immersed within these representations to compare the different conditions directly. Furniture was also added, which served as an additional option for the viewer when switching between scenes. It indicates not only each room's function but also scales.

Finally, the building is presented as it is today (Fig. 13.11). Photogrammetry, CAD and laser scan models are placed into the game engine at one-to-one scale. Like the previous scene, these models can be switched—hence, scripted to turn on and off—in order for the user to directly compare these during dissemination. One of the attractions of this scene is that the user can fly around the building. Gravity does not apply, and there are no colliders on the building—so this experience defies all rules of reality.

These tangible elements are enhanced with oral history interviews and interviews with the makers of the experience. Different parts of interviews that relate to different parts or representations of the building were selected to play within the scene. It results in multi-dimensional scenes that form dynamic representations of the building.

13.4.2.2 Non-narrative

Non-narrative prepares each piece of documentation individually. They are not placed within a game engine but instead kept as their original fines. For example, an obj. for a 3D model or a video file.

13.4.3   Dissemination

The dissemination stage adds value through the immersive nature of the experience, within which users transend time and space to explore and understand the Gordon Wilson Flats. Two modes of dissemination were used as together they present a range of representations and present greater opportunity for user's to construct meaning throughout their experience—as each of these encounters allows users to engage with both tangible and intangible aspects of the Gordon Wilson Flats. As an immersive medium, Virtual Reality permits people to experience the building at a one to one scale, with documentation shown among the virtual space's utilised during the dissemination of this research. As a result, they can form their interpretations and thus opinion on the building.

13.4.3.1   Individual Immersion

Following the development of the Gordon Wilson flats narrative, *SteamVR* and the *HTC Vive* system were used to disseminate the narrative environments (Fig. 13.12). The HTC Vive is a head-mounted display that includes ear audio speakers. This system also includes dual hand controllers; these give the user the ability to walk around and interact with parts of the environment that interest them most. Isolated within the environment, the user is free from the influence of others and is guided through space by their interests. They only stop to look at what they are drawn to or spend time in particular scenes longer than others. As a result, each user has a different experience, and they can derive understanding in different ways. Each user's attention can reside on different objects, and the points of interaction allow them to move through the different representations within a timeframe that works for them. It gives each user the chance of experiencing the building in each of its representations without the subjective influence from another user or varying site, context or decay simultaneously (Schnabel and Aydin 2015).

Fig. 13.12   Use of individual immersion system

Fig. 13.13 Use of social immersion

13.4.3.2 Social Immersion

Taking the non-narrative elements, Social Immersion presents them using the Hyve3D. It is a system that projects models or videos onto a spherical canvas and allows users to interact with the virtual context. The shape and scale of the concave screen create a dome-like space that immerses the viewer within the projection. A rendering engine distorts the content, which is projected onto a spherical mirror to then reflect off onto the curved canvas, making a 3D scene that appears in proportion. When bodies are placed within this system, real and virtual worlds are merged. The result is a semi-immersive 3D social Virtual Environment that does not require any Virtual Reality headsets or controllers (Fig. 13.13).

The spherical screen forms a space that is covered by projections and is large enough to be comfortably populated by a group of people. Unlike individual immersion, where only one person can explore the environment at any time, Social Immersion encourages multiple people to explore the projections together in real-time. Social Immersion facilitates engagement, not only through the semi-immersive and interactive environment but through shared experience. People can and are encouraged to discuss what they see within the group. They can share their past perceptions and current interpretations of the heritage with others, which contributes to the intangible value (Schnabel et al. 2016).

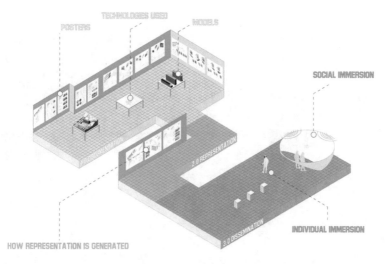

Fig. 13.14 A conceptual representation of the intented path for visitors, which was to follow the making of the Gordon Wilson Flats Digital Heritage and therefore build meaning throughout the path, following the project's methodology

13.5 Exhibiting Digital Heritage

Either experienced in isolation or together, each Virtual Reality experience presents a meaningful representation of the building. The latest iteration of this work saw these representations brought together in an exhibition. The Gordon Wilson Flats Virtual Reality experiences were exhibited as part of "Immersive Legacies: 320 The Terrace". This exhibition was held in the capital city of Wellington, New Zealand, in the Wellington Museum.[1] The exhibition was open for two weeks and was featured as part of 'Wellington Heritage Week'[2]—a significant, annual week-long event that features a range of heritage in Wellington. The exhibition hosted a broad audience, including international, national, and local visitors to reach a wide demographic of all ages.

The exhibition aimed to follow the making and methodology of digital heritage, using the Gordon Wilson Flats digitisation project as an example (Fig. 13.14). The Immersive Legacies Exhibition aimed to communicate the methodology of digital heritage and the role of technology within the project's making of meaning. Figure 13.15 illustrates the floorplan of the exhibition and the intended path of visitors for viewing the exhibition. An intended sequence, however, contradicts the purpose of digital heritage. The Immersive environments that present the Gordon Wilson Flats are un-mediated, and traditionally exhibitions in museums are mediated (Aydin and Schnabel 2016). This paradox was navigated as the aim of the exhibition was to show

---

[1] museumswellington.org.nz/wellington-museum/.

[2] wellingtonheritageweek.co.nz/event/immersive-legacies-320-the-terrace/.

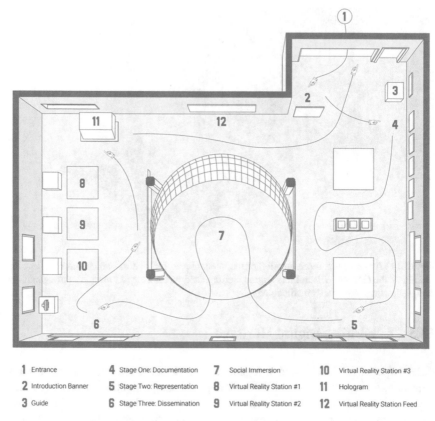

Fig. 13.15 Floor plan and intended sequence

1	Entrance	4	Stage One: Documentation	7	Social Immersion	10	Virtual Reality Station #3
2	Introduction Banner	5	Stage Two: Representation	8	Virtual Reality Station #1	11	Hologram
3	Guide	6	Stage Three: Dissemination	9	Virtual Reality Station #2	12	Virtual Reality Station Feed

the making of digital heritage. Social Immersion and Individual Immersion featured as the centrepiece of this process.

Exhibition content is spread across Milgram's Reality-Virtuality Continuum, as some experiences are complete Virtual Reality and others are real objects. The exhibition began with documentation (Fig. 13.16), which included historical information; displays of the laser scanner, 360° camera, drone and other historical material. Physical models were also included; small interactive models that visitors to the exhibition could interact with, and a 1:100 detailed model that illustrated the original colours of the building. These models corresponded to the models included in the Virtual Reality narrative experiences. In that, the interactive models are the same as the virtual models that users can engage within the construction scene, and there is also a representation of the original colours in this scene. At the back of this space is a panel which explains representation, and how the physical objects that the visitor has just observed and interacted with are translated into a digital realm, which leads the visitor to the modes of dissemination and virtual environments.

Beginning with Social Immersion (Fig. 13.17), a 360° video immerses visitors

Fig. 13.16 Physical models and panels

Fig. 13.17 Social immersion (left) and individual immersion (right)

in a recent walkthrough of the flats. Next, there are three HTC Vive headsets for the individual immersive experience. Each station plays one scene, beginning with construction, followed by the apartments, then the flythrough (Fig. 13.17). Finally, there is a hologram which plays animations of the different representations of the Gordon Wilson Flats. It includes the CAD and laser scan representations to show the contrast and again give visitors an idea of what they will experience in the individual immersive experience.

Recordings of interviews, with those who entered the flats after the building closed, played throughout the exhibition. The interviews are concentrated within the Social Immersion but are intended to be throughout the space by visitors. Thia audio focuses on the experience of the Gordon Wilson Flats creators within the building, but also why they were inside it—which was to record and digitally preserve the building. The team discusses digital tools and how they were used during the documentation and representation processes. With sound, two-dimensional written content, and interactive models, the virtual experiences are enriched with another dimension by these encounters throughout the exhibition.

This sequence of information, accompanied by recordings of interviews playing throughout the space, shows that even in the mediated space of the museum, curators have attempted to replicate the conditions of digital heritage. These different forms of media, which are represented across realms, are there to support the building of interpretation—a range of interpretations for a wide array of visitors while moving throughout the path intended by the exhibition curation.

13.6 Discussion

The Immersive Legacies Exhibition illustrates how representations of reality, generated using digital technology, can be translated throughout virtual environments. Ranging from a real environment to a Virtual Environment—with mixed reality in-between—this chapter has illustrated that although the content or experience of digital heritage varies in each of these realities, multimedia experiences construct meaning. Derived from the digital representation of the site, each mode of dissemination presents a unique aura that is a result of the process. The many outcomes of the methodology show how realities that are reconstructed do not need to replicate the reality that is experienced in a real environment. Instead, new tools and techniques are employed to not only produce a tangible experience but to communicate intangible significance. These outcomes transend time and place to present authentic representations of place. The result offers visitors to the exhibition and users of each virtual experience the opportunity to experience the Gordon Wilson Flats and make their interpretations of heritage. This section will return to the realms along Milgram's Reality-Virtuality Continuum, to discuss how each of these realities presents a valuable and authentic experience, both within and outside of an exhibition context.

Figure 13.18 illustrates the content within the exhibition where each experience

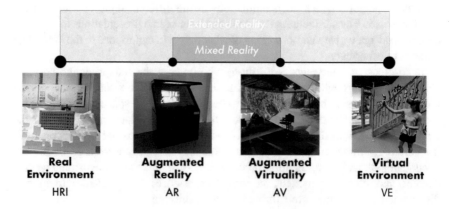

Fig. 13.18 Virtual experiences within the immersive legacies exhibition

created from this research sits along with it. During the exhibition, the engagement and education of these were intended to be enhanced by interpretative media around the space. These included printed panels, physical models and a hologram, which are classified as Augmented Reality. These illustrate the documentation and representation processes, thus do not hold the layers of information that have been built up over the process. They only represent moments within this process, and as a result, they do not communicate a connection between the tangible and intangible and are only meaningful in the context of the exhibition as they support the context of the creation of these immersive experiences.

Unlike the first two realms utilised in the exhibition, Social Immersion and Individual Immersion connect the building's tangible and intangible characteristics. Although this is done in different ways, the result of these realities within the exhibition illustrates the ability of these realms to present authentic experiences of heritage architecture. The first of these, Social Immersion, fulfils this chapter's criteria of authenticity, as virtual tangibility experienced by users and intangible value is created during this experience. Virtual tangibility in this augmented Virtuality experience relates to spatial free-rotational drawing on an *Apple iPad* to interact with three-dimensional models, or a laptop trackpad to navigate 360°. As a mode of dissemination uses representational material that is non-narrative, the social nature of this experience allows groups of visitors to discuss and generate their narratives and interpretations together—generating intangible value. Individual Immersion features completely immersive spatial interactions using an HTC Vive headset and its controllers. These environments present an established narrative that allows users to experience the passing of time and communicates the context of the building's decay. Virtual tangibility is established in the experience, not only through scripting that applied colliders and mass to objects, so that they can be experienced in a similar way to that of real environments but with the use of physical controllers which require the user to press buttons to trigger feedback in the virtual scene. Unlike Social Immersion, a user's interpretation is entirely determined by their own experience within each of the scenes. It comes from their engagement with the range of multimedia—oral histories, ambient sound, photographs and original documentation—that is included in the scenes.

As tangible architecture is translated into virtual realms, intangible value is added when the process and outcomes are embraced and embedded with multimedia to establish a range of interpretations for users further. When interaction, in a tangible sense, is made possible in Virtual Realities, users are given agency (Murray 1997). As a result, visitors to the museum were more engaged with the augmented Virtuality and Virtual Reality experiences. With a range of media, these experiences are open to different interpretations. Agency is, therefore, offered due to the opportunity for multiple interpretations but also because of the virtual tangibility offered by Social Immersion and Individual Immersion. Due to the draw of Virtual Reality, it was found that people went straight to these experiences, missing the interpretative media. However, exhibition staff found that visitors spent a significant amount of time in the narrative and non-narrative scenes, investigating the content and interacting with different forms of media. Therefore, on their own, these experiences provide meaning.

Visitors could go back through the exhibition to look at the physical media; however, meaning could be derived from only the Social and Individual Immersive experiences.

What the visitors' path and experience in the exhibition space shows is that although the exhibition fosters an alternative space to digital heritage, the unmediated experience of digital heritage is enhanced by the museum context. Visitors did not use the physical media in the space as intended, but the Social and Individual Immersive experiences engaged them. These led them to interact with the media inside these spaces, and from what they learned within these realities further engage with the physical content in the exhibition or discuss the building and its history with the exhibition's volunteers. Ultimately, the exhibition enriches how digital heritage offers interpretation and engagement.

The Immersive Legacies Exhibition shows that, while these experiences are meaningful on their own, placing them in their broader context creates greater value. It is especially true because this exhibition took place in Wellington, New Zealand. As the city of the Gordon Wilson Flat's location and debate, this exhibition presented an opportunity for the city's curious residents and visitors to explore the inaccessible building. While doing this, they also became more informed about the building and its origins and are enabled to take part in the debate of the cities and their own heritage. It is clear that the methodology of documentation, representation and dissemination does not only construct a meaningful outcome, but it presents a meaningful conceptual model for curating digital heritage that encourages audience agency.

13.7 Conclusion

When the reproduction of heritage architecture is discussed in the digital age, Benjamin's concerns are evoked within a new context. This chapter has followed the methodology of a digital heritage case study of the Gordon Wilson Flats to illustrate that, although virtual translations remove time and place, they do not remove aura. These can be reconstructed to evoke the experience and emotions of tangible and intangible aspects of heritage, and thus authenticity. Meaning is hence constructed throughout the digital heritage methodology of documentation, representation and dissemination. Throughout the Reality-Virtuality Continuum, each stage adds layers of intangible information to the tangible architecture—translating it into digital realms in a way that forms an authentic experience of the building. It has been shown that in order for these technologies to make meaningful representations of reality, they do not reproduce or preserve reality, rather reinterpret it. It is through this process of abstraction that communicates a sense of the real, and hence aura. As a result, architectural legacies of the decaying or forgotten buildings can be translated to be freely available and accessible for the broader public to learn and to experience heritage artefacts in a contemporary context. These new opportunities for interpretation present agency to the public that allows them to take part in their own making of heritage, which ultimately questions the role of GLAMS.

References

Affleck J, Kvan T (2005) Reinterpreting virtual heritage. In: 10th international conference on computer-aided architectural design research in Asia, New Delhi, India, pp 169–178

Affleck J, Kvan T (2008) Memory capsules: discursive interpretation of cultural heritage through new media. In: Kalay YE, Kvan T, Affleck J (eds) new heritage: new media and cultural heritage. Routledge, London, pp 92–111

Aydin S, Schnabel MA (2016) The museum of gamers: unmediated cultural heritage through gaming. In: Borowiecki K, Forbes N, Fresa A (eds) Cultural heritage in a changing world, pp 125–141. https://doi.org/10.1007/978-3-319-29544-2_8

Aydin S, Schnabel MA (2017) Glitch in the museum: a digital heritage project rejecting authorised heritage institutions. LIVENARCH V-2017: Rejecting/Reversing Architecture. Trabzon, Turkey, p 6

Batchen G (2001) Each wild idea: writing, photography, history. The MIT Press, London and Cambridge

Benjamin W (1969) The work of art in the age of mechanical reproduction. In: Arendt H (ed) Illuminations. Schocken Books, New York, pp 217–251

Bold J (2017) Reconstruction: the built heritage following war and natural disaster. In: Bold J, Larkham P, Pickard R (eds) Authentic reconstruction: authenticity, architecture and the built heritage. Bloomsbury Publishing, London, UK and New York, NY, pp 13–36

Bouchenaki M (2003) The interdependency of tangible and intangible cultural heritage. Convention for the Safeguarding of the Intangible Cultural Heritage, 1–5, Victoria Falls, Zimbabwe.

Cabral M (2001) Exhibiting and communicating history and society in historic house museums. Museum Int 53:41–46

Centofanti M, Brusaporci S, Lucchese V (2014) Architectural heritage and 3D models. In: Giamberardino P, Iacoviello D, Natal Jorge R, Tavares J (eds) Computational modeling of objects presented in images, p 15. https://doi.org/10.1007/978-3-319-04039-4_2

Champion EM (2008) Otherness of place: game-based interaction and learning in virtual heritage projects. Int J Heritage Stud 14(3):210–222

Gatley J (2000) Wilson, Francis Gordon. Dictionary of New Zealand biography. https://teara.govt.nz/en/biographies/5w36/wilson-francis-gordon. Accessed 20 June 2020

George D, Te M (2020) Victoria University plans to demolish heritage-listed Gordon Wilson Flats to create 'new front door', Stuff. https://www.stuff.co.nz/national/education/122257632/victoria-university-plans-to-demolish-heritagelisted-gordon-wilson-flats-to-create-new-front-door. Accessed 30 July 2020

Gordon Wilson Flats (1961) Wellington: the work of the architectural division, ministry of works. J New Zealand Inst Arch 28(1):1–8

Gordon Wilson Flats, 314 The Terrace, Wellington: Heritage Assessment (2015). https://wellington.govt.nz/~/media/your-council/plans-policies-andbylaws/district-plan/changes/active-changes-variations/files/plan_change_81/A3_2.pdf. Accessed 20 June 2020

Guillet AL (2007) Docomomo international: modernity as heritage. J Architect Conserv 13:151–156

Jones S, Stuart J, Mhairi M, Hale A, Cara J (2018) 3D heritage visualisation and the negotiation of authenticity: the ACCORD project. Int J Heritage Stud 24(4):333–353. https://doi.org/10.1080/13527258.2017.1378905

Kember S (1998) Virtual anxiety: photography, new technologies and subjectivity. Manchester University Press, Manchester and New York

Kernohan D (1996) Introduction. In: Wilson J (ed) Zeal and the crusade. Te Waihora Press, Christchurch, pp 9–14

Lewi H (2013) Going public: the modern heritage house on display. Hist Environ 25:62–74

Lillemose J (2006) Conceptual transformations of art: from dematerialisation of the object to immateriality in networks. In: Kysa J (ed) Curating immateriality. Autonomedia, New York, NY

Martin M, Charlton J, Connor AM (2014) Augmented body: changing interactive body play. In: Proceedings of the 2014 conference on interactive entertainment. Interactive entertainment, Newcastle, Australia, pp 1–4. https://doi.org/10.1145/2677758.2677790

Milekic S (2007) Toward tangible virtualities, theorising digital cultural heritage. In: Cameron F, Kenderdine S (eds) Theorising digital cultural heritage: a critical discourse. The MIT Press, London, UK and Cambridge, MA, pp 369–388

Milgram P, Takemura H, Utsumi A, Kishino F (1995) Augmented Reality: a class of displays on the reality-Virtuality continuum. In: Proceedings volume 2351. Telemanipulator and Telepresence Technologies. https://doi.org/10.1117/12.197321

Murray JH (1997) Hamlet on the holodeck: the future of narrative in cyberspace. MIT Press, Cambridge, MA

Rahaman H, Tan B (2011) Interpreting digital heritage: a conceptual model with end-users' perspective. Int J Architect Comput 9:99–113

Richin F (2009) After photography. W.W. Norton and Company, New York

Rogers J, Schnabel MA, Lo TT (2018) Digital culture: an interconnective design methodology ecosystem. In: Fukuda T, Huang W, Janssen P, Crolla K, Alhadidi S (eds) Learning, adapting and prototyping, vol 1. Association for Computer-Aided Architectural Design Research in Asia, pp 493–502

Rogers J, Schnabel MA, Moleta T (2019) Reimagining relativity: transitioning the physical body into a virtual inhabitant. In: Haeusler MH, Schnabel MA, Fukuda T (eds) Intelligent and informed, vol 2. Association for Computer-Aided Architectural Design in Asia, pp 727–736

Roussou M, Drettakis G (2003) Photorealism and non-photorealism in virtual heritage representation. In: Chalmers A, Arnold D, Niccolucci F (eds) First eurographics workshop on graphics and cultural heritage. Brighton, UK. 10.1.1.58.9500

Rushton H, Silcock D, Rogers J, Schnabel MA (2018a) The tangible and intangible: interpreting modern architectural heritage in virtual realities. In: Segantini MA (eds) AMPS series 15, Tangible—Intangible Heritage(s)—design, social and cultural critiques on the past, the present and the future, vol 1. University of East London, London, pp 130–140

Rushton H, Silcock D, Schnabel MA, Moleta T, Aydin S (2018) Moving images in digital heritage: architectural heritage in virtual reality. In: Akçay A (ed) AMPS series 14, moving images—static spaces. Altınbaş University, Istanbul, pp 29–39

Schnabel MA, Wang X, Seichter H, Kvan T (2007) From virtuality to reality and back. In: Sharon Poggenpohl (ed) International association of societies of design research. School of Design, The Hong Kong Polytechnic University. 988-99101-4-4

Schnabel MA, Aydin S (2015) Amphiboly of digital heritage. In: Guidi G, Scopigno R, Torres JC, Graf H (eds) Proceedings of the 2nd international congress on digital heritage, vol 2. VSMM, EUROGRAPHICS, CIPA ICOMOS/ISPRS, IEEE, pp 129–132

Schnabel MA, Aydin S, Moleta T, Pierini D, Dorta T (2016) Unmediated cultural heritage via HYVE-3D: collecting individual and collective narratives with 3D sketching. In: Chien S, Choo S, Schnabel MA, Nakapan W, Kim MJ, Roudavski S (eds) Living systems and micro-utopias: towards continuous designing. Association for Computer-Aided Architectural Design Research in Asia, pp 683–692

Schnabel MA (2009) Framing mixed realities. In: Schnabel MA, Wang X (eds) Mixed reality in architecture, design and construction. Springer, Dordrecht, pp 3–11. https://doi.org/10.1007/978-1-4020-9088-2_1

Seichter H (2005) Assessing virtual tangibility–usability evaluation methods for augmented reality urban design. In: Martens B, Brown A (eds) CAAD Futures 2005—learning from the past, a foundation for the future. Special Publication of Papers Presented at the CAAD Futures 2005 Conference. IRIS-ISIS Publications, Vienna, pp 151–159. 10.1.1.720.9642

Silcock D, Rushton H, Rogers J, Schnabel MA (2018) Tangible and intangible digital heritage: creating virtual environments to engage public interpretation. In: Kepczynska-Walczak A, Bialkowski S (eds) Computing for a better tomorrow, 36th annual conference on education and research in computer aided architectural design in Europe, vol 2. Lodz University of Technology, Lodz, Poland, pp 225–232

Sontag S (1978) On photography. Allen Lane, London

Uzzel DL (1994) Heritage interpretation in britain four decades after tilden. In: Harrison R (ed) Manual of heritage management. Butterworth-Heinemann, Oxford, U.K., pp 293–302

Uzzell DL (1998) Interpreting our heritage: a theoretical interpretation. In: Uzzell DL, Ballantyne R (eds) Contemporary issues in heritage and environmental interpretation: problems and prospects. The Stationary Office, London, UK, pp 11–25

Van Zanten W (2004) Constructing new terminology for intangible cultural heritage. Museum Int 56(1–2):36–44

Vecco M (2010) A definition of cultural heritage: from the tangible to the intangible. J Cult Heritage 11(3):321–324

Chapter 14
Getting the Measure of Brochs: Using Survey Records Old and New to Investigate Shetland's Iron Age Archaeology

Li Sou, Julie Bond, Stephen Dockrill, James Hepher, Al Rawlinson,
Tom Sparrow, Val Turner, Lyn Wilson, and Andrew S. Wilson

Abstract Brochs are monumental Iron Age (c.400–200 BC) drystone towers or roundhouses. They are only found in Scotland, particularly the Atlantic north and west. Whilst the structural layout of brochs has long been debated, few measured surveys have been conducted. Three significant broch sites form the tentative World Heritage site of "Mousa, Old Scatness and Jarlshof: the Zenith of Iron Age Shetland" (UNESCO in Mousa, Old Scatness and Jarlshof: the zenith of Iron Age Shetland, UNESCO (2019) Mousa, Old Scatness and Jarlshof: the zenith of Iron Age Shetland. http://whc.unesco.org/en/tentativelists/5677. Accessed 9 Aug 2019). All three sites have undergone new surveys as part of a collaborative doctoral partnership research project. This chapter presents a diachronic perspective using digital documentation techniques to detect stone displacement and weathering at the site of Old Scatness using historic imagery, including photographs from the Old Scatness excavations (1995–2006) and regular condition monitoring undertaken by Shetland Amenity Trust to undertake retrospective digital structure-from-motion (SfM) photogrammetry. Whilst point clouds and 3D meshes were successfully generated from low-resolution digital images, analogue film transparencies without metadata could not produce accurate geospatial data without manually trying to extant reference data. It was possible to detect displacements in stonework over time by comparing two meshes together and measuring the distances between vertex point pairs. The reliability and accuracy of these results were dependent on how well pairs of meshes could be aligned.

L. Sou (✉) · J. Bond · S. Dockrill · T. Sparrow · A. S. Wilson
University of Bradford, Bradford, UK
e-mail: li_sou@hotmail.co.uk

J. Hepher · A. Rawlinson · L. Wilson
Historic Environment Scotland, Edinburgh, UK

V. Turner
Shetland Amenity Trust, Lerwick, Shetland, UK

© Springer Nature Switzerland AG 2022
E. Ch'ng et al. (eds.), *Visual Heritage: Digital Approaches in Heritage Science*,
Springer Series on Cultural Computing,
https://doi.org/10.1007/978-3-030-77028-0_14

271

Keywords Laser scanning · Photogrammetry · Structural analysis · Broch ·
Conservation · Shetland · Archive data · Data reuse · Retrospective

14.1 Background to Old Scatness

The broch at Old Scatness was completely unknown until it was accidentally revealed
in 1975 during the construction of a new access road for Sumburgh airport (Dockrill
and Bond 2015). This site was the focus of a major academic research and training
excavation project from 1995 to 2006, undertaken by the University of Bradford in
partnership with Shetland Amenity Trust (for monographs see Dockrill et al. 2010,
2015). Excavations revealed a complex multi-phase site consisting of the Iron Age
broch (Structure 9 in the excavations), contemporary and later Iron Age roundhouses,
as well as evidence of reuse during the Norse and post-Medieval periods. The Old
Scatness and Jarlshof Environs Project took place over a significant period for image
capture technology, with analogue site photography used throughout the project.
The majority of the project's photographic record was captured using Agfa 200
ASA film, which was stored and archived as colour positive slides. The advent of
digital cameras becoming more widely available in the early 2000s meant that digital
imagery was also taken in the later stages of the project. These photographs captured
the Iron Age structures as they were excavated, providing an important contrast to the
extant sites at Mousa and Jarlshof. Their appearance was recorded prior to necessary
consolidation works being undertaken by Shetland Amenity Trust to ensure that the
structures were safe and stable. Digital documentation of Old Scatness is of key
importance for conservation monitoring, and as a tool to help to inform and educate
visitors about the Iron Age societies who developed broch sites and constructed
complex drystone architecture across the Late Iron Age in southern Shetland, given
the different forms of Iron Age architecture that are represented at this multi-phase
site. With such a varied excavation archive, retrospective analysis was considered an
important approach to test and to determine if stability issues and weathering in the
past could be recognised and flagged to help to inform the future conservation of this
and similar sites.

14.2 Retrospective Photogrammetry and Chapter Intentions

There have been several successful archaeological projects that have used retrospective photogrammetric processing steps, with a particular focus on producing 3D
datasets of sites that have since been lost or greatly changed (for example, Gruen
et al. 2003; Discamps et al. 2016; Green 2019; Wilson et al. 2019). The Omega
House project was successful in using a combination of both old and new imagery in
photogrammetry to produce composite 3D models, some only using the old images

for texture (Wallace et al. 2017), and the *Curious Travellers* project, composite photogrammetric models have been produced through web-scraped images of archaeological sites (Faber et al. 2017; University of Bradford 2017; Wilson et al. 2019). A distinction with this project was that it explored the results of retrospective photogrammetry solely using historic imagery, to present the appearance of the structures at a given time point.

This chapter demonstrates through five case studies the application of digital documentation to investigate the extent to which progressive changes to Iron Age drystone structures at the archaeological site of Old Scatness can be recognised over time, represented through loss of material, cracks, deformations, stone detachment and erosion. By doing so it aims to evaluate the pros, cons, successes and failures of attempting to recycle historic data for processing using modern digital documentation techniques, for any researchers who may find similar archive data in the future and if they want to consider the applicability and usefulness of such methods in determining conservation issues with similar, drystone archaeological sites.

Firstly, two types of photograph contained in the Old Scatness excavation and conservation archive are examined for their potential for retrospective photogrammetric processing; film slides and low-resolution JPEG digital images taken at different times. The paper then presents a method that attempted to detect changes due to stone displacement and weathering between two 3D datasets using alignment and by quantifying the direction of, and the measured distances between their nearest points. Control data was captured by the authors in 2018 using terrestrial laser scanning and photographic survey using full-frame digital photography. The same analytical method was then applied to inspect the differences between the 3D outputs created from images taken in 2003 and 2015, through a series of case studies examining specific areas of the broch at Old Scatness. In doing so, different findings on the benefits, issues, and reliability of such analyses were revealed, highlighting the usefulness of the measurement technique and its applicability for future retrospective 3D processing.

14.3   Retrospective Structure-From-Motion (SfM) Photogrammetry from Film Slides

During the excavations, archive film photographs of Old Scatness were taken once contexts were fully excavated. Consistent composition was assured by these archive photographs each being taken by Dockrill as project director. Multiple photos of the same contexts were taken to ensure good quality photos were captured using Agfa 200 ASA colour negative film, as it was not possible to check and process the film on site. A Nikon F3 camera was used with a combination of Nikon 28 mm wide angle, Nikon 35 mm wide angle and Nikon zoom 28–70 mm lenses, however, as no metadata was recorded during the taking of the photographs, it is not possible to determine which exact lens and settings were used for each shot, as the zoom lens parameter falls into the same range as the other lenses. Such information may have been useful for SfM photogrammetry, as software such as Agisoft Photoscan aligns images whilst taking into account lens distortion for many makes and models of camera and lenses, if such metadata is available.

Most of the film photos were limited by the different angles of the features recorded and were therefore not suitable for SfM photogrammetry, which requires sufficient overlap in the images of the feature to be recorded and modelled. However, a set of post-excavation photos of Structure 24, a small Late Iron Age corbelled cell, appeared to show variations in the angles of the photos taken and clearly had photos taken from different locations around the cell. These photos were digitised using an Epson Perfection V850 Pro scanner and imported into Agisoft Photoscan Professional Edition 1.4.4 build 6848 (hereon referred to as Photoscan) for SfM processing. Following guidance on retrospective photogrammetry (Wallace 2017), only 18 images that had clearly been taken from different positions were used, as sets of images that are too similar confuse the software to only focus on them and force the alignment around them. Only the areas of Iron Age stonework were selected for modelling, with scale bars masked due to their inconsistent placement in the photos (Fig. 14.1).

The point cloud that was generated appeared as a flat plane, with Photoscan apparently unable to accurately calculate the camera positions (Fig. 14.2). There was clearly insufficient overlap in the remaining images to enable point matching. It is possible that the different lenses used with a zoom have led to varied focal lengths that the software has technically calculated correctly, but which has led to the camera positions being presented so differently although on the photos, it appears that the camera positions were always from a similar distance. This hypothesis needs testing to determine if this is a major issue for retrospective photogrammetry. The same dataset was processed in 3DF Zephyr 4.003 (3Dflow SRL 2019) and COLMAP 3.4 (Schönberger and Frahm 2016; Schönberger et al. 2016), however, they were also unable to fully process these images.

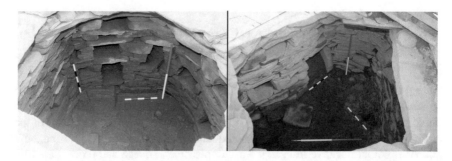

Fig. 14.1 Examples of two digitised slides of Structure 24 at Old Scatness. Note how the scale bars in the photos were placed in different positions, meaning that they were challenging for scaling and also prevented the floor from being processed (S.J. Dockrill)

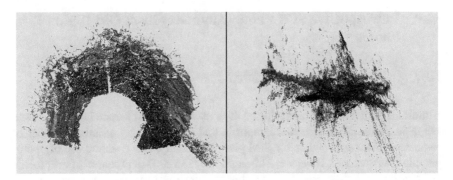

Fig. 14.2   Left, top-down view of the resulting dense point cloud from SfM photogrammetry. Right, side view of the dense point cloud. It is clearly inaccurate and affected by the plane effect (L. Sou)

The overlap in the shots of Structure 24 was taken from too similar an angle, position and distance which caused a flat plane effect in both Photoscan and 3DF Zephyr, since many had been taken from a photographic platform that had been erected on site. Though other camera positions existed for the other sides of the cell (such as the right-side image in Fig. 14.1), there were an insufficient number of these to match the large number taken from one position (18 out of a total of 42 images were views from the position of the left-side image in Fig. 14.1), which both software focussed on in the SfM process, discarding the other images. Even when the numbers of these duplicates were drastically reduced and the images masked, both software packages continued to use only images taken from one position of Structure 24 in SfM processing. When the images from this same position were removed completely the remaining images failed to process in SfM, even though some of these remaining images did show the duplicated area from more oblique and different angles. COLMAP only matched two image pairs. In conclusion, using only the photos of Structure 24 from the 2000 excavation season, it was not possible to generate a detailed 3D point cloud due to a lack of overlap in the images. More photos from different positions were needed. Knowing the exact camera settings and lenses used in each shot would have also aided in a successful attempt at modelling from film photographs. Such data would need to be retrieved from old excavation archives to make successful retrospective SfM photogrammetric models from film photographs.

14.4 Retrospective SfM Photogrammetry from Old Digital Photos

14.4.1 Digital Photos from 2003

Almost all digital images taken during the excavation project shared the same issue as the post-excavation film photographs in that there was only a limited number of camera positions and angles for SfM photogrammetry, based on the use of photographic towers on site. However, 21 images from the 2003 field season of the broch's northern cell, stairs and outer line of orthostats appeared to overlap and show multiple camera positions and angles of this area (Fig. 14.3). The potential for them to be used in SFM photogrammetry was recognised during archive research based upon standard guidance on optimum camera settings for maximum quality for photogrammetry (The Survey Association 2016; Historic England 2017; Agisoft 2018; Frost 2018). The 2003 photographs were taken using an Olympus E-10 digital camera, incorporating metadata on lens type and focal length within their files, such that it was considered very likely that a point cloud could be created from the images, despite the fact that these early digital images were limited by low resolution (4 megapixel resolution), and compressed JPEG format.

The 21 images had their white balance corrected in Adobe Camera RAW, before they were uploaded into Agisoft Photoscan Professional Edition, where a sparse point cloud was generated successfully and points aligned using the high accuracy setting, using 40,000 maximum key points and 4000 maximum tie points. After processing, 11,395 points were aligned, with the sparse cloud clearly producing 3D details of the structure (Fig. 14.4). A further dense point cloud was produced using the high-quality setting, to produce as detailed a 3D dataset as possible from the images.

2,211,724 points were generated in a full coloured 3D model, of far better quality and accuracy than any of the digitised slide images from the Old Scatness excavations detailed above. Once the dense point cloud was scaled using the 50 cm black and white scale that was physically present on the broch wall in the images, the error value across the entire point cloud was 1 mm. The scale bar included in the photographs was useful as it was not moved between shots, as the date and the time of each image recorded in their metadata showed that the photographs were taken consecutively, so it was highly unlikely for the scale to have been moved in such a short amount of time.

The dense point cloud was exported as an E57 file with no decimation. The model was imported into Cloud Compare version 2.10.2 (Zephyrus), where the statistical outlier removal (SOR) tool was used to filter and remove points further than the average distance between point neighbours. The number of points used for mean distance estimation was set to 8, as it was found that a higher number would be more accurate, in using more points. The standard deviation multiplier threshold (nSigma) across the SOR calculation was set to 1, as it was found that this setting ensured a sufficient number of points remained within the distance range to preserve detail of features in the point cloud. Most noisy, erroneous loose points were removed. A lower

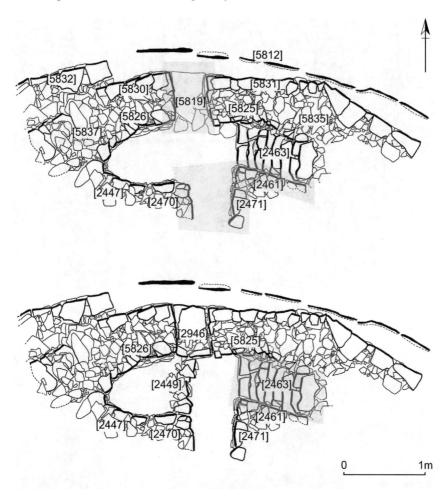

Fig. 14.3 Plan drawings of Structure 9's northern cell, before (top) and after (bottom) the post-construction blockade was removed. Areas discussed in the chapter are highlighted in yellow. *Source* Dockrill (2015)

setting removed too many points whilst a higher number retained too many clearly inaccurate points. Setting the standard deviation to 1 helped to remove obviously inaccurate, extraneous points which were produced as a result of the limited camera angles in the photographs, which caused "streaking" across areas of the point cloud. Some manual editing and cleaning were undertaken; however, it was not possible to meticulously remove every extraneous point in this manner in the duration of the research project. As such, the SOR filter settings were deemed sufficient for the purpose of initially cleaning the point clouds prior to comparison.

The 3D dense point cloud generated from the images appeared accurate, with the stonework in spatially correct positions. The resultant model is not very large, only capturing in detail the following: (1) the northern circuit of the broch's exterior

Fig. 14.4 Sparse point cloud successfully generated of the northern wall of Structure 9. The small yellow scale bar in the centre measures 50 cm (L. Sou)

Fig. 14.5 Dense point cloud produced of Structure 9 northern intramural cell, outer and inner walls and exterior orthostats (foreground). The yellow scale bar is 50 cm (L. Sou)

wall directly in front of the blocked external entrance to the northern cell; (2) the intramural stair that led upwards from the cell and (3) the blocked entrance passage leading to the broch's centre. The uppermost surviving courses of stonework of the interior wall, and the north-western external wall circuit of the broch were of lower resolution within the point cloud, with apparent edge artefacts and more noisy inaccurate 3D data. Data points were unsurprisingly lacking from areas where there was insufficient overlapping imagery at the base of the cell and the vertical profile of the steps that were obscured by the wall tops of the outer wall within the photographs. The higher levels of stonework on the inner wall were well represented in the model, as evidently there was sufficient overlapping coverage of imagery. This therefore means that currently the photogrammetric model produced from the 2003 images is the earliest 3D record of the site to have been retrospectively created. This record is significant as it represents the appearance of the stonework as freshly excavated in 2003. Based on the success of this pilot a similar dataset was sought for comparison.

14.4.2   Digital Photos from 2015

Shetland Amenity Trust conducted a condition monitoring survey of Old Scatness in 2015, with a digital photographic record of all exposed structures at the site. As with the 2003 digital photographs, these were not taken with photogrammetric processing in mind, rather as a visual record of the condition and appearance of the captured features and structures at that moment in time. The images from this collection that featured the northern circuit of the broch were processed with SfM photogrammetry as above, in Photoscan to further assess the usability of archived digital images for retrospective photogrammetry. It was noticed that the prevailing weather conditions were not ideal for SfM photogrammetry, with some photographs having been taken on bright sunny days and others in the rain, which was not conducive to an even colour texture. However, as the coverage was comprehensive, it was recognised that there were likely to be areas of overlap in the imagery as captured, and the data was suitable for scaled modelling because of the consistent use scale bars within the imagery.

The photos had to be divided into two sets to be separately processed, as the images for the complete area of the northern cell would not align in a single batch. As such, two separate chunks were made; one of the exterior northern wall circuit (Fig. 14.6) and one of the intramural stair and interior blocked entrance within the cell (Fig. 14.7). SfM processing of the broch's north wall was successfully scaled, but the dense point cloud generated appeared inaccurate, as "wavy" distortions were visible on the stonework (see Fig. 14.6). Correcting the scale of the point cloud using the scale bars in shot increased the point density of the dataset. The "wave pattern" distortion was still present but in thinner, more abundant lines. It is possible that this distortion was the result of the low-resolution compressed JPEG format of the images and that by increasing the scale of the point cloud, or using the high-quality dense cloud generation option, more points were sampled which exaggerated the

Fig. 14.6 Dense point cloud of Structure 9 northern cell and outer wall, produced in Agisoft Photoscan Professional Edition, from digital images taken in 2015, saved as JPEGs. Note how the outer wall (foreground) has a distinct wave pattern of distortion. The red and white scale bar (centre left) is 1 m in total height (L. Sou)

Fig. 14.7 Dense point cloud of Structure 9's blocked northern entrance and staircase, created from images taken in 2015. Note the 1 m scale bars used to aid in the alignment and scaling of the images and SfM processing (L. Sou)

distortion effect. A future controlled study is recommended to test these theories, which cannot be confirmed with certainty from the two case studies presented here. The extent to which such distortions can cause problems for analysis of weathering or stone displacement on site is discussed below.

The two dense point clouds created from the 2015 images are notably noisy, with a large amount of point streaking, where point placement is inaccurate due to the limited camera positions processed during the camera alignment. An extreme example of this was demonstrated above in the processing of the digitised film slides of Structure 24. Whilst the point cloud of the external wall also contained other features, including the blocked entrance, it was clear on close observation of the points in that area that the alignment was poor and inaccurate, as the appearance of the stonework was warped and not true to its appearance in the photographs (Fig. 14.6). Whilst the second point cloud is also noisy, the stonework is much better defined around this region. Due to the level of variation between these two dense clouds, it was decided not to align them, as this would introduce further inaccuracy due to the discrepancies between the datasets. As such, they were exported as separate E57s into CloudCompare for cleaning, as with the point cloud produced from images taken in 2003 (see above section).

14.5   Control Experiment, Detecting Stone Displacement Through Mesh-to-Cloud Distance

The case studies above have presented how old digital images of Old Scatness can be retrospectively processed successfully using SfM photogrammetry, whilst film photos were more problematic. As 3D datasets were generated from two different years, over a decade apart, comparing them for changes would be expected to have great value in detecting information on potential structural issues that could be used to inform future conservation approaches to mitigate against such effects. In order to evaluate the accuracy of the point cloud data generated from the 2003 and 2015 archive photographs, these were compared to the high-resolution 3D data from Old Scatness acquired in 2018.

Hypothetically, as the 2018 laser scan and photographic survey of the site were captured with detailed digital documentation in mind, there should be no difference in distance or any movement between a laser scan point cloud and a high-resolution 3D mesh created from SfM photogrammetry. To test this assumption, a single laser scan taken using a FARO Focus X330 from the centre of the northern cell of the broch was selected for comparison, as registering several scans together would have introduced error margins between the alignments. The single scan was exported from FARO SCENE 7.1.1.81 following processing to remove dark scan points, edge artefacts and stray points from the point cloud. The cleaned point cloud was then exported in E57 format. The photogrammetric model was produced from uncompressed full-frame TIFF images taken from a Nikon D750 with optimised settings for such processing;

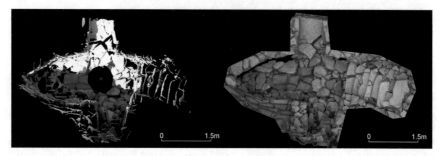

Fig. 14.8 2018 datasets prepared for comparison. Left, single laser scan from the centre of the cell. Right, cropped mesh produced from SfM photogrammetry of high-resolution photographs (L. Sou)

with one aperture and shutter speed setting used throughout all recording shots, on a 28 mm prime lens with a photographic mast set at a consistent height to ensure all features would be sharply in focus. This was processed in Agisoft Photoscan Professional edition 1.4.4 build 6848, with high-quality settings used throughout. The resulting 3D model was exported as a PLY mesh and imported into CloudCompare for alignment with the laser scan point cloud. The mesh covered a wider extent than the single laser scan (see Fig. 14.8), so was used as the reference cloud in alignment, as following processing recommendations in CloudCompare (2015). The initial point pair alignment RMS (square root of the mean square errors) was 1.18 mm. As the mesh covered a much larger area, it was cropped to fit only the features recorded in the laser scan, so only overlapping areas remained.

A fine Iterative Closest Point (ICP) registration was then conducted with overlap set to 50% between both datasets, due to the laser scan point cloud still lacking data in several areas compared to the point cloud due to it being taken from a single scan position (see Fig. 14.8). The final RMS from the ICP registration was 0.91 mm, computed on 49,999 points. This considered the noise of the datasets, registration errors and density variations of both point clouds (CloudCompare measures meshes through their vertex points as a point cloud) (CloudCompare 2016). A low error margin was expected from these two highly detailed datasets, which were specifically collected with spatial analysis in mind. A cloud-to-mesh distance measurement between the two 3D datasets was then calculated, using the mesh as reference (Fig. 14.9). Most areas were within this distance tolerance—coloured yellow and green in Fig. 14.9. The majority of those areas coloured blue and red were where no data was available in either the mesh or point cloud. Cropping the SfM mesh to fit the exact areas of overlap with the laser scan point cloud was not feasible due to this process requiring a substantial amount of manual editing, so such gaps were left in the models. Many gaps between stones also exceeded the 10 mm distance between the two datasets, likely as less points were recorded in these areas, so an increase in distance was more likely.

When the maximum distance of the scalar field was set to 1 mm, it was found that most points between the two datasets exceeded this (Fig. 14.10). The RMS of the fine ICP registration was 0.91 mm so it was expected for differences lower than this

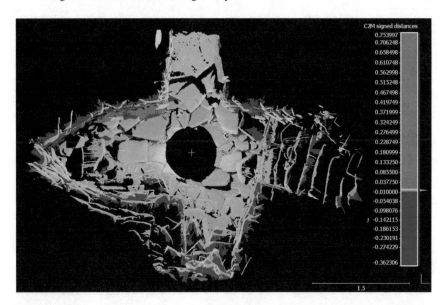

Fig. 14.9 Scalar field showing distances between the 2018 laser scan point cloud and SfM mesh, with maximum distance set to 10 mm. Scale in metres. Plan view, looking north (L. Sou)

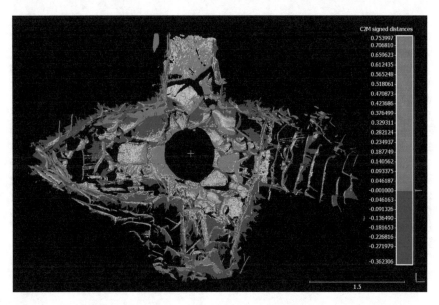

Fig. 14.10 Scalar field showing distances between the 2018 laser scan point cloud and SfM mesh, with maximum distance set to 1 mm (L. Sou)

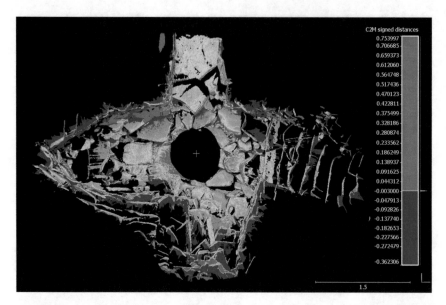

Fig. 14.11 Scalar field showing distances between the 2018 laser scan point cloud and SfM mesh, with maximum distance set to 3 mm (L. Sou)

range to not be detected. Adjusting the maximum distance to 2–3 mm showed that more stonework was very closely aligned within this tolerance (Figs. 14.11, 14.12). A possible explanation for such differences being found between two datasets that were expected to be identical may be due to a movement of the gravel bags in the centre of the cell, resulting from when the laser scanner tripod was placed on them. Laser scanners can also acquire noisier data when the feature recorded is closer than its minimum recommended operating range. For example, the FARO Focus3D X330 has a specified range of 0.6–330 m indoors and outdoors (FARO 2016).

The scalar field shows a higher distance between the datasets in the region of the scanner (where no data is visible in the centre of the figure, since the scanner cannot scan beneath itself). Also, such differences may be within the accuracy tolerances of the processing techniques used. This suggests that sub-millimetre level differences cannot be easily or confidently detected using mesh-to-cloud distance measurements, however, differences above this parameter are possible.

The mesh-to-cloud distance measurement was therefore used for the other case studies, with meshes being generated from the point clouds to be analysed.

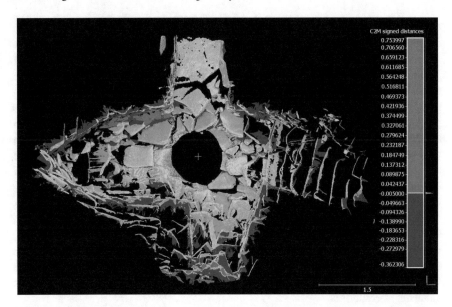

CZM signed distances
0.753997
0.706560
0.659123
0.611685
0.564248
0.516811
0.469373
0.421936
0.374499
0.327061
0.279624
0.232187
0.184749
0.137312
0.089875
0.042437
-0.005000
-0.049663
-0.094326
-0.138990
-0.183653
-0.228316
-0.272979

-0.362306

1.5

Fig. 14.12 Scalar field showing distances between the 2018 laser scan point cloud and SfM mesh, with maximum distance set to 5 mm (L. Sou)

14.6 Case Study 1—the Blocked Inner Entrance to the Broch

Comparison of the 2015 photos with the laser scan data shows that many changes have occurred since the excavations were completed. Inside the cell, many gravel bags were placed on exposed stonework to protect it. To allow the point clouds produced from images between 2003 and 2015 to be compared, features missing in the earlier photos were digitally removed from the point cloud of the 2015 data, as the difference in point-to-point measurement would be too large and therefore dominate the distance measurements over more subtle changes that may have been caused by weathering or other factors. Similarly, the floor was removed, as this was a later artificial surface placed to protect the underlying archaeology. In order to monitor small, subtle changes possibly caused by weathering, the more obvious differences had to be removed from the later dataset.

After the point, clouds produced from images taken in 2003 and 2015 were cleaned, and as many clearly different features or those not present in both clouds were removed, the data were processed into meshes of specific areas surrounding the north cell. Three areas were found with sufficient overlap between the 2003 and 2015 3D data. This first case study examines the area of the blocked inner entrance to the broch.

The meshes were produced in Photoscan Professional Edition after the dense clouds were cleaned, so that only overlapping areas between the clouds were made into meshes, just as with the analyses conducted above. The surface type was set to arbitrary 3D, the face count set to 0 so that it would use all points in the dense cloud, due to the low resolution of the dense cloud produced from the 2003 photos. Interpolation was disabled to ensure that any gaps in the dataset remained unfilled. The gradual selection tool, only applicable to meshes, was used in Photoscan to select small non-connected components of the mesh, which were then removed from the dataset. The resulting mesh had 790,140 vertex points. The 2015 mesh was produced using the same method, however, was decimated to be comparable with the 2003 mesh. This mesh, using the 2015 data, had 1,303,373 vertex points, and thus served as the reference dataset, being a denser dataset. It was very noticeable how poor the resolution of the meshes were, as details of the stonework were blurred and not sharply rendered (Figs. 14.13, 14.14). The initial point pairs were aligned by bounding box, as the cropped datasets were both only focussed on overlapping areas of the blocked entrance of Structure 9. ICP fine registration was then conducted with 50% overlap and 1-0e-5 RMS difference. The cloud-to-mesh distance was calculated, with the mesh of the larger 2015 dataset as reference, and signed distance selected, to produce distances with ± values between the two clouds. Positive values indicate vertices that were in front of the reference mesh (the 2015 dataset), whilst negative values lay behind this.

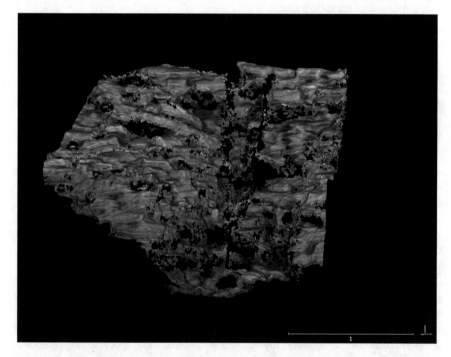

Fig. 14.13 RGB coloured mesh produced from dense cloud of 2003 images, looking southeast. Note the low resolution and lack of sharp details in the edges of the stonework. Scale in metres (L. Sou)

Fig. 14.14 RGB coloured mesh created from dense point cloud of 2015 images, looking southeast. Whilst more detailed and denser than the 2003 mesh, it is still noticeable that regular wavy patterns appear in the 3D mesh, likely a result of the low-resolution format of the images and lack of varied camera angles. Scale in metres (L. Sou)

With the scalar field colour display range set between ±50 mm, this shows that most vertex points are within this range (Fig. 14.15). The 2003 mesh, despite being cleaned through gradual selection with the smallest component sizes with the fewest connected vertices removed, still had a substantial amount of unreliable, noisy data. Despite this, the scalar field suggests that in most areas of the passageway, there had been no stone movement in excess of 50 mm, however, the blockade and some of the large, angled stones that were not laid flat, appear to have been subject to some large movements.

Through comparison of the original photographs to the scalar field results, it was found that of the areas coloured blue, which indicate features from the 2003 mesh were behind the 2015 mesh and which could be suggestive of stone settling and forward-facing collapse, most were areas where no data was present in the 2015 model. For example, the blue area to the top right of the mesh in Fig. 14.15 is due to a lack of data of the tops of those large protruding stones from 2015. The western inner passage wall was not covered well in the 2015 series of photographs due to a scale bar obscuring it; however, it is clear that stones have fallen forwards into the bottom of this area, with the original photographs confirming these changes (Fig. 14.16). Other than this finding, the 50 mm distance was too wide to detect more

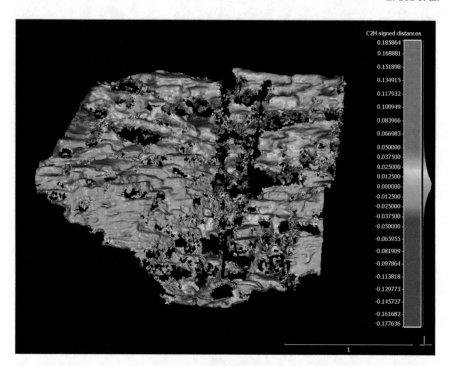

Fig. 14.15 Cloud-to-mesh distance measurements between meshes of the 2003 and 2015 photo data, looking southeast, displayed as a scalar field with red indicating distances exceeding 50 mm positively, and blue indicating distances exceeding 50 mm negatively. Yellow-green indicates areas of little (less than 50 mm) variation. The red and blue shown on the left edge of the mesh presents an area that was missing in the 2015 mesh. Scale in metres (L. Sou)

Fig. 14.16 Left, top-down view entrance passage in 2003. Right, side view entrance passage in 2015. Note how a stone from the wall top on the western side of the passage has fallen into the passage itself and is located beside the range pole (circled in yellow) (V.E. Turner, Shetland Amenity Trust)

subtle displacements, such as individual stone cracking.

With the scalar field set to show distances between ±10 mm, much more variance is visible, however, it also shows that there are areas of very little movement between the two meshes (Fig. 14.17). As detected in the cloud-to-cloud distance comparison between point clouds, the front faces of many stones at the entrance of the eastern inner passage wall were shown to be very similar in both meshes. This demonstrates the good stability of this section of the passageway over 12 years, and that the level and even stacking of flat stones in the construction is likely to be the main factor in this, however, even with finer distances viewed, stone cracks cannot be seen. The areas of red and blue which indicate differences over 10 mm between these stones are likely to have been caused due to the low resolution of the 2003 photographs, which presented the stone voids inaccurately, as seen in the mesh (see Fig. 14.13).

In contrast to the relative stability of the eastern side of the passageway, the scalar field does appear to demonstrate that many of the stones located on the top of the wall have slumped downwards, which suggests that their position is roughly 10 mm lower than their position relative to the 2003 mesh, as the tops of the stones are defined in blue. The fronts of many of these stones show as a band of green, then red, which is

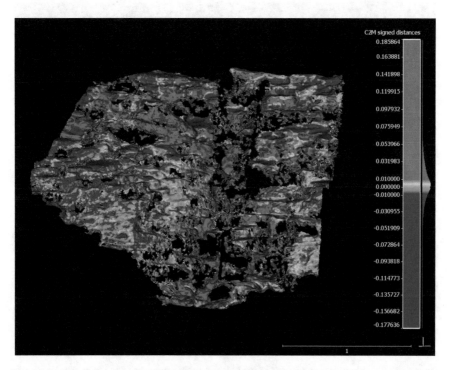

Fig. 14.17 Cloud-to-mesh distance measurements between meshes of the 2003 and 2015 photo data, looking south-east, displayed as a scalar field with red indicating distances exceeding 10 mm positively, and blue indicating distances exceeding 10 mm negatively. Yellow-green indicates areas of little (less than 10 mm) variation. Scale in metres (L. Sou)

the pattern expected if a stone is sliding downwards and forwards, as the base enters a new position where there was no stone in the 2003 mesh, whilst the central area stays within the 10 mm bounds of movement across 12 years. This movement is apparent on many of the upper stones on the western side of the entrance (Figs. 14.18, 14.19). The placement of gravel bags mid-way up the exposed north-western side of the broch sometime after the excavation, which are currently in-situ, indicates that stone movement was recognised to be a potential risk for those areas. This retrospective analysis of different epochs of photogrammetric data has shown that the outward movements of the stone are occurring on the western edges of the passageway too.

Collectively this data demonstrates that retrospective analysis of different photogrammetric datasets derived from archive data can successfully identify directional movement of stones between these two datasets, where stone "loss" and "gain" occur depending on whether the later mesh has vertices in front of or behind those of the earlier mesh. Despite neither dataset originally being recorded for such a purpose, and the low resolution of the meshes created, this technique was successful at detecting and, at a low resolution, measuring stone displacement.

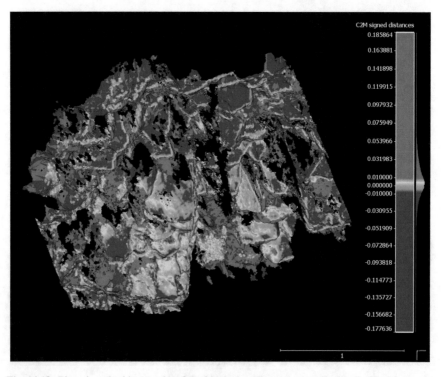

Fig. 14.18 Plan view (looking south) of the blocked north entrance to the broch. The blue areas indicate a downwards movement of over 10 mm. Note how many stones on the wall top appear to have this pattern, whilst the sides have not moved substantially (indicated in green). Scale in metres (L. Sou)

C2M signed distances
0.185864
0.163881
0.141898
0.119915
0.097932
0.075949
0.053966
0.031983
0.010000
0.000000
-0.010000
-0.030955
-0.051909
-0.072864
-0.093818
-0.114773
-0.135727
-0.156682
-0.177636

1.5

Fig. 14.19 Oblique view of subsiding stones from the wall tops of the entrance passage (right). Note the blue, green, red pattern as the stones slip downwards and forwards, as the wall top is not level but angled downwards with fewer stones at the front. Scale in metres (L. Sou)

14.7   Case Study 2—the North Cell Staircase

Given that the first case study was successful in examining the movement of stonework in the blocked staircase entrance to the broch, the same method was applied to the northern staircase, which appeared to show differences in the 2003 and 2015 images, although it was difficult to discern to what extent they did vary, from 2D imagery alone (Fig. 14.20) due to the different camera angles used.

Two 3D meshes were generated of the north cell staircase, context [2463], from point clouds produced from the 2003 and 2015 images using the same method detailed above. These were found to be extremely low in resolution (Fig. 14.21). Evidently, there were not enough overlapping images taken from different positions to produce detailed SfM photogrammetric models.

Once the two meshes were aligned using ICP fine registration, the mesh-to-cloud distances were computed. The maximum distance was initially set to 50 mm, to see if any major stone movements had taken place (Fig. 14.22).

Fig. 14.20 Left, top-down view photograph of the north stair taken in 2003. Right, side view the same stair in 2015. Note how the wooden pinnings supporting the fourth step are in different positions, suggesting stone movement, small loose stones are in different positions. The angle of the photographs is different, as is the perspective of the shots, which makes like for like visual comparison of the steps difficult through studying only the original photographs, although there are some certain differences in loose stones being in different locations (V.E. Turner, Shetland Amenity Trust)

The scalar field showed that there was a substantial amount of distance between the two meshes on the upper stairs of over 50 mm. This was most likely caused by stone displacement, as the top stone was not laid flat when it was revealed at excavation and this has most likely slumped downwards over 12 years. The areas of red in Fig. 14.22, which indicated forwards and upwards movement of the stone across time, may have been due to issues in accuracy of the two meshes and their low resolution rather than indicating genuine upwards movements. This method of analysis cannot instantly indicate rotational movement of stonework as the scalar field would present such movements through different distances, which would require more detailed study to enable patterns of rotation to be identified.

The 10 mm maximum distance scalar field (Fig. 14.23) showed that the difference between both the meshes and the downwards slumping of the stone steps is much more apparent. These distance measurements indicated the level of difference was most extreme at the top of the staircase, which is also the area most likely to have more displacement due to the stones being looser, more exposed and not being laid flat, whilst there were smaller differences on the mid-lower stones. This would be expected as the stones were set between each other and were laid in a more level alignment, so less movement was likely. The stones at the very base of the staircase appeared to have moved forward, according to the distance comparisons between the meshes. This can be interpreted as the lower stones being pushed forwards due to the slope of the stair, as the upper stones were forced downwards over time by gravity.

These results appear to suggest that movement had taken place in this northern area of the broch. Although the retrospective nature of the SfM processing meant

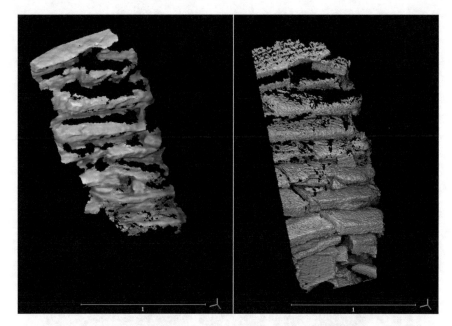

Fig. 14.21   (Left) 2003 images processed into 3D mesh of the stairs. (Right) 2015 images processed into 3D mesh of the same area. Both images aligned in the same position. It is clear much data is missing from the 2003 model and the definition of the stone details is very poor. The 2015 model also did not capture the surface of the stone accurately, as wavy patterns appeared in the mesh, as with other stonework throughout the retrospective processing of these archived photos, likely due to image file decimation (though this needs confirmation). Scale is in metres (L. Sou)

that the interpretations made could not be confirmed with certainty, from analysis of both the original images and from distance measurements being made, the pattern of distances between the stonework did imply that displacement had taken place, and the interpretations for how the movement had occurred is likely (Harkness et al. 2002; Mundell et al. 2008; Douglas in prep). The stairs were interpreted as being constructed on top of a rubble core with the walls either side of them being built at the same time as the steps (Dockrill 2015). It may be possible that the uneven nature of its foundation may have also been a factor in its movement over time. The noticeable movement of smaller loose stones between images taken in 2003 and 2015 also suggests this. A caveat to these interpretations is the poor resolution of the 3D data created, however, since clear differences in distance on the steps could not be detected on the basis of comparing the still photographs on their own, this case study also shows that retrospective photogrammetry can reveal potential structural issues, even with relatively small numbers of images at low resolutions. Without further detailed conservation/engineering assessment it is not possible to discuss whether the movements that have been examined in this study are of immediate concern. However, by highlighting the potential of using archive imagery for retrospective SfM photogrammetry analysis, we offer conservators, site managers

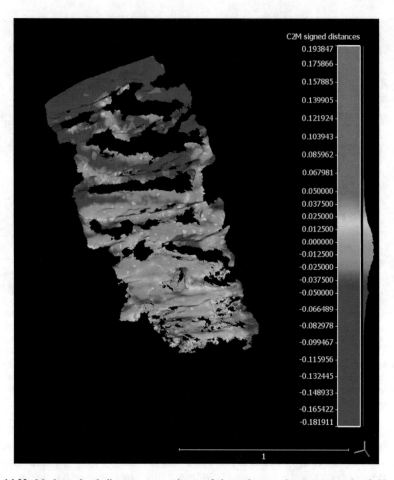

Fig. 14.22 Mesh-to-cloud distance comparisons of the staircase, shown as a scalar field with maximum distance set to 50 mm. Stone displacement is clear on the upper stone flag stairs, coloured blue, as negative movement had occurred between 2003 and 2015. This indicates that the 2015 mesh in this area was beneath the 2003 mesh, suggesting downwards subsidence over time (L. Sou)

and future researchers a valuable tool to be able to examine specific areas of sites and monitor them diachronically, to see if displacement issues are apparent, and to act on them if necessary.

Whilst certain changes are visible with this type of data analysis, the results also suggest that this technique of analysis on retrospective data may be too coarse to detect changes in stonework that are the result of weathering and erosion to stone. However, this will be dependent on the accuracy and detail of the SfM point clouds and 3D meshes that are generated from old images and their coverage and overlap of the features recorded. Analysis was determined using the following parameters adjusted to a finer resolution of 1–5 mm, to see if smaller differences could be shown and recognised between the meshes of the stairs, however, most of the distances

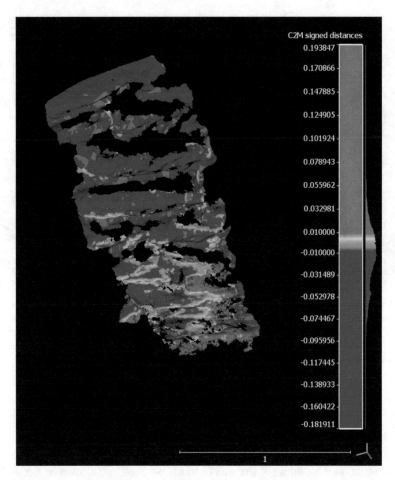

C2M signed distances

0.193847
0.170866
0.147885
0.124905
0.101924
0.078943
0.055962
0.032981
0.010000
-0.010000
-0.031489
-0.052978
-0.074467
-0.095956
-0.117445
-0.138933
-0.160422
-0.181911

1

Fig. 14.23 Mesh-to-cloud distance comparisons of the staircase, shown as a scalar field with maximum distance set to 10 mm (L. Sou)

shown were too large to highlight more subtle changes, in areas where there was less variation (Fig. 14.24). This dataset was notably noisy, and the mesh generated from the 2003 photos was particularly poor in resolution and accuracy. To determine whether better, more accurate data could be successful in detecting distance variation as a result of weathering rather than stone displacement, a final case study analysis was made of the point clouds from the area of the broch that aligned most successfully from these case studies, which was the north external wall.

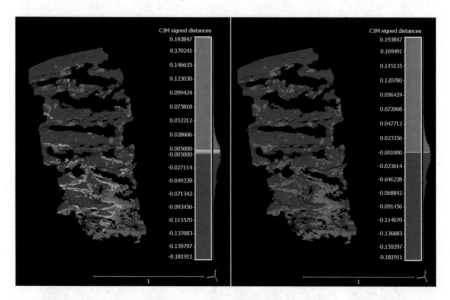

Fig. 14.24 Left, top-down view 5 mm maximum distance scalar field of the meshes. Note how there is little difference between this and the 10 mm max. scalar field. Right, side view 1 mm maximum distance scalar field. This shows that all points in the meshes exceed distance of 1 mm between each other, which was expected due to the low resolution of the data. Therefore, finer distances cannot be analysed with this technique on such data. Scale is in metres (L. Sou)

14.8 Case Study 3—the Exterior Entrance to the Broch and Outer Wall

The third analysis was conducted on a localised area of the broch's external entrance in the north wall, comparing the point clouds produced from images from 2003 to 2015. This entrance was found blocked when first excavated and the blocking stonework was subsequently removed, leaving the inner wall element contexts east [5825] and west [5826] of the entrance [5819] and outer walls [5830] to the west and [5831] east (Dockrill 2015) (see Fig. 14.3). It was found through an initial alignment made on the large flag stone at the base of the passage (context [5819]) that the two point clouds (Figs. 14.25, 14.26) aligned extremely well in this area, using the same method outlined above (Fig. 14.27). This area may have been the most unlikely to have moved due to the low and level position of the stones, making it an appropriate candidate to observe fine differences potentially due to weathering.

To analyse the single flagstone in greater detail, both the point clouds produced from 2003 to 2015 images were cropped of all other features. High-resolution meshes were created from these and the two meshes were aligned to ensure the alignment was reliably accurate with little error.

As found with the above case study, creating the meshes emphasised the low resolution of the data and possible issues with compression, as much of the 3D

Fig. 14.25 Dense point cloud produced from images taken in 2003, of the external wall of Structure 9, the Iron Age broch, looking south. Compared to the point cloud generated of the blocked north inner entrance and staircase (see below), the level of detail in the stonework is high, due to the better overlapping coverage of this feature in the photographs taken. Large flagstone selected for analysis indicated by arrow. Scale in metres (L. Sou)

Fig. 14.26 Dense point cloud produced from images taken in 2015, of the external wall and passage of Structure 9, the Iron Age broch, looking south. Note how there are large areas where data is missing due to lack of overlap in the images used. Despite this, the point cloud was denser than the one produced from 2003 photos, as the images were higher in resolution. Scale in metres (L. Sou)

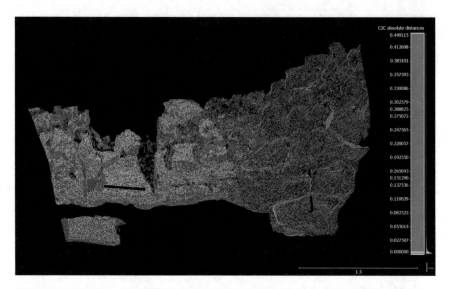

Fig. 14.27 Scalar field of absolute distances measured between the 2003 and 2015 image point clouds after ICP fine registration and estimated 20% overlap set, as it was expected many points would not overlap due to variations and differences expected between 12 years of exposure to the elements. The RMS, the square root of the mean square errors from the cloud-to-cloud alignment out of 49,999 sampled points, was 6.39 mm. Scalar field shows all distances above 6.39 mm in red. Note how there was very little difference in the point clouds around the faced outer wall passage apart from where data was missing and where a small stone was dislodged sometime in the 12 years between when the photographs were taken. Scales in metres (L. Sou)

representation of the surface of the stone looked very uneven (Fig. 14.28), whilst in the photographs and point clouds it looked much flatter (see Figs. 14.25, 14.26).

These meshes were aligned in CloudCompare using the same methods as above and a cloud-to-mesh distance calculation was conducted. The total RMS from the ICP registration of the two meshes was 2.16 mm computed on 29,950 points. This was significantly lower than the RMS values produced from aligning the larger point clouds in the above case studies, indicating much lower error margins, however, this still did not reach sub-millimetre levels of accuracy, and visually the alignment looked poor (Fig. 14.28). A cloud-to-mesh distance calculation was conducted between the two meshes (Fig. 14.29).

It is clear that the uneven, regular wave pattern found across the 3D data generated from the 2015 photographs impacted on the distances measured. Four distinct bands of the waves can clearly be seen rising above the 2003 mesh as red lines in the scalar field. At a resolution of 1 mm maximum distance, this is apparent. Due to this regular wave pattern being found in the 2015 3D data, and only being clearly apparent in the 3D meshes generated, it was not possible to examine the data at a finer resolution. Significantly, this pattern was not detected on visual inspection and in distance measurements between the dense point clouds studied above. This research has therefore shown that the 3D meshes helped to highlight problematic

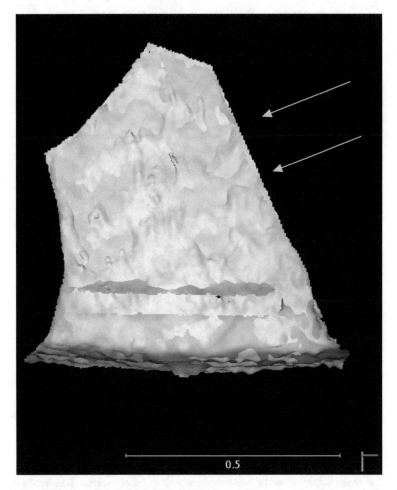

Fig. 14.28 Aligned meshes of the flagstone at the front of the external entrance to the broch in 2003 and 2015. Note the poor resolution of the mesh, as the surface of the stone was processed very unevenly in both meshes. The pattern of bumpy waves was more apparent in the 2015 mesh, as seen across the other point clouds and meshes generated from those photographs. Direction of the waves indicated by arrows. Scale in metres (L. Sou)

datasets which were not observed in the dense point clouds. The control case study with the 2018 survey data showed no evidence of this issue, which indicated that the problem was associated with the digital images from 2015. Whether this is due to compression settings in their file format, the limited angles the images were taken from or the scale bars being used to correctly scale and align the photographs for SfM photogrammetry needs further investigation.

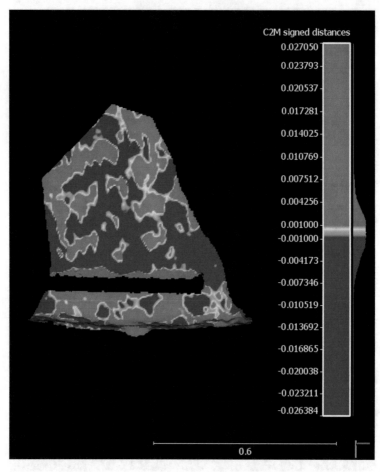

Fig. 14.29 Scalar field showing distance movement between the two meshes. Blue indicates negative movement and red positive with the maximum distance was set to 1 mm. Scale in metres (L. Sou)

14.9 Conclusion

This chapter has shown that retrospective photogrammetry using archive digital photographs can produce 3D data that can be used in the detection of stone displacement in drystone architecture, as at the broch of Old Scatness. However, without metadata, scale bars and sufficient varied camera angles and positions capturing the feature of interest, analogue film photographs could not be successfully processed with accuracy, demonstrating the importance that such information needs to be made available where possible. Comparison of smaller areas of point clouds and meshes produced using archived digital imagery was successful in enabling diachronic change to be examined. The error values produced in the process of 3D model creation and alignment were found to increase with comparisons of larger areas of 3D data, however the smallest RMS error with old data was found to be over 2 mm, so very subtle changes could not be identified. The control case study demonstrated this as the fine registration RMS was 0.91 mm, even when theoretically there should have been no difference between the laser scan point cloud and photogrammetric model. The case studies demonstrated several instances where changes in distances between meshes were likely to be the result of displacements in the 12 years between the two image sets from 2003 to 2015 being taken, and the technique of analysing cloud-to-mesh distances was particularly successful in detecting large displacements in stone of over 5 mm in scalar fields, with some of these changes evident within the photographs. However, where camera angles varied more between the two image sets, the Cloud-Compare cloud-to-mesh distance measurement calculation was especially useful in indicating the direction of the variations, as in the case of the north cell stair. From these analyses, it was evident that many of the non-level, sloping vertically stacked stones had been moving downwards over time. This may be due to weight-bearing issues of the stone, a lack of or loss of stone pinnings, or other factors that will require further investigation to better understand and support consolidation works in the future.

The case studies have demonstrated that a retrospective approach to SfM photogrammetry is possible, but only when legacy photographs possess the required attributes and metadata. This highlights the present need for digital metadata to be archived with archaeological photography with sufficient information about the context from which it was taken, so future researchers may face fewer issues in retrospective processing. Whilst much metadata is automatically recorded in modern digital cameras, practical actions can also be useful, such as archaeologists ensuring scale bars remain in the same position for every post-excavation shot to maximise the usability of their photographs. Retrospective SfM photogrammetry has benefits to conservation monitoring of structures to detect some structural changes over a period of time, and more research into retrospective SfM processing of old archaeological images is required to further understand the potentials and limits of these valuable datasets.

References

Agisoft (2018) Agisoft photoscan user manual: professional edition, version 1.4. Agisoft, St. Petersburg, p 113

CloudCompare (2015) Cloud-to-mesh distance. https://www.cloudcompare.org/doc/wiki/index.php?title=Cloud-to-Mesh_Distance. Accessed 5 Sept 2019

CloudCompare (2016) Meaning regitration RMS. http://www.danielgm.net/cc/forum/viewtopic.php?t=1631. Accessed 5 Sept 2019

3Dflow SRL (2019) 3DF Zephyr. https://www.3dflow.net/3df-zephyr-pro-3d-models-from-photos/. Accessed 8 Sept 2019

Discamps E, Muth X, Gravina B, Lacrampe-Cuyaubère F, Chadelle J-P, Faivre J-P et al (2016) Photogrammetry as a tool for integrating archival data in archaeological fieldwork: examples from the Middle Palaeolithic sites of Combe-Grenal, Le Moustier, and Regourdou. J Archaeol Sci Rep 8:268–276. https://doi.org/10.1016/j.jasrep.2016.06.004

Dockrill SJ (2015) The pre-broch sequences and broch construction. In: Dockrill SJ, Bond JM, Turner VE, Brown LD, Bashford DJ, Cussans JEM et al (eds) Excavations at Old Scatness, Shetland, vol 2. The Broch and Iron Age Village. Shetland Heritage Publications, Lerwick, pp 31–63

Dockrill SJ, Bond JM (2015) An introduction to the archaeological excavations at Old Scatness. In: Dockrill SJ, Bond JM, Turner VE, Brown LD, Bashford DJ, Cussans JEM et al. (eds) Excavations at Old Scatness, Shetland vol 2. The Broch and Iron Age Village. Shetland Heritage Publications, Lerwick, pp 1–29

Dockrill SJ, Bond J, Turner V, Brown LD, Bashford DJ, Cussans JE et al. (2010) Excavations at Old Scatness, Shetland, vol 1. The Pictish village and Viking settlement. Shetland Heritage Publications, Lerwick

Dockrill SJ, Bond JM, Turner VE, Brown LD, Bashford DJ, Cussans JE et al. (2015) Excavations at Old Scatness, Shetland, vol 2. The Broch and Iron Age village. Shetland Heritage Publications, Lerwick

Faber E, Sparrow T, Murgatroyd A, Wilson AS, Gaffney V, Gaffney C et al (2017) Curious Travellers: Preserving endangered heritage across the world. Curr World Archaeol 1

FARO (2016) FARO laser scanner Focus3D X 330 tech sheet. In: FARO (ed). FARO, Lake Mary, Florida

Frost A (2018) Applied digital documentation in the historic environment. In: Wilson L, Rawlinson A, Gonzalez A, Hyslop E (eds) Short guides, 1st edn. Historic Environment Scotland, Edinburgh, p 84

Green J (2019) Legacy Data in 3D: the Cape Andreas Survey (1969–1970) and Santo António de Tanná Expeditions (1978–1979). In: McCarthy JK, Benjamin J, Winton T, van Duivenvoorde W (eds) 3D Recording and interpretation for maritime archaeology. Springer International Publishing, Cham, pp 29–43

Gruen A, Remondino F, Zhang L (2003) Image-based automated reconstruction of the Great Buddha of Bamiyan, Afghanistan. Paper presented at the computer vision and pattern recognition workshop. CVPRW '03, Madison, USA

Harkness RM, Bush DI, Powrie W, Zhang X (2002) Deformation and failure modes of drystone retaining walls. Geotechnique 52:435–446. https://doi.org/10.1680/geot.2002.52.6.435

Historic England (2017). Photogrammetric applications for cultural heritage. Guidance for good practice. Historic England, Swindon, p 128

Mundell C, McCombie P, Heath A (2008) Large scale testing of drystone retaining walls. In: VI international conference on structural analysis of historic construction, SAHC08, Bath, 2–4 July 2008

Schönberger JL, Frahm J-M (2016) Structure-from-motion revisited. In: Proceedings of the IEEE conference on computer vision and pattern recognition, pp. 4104–4113

Schönberger JL, Zheng E, Pollefeys M, Frahm J-M (2016) Pixelwise view selection for unstructured multi-view stereo. Paper presented at the European conference on computer vision, Amsterdam

The Survey Association (2016) Client guide to photogrammetry. TSA client guides. The Survey Association, p 17

UNESCO (2019) Mousa, Old Scatness and Jarlshof: the zenith of Iron Age Shetland. http://whc.unesco.org/en/tentativelists/5677. Accessed 9 Aug 2019

University of Bradford (2017) Curious travellers: visualising heritage. http://www.visualisingheritage.org/CT.php. Accessed 30 Jan 2018

Wallace C, Dedík L, Minaroviech J, Moullou D (2017) 3D modeling and virtual access of omega house in the athenian agora. Paper presented at the conference on cultural heritage and new technologies (CHNT) 22, Vienna, Austria

Wallace C (2017) Retrospective photogrammetry in greek archaeology. Stud Dig Heritage **1**(2):20. https://doi.org/10.14434/sdh.v1i2.23251

Wilson AS, Gaffney V, Gaffney C, Ch'ng E, Bates CR, Sears G et al (2019) Curious travellers—repurposing imagery to manage and interpret threatened monuments, sites and landscapes. In: Dawson M, James E, Nevell M (eds) Heritage under pressure—threats and solutions: studies of agency and soft power in the historic environment. Oxbow, Oxford, pp 107–122

Chapter 15
Digital Refit Analysis of Anthropogenically Fragmented Equine Bone from the Schöningen 13 II-4 Deposits, Germany

Andrew D. Holland, Jarod M. Hutson, Aritza Villaluenga, Tom Sparrow, Andrew Murgatroyd, Alejandro García-Moreno, Elaine Turner, Adrian Evans, Sabine Gaudzinski-Windheuser, and Andrew S. Wilson

Abstract Excavation of the Schöningen lignite mine in Germany produced the earliest examples of hunting spears to date, and a large assemblage of anthropogenically fragmented faunal remains deposited in anaerobic lacustrine silt sediments during the Middle Pleistocene. The exceptional preservation of the assemblage makes the site of prime importance to our understanding of the behavioural, social and economic patterns of hominins in the Lower Palaeolithic of the Middle Pleistocene in Europe. This chapter describes the digital refitting analysis, part of the AHRC-funded *Fragmented Heritage* project, undertaken to address the logistical challenge posed by manually comparing individual bone fragments within the assemblage to identify refitting sequences. This logistical refit challenge uses the Schöningen assemblage to investigate the effectiveness of a digital refit approach to the analysis of large faunal assemblages. We describe the process from digitisation of the bone fragments by macro structured light scanning, digital segmentation of refitting surfaces, and digital comparison of the refitting and non-refitting surfaces to

A. D. Holland (✉) · T. Sparrow · A. Murgatroyd · A. Evans · A. S. Wilson
Visualising Heritage, School of Archaeological and Forensic Sciences, University of Bradford, Bradford, UK

J. M. Hutson · A. Villaluenga · A. García-Moreno · E. Turner · S. Gaudzinski-Windheuser
MONREPOS Archaeological Research Centre and Museum for Human Behavioural Evolution, Neuwied, Germany

J. M. Hutson
Department of Paleobiology, National Museum of Natural History, Smithsonian Institution, Washington, D.C, USA

A. Villaluenga
University of the Basque Country (UPV-EHU), Prehistory Research Group, Vitoria-Gasteiz, Spain

A. García-Moreno
Prehistory and Archaeology Museum of Cantabria (MUPAC), Santander, Spain

S. Gaudzinski-Windheuser
Institute of Ancient Studies, Johannes Gutenberg University, Mainz, Germany

© Springer Nature Switzerland AG 2022
E. Ch'ng et al. (eds.), *Visual Heritage: Digital Approaches in Heritage Science*,
Springer Series on Cultural Computing,
https://doi.org/10.1007/978-3-030-77028-0_15

produce statistical matches. We discuss how taphonomic data can be visualised from the analysis and can be used to inform interpretation of the taphonomic histories of these faunal remains and the human behaviours associated with the formation of this unique assemblage.

Keywords Digital refit · Structured light scanning · Lower Palaeolithic · Faunal assemblage

15.1 Introduction

The Schöningen lignite extraction mine in Germany has yielded large assemblages of organic materials deposited in anaerobic lacustrine silt sediments during the Middle Pleistocene (781kya to 126kya). The preservation of the remains is exceptional and offers detailed information about organic material, hunting weapons, prey carcases and evidence of their butchery, making the site of Schöningen of prime importance to our understanding of the behavioural, social and economic patterns of hominins in the Lower Palaeolithic of the Middle Pleistocene in Europe.

The primary prey species at the site were large equids, which represented between 85 and 95% of the individuals (Starkovich and Conard 2015). This imprecise estimate reflects the fragmentary nature of the remains following their perimortem processing to extract the marrow (Voormolen 2008a, b; van Kolfschoten et al. 2015). The number of fragments of equine bone within the deposits offers a refit analysis problem comparable to that of lithic refit analysis on other butchery sites such as Boxgrove (Rees 2000; Ashton 2007); a manual refit process, comparing each surface to every other surface in the assemblage, would be prohibitively time consuming. Yet, refitting the bone fragments is important to produce accurate numbers for the minimum number of skeletal elements (MNE), which is key to the calculation of measures of abundance such as minimum number of individuals (MNI). These in turn are used to assess the taphonomic histories of the faunal assemblage and the human behaviours associated with its formation (García-Moreno et al. 2015; Hutson et al. 2013).

The wider *Fragmented Heritage* project aims to demonstrate how the power of computer aided automation can be applied to the problem of refit analysis for lithics. The osseous remains from Schöningen 13 therefore offered an opportunity to extend computer-based refit to skeletal material from a similar context to that of the lithic material already being analysed by the *Fragmented Heritage* project. This research explored some of the factors that can inform the adaption of the *Fragmented Heritage* digital refit system to the refitting of fragmentary osseous material. As such, digitisation of the complete Schöningen 13 faunal assemblage was not considered to be achievable until the refit methodology had reached a more mature form, but an initial study of a subsample of the faunal remains would form an ideal case study. A subsampling strategy for the faunal remains was developed, and the author carried out digitisation of the fragmentary skeletal material whilst it was being studied at the

MONREPOS Archaeological Research Centre and Museum for Human Behavioural Evolution, in Neuwied, Germany.

15.2   Site Description

The archaeological deposits at Schöningen were located within a large open cast lignite extraction mine to the east of the village of Schöningen near Helmstedt in Lower Saxony, Germany (Fig. 15.1). The site is divided into two large quarries (northern and southern).

Schöningen site 13, within the southern quarry, was comprised of a sequence of six paleochannels eroded into the glacial till deposits associated with the Elsterian glaciation (Fig. 15.3). These, in turn, overlie the Palaeogene lignite deposits that were being extracted. The six channels, numbered I to VI, intercut each other (with channel I being the stratigraphically earliest) and are filled with lacustrine silts and later peat formation. The six channels therefore represent a sequence of laterally stacked shallow channels of an interglacial lake, forming a deltaic littoral, wetland environment (Mania 1995; Thieme 1999; Lang et al. 2012).

From 1994 onwards, removal of the quaternary deposits overlying the Palaeogene lignite in the southern quarry exposed a series of waterlogged Middle Pleistocene deposits in which significant archaeological material was identified (Fig. 15.2).

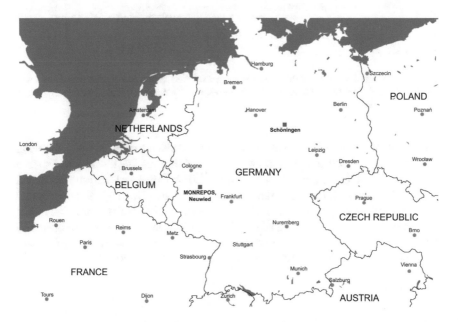

Fig. 15.1 Map showing location of Schöningen, Germany (Used with kind permission of Andrew Holland 2017, p. 201)

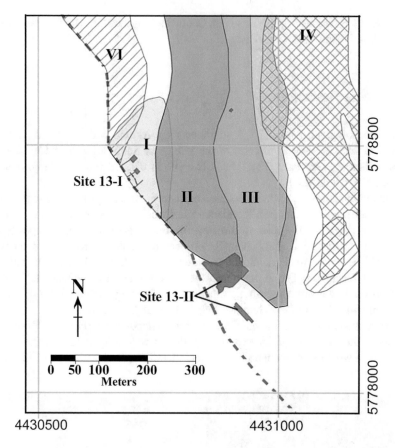

Fig. 15.2 General site plan for the southern quarry of the Schöningen lignite extraction mine including Schöningen 13-II (Used with kind permission of Andrew Holland 2017, p. 202, after Serangeli et al. 2015)

Layer 4 of channel II (Schöningen 13 II-4) produced eight wooden throwing spears made of spruce and pine. These were dated through U/Th dating to 290 ± 5 KaBP (Marine Isotope Stage 9) (Sierralta et al. 2012; Urban and Sierralta 2012) and represent the earliest throwing spears recorded anywhere (Thieme 1997). In association was a very large assemblage of faunal remains (c. 15,000 elements). The faunal remains from the site are dominated by a large equine species (*Equus mosbachensis*) although large bovids and cervids are also present within the assemblage in smaller numbers (van Kolfschoten 2012, 2014; García-Moreno et al. 2015).

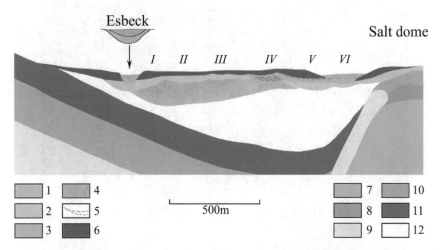

SW   Exposure at the open-cast mine, Schöningen, 1995   NE

Fig. 15.3 Reconstructed section drawing of the deposits of Schöningen 13 in the southern quarry of the Schöningen lignite extraction mine. Key: 1. Elsterian glacial tills; 2. Saalian glacial deposits; 3. Lacustrine deposits; 4. Limnic telmatic sequences; 5. Soil complexes; 6. Loess deposits; 7. Evaporites; 8. Gypsum cap-rock; 9. Buntsandstein; 10. Triassic limestone (Muschelkalk); 11. Triassic deposits (Keuper); 12 Palaeogene deposits (Used with kind permission of Andrew Holland, 2017, p. 203, based on Mania 1995)

15.3 Taphonomy

Preservation of the organic materials from the Middle Pleistocene layers of the Schöningen 13 site is exceptional and due to the wet anaerobic nature of the lacustrine silt sediments into which they were deposited. Additionally, the underlying limestone geology imparts a high carbonate concentration to the pore water environment, producing stable, reducing conditions which have limited the dissolution of bone mineral (Serangeli et al. 2015), and inhibited access to the underlying collagen structure (Kuitems et al. 2015). Consequently, the surfaces of the equine bone from Schöningen 13 II-4 were very well preserved, allowing the marks of carcass processing to be assessed against evidence for pre- and post- depositional taphonomic change (Starkovich and Conard 2015). 98% of the equine remains are ascribed to weathering stage A (i.e. "not to slightly weathered") (Voormolen 2008b), indicating that the bones were rapidly deposited within the silt. Furthermore, 95% of the bones show no sign of post-depositional taphonomic damage to the bone surface with only 2.8% of the specimens showing slight rounding of the fracture surfaces. Fluvial transport and erosion of the surface of the bone is not a significant factor in the assemblage, with only 1.5% of bone fragments exhibiting sediment friction striation damage to the bone surfaces (Voormolen 2008a; Starkovich and Conard

Fig. 15.4 MechInnovations MechScan macro structured light scanner (Used with kind permission of Andrew Holland 2017, p. 234)

2015). The surfaces of the bones were stained mid to dark brown in colour from the surrounding organic rich silt and peat sediments.

In terms of the fracture patterns, green bone fractures occur in a large percentage of the assemblage; these are associated with impact notches and scarring, indicating that the bone was intentionally fractured close to the animal's death, a pattern that has been linked to marrow extraction (Voormolen 2008a). Whilst dry bone fractures were also identified within the assemblage, these fractures occur almost exclusively (82.6% of dry bone fractures) on fragile osseous structures particularly in the axial skeleton (vertebral processes, ribs etc.) and are associated with sediment compaction and deformation from the weight of overlying sediments (Voormolen 2008b).

15.4 Methodology

As part of the post excavation analysis and documentation of the Schöningen 13 II-4 faunal assemblage at the MONREPOS, a number of fracture refits had been manually identified. The research aimed to examine whether refitting fracture surfaces could be identified from digitised fragmentary skeletal material. In order to test this, the sub-sample needed to include material that was known to refit. The sub-sample of material considered for scanning therefore included all those fragments where manual refits had been already identified (Table 15.1). Additionally, in order to demonstrate that digitised material did not generate false positive results for otherwise non-refitting fracture surfaces, a further two fragments that were known from manual refit testing not to match any of the surfaces within those in the sub-sample were also included.

Initially the criteria for the sub-sample included both green bone fractures and dry bone fractures, in order to further examine the effect of taphonomic change on

Table 15.1 Refitting bone fragments from Schöningen 13 II-4, Germany

Sample	Site no	Local find no	Description
SCH_7574	13II-4	698/13–8	Equine femur fragment
SCH_7707	13II-4	699/13–4	Equine femur fragment
SCH_7094	13II-4	696/12–13	Equine femur shaft fragment
SCH_5167	13II-4	691/17–5	Equine distal femur
SCH_6056	13II-4	693/15–26	Equine right radius shaft fragment
SCH_6540	13II-4	694/16–29	Equine right radius shaft fragment
SCH_6726	13II-4	694/20–24	Equine right radius mid-shaft fragment
SCH_12487	13II-4	695/20–4	Equine right radius distal end
SCH_2926	13II-4	687/21–1	Equine right radius shaft fragment
SCH_3058	13II-4	687/24–15	Equine right radius shaft fragment
SCH_2499	13II-4	686/25–5	Equine right radius shaft fragment
SCH_3134	13II-4	687/27–8	Equine right radius shaft fragment
SCH_2525	13II-4	686/26–28	Equine left radius shaft fragment
SCH_1158	13II-4	683/28–19	Equine left radius shaft fragment
SCH_5140	13II-4	691/16–6	Equine left radius shaft fragment
SCH_4283	13II-4	689/19–75	Equine left radius shaft fragment
SCH_6835	13II-4	695/11–17	Equine left radius distal end
SCH_4772	13II-4	690/18–52	Equine left radius distal end
SCH_6880	13II-4	695/13–20	Equine left ulna (olecranon process)
SCH_6599	13II-4	694/17–3	Equine left ulna (prox artic surfaces)
SCH_6599_b	13II-4	694/17–3	Equine left ulna
SCH_17702	13II-4	689/22–15	Equine left radius shaft fragment
SCH_3702	13II-4	688/21–16	Equine left radius shaft fragment

digitisation and the resultant digital refit. The dry bone fractures within the assemblage occurred on small and fragile osseous structures meaning that manual refit had not identified any refitting bone fracture pairs by the date of digitisation; therefore, the sub-sample was limited to green bone fractures.

The samples had been cleaned and dried during the post-excavation processing of the site archive. The samples were dry, but some had accumulated a fine coating of dust in the interim, which was gently removed with a soft brush prior to digitisation.

15.5   Sample Digitisation

The Schöningen 13 II-4 samples were digitised over a week at MONREPOS in Germany using a MechInnovations MechScan (MechInnovations Ltd, Leamington Spa, UK) macro structured light scanner with an 8 cm field of view calibrated via a 1.3 mm calibration pattern board and a MechInnovations high precision computer controlled turntable (MechInnovations Ltd, Leamington Spa, UK) controlled using FlexScan3D version 3.3 (LMI Technologies Inc., Delta, BC, Canada) software system.

To capture the 3D surface shape of an object, structured light scanners use the deformation of a series of binary structured fringe images projected onto an object (Inokuchi et al. 1984; Pribanić et al. 2010; Salvi et al. 2010) to identify its shape and position in 3D space through the use of machine vision cameras (Inokuchi et al. 1984; Salvi et al. 2004). Phase-shifting the structured fringe patterns over the object's surface uses the full spatial resolution of pixels on the camera sensors and results in higher quality scans. As phase-shifting of the pattern uses multiple camera images in rapid succession and averaging of point information between patterns, structured light systems exhibit greater adaptability to ambient light conditions and darker coloured objects (Bathow et al. 2010; Ekstrand et al. 2013). This includes the dark brown surface colour of the Schöningen samples. To further mitigate the impact of ambient light on the dark coloured samples, black-out curtains were used to limit the light on the samples during scans, resulting in better structured light pattern recognition within the machine vision element of the scanner and thus improving scan quality.

Using the turntable to automate the scanning, individual scans were recorded every 30° of rotation. Additional, manually oriented scans were added as required to ensure full coverage of each sample's surface. After each scan, FlexScan3D calculates the 3D points from the fringe pattern images of the two cameras and produces a point cloud for each scan pass. Noise filtering was applied at this stage, and FlexScan3D temporarily meshes the point clouds from each scan pass with a triangulated irregular network meshing and attempts to automatically align all the scan passes using a basic mesh to mesh geometry matching algorithm. As the number of scan passes increases, both the number of possible solutions to the mesh to mesh matching and the level of uncertainty due to imprecision resulting from mesh variation increases and additional scans follow a pattern of diminishing returns (Friess 2012). Therefore, prior to combining scans into a single 3D model, a fine alignment was applied using an iterative least squares alignment on the underlying point cloud data for each scan pass. This produces a mesh to mesh distance statistic which is an indicator of model and scan quality.

To create a single model, the scan passes were then combined and finalised, the point clouds of the scan passes were merged into a single reconstructed model and the resulting combined point cloud was meshed with an irregular triangulated network meshing operation and small holes were automatically filled. The finalised models were exported, using the sample and fragment numbering system in the filename, to both an.obj and an.stl file format for later analysis.

15.6 Refit Analysis

Refit quality assessment for the samples was carried out in CloudCompare V2 version 2.6.1 (CloudCompare.org, Paris) and MeshLab version 1.3.3 (ISTR/CNR, Pisa/Rome). The two.obj models for each previously identified refit were imported into CouldCompare V2, moved to the centre of the virtual space and orientated to the local X, Y, Z axes. The fragment with the lowest fragment number was chosen to be the reference fragment (i.e. to remain in a fixed position), and the other fragment was orientated using the *Translate-Rotate* tool so that their refitting surfaces were roughly aligned, and then further alignment was carried out using the *Point-Pair Registration* tool.

Computer modelling systems were found to be poor at characterising refitting fracture surfaces and distinguishing them from surrounding bone. In the wider *Fragmented Heritage* project this problem was the subject of extensive research in computer modelling theory and 3D computational mathematics. Due to this computational challenge, the computer programmes cannot yet determine which areas of two 3D models to compare to produce a refit analysis. The presence of large digitised areas of the external cortical surfaces of the bone fragments within the scans dominate alignment calculations over the smaller fracture surfaces and confuse the alignment algorithms. To overcome this, the 3D models of the fragments were manually edited using the *Segment* tool to remove the external and internal cortical surfaces and leave only the fracture surfaces. Following this segmentation an Iterative Closest Point (ICP) alignment algorithm was applied using the *ICP Fine Registration* tool to produce a fine alignment with a Root Mean Square difference between iterations of less than $10e^{-6}$ and a final overlap between the refitting surfaces of at least 75%.

A statistical analysis of the distances between the two fracture surfaces was carried out using the *Cloud to Mesh Distance* analysis tool. To facilitate this, the segmented surface of the fragment with the higher fragment number was converted to a cloud point using the *Points Sampling on Mesh* tool. The tool produced a regularly distributed high density point cloud with point positions corresponding to the surface of the source mesh. The *Cloud to Cloud Distance* tool calculates the Euclidean distance between each point and its nearest neighbour within a spherical neighbourhood domain of the reference cloud, whilst the Cloud to Mesh Distance tool calculates

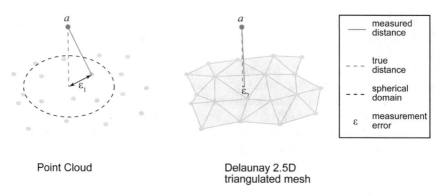

Point Cloud   Delaunay 2.5D
                                     triangulated mesh

Fig. 15.5 Comparison of cloud to cloud and cloud to mesh distance analysis methods

the distance from a point to the intersect with the reference mesh (Fig. 15.5). The distance between a point and its nearest neighbour, which may be offset to one side, does not provide the true distance between the two clouds and therefore introduces small imprecision error to the overall results. Cloud to Mesh Distance analysis overcomes this as the distance is calculated to the mesh surface rather than a point that might be offset and therefore Cloud to Mesh Distances provide more accurate results.

Measured distances between a point and its nearest neighbour in Cloud to Cloud Distance analysis may not as accurately reflect the true distance (left); Cloud to Mesh Distance analysis produces a measurement from the point to the nearest mesh surface resulting in more accurate data (i.e. $\varepsilon_1 > \varepsilon_2$) (Used with kind permission of Andrew Holland 2017, p. 254; after CloudCompare.org 2015, page 30).

The statistical analysis produced both mean and standard deviation signed distances between the cloud points and the mesh surface and applied them as a symmetrical scalar field colour scale to the surface of the point cloud, with the colour thresholds set at ±0.1 mm. The long tails of outliers for the distance distributions were removed from the data using the *Filter Points by Value* tool. The upper and lower bounds for the outlier removal were calculated based on the outlier data labelling rule with a *g* value of 2.2, and the calculated mean and standard deviation of the distances between the two surfaces were recorded.

As a further quality measure for the refit of the fracture surfaces, the percentage of the refitting surface at a distance from the corresponding fracture surface within a range of ±0.1 mm was calculated. Surface area calculations can only be reliably applied to meshed surfaces, as point clouds do not have any surface dimensions. Two clones of the point cloud produced in the *Cloud to Mesh Distance* analysis (Fig. 15.5) were made using the *Clone* tool. One of the cloud points was filtered using the *Filter Points by Value* tool to remove all values outside of the -0.1 to 0.1 mm range. Both clouds were meshed using the *Delaunay 2.5D (Best Fitting Plane)* tool from the *Mesh Tools* menu. This produced two comparable surfaces meshed using the same Delaunay triangulation process, applied to the 3D point cloud which had been projected on the best fitting plane, determined through a least squares process.

The resultant surfaces were exported as.obj models and imported into MeshLab. The MeshLab *Compute Geometric Measures* tool from the *Quality Measure and Computations* filter was used to determine the total surface area of each mesh in order to allow comparison of the results with those for the whole bone samples. The surface areas were recorded, and the percentage was calculated.

15.7 Results and Discussions

The research was intended as a pilot study to see if digitisation and refit analysis could be used to support the analysis of large faunal assemblages with the ultimate aim of providing data to support the development of a fully automated system for digital refit.

The research was part of a larger study to explore the impact of taphonomic change to bone on digital analysis (Holland 2017) including an examination of whether digital refit analysis could confirm the timescales for anthropogenic fragmentation of the bone for marrow extraction suggested by other investigators of the Schöningen assemblage.

Voormolen (2008a,b) and van Kolfschoten et al. (2015) suggested that the Schöningen 13 II-4 samples were intentionally fragmented to extract marrow from the bones and therefore the fragmentation occurred at or around the point that the animals were killed. The fracture of fresh bone results in distortion of the bone fragment (and therefore its fracture surface) at the point of fracture, as the stress on the bone exceeds the yield strength and the bone deforms plastically prior to fracture (Currey 2006). The robust nature of the equine bones would have required the application of a fast loading of stress to the bone in order to fracture the bone to access the marrow. The faster rates of stress loading on bone result in smaller post-yield areas, and therefore we expected to see moderate levels of distortion (Hansen et al. 2008; Ural et al. 2011) characterised by curved fracture surfaces. By comparison bone that is not fresh when broken, fractures in flatter fracture plains and with little plastic distortion to the bone surface (Currey 2006).

Visualisation of the Schöningen samples clearly showed this pattern of high-speed loading of green bone with curved fracture surfaces (Fig. 15.6).

Additionally, the dark colour of the bone fragments made examination of the taphonomic changes to the cortical surfaces of the bone difficult to compare in the real samples, whereas visualisation of the samples allowed substitution of the obscuring dark brown colour with a mid-grey colour where the taphonomic features of the surface became clearer.

The outer cortical surface of the Schöningen samples exhibited characteristics of the early stages of taphonomic degradation in low oxygen and high pH burial conditions. Cracking and exfoliation of the outer most layer of circumferential lamellae was easily identified in the digitised samples (Fig. 15.7). The pattern of taphonomic change is comparable to the earliest stages of samples experimentally degraded in

70

Fig. 15.6 3D macro structured light model of Schöningen bone sample showing curved fracture surfaces resulting from fragmentation of the bone whilst it was still fresh. Scale in mm (Used with kind permission of Andrew Holland 2017, p. 408)

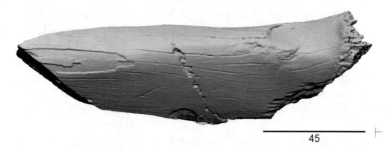

45

Fig. 15.7 3D macro structured light model of Schöningen bone sample showing cracking and exfoliation to the outer cortical bone surface similar to the changes seen in bone from high pH burial environments. Scale in mm (used with kind permission of Andrew Holland 2017, p. 409)

controlled alkaline environments undertaken as part of the wider research (Holland 2017).

The fracture surfaces exhibited very little taphonomic alteration at the gross level, and the margins of the fracture surfaces remained sharp with none of the rounding of the margins due to erosion or animal gnawing of samples left exposed on the surface suggesting that the fragments were rapidly incorporated into the anoxic alkaline environment of the lacustrine silts that aided their preservation and pre-fossilisation (Serengeli et al. 2015; Kuitems et al. 2015). This taphonomic history was reflected in the refit data of the Schöningen refitting bone fragments.

The results of the refit analysis showed that of the eleven refitting fracture surfaces between the twenty-one selected bone samples from the Schöningen 13 II-4 faunal assemblage, eight of the refit pairs gave good quality data and three failed to refit (Table 15.2).

The data for eight successfully identified refit pairs showed that refit quality was good for taphonomically altered bone in alkaline environments and that whilst the percentage of the refitting surfaces that were within a tight refit match (i.e. ±0.1 mm) was as low as 19% in some samples; there was still sufficient variation in the surface morphology of the fracture surface to positively identify a refitting surface in thick cortical bone.

Table 15.2 Refit analysis results for Schöningen samples with known refits from manual refit analysis

Reference model	Compared model	Mean refit distance (mm)	Refit distance variation (2σ)	% of fracture surface within ± 0.1 mm
SCH_7574	SCH_7707	0.13	1.11	26.08%
SCH_7094	SCH_5167	Refit failed		
SCH_6056	SCH_6540	Refit failed		
SCH_6726	SCH_12487	0.44	1.38	28.33%
SCH_2926	SCH_3058	0.05	0.42	47.43%
SCH_2499	SCH_3134	0.02	0.64	26.82%
SCH_2525	SCH_1158	0.11	0.45	60.16%
SCH_5140	SCH_4283	0.06	0.47	39.71%
SCH_6835	SCH_4772	0.12	1.08	19.70%
SCH_6880	SCH_6599	0.17	0.95	31.44%
SCH_6599	SCH_6599_b	Refit failed		
Mean		0.139	0.812	34.96%
Standard Deviation		0.132	0.365	13.35%

To ensure that these positively identified refits were not due to lack of methodological sensitivity to false positives, fracture surfaces were segmented from the two bone fragments known not to manually refit and these were tested for refit against each of the fracture surfaces of the other samples using the same process refit method. None of these fracture surfaces provided a positive match providing confidence in a low likely rate of false positives if the refit analysis process was automated for larger sample sets.

The three manually refitting pairs that failed digital refit were all characterised by fractures at the articular ends of the bones where the proportion of the refit surface that was made up of cortical bone was small and the fracture plains were primarily across trabecular bone. The structure of trabecular bone, being made up of a spongy matrix of thin bone pieces, was found not to offer large enough refit surfaces to provide a good surface to surface comparison for digital refit analysis. When the trabecular bone parts of the digital models were segmented out, the remaining thin cortical bone did not have enough surface area to provide a good statistical analysis. All three pairs of refitting bone fragments could be refitted together by hand but not digitally, suggesting that in a larger automated system, these types of refit pairs are likely to be under-reported. Our results, therefore, suggest that automated digital analysis of large faunal assemblages such as that from Schöningen 13 II-4 could rapidly identify refitting pairs within areas of the skeleton with greater cortical thicknesses (e.g. long bone diaphyses) where marrow extraction would also have been targeted. In combination with manual sorting of bone fragments by structure type this would reduce the level of manual refit testing needed by a specialist to just those fragments with predominantly trabecular bone or thin cortical bone.

Brittle fracturing materials such as flint in lithic tools or bone fragmented when dry have very small refit distances as the ultimate strength of the material is reached either at or immediately after the yield strength, meaning that there is no post-yield area of plastic deformation during the fracture sequence. The two sides of the fracture are, therefore, identical except for any further taphonomic alteration to the fracture surfaces themselves. In fresh bone which retains some elastic properties from the wet collagen, the bone when loaded first deforms elastically to relieve the stress and then plastically until it reaches the ultimate strength of the bone and the bone fractures. However, as the stress load is relieved by this plastic deformation during the fracture sequence the fragments on either side of the propagating fracture plane undergo differing degrees of load relief and thus variations in the degree of plastic deformation (Currey 2006). The differing plastic deformations either side of a fracture leads to slight variation in the shape of the fracture surface and therefore to poorer refitting distances compared to brittle materials. Refit distances therefore can provide evidence for the taphonomic history of bone fragments. The larger refit distances within the Schöningen refitting data may be interpreted as being due to differing plastic distortion in each fragment imparted during fast loading of the bone at the moment of fracture indicating that the bone was fresh (i.e. still had surviving wet collagen structure) when it was fragmented supporting the suggestion that the bone was intentionally fractured to extract the marrow.

Whilst differing load forces applied to the bones should lead to some variation within the degree of plastic deformation and therefore the refit distance, the variation within both the refit distance and the percentage of the refitting surface within 0.1 mm is larger than expected when compared to experimentally fractured samples of fresh bone in the wider research (Holland 2017). Comparing the widely distributed find locations for the now known to correspond refitting fragments reflects the suggestion of Van Kolfschoten (2012, 2014) and García-Moreno et al. (2015) that some limited sediment friction striation damage of the bones was likely due to a period of post deposition transportation within the wetland environment of Schöningen. The refitting fracture surfaces were therefore subject to limited but differing tapho-nomic alteration which resulted in surface level changes to the fracture surfaces. Such surface level changes to the fracture surfaces would further increase the variation and alignment of the two corresponding fracture surface morphologies and lead to the degree of variance in the quality of the refit and refit distances seen in the refit data.

Currently manual refit analysis has only provided refit data for smaller assem-blages where the number of fragment to fragment comparisons that are required is within the timescales and resources available to a research project, as the number of fragments in an assemblage increases, the number of fragment to fragment compar-isons required for manual refit grows exponentially. The analysis time and resource requirements of manual refit therefore limits analysis to smaller assemblages where the level of archaeological interpretation is also constrained by the small sample numbers. Larger assemblages offer the potential for higher level archaeological inter-pretations that identify more finely resolved patterns of human behaviours associated with faunal resource exploitation in the past, but the resource requirement of manual refit is a barrier to these areas of research.

Our study shows that digital methods of refit can identify refitting surfaces between faunal remain fragments, and the wider *Fragmented Heritage* project is exploring the automation of digitisation and analysis to provide automated digital refit processes that will reduce the researcher time requirement for the fragment to fragment comparison of manual refit, offering an expanded potential for archaeological interpretation of larger faunal assemblages. Whilst trabecular bone refit analysis remains a challenge for digital methods, limiting the researcher time requirement of manual refit comparisons to only trabecular bone fracture surfaces significantly expands the potential assemblage size available for archaeological interpretation.

Additionally, manual refit analysis is limited to qualitative analysis of refits only, and this research shows that digital refit analysis provides quantitative data in the form of both the quality of refitting surfaces and the refitting distance between refitting surfaces. These data offer potential insights into the taphonomic histories of these faunal assemblages that will contribute to greater archaeological understanding of their exploitation by humans in the past and their post-depositional preservation.

15.8 Conclusion

Visualisation of bone is a valuable technique for the exploration of large faunal assemblages offering potential to aid assessment of taphonomic alteration to bone and the possibility of digital refit analysis. This research has shown that analysis of visualised bone fracture surfaces can identify corresponding refit surfaces in cortical bone but is less applicable to fracture surfaces across trabecular bone. Development of automated digital refit systems, therefore, has potential applications in the analysis of large faunal assemblages supplemented by manual refit analysis limited to bone fragments with trabecular bone structures (e.g. articular ends of long bones) significantly reducing the resource requirements compared to purely manual refit analysis.

Digital refit offers the potential to explore the taphonomic histories of faunal remains and to elucidate behavioural, social and economic patterns of hominins exploiting food sources through processes such as marrow extraction.

The research also demonstrated that refit analysis results are influenced by post-deposition taphonomic alteration to bone but, where the preservation of bone is limited by the post-deposition environment, refit analysis can still provide useful results even over the significant time depths of the European Lower Palaeolithic and Middle Pleistocene.

Acknowledgements This research was a collaboration between the School of Archaeological and Forensic Sciences at the University of Bradford and the Archaeological Research Centre and Museum for Human Behavioural Evolution (MONREPOS) in Neuwied, Germany. The research was funded through an AHRC doctoral award as part of the AHRC Digital Transformations funded

Theme Large Grant *Fragmented Heritage* (AH/L00688X/1) and through in-kind contributions from MONREPOS.

References

Ashton NM (2007) Refitting and technology in the British Lower Palaeolithic: where are we? In: Schurmans U, De Bie M (eds) Fitting rocks: lithic refitting examined, vol 1596. Oxford, pp 45–53

Bathow C, Breuckmann B, Scopigno R (2010) Verification and acceptance tests for high definition 3D surface scanners. In: Proceedings of the 11th international conference on virtual reality, archaeology and cultural heritage. Eurographics Association, Aire-la-Ville, Switzerland, pp 9–16

CloudCompare.org. (2015) CloudCompare version 2.6.1: user manual. Cloudcompare.org, Paris

Currey JD (2006) Bones: structure and mechanics, New. Princeton University Press, Princeton, New Jersey

Ekstrand L, Wang Y, Karpinsky N, Zhang S (2013) Superfast 3D profilometry with digital fringe projection and phase shifting techniques. In: Zhang S (ed) The handbook of 3D machine vision: optical metrology and imaging. CRC Press, Boca Raton, pp 233–251

Friess M (2012) Scratching the surface? The use of surface scanning in physical and paleoanthropology. J Anthropol Sci 90:7–31

García-Moreno A, Hutson JM, Villaluenga A, Turner E, Gaudzinski-Windheuser S (2015) Counting sheep without falling asleep: using GIS to calculate the minimum number of skeletal elements (MNE) and other archaeozoological measures at Schöningen 13II-4 "Spear Horizon." In: Giligny F, Djindjian F, Costa L, Moscati P, Robert S (eds) CAA 2014—21st century archaeology: concepts, methods and tools. Proceedings of the 42nd annual conference on computer applications and quantitative methods in archaeology. Archaeopress Archaeology, Oxford, pp 407–412

Hansen U, Zioupos P, Simpson R, Currey JD, Hynd D (2008) The effect of strain rate on the mechanical properties of human cortical bone. J Biomech Eng 130(1):011011

Holland AD (2017) Examining the taphonomic challenges to the 3D digitisation of fragmented bone. Ph.D. Thesis. University of Bradford

Hutson JM, Villaluenga A, García-Moreno A, Turner E, Alt K, Gaudzinski-Windheuser S (2013) A landscape perspective of hominin behaviour at Schöningen 13II-4 "Spear Horizon." In: Abstracts of the ESHE Meeting, Viena, Poster Number 125, p 117

Inokuchi S, Sato K, Matsuda F (1984) Range imaging system for 3-D object recognition. In: Proceedings of the international conference on pattern recognition, vol 48, pp 806–808

van Kolfschoten T (2012) The Schöningen mammalian fauna in biostratigraphical perspective. In: Behre K-E (ed) Die pleistozänen Fundstellen in Schöningen - eine Einführung. Römisch-Germanischen Zentralmuseums, Mainz, pp 113–124

Kuitems M, van der Plicht J, Drucker DG, van Kolfschoten T, Palstra SWL, Bocherens H (2015) Carbon and nitrogen stable isotopes of well-preserved Middle Pleistocene bone collagen from Schöningen (Germany) and their paleoecological implications. J Hum Evol 89:105–113

Lang J, Winsemann J, Steinmetz D, Polom U, Pollok L, Böhner U et al (2012) The Pleistocene of Schöningen, Germany: a complex tunnel valley fill revealed from 3D subsurface modelling and shear wave seismics. Quatern Sci Rev 39:86–105

Mania D (1995) Die geologischen Verhältnisse im Gebiet von Schöningen. In: Thieme H, Maier R (eds) Archäologische Ausgrabungen im Braunkohlentagebau Schöningen. Hahnsche Buchhandlung, Hannover, pp 33–43

Pribanić T, Mrvoš S, Salvi J (2010) Efficient multiple phase shift patterns for dense 3D acquisition in structured light scanning. Image vis Comput 28(8):1255–1266

Rees DA (2000) The refitting of lithics from unit 4C, area Q2/D excavations at Boxgrove, West Sussex. England. Lithic Technol 25(2):120–134

Salvi J, Pagès J, Batlle J (2004) Pattern codification strategies in structured light systems. Pattern Recogn 37(4):827–849

Salvi J, Fernandez S, Pribanic T, Llado X (2010) A state of the art in structured light patterns for surface profilometry. Pattern Recogn 43(8):2666–2680

Serangeli J, Böhner U, van Kolfschoten T, Conard NJ (2015) Overview and new results from large-scale excavations in Schöningen. J Hum Evol 89:27–45

Sierralta M, Frechen M, Urban B (2012) 230Th/U dating results from opencast mine Schöningen. In: Behre K-E (ed) Die pleistozänen Fundstellen in Schöningen - eine Einführung. Römisch-Germanischen Zentralmuseums, Mainz, pp 143–154

Starkovich BM, Conard NJ (2015) Bone taphonomy of the Schöningen "Spear Horizon South" and its implications for site formation and hominin meat provisioning. J Hum Evol 89:154–171

Thieme H (1997) Lower Palaeolithic hunting spears from Germany. Nature 385(6619):807–810

Thieme H (1999) Altpaläolithische Holzgeräte aus Schöningen, Lkr. Helmstedt: Bedeutsame Funde zur Kulturentwicklung des frühen Menschen. Germania 77(2):451–487

Ural A, Zioupos P, Buchanan D, Vashishth D (2011) The effect of strain rate on fracture toughness of human cortical bone: a finite element study. J Mech Behav Biomed Mater 4(7):1021–1032

Urban B, Sierralta M (2012) New palynological evidence and correlation of Early Palaeolithic sites Schöningen 12 B and 13 II, Schöningen open lignite mine. In: Behre K-E (ed) Die pleistozänen Fundstellen in Schöningen - eine Einführung. Römisch-Germanischen Zentralmuseums, Mainz, pp 77–96

van Kolfschoten T (2014) The Palaeolithic locality Schöningen (Germany): a review of the mammalian record. Quatern Int 326–327:469–480

van Kolfschoten T, Buhrs E, Verheijen I (2015) The larger mammal fauna from the Lower Paleolithic Schöningen Spear site and its contribution to hominin subsistence. J Hum Evol 89:138–153

Voormolen B (2008a) Ancient hunters, modern butchers: Schöningen 13II-4, a kill–butchery site dating from the North West European Lower Palaeolithic. Ph.D. thesis. Leiden University

Voormolen B (2008b) Ancient hunters, modern butchers. Schöningen 13II–4, a kill–butchery site dating from the Northwest European Lower Palaeolithic. J Taphonomy 6(2):71–247

Chapter 16
Industrial Conservation: Digital Data Applications in Heritage Science and Engineering Contexts

Lyn Wilson, Alastair Rawlinson, Adam Frost, James Mitchell, Damian Liptrot, and Dominic Liptrot

Abstract The conservation and recording of industrial heritage can be challenging, due to the often-complex constructions, the use of mixed materials, differential corrosion or decay and exposed locations, amongst other factors. Engineering solutions and heritage science analyses are often required to facilitate the conservation process for structures such as statues, fountains and bridges. Using terrestrial laser scanning, structured light scanning and structure-from-motion photogrammetry, accurate 3D datasets can be generated which have a multitude of applications, being integrated with scientific analysis or used to facilitate engineering processes. They can be interrogated to generate quantifiable measurements and to create visualisations of current and potential condition. In combination with CNC manufacturing and 3D printing, digital data can aid the reverse engineering of missing structural components. 3D models can also form the basis of digital resources for learning and engagement with industrial heritage. This chapter discusses general principles of digital documentation within an industrial heritage context, drawing on case studies from around the United Kingdom. These include the Grand Fountain in Paisley, Coalbrookdale Fountains in Lurgan and Wigan, Ross Fountain in Edinburgh's Princes Street Gardens, The National Wallace Monument in Stirling, Linlathen Bridge in Dundee and the Forth Bridge UNESCO World Heritage Site, near Edinburgh.

Keywords Conservation · Industrial heritage · Digital documentation · Laser scanning · Structured light scanning · Photogrammetry · Heritage science · Engineering

L. Wilson (✉) · A. Rawlinson · A. Frost
Historic Environment Scotland, The Engine Shed, Forthside Way, Stirling FK8 1QZ, UK
e-mail: Lyn.wilson@hes.scot

J. Mitchell
Industrial Heritage Consulting Limited, Rothesay, Isle of Bute PA20 0QF, UK

D. Liptrot · D. Liptrot
Lost Art Limited, 1 Yewdale Crescent, Wigan WN1 2HP, Lancashire, UK

© Springer Nature Switzerland AG 2022
E. Ch'ng et al. (eds.), *Visual Heritage: Digital Approaches in Heritage Science*,
Springer Series on Cultural Computing,
https://doi.org/10.1007/978-3-030-77028-0_16

16.1   Introduction

The Nizhny Tagil Charter for Industrial Heritage defines industrial heritage as "the remains of industrial culture which are of historical, technological, social, architectural or scientific value. These remains consist of buildings and machinery, workshops, mills and factories, mines and sites for processing and refining, warehouses and stores, places where energy is generated, transmitted and used, transport and all its infrastructure, as well as places used for social activities related to industry such as housing, religious worship or education" (TICCIH 2003). The Charter also identifies the importance of recording industrial heritage as a fundamental part of its study, via "descriptions, drawings, photographs and video film of moving objects" (ibid.).

Industrial heritage presents unique challenges for conservation and recording, due to the often-complex constructions, the use of mixed materials, differential corrosion or decay and exposed locations, amongst other factors. Subsequently, the application of digital documentation in this area has grown in importance in recent years. Techniques are rapid, non-contact and accurate, facilitating the creation of objective 3D datasets which have a range of applications. Laser scanning, structured light scanning and structure from motion photogrammetry are currently the most common techniques used to digitally document industrial heritage, generating 3D point clouds. From these, 3D surface models with high resolution image textures can be derived.

The possibility of integrating data obtained from scientific analyses with these 3D models offers considerable opportunity to assist with conservation decision-making. Infrared thermography, 3D moisture mapping and ground penetrating radar, for example, all produce imagery which can be mapped onto models to allow visualisation and interrogation in a 3D environment.

From point clouds, precise measurements can be taken and quantifiable information for engineering processes provided in advance of and during conservation work. This offers the opportunity for remote, virtual access to the industrial structure for assessment, potentially reducing costs and providing risk-free evaluation. Digital models can be processed to make them suitable for 3D printing or CNC manufacturing. In turn, these physical models can be used for reverse engineering and the creation of lost structural or decorative industrial heritage components. Visualisations derived from 3D point clouds or surface model data are of direct use in conservation projects, for envisioning as-is, as-was and future condition. Moreover, visualisations can be a means of engagement with industrial heritage, for learning, interpretation and tourism purposes.

This chapter will examine a range of unique case studies undertaken by the authors, drawing together experiences and lessons learned. Each project presented novel challenges for digital documentation and other non-destructive testing methodologies such as the scale of operation, physical access, working tolerances and coordination with other techniques. Some common themes that emerged between these case studies can be identified in the following areas: Condition and materials investigation, determining assembly or construction methods, historic paint schemes, or monitoring decay. Reproduction, in reinstating components that are lost or damaged using techniques such as CNC milling, casting and hand finishing. Recording, using digital documentation to produce highly accurate 3D records that enable visualisation for remote virtual access and inspection. Engagement and outreach, with the aim of sharing the physical and digital outcomes from these projects to engage with communities. This encompasses the promotion of the conservation process during the projects (such as through displaying project insights and narratives on construction hoarding) and in creating wider learning opportunities. All of the projects have sought to protect and promote industrial heritage using cutting edge technologies to support efficient and informed conservation decisions.

16.2 Background

The recent role of digital documentation in helping protect and promote industrial heritage has had an influence around the world, enabling new ways of recording and novel methods to facilitate conservation work. Miles Oglethorpe and Miriam McDonald, in *Industrial Heritage Re-Tooled* (Douet 2013), identify the developing role of digital recording technologies as having 'transformed' field recording. Building on the use of Electronic Distance Measurement (EDM) survey and GNSS since the 1980's, early commercial Terrestrial Laser Scanners were developed in the late 1990's as a technique for rapidly recording complex, often irregular environments to a high degree of accuracy that would be challenging for traditional methods. Oglethorpe and McDonald further highlight, with the ability to now record millions of measurable 3D points rapidly, there is an increasing onus on post-survey work, and new challenges in managing and migrating these potentially enormous datasets.

There are a number of illustrative cases showing the use of digital documentation to create a detailed record of industrial sites which are unique, significant and testing for traditional survey methodologies often due to their challenging designs and varied condition. This can be seen in England with Historic England's use of terrestrial laser scanning to document The Iron Bridge (erected 1779 in Shropshire), a pivotal structure for the use of cast iron in construction (Historic England 2018). Likewise, Historic England's preceding project to record The Lion Salt Works in Cheshire made use of terrestrial laser scanning, to ensure that the partially collapsed and irregular structure was accurately recorded (English Heritage 2007).

In the United States, the National Park Service created the Historic American Engineering Record (HAER) in 1969, as a dedicated resource to record industrial heritage, including building fabric but particularly with a focus on machinery and processes. HAER illustrate the role of laser scanning in their documentation work, looking at the advantages and disadvantages of the technology within the broader remit of recording sites and structures relating to engineering and industry (National Park Service 2016).

The Taipei Declaration for Asian Industrial Heritage (2012), as a result of the TICCIH Congress 2012 in Taiwan, identifies the distinct development of industrial heritage in Asia to its Western counterparts. To promote international dialogue and the adoption of digital documentation methods, as part of the Scottish Ten project Historic Environment Scotland worked with project partners The Glasgow School of Art and CyArk to digitally document a number of the sites of Japan's Meiji Industrial Revolution (The Scottish Ten 2019). These sites included Nagasaki's Giant Cantilever Crane, a Scottish engineered crane, and Kosuge Slip Dock, which featured machinery sourced in Aberdeen by Thomas Blake Glover in 1868. The Japanese partners included The Government of Japan's Cabinet Secretariat, the Agency for Cultural Affairs, Nagasaki City, Mitsubishi Heavy Industries and Keisoku Research Consultant Company. Four of the sites scanned as part of this project were included in the Sites of Japan's Meiji Industrial Revolution World Heritage nomination and inscribed as a World Heritage Site in 2015 (UNESCO 2015).

In Taiwan, the work of Tsung-Chiang et al. (2015) demonstrates the use of terrestrial laser scanning to document the Taiwan Tile Corporation's Takao Factory, which suffered damage in the 2010 Chia-hsien earthquake. The results of the scanning survey were used in a novel way to show the spatial relationship between the fallen brickwork using a fuzzy c-mean algorithm, which was too bulky for conservators to handle for reassembly. This helped to determine the original positions of the fallen masonry within the structure.

It is important to emphasise that the methods and techniques of digital documentation are most effectively illustrated with case studies and practical applications. Bringing these together in an accessible guidance document was the aim of the Historic Environment Scotland Short Guide 13: Applied Digital Documentation in the Historic Environment (Frost 2018). The guide also looks at how the discipline of digital documentation has been used in a range of areas to support and promote the historic environment using established and emerging technologies, and engaging specialists through to wider audiences.

16.3   Inspection and Analysis

This section presents the results from use of 3D documentation for the inspection and analysis of monuments. It focuses on two case studies; the bronze Wallace Monument statue in Stirling and the Grand Fountain in Paisley.

16.3.1   The Wallace Monument Bronze Statue

To document the Wallace bronze prior to its removal for conservation (Mitchell 2019), we scanned it using several capture techniques to acquire an accurate, measurable dataset that would be useful for additional inspection and analysis purposes. Due to the inaccessibility of the monument before the erection of scaffolding, we employed a combination of high-resolution terrestrial laser scanning in tandem with close-range structured light scanning via a Mobile Elevated Work Platform (MEWP). This dataset provided a detailed geometric baseline for the statue and its niche (Fig. 16.1), which enabled the engineering team to make qualitative and quantitative observations and more informed decisions in planning the removal of the bronze from the monument.

To use the 3D data for quantitative analysis, we separated the bronze cast geometry from its stone corbel foundation and rear supports. It was then processed into water-tight manifold geometry through a combination of manual re-topologising, cleaning and hole-filling. This was to compensate for some areas, such as the back of the bronze, not having complete coverage due to access constraints. The preparation of the geometry therefore included assumptions about the surface in these areas, though these adjustments were informed by visual observations during the capture process and formed only a small part of the overall geometry.

One of the key considerations for planning the removal of the bronze was weight estimation, which would dictate the design tolerances of lifting apparatus and the logistics of removal. This estimation has previously been achieved for hollow casts

Fig. 16.1 Rendered image of 3D scan data showing the bronze cast, monument niche, corbel and crown

through estimating the surface area of the cast, then multiplying by the approximate thickness of the cast across its surface. The same approach was taken here to achieve an initial estimate, and our 3D inspection software was used to compute the surface area, returning a value of 17.95 m^2 for the manifold bronze topology. With an assumed cast thickness of 20 mm, and a reference weight value for copper of 8730 kg/m^3 (BS648 1964), the estimate shown below was calculated at just over 3100 kg. This aligned with previous expectations about the approximate weight of the bronze based on similar assumptions.

$$\left(17.95\,\mathrm{m}^2 \times 0.020\,\mathrm{m}\right) 8730\,\mathrm{kg/m}^3 = 3134\,\mathrm{kg}$$

This estimate excluded any possible internal structure, armature, or filling. As the project progressed, after the erection of the scaffolding, it was possible to do further non-destructive testing to inspect the internal space of the cast. To reveal more about the internal composition, radiography was undertaken and interpreted by specialist contractor IRISNDT and confirmed the existence of material on the interior of the cast, predominantly in the form of swarf from the casting process. No supporting armature was identified throughout the body or head of the cast, except for a linear support for the sword. Due to the greater thickness of the cloak, the radiography could not penetrate the thicker material or reveal its internal areas.

Later investigation revealed that the internal armature, or iron skeleton had all but disappeared, or at least returned to its natural state as oxide of iron. It is assumed that the armature had been formed in wrought iron, as it would have almost certainly been formed by a blacksmith in the employ of the foundry. In fact, the statue was found to be filled with a mixture of materials that had previously confounded the radiographers. The fill consisted of mixed sands, gravel, pieces of wood, and even half bricks.

As the statue had no internal frame it was decided it would be too risky to lift in a single piece, so it was decided to dismantle it in sections that would be individually safe. As far as possible, and indeed as it turned out, with remarkable accuracy. The statue had been originally been constructed in seven pieces and lifted into place in at least four.

The sand fill had been used to fill the lower parts up to each previously wedged joint level. Then a casting bed was formed and molten bronze poured inside to seep out of the joint to the outside, where it was dressed and tooled, probably by the sculptor, to be invisible from the outside. This was repeated up to neck and the raised arm shoulder level, where another technique was employed. The lower neck was packed with clay as was the raised arm socket wrist then sword. These joints were pegged with bronze keys then the joint made by pouring in molten lead, tamped home when it cooled.

However, we believe that the sand was meant to be discharged through vents in the underside of the feet. It could have been that some of the fill, being composed of larger objects, blocked the exits and therefore could not be discharged. Alternatively, the sand was not dry enough at the time. We will never know, but the result was that the stone corbel was carrying 0.75 T more than it was intended.

In addition to the utility of the scan data for quantitative applications, we found significant value in inspecting the wider 3D dataset including the cast, its niche and the surrounding stonework such as its supporting corbel and decorative crown above the cast. Qualitative inspection and manipulation in 3D revealed spatial relationships, clearances for access and provided reference material for use throughout the project to demonstrate areas of interest. Some key interactions in this inspection included viewing and manipulating the data in orthographic display, producing images in elevation from different aspects, slicing sections through the data to view profiles and linear measurements. This helped to reveal the plumbness of the cast relative to the building, the centre of its mass and position relative to the corner of the monument's upstanding walls, and the clearance between the cast and the niche at various points. This informed decisions about possible lifting apparatus without direct access to the site and before the erection of scaffolding.

As it was decided to dismantle the statue, the single lifting frame idea was abandoned and soft strapping of individual parts was adopted. However, the original method of assembly was not possible and so a stainless-steel space frame was built up internally, fixed through the outer skin the filled with bronze brazing, to be dressed in the manner of the original. This frame was terminated at the neck with a lifting eye, which allowed a one-piece lift. The head, arm and sword were refitted using the original method. Following the erection of the scaffolding for the conservation works the cast was re-scanned using structured-light scanning to gain greater coverage which was previously inaccessible due to access (Fig. 16.2).

Ultimately throughout the conservation process, the scanning helped to document and inform decision making. Using it has allowed us to create a new record of the cast (and to some degree the surrounding stonework) in significant detail, to an extent not previously recorded, and can also serve as a reusable digital asset in the future for a potential range of outputs to assist with engagement, especially given the inaccessibility and detail of the bronze in its elevated position.

16.3.2   Grand Fountain, Paisley

An unusual, large-scale cast iron spray fountain located in Paisley Fountain Gardens in the west of Scotland was surveyed by Historic Scotland in 2006, prior to an extensive programme of conservation. The fountain was made by Glasgow's George Smith and Co.'s Sun Foundry and is adorned with a large number of decorative castings including four 2.4 m long walruses (Davey et al. 2006). The fountain itself is the only known example of a pattern No.1 fountain by the Sun Foundry and was noted to have a uniquely designed decorative paint scheme which significantly surpassed what might be expected on such a structure (ibid.). As such, the fountain is A-listed, the highest level of protection which can be afforded to a building or structure in Scotland. The Fountain Gardens were opened in 1868, and it is widely recognised that the fountain is one of the most significant nineteenth century cast iron ornamental spray examples in Scotland (Fig. 16.3).

Fig. 16.2 Rendered image of the Wallace monument bronze structured-light scanning data, shown with diffuse albedo textures

By 2006, the fountain had suffered substantial corrosion, frost heave damage and structural movement and was largely derelict. The importance of the structure merited a detailed assessment, and it was at this time that the decorative paint scheme was further investigated.

From historic photographs, it was known that the current paint scheme was not original. Archival accounts indicate that Daniel Cottier, a respected nineteenth century artist and designer, best known for his interior decoration in Glasgow, was responsible for the fountain's decoration (Mitchell 2014a). Paint samples were taken from the lower levels of the fountain, which revealed parts of the original paint scheme (Davey et al. 2006). The fountain had been re-painted at least four times over the years, with areas of gilding also evident. By undertaking microscopic paint analysis (Fig. 16.4), in combination with examination of archival photographs, it

Fig. 16.3 Left: Image of the fountain as illustrated in Cook and Cook (2012), Right: Paisley Grand Fountain prior to conservation

Fig. 16.4 Cross-section through decorative paint scheme viewed under optical microscope, showing first primer and undercoat intact, but paint above disturbed by heat treatment (Pearce 2007)

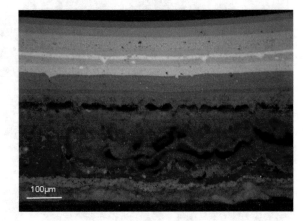

was possible to identify parts of the original colour scheme, which was found to differ considerably from the one which existed at the time of conservation (ibid.). Microscopy indicated the use of gold, bronze and tinted glazes which would have produced a striking surface finish (Mitchell 2014a). Gold leaf was applied by oil-gilding on a yellow base to highlight areas of the fountain. Evidence of finishing glazes and varnishes were also noted under the microscope which would have given the fountain a high degree of lustre (Pearce 2007).

Concurrent with the paint analysis, a detailed laser scan of the fountain was undertaken to capture the current condition prior to conservation. For this, a time-of-flight laser scanner (Leica ScanStation) was used to capture the entirety of the fountain and its contextual setting, and a close-range articulated arm scanner (Perceptron Romer V5) used for higher resolution detailed scans of particular cast components (Wilson et al. 2010). The point cloud produced is shown in Fig. 16.5. This was further processed into a triangulated mesh model.

Given the significance of the fountain and the recent discoveries of the unique and rich decorative scheme, the next step was to explore the digital combination of the original paint scheme with the 3D model. This involved the conservation scientist who had undertaken the microscopic paint analysis working with the 3D modeller to develop a visual representation true to the original decorative scheme and based on objective scientific analysis. The final result (Fig. 16.6) was rendered as an animation, illustrating not only the original colours but also the extensive use of lustre varnishes which would have been very difficult to visualise through non-digital means.

Visualisations of the original decorative scheme were an integral part of a successful funding application for conservation of the fountain. There was a positive emotional response to the visualisations and increased the level of engagement with

Fig. 16.5 Point cloud obtained from laser scanning of Paisley Grand Fountain

Fig. 16.6 Visualisation of the original paint scheme based on scientific analysis of original paint scheme and 3D model derived from laser scan point cloud

the conservation effort. The work was completed in 2014 and the fountain is once again a central focal point within Paisley (Mitchell 2013a, b; 2014a–d).

16.4   Reverse Engineering—Coalbrookdale Fountains, Lurgan and Wigan Case Study

In the 1920s the Coalbrookdale fountain in Mesnes Park, Wigan, was removed (The Friends of Mesnes Park 2019). As part of a regeneration project a recreation of a fountain to match the original was commissioned. A sister fountain to the one in Wigan was installed in Lurgan, Northern Ireland. A team from Lost Art, Industrial Heritage Consulting and CDDV travelled to Lurgan to survey and digitally document the fountain with the aim of using the survey data to aid in the recreation of the Mesnes fountain.

The project was commissioned by Wigan Council, following a quality/price based competitive tender process and supported by the Heritage Lottery Fund. Originally purchased at a cost of £150, the 14 ft high fountain featured both stylised and figurative elements, with a sculptural boy holding a serpent standing atop the assembly and providing the uppermost water outlet. The central structure containing 2 basins is further and unusually located within a 25 ft diameter basin featuring a cast iron kerb. The complete construction had been removed and required recreating and installing, along with newly designed pumping and purifying systems, reflecting modern health standards and environmental concerns.

The fountain was laser scanned using a Leica HDS 6100 laser scanner from 20 different locations around its circumference. The team also made use of an extending tripod to raise the laser scanner to a height of 4.2 m. This allowed detailed scans of the upper areas of the fountain and reduced occlusions. Key sculptural details were also scanned at a higher resolution using an Artec MHT structured light scanner (Fig. 16.7), a MEWP (mobile elevated working platform) was used to gain access to the higher-up areas. The details were captured at a surface resolution of less than 1 mm.

The laser scan data was registered in Leica Cyclone and a triangulated 3D model was created using 3D Reshaper software. Elevations and profiles of the fountain were drawn in AutoCAD (Fig. 16.8) using the Leica Cloudworx plugin. The Artec MHT data was processed in Artec Studio V9 this produced high resolution 3D models as an output.

The terrestrial laser scan data was used to produce a series of CAD drawings showing elevations, details and sections. The high-resolution 3D models were used to create scaled rendered images of each detail.

As well as being used to create scaled 3D images the high-resolution 3D models were processed and cleaned to make then suitable for use in CNC milling software.

Following the 3D scanning onsite at Lurgan, the data for the fountain top figure was cleaned to fill in any blank areas to remove defects and to smooth details removed

Foot

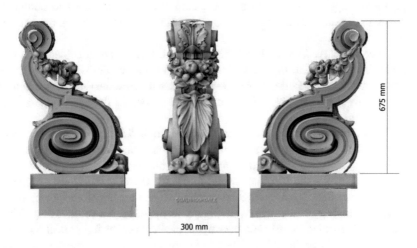

Fig. 16.7   Foot detail scanned with an Artec MHT structured light scanner

Fig. 16.8   Elevation of the fountain drawn in AutoCAD using the Leica Cloudworx plugin

by factors such as paint overlay. The finalised data was input into the CNC machine under the direction of Bridge Patterns of Shipley and a High-Density Model Block positioned appropriately. The size and complexity of the data and output model meant that, using 2 mm then 1 mm cutters for the process, the block remained in the machine for 3 days.

Once the carved model had been machined, this was then coated with sanding sealer in order to seal the model board. The finished model was then delivered to Ruth Davies of the Pollock Davies company, who corrected for over a century of attrition by hand carving in fine detail to areas such as the eyes, fingers and toes (Fig. 16.9).

The completed model was then delivered to JT&E Castings, Wigan where it was used to produce a loose pattern casting sand mould (Fig. 16.10). Given the complexity of the model, foundryman Andy Bradley produced over 20 sand drawback pieces to create undercuts that would allow for the correct external shape of the casting. Additionally, an internal core was produced to allow for a casting thickness of approximately 15 mm across the figure, as opposed to a solid casting. This was extended to include the arm and the serpent elements of the figure to allow the water carrying pipe to be included. The whole process therefore reflected an excellent integration of new technology with traditional skills and craftsmanship.

Fig. 16.9 Final CNC milled figure which has had details corrected and has been sealed

Fig. 16.10   CNC milled and finished model being used to create a loose pattern sand mould

16.5   Physical Interventions—Linlathan Bridge

The Linlathen East Bridge is the oldest surviving iron bridge in Scotland with construction dating from 1795 to 1819 (Paxton and Shipway 2007). It is made from wrought and cast iron and spans the Dighty Burn to the east of Dundee. The bridge had fallen into a state of disrepair and neglect. In 2005 Dundee City Council engaged the City Engineers Division to explore the possibility of restoration. Glasgow School of Art's Digital Design Studio were commissioned to conduct a 3D laser scan survey of the bridge in its then current condition.

The detailed laser scan survey was carried out using a Leica Scan Station and included laser scans from the water under the bridge to ensure maximum coverage. The 3D survey data was used to develop comprehensive 2D CAD drawings of the existing structure detailing all remaining structural and detail elements. A photorealistic 3D model of the bridge and surrounding landscape was also produced. This model was used to visualise the disassembly of the bridge and highlighted the order in which this work would be carried out (Fig. 16.11). Using the 3D survey data as a base a new 3D model of the proposed restoration was created and this was used to help secure financial support for the restoration project (Fig. 16.12). The laser scan showed significant movement evidenced by a loss of symmetry. This flagged up the need for remedial action in the repairs to the abutments and in strengthening key joints on the iron structure.

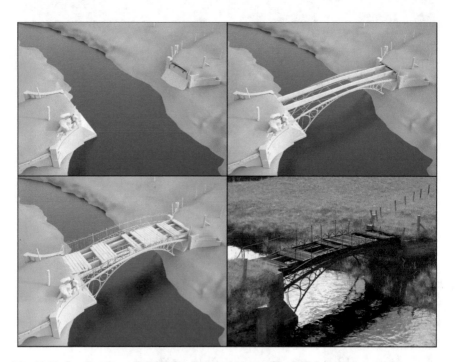

Fig. 16.11 Detailed 3D model showing disassembly as well as 'as is' condition

Fig. 16.12.   3D visualisation of proposed restoration

16.6   Visualisation—The Ross Fountain

The Ross fountain has acted as a focal point of Edinburgh's West Princes Street gardens since its installation in 1872. Its location, a short distance north-west of Edinburgh Castle, offers iconic views of Edinburgh's Princes Street gardens and encourages photography from a range of visitors. The gardens are adjacent to and readily accessible from Princes Street, which receives significant footfall all-year-round at over 40,000 visitors per-day on average (Edinburgh by numbers, 2018). The gardens are at the heart of the Old and New Towns of Edinburgh UNESCO World Heritage Site, are listed in the Inventory of Gardens and Designed Landscape in Scotland (The City of Edinburgh Council 2019), and contain several other significant historical monuments. Commitment to their maintenance and conservation is outlined in the City of Edinburgh Council's Princes Street Gardens Management Plan 2017–2020 (The City of Edinburgh Council 2018).

The Ross fountain colour scheme has changed and received subsequent conservation in 2001 (Canmore 2019), and the proposed 2017–2018 scheme of conservation works offered an opportunity to instate a new painted colour scheme reflecting the fountain's French origins at Antoine Durenne's Sommevoire foundry. This presented two main challenges: one being how best to align the proposed colour scheme to an authentic contemporary design and another concerning planning and approval. For the former of the two challenges, heavy reference to the contemporary C19th French fountains, such as those at Place de la Concorde in Paris provided a host of consistent examples from which to draw parallels in terms of paint colour and its specific application to the cast iron elements. For planning purposes, this visualisation was designed as a representative proposal that could be presented to project stakeholders.

Digital documentation of the Ross Fountain was carried out in two stages, the first using a Leica P40 and Z + F 5010C terrestrial laser scanners and the second using photogrammetry using a Nikon D810 DLSR camera. A total of 20 individual 360-degree scans at a resolution setting of 3.1 mm at 10 m were taken from ground level as well as 8 from an extending tripod at a height of 4 m. Full colour image for each scan were taken using on-board cameras. 1450 photographs were taken from points all around the fountain and a 5 m extending pole was used to capture details of the upper fountain.

The laser scan data was registered using the cloud to cloud method in Leica Cyclone software. This data was then transferred to Reality Capture software where it was then aligned with the photogrammetry images (Fig. 16.13). The result was a combined dataset which was then used to create a high resolution phototextured model of the complete fountain.

To set the visualisation on an accurate foundation, our methodology to illustrate the proposed colour scheme needed to use the accurate and high-resolution 3D geometry from the digital documentation data. However, the approach also had to be quick and light-weight enough for the 3D artist to allow rapid alterations where material shader boundaries would likely move and change across different fountain elements (e.g. figurative clothing, skin, floral decorative elements, edges and highlighted details, etc.).

The visualisation brief was for an illustrative image to show the proposed colour scheme. It would be used as a working prototype to adjust initial ideas, refine specific

Fig. 16.13 Alignment of 3D laser scans and DSLR photographs in Reality Capture software

areas, anticipate the visual relationship between the paint colours and a simulated lighting environment, and present a finalised concept. To achieve this, we opted to compose a setup with pre-rendered masked layers to allow quick, pixel-level adjustment on the final image. This allowed the introduction or removal of any of the four primary material types (verdigris green, dark brown/bronze, gold and sandstone) to different elements of the fountain without the requirement to undertake more time-consumptive 3D operations such as UV unwrapping, vertex painting, or projection on the complex dataset. To compose the initial view, a generic grey diffuse material was applied to the processed and cleaned 3D geometry, and rendered with ambient occlusion for an orthographic view, showing the west elevation of the fountain (Fig. 16.14).

With an initial composition showing the detailed geometric elements of the fountain, our methodology required four different material shaders to be defined. These

Fig. 16.14 Orthographic render of Ross fountain, visualised with an 'ambient occlusion' map to show the geometric data captured by digital documentation

were outlined early on as the following: verdigris green paint, metallic bronze paint, gold paint and sandstone. We created these within a physically correct path tracing rendering engine, adjusting the material shader properties to reflect those of the material types defined.

Although the fountain is cast-iron, its surfaces would be treated with paints and finishes with different levels of specular reflection and glossiness. Metals also behave differently to dielectrics in the reflection of light, which would significantly influence the appearance of the dark glossy metallic bronze paint and gold painted surfaces. In addition, a large component of how glossy materials reflect light is their characteristic specular reflection, which meant that the representative rendered image would need a lighting environment to better capture the behaviour of the materials. We opted to use a spherical High-dynamic Range Image (HDRI) to light the scene, with an analogous outdoor slightly overcast environment. Throughout the material creation process, these materials were test-rendered and compared against the source reference material, allowing tweaks and adjustments to be made to bring the finished scheme closer to the paints used on the identified fountains. The completed material shaders were subsequently applied to the fountain and rendered as several passes, then loaded into a single composition to allow features to be masked by material type. We then created and applied the masks based on initial rules (such as clothes and fabric would be verdigris green, skin to be bronze, decorative elements to be gold) and then refined—guided by the scheme reference material. The finalised image (Fig. 16.15) that was produced served as a reference for visualising the proposed colour scheme.

16.7 Learning and Engagement—Go Forth!

The Forth Bridge, near Edinburgh, is one of the world's great engineering marvels. Opened in 1890, its cantilever design by John Fowler and Benjamin Baker was the world's first major mild steel structure and represented a major step forward in civil engineering, made possible by innovations in construction technologies pioneered by William Arrol of Glasgow (The Forth Bridge 2019). As part of the UNESCO World Heritage Site nomination (Oglethorpe 2014), digital documentation was undertaken on one cantilever to create an accurate record of the bridge's as-built condition. The bridge was successfully inscribed onto the World Heritage list in 2015, and a full programme of digital documentation on the entire structure was then taken forward with the support of the Scottish Government. The objective was not only to develop a conservation and maintenance digital asset but also to create learning resources focusing on the promotion of STEM subjects (Science, Technology, Engineering and Maths) which every school-aged child in Scotland could access (Games and apps created using 3D scans of forth bridges 2017).

Digital documentation was a huge technical challenge, given its complex steel geometry, the situation of the bridge over the River Forth, at height, and the fact that over 200 trains pass over the bridge each day (Wilson 2016). Laser scanning was

Fig. 16.15 Composite orthographic render of Ross fountain, showing proposed paint scheme

coordinated closely with the bridge operators, Network Rail, and involved overnight access to the tracks when trains were not running, cantilever rigs being suspended over the sides of the bridge with laser scanners attached and both boat-mounted and rope-access scanning (Fig. 16.16). A survey control network was first established using a Leica MS50 multistation. A combination of laser scanning technologies was next used, including Leica Geosystems P40, FARO X350 and Z + F 5016 laser scanners. The Leica Geosystems Pegasus mobile mapping scanner facilitated the boat-mounted scans. High resolution photography was undertaken to supplement the laser scans using Nikon D810 cameras. 360° photography and video were captured using an Insta 360 camera.

Registration of the individual scans was also a challenge, given the scale of the project and the file sizes. In total, the 3D dataset comprised some 1426 laser scans and over 23 billion geometrically accurate data points. The point cloud was georeferenced

Fig. 16.16 Photo montage of laser scanning the Forth Bridge

to a real-world coordinate system using the survey control network data. Combined, this represented some 6 TB of data (Fig. 16.17).

To translate these massive 3D datasets, which required specialist software and high specification workstations, into resources that could be accessible for young learners on basic computer systems, a specialist in digital learning was engaged. A suite of resources was envisioned with the 3D point clouds and digital models at their core which corresponded directly to Education Scotland's Curriculum for Excellence learning outcomes in technical and social subjects. Each resource was carefully storyboarded by the digital learning expert who worked closely with a team of 3D modellers to ensure the resources developed correctly.

An excellent archival photographic and documentary record exists for the Forth Bridge and this source material allowed narrative about a day in the life of David, a young boy who worked on the bridge construction as a riveter to be developed. The learners undertake a range of game-based challenges based around David's daily

Fig. 16.17 Registered georeferenced point cloud of the Forth Bridge

Fig. 16.18   Go Forth and Discover PC game-based learning resource

tasks to gain an understanding of the social and environmental conditions he would have lived with. These are collated as a PC-based game with 3D models of the bridge throughout entitled 'Go Forth and Discover' (Fig. 16.18).

To target computing and technical learning outcomes, two further resources were developed to teach young learners about digital design and coding. 'Go Forth and Create' uses simplified 3D models of the Forth Bridge within MIT's Scratch coding software, encouraging learners to build narratives and animations using block-based coding (Fig. 16.19). 'Go Forth and Design' again uses simplified versions of the 3D models within Autodesk's TinkerCAD software, to allow learners to design and build their own bridges, using pre-created components. Both software packages are used extensively in Scottish schools.

To accompany each digital resource, a detailed pdf lesson plan was developed to enable teachers to understand how best to use the resources and what outcomes learners should be attaining. The Go Forth suite of learning resources were launched in October 2018 and are now available to all school learners in Scotland through Education Scotland's Glow learning portal. They can also be accessed freely here: https://www.theforthbridges.org/visit/go-forth-digital-learning-resources/.

16.8   Conclusions

The common areas between these industrial heritage projects are strands that could help to inform a procedural toolset for consideration in future conservation projects. The themes identified in the introduction bring together condition and materials investigation, reproduction, digital documentation and outreach and education. As

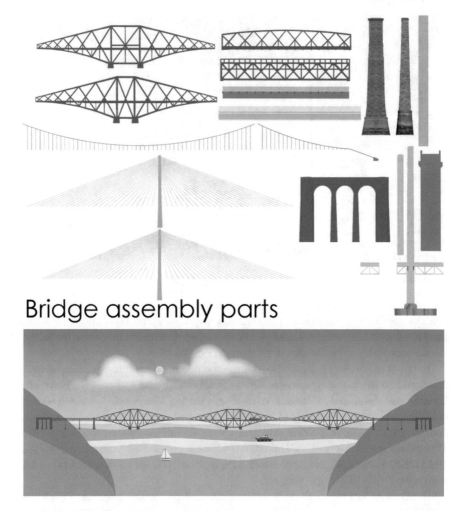

Fig. 16.19 Go Forth and Create Scratch coding learning resource

digital documentation and other technologies continue to evolve at a rapid pace, the adaptability of techniques and how they are flexibly used to support the overarching themes is essential.

The authors have used digital scanning and the resultant accurate 3D data in the conservation and recording of industrial heritage structures for over ten years now, and the ever-improving technology means that it has become an invaluable tool. It is worth reflecting on the fact that these 3D digital scanning technologies were originally devised to serve contemporary industry (for example, digital surveys of oil and gas installations), but now, they are being deployed to serve historic industrial sites and structures. The conservation of three of the largest ornamental fountains in the UK has allowed a detailed record to be made—not only of individual parts but given a better understanding of how movement such as subsidence, has affected the interrelated parts of the structures. The 3D data has also allowed direct router cutting of parts such as figures which are used as casting patterns. The objectivity of this precludes "artistic interpretation" where a perfect replica is required, needing only some light finishing by hand. The information gathered both by 3D scanning and 3D radiography on the large Wallace bronze statue, before its removal, guided the approach taken by the conservators and mitigated risk by informing the dismantling process. The laser scanning data generated for the Linlathen Bridge similarly assisted the conservation process. The Go Forth learning resources are a highly novel application for digital data generated for industrial heritage structures with significant potential to encourage learning in STEM areas.

There is no doubt that digital scanning of industrial heritage structures has moved on from being "something of interest" to a real tool where measurement of difficult and irregular shapes has been invaluable in the making of patterns and in some cases, direct manufacture of patterns or parts from the data. Techniques have become increasingly more refined as new applications emerge. Of critical importance, digital technologies must be seen as valuable additions in conservation toolkits, which work incredibly well in parallel with traditional skills. Within the industrial heritage sector, there is more work required to promote the benefits of applying digital technologies, not only to create an accurate record but also to detect issues before physical conservation work commences, to assist in restorations and to stimulate learning and engagement.

Acknowledgements The authors would like to thank the following for their contributions to this chapter and the projects discussed within: Dr Miles Oglethorpe (Historic Environment Scotland and President, TICCIH), James Hepher (Historic Environment Scotland), Alan Simpson (Historic Environment Scotland), Jenni Mackay (Education Scotland), Centre for Digital Documentation and Visualisation LLP team, Transport Scotland, Network Rail Scotland, National Records of Scotland, Education Scotland, Dundee City Council, Renfewshire Council, City of Edinburgh Council, The National Wallace Monument, Ross Development Trust.

References

British Standards Institution (1964) BS648: 1964: schedule of weights of building materials. https://www.thenbs.com/PublicationIndex/documents/details?Pub=BSI&DocID=201785. Accessed 25 Oct 2019

Canmore (2019) Edinburgh, West Princes Street Gardens, Ross Fountain. Field visit: 11 June 2001. https://canmore.org.uk/site/111804/edinburgh-west-princes-street-gardens-ross-fountain. Accessed 23 Oct 2019

Cook J, Cook J (1868 Republished 2012) Inaugural ceremonies in honour of the opening of the Fountain Gardens, Paisley. RareBooksClub.com, Paisley

Davey A, Jenkins M, Mitchell D, Pearce M (2006) Paisley Fountain Gardens: preliminary survey report. Fountain, bronze statue and boundary ironwork. Unpublished Historic Scotland Report, Edinburgh

Douet K (ed) (2013) Industrial heritage re-tooled: the TICCIH guide to industrial heritage conservation. Routledge

English Heritage (2007) 3D Laser scanning for heritage. case study 11: surveying industrial archaeology: scanning Lion Salt Works, Marston. https://www.cices.org/pdf/newcastle%20uni%203d%20laser%20scanning.pdf

Frost A (2018) Short guide 13: applied digital documentation in the historic environment. https://www.historicenvironment.scot/archives-and-research/publications/publication/?publicationId=9b35b799-4221-46fa-80d6-a8a8009d802d

Games and apps created using 3D scans of forth bridges (2017). https://www.bbc.co.uk/news/uk-scotland-edinburgh-east-fife-38494716. Accessed 16 July 2019

Go forth! digital learning resources. https://www.theforthbridges.org/visit/go-forth-digital-learning-resources/. Accessed 16 July 2019

Historic England (2018) 3D Laser scanning for heritage: advice and guidance on the use of Laser scanning in archaeology and architecture. Historic England

Mitchell J (2013a) Paisley's grand fountain, Part 1. ICON News 48:17

Mitchell J (2013b) Paisley's grand fountain, Part 2. ICON News 49:14–15

Mitchell J (2014a) Paisley's grand fountain, Part 3. ICON News 50:14–16

Mitchell J (2014b) Paisley's grand fountain, Part 4. ICON News 51:17–18

Mitchell J (2014c) Paisley's grand fountain, Part 5. ICON News 52:15–17

Mitchell J (2014d) The fountain flows again. ICON News 54:13–16

Mitchell J (2019) Conservation of the Wallace Bronze. ICON News 85:16–20

National Park Service (2016) Guidelines (HABS/HAER/HALS). https://www.nps.gov/hdp/standards/guidelines.htm.Accessed 19 Sep 2019

Oglethorpe M (2014) The Forth Bridge: UNESCO World Heritage nomination dossier. Historic Scotland, Edinburgh

Paxton R, Shipway J (2007) Civil Engineering heritage: Scottish Highlands and Islands. London

Pearce M (2007) Fountain Gardens, Paisley: evidence of the cottier paintwork of the fountain. Unpublished Historic Scotland Report, Edinburgh

The City of Edinburgh Council (2018) Edinburgh by Numbers. https://www.edinburgh.gov.uk/strategy-performance-research/edinburgh-numbers-1/1. Accessed 19 Sep 2019

The City of Edinburgh Council (2019) Parks and gardens—Princes Street Gardens. https://www.edinburgh.gov.uk/downloads/file/22597/princes-street-gardens-management-plan. Accessed 19 Sep 2019

The Forth Bridge. https://www.theforthbridges.org/forth-bridge/. Accessed 16 July 2019

The Friends of Mesnes Park. http://www.friendsofmesnespark.co.uk/history.html. Accessed 23 Oct 2019

The Scottish Ten. https://www.engineshed.scot/about-us/the-scottish-ten/sites/nagasaki-japan/. Accessed 23 Oct 2019

The Taipei Declaration for Asian Industrial Heritage (2012). https://ticcih.org/about/charter/taipei-declaration-for-asian-industrial-heritage/

TICCIH (2003) The Nizhny Tagil Charter for the industrial heritage, July 2003. http://ticcih.org/about/charter/. Accessed 23 Oct 2019

Tsung-Chiang W, Yi-Chun L, Min-Fu H (2015) A study of 3D modeling for conservation work of large-scale industrial heritage structures: using the south chimney of Taiwan tile corporation's Takao Factory as a case study. J Asian Arch Build Eng 14(1):153–158. https://doi.org/10.3130/jaabe.14.153

UNESCO (2015) Nomination file 1484. Sites of Japan's Meiji industrial revolution. Kyushu-Yamaguchi and related areas. World Heritage Nomination. https://whc.unesco.org/en/list/1484/documents/

Wilson L, Mitchell DS, Davey A, Pritchard D (2010) Digital documentation of historic ferrous metal structures: 3D Laser scanning as a conservation tool. In: Mardikian P, Chemello C, Watters C, Hull P (eds) Metal 10, international conference on metal conservation. Interim meeting of the international council of museums committee for conservation metal working group, October 11–15 2010, Charleston, USA. Clemson University Press, Charleston, pp 279–286

Wilson L (2016) Forth Bridge goes digital. In: Focus: informing the conservation of the historic environment. Historic Environment Scotland, Edinburgh, pp 16–17

Chapter 17
Archival Photography, UAV Surveys and Structure-from-Motion Techniques for Local Heritage Management

Tabitha K. Kabora and Katie Campbell

Abstract Unmanned aerial vehicle (UAV) surveys provide a viable methodology for conducting archaeological surveys, and Structure-from-Motion (SfM) techniques allow for the development of high-resolution maps, digital elevation models (DEMs) and 3-dimensional models of heritage sites. The archaeological site of Engaruka in Tanzania, covering c. 20 km^2, was utilised in a series of projects to assess the potential of UAV surveys and SfM techniques to develop high-resolution imagery, combined with DEMs generated from archival aerial photographs. Data were processed using SfM software to create a DEM with a resolution of up to 3 m, providing a considerable improvement on the current 30 m resolution Advanced Spaceborne Thermal Emission and Reflection Radiometer (ASTER) Global DEM (GDEM). Rigorous analysis using GIS indicated issues to consider when applying this technique to analogue photos. Further aerial surveys were then undertaken to establish the feasibility of using the innovative UAV survey techniques on the ground to generate aerial photographs and the use of SfM to develop high-resolution maps and DEMs at 0.25 m resolution, compared with the 0.7 m resolution Quickbird satellite image. These facilitate the remote analysis of smaller archaeological features that would otherwise not be identifiable, supporting further research and monitoring of these heritage sites.

Keywords Aerial and UAV surveys · Structure-from-motion · Archival and digital photographs · Engaruka archaeological site · Heritage management

T. K. Kabora (✉)
Department of Environment and Geography, University of York, Heslington, York YO10 5NG, UK
e-mail: tabitha.kabora@york.ac.uk

K. Campbell
Institute of Archaeology, University of Oxford, 36 Beaumont Street, Oxford OX1 2PG, UK
e-mail: katie.campbell@arch.ox.ac.uk

© Springer Nature Switzerland AG 2022
E. Ch'ng et al. (eds.), *Visual Heritage: Digital Approaches in Heritage Science*,
Springer Series on Cultural Computing,
https://doi.org/10.1007/978-3-030-77028-0_17

17.1 Introduction

The documentation of heritage artefacts and architecture forms an integral part of global and local heritage management as it supports research, conservation, and management efforts. This chapter considers the use of historical analogue aerial photographs, alongside more conventional unmanned aerial vehicle (UAV) survey with rigorous testing of their comparative accuracy to evaluate their effectiveness for these purposes, and the limitations of the new data created. Historical analogue aerial photographs from light aircraft surveys have been used in the past to document landscapes for a variety of reasons and often include comprehensive imagery of archaeological and heritage sites. These historical datasets present an opportunity for the development of new digital resources and three-dimensional models of landscapes, providing the potential to model a landscape before mechanised agriculture caused major alteration or before heritage sites experienced erosion or destruction. However, the challenge lies in digitising and creating new digital elevation models (DEMs) from these legacy analogue data, with a lack of metadata concerning their creation presenting one of the greatest issues. Digitising historical analogue aerial photograph is particularly important for study sites such as Engaruka, Tanzania, which lack high resolution DEMs for analysis and monitoring of the archaeological site. These new datasets, based on analogue imagery, could complement (UAV) surveys and Structure-from-Motion (SfM) photogrammetry techniques, providing greater potential for community inclusion and engagement in heritage management, communicating landscape change and the importance of monitoring and management of heritage sites through the development of orthomosaic and aerial photographs. This chapter explores the potential of different aerial survey datasets, digital technologies, and visualisation techniques for the development of high resolution DEMs and orthomosaics for the Engaruka archaeological site.

Digital technology and visualisation techniques, such as digital aerial imagery, SfM and mapping software, have become important tools for the research, monitoring and management of heritage and archaeological sites particularly in the face of global and local challenges such as site degradation over time, damage from conflicts and climate change (Sužiedelytė-Visockienė et al. 2015; Remondino and Rizzi 2010). The identification, location and quantification of the heritage resource can be achieved through a variety of documentation techniques, which include topographic surveying for spatial data, tacheometry, laser scanning and photogrammetry (Jorayev et al. 2016; Sužiedelytė-Visockienė et al. 2015), as well as remote sensing techniques. For example the increased availability of satellite imagery has enabled projects such as the EAMENA project (Bewley et al. 2016) to utilise satellite imagery to map archaeological sites that are at risk from damage from war and natural disasters. Certain techniques used for documentation of archaeological sites such as high- and low-resolution mapping, topographical survey and tacheometry can be time-consuming, costly and labour-intensive, especially when dealing with heritage and archaeological sites across expansive landscapes. In addition, the lower resolution of aerial photographs from fixed-wing aircraft, satellite imagery and topographical maps may not allow for identification and analysis of smaller archaeological features present in the landscape.

This chapter aims to demonstrate some of the challenges, benefits and technologies involved in using digital techniques to represent, monitor and understand archaeological landscapes to better protect them, with a particular focus on the archaeological site of Engaruka. By exploring various methods for the digitisation and analysis of these heritage sites, we aim to formulate a number of suitable processes that would support heritage management and assess their effectiveness. The methodology presented in this chapter demonstrates how SfM techniques can make use of archival analogue imagery for the creation of high-resolution orthomosaic maps and DEMs. The practicability of UAVs and SfM techniques to support research and management of these sites through digitisation and visualisation of archaeological features is also discussed. Techniques presented in this research have far-reaching applicability beyond the study site with the methodologies and workflows discussed relevant across a broad range of disciplines and provide a valuable resource for a variety of practitioners.

17.2 Background

17.2.1 Summary of Aerial Imagery Technologies

The use of aerial imagery as a tool to understand, quantify and protect archaeological sites began almost at the same time as manned flight. British archaeologist O.G.S. Crawford pioneered the discipline in the UK, publishing aerial photographs of Oxfordshire in *Antiquity* Journal's inaugural volume (Crawford 1927) and aerial imagery remained important to the discipline throughout the twentieth century. Increased availability of global satellite imagery in the 1990s and early 2000s, with the declassification of the US government's Corona imagery in 1995 and 2002, and the subsequent release of newer Advanced Spaceborne Thermal Emission and Reflection Radiometer (ASTER) Global Digital Elevation Model (GDEM) imagery led to an explosion of its use in a wide range of disciplines including archaeology (Keay et al. 2014), landscape survey and environmental monitoring (Narama et al. 2010). In archaeology, satellite images were used to visually identify archaeological sites and in environmental science to monitor issues such as deglaciation and vegetation change (Narama et al. 2010). By the early 2000s, some disciplines were creating DEMs from satellite imagery to monitor issues such as landslides (Barlow et al. 2006), large-scale geological features which suited the relatively low resolution of DEM the imagery was capable of producing, and of enough importance to facilitate the complex stereoscopy required to create such models. Although the satellite imagery itself was used to identify and monitor archaeological sites from the late

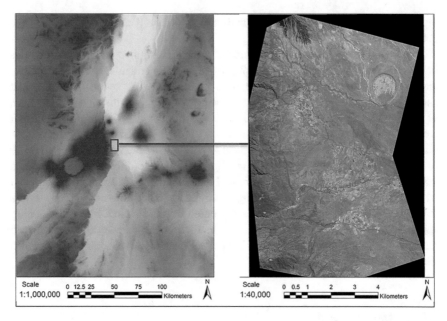

Fig. 17.1 ASTER DEM (Left, Imagery © 2015 NASA LP DAAC) and Quickbird satellite image (Right, Imagery © 2002 DigitalGlobe, Inc) of the Engaruka landscape; the ASTER DEM has a resolution of 30 m while the Quickbird satellite image has a resolution of 0.7 m (DigitalGlobe 2002; NASA_LP_DAAC 2011). The green bounding box indicates the extent covered by the Quickbird satellite image in the ASTER DEM

1990s, the images were rarely used to create topographic maps due to their insufficient resolution for the creation of detailed elevation models, and the complexity of this technique (Fig. 17.1).

In addition, the resolution of the satellite imagery and DEMs may not allow for identification and analysis of archaeological features present in the landscape (Fig. 17.1). For example, the NASA ASTER GDEM that covers the Engaruka site has a resolution of 30 m (NASA_LP_DAAC 2011) and at this lower resolution small archaeological features would be difficult to identify. UAV surveys provide an alternative and provably viable methodology for conducting archaeological surveys and for the development of high-resolution maps and DEMs. Aerial surveys also provide a bridge in the resolution scale between satellite imagery and terrestrial topographic surveys, such as high-resolution terrestrial laser scanning, combined with the flexibility in the resolution generated for multi-scale mapping (d'Oleire-Oltmanns et al. 2012). Thus, it was only with the appearance of relatively cheap and user-friendly UAVs in the 2000s, followed by SfM software, that the utility of high-resolution imagery for the identification and monitoring of archaeological sites, features and landscapes started to become widespread. Initially UAV-derived images were limited in quality due to the challenges in orthorectification of images and creating mosaics as well as issues caused during data collection such as turbulence (Lazzari and Gioia

2017). However as technologies improved and with the introduction of photogrammetry software packages, UAV survey images improved in quality and the technique became an important method for monitoring and mapping archaeological sites (Lazzari and Gioia 2017). Studies such as by Westoby et al. (2012) explored the benefits of these SfM techniques and outlined the workflows involved in the development of DEMs. These studies also highlighted the logistical advantages of SfM techniques as well as the quality of DEMs developed.

17.2.2 Aerial Surveys

UAV surveys have benefits over traditional piloted aerial surveys in terms of costs and resolution of the images generated, as well as its portability, flexibility, and low-flying altitude (Luo et al. 2019; Rippin et al. 2015; Javernick et al. 2014; Snavely et al. 2008) and have recently gained importance in environmental and ecological disciplines (Anderson et al. 2019; Rippin et al. 2015; Hugenholtz et al. 2013). Further benefits of the technique have been demonstrated by studies which compare topographical models made using UAV surveys and SfM against more expensive methods like LiDAR (De Reu et al. 2016), showing that they produce three dimensional models of archaeological sites with great accuracy (Nikolakopoulos et al. 2017). The rapid development of aerial surveys and SfM photogrammetry, alongside simplified workflows also allowed a wide range of users to access data and expand digital resources without relying on agencies and organisations with high budget equipment to process the data (Anderson et al. 2019), while the technique's ease of use and cost-effectiveness have also been highlighted (O'Driscoll 2018).

Documentation techniques are of importance for heritage management, in particular for the monitoring and conservation of archaeological sites that are at risk from gradual degradation, damage in war and natural disasters. The utility of UAV surveys for heritage management ranges from site detection, landscape scale monitoring and assessment and high-resolution mapping, proving particularly useful for the management of archaeological sites that are in remote or difficult to access areas (Luo et al. 2019; Chiabrando et al. 2011). Studies have also compared UAV images made from historical/archival photos to assess the on-going condition of archaeological sites and catalogue features (Lazzari and Gioia 2017), while a broad audience can be reached through data made available via platforms such as SketchFab (O'Driscoll 2018) which makes the data publicly available in an easily understandable package and is of use for public awareness programmes.

17.3 Methodology

Engaruka in Northern Tanzania appears to have developed in the late fifteenth century with radiocarbon dating showing intense use until the late 18th, before its complete abandonment in the nineteenth century. Agricultural cultivation at the site employed terracing and irrigation canals and is among the oldest of these systems so far identified in eastern Africa. The site covers an area of more than 20 km² and sits on the edge of the Great Rift Valley in a semi-arid area that was able to support agriculture due to the river systems which flow from the Crater highlands into the Rift valley (see Fig. 17.1). The water supply was intensively managed with a series of terraces and irrigation channels, which supported several settlements in the area (Fig. 17.2) (Sutton 2004). Recent excavations have demonstrated that the terraces were formed by sediment capture, and ongoing work focuses on these agricultural practices and

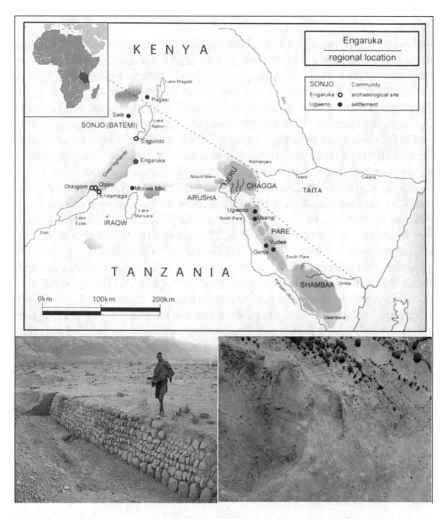

Fig. 17.2 Top: Engaruka location map (Stump 2006a), Left: Excavated stone-lined water channel (Stump 2006b, 196), Right: stone bounded terraces at Engaruka, visible on an aerial photograph from the 1960s (AAREA Project Archive). Images reproduced with permission from Stump, D)

their sustainability, rather than investigation of settlement sites (Lang and Stump 2017; Stump 2006a).

Engaruka is the largest site of its type abandoned before the arrival of Europeans in the mid-nineteenth century and so provides a unique opportunity to explore precolonial agricultural practices, which have the potential to play an important role in debates around present-day agricultural sustainability (Stump 2010a, b). However, the irrigation systems at Engaruka are not yet fully understood in terms of how they were formed and how they functioned (Fig. 17.2). To this end geoarchaeological and botanical analysis of the local sediment, alongside hydrological models are being employed to explore how and under what circumstances the irrigation systems were constructed. Initial results indicate that the site may represent a more sustainable method of agriculture, adapted to this environment (Lang and Stump 2017) and archaeobotanical evidence shows that a wider range of crops were grown than initially assumed (Thornton-Barnett 2018). DEMs and aerial survey perform several functions at Engaruka that support heritage management: the identification and mapping the extent of the site; monitoring degradation and encroaching development; and providing a base map for hydrological modelling to understand past agricultural and irrigation processes.

At present the most accurate topographic model available for Engaruka is the NASA ASTER Global DEM (NASA_LP_DAAC 2011; NASA_JPL 2012) which has a resolution of 30 m. However, higher resolution DEM models can be created with SfM software (Pulighe and Fava 2013; Kjellman 2012), something which proves invaluable for such targeted archaeological analysis and the monitoring of environmental degradation. Historical analogue photos of the site also provided the opportunity to create a higher resolution DEM of an earlier landscape, and the case studies presented here use SfM photogrammetry techniques on historical and UAV derived images, using the commercial software package AgiSoft PhotoScan Pro (Version 0.9.0) (AgiSoft 2010), renamed Agisoft Metashape in 2019. Both image sets were input into the software which identifies and matches features within and between images to find common points. These common points are then used to extrapolate the spatial relationships and produce a dense point cloud which can then be georeferenced with geographical coordinates to develop high resolution DEMs (Lazzari and Gioia 2017). These outputs aid archaeological research, creating a visual basemap of the site for monitoring and protection, and are invaluable to archaeologists working at the site, NGOs concerned with agricultural conservation in the region, and state bodies in charge of heritage protection. They enable different groups to test theories on the site's function and sustainability using this digital model and assess the effectiveness of preservation strategies employed. The DEM model presented below will also be of interest to geographers, geologists and hydrologists, but the models created from historical photos should also be tested to demonstrate their accuracy relative to the source data. As the DEM creation process is cost-effective and repeatable, the original source photographs and detailed workflows enable interested parties to repeat the process and investigate the conclusions reached below.

17.3.1 Study Site

Engaruka

Engaruka comprises approximately 2000 ha, with stone-bound fields, dry-stone terraces and stone-bound irrigation canals as well as dry-stone habitation terraces on the hill slopes (Westerberg et al. 2010; Stump 2006a; Sutton 1998). The field system is made up of three sections (Fig. 17.3), the north, central and south fields with each section having distinct differences from the other (Stump 2006a; Sutton, 1998). The north fields, located north of the Engaruka River, and the south fields, located south of the Olemelepo irrigation furrow, were most similar. These fields were made up of agricultural terraces which functioned as sediment traps with walls measuring 0.3–3.0 m high. Permanent stone-bound irrigation off-take canals were also present in these fields with further tributary canals distributing water throughout the terraces (Stump 2006a). In contrast, the central fields had no irrigation furrows except on the small hills, and the fields were bounded by single layers of stone. The main irrigation off-takes were on the perennial river of Engaruka and the now ephemeral rivers of Olemelepo and Intermediate gorge; but apart from Engaruka,

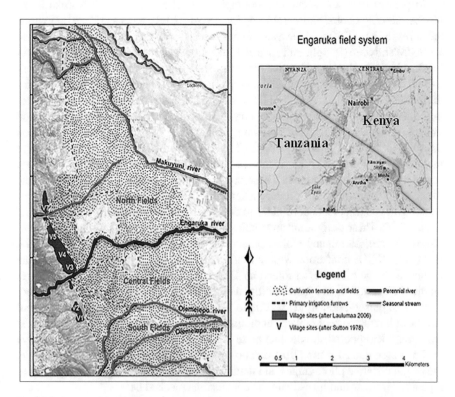

Fig. 17.3 Extent of the Engaruka system with river sources, primary irrigation off-takes and village settlements

these other river sources have dried up, which could be a possible reason for the abandonment of the system (Fig. 17.3).

The extensive field terracing and irrigation canal system of Engaruka provide interesting areas of study into the sustainability of historical water management systems (Fig. 17.3), elucidating historical agronomies that employed irrigation and terrace agriculture due to the preserved archaeological infrastructure. Historical and ethnographic evidence of agriculture and water management systems exist across East Africa, but these accounts lack physical evidence due to the use of earthworks such as earth bunds and organic materials like wood, which are lost over time through natural degradation and human activity (Stump and Tagseth 2009; Adams and Anderson 1988). For example, Kerio valley in Kenya and Mt. Kilimanjaro in Tanzania, both had canals which were either simple dirt ditches or hollowed out trees, while stone-bounded canals were only used in places of stress. In these cases, historical water management practices have been reconstructed, through oral history, archival records, and some continued use of antecedent practices believed to have been passed down through the generations.

17.3.2 Case Study 1 Using Archival Imagery and SfM Technology to Develop DEMs

Analogue to Digital

Analogue aerial imagery of Engaruka, recorded from light aircraft in the 1960s, was digitised to explore the potential of SfM software, to create DEMs from historical aerial photographs, and so create a 3D model of the landscape in the 1960s. AgiSoft PhotoScan enables the creation of a DEM of up to 3 m resolution, providing a considerable improvement on the current ASTER GDEM, which has a resolution of up to 30 m. However, any DEM created by this method must be thoroughly interrogated for accuracy before it can be used as the basis for further modelling or the monitoring of environmental degradation. Therefore, the second part of the process involved the comparison of the AgiSoft-created DEM with the ASTER elevation model by using map algebra tools in ArcMap. The terrain model and subsequent GIS analysis have been created within a broader critical background of visualisation for geographic and archaeological analysis (Wheatley and Gillings 2002). The digital outputs included a DEM based on the 1960s aerial photos as well as a series of analytical models, comparing the accuracy of this model with the ASTER GDEM, which aims to provide a comprehensive overview of the process for critical reflection and enables the workflow to be repeated, tested and hopefully improved upon. This methodology aims to combine the methods common for the processing of UAV aerial imagery and apply it to historic aerial photographs, which have the capacity to provide a higher resolution of model than Corona satellite imagery, and can therefore provide elevation models of greater precision, and more appropriate for the analysis and monitoring of anthropogenic features.

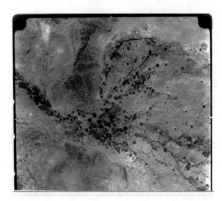

Fig. 17.4 A pair of the 1960s aerial photographs, note the colour variation and black targets which were masked before processing (Images from Sassoon's 1967 flight reproduced with permission from the BIEA)

Methodology

The source data for creating the DEM is a series of aerial photos taken in the 1960s from a light aircraft, which were subsequently printed, chopped in half and eventually scanned (Fig. 17.4). The aerial photographs were part of a collection from an aerial survey commissioned by Hamo Sassoon, courtesy of the Air Survey Division of the Ministry of Lands, Settlement and Water Development in Tanzania, and then archived with the British Institute in East Africa (BIEA), where the images were digitised (Sassoon 2009). Four pairs of photographs were selected to test whether it would be possible to create a higher resolution DEM as a basis for hydrological modelling (Fig. 17.4). The first step was to stitch and colour match the two parts of each photo in Adobe Photoshop so that they could then be input to SfM software. A mask was then created to ensure the corner targets were not included in the photo-matching.

Following the AgiSoft PhotoScan workflow, a meshed terrain model was created and georeferenced against the 2002 Quickbird satellite imagery of the area, before being exported to ArcGIS as a DEM (Fig. 17.5). A lowest resolution terrain model (which matches fewer pixels from the input images) was created at first and then a model at the highest resolution offered by the software. Both these models were then given an absolute height from the ASTER DEM and map algebra tools used to ascertain their relative accuracy.

Interrogations of the source data as well as the results of each step of the DEM creation process are important to reduce error in the subsequent hydrological modelling. Other studies such as by Pulighe and Fava (2013) report the successful creation of a DEM with a root mean squared error (RMSE) of 4.9 m, which is significantly better than the 12.95 m RMSE for the ASTER data for their study area in Sardinia, showing the validity of this technique. Other studies such as by Wise (2007) argue that it is important to look at not only error in the DEM but also the algorithms used for hydrological analysis as there is a complex relationship between these,

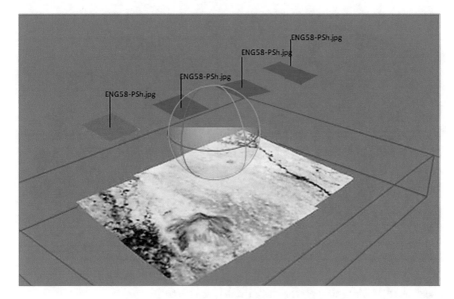

Fig. 17.5 Creating the terrain model in AgiSoft PhotoScan, this was then georeferenced and exported as a DEM

which can cause cumulative error. The investigation of elevation models created from Ordnance Survey maps to produce surface runoff predictions conducted by Wise (2007) demonstrated that the eventual models can differ by 200%. The importance of interrogating the source data as well as creating different iterations of the model to test it at every stage is therefore an important process to ensure eventual hydrological models are as accurate as possible.

Results and Testing for Accuracy

Visual analysis of the DEMs and orthophotos created in AgiSoft suggest that there has been some lens distortion or other anomalies affecting the output; however, these took a different form in the low and high resolution DEMs (Figs. 17.6 and 17.7).

The highest resolution DEM picks out more topographic features in the landscape, with river gullies discernible at this resolution. Trees seem also to be adding extra anomalies on the mesh, particularly in the north of the sample area. However, the highest resolution DEM also contains anomalies which do not seem to correspond to natural features and follow a different pattern to those in the lower resolution DEM (Fig. 17.7).

To gain more quantitative data on how accurate or otherwise the AgiSoft-created DEMs are, map algebra was employed to work out their accuracy relative to the ASTER DEM. The AgiSoft-created DEMs were first resampled to the same resolution as the ASTER DEM and then the differences in absolute heights between the two were calculated. This layer was then queried to highlight areas that correspond with certain height differences to illustrate how much of the DEM lies within a certain

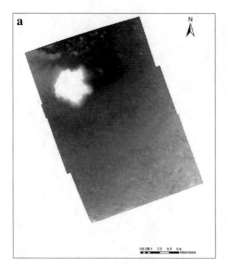
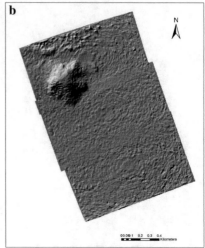

Fig. 17.6 a Lower resolution DEM, with ovoid pattering visible in the DEM **b** Hillshade of lower resolution DEM which highlights anomalies in elevation model

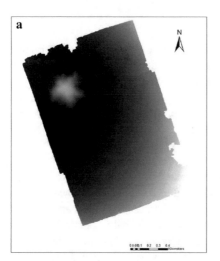

Fig. 17.7 a High resolution AgiSoft-created DEM, note the visibility of river channels which are not discernible in the lower resolution DEM and the curved patterning of interpolation artefacts from creating the DEM; **b** Hillshade of high quality AgiSoft-created DEM, which clearly shows water courses in the area

range of error. Comparative analysis of the DEMs demonstrate that the lower resolution DEM is better matched to the ASTER model, and that both models follow a similar pattern, although neither are particularly convincing in terms of relative accuracy to the ASTER as a basis for hydrological modelling.

Analysis

The anomalies and inaccuracies described above are hard to attribute to a precise cause, although the most likely candidates are lens distortion, or a stretching effect caused by uneven georeferencing. Both the highest and lower quality DEMs seem to follow a similar error pattern, with the most accurate parts of the DEM largely corresponding to the parts of the model which could be easily georeferenced with the 2002 Quickbird satellite image. Georeferencing the AgiSoft DEM proved complicated due to significant landscape change since the 1960s aerial photographs were taken. Therefore, most of the points which could be matched between the two images were in similar locations, on the western side of the test area, which is likely to have compounded any error.

The relative accuracy of the lower resolution model compared to the higher resolution one, while following roughly the same pattern of accuracy, suggests that the higher quality terrain modelling is exacerbating error. This indicates that the problem is likely in the source data rather than caused by human error, unless this error is in the first processing and stitching phase. Further investigation would be required to identify the possible causes of error. This process and review of relevant literature has shown that an elevation model can be created from analogue photographs; however, the consistent accuracy of such models remains debatable. Certainly, the number of steps required to create the model leads to a high potential for human error, which could exacerbate existing errors from lens distortion. At this point, the ASTER DEM remains the most reliable model available, although it is not yet clear what results will be produced when using the ASTER elevation model for hydrological analysis.

There are however several directions which could be considered for the next step in this process. One option would be to stitch a larger number of photos together to test whether the number and location of georeferencing points are causing a stretching effect on the resulting DEM. This would likely also improve any fish-eye effect or lens distortion over a larger area. Testing a relatively larger area would also give a better idea of whether the photo overlap is cancelling out or exacerbating photo differences. Smoothing the DEM will also remove some of the interpolation artefacts and this process could be investigated to see what difference it might make to the final DEM (Wise 2007). Ground truthing, by obtaining a small number of spot heights over transects or on easily recognisable points in the landscape (Pulighe and Fava 2013), would also enable a more precise way of checking DEM heights. Regardless of the likely causes of the error, the DEMs created in AgiSoft show that it is possible to create a workable (if inaccurate) DEM from analogue legacy data as well as a clear means of testing the output.

17.3.3 Case Study 2 Modern UAV Surveys with SfM to Develop New Aerial Imagery Maps

Aerial Surveys

The aerial survey conducted in Engaruka involved deploying a DJI Phantom 2 quadcopter mounted with a high-definition GoPro Hero3+ Silver Edition camera and the resultant images analysed using SfM software packages to generate point clouds before being input into ArcMap 10.2 to produce DEMs (see below).

The Engaruka field system covers an extensive area which would have required multi-day data acquisition to ensure the site is fully covered; however, time constraints and rough terrain limited the aerial survey to specific areas of interest in the south and north fields (Fig. 17.3). Surveys were conducted in 2016 in both areas with north–south flight direction to take into consideration the influence of inconsistent light exposure which might affect processing of the aerial images. The aerial photographs were taken at a near vertical angle (<3°) to minimise the possibility of point cloud noise that the vegetation could generate. An overlap of 60% and a minimum side-overlap of 30% (with side-overlaps of 60% preferable) was the target for the images over a series of survey lines covering the site (Fig. 17.8).

This overlap was achieved by limiting the distance between flight paths for each sector within the sites being surveyed, with flight paths approximately 20 m apart. Each section of the specific sites in the North and South fields was divided into sectors for ease of survey where each sector had approximately 10 ground control points (GCPs) to provide referencing points for the images in post-processing. Studies by James et al. (2017) have shown the importance of ensuring that the GCPs cover the area studied adequately. Survey height was approximately 25 m to ensure fine resolution of the images produced and a handheld electronic tablet device monitored the quadcopter's height and speed.

Fig. 17.8 Aerial Survey photograph overlays showing an overlap of 60% (red and blue rectangles) and a minimum side-overlap of 30% (blue and green rectangles)

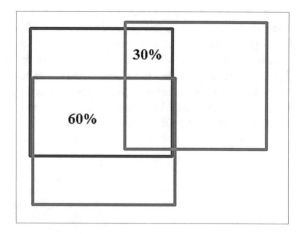

Analysis

The results of these surveys were post-processed by georectifying the data for inclusion into multi-scale GIS databases. Post-processing involves the comparison of time-coded signals from the GPS (rover) device, which are used to determine the coordinate positions measured in the field, with those received by a fixed reference (base) station with known coordinates in the same region. By comparing the coordinate data from the rover GPS devices with those from base stations, the data was georectified to improve the accuracy of the coordinates collected.

The aerial survey images were processed using the established workflows in the PhotoScan software (Fig. 17.9). The images were georectified using GCPs visible within the landscape and georeferenced orthomosaic images were then exported for use in ArcGIS 10.2 as tagged image file format (TIFF) and DEM.

The data from the archaeological excavations, topographical surveys and aerial surveys were processed using ESRI ArcGIS 10.2 to develop maps of the archaeological features and surrounding landscape. In addition, the DEMs created were analysed using the ArcGIS raster calculator tool to determine the accuracy of the photostitched images. DEMs are single dataset files containing elevation data and are stored in a GIS database as raster or GRID image file or Triangular Irregular Network (TIN) format, which are vector surface models. The DEMs created were analysed by comparison with existing DEMs which are georeferenced to a known geographic or projected coordinate system, comparing pixels in each images with attributed height values. The DEMs primarily used for most of the analysis in this research were obtained from the USGS EarthExplorer the ASTER GDEM V2 and the Shuttle Radar Topography Mission (SRTM) Void Filled (NASA_LP_DAAC 2011; NASA_JPL 2012).

To test the accuracy of the UAV-derived orthomosaic model and DEM, the model was first re-projected to ensure it was in the same projection system as the ASTER GDEM and resampled using Raster processing tools to ensure the resolutions were the same. Using the Map Algebra tool, the difference between the UAV-derived model and ASTER GDEM was calculated to highlight areas that correspond.

Results

The aerial surveys conducted in 2016 were used to develop high resolution imagery using SfM techniques. In a comparison with the ASTER GDEM, SRTM Void Filled and Quickbird satellite imagery, the photo-stitched aerial survey imagery had the highest resolution at 0.25 m in comparison to the satellite imagery that had a resolution of 0.7 m and the GDEM and SRTM at 30 and 90 m respectively (Table 17.1). While a resolution of 0.25 m is not the highest resolution that can be achieved using this methodology, computer processing restrictions meant that this was the most feasible strategy. The higher resolution of 0.25 m still allows for smaller archaeological features to be assessed within the context of the wider landscape.

The UAV-derived image when compared against the ASTER GDEM showed a mostly positive correlation (Fig. 17.10) with most of the model within 20 m of the ASTER. The model showed greater inaccuracy towards the outer edges of the

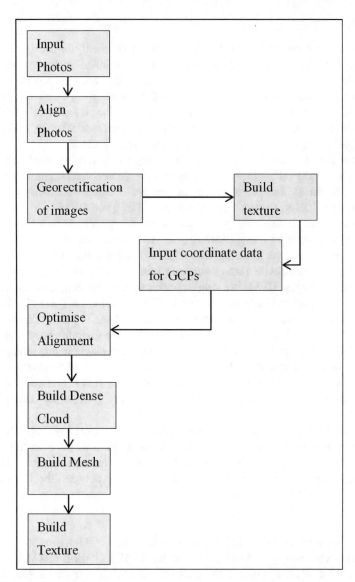

Fig. 17.9 PhotoScan workflow for photo-stitching and georectification of aerial survey image data

Table 17.1 Comparison of resolution of image datasets for analysis of topography and archaeological features

Dataset	Resolution (m)
SRTM void filled	90
ASTER GDEM	30
Quickbird satellite image	0.7
Aerial survey image	0.25

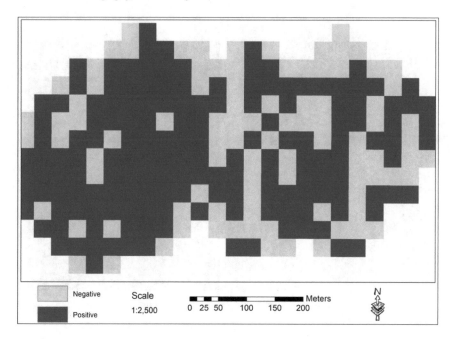

Fig. 17.10 Correlation of the UAV-derived DEM showing the areas within 20 m of the ASTER GDEM

DEM, with further anomalies also noted in patches within the model and DEM generation, the areas in which these different images overlapped were likely to carry over inconsistencies.

The areas of negative correlations to the ASTER shown in Fig. 17.10 could be due to inaccuracies that occurred during processing as multiple model chunks were processed individually and then stitched together to create the final orthomosaic and DEMs. In addition, as the DEM had to be resampled to match the resolution of the ASTER, this stretching process could have also resulted in further inaccuracies.

Analysis of the aerial survey images reveals additional details on the pattern of placement of irrigation canals and sediment trap fields within the landscape. Adjusting the colour spectrum on the images also allows for more features to be observed (Fig. 17.11) showing sequences of fields that were otherwise unclear. The irrigation canals were angled to take advantage of gravity to support the movement of water, with canals built heading downslope and the angle of the off-take for the irrigation canal improves discharge while minimising possible damage to the channel walls.

The irrigation canals were set at oblique angles to the natural water channels, with the approximate angle for the off-takes at 120° (Fig. 17.11). The stone-bound fields were also angled away from the irrigation canals which allows water to be diverted into the stone-bound sediment trap fields at a fast enough rate to cover the field without causing damage to the field walls. The irrigation canals were also spaced

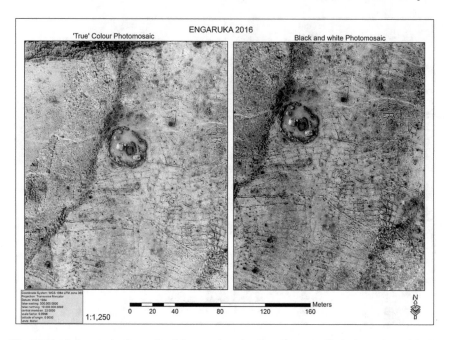

Fig. 17.11 Orthomosaic photo of aerial survey imagery from Engaruka, in the South fields at scale of 1:1,250. The high resolution imagery reveals a series of stone-bound fields and irrigation canals with little degradation of the image as compared to satellite imagery at the same resolution

out along the water channels to ensure adequate coverage of the fields before any additional water was carried out of the system downstream. The creation of these orthomosaics thus enable more detailed observation of the archaeological features across the site and support interpretations of the features and their relation to the wider landscape.

17.4 Discussion

These two case studies on the Engaruka archaeological site demonstrate the utility of SfM technologies for the creation of DEMs and support archaeological interpretations of features. By being able to identify archaeological features and monitor changes over time these techniques can contribute to the protection and management of the archaeological site. The use of UAVs and SfM techniques are a particularly suitable method to investigate and monitor a site such as Engaruka because of its extent, and the differences in elevation caused by terracing, as well as the complexity of the field system and channels, which make it more challenging to identify and map features during field surveys. The various approaches outlined above indicate that several different aerial techniques can be used to provide meaningful, precise and accurate mapping of sites of this type, for the purposes of effective monitoring of environmental changes at the site as well as answering archaeological questions. Using aerial photographs to monitor and understand archaeological sites is not a new development (Crawford 1927) but advances in satellite and drone technology, leading to decreasing cost and increased availability for archaeologists have broadened their application and uses.

The first case study shows that historical aerial photos can have an application, beyond just a visible assessment of the site, and it is anticipated that this approach could be transformative in a wide range of applications, as long as the accuracy of the created model is thoroughly tested. In this chapter, a suitable methodology for testing this accuracy is presented and demonstrates that the creation of a DEM was possible, but when tested against the ASTER GDEM it became clear that there was a consistent error. This error may be caused by a combination of factors, with the major issue being the lack of digital metadata from a scanned image which consequently lacks information such as lens type and camera calibration as well as height and geographic coordinates which is used by SfM software to create a more accurate model. Distortions may also have been caused during scanning, and the many steps required to prepare the photos before they could be processed in PhotoScan also provides the potential for cumulative errors to become a factor. This example indicates that the creation of reliable and precise DEMs from analogue photographs is possible, but problems may occur without the metadata traditionally stored in a digital image. In order to interrogate and improve upon this process, the DEMs accuracy can be tested in ArcMap, and an effective method for this process is demonstrated here. Studies of this type are scarce but have found similar issues in working with historical and archival aerial photos (Lazzari and Gioia 2017). Although the DEM created was not suitable for hydrological modelling, which requires an accurate basemap due to both precision and accuracy required for monitoring flow patterns, it was still of use for the monitoring of the site as the high-quality imagery provides a relative accuracy, indicating river channels across the site. In cases where landscapes have been heavily altered by mechanical farming techniques or extensive irrigation, these channels can often disappear, leading to difficulties in reconstructing past agricultural techniques or natural resources. Photographs from the early- or mid-twentieth century are often uniquely placed, due to their relatively high quality and increasing uniformity in terms of capture from light aircraft, but crucially often represent landscapes that are on the brink of change as mechanised agriculture transformed landscapes and irrigation canals diverted or subsumed previous water courses.

The second case study further demonstrates that SfM techniques can rapidly produce highly detailed models to support archaeological interpretation. UAV surveys and the orthomosaics produced can be used to provide up-to-date information on the status and condition of extensive archaeological sites where other topographical survey techniques would be time-consuming and can be further used to update existing maps (Koeva et al. 2018). In addition, the greater mobility and wide view of the UAVs provide exploratory opportunities for heritage managers and researchers to view expansive sites, access difficult terrain or conduct reconnaissance for research and monitoring at lower costs and shorter timescales as compared to traditional topographical surveys.

17.5   Conclusion

The case studies outlined above demonstrate that the use of SfM technologies, UAV surveys and historical photos can be beneficial to heritage management and archaeological research. The increasing availability of these technologies as well as the ease of generation of the orthomosaics through simple workflows mean that these methods present heritage managers with new opportunities to document, monitor and research archaeological sites. However, there are some challenges presented by these methods; the storage and digitisation of the archival photographs can be expensive and storage of digital material in an accessible format and repository needs to be taken into consideration. In addition, the initial costs of the UAV equipment and processing software as well as training for staff can prove prohibitive, but advancements in the use of these techniques have seen the development of low-cost survey equipment as well as open-access software for SfM processing. The small sample of historical aerial photographs generated a DEM, but the absence of data on the camera calibration used in the 1960s presented challenges to its accuracy. Digitally adjusting archival images to make them suitable for SfM processing can also create further anomalies through the stitching and resizing processes in particular. Future research could explore expanding the sample set of historical analogue photos digitised to create DEMs that cover larger areas. In addition, although it appears that the original metadata from this flight has been lost, archival research to determine details on the camera type and calibration might enhance processing quality, although other details such as the height of the aircraft would be more difficult to determine.

While there remain challenges, the methodologies outlined in the case studies provide a useful and repeatable way to explore the potential of analogue legacy data in terrain modelling, and this project underlines the need for continued analysis of outputs at every stage of the workflow to ensure the validity of the DEM. The use of historic photographs presents a new and exciting avenue, with the potential to transform monitoring and modelling of historic landscapes in regions where these images exist. Ongoing declassification of military and other monitoring imagery (see for example Hammer and Ur 2019) means that the potential for these is increasing and would support future heritage management as well as better understanding historic landscapes and their change over time. This potential is strengthened by the increased availability of user-friendly software. The UAV surveys and the orthomosaics produced can further be used to provide up-to-date information on the status and condition of extensive archaeological sites where other topographical survey techniques would be more time-consuming.

The use of aerial imagery and orthomosaics is also useful in engaging local communities in heritage management, being far more accessible than archaeologically interpreted visualisations and enabling the public and local communities to visualise and understand interventions and practices, particularly in cases where the archaeological sites are extensive and complex. This can support collaborative decision-making between local communities and heritage managers. UAV surveys and SfM technologies have broad academic and practical impacts not only for heritage research but also in capacity building for heritage management for local communities.

Acknowledgements The Archaeology of Agricultural Resilience in Eastern Africa (AAREA) project is funded by the European Research Council, Grant Agreement No. ERC-StG-2012-337128-AAREA awarded to D. Stump in February 2014. The research was also supported by the British Institute in East Africa under the Thematic Research Grants 2015/2016 awarded to Kabora, T.K. Research in Tanzania was carried out under a research permit issued by the Tanzanian Commission for Science and Technology. The authors would also like to thank the anonymous reviewers for their comments and critiques that helped improve this chapter.

References

Adams WM, Anderson DM (1988) Irrigation before development: indigenous and induced change in agricultural water management in East Africa. Afr Aff 87(349):519–535. https://doi.org/10.2307/722892

AgiSoft (2010) AgiSoft PhotoScan Professional (Version 0.9.0). http://www.agisoft.com/features/professional-edition/

Anderson K, Westoby MJ, James MR (2019) Low-budget topographic surveying comes of age: structure from motion photogrammetry in geography and the geosciences. Prog Phys Geogr Earth Environ 43(2):163–173. https://doi.org/10.1177/0309133319837454

Barlow J, Franklin S, Martin Y (2006) High spatial resolution satellite imagery, DEM derivatives, and image segmentation for the detection of mass wasting processes. Photogramm Eng Remote Sens 72.https://doi.org/10.14358/PERS.72.6.687

Bewley R, Wilson A, Kennedy D, Mattingly D, Banks R, Bishop M et al (2016) Endangered archaeology in the Middle East and North Africa: Introducing the EAMENA project. In: CAA2015. Keep the revolution going: proceedings of the 43rd annual conference on computer applications and quantitative methods in archaeology. p 919

Chiabrando F, Nex F, Piatti D, Rinaudo F (2011) UAV and RPV systems for photogrammetric surveys in archaelogical areas: two tests in the Piedmont region (Italy). J Archaeol Sci 38(3):697–710. https://doi.org/10.1016/j.jas.2010.10.022

Crawford OGS (1927) Air-photographs near Dorchester, Oxon (Plates I-II). Antiquity 1(4):469–474. https://doi.org/10.1017/S0003598X00000946

d'Oleire-Oltmanns S, Marzolff I, Peter KD, Ries JB (2012) Unmanned aerial vehicle (UAV) for monitoring soil erosion in Morocco. Remote Sens 4(11):3390–3416

De Reu J, Trachet J, Laloo P, De Clercq W (2016) From low cost UAV survey to high resolution topographic data: developing our understanding of a medieval outport of Bruges. Archaeol Prospect 23(4):335–346. https://doi.org/10.1002/arp.1547

DigitalGlobe (2002) 'QuickBird scene, 000000021552_01_P001, Level Standard 2A' Level Standard 2A. DigitalGlobe, Longmont, Colorado

Hammer E, Ur J (2019) Near eastern landscapes and declassified U2 aerial imagery. Adv Archaeol Pract 7(2):107–126. https://doi.org/10.1017/aap.2018.38

Hugenholtz CH, Whitehead K, Brown OW, Barchyn TE, Moorman BJ, LeClair A et al (2013) Geomorphological mapping with a small unmanned aircraft system (sUAS): feature detection and accuracy assessment of a photogrammetrically-derived digital terrain model. Geomorphology 194:16–24. https://doi.org/10.1016/j.geomorph.2013.03.023

James MR, Robson S, d'Oleire-Oltmanns S, Niethammer U (2017) Optimising UAV topographic surveys processed with structure-from-motion: ground control quality, quantity and bundle adjustment. Geomorphology 280:51–66. https://doi.org/10.1016/j.geomorph.2016.11.021

Javernick L, Brasington J, Caruso B (2014) Modeling the topography of shallow braided rivers using Structure-from-Motion photogrammetry. Geomorphology 213:166–182. https://doi.org/10.1016/j.geomorph.2014.01.006

Jorayev G, Wehr K, Benito-Calvo A, Njau J, de la Torre I (2016) Imaging and photogrammetry models of Olduvai Gorge (Tanzania) by unmanned aerial vehicles: a high-resolution digital database for research and conservation of early stone age sites. J Archaeol Sci 75:40–56. https://doi.org/10.1016/j.jas.2016.08.002

Keay SJ, Parcak SH, Strutt KD (2014) High resolution space and ground-based remote sensing and implications for landscape archaeology: the case from Portus, Italy. J Archaeol Sci 52:277–292. https://doi.org/10.1016/j.jas.2014.08.010

Kjellman E (2012) From 2D to 3D: a photogrammetric revolution in archaeology? Universitetet i Tromsø

Koeva M, Muneza M, Gevaert C, Gerke M, Nex F (2018) Using UAVs for map creation and updating. A case study in Rwanda. Survey Rev 50(361):312–325. https://doi.org/10.1080/00396265.2016.1268756

Lang C, Stump D (2017) Geoarchaeological evidence for the construction, irrigation, cultivation, and resilience of 15th–18th century AD terraced landscape at Engaruka, Tanzania. Quat Res 1–18.https://doi.org/10.1017/qua.2017.54

Lazzari M, Gioia D (2017) UAV images and historical aerial-photos for geomorphological analysis and hillslope evolution of the Uggiano medieval archaeological site (Basilicata, southern Italy). Geomat Nat Hazards Risk 8(1):104–119. https://doi.org/10.1080/19475705.2017.1310762

Luo L, Wang X, Guo H, Lasaponara R, Zong X, Masini N et al (2019) Airborne and spaceborne remote sensing for archaeological and cultural heritage applications: a review of the century (1907–2017). Remote Sens Environ 232:111280. https://doi.org/10.1016/j.rse.2019.111280

Narama C, Kääb A, Duishonakunov M, Abdrakhmatov K (2010) Spatial variability of recent glacier area changes in the Tien Shan Mountains, Central Asia, using Corona (~1970), Landsat (~2000), and ALOS (~2007) satellite data. Glob Planet Chang 71:42–54. https://doi.org/10.1016/j.gloplacha.2009.08.002

NASA_JPL (2012) 'NASA Shuttle Radar Topography Mission (SRTM) Void-Filled 3 arc second. Version 2. 03°S, 35°E.' NASA EOSDIS Land Processes Distributed Active Archive Center (LP DAAC), USGS Earth Resources Observation and Science (EROS) Center, Sioux Falls, South Dakota. https://lpdaac.usgs.gov. Accessed 11 Jan 2015

NASA_LP_DAAC (2011) 'ASTER Global Digital Elevation Model (GDEM) 1 arc second. Version 2. 03°S, 35°E'. NASA EOSDIS Land Processes Distributed Active Archive Center (LP DAAC), USGS Earth Resources Observation and Science (EROS) Center, Sioux Falls, South Dakota. https://doi.org/10.5067/ASTER/ASTGTM.002. https://lpdaac.usgs.gov. Accessed 11 Jan 2015

Nikolakopoulos KG, Soura K, Koukouvelas IK, Argyropoulos NG (2017) UAV vs classical aerial photogrammetry for archaeological studies. J Archaeol Sci Rep 14:758–773. https://doi.org/10.1016/j.jasrep.2016.09.004

O'Driscoll J (2018) Landscape applications of photogrammetry using unmanned aerial vehicles. J Archaeol Sci Rep 22:32–44. https://doi.org/10.1016/j.jasrep.2018.09.010

Pulighe G, Fava F (2013) DEM extraction from archive aerial photos: accuracy assessment in areas of complex topography. Eur J Remote Sens 46(1):363–378. https://doi.org/10.5721/EuJRS20134621

Remondino F, Rizzi A (2010) Reality-based 3D documentation of natural and cultural heritage sites—techniques, problems, and examples (journal article). Appl Geomat 2(3):85–100. https://doi.org/10.1007/s12518-010-0025-x

Rippin DM, Pomfret A, King N (2015) High resolution mapping of supra-glacial drainage pathways reveals link between micro-channel drainage density, surface roughness and surface reflectance. Earth Surf Process Landf.https://doi.org/10.1002/esp.3719

Sassoon H (2009) New views on Engaruka, Northern Tanzania: excavations carried out for the Tanzania government in 1964 and 1966. J Afr Hist 8(2):201–217. https://doi.org/10.1017/S0021853700007027

Snavely N, Seitz S, Szeliski R (2008) Modeling the world from internet photo collections. Int J Comput Vision 80(2):189–210. https://doi.org/10.1007/s11263-007-0107-3

Stump D (2006a) The development and expansion of the field and irrigation systems at Engaruka, Tanzania. AZANIA J Br Inst East Afr 41(1):69–94

Stump D (2006b) Towards an applied archaeology of east African intensive agricultural systems. Doctoral Dissertation, UCL (University College London)

Stump D (2010) "Ancient and backward or long-lived and sustainable?" The role of the past in debates concerning rural livelihoods and resource conservation in eastern Africa. World Dev 38(9):1251–1262

Stump D (2010) Intensification in context: archaeological approaches to precolonial field systems in Eastern and Southern Africa. Afr Stud 69(2):255–278. https://doi.org/10.1080/00020184.2010.499201

Stump D, Tagseth M (2009) The history of precolonial and early colonial agriculture on Kilimanjaro: a review. In: Clack T (ed) Culture, history and identity: landscapes of inhabitation in the Mount Kilimanjaro area. Archaeopress, Oxford, pp 107–124

Sutton J (2004) Engaruka: the success and abandonment of an integrated irrigation system in an arid part of the Rift Valley, c. 15th to 17th centuries. In: Widgren M, Sutton JEG (eds) Islands of intensive agriculture in the Eastern Africa. James Curry, Oxford, pp 114–132

Sutton JEG (1998) Engaruka: an irrigation agricultural community in Northern Tanzania before the Maasai. AZANIA J Br Inst East Afr 33:1–37

Sužiedelytė-Visockienė J, Bagdžiūnaitė R, Malys N, Maliene V (2015) Close-range photogrammetry enables documentation of environment-induced deformation of architectural heritage. Environ Eng Manag J 14:1371–1381. https://doi.org/10.30638/eemj.2015.149

Thornton-Barnett S (2018) Persevering with great abandon: an archaeobotanical investigation of resilience and sustainability in Eastern African irrigated terrace agriculture. University of York

Westerberg L-O, Holmgren K, BÖrjeson L, HÅkansson NT, Laulumaa V, Ryner M, et al (2010) The development of the ancient irrigation system at Engaruka, northern Tanzania: physical and societal factors. Geogr J 176(4):304–318.https://doi.org/10.1111/j.1475-4959.2010.00370.x

Westoby MJ, Brasington J, Glasser NF, Hambrey MJ, Reynolds JM (2012) 'Structure-from-Motion' photogrammetry: a low-cost, effective tool for geoscience applications. Geomorphology 179:300–314. https://doi.org/10.1016/j.geomorph.2012.08.021

Wheatley D, Gillings M (2002) Location models and prediction. In: Wheatley D, Gillings M (eds) Spatial technology and archaeology. Taylor & Francis, London, pp 165–181

Wise SM (2007) Effect of differing DEM creation methods on the results from a hydrological model. Comput Geosci 33(10):1351–1365. https://doi.org/10.1016/j.cageo.2007.05.003

Chapter 18
A Rapid Approach to the Digital Documentation of Bradford's Rich Industrial Heritage

Joe Moore, Chris Gaffney, Tom Sparrow, Henry Irving, Saira Ali, Richard Middleton, Sheena Campbell, Jon Ackroyd, Adrian Walker, Sydney Simpson, Joe Ritchings, and Andrew S. Wilson

Abstract The industrial heritage for the City of Bradford Metropolitan District is of international significance, with the city formerly being the centre of the world's worsted trade during the nineteenth century. The intensification of textile production during the industrial revolution resulted in exponential growth of all aspects of the city, the legacy seen in the townscape heritage of the city today. The structures from this period have played a key role in defining the city's identity. Since the decline of the textile industry the fabric of many of these buildings from the city's golden age are under threat and at high risk of loss due to weathering, vandalism and fire. Given the varied nature and condition of these structures, a rapid approach has been applied that complements initiatives in train with Bradford Council to regenerate the 'Top of Town'; that are reflective of Historic England's 'Engines of Prosperity' report into the regeneration of Industrial Heritage; and with the Management of Saltaire World Heritage site. This chapter focuses on the digital documentation of a conservation area which is highly vulnerable, producing a dataset to aid conservation, management, interpretation and promotion of Bradford's rich heritage.

Keywords Industrial archaeology · Textile industry · Cultural heritage · Geospatial recording · Mobile mapping · Simultaneous localisation and mapping (SLAM) · LiDAR

J. Moore · C. Gaffney · T. Sparrow · A. S. Wilson (✉)
Visualising Heritage, School of Archaeological & Forensic Sciences, University of Bradford, Bradford, UK
e-mail: A.S.Wilson2@bradford.ac.uk

J. Moore
e-mail: J.Dwyer-Moore@student.bradford.ac.uk

H. Irving
School of Cultural Studies and Humanities, Leeds Beckett University, Leeds, UK

S. Ali · R. Middleton · S. Campbell · J. Ackroyd · A. Walker · S. Simpson · J. Ritchings
Department of Place, City of Bradford Metropolitan District Council, Bradford, UK

375

E. Ch'ng et al. (eds.), *Visual Heritage: Digital Approaches in Heritage Science*,
Springer Series on Cultural Computing,
https://doi.org/10.1007/978-3-030-77028-0_18

18.1 Introduction

The application of a variety of LiDAR-based methods on heritage assets is now a commonplace practice through all levels of the heritage sector and is often the first port of call when recording built heritage. Traditional LiDAR recording methodologies for the built environment, either using a Total Station Theodolite or Terrestrial Laser Scanning, require a significant amount of time spent in the field and in post-processing, though have the capability of producing virtual representations of the assets with millimetre accuracy. Recent advancements in Mobile Mapping Systems have provided a means of recording large and complex environments, with a drastically reduced amount of time spent in the field and during processing, though the resulting dataset has reduced accuracy and increased noise levels when compared to more traditional methods. This chapter offers a case study where, when dealing with heritage at risk, a primary geospatial record captured rapidly can be preferred over a more accurate but time-consuming method (Fig. 18.1).

Fig. 18.1 Locations maps showing Bradford, the four conservation areas within the city centre of Bradford, West Yorkshire, including the Goitside conservation area. The blue points indicate listed structures. Base map—Ordnance Survey (2019)

18.2   Background

A globally significant nineteenth-century industrial townscape known as the Goit-side conservation area in Bradford, West Yorkshire, was recorded from street level, producing the first high level geospatial record of the whole conservation area captured from the public realm, providing a virtual representation of a snapshot in time. The work was undertaken as part of an AHRC funded PhD project on the digital documentation of industrial heritage at risk within the district, based within the Visualising Heritage Team of the School of Archaeological and Forensic Sciences at The University of Bradford.

The heritage of Bradford is unquestionably rooted within the industrial revolution and the role it played in the world's textile trade. During the nineteenth-century Bradford witnessed an unprecedented boom in urban development as a direct result of the textile industry, during which it became the fastest growing town in Europe (Reynolds and Baines 1978) with an estimated two-thirds of England's wool being processed in Bradford (Duxbury-Neumann 2015) and as a consequence became known as 'Worstedopolis' (Cudworth 1888). Over 200 mills were constructed in the first half of the century, with a resulting rise in the population from c. 13,000 to over 100,000 in the same period (Jowitt 1991). Today, Bradford's former glory as the wool capital of the world is a legacy rooted in the surviving architecture of the city and surrounding mill towns. Throughout the district of Bradford, there are over 5800 listed building, 31% of which date from 1700 to 1840, and 32% from 1840 to 1900, though regardless of the exemplary significance the textile trade had on the district, only 3% of the total listings are attributed to mills and warehouses (CBMDC 2012: pp. 2–3).

Within the city centre there are four conservation areas, each with their own unique features which have led to their definition as areas of special architectural and histor-ical interest. Of the four, Goitside stands out from the rest. Designated a conservation area in 1992 on the premise that, regardless of the substantial redevelopment the area has borne witness to, it still retains many nineteenth- and early twentieth-century industrial buildings, along with a few older structures which demonstrate the area's development as the earliest industrial heart of the city. Furthermore, it represents a relatively complete and well-preserved landscape which was typical of the industrial, commercial and social elements of the late nineteenth-century and early twentieth-century City of Bradford (CBMDC 2005a: p. 4). Many of the structures found within the boundary are relatively simple in design, built purely as functioning spaces for the production and storage of the produce of the textile industry. This is of stark contrast to the other three conservation areas within the city centre and is manifested in the number of listed buildings that each area contains. Little Germany offers a good contrast to the Goitside area, an area rapidly formed as a merchant's quarter with the juxtaposition of the Midland Railway terminus and the most successful of the textile merchants. Dealerships involved in the storage and sale of the produce coming out of Goitside resulted in many of the structures being architecturally ornate, designed to impress potential clients (CBMDC 2005b: pp. 8–9). Whilst the two areas differ in

architectural design, both are arguably equally significant historically to the industrial heritage of Bradford. However, the simplistic nature of many of the buildings
found within Goitside have led to a somewhat unappreciated outcome, regardless of
the high significance they played in the foundation of the city's prosperity, with only
five listed buildings found within the conservation area (CBMSC 2005a: p. 31). In
contrast, Little Germany boasts fifty (CBMSC 2005b: p. 10).

The Little Germany area has witnessed successful redevelopment of many of
the buildings found within the conservation area, and whilst a few structures within
the area are vacant, there have been many successful conversions of the structures
found within (CBMSC 2005b: p. 28). The Goitside area, in comparison, suffers
from a high level of underused space, with a significant proportion of the buildings
currently sitting vacant, a trend which is only worsening with time (CBMSC 2007:
p. 6). From a building conservation perspective, vacancy is the top contributor to the
deterioration of a structure (Historic England 2018a), with the Goitside conservation
area deemed to be in a 'very bad' condition and within the Heritage at Risk Register
(Historic England 2019). For this reason, the Goitside area was selected to test the
applicability of new technology in the documentation of an area of underrepresented
heritage of high significance that was in need of rapid geospatial documentation. This
provided a level of digital documentation to mitigate against further loss of historic
fabric, whilst acting as a test-case for the application of a SLAM based LiDAR
scanner where speed is preferred over accuracy.

18.3   Method

Data capture was achieved using the ZEB Horizon mobile mapping system
(GeoSLAM 2019a), the first such device purchased by an academic institution in
the UK and owned by the Visualising Heritage team within the School of Archaeological and Forensic Sciences, University of Bradford. The ZEB Horizon is a class
1 eye-safe Simultaneous Localisation and Mapping (SLAM) LiDAR-based system,
collecting data at a rate of 300,000 pt/s, with a range of 100 m and an accuracy
quoted at ±30 mm, though normally defined at a specific distance from the scanner,
in this case, no further criteria of the accuracy are given beyond that value. Colourisation of the point cloud is possible with the use of the integrated ZEB cam, though
technical issues with the camera were encountered during this fieldwork, leading to
the lack of colourised data. Through a combination of the inbuilt inertial measurement unit (IMU) providing data concerning the orientation and travel direction of
the scanner, and the VLP-16 puck LiDAR data to map the surrounding environment,
GeoSLAM's SLAM algorithm produces a point cloud of the traversed environment
through the user holding the device and moving freely through the environment at
a steady pace, offering a high level of mobility and flexibility in the types of environments that can be documented, allowing the user to manoeuvre into positions to
ensure as complete as possibly coverage of the given subject and quickly pass through
and record large areas of complex geometry. By comparison, tripod-mounted laser

scanning methodologies rely on data collection from a network of fixed locations throughout and around the given subject, requiring multiple scans to ensure complete coverage, equating a significantly larger time investment to gain the same level of coverage, especially when dealing with complex environments such as entire historic townscapes or building interiors. A comparative overview of the different scanning methodologies commonly applied to cultural assets can be seen in Historic England (2018b: pp. 7–19).

For the purpose of this survey, all of the data was captured from the public realm. Access to private property, mainly parking lots and internal spaces of buildings, was intentionally avoided. This choice was made to explore the capabilities of data capture where no prior arrangements with third parties were needed, thus enabling rapid deployment for geospatial data capture should situations that require immediate action arise. Although the same rapidity enables the capture of internal spaces in small time slots, avoiding large disruptions to property/business owners should access be agreed. To ensure continuity and quality assurance between the scans, a standard operating procedure has been established for the operation of the ZEB Horizon. Firstly, where possible, all data is captured in a loop, returning to the exact spot from which the scan started, as suggested by GeoSLAM. Though it is possible to process data which has not closed at the same location as the start, for instance because of weather conditions forced data capture to be cut short, returning to the start location is the preferred method to ensure as tight as possible dataset for the SLAM processing. During a scan, multiple passes of the same location provide further data to help tighten the dataset during processing, increasing the accuracy of the resulting point cloud. As an extra measure, though somewhat difficult in various environments, the traveling speed during collection is kept as constant as possible (although roads, people, obstacles, etc., can make this difficult). The length of time taken for any one scan is suggested to be no longer than 30 min. No control points were established or used for the purpose of this work.

Prior to the fieldwork commencing, a strategy was devised that divided the area into four separate routes to traverse, although one scan had to be cut short because of weather conditions, requiring an extra scan to capture the missing data. Whilst all attempts were made to ensure the speed of travel during the scans were consistent, this was not always possible for various reasons. During one scan it started to rain towards the end of the scan, and as the Horizon has no waterproofing, the walking speed was increased to ensure that the loop was closed. Whilst this does not seem to have had any detrimental effects on the data, a small area of the conservation area that was planned for capture during this scan was missed, leading to one further scan than was originally planned. Secondly, pedestrians and traffic made walking at a constant speed near impossible because of the need to cross roads, although again, this had no noticeable detrimental effects on the data.

All primary processing of the data is, by necessity, done in the GeoSLAM HUB software package. This has the option to export the point cloud in a variety of formats, and through the use of the GeoSLAM Draw software, produce a range of CAD ready outputs depending upon the requirements of the project, with the capability to anno-tate and analyse the data (see Fig. 18.6), achieving the standard requirements of

any architectural survey and enabling the export of annotated and stylised eleva-
tion/plan in .DWG format. Furthermore, point cloud data can also be exported in a
variety of formats, usable as is, or imported into other software for further processing.
Whilst merging of datasets is possible by an inbuilt feature of the GeoSLAM software, in this instance the point clouds were individually exported and aligned using
the open-source software CloudCompare (2019). The recorded street level survey
was augmented with aerial LiDAR data from 2007 collected by the Environmental
Agency (2019). The benefit of this was two fold; Firstly, it provided a means of
georeferencing the collected dataset, whilst also providing a level of coverage for
the roof spaces which were the largest voids in the dataset.

18.4   Results

The resulting dataset is a combination of five scans of varying lengths, which in total
equate to 1 h and 16 min of scan time. The total area covered is roughly $124,000m^2$
represented by 593,611,574 points. The length of the individual scans varied, with
the longest being just under 25 min, and the shortest just over 3 min. Figure 18.2
provides an aerial view of the conservation area surveyed, along with the trajectories
taken. Scanning took place over three days, although it would have been possible to
do it in one day had weather conditions been favourable. Data was captured in an
opportunistic manner, with the proximity of the conservation area to the University
aiding in this process. Processing time was not kept track of, although the workflow
is very standardised in the GeoSLAM software, requiring the user to simply drag and
drop the compiled scan file onto the software interface. In this instance, none of the
scans required any additional re-processing beyond the default settings (Fig. 18.3).
     Scanning from only the public realm has resulted in some key areas of the data
being quite sparse. The private/public status of some areas was unknown during
scanning, so the decision was made not to access any area in doubt. As a result,
some areas of highly significant structures do not have optimal coverage and there
is a reduced level of accuracy for the given points, examples of which can be seen in
Fig. 18.5. Equally, areas which were not physically accessible to within a reasonable
range resulted in the same limited level of coverage and questionable point accuracy.
Though the ZEB Horizon has a range of 100 m, data that is only captured at the upper
end of this range with no closer interaction results in a reduction in point density
and reduced accuracy and precision. The individual laser pulses originate from a
central point, and as they travel away from the scanner they diverge, resulting in the
distance between points captured at the upper range being larger, providing less data
for the processing algorithm and in turn, reduced accuracy. Due to the nature of data
captured with the Zeb Horizon system, the same area is passed multiple times, and in
this case, on multiple scans. The range at which specific areas are encountered varied
between the scans, so where a structure or feature had been passed closely on one
scan, it will have been recorded from a distance on another, resulting in a combined
coverage which is highly noisy. This can be reduced with post-processing.

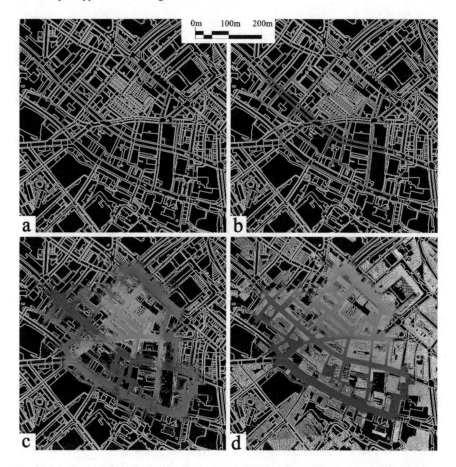

Fig. 18.2 **a** Goitside conservation area boundary. **b** The traversed path taken during the recording of the area. **c** The resulting point cloud data from an aerial perspective, colourised by scan index. **d** The merged complete dataset inclusive of the Environmental Agency (2019) aerial LiDAR data from 2007. Base map—Ordnance Survey (2019)

Once processed, the five point clouds were exported and aligned to each other by eye and merged into one dataset within CloudCompare opensource software, with the resulting dataset then aligned with the Environmental Agency aerial LiDAR data. Whilst the issue of combining datasets which have very little overlap (like elevations and roofing) are always present (Fryskowska et al. 2015), this was somewhat mitigated in this instance by the presence of some roof data captured during the survey, enabling a level of certainty to be determined. Equally so, the Environmental Agency data has a vertical accuracy of ± 15 cm, making any slight misalignment in the z axis inconsequential. The data was already classified, so all data but the roofs were filtered out. Whilst the inclusion of the aerial LiDAR data is not strictly necessary, the benefit was twofold, as it provided a sparse coverage for the largest voids in the dataset (the

Fig. 18.3 Visualisation of
the radial resolution
behaviour of laser scanners
(From Hett et al. 2018)

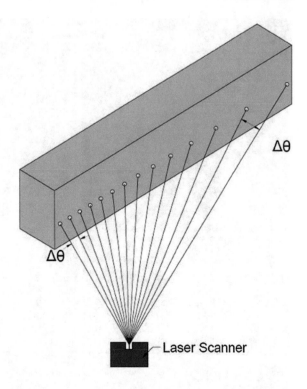

roof space), it also provided a means for georeferencing the captured data. However, the most recent aerial point cloud data available is outdated, resulting in the presence of roof data for some structures that are no longer standing, whilst other localities that include structures that have since been built upon are void.

The GeoSLAM data posed some challenges during registration. During alignment, the lengthwise scans were fractionally misaligned. These errors have two potential causes; the SLAM algorithm and the challenge of data captured from a longer distance, resulting in reduced accuracy, or it could be in relation to the pattern of data capture, although it is likely to be a combination of the two. Further reprocessing should reduce or completely remove this error. Given the area covered by the total dataset, and the initial error margin of the scanning system, the errors produced by the misalignment are negligible depending upon the scale at which the dataset is employed. In this instance, the scale of documenting an entire townscape is likely to be unaffected by the presented errors within the dataset (Fig. 18.4).

Further post-processing of the data was minimised in order to produce a detailed record of the area, whilst providing a true representation of what can be attained in the shortest time possible. However, it is possible to apply various methods of noise filtration and sub-sampling to the dataset to elucidate further detail with additional time.

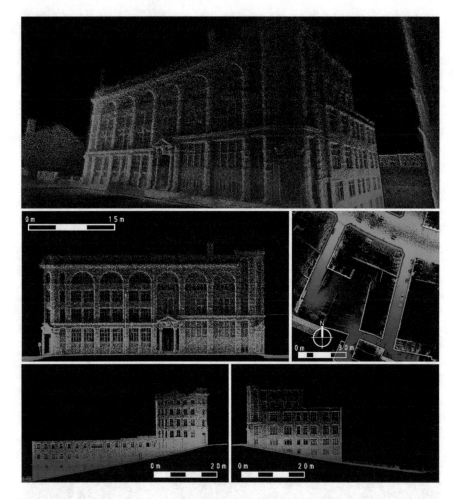

Fig. 18.4 Point cloud visualisations of one of the Grade II listed structures found within the Goitside conservation area (List Entry Number: 1133679) colourised by elevation. (top) street level view from a viewer-based perspective. (mid-left) Orthographic projection of the front elevation. (mid-right) Plan of the structure. (bottom left) Orthographic projection of the eastern elevation (bottom-right) Orthographic projection of the western elevation

18.5 Discussion

The key aim of this research was to generate a rapid 3D dataset with the goal of providing support and protection by means of virtual documentation to one of the most at risk areas of Bradford. The success of this research serves as a proof of concept for the application of SLAM technology in the Industrial Heritage setting of a globally significant nineteenth-century heritage townscape, producing the first rapid geospatial survey of 124,000 m², inclusive of the five listed structures along

Fig. 18.5 Rendered image of the highly significant unlisted structure of Hollings Mill (centre of the image), previously owned by Sir Titus Salt, who later went on to construct Saltaire—inscribed as a UNESCO World Heritage Site in 2001. Only one gable end is accessible from the public realm, leading to a sparse covering of data for most of the structure. The data is colourised by elevation, with Environmental Agency (2019) aerial LiDAR data represented in white

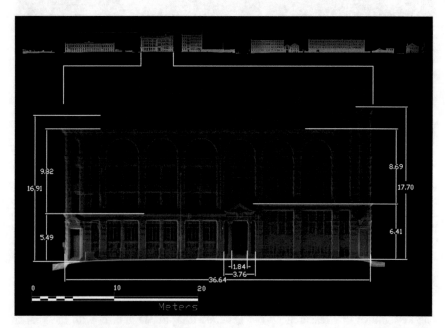

Fig. 18.6 Elevation detail of the Grade II listed structure 1,133,679, above which the entire elevation of the street it sits on (Sunbridge Road). Several example measurements are displayed to provide a visualisation of what is possible from the presented dataset

with all the other significant unlisted structures. When considering the requirements of the industrial heritage of Bradford from a cultural heritage perspective, there are two main issues which arise. Primarily, the sheer abundance of significant assets unquestionably results in the architecturally ornate examples being favoured over the utilitarian yet no less significant examples. Secondly, the large amount of both that are deemed at risk. The method applied here addresses these issues, providing a means of rapidly recording assets which are threatened by relentless decay and under threat from instant and complete loss through fire, whilst being highly time-efficient enabling focus to be allocated to the less ornate examples, aiding in the production of a large number of historically significant structures relating to Bradford's Industrial past (Fig. 18.5).

The area covered over the combined course of 1 h and 16 min of fieldwork shows the unprecedented advantages that can be attained through the application of a SLAM-based method within large areas containing multiple at risk heritage assets. The ZEB Horizon system is quoted to be eight times faster than other methods (GeoSLAM 2019b), although it is impossible that this area could have been recorded in 10 h by other currently available methods to the same level of detail, and would have thus remained undocumented. Equally so, the documentation of an area as opposed to a singular asset has enabled the context and interrelationships of the structures within the area to be recorded, placing them within their surrounding environment. To compliment the speed of deployment, the speed at which a finished output can be produced is unparalleled. This dataset can be used to digitally interrogate and investigate the Goitside area of Bradford's city centre in numerous ways that would otherwise have been impossible to do prior to scanning, and would most likely have remained that way without access to the GeoSLAM Horizon system, opening up a fresh dataset for the conservation and monitoring of the area as a whole. Entire street elevations can be exported in orthographic projections, enabling scaled visualisation and real-world measurements of all recorded structures, an example of which is provided in Fig. 18.6, which was produced in a matter of hours from scan to finished product. Whilst the .DWG outputs of the GeoSLAM software are quite stylised, in most cases they provide enough detail for the creation of more traditional linework if required. However, due to the level of detail attainable and the presented errors within the data, outputs of the dataset are generally restricted to a scale no finer than 1:100.

The resulting dataset will now make it possible to digitally investigate the area for years to come, regardless of what fate awaits the physical structures. Equally so, the ease of deployment and rapidity of data collection opens up the possibility for the capture of subsequent scans that offer the potential to monitor change over time, with a high degree of reproducibility. This approach produces a series of snapshots in time for the monitoring and documentation of change within the area, capable of charting both redevelopment or the effect of neglect, vandalism and dilapidation. However, the limits of noticeable change will be restricted by the level of detail that is attainable from the dataset, with surface changes more difficult to record solely from the scan data, but enabling larger changes to be over time. Irrespective of the reason behind conducting a survey, the method employed must be appropriate to the desired outputs. In this instance, any record was far superior to having no record at all. Whilst the dataset may not be ideal for applications which require fine detail, the integration of other documentation methods will only act to strengthen the record. Where additional detail is required, the use of Structure from Motion (SfM) Photogrammetry or Terrestrial Laser Scanning can easily be integrated into this dataset, providing an enriched record for both the individual asset being detailed by placing it within the surrounding environment, whilst also adding further depth to the presented dataset as a whole.

Ultimately, the ease of deployment, rapidity of data capture and rapid processing opens opportunities to heritage assets which were previously not considered worthy of the time or money for detailed survey, as is the case with multiple highly significant but underappreciated industrial structures of Bradford's former textile trade. It is often the case that heritage assets only become assets where there are too few examples left. It is now possible to economically record multiple assets in their landscape setting, inclusive of the seemingly less significant heritage assets, which, over time, will eventually become appreciably more significant as fewer remain. It is worth noting that the data presented here is still a working dataset, with the intended purpose of acting as a primary record for the integration of other methods as described, including the rescanning of external areas to enable the documentation of finer architectural details, whilst also investigating and recording the internal spaces for some of the key structures.

18.6 Conclusion

The method applied here clearly has great value in the documentation of not just Bradford's built heritage, but all built heritage assets, and as demonstrated, enables vast areas to be recorded in a matter of hours. In this instance, a highly significant but underappreciated environment which had no prior geospatial record has been documented with a reasonably high level of detail to enable meaningful data extraction of real-world measurements from the 3D dataset, with a drastically reduced amount of time invested that would otherwise been necessary and unlikely to have materialised. This approach is perfectly suited to the Industrial Heritage environment of Bradford, whereby no single asset stands alone, but is part of an interrelated collection of assets, enabling this to be accurately documented, providing a deeper record of Bradford's heritage than a series of singular records for each asset, whilst not overlooking the utilitarian architecture that was critical to the formation of Bradford during the Industrial Revolution. It provides a dataset from which future subsamples can be drawn, dependent upon the desired requirements, providing a snapshot in time of the Goitside conservation area to address the need for accurate information of an area at risk. The authors wish to acknowledge support via the AHRC Heritage Consortium and the EU-SCORE project, with this research serving as pilot work for the *'Virtual Bradford'* digital twin Walker and Wilson (2021).

References

City of Bradford Metropolitan District Council (2005a) Goitside conservation area assessment. https://www.bradford.gov.uk/media/3237/goitsideconservationareaassessment.pdf. Accessed 23 Sep 2019

City of Bradford Metropolitan District Council (2005b) Little Germany conservation area assessment. https://www.bradford.gov.uk/media/2457/littlegermanycaa.pdf. Accessed 15 Sep 2019

City of Bradford Metropolitan District Council (2012) Report of the assistant director planning, transportation & highways to the meeting of the regeneration and economy overview & scrutiny committee to be held on 2nd February 2012. https://bradford.moderngov.co.uk/Data/156/201 20202/Agenda/Report%20-%20Heritage,%20Listed%20Buildings%20and%20Regeneration. pdf. Accessed 14 Sep 2019

CloudCompare (2019) Home page. https://www.danielgm.net/cc/. Accessed 26 Oct 2019

Cudworth W (1888) Worstedopolis: a sketch history of the town and trade of Bradford, the metropolis of the worsted industry. The Old Bradfordian Press, Bradford

Duxbury-Neumann S (2015) Little Germany: a history of Bradford's Germans. Amberley, Stroud

Environmental Agency (2019) LIDAR point cloud. https://data.gov.uk/dataset/977a4ca4-1759-4f26-baa7-b566bd7ca7bf/lidar-point-cloud. Accessed 18 Oct 2019

Fryskowska A, Walczykowski P, Delis PB, Wojtkowska M (2015) ALS and TLS data fusion in cultural heritage documentation and modelling. ISPRS Int Arch Photogramm Remote Sens Spat Inf Sci XL-5/W7:147–150

GeoSLAM (2019a) ZEB HORIZON. https://geoslam.com/solutions/zeb-horizon/. Accessed 28 Sep 2019

GeoSLAM (2019b) The ZEB family. https://microsolresources.com/wp-content/uploads/2019/06/ GeoSLAM-Family-Brochure.pdf. Accessed 10 Oct 2019

Hess M, Petrovic V, Yeager M, Kuester F (2018) Terrestrial laser scanning for the comprehensive structural health assessment of the Baptistery di San Giovanni in Florence, Italy: an integrative methodology for repeatable data acquisition, visualisation and analysis. Struct Infrastruct Eng 14(2):247–263

Historic England (2018a) Vacant historic buildings: guidelines on managing risks. Historic England, Swindon

Historic England (2018b) 3D laser scanning for heritage: advice and guidance on the use of laser scanning in archaeology and architecture. Historic England, Swindon

Historic England (2019) Heritage at risk. North East & Yorkshire Register 2019. https://historicengl and.org.uk/images-books/publications/har-2019-registers/ne-yo-har-register2019/. Accessed 14 Sep 2019

Jowitt JA (1991) Textiles and society in Bradford and Lawrence, USA, 1880–1920. Bradf Antiq 5:3–24

Ordnance Survey (2019) OS MasterMap Topography®, Bradford. https://jisc.geostore.com/jisc/. Accessed 15 Sep 2019

Reynolds J, Baines WF (1978) One hundred years of local history: the Bradford historical and antiquarian society, 1878–1978. The Society, Bradford

Walker, A and Wilson, A.S. (2021) 'Virtual Bradford' – an open digital twin for the City of Bradford. https://www.local.gov.uk/case-studies/bradford-district-council-digital-twin (accessed 10th March 2022).

Part IV
Cultural Connections and Creative Industries

Chapter 19
Manual/Digital Interactions in 'Project code-named Humpty'

Kate Johnson, Adrian Evans, Tom Sparrow, Leon Black, Rob Harman, Dongmin Yang, and Andrew S. Wilson

Abstract 'Project code-named Humpty' is a performative art piece involving the creation, fragmentation, and reconstruction of a 2.7 m high classically inspired sculpture. It was conceived to complement an archaeological science research project setting out to explore the use of digital scanning technologies in artefact reconstruction. The statue's form was free sculpted in clay over a period of four years. It was cast in a self-supporting cementitious material specifically for the purpose of ceremonial fragmentation and subsequent reconstruction by archaeologists. In this chapter, we explore the project's human/machine intentions, interactions, development processes and their wider implications leading to fragmentation. We explore how 3D terrestrial laser scanning with photogrammetry was used to chart the creation of the sculptural form and how scans informed finite element analysis, essential for safe casting and fragmentation. We show how structured light scanning was essential to create a digital backup of the mould and how drone imagery documented fragmentation tests and 360° imaging recorded studio and quarry activity.

Keywords Sculpture · Statue · Fragmentation · Digital scanning · Photogrammetry

K. Johnson (✉)
Department of Media, Design and Technology, Faculty of Engineering and Informatics, University of Bradford, Bradford, England
e-mail: k.m.johnson1@bradford.ac.uk

A. Evans · T. Sparrow · R. Harman · A. S. Wilson
School of Archaeological and Forensic Sciences, Visualising Heritage, University of Bradford, Bradford, England

L. Black
Centre for Infrastructure Materials, School of Civil Engineering, University of Leeds, Leeds, England

D. Yang
Discipline of Mechanical Engineering, School of Engineering, University of Edinburgh, Edinburgh, United Kingdom

© Springer Nature Switzerland AG 2022
E. Ch'ng et al. (eds.), *Visual Heritage: Digital Approaches in Heritage Science*,
Springer Series on Cultural Computing,
https://doi.org/10.1007/978-3-030-77028-0_19

391

19.1 Introduction

'Project code-named Humpty' [P c-n H] was conceived by artist Kate Johnson in 2014 to complement the wider concerns of the School of Archaeological and Forensic Sciences' beacon project 'Fragmented Heritage' [FH]. With significant challenges facing cultural heritage under threat, one of FH's goals was to enhance existing fragment refitting methodologies using the latest digital tools.

Between 2013 and 2014 Johnson engaged with FH team activities including flint knapping and assemblage of *structured light scanning* equipment. An initial idea was to make a piece combining flint knapping and 3D printing.

In May 2014, following a visit to a favourite coastal location in Anglesey, Johnson proposed the concept of a performative artwork with a statue as its protagonist. She would sculpt a larger than life size sculpture and fragment it at a cliff site for the FH team to reconstruct. Archaeological practice would thereby form part of the artwork narrative. An artefact history would play out over time (Johnson 2015, 2020).

The FH team agreed to the concept and stipulated a preference for the statue to be three metres tall. As the artwork and collaboration evolved, digital tools and technologies entwined with manual processes ensuring a successful fragmentation.

This chapter focuses on these processes leading to fragmentation. Firstly, P c-n H is placed within a broad art and archaeological context.

19.2 Context

The human body and landscape have been dominant features in Johnson's narrative work (1993, 2000, 2011). Destruction has featured in some of her art processes since 1982 (Johnson 2000). Replication of a free-sculpted life-size figure was undertaken as part of the process in 'Vesuvian Man' (Johnson 2000). In 'Man and Machine', (Johnson 2011), manual clay sculpting processes were combined with *digital scanning*, reverse engineering, and computer numerical control [CNC] milling (Johnson 2015).

There have been private performative elements in Johnson's earlier work (2000), but P c-n H is Johnson's first shared 'performance'. Performance and archaeology are explored by archaeologists Mike Pearson and Michael Shanks (2001). The convergence between art and archaeology is explored by Renfrew (2003), Russell and Cochrane (2014), and Douglas Bailey (2014), amongst others. P c-n H sees Johnson using film for the first time. A series of short filmic chapters capture elements of P c-n H's performative narrative. They have been screening intermittently in public spaces since March 2018 (https://www.bradford.ac.uk/project-code-named-humpty/). Sculpture and film are explored by Jon Wood (2018).

P c-n H embraces some of the earliest and most recent materials and tools associated with making. We have evolved from the technology upon which we critically rely (Taylor 2010). The capacity to develop tools and processes optimised human chances of survival and promoted cognitive development (Valamoti 2011).

Around 40,000 to 35,000 years ago humans showed signs of symbolic behaviour making what we might now describe as 'art' (Renfrew 2003), (Spivey and Murphy 2005). Manipulation of clay to fashion a human form occurs as far back as the Gravettian industry of the Upper Paleolithic c.28,000–21,000 BP. Examples of fired clay Venus figurines have been found in large numbers at Dolní-Věstonice (Spivey and Murphy 2005), (Weston 2016). The materiality of clay is recently explored by Anthony Gormley with choreographer Sidi Larbi Cherkaoui in a ballet entitled 'Icon' (Winship 2018). Earth-sourced red ochre has been in use for over 100,000 years as a pigment or dye (Cox and Dyas, 2019). It has been found in cave painting, on figurines and on human bones. It was likely used as body ornament in the Neolithic period (Croucher 2012) and still used today as such by the Maasai (Cox and Dyas 2019). Red ochre has been associated with rebirth or resurrection (Mailly 2017) and it was used in the P c-n H fragmentation 'ritual'.

3D digital scanning technologies have revolutionised archaeological practice, supplementing drawing and photography, to capture essential artefact information. Since 2011, modern laser scanning technologies have advanced in 'speed, resolution, mobility and portability' as well as in their ability to integrate with other sensor solutions (Historic England, 2018). This makes them now an essential part of heritage practice. Making 3D replicas using *structure-from-motion photogrammetry* is also a significant contemporary archaeological practice. Web-scraped and donated imagery enabled 3D replication of the earthquake ravished Vatsala Temple, Nepal (Wilson et al. 2019) and the terrorised Temple of Bel, Palmyra (Faber et al. 2017). *3D digital artefact replication* has enabled remote sharing of artefacts and associated data. Artefacts can be 'transported' safely and inexpensively, in many cases ruling out the need of a 'physical' surrogate. Digital artefact refit testing can happen without unnecessary handling of delicate fragments. Artefact information can be preserved at a specific point in time allowing for comparisons to be made. Augmented and virtual reality visualisations of artefacts can be made and put in contexts which no longer remain. In the BReaTHe project, visual reality imagery of lost places is helping displaced or refugee communities cope with loss (Evans et al. (2020).

Digital technologies have changed sculptural practice. Douglas Gordon's Breaking Burns (2017) employed digital scanning replication processes (Cooper 2017). Marc Quinn's statue of the protestor Jen Reid (2020) is a 3D print from a 3D scan (Emelife 2020). Many sculptures arriving for 'manufacture' now arrive in digital form, either destined for same scale replication, [sometimes with variations included in each replica], or for enlargement using digital processes. A monumental sculpture no longer needs to be made at its true scale before replication happens. Neither does it need to be manually 'sculpted'.

According to some, we are now in a 'post-digital' age. 'Postdigital art is emerging from a vital dialogue between high tech and high touch experiences. It invites the rediscovery of ten fingers by adding the human touch to digital technologies' (Alexenberg 2011, p. 35). In the space of a decade, 'aesthetic and conceptual trends have emerged that go beyond the novelty of the technology in and of itself' said Ron

Labaco in an interview with Lilia Ziamou (2014). 'We are now at a point in digital fabrication in which practitioners are combining the different technologies together for greater creative expression, in many cases with more traditional methods of making' (Ziamou 2014). Labaco cites Stella and Mann as artists combining manual and digital technologies. Grayson Perry is another significant proponent.

In terms of theme, P c-n H explores human/artefact relationships and the complexities of artefact histories. (Johnson 2015, 2020). 'Images lend themselves equally to being displayed and venerated and to being desecrated and destroyed' said Belting in 1994 (in Taylor 2010, p. 173). Complex artefact histories over deep time beg the question; can any work ever be finished? 'No work is ever truly finished' said Ingold (2013, p. 96).

'Iconoclasm' as an act of physical destruction has a long history. It is a subject which 'we cannot afford to ignore or avoid' (Boldrick 2013a). For Brubaker, it is 'a powerplay directed against the past and its baggage' (Brubaker 2013). It 'perhaps existed as far back as we can dig into the record of human life on earth' (Chapman and Gearey 2013). 'It might be productively re-conceived as a form of sign transformation' (Clay 2012). 'Deconstructions recontextualize artifacts in a meaningful way' (Cunningham 2013, p. 54). Destruction of statues as a sign of protest has happened throughout history and continues today (Johnson 2020).

Not all acts of destruction have violent intent. Lucian writes of a 'stain' left on a 'now lost statue of Aphrodite by Praxiteles at Knidos' after a young man's night of passion with the sculpture. (Jenkins 2015). In 'Parts and Wholes' (2007), Chapman and Gaydarska cite Grinsell's paper of 1960 which advances the concept of ceremonial 'killing' of objects at funerals. For Chapman, this would seem to be a positive behaviour, promoting enchained relationships. Fragmentation is widely found in the archaeological record (Klima 1963, Vandiver et al. 1989 as cited in Chapman and Gaydarska 2007). It is a widely debated subject in theoretical archaeology. 'Fragmentation theory' was advanced by Chapman (2000), (Chapman and Gaydarska 2007); and revisited, (Brittain and Harris 2010).

Rituals of joyous destruction, more commonly involving burning, exist today in annual festivals (Johnson 2020). At 'Las Fallas' in Valencia, carefully constructed 'ninots' are stuffed with fireworks and burnt at the 'La Nit de Foc', the final night of festivities (Howe 2016). Since 2001, artist David Best has created 'cathartic temples'. These he ritually sets alight at the annual Nevada Burning Man Festival (Bromwich 2015). 'Up Helly Aa', in Lerwick celebrates the ritual burning of a 'lovingly made' Viking longboat replica (Mallet 2019).

Destruction, as part of the creative process, is a persistent feature of modern and contemporary art (Johnson 2015, 2017, 2020). Around 1907–08, Cubist artists Braque, Picasso, Gris, and Léger rejected rational spatial systems and shattered previous depictions of form. In 1919, Duchamp scrawled a moustache over a postcard reproduction of Mona Lisa. In the 1960's Gustave Metzger, 'archetypal humanist/anarchist', (Rosenthal 2009) advanced auto-destructive art. He disseminated the concept in the interdisciplinary Destruction in Art Symposium, (DIAS) of 1966 (Copeland 2010). His was art which would 'fall apart, breakdown or disappear' (Dwyer 2017). 'Auto-destructive art is to do with rejecting power' said Metzger in 2012 (Dwyer 2017). In the 1980s, Paolini explored destruction of a classical archetype (Paolini 1984). In 'Cold, Dark, Matter', Cornelia Parker had the British Army explode a garden shed. She hung the resulting fragments suspended around a lightbulb (Parker 1991). In Michael Landy's 'Break Down' (2001), the artist reversed automated production and consumption mechanisms by the systematic and orderly dismantling of all 7,227 of his possessions, including works of art (Boldrick 2013b). In the Chapman brothers' 'One Day You Will No Longer Be Loved II (No.6)' (2009), the artists painted over another artist's work (Barber and Boldrick 2013).

In P c-n H, the processes of destruction do not operate on the work of others nor of any appropriated or found object (Johnson 2020). Destruction is not the end of the P c-n H sculpture's form or story. It marks the end of one form of the statue; one part of the 'story', prior to reconstruction and the statue's future history.

Evidence that prehistoric humans reconstructed artefacts is seen in vessels from Tell Sabi Abyad circa 6600 BCE; 'visual reminders of the object's tormented cultural biography' (Nieuwenhuyse and Dooijes 2008, p. 159). 'Kintsugi', (Johnson 2015), ['golden joinery'], possibly dates to the late C15th (Azzarito 2017). It is a Japanese technique of mending pottery with gold. It is linked with the Japanese philosophy of 'wabi-sabi' meaning to see beauty in the flawed or imperfect (Richman-Abdou 2019). Twice dismantled and reconstructed, the Portland Vase, originally smashed in 1845, demonstrates how complex artefact reconstruction stories can be (British Museum 2019). Reconstruction of the 3,000-year-old Tell Halaf statues destroyed in a WWII bombing raid on Berlin demonstrates that sculptural objects can be reconstructed without digital technologies, albeit very slowly. Lutz Martin, co-ordinator of the nine-year reconstruction effort, said, the only tools were 'our eyes, our brain, our endurance and our patience' (Magnay 2011). Virtual reality technologies have now allowed the reconstructed Tell Halaf sculptures to be seen in their original architectural surroundings (Grellert and Schmid 2014).

P c-n H incorporates hard-wired artefact/ human behaviours. It echoes and builds on discussion in both art and archaeology. By employing artefact reconstruction as part of the artwork's concept and harnessing archaeological conservation practices as part of its story, P c-n H embraces a scientific usefulness absent in much contemporary art.

19.3 Methodology

A 400 mm tall model was sculpted in stoneware grey clay [SGC] supported by a wooden armature—a ⌀ 8.6 mm pole with two horizontal ⌀ 6.7 mm supports attached to a 380 mm × 380 mm plywood plinth. Experiments with imagery and pose were undertaken over a three-month period. Work ceased when the figure resembled a humanoid male caught in an arrested walking pose. The final form underwent *3D capture using photogrammetry*. Around 50 photographs were taken and uploaded to the former online software package which processed 3D digital data and allowed the model to be seen in 3D through a mobile phone app. Three coats of 50/50

Fig. 19.1 Model (400 mm high). Iterations (left to right: 1 July 2014, 1 July 2014, 3 July 2014, 3 July 2014, 14 July 2014, 15 July 2014, 22 July 2014, 22 July 2014, 10th December 2014 Photographs by Kate Johnson. First published in Johnson (2020) and reproduced here with permission from the organisers of the 6th International Conference in Visual Culture)

water/Polyvinyl Acetate [PVA] were applied to seal the clay and hinder cracking (see Fig. 19.1).

An armature was constructed to support the 3 m high sculpt. A vertical steel pole, 2438 mm × ø 50 mm, was welded onto the base of a steel framework 'cage' measuring 1070 mm × 1070 mm × 150 mm. The 'cage' was 'cast into concrete. Two flat steel plates, each containing four apertures, were welded onto the vertical steel pole at 1820 mm and 2390 mm. The apertures allowed flexible 5 mm × 5 mm aluminium armature wires to be threaded. These were to support each of the arms and legs. Open weave jute hessian was wrapped around the metal pole and aluminium wires and made rigid with clay slip forming a solid core. Over forty months, clay was manually built up over the core and the statue's form was free sculpted [by eye and hand alone] in SGC. A wire loop tool was used for detail. After each day's work, the clay was moistened and wrapped to hinder cracking and *Smartphone photography* was used to record and evaluate a day's work (see Fig. 19.2).

A material was developed to cast the sculpture. Over 60 160 mm × 40 mm × 40 mm bricks were produced and tested (see Fig. 19.3). A mix containing architectural quality white Portland cement and white marble dust [PCMD] was duplicated and tested in another institution's laboratory. There, five tests for compression and three for flexural strength, confirmed a characteristic material strength of 64 megapascals [MPa] (Johnson 2019, 2020).

Four *digital 3D scans* were made during the clay sculpt as a record of the form and changes (https://www.bradford.ac.uk/project-code-named-humpty/). 3D capture was achieved by *terrestrial scanning with Structure from Motion [SfM] Photogrammetry*. Scanning was undertaken using a FARO Focus 3D X330 terrestrial laser scanner and a FARO Freestyle handheld scanner. Photographic documentation for SfM photogrammetry was undertaken using a Nikon D750 with a 24 mm lens. The documentation process varied depending on what the scans would be used for. The

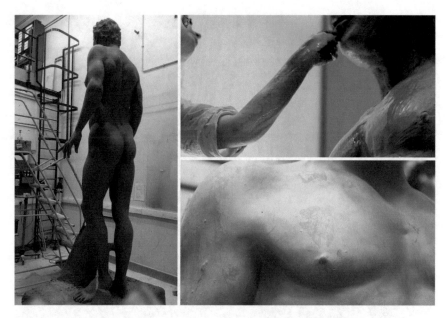

Fig. 19.2 Working in grey clay on the monumental sculpture (2700 mm high) (Smartphone photo of the completed clay form by Kate Johnson, February 2018 (left) film stills from Chapter One [filming by Jimi Lund] (right). Bottom right image first published in Johnson (2020) and reproduced here with permission from the organisers of the 6th International Conference in Visual Culture)

process varied from a few scans taken from a normal tripod to a more combined approach using a telescopic tripod, handheld laser scanner and pole based SfM photogrammetry to allow for an integrated data processing pipeline. The data was processed using FARO Scene, Reality Capture and Blender.

The first scan, (see Fig. 19.4 *left*) was uploaded to 'Sketchfab' and shared with Johnson over an online platform.

A second scan, charted progress since the first scan. In Fig. 19.4 [*centre*], it is seen in point cloud alongside the first scan, which is meshed. For this to be uploaded to 'Sketchfab' for online viewing, the point cloud had to be decimated. The frontal view of both scans shows changes in scale, proportion, and form. A third scan of the head and shoulders was undertaken shortly afterwards to improve their capture.

A fourth scan was undertaken to predict the sculpture's volume once cast. The visible armature, arm supports and triangular clay 'counterweight' mass, were 'removed' digitally within Blender. Any holes were filled and the area where supporting materials had been removed were closed using the surrounding sculptural form data as a guide. This scan gave a prediction of the cast's volume (=0.286 m^3) and weight (0.686 metric tonnes, based on a cubic metre of concrete being 2,400 kg/m^3).

The raw scan data was decimated and converted into a solid file and sent for *Finite element analysis* [FEA] to predict real forces as a Drawing eXchange Format

Fig. 19.3 Material Development (Smartphone photo by Kate Johnson)

[DXF] file. For FEA, the DXF file was imported into Abaqus FEA (Abacus Inc.) and assigned with material properties. The material properties of C30 concrete were chosen as one with a compression resistance of 30 N/mm^2 in 28 days with the mechanical properties of the sculpture set out in Table 19.1 [Engineering ToolBox, 2008 www.engineeringtoolbox.com/concrete]. A maximum principle stress criterion was used for assessing the risk of fracture, i.e. there would be risk of failure if the maximum principle stress met any of the tensile or compressive strength values.

The first FEA analysis tested whether the sculpture could stand unaided when cast (see Fig. 19.5). Further tests were undertaken for wind loading. Two methods, Generic Formula (ASCE/SEI 7–05 2006) and Eurocode (European Standards Institution 2005) were considered for the calculation of wind loading. A concentrated force was applied to the top of the sculpture from two different directions, face-wind and back-wind (see Fig. 19.5).

Table 19.1 Mechanical properties of the sculpture (ToolBox 2008)

Density	Young's modulus	Poisson's ratio	Compressive strength	Tensile strength
2400 kg/m^3	29 GPa	0.18	20 MPa	2 MPa

FEA analysis was also undertaken to demonstrate potential issues with any attempts to lift the sculpture from horizontal to vertical. FEA analysis suggested it was safe to hoist the sculpture under the arms (see Table 19.2).

A final scan of the clay captured the point that work on the clay ceased. Scanning was undertaken using the FARO X330, at 1/5 resolution, 4 × quality (8102 × 3414) with colour capture to allow this data to be processed with photographs taken with a Nikon D750 and 24 mm lens (see Fig. 19.4 *right*).

FEA analysis indicators promoted further tests of the casting material. A large block PCMD, 550 mm × 300 mm × 300 mm, weighing 101 kilos, was cast from a plywood mould. Six thermocouples were mounted at defined locations within the mould cavity to monitor the temperature distribution profile over 28 days. When fully cured and demoulded, the block cast was dropped from an 18 m height at a North Yorkshire quarry. It took two attempts to fracture.

The test drop was filmed using a *modified action camera* (QUMOX SJ4000) with a 5.8 GHz video sender to transmit the video feed for viewing and recording in near real time on an Android tablet. This was necessary as there was a strong possibility that the camera might be damaged during the drop thereby rendering the footage unrecoverable. The camera was mounted to the block inside a custom *3D printed* holder. This was sandwiched between two metal plates to protect the camera from impact. The camera had its standard fisheye 170-degree lens replaced with a 72-degree 'distortion' free lens to capture a more naturalistic view. This allowed for the lens to be recessed within the case to protect it during the drop without the case being in shot. A second camera (GoPro Hero 5) was mounted to the bucket of the quarry's telehandler. It filmed the block as it was tipped by the telehandler over the edge of the quarry. A *Drone,* DJI Mavic Pro, also captured this test in film. Analysis of fracture behaviour was undertaken. Fragments underwent *3D scanning* to test how well the casting material scanned [essential for reconstruction].

A disassemblable mould of 35 interlocking pieces was constructed to replicate the clay original (see Fig. 19.6 *centre*). The piece-mould sections were made from Jesmonite, a polymer-modified plaster, reinforced with Quadaxial Stitched Glass [QSG]. Dense urythene [Brush-On 60] with [Ure-fil 11] filler was employed for areas with undercuts around the groin, buttocks, fingers, and toes. Silicone rubber [Silastic 3481] was used for the statue's head (Johnson 2019, 2020). These flexible materials were held within an outer shell made from Jesmonite, (Johnson 2019,

Table 19.2 Analysis result of the modelling of hoisting process	Angle α	Maximum Principal stress (Tensile, MPa)	Location
	15°	3.5	arms
	30°	2.5	arms
	45°	1.4	ankle
	60°	2.0	ankle
	75°	3.5	ankle

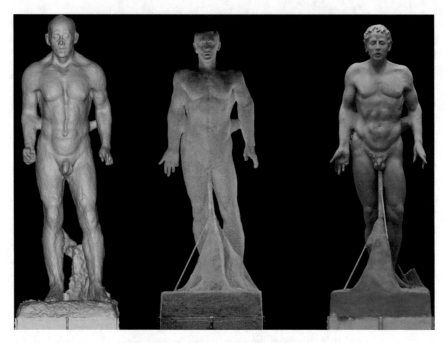

Fig. 19.4 Scan images (Scans by Tom Sparrow, Visualising Heritage)

2020). The piece mould sections were grouped to form three main sections: 'legs', 'torso with arms', and 'head' (Johnson 2019, 2020).

Once the clay sculpture was completely encased, mould pieces were removed. Clay deposits were cleaned off and flanges trimmed. 3 coats of 50/50 methylated spirits/shellac sealed each mould piece. Each mould piece was scanned using a *structured light scanner* to 'back-up' mould information in case of mould damage during casting. Some of the mould piece scan data were scaled down so these digital surrogates could be *3D printed* as a test. After scanning, the statue's mould pieces were assembled into their sections and internal seams were sealed with bees' wax (see Fig. 19.6, *left*).

360° imaging captured studio activity post mould removal with a Sony A7r mirrorless camera, a Nikon 16 mm Fisheye lens and a Nodal Ninja NN5 panoramic head. It was processed using Autopano Pro V2.6 (Kolor) (see Fig. 19.7).

To cast the statue, a concrete plinth, 1100 × 1100 × 200 mm, was made. The plinth included a recess measuring 500 × 600 × 75 mm. A vertical rectangular wooden frame 'cage', 2900 mm × 1400 mm × 1400 mm, with four detachable panels on each face, was designed and constructed to surround the plinth base.

Mould pieces were transported to a heavy structures laboratory in their three bolted sections. The wooden frame 'cage' and panels were transported in pieces and assembled on site as required. The wooden frame 'cage' was hoisted into place

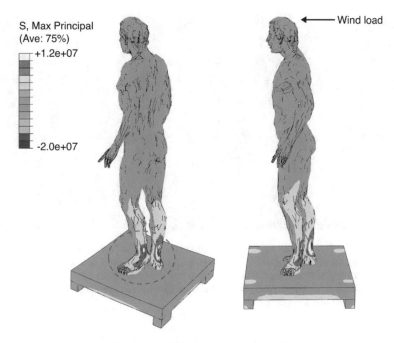

Fig. 19.5 The distribution of maximum principle stress under gravity (left) and the sculpture model under wind loading (right) (FEA images by Dongmin Yang from scans by Tom Sparrow, Visualising Heritage)

around the plinth. Rebar was positioned and attached to the plinth recess to run through both ankles of the cast.

Outer mould seams on the three mould sections were filled with a clay paste. The 'legs' section was fixed to the concrete plinth with Jesmonite and QSG. A ⌀100mm aperture was drilled into the back of the 'head' section to which a 60 mm long 'funnel' tube was attached. The 'head' section was bolted to the 'torso and arms' section and both were wrapped in hessian reinforced with Jesmonite to form an outer 'mother mould'. As one component, they were hoisted onto the 'legs' section and bolted, then bound, to it.

Sharp sand was compressed around the 'legs' section confined by the 'cage's' panels. PCMD materials were organised into 'batches'. On the day of casting, 'batches' were mixed sequentially in a screed mixer/pump machine and pumped steadily through the mould aperture in the statue's head.

The mould filled to the upper chest at which point PCMD burst out through the panelled 'cage' base (Johnson 2020). Failure of the first cast yielded valuable information and informed a second casting (see Fig. 19.8). Excavation revealed that the mould had lifted from the base under intense pressure and the sand had failed to restrain PCMD. Part of the 'legs' section mould had sprung apart. The major seam between the 'torso and arms' and 'legs' had also failed. Internal section seams, filled with bees wax, had held.

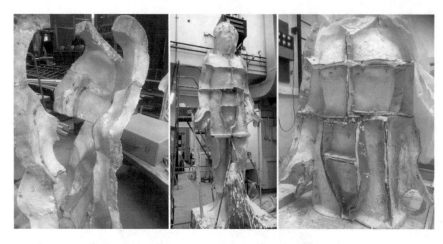

Fig. 19.6 Mould development. Mould torso front and back sections *(left) first published in* Johnson (2020); fabrication of the piece mould approaching completion *(centre first published in* Johnson (2020)—both images *reproduced with permission from the organisers of the 6th International Conference on Visual Culture)*; mould flange reinforcements after first casting attempt failure *(right)* (Smartphone photos by Kate Johnson)

The mould sections were disassembled. Each mould piece underwent cleaning, refinishing, and sealing. Some pieces needed mending and strengthening. Mould sections were rebolted along their flanges. Flanges were reinforced with 1.5 mm aluminium sheet to prevent any springing (see Fig. 19.6 *right*). The 'legs' mould section base underside was built up by 15 mm at the statue's front to minimise the forward lean detected by FEA analysis. An outer 'mother mould' of Jesmonite and high-density plaster reinforced with diamond steel mesh ['legs'] and hessian ['torso and arms'] was constructed around the three major mould sections up to a depth of 300 mm. Each section was strapped using a polypropylene tensioner to prevent any issues arising from pressure.

Further tests of PCMD were undertaken to establish reliability of the mix and its curing time. ø40mm dowels were cast from PCMD and tested for flexural strength. Red missen sand was tested to restrain the casting mix. Closed cell neoprene sheeting was tested to restrain liquid under pressure. A high strength cementitious bonding agent was tested in a ø150mm cylinder of the casting material.

A 4000 mm × 4000 mm × 150 mm concrete 'floor' was cast in an outdoor location and a 4000 mm tall scaffold build around it. The scaffold was draped with a transparent waterproof tarpaulin creating a casting 'tent'. A concrete plinth measuring 1200 mm × 1200 mm was cast. It housed a central cast upper side recess 600 mm × 500 mm × 100 mm and two parallel recesses, 120 mm wide, running the length of the plinth, cast into its underside. The underside recesses were to allow fork lifting and hoisting. *No* steel rebar was attached to the plinth upper side recess to support the cast statue's ankles. They had been pushed out of place under pressure in the first casting attempt.

The original wooden frame 'cage' was reused and bolted to the plinth on each face (see Fig. 19.8). The 'legs' mould section was mechanically positioned on the plinth and bolted to it through a 3 mm d steel grid and 10 mm d neoprene sheeting. PCMD materials were twice weighed and sealed in waterproof containers. On casting days [5 in total], a forced action mixer was operated with exact timings for each mix. On day 1, PCMD was poured through a funnel and tube into the 'legs' section. Once the 'legs' section was filled, the wooden 'cage' lower frame panels were screwed to the frame. Moist red 'missen' sand was compacted around the mould, constrained by the frame panels to take up the heat generated by the curing mortar. The mix was left to cure over 36 h.

Once cured the 'torso and arms' section was mechanically positioned and bolted to the 'legs' mould section through a 10 mm d layer of neoprene. The 'mother moulds' were also joined with high-density plaster substantially reinforced with plaster, hessian and finally Jesmonite and QSG. The 'torso and arms' section was cast over three separate days. Each day's casting was left for a minimum of 36 h, allowing curing and mix cooling to take place. Wooden 'cage' panels were screwed to their frame and moist red 'missen' sand was compacted around the exterior of the 'mother mould', both in line with the level of PCMD in the mould. The same procedure was undertaken to fix and cast the head. A bonding agent and precast dowels were used between each major section cast (Johnson 2020). Once the cast head section was surrounded by compacted moist sand, the fully panelled wooden 'box' was strapped using a polypropylene tensioner and left for a week to PCMD to cure.

The sand and the 'mother mould' were removed in stages, the latter using a combination of handheld chisels and electric cutting tools. Inner mould pieces were unbolted in stages. Wooden frame panel sections were removed or added as required to enable the painstaking process of cast surface finishing. Hand-held steel rifflers, sanding blocks and hand-held electrical grinding machinery were used for this purpose.

Once surface finishing was complete with all the seam flashing removed, (Johnson 2020), the sculpture was briefly unveiled and *digitally scanned* with the FARO X330. This enabled comparison between the clay form and its replica. Figure 19.9 illustrates some changes in the form. The face is visibly thinner in a visualisation of point to point comparisons and distance calculations.

The statue was secured to the wooden frame 'cage' with cross braces. Wooden panels were screwed in place and the 'box' with statue was hoisted onto a flatbed lorry and transported to the same North Yorkshire Quarry used for the block cast test. 1838 mm × 1300 mm portrait format posters featuring the clay face of the original statue and *digital quick response [QR] codes* linking to the P c-n H website, were stapled to the sides of the 'box'.

The boxed cast was taken into the quarry and mechanically lifted on to plinth which had been cast at the quarry ledge. A sudden lurch of the boxed cast was observed during the journey over rough terrain to the awaiting plinth. A lower panel section of the wooden frame box was removed. Both ankles had cracked cleanly, but

Fig. 19.7 360-degree image of mould making process with clay sculpture fragmented by demoulding (Image by Tom Sparrow, Visualising Heritage)

Fig. 19.8 Cast in its casting frame (Photo by Kate Johnson first published in Johnson (2020) and reproduced here with the permission of the organisers of the 6th International Conference on Visual Culture)

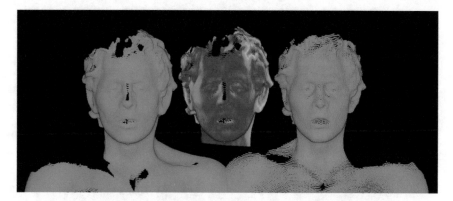

Fig. 19.9 A side by side view of clay original (left) and cast (right) with a visualisation of point to point comparison (middle) (Image by Adrian Evans, Visualising Heritage, from scans by Tom Sparrow and Adrian Evans)

the statue remained standing. The fractured cast remained supported upright in its 'box, for a week.

A week later, all the side panels were removed from the wooden frame leaving the wooden 'cage' around the figure. Straps were secured under the statue's arms and around its chest allowing safe removal of the remaining wooden structure (see Fig. 19.10). The statue was lifted by a telescopic handler from its plinth with hoist strap looped over a bucket claw tooth. It was extended out beyond the quarry ledge and the statue was released (Johnson 2020).

Fragmentation was filmed from four vantage points using a Sony FS5, two Blackmagic URSA mini 4 K cameras and a GoPro Hero 6. A spectator filmed using a retro Super 8 camera. Digital photography was taken throughout the event by spectators. *360° capture* was undertaken by GoPro Hero 5 cameras which were set up on a custom 3D printed rig and set record just prior to the drop. The rig was placed in front of the drop landing site and closer to impact than people present were able to be.

The statue's scattered fragmented form was recorded through *scanning and SfM photogrammetry*. This provided an accurate record of the dispersal of fragments. The DJI Mavic Pro drone filmed on the day of fragment retrieval.

19.4 Discussion

A free sculpt approach is relatively unusual in modern times for a piece on this scale. This approach was deliberately chosen to contrast with the speed of the statue's subsequent fragmentation and to challenge a recent tendency in contemporary art to appropriate the work of others. It allowed for a responsive and spontaneous evolvement of the form. 'In handling a thing, moving it around, feeling it, looking at it, we

Fig. 19.10 Fragmentation event September 28th, 2019 (Photo by Carlton Reeve)

come to understand how our body works, how the different parts interrelate, how we can be coordinated' (Hodder 2012, p. 30).

Sculpt decisions were made to the statue's form in response to PCMD tests and FEA analysis. The casting material strength meant a hand could have projecting finger articulations instead of a closed fist. FEA results meant that the statue's ankles could be narrowed, and his left foot raised at the heel.

Digital scanning indirectly facilitated risk-taking throughout the sculpt, mould making and fragmentation processes. The knowledge that *scanned data,* whether of the clay form, the cast statue or the mould could 'retrieve' irreparably damaged parts promoted experimentation in mould making and meant it was psychologically easier to fragment the cast statue. *Structured light scanning* of mould pieces meant a backup of pieces could be made without touching or damaging the originals.

Digital scanning captured and quantified processes of change as Fig. 19.9 demonstrates. When the head mould pieces were removed post casting, it was evident that casting material had emerged through the head neck seam and channelled between the silicone flexible mould and its outer shell. Figure 19.9 shows exactly the impact this had on the cast. It would be difficult to confirm these changes without cloud point analysis. The ability for scanning to monitor change has substantial implications for heritage conservation ensuring that timely interventions can be made to protect artefacts and edifices.

With hindsight, more scans of the sculpting process would have been interesting as a record of decision making and clay behaviour over time. However, *scanning* was not straightforward. The sculpture studio had uneven lighting and the clay form needed to remain moist to prevent cracking (see Fig. 19.2). Spraying could not be undertaken during scanning because of the challenge of specular reflectance and highlights, which would have compromised the results. Scanning therefore had to be undertaken rapidly and not in ideal conditions. The mould pieces presented scanning issues too. Jesmonite scanned reasonably well but the silicone rubber parts proved difficult to scan, primarily because they featured complex convex parts of anatomy which are inherently difficult to scan. Structured light scanners need projection and surface visibility by both cameras to be able to resolve any features; the inside of the nose proved particularly difficult due to the geometry of the mould, meaning that the nose was occluded from the scanner.

Scanning, drone filming and *360° imaging* allowed, and will allow, the statue and its studio and quarry surroundings to be viewed and understood in ways which would otherwise be impossible due to physical or human constraints. Scanning of the 3D statue sculpt allowed virtual rotation of 3D form and sculptural progress to be shared remotely. *360° imaging* will inform a virtual reality experience giving a precarious vantage point of the statue's landing.

The final scan of the clay obtained detail, not easily achieved with the FARO X330 and better colour (texture) information. Scans can reveal surface detail beyond what the human eye is capable of perceiving.

Data from the final scan could have informed CNC milling in marble negating the need for a mould and casting. However, this option was rejected due to prohibitive cost and the fact that there may too have been a loss of detail in finishing a CNC milled piece.

Jesmonite proved to be suitable as a mould making material, meaning mould strength of the disassemblable sections could be achieved with less weight. Silicone rubber cast the statue's head with good definition but a denser urythene could have performed better.

The first casting attempt failed largely because of the unknowns of casting a monumental scale statue in an unknown material. Mould to base joining preparations were rushed and mould mixing equipment had not been tested with the unusual casting mix before the day of casting. Meticulous preparations informed the successful second casting with a sequential casting of sections.

The inclusion of an internal armature in casting the statue would hinder its successful fragmentation. It would hold the cast together upon impact. Prior to polymer casting processes introduced in the second half of the C20th, complex armatures, ['an essential procedure' (Mills 1967)] were employed in the creation and casting of any large-scale figurative form. Here no armature should be used.

However, *FEA test* results favoured the inclusion of steel rebar inside the ankles to ensure the statue's stability in a high wind situation [typical at the quarry]. Rebar was included in the first casting but proved highly problematic to position. During casting, the rebar was forced out of place by the casting material. The decision not to include internal armature in the second casting proved to be the right decision. The statue was able to stand for a period of three weeks without any internal or external support while fine finishing was undertaken, proving PCMD strength.

FEA determined the position of the centre of mass of the statue. The origin of the coordinate was in the centre of the base and the centre of mass was found to be 1.04 m above the base and 3–3.5 cm away from the sculpture's geometric centre. This meant that the statue had a forward lean. In preparing the mould for the second casting the 'legs' section base was built up from back to front with a rise of 10 mm. This offset the forward lean minimally and helped mitigate against ankle stresses in the second casting.

Transportation of the cast caused the ankles to shear in the cast's final leg to the quarry. This changed plans for a fragmentation method (Johnson 2020). *FEA,* having determined the effect of potential wind load at the quarry, showed also that the statue could withstand a hoist under the arms for safety from a strong gust of wind. The inclusion of the hoist was essential to support the statue at the quarry edge.

Scanning of the fragments in the quarry has yielded useful fragment dispersal information in terms of understanding fragment scatterings in the archaeological record.

19.5 Conclusions

Digital technologies have been employed in P c-n H to date in four distinct ways. Firstly, they have provided accurate information throughout key stages of the project. Secondly, they have recorded and archived the sculptural form and mould. Thirdly, they have enabled evaluation or prediction of outcomes such as finite element analysis. Finally they have, and will offer significant potential to enhance interpretation and understanding alongside exhibition and in support of visualisation experiences. Going forward, the use of high fidelity digital technologies will inform manual reconstruction.

Manual technologies have been employed to create a certain aesthetic, in this case a 'modern classical' (Modern Classicisms 2017) aesthetic inspired by the classical Greek 'Riace' bronzes and the High Renaissance free-sculpted marble nudes by Michelangelo. The mould was crafted and hand finished for aesthetic reasons. The demoulded cast was fine finished using hand-held tools to resemble a finished carved statue.

The extent to which P c-n H incorporates both manual and digital technologies would suggest that it fits comfortably within the kind of emerging 'Postdigital' framework described by Alexenberg (2011) and Labaco, in interview, (Ziamou 2014), where manual and digital crafting are not mutually exclusive, but bound within a wider context underpinning our humanity. With digital systems well entrenched in our everyday lives, the wonder or threat that digital systems might engender, may no longer exist.

And what of the future? If one considers that *digital 3D scanning* can store information without requiring a physical space; capture change; recreate what is lost; visualise the non-existent; speed up lengthy reproduction and reconstruction processes; share information; it is not surprising that it is becoming a dominant methodology in artistic and heritage related processes.

With smartphone cameras becoming ever more sophisticated, the potential to 'capture' the data of an art piece on show in a public space, is increasingly easy. Thomas Flynn uses Sketchfab.com to showcase his collection of uploaded digital scans of cultural artefacts. These can be rotated allowing a 3D view. A virtual reality and download option is available (www.sketchfab.com/nebulousflynn). Another example is 'Scan the World' (Beck 2019). Appropriation of existing artworks is not likely to cease which begs the question whether future artistic production will become an endless history of snatched digital iterations?

What about stored cultural artefacts. If unexhibited works can be replicated and 'stored' digitally, will the originals, taking up a fusty space somewhere, still be wanted? This was an issue raised recently in relation to the Spode Work mould store (Brownsword and Weyrich 2019). In this future scenario, might the value of an original hand wrought work increase in value or might the digital replications become of greater value. It is interesting to speculate what will become of the art market.

If each digital reproduction embodies a change, however slight, then each replica becomes an original and of potentially of monetary value. Foster & Jones (https://replicas.stir.ac.uk/principles-and-guidance/) are triumphing the right of any replica to be recognised as original objects of value as they each have their own stories to tell.

This chapter ends by sharing a reflection on P c-n H's narrative journey. Although at the outset the P c-n H was conceived with distinct phases of creation, destruction and reconstruction, these phases cannot now be seen so distinctly. Destruction occurred as part of creation when clay cracked, scan data had to be decimated and projecting armature wires hammered back into the developing clay form. Reconstruction became part of creation when these failures had to be rectified. Creation became part of destruction when, to ensure fragmentation, a suitable casting material had to be formulated, test blocks required filming and launch logistics solved. Reconstruction formed part of destruction as the statue was made to look whole prior to its fall. Both creation and destruction will form part of the statue's reconstruction as associated challenges are overcome. Such a rich entanglement could have only been achieved with a healthy interplay of manual and digital technologies.

Acknowledgements Many people have contributed to P c-n H to date. Firstly, we are very grateful to AHRC, the Arts and Humani[es Research Council who in 2017 awarded follow-on funding to support '*Project code-named Humpty*' (AH/R004846/1), linked to the AHRC Digital Transformations Theme Large Grant '*Fragmented Heritage*' (AH/L00688X/1). Highlight Digital Transformations, linked to the 'Fragmented Heritage' Project, funded under the Arts and Humanities Research Council's Digital Transformations Theme Large Grant. Theme Leader Fellow, Andrew Prescott has offered continued encouragement and support for which we are very thankful.

We are also most grateful to colleagues at the University of Bradford who stepped in for a second casting attempt. Paul Metcalfe, PhD student in Archaeological Sciences assisted with mould reinforcements and demoulding and sanding. Roger Clarke, Research Fellow, helped with scaffolding logistics, safe electrical supplies and demoulding. Both gave time handling mixers and helping move heavy loads of material. We also thank David Barker, Ian Mackay, Mick Jagger, and Stephen Robinson from the University of Bradford engineering workshop for their assistance and suggestions from the outset of the project.

Generous help has been given to the project by project partners Bradford UNESCO City of Film to support public dissemination of filmic outputs to the 'big screens' in Bradford and Leeds and David Wilson, Jo Willis and Julie Gatenby have given their time in kind. We also very much thank Jeremy Bradford and Jimi Lund for collaborating on filmic outputs. Their enthusiasm, patience and ability to produce work sometimes at very short notice are highly commended. We want to thank those who accompanied us on the day of the statue's fragmentation, for their participation, support and for contributing photographic records to the artwork archives: Jeremy Bradford, Mark Goodall, Andrea Johnson, Anthony Johnson, Daniel Johnson, Karen Johnson, Maureen Johnson, Michael Johnson, Jimi Lund, Paul Metcalfe, Steven Morant, Robert Peden, Dominic Phillips, Oliver Phillips, Carlton Reeve, Danielle Taylor, Jill Thompson, Alastair Wood and Callum Wood.

Johnson has benefited from the mentorship of Steven Morant, Alison Smith and Graeme Willson. Michael Neilson has given his time and invaluable advice on replication. Technical suggestions have been given by Jamila Abdalmid, Leslie Arkless, Philip Caton-Rose, David Elliot, Mark Goodall, Stephen Holmes, David Hughes, Anthony Johnson, Christopher Hazell, Dennis Lam, Rajnikant Patel, Kashif Shehzad, Marvin Wildman, Joanna Wood, Steve Wong, and Kan Zhou. Along the way, kind support has been given by Nick Ashton, Karina Croucher, Robert Cross, Rob Davies, Nigel Downs, Abbey Ellis, Sally Foster, Lisa Fowlie, Kirstie Gregory, Martin Henig, Susan Hinchliffe, Lisa le Feuvre, Christine Finn, Tahir Khan, Michael Kissane, Andrew Kurziel, Milena Melfi, Stephen Milne, Kate Morton, Colin Neville, Helen Pheby, Verity Platt, Martin Priest, Lijun Shang, Simon Skirrow, R.R.R. Smith, Holly Squire, Suzanne Turner, Richard Telford, Cristina-Luminita Tuinea-Bobe, Dimitrios Vgenopoulos, Jonathan West, Neil Wilkin and Jon Wood.

Many teams at the University of Bradford have helped operations: Purchasing; RKTS and Contracts; Health and Safety; Marketing, Estates; Joinery, and Security. Their help has been essential, and we are very grateful.

The project has received support from external companies and their representatives. Robert Kettleborough from Buro Happold Leeds contributed invaluable structural engineering input for plinths, crate and fastenings. Bob Orange, Richard Green, Kevan Mason and others from Hanson's Quarries warmly welcomed and accommodated us at Coldstones Quarry in North Yorkshire for the fragmentation tests and main event. They ensured a safe and dramatic occasion. We are very grateful to them. We also want to express gratitude to Matthew Gabriel and Russell Greally of Christeyns, Bradford, Stuart Nowell of Supapak Ltd. Shipley, and John Wilson of Lafarge Cement for generous donations of materials and substances. Grateful thanks also go to Paul Wood, Darren Wood, Wesley Broadbent and Eddie Kent from Woods Logistics and Lifting Ltd. Darren's skill to hoist the statue at the quarry edge was much admired.

Many companies have efficiently provided materials or services: Arco Ltd, Arrow Commercial Centre, Huddersfield, Ltd, Bentleys Advanced Materials, Blade Scaffold Ltd., Broadford Tool Hire Bradford, L Cornelissen & Son, London, Huws Gray Ltd., Fisher Scientific UK Ltd., Flints Hire and Supply Ltd., HSS Hire Service Group Plc., HC Slingsby Plc Baildon, JB63 Ltd., JT Atkinson,

Bingley, Lancaster and Winter Ltd., Manningham Concrete Ltd., Quick Fix, Bingley, Rapid Electronics Ltd., RS Components Ltd., JM Stubbs Construction Services, Taylors Timber Centre Ltd., Bradford, Alec Tiranti Ltd., Travis Perkins Trading Company Ltd. and Uriah Woodhead and Sons Ltd.

References

Alexenberg M (2011) The future of art in a postdigital age (2nd ed). Intellect
ASCE/SEI (2006) Chapter 6, Wind loads [Standard] In: Minimum design loads for buildings and other structures. American Society of Civil Engineers, pp 21–80
Azzarito A (2017) The Most Glamorous way to fix a broken ceramic [website post]. Architectural digest. https://www.architecturaldigest.com/story/kintsugi-japanese-art-ceramic-repair
Bailey D (2014) Art//Archaeology//Art: letting-go beyond. In: Russell IA, Cochrane A (eds) Art and archaeology: collaborations, conversations, criticisms. Springer, pp 231–249
Beck J (2019) Scan the world [Conference Paper]. Celebrating reproductions: past, present and future. V&A, London
Boardman C, Bryan P. 3D Laser scanning for heritage [technical guidance leaflet] Historic England. https://historicengland.org.uk/images-books/publications/3d-laser-scanning-heritage/heag155-3d-laser-scanning/
Boldrick S (2013) Introduction: breaking images. In: Boldrick S, Brubaker L, Clay R (eds) Striking images, iconoclasms past and present. Ashgate, Farnham, pp 1–12
Boldrick S (2013) Art transformed: matter and translation in contemporary art. In: Barber T, Boldrick S (eds) Art under attack, histories of British Iconoclasm. Tate Publishing, London, pp 154–163
Brubaker L (2013) Making and breaking images and meaning in Byzantium and Early Islam. In: Boldrick S, Brubaker L, Clay R (eds) Striking images, iconoclasms past and present. Ashgate, Farnham, pp 13–24
Brittain M, Harris O (2010) Enchaining arguments and fragmenting assumptions: reconsidering the fragmentation debate in archaeology. World Archaeology 42(4):581–594. https://doi.org/10.1080/00438243.2010.518415
Bromwich K (2015) The man who builds art—and burns it. The Observer
Brownsword N, Weyrich T. Mould store: exploring the preservation of the former spode factory's post-industrial heritage through digital technologies [Conference Paper]. Celebrating reproductions: past, present and future. V&A, London
British Museum (2019) The Conservation history of the Portland Vase. British Museum. https://www.britishmuseum.org/collection/object/G_1945-0927-1
Chapman H, Geary B (2013) Iconoclasm in European prehistory? Breaking objects and landscapes. In: Boldrick S, Brubaker L, Clay R (eds) Striking images, iconoclasms past and present. Ashgate, Farnham, pp 25–37
Chapman J, Chapman D (2009) One day you will no longer be loved II (No. 6) [Painting]. Art under Attack. Tate Britain, October 2, 2013–January 5, 2014
Chapman J (2000) Fragmentation in archaeology: people, places and broken objects in the prehistory of South Eastern Europe. Routledge, London
Chapman J, Gaydarska B (2007) Parts and wholes: fragmentation in prehistoric context. Oxbow Books, Oxford
Clay R (2012) Smells, bells and touch: Iconoclasm in Paris during the French Revolution. J Eighteenth-Century Stud 35(4):521–533. https://onlinelibrary.wiley.com/doi/abs/10.1111/j.1754-0208.2012.00537.x
Cooper N (2017) Black burns: Douglas Gordon reinvents Scotland's beloved poet [Interview]. The list. https://edinburghfestival.list.co.uk/article/93000-black-burns-douglas-gordon-reinvents-scotlands-beloved-poet/

Copeland M (2010) In: Carrion-Murayari G, Gioni M (ed.) Gustav Metzger. New Museum, pp 18–27

Cox B (Writer), Dyas M (Director) (2019) The moth and the flame (Episode 3.) [TV documentary series episode]. In: Cohen A (Executive Producer), Peck D (Series Producer) (eds) Forces of Nature. BBC One Documentary Television

Croucher K (2012) Death and dying in the Neolithic Near East. Oxford University Press

Cunningham T (2013) Deconstructing destructions. In: Driessen J (ed.) Destruction, archaeological, philological and historical perspectives. UCL Presses Universitaires de Louvain

DwyerC (2017) Gustav Metzger, whose creations were works of destruction, dies at 90. NPR. https://www.npr.org/sections/thetwo-way/2017/03/03/518350960/gustav-metzger-whose-creations-were-works-of-destruction-dies-at-90?t=1597241680202

Emelife A (2020) Hope flows through this statue: Marc Quinn on replacing Colston with Jen Reid, a black lives matter protestor [Article]. The Guardian. https://www.theguardian.com/artanddes ign/2020/jul/15/marc-quinn-statue-colston-jen-reid-black-lives-matter-bristol

European Standards Institution. (2005) Eurocode 1: actions on structures—Part 1–4: general actions—wind actions. [Standard] Authority The European Union Per Regulation 305/2011, Directive 98/34/EC, Directive 2004/18/EC

Evans A, Croucher K, Greene O, Wilson AS. (2020) Virtual heritage for resilience building (Version 1) [Poster]. Zenodo, https://doi.org/10.5281/zenodo.3950360

Faber E, Sparrow T, Murgatroyd A, WIlson AS, Cuttler R, Gaffney V, Gaffney C (2017) Special report curious travellers: preserving heritage across the world. Current World Archaeology 82(11). https://www.world-archaeology.com/issues/special-report-curious-travellers/

Grellert M, Schmid J (2014) Oriental adventures: the excavations at Tell Halaf—Syria a virtual reconstruction. In: International conference on cultural heritage and new technologies, Vienna. http://www.chnt.at/wp-content/uploads/eBook_CHNT19_Grellert_Schmid.pdf

Hodder I (2012) Entanglement: an archaeology of the relationships between humans and things. Wiley Blackwell

Howe S (2016) Las Fallas: destruction, satire and indulgence [Online travel blog]. Urban Travel Blog. http://www.urbantravelblog.com

Ingold T (2013) Making: anthropology, archaeology art and architecture. Routledge

Jenkins I (2015) Defining beauty, the body in ancient Greek art. The British Museum

Johnson KM (1993) Kate Johnson: sculpture-paintings [Exhibition of 2D paintings with 3D projections]. Gallery 1616, Chicago, September 11–October 23

Johnson KM (2000) Kate Johnson: five apocalyptic pieces [Exhibition of Drawings and Sculpture]. Exhibited at Falmouth City Art Gallery, March 18–April 15, 2000

Johnson KM (2011) Man and machine—sculpture and engineering [Web log post]. http://blogs. brad.ac.uk/bsf/2011/09/10/man-and-machine-sculpture-and-engineering/

Johnson KM (2015) Creation, destruction, and transformation: 'Project code-named Humpty'. Theoretical Archaeology Group Conference 2015 University of Bradford. https://antiquity.ac. uk/sites/default/files/downloads/tag/TAG_2015_handbook_schedule.pdf

Johnson KM (2017) Burn, break, bulldoze: is it ever OK to destroy a piece of art? [Article]. The Conversation. https://theconversation.com/burn-break-bulldoze-is-it-ever-okay-to-destroy-a-piece-of-art-81073

Johnson KM (2019) Mould making, materials and casting in 'Project code-named Humpty'—a contemporary art and archaeological science collaboration [Study Day Presentation]. Lasting Impressions, Making and Remaking the Replica, Pitt Rivers Museum, Oxford

Johnson KM (2020) Project code-named Humpty: gesture and the performative body. GKA Visual 2020, Paris [Virtual]. https://gkacademics.com/project-code-named-humpty-gesture-and-the-per formative-body/

Landy M (2001) Breakdown [Art happening]. Oxford St. London, February 10–February 24 2001. https://www.artangel.org.uk/project/break-down/

Lewis-Williams D. The mind in the cave. Thames and Hudson

Mallet AR (2019) Embrace your inner Viking at Shetland's fire festivals [Online blog]. The Blog. https://www.visitscotland.com/blog/events/up-helly-aa-viking-fire-festival/

Mailly H (2017) Re:Utilitarian use of red ochre in the archaeological record [Discussion post] ResearchGate. https://www.researchgate.net/post/Utilitarian_Use_of_Red_Ochre_in_the_Archaeological_Record2

Magnay D (2011) How a 27,000 piece jigsaw puzzle was solved. CNN. http://edition.cnn.com/2011/WORLD/europe/02/23/tell.halaf.reconstruction/index.html?iref=allsearch

Mills JW (1967) The technique of casting for sculpture. B T Batsford Ltd, London

Modern Classicisms (2017) Classical art and contemporary artists in dialogue [A Symposium]. Kings College, London

Nieuwenhuyse O, Dooijes R (2008) A new life for old pots. early pottery repairs from 7th Millenium Tell Sabi Abyad. Leiden J Pottery Stud 24:159–170. https://www.academia.edu/419102/A_New_Life_for_Old_Pots

Paolini G (1984) L'Altra Figura [Installation art]. Art gallery of New South Wales. Sydney, Australia. https://artsandculture.google.com/asset/l-altra-figura/mAGNJt5rwKMjGw?hl=en-GB

Parker, C (1991) Cold dark matter: an exploded view [Installation art]. In: Tronzo W (ed.) The fragment, an incomplete history. The Getty Research Institute Publications Program

Pearson M, Shanks M (2001) Theatre/Archaeology. Routledge

Renfrew C (2003) Figuring it out. Thames and Hudson

Richman-Abdou K (2019) Kintsugi: the centuries-old art of repairing broken pottery with gold. My Modern Met. https://mymodernmet.com/kintsugi-kintsukuroi/

Rosenthal N (2009) Octogenarian artist out to save the world. Financial times. https://www.ft.com/content/f2d8295e-98e3-11de-aa1b-00144feabdc0

Russell IA, Cochrane A (2014) Art and archaeology: collaborations, conversations, criticisms. Springer

Spivey NJ (Writer), Murphy N (Director) (2005) More human than human (episode one) [TV documentary series episode]. In: Thomas K (Executive Producer), Hedgecoe M (Producer). How art made the world. BBC One Documentary Television

Taylor T (2010) The artificial ape: how technology changed the course of human evolution. Palgrave Macmillan

Valamoti SM (2011) (2010) Ground cereal food preparations from Greece: the prehistory and modern survival of traditional Mediterranean fast foods. Archaeol Anthropol Sci 3:19–39. https://doi.org/10.1007/s12520-011-0058-z

Weston M (2016) Venus figures, evidence of women's work. Academia. https://www.academia.edu/31112020/Venus_Figurines_Evidence_of_Womens_Work

Wilson AS, Gaffney V, Gaffney C, Ch'ng E, Bates R, Sears G, Sparrow T, Murgatroyd A, Faber E, Coningham AE (2019) Curious travellers: repurposing imagery to manage and interpret threatened monuments, sites and landscapes. In: Dawson M, James E, Nevell M (eds) Heritage under pressure, threats and solutions: studies of agency and soft power in the historic environment, pp 107–122

Winship L (2018) Icon review—Antony Gormley's amazing feat of dancing, churning clay the guardian. https://www.theguardian.com/stage/2018/dec/02/icon-review-antony-gormley-clay-goteborgsoperans-danskompani-sidi-larbi-cherkaoui-sadlers-wells-london

Wood Christie J (eds) (2018) Sculpture and film—subject/object: new studies in sculpture. Taylor and Francis Ltd

Ziamou L (2014) Art and design in the postdigital world: a conversation with Ron Labaco [Interview] Huffpost. https://www.huffpost.com/entry/art-and-design-in-the-pos_

Chapter 20
Error Bred in the Bone

**Karina Thompson, Keith Manchester, Jo Buckberry, Tom Sparrow,
Andrew D. Holland, and Andrew S. Wilson**

Abstract This chapter describes a collaborative project funded by Grants for All,
Arts Council England, led by artist Karina Thompson, together with researchers
from the Biological Anthropology Research Centre (BARC), School of Archaeological and Forensic Sciences, University of Bradford. The artworks took digitised
historic clinical radiographs and digitised human skeletal pathological data from the
landmark *Digitised Diseases*, and *From Cemetery to Clinic* digital bioarchaeology
resources developed by colleagues from Visualising Heritage as a starting point.
In addition to a series of small-scale installations displayed alongside the Biological Anthropology Research Centre teaching collection, large-scale exhibition pieces
were displayed as part of national and international exhibitions. Collectively these
works draw attention to the potential of digital bioarchaeology, whilst ensuring the
importance of humanising the documentation of disease through time.

Keywords Digital bioarchaeology · Conservation · Ethics · Art textiles ·
Bioarchaeology of care

20.1 Introduction

This chapter presents an important conceptual artwork that transitions from physical evidence (archaeological human remains exhibiting pathological lesions characteristic of leprosy; and historic radiographs of patients with Hansen's disease), to

K. Thompson (✉)
Faculty of Arts, Business and Social Sciences, University of Wolverhampton, Wolverhampton,
United Kingdom
e-mail: k.thompson8@wlv.ac.uk

K. Manchester · J. Buckberry · T. Sparrow · A. D. Holland · A. S. Wilson
Biological Anthropology Research Centre, School of Archaeological & Forensic Sciences,
University of Bradford, Bradford, United Kingdom

T. Sparrow · A. D. Holland · A. S. Wilson
School of Archaeological & Forensic Sciences, Visualising Heritage, University of Bradford,
Bradford, United Kingdom

© Springer Nature Switzerland AG 2022   415
E. Ch'ng et al. (eds.), *Visual Heritage: Digital Approaches in Heritage Science*,
Springer Series on Cultural Computing,
https://doi.org/10.1007/978-3-030-77028-0_20

the digital (3D scanning of archaeological bones and digitisation of historic clinical radiographs), and back to the physical (visual artworks) using digital textile manufacturing processes as a means of creating them.

The purpose of this chapter is to explain the important overlap between emerging visual heritage methodologies and the relevance of involving visual artists to help to reveal new insights as we present aspects of these important collections of archaeological human remains and historical medical archives to a wider public through the creation of artworks.

There are over 4000 skeletons of archaeological provenance curated in the Biological Anthropology Research Centre (BARC), School of Archaeological and Forensic Sciences, University of Bradford. Until recently this curated resource has largely been sheltered from public attention, with these human remains normally only accessible to students of biological anthropology and bone fide researchers. With the creation of the web-based resources - *Digitised Diseases* and *From Cemetery to Clinic* – the status quo has been disrupted. When launched, Digitised Diseases was described as the largest and most comprehensive digital bioarchaeology resource (Killgrove, 2015). In fact the visibility and usage of these resources by students, academics and researchers in North America has now overtaken online use within the UK. Whilst digital bioarchaeology as an emerging discipline offers much potential, particularly given the strict access policies to physical collections, new ethical debates have emerged about display of human remains, re-use of imagery and 3D printing of human skeletal elements (Clegg, 2020). The importance of contextualising digital bioarchaeological content is seen as paramount, with the approach that we took with *Digitised Diseases* - with use of clear descriptors and clinical synopses –upheld as best practice at the World Archaeology Congress, Kyoto accord (Hassett et al. 2018).

For many people in contemporary society, human skeletal remains, represent the remains of once living people of antiquity, and it is essential to understand that their lives, emotions, and relationships were the same as those affecting people today. It is our ethical duty to understand this and to ascribe to these remains as we respectfully study them today, our sensibility to their happiness, troubles in times of stress, illness, and the psychological impact that their suffering and death would have had on their kin.

One of the main aims of this project was to investigate how the BARC collections and the digitised content in the *Digitised Diseases* and *From Cemetery to Clinic* resources could be used as an inspirational starting point for artworks that, in turn, could help to explain the context of those remains and raise awareness of the lived experience of the individual whose remains BARC now curates.

The BARC collection is an extensive collection of more than 4000 human skeletal remains dating from the Neolithic period to the nineteenth century. Whilst much of the work of BARC uses traditional archaeological, palaeopathological, and osteological research techniques, the use of 3D laser scanning of pathological skeletal lesions, structured light scanning, structure-from-motion (SFM) photogrammetry, computed radiography and CT, have become increasingly used as methods to study, analyse, interpret and to disseminate aspects of the collection to a wider audience through digital means.

In this endeavour, we are mindful of important ethical frameworks that guide work with human osteology collections (Clegg 2020). Similarly, in artistic collaborations such as 'The Heart of the Matter' which began as a collaboration between artist Sofie Layton and bioengineer Giovanni Biglino it is recognised that there is a danger of forgetting that each datapoint is an individual (Coates, 2018). The BARC collection represents evidence of disease from the pre-antibiotic era before medical intervention and understanding had been effectively developed, consequently pathological conditions largely progressed without effective treatment. It is human nature that we are interested in the extreme pathological aspects of the BARC collection; a fractured femur with gross deformity, a spine with a fulminating cancerous lesion, a skull of an individual with Down's syndrome. These individual skeletal abnormalities are isolated manifestations of specific objective diseases, but in their very isolation, do not indicate the totality of subjective sufferings of pain, disability and constitutional symptoms which constitute illness.

Collaboration between Thompson and the University of Bradford arose by a chance meeting, when in 2013, the international exhibition of Art Textiles, *Cloth and Memory 2* (Millar et al. 2013), was mounted in the Spinning Room of Salts Mill, within the World Heritage Site of Saltaire, West Yorkshire. Amongst the innovative artworks created, mostly thematically based on industrial or social issues, was one created by Thompson entitled *1 hour's production = 1 ½ miles = 15 lengths*. The artwork was created as a visual representation of physiological cardiovascular stress under the physical exertion of running 1 ½ miles, which served as metaphor for the length of cloth manufactured in the Mill every hour of the working day during the nineteenth century when Bradford was the centre of the World's worsted trade and Sir Titus Salt pioneered his method for spinning high quality cloths from alpaca and angora wool at his mill. The biometric data recorded from continuous electrocardiography and intermittent echo cardiac imaging, was digitally machine embroidered onto 100 m of locally made woollen cloth (Fig. 20.1).

During the exhibition, Professor Keith Manchester expressed concern about the normality of the ECG tracing embroidered into the length of the piece. During discussion about the ECG, a mutual interest between Thompson and Manchester became apparent. The potential application of Art Textiles based upon the skeletal and radiographic collections in BARC was explored in a visit to the collection to develop a collaborative project at the interface of science/ art. Thompson became 'artist in residence' at BARC for the project which was awarded an Arts Council England grant, generously augmented by financial assistance from Maggie Silver of Salts Mill.

20.2 Methodology

Paleopathogical perspectives

Digitised Diseases is an open access resource featuring human bones which have been digitised using 3D laser scanning with high resolution texture photography, CT

Fig. 20.1 *1 hour's production = 1 ½ miles = 15 lengths* installed as part of *Cloth and Memory2* in the Spinning room at Salts Mill, Saltaire, West Yorkshire 2013. Photo credit Karina Thompson

and X-radiographs. The resource focuses on visual evidence of a wide range of pathological 'type specimens' from archaeological and historical medical collections, and specifically examples of chronic diseases which affect the human skeleton for which many of the physical changes are not directly observable within clinical practice. Of major interest to many are the high-definition photorealistic digital representations of 3D bones that can be viewed, downloaded and manipulated on computer, tablet, or smartphone (DigitisedDiseases, 2013).

By combining new clinical descriptions alongside the 3D data, this resource offers the opportunity to inspire an emotional response, understand past human experiences, and offer people the chance to come face-to-face with the realities of the disease and how people in the past may have responded to the social stigma of the disease. The 3D digital archive also preserves fragile dimensional information that is otherwise under threat from attrition through handling and is aimed as a virtual training and research tool for clinicians, human osteologists, palaeopathologist, archaeologists and the wider public.

The *From Cemetery to Clinic* project, was a pilot for the larger *Digitised Diseases* resource, both funded by Jisc through their Content programme 2011–13, Rapid Digitisation and Mass Digitisation calls. It was designed to create a unique interactive resource on the pathological manifestations of Leprosy (Hansen's disease) in skeletons excavated from the mediaeval leprosarium of St. James and St Mary Magdalene, Chichester in 1986–87 and 1992 by Chichester Archaeology Unit (Magilton et al. 2008).

Leprosaria were founded circa 1118 AD to care for 8 leper brethren and was used until at least 1418 (Magilton et al. 2008). Of the 384 individuals excavated, a minimum of 75 show skeletal lesions due to Leprosy. The Chichester collection is one of two large-scale excavated and published archaeological assemblages of leprosarium patients in the U.K. None of the child skeletons from Chichester had definitive skeletal changes of Leprosy.

The *From Cemetery to Clinic* resource became a useful tool for becoming familiar with the collection in BARC, and understanding the significance of the skeletal lesions and their clinical interpretation. This was true also for the understanding of the Andersen X-ray archive. Dr Johs Andersen was a Danish clinical leprologist and surgeon who had devoted his life to the care and treatment of patients with Hansen's disease in Ethiopia and the Indian Subcontinent, and much of his work was in the days prior to effective drug treatment of the disease in the 1970s and 80s. Therefore, many of the X-rays in this archive are of 'untreated' disease. On his retirement from clinical practice he donated his entire radiographic collection to the University of Bradford via Professor Keith Manchester.

An artist's approach

The visual and tactile nature of textiles makes it a powerful medium for art pieces exploring the themes of memory and the body. To critic and writer Catherine Dormor its potency is powerful. 'Cloth surrounds us from the moment of birth, making it probably unsurprising that it constantly exceeds the cognitive, verbalized meanings, metaphors and concepts that are applied to it' (Dormor in Millar and

Kettle 2018: 124). In her introduction to the catalogue of *Cloth and Memory 2*, the exhibition that introduced Thompson to Manchester, Millar explained 'The haptic relationship between our bodies and textiles which accompany us provides an alternative language of memory, one that can be used by the artist to locate memory in an object, a material thing. In this way memory is recreated in a re-visitable manner, but it is a transformed memory' (2013: 15).

McCullough (1998), Treadaway (2009) and Harris (2012) all point to the dilemmas of craft practitioners who balance both digital and traditional materials and processes in their visual artworks. At the start of the residency whilst there were leading exponents of digital making in 3D craft processes for example Eden(2011), Wallace (2011), Neal (2013) and the technologies were beginning to be commonly used in the fields of ceramics, jewellery and furniture making, there were very few textile artists engaging with digital stitch (Kettle, 2012; Brennand Wood, 2011) and no-one else obviously using the technology in direct response to archaeological artefacts and data.

Thompson's machine-stitched wallpieces and installations frequently draw on scientific imaging and data-capture systems to explore the impact of disease on the human body and the power of medicine to diagnose and, in some circumstances, repair physical damage. Her first digitally embroidered art works were a series of pieces for the Centre for Clinical Haematology, Queen Elizabeth Hospital Birmingham in 2009. Based on activities in the centre they featured the illegibility of the data from the patient perspective of genetic diagnostic tests, microscopic images of blood cells and chromosomes and the molecular structure of drug treatments. Her exploration of echocardiograms and other cardiac tests began in 2010 and pinnacling with the 100 m long piece for *Cloth and Memory 2*.

Critic Barbara Bole (2006: 4) has written 'the privileged place of art arises from the capacity to create an opening, a space in which we are forced to reconsider the relations that occur in the process or tissue of making life'. Thompson actively seeks to find these 'openings' to question how we communicate with the world around us. Although she creates 'real world' artworks, the role of digital technologies is fundamental to their inspiration and production. Whilst actively collaborating with specialists to inform themes within her work, as an artist, Thompson appreciates and understands that there is more than just the aesthetics of the artwork itself. In creating an artwork, it is necessary to spend time with the expert in the field, in order to understand the information or data that is considered, or used as the theme within the creative process. Collaborations have ranged from electrocardiographers, cytogeneticists, industrial historians and in this case, palaeopathologists.

20.3   Methods

Digital print and digital stitch were key textile techniques used in the creative process for this project. Digital print is self-explanatory; image files printed out onto fabric that can then be stitched upon. The digital stitch is a more complicated process. There are similarities with CNC (Computer Numerical Control) milling, where a surface is moved by machine on both the X and Y axis lying beneath a fixed point which allows change on the Z axis. In the case of digital embroidery, fabric is held taut in a hoop which is moved by the machine under the moving sewing needle. This process allows for very accurate, repeatable stitchery.

Imagery is manipulated in *6D Embroidery System* specialist software which generates embroidery files to instruct the machine where to stitch. This might be in the form of linear lines or areas of dense stitch, sometimes termed pattern fill. The embroidery file can be generated by hand-plotting of lines or areas, or using in-built selection tools or wizards to process a whole jpeg image. Once the embroidery files have been digitised, they are then like a series of screens for a multi-coloured screen print. They can be used in the correct order or mixed up, deliberately mis-stitched in an off-registered spot or some colours actually omitted, to create the artwork. The files are transferred to a Pfaff Creative Sensation digital embroidery machine using a USB stick for stitchout. Additional stitchery on a Pfaff PowerQuilter similar to free hand drawing, called free motion work, can also be used to embellish surfaces and textures (Figs. 20.2 and 20.3).

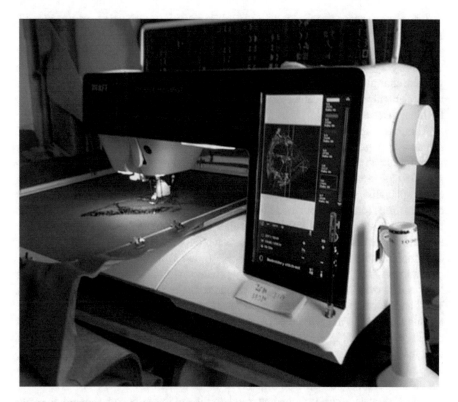

Fig. 20.2 Pfaff Creative Sensation digital embroidery sewing machine in the studio of Karina Thompson 2012. Photo credit Karina Thompson

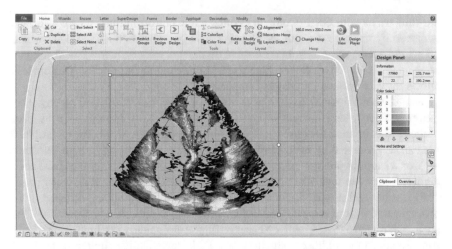

Fig. 20.3 6D Embroidery Software screen grab showing embroidery file being created. Photo credit Karina Thompson, with permission from VSM software to use the imagery of their software

Once images have been selected and digitised a series of trial pieces are produced. At this stage the sampling is playful and intuitive—adapting the ethos of furniture designer Hans Wegner (1949) that 'we must play, but play seriously' to experiment with imagery, abstracting it so that it is reduced but still communicates what is wanted, changing colours, textures, and scale. However, it requires a delicate balance to experiment when the subject matter of these creations may be images relating to terminal disease.

This body of samples was used as the basis for a dialogue with the BARC researchers to garner opinion as to the accuracy and validity of the interpretation. The work is seen as only having value if the meaning and relevance of the subject represented in the creation are correct and justified. This critical review, through the eyes of the specialist, enables assessment of the salient features of the samples and these conversations form the basis for decisions on the nature of the final, finished output. It is these pieces which must interest, stimulate and be emotive for the viewer whether they are members of the general public, osteologists and digital bioarchaeologists, or clinicians with specialist knowledge.

Dialogue is key with interdisciplinary projects within the digital humanities and feedback is critical for collaborative research at the interface of art and science. The first information gathering session for Thompson at BARC was a postgraduate teaching session. This session explored how debilitating some of the pathological conditions manifest in the skeletons within the BARC collection might be and how they may be interpreted—with disability caused by malunion of a fractured femur; and the chronic pain and limitation of movement caused by arthritic hip joints, two conditions that were considered together with the students.

Bole (2006: 4) suggests that when 'our handling of things becomes habitual, …we forget the wonder of it all'. As an artist and not an osteologist, seeing human skeletal remains which were being examined within the Laboratory setting was initially uncomfortable for Thompson 'I was slightly queasy with the thought that these "things" on bubble wrapped tables before me were actually part of someone; that once they were inside a human, wrapped in muscle and tendons; that arteries fed blood to them; that they were tucked away inside their owners until their flesh rotted away and then they were uncovered in an archaeological excavation…and all around me people seemed unphased by how remarkable this all was'.

The dialogue between Thompson and staff at BARC was integral to the development of the project collaboration. One has to look beyond collective experiences in terms of contemporary twenty-first-century living to consider subjectively, the impact that injuries and disabilities would have had on the dependants and kin of these individuals in antiquity, a process that is mirrored with the Bioarchaeology of Care approach (Roberts 2017; Tilley 2015; Wilson et al. 2017). Trying to develop a clinical objectivity to bear witness, and 'to produce a rift which, in turn, affirms a way of seeing things differently' (Guattari, 2000 cited McKeown, 2013, p. 222). It is paramount for these artistic outcomes to attempt a clinical interpretation of the skeletal remains and in turn understand the lives, disabilities, and suffering of past peoples.

Most of the human skeletal remains within the BARC collection are curated in custom-made acid-free cardboard boxes. There is an established curatorial protocol to the order in which the bones are bagged and packaged within these archival boxes to minimise damage. These preventive conservation measures are of particular importance with fragile pathological lesions. As an artist with limited knowledge of osteology, it was not possible for Thompson to differentiate the normal skeletal anatomy from the pathologically affected bones. Similarly, although the bones selected for the *Digitised Diseases* and *Cemetery to Clinic* resources had already been 'curated' with a written palaeopathological description, this text was for a specialist audience who would be familiar with the terminology and implications of the disease as represented in the 3D digital models. The accompanying clinical synopses, together with dialogues with BARC researchers was invaluable to gaining knowledge and understanding for interpretation of symptoms and physical signs in the living person—putting 'flesh and blood' on these ancient human remains. The digitisation of the original X-radiographs meant that they could easily be imported into digital programmes for the creation of final artworks.

20.4   Results & Discussion

A theme that Thompson chose to explore was the dilemma of interest in severity of disease, illness or trauma within the collection whilst remembering the human impact that the condition would have had on that individual's life. In his poem, *A postcard from the volcano* Wallace Stevens (1936) describes the act of remembrance of one generation for the remains of a much earlier one. Miklitsch (1979: 119) summed up this aspect in his critique of the poem.

"The children will go on picking up bones. In their naïve curiosity they will see not the man but the ghost, not the being but the bones. This is the fate of the dead; the knowledge that they will be forgotten, that those who come after them will not remember that they were once " quick as foxes on the hill".

Through conversations with Dr Jo Buckberry a pelvis was identified as one of the important 'type specimens' within the collection which shows signs of Paget's disease—a painful and debilitating condition that would have limited the movement of the patient. In Thompson's large-scale wall piece '*As quick as foxes on the hill*' a quote from the Stevens' poem was printed over the X-radiograph image of the pelvis, with stitchery used to 'emboss' the surface (Fig. 20.4).

Hansen's Disease and the Andersen Archive, digitised as part of *From Cemetery to Clinic*, became a particular focus for the direction of the project. It was easy to appreciate that the deforming sequelae of the disease in the hands; the absorption of the phalanges, and the clawing disfigurement of the hands associated with the peripheral nerve damage in the disease, would have made grasping and manual dexterity almost impossible. The combined skeletal and X-radiograph studies of the collection allowed a clinical interpretation of this most deforming disease. As an

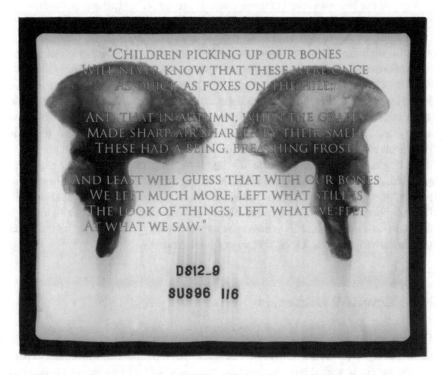

Fig. 20.4 *As quick as foxes on the hill,* 2015, digital print on cotton, free motion stitch, rayon thread, cotton wadding and backing, approx. 175 × 145cms. Photo credit River Studio

artist reliant on the use of her hands to create works of art, Thompson found these the most emotive skeletal specimens and X-radiographs.

In discussion with Buckberry and Manchester, Thompson chose a number of X-radiographs that illustrated the physiology of the disease. *The Leprous Hands* became a series of pieces showing the visual disintegration of the imagery of the historic X-radiographs as a metaphor for the degeneration of the hands. Each hand was slightly larger than life, allowing for clear representation of the musculature and skeletal features. This series contained small artworks featuring individual pairs of hands that were installed in the teaching laboratories alongside items of the BARC collection and large-scale wall pieces featuring up to eighteen versions of pairs of hands that were exhibited in gallery settings.

In *The Leprous Skull* a dramatic image of the X-radiograph of a medieval skull showing initial signs of rhino-maxillary syndrome, was printed onto fabric. The excavation plan of the cemetery site associated with the Medieval hospital of St James and Mary Magdalene from where it was excavated, which had been digitised as part of the *From Cemetery to Clinic* project, was quilted onto the background of the image, giving a shadowy texture (Fig. 20.5).

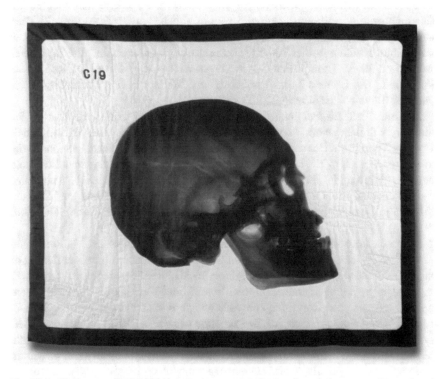

Fig. 20.5 *The Leprous Skull*, 2015 digital print on cotton, free motion stitch, rayon and lurex thread, cotton wadding and backing, approx. 175 × 145 cms. Photo credit River Studio

The dissemination of final artworks took two routes. Initially, a series of formal and informal displays and discussions with Paleopathologists, Osteologists and Digital Bioarchaeologists was held and Thompson delivered a paper on her experience at the 'Skin and Bones' session of the Anatomical Society Summer Meeting 2014. BARC holds a monthly 'bone clinic' allowing for informal discussion about a case within the collection. Thompson did a planned 'take over the meeting', with installation of large-scale pieces in the corridors of the University and smaller pieces installed alongside items of the collection in June 2015. 34 people attended the session with comments being positive and used by Thompson to help inform further work (Fig. 20.6).

Secondly, the art works were included in a series of exhibitions across Europe which allowed the general public to see the work and become aware of the project. '*As quick as foxes on the hill*' and '*600 diagnoses a day*' from the '*Leprous Hands series*' were included in the Quilt Art exhibitions '*Dialogues*' and '*Small Talk*' (Marks, 2015). This show toured 13 venues across Europe and was seen by at least 5,600 people. '*The Leprous Skull*' was shortlisted for the '*Fine Art Quilt Masters Award*', Europe's premier competition for large-scale art textiles in 2015. The two public showings of the competition attracted in excess of 38,000 members of the general public. '*The Leprous Skull*', along with the largest of the Leprous Hands piece were included in the exhibition '*What have I got to do to make it Okay?*' (Cooper, 2015). This high profile exhibition featured 5 well-established artists from the UK, USA and Ireland and toured to 6 international venues. In total, 46,000 people visited the exhibition with a further 700,000 seeing the work online or in editorial articles (McGregor, 2018). Thompson included '*As quick as foxes on the hill*', '*The Leprous Skull*', and '*The Leprous Hands*' in her gallery '*Pattern within*' at the Festival of Quilts 2019 which had at least 20,000 visitors.

Editorial feedback was extremely positive with many critics mentioning the humanity within the work. 'Trying to portray this serious subject has proved a challenge for Thompson. Her solution has been imagery that shows what happens as the bones are resorbed by the body when leprosy is contracted, resulting in delicate and haunting embroideries that demand further scrutiny' (Marks 2015: 81). 'The image is simultaneously bold and ghostly....heart-breaking, private and intimate' (Wilson 2016: 49). 'Thought provoking, full of unique ideas and skilled work' (Crawford 2016: 38).

Feedback from the general public showed many similar responses. Visitors would often compare their hands with those on the artworks examining the shortening of phalanges or clawing deformity of the leprous hands. In gallery feedback, words such as 'thought provoking', 'emotional' and 'interesting' were commonly used. There is anecdotal evidence from the gallery showings of visitors breaking into tears in front of '*The Leprous Hands*' on two separate occasions. When asked about their reaction, the response was that they had not considered the implications of what they thought was a medieval disease consigned to history, yet clearly still present in modern times. Poignantly, a third audience member on crutches also wept in front of '*As quick as foxes on the hill*'. The artworks on display within BARC also stimulated conversation with visitors to the human remains collections at Bradford, a unique

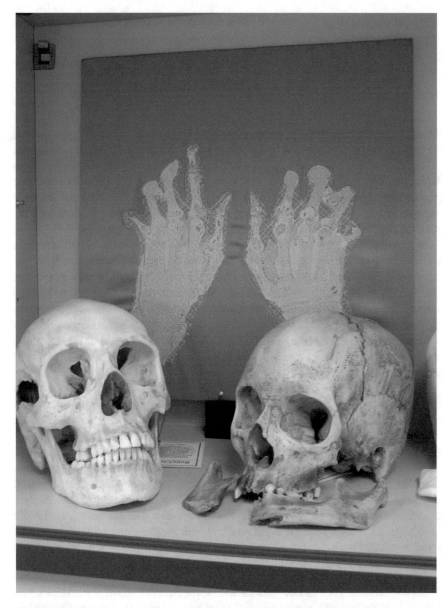

Fig. 20.6 Untitled piece from *The Leprous Hands* series installed alongside osteological remains from the teaching collection at BARC Photo credit Karina Thompson

way of reminding all of the personal and unique qualities of the remains that we have responsibility to curate.

20.5 Conclusion

This collaborative project explored how bones and data from digitised human skeletal remains, could inspire artworks that would highlight the humanity of those bones. By taking time to study the digitised resource, and in discussion with researchers from BARC, a fuller understanding was developed that served as the basis for a series of experimental samples, which in turn evolved into the final textile artworks that were seen by at least 70,000 members of the general public, thereby also widening the reach of the collections normally only visible to students and researchers.

Whilst there is no substitute for the tactile experience of using real-world artefacts and osteological remains in a teaching environment, these interactions are often at the cost of irreparable damage by the handling of such fragile Archaeological items (Wilson 2014). The nature of the osteological evidence from the *Digitised Diseases* resource meant that the collection was easy to explore and study. Points of interest in the high-definition images could be closely examined and discussed, sometimes at a considerable distance from the collection itself. The digitisation of the collection meant that imagery could easily be used in digital programmes to be adapted and translated into artworks.

But here lies a contradiction; the artworks are tangible, analogue, real world objects that can be touched, based on tangible, analogue, real world objects that can also be touched. But without the digital technologies they would not have been created. It was the digitisation of the collection that allowed Thompson to 'discover' these objects. The *Digitised Diseases* resource allowed the osteological evidence to be selected and viewed as photorealistic textured 3D models. Furthermore, it was digital technologies that allowed the digital model to be converted into another digital image and subsequently an embroidery file, which was then printed and stitched onto fabric returning them again to the analogue world. The symbiotic, circularity of these relationships were the keystones in expressing the physicality of the human remains themselves—'the boundary between analogue and digital virtual objects has solidified into physical forms' (Harrison, 2013, p.xiii).

Acknowledgements The authors wish to thank G4A Arts Council England/ Maggie Silver, Salts Mill/ Pfaff sewing machines for project funding and support in kind to Thompson and Jisc 2011-13 Rapid Digitisation scheme for *'From Cemetery to Clinic'* and the Jisc 2011-13 Mass Digitisation scheme for *'Digitised Diseases'* led by Wilson, University of Bradford. *Digitised Diseases* was a partnership with The Royal College of Surgeons of England, The Museum of London and MOLA, together with contributions from partners York Museums, York Minster, The Novium. Further contributions and acknowledgements are found at www.digitiseddiseases.org.

References

Bolt B (2006) Materializing pedagogies? Working papers in art and design, vol 4. ISSN 1466-4917, University of Hertfordshire

Brennand Wood M (2011) Pretty deadly, digital embroidery, private collection

Churchill College Cambridge, Chairs by Wegner [online], Churchill College Cambridge. https://www.chu.cam.ac.uk/about/art-collection/chairs-wegner/. Accessed 9 Aug 2019

Clegg M (2020) Human remains: curation, reburial and repatriation. Cambridge University Press

Coates L (2018) Making peace with our faulty hearts. The Lancet 392(10146):451–530

Crawford J (2016) The Journal of Spinners, Weavers and Dyers, issue 258 Summer, p 38

Digitised Diseases (2013) www.digitiseddiseases.org. Accessed Jan 2021

Eden M (2011) The Mnemosyne, laser-sintered vessel, Carnegie Museum of Art, Pittsburg, Pennsylvania, UK

Guattari F (2000) The three ecologies. The Althone Press, London

Harrison D (2013) Digital media and technologies for virtual artistic spaces. IGI Global, Hershey, PA

Harris J (2012) Digital practice in material hands: How craft and computing practice are advancing digital aesthetic conceptual methods. Craft Research 3: 91–112. Cited in Niedderer K, Townsend K (2014) Designing craft research: joining emotion and knowledge, The Design Journal, Vol 17, issue 4, pp 624–648. Bloomsbury Press, London

Hassett BR, Rando C, Bocaege E, Durruty MA, Hirst C, Smith S, Ulguim PF, White S, Wilson A (2018) Transcript of WAC 8 digital bioarchaeological ethics panel discussion, 29 August 2016 and resolution on ethical use of digital bioarchaeological data. Archaeologies 14(2):317–337

Kettle A (2012) Untitled, digital embroidery. Telling Fortunes, Platt Hall, Manchester

Killgrove K (2015) How 3D printed bones are revolutionizing forensics and bioarchaeology, https://www.forbes.com/sites/kristinakillgrove/2015/05/28/how-3d-printed-bones-are-revolutionizing-forensics-and-bioarchaeology/. Accessed 21 Dec 20

MacGregor S (2018) Make it okay: exhibition report, s.l.: s.n.

Magilton J, Lee F, Boylston A (2008) Lepers outside the gate: excavations at the cemetery of the hospital of St James and St Mary Magdalene, Chichester, 1986–1987 and 1993. Council for British Archaeology, New York

Marks S (2015) Dialogues and small talks, exhibition catalogue. Quilt Art, Edinburgh

McCullough M (1998) Abstracting craft: the practiced digital hand. MIT Press, Cambridge MA and London. Cited in Niedderer K, Townsend K (2014) Designing craft research: joining emotion and knowledge. The Design Journal, vol 17, issue 4, pp. 624–648. Bloomsbury Press, London

McKeown A (2013) Virtual communitas, "Digital Place-Making," and the process of "Becoming". In: Harrison D (ed.), Digital media and technologies for virtual artistic spaces. IGI Global, pp. 218–236. https://doi.org/10.4018/978-1-4666-2961-5.ch016

Miklitsch R (1979) Poems 98, The Wallace Stevens Journal, vol 3, number 3/4, pp 119–121. John's Hopkins University Press, Baltimore

Millar L (ed) (2013) Cloth and memory 2, exhibition catalogue. Salts Estates Ltd., Saltaire

Neal G (2013) Anne table, walnut, exhibited at collect. Saatchi Gallery, London, May 10–13

Roberts CA (2017) Applying the 'Index of Care' to a person who experienced leprosy in late Medieval Chichester, England. In: Tilley L (ed), New developments in the bioarchaeology of care, Springer, pp 101–124

Stevens W (2015) The collected poems: the corrected edition. Vintage Books, New York

Tilley L (2015) Theory and practice in the bioarchaeology of care. Springer, New York

Treadsway C (2009) Hand e-craft: An investigation into the hand use in digital creative practice. In: Proceedings of the Seventh ACM Conference on Creativity and Cognition. ACM, Berkeley CA, pp 185–194. Cited in Niedderer K, Townsend K (2014) Designing craft research: joining emotion and knowledge. The Design Journal, vol 17, issue 4, pp 624–648. Bloomsbury Press, London

Wallace J (2010) Personhood in Dementia [Digital jewellery]. https://openlab.ncl.ac.uk/things/per sonhood/. Accessed 29 Nov 2016

What Have I Got To Do To Make It Okay? (2015–2017) [exhibition] Curated by Liz Cooper, Pumphouse Gallery, Battersea, London

Wilson I (2016) Making it okay, Surface Design Journal, Fall 2016, Albuquerque. Surface Design Association, New Mexico

Wilson AS (2014) Digitised diseases: preserving precious remains. Br Archaeol 136:36–41

Wilson AS, Manchester K, Buckberry J, Storm R, Croucher K (2017) Digitised diseases: seeing beyond the specimen to understand disease and disability in the past, pp 301–315

Chapter 21
Fad Touch: Creative Economy Engagement

Daniel Pett, Catriona Cooper, Abi L. Glen, Melanie Pitkin, and Jennifer Wexler

Abstract The purpose of this chapter is to discuss the outcomes of the Fitzwilliam Museum's Arts and Humanities Research Council funded (AHRC) Creative Economy Engagement Fellowships, a practice-driven research, development programme and knowledge transfer activity. The guiding principles and methods behind these Fellowships were to make use of low cost, replicable 3D scanning of the Museum's collection, whilst working with an educational technology startup and a 3D printing artisan workshop to determine how their technologies could be exploited whilst focusing on user-centred design. This chapter demonstrates how Early Career Researchers (ECRs) can gain valuable career progression and creative industries experience whilst combining digital technologies, audience engagement and research and implement them in a short time frame.

Keywords Creative industries · 3D printing · Museology · Egyptology · Archaeology

21.1 Introduction

The heritage sector has often been at the forefront of emerging technology and is championed as having the potential for exciting or engaging case studies. 3D printing is a prime example of a technology that has been an early focus of experimentation in the museum and heritage sector (Coates 2019) with early adopters presenting the potential as early as 2014 (Reilly 2015). The potential of these technologies, techniques and associated interventions led to the Fitzwilliam Museum

D. Pett (✉) · A. L. Glen · M. Pitkin
The Fitzwilliam Museum, University of Cambridge, Cambridge, UK
e-mail: dejp3@cam.ac.uk

C. Cooper
Royal Holloway, University of London, London, England

J. Wexler
The British Museum, London, England

(FM) obtaining funding from the Arts and Humanities Research Council's Creative Economy Engagement (CEE) scheme (AH/S012583/1) to establish four post-doctoral fellowships (each for 6 months in duration)—identified as CEEF by the museum.

These four short term posts (6 months long) aimed to provide the opportunity for Early Career Researchers (ECRs) to work with small/medium enterprises (SMEs) as creative industry partners to explore the interface between 3D printing and associated educational technologies and museological practices, and the public engagement programmes of the University of Cambridge's (UCAM) principal art museum.

This novel approach had not been implemented before in UCAM museums and provided significant individual contributions to original research (Egyptological studies), major exhibitions (*Feast and Fast (F&F)* and prototypes for the *Being an Islander (BAI)* exhibition (now delayed by Covid19) and a large-scale conference in 2019 held at the Judge Business School.

The Museum's partners in this endeavour were Museum in a Box (MiaB) and ThinkSee3D (TS3D); both SMEs use 3D materials derived from cultural heritage to provide new and meaningful interactions for museum and non-museum going audiences. To enable this programme of research, three fellowships were assigned a specific practise-led research programme of activity, with the remaining fellow-ship focusing on existing practices and theory, and to provide guidance for the other fellows and ideally the museum/heritage sector on the use of 3D printing. The fellowships were divided into:

CEEF1: Development of guidance for the museum sector for the use of 3D replicas.

CEEF2: Development of 3D interventions to engage diverse audiences with the Egyptian Coffins research via a 'Pop-Up Museum'.

CEEF3: Development of prototype subscription models for Museum in a Box and an intervention for the *F&F* exhibition.

CEEF4: Development of a prototype Museum in a Box collection for the **BAI** exhibition.

The researchers' projects were influenced by current industrial and academic challenges in the heritage sector, in line with the AHRC Heritage Priority Strategy document (AHRC 2018) and aimed to enhance the mission and guiding principles of FM public engagement activity.

Through three of these fellowships, 3D prints were offered to create tactile expe-riences of museum objects, with the concept of storytelling, narrative discussion and development of new content as a key component. Storytelling is at the heart of the mission for many museums (Adler & Johnsson 2006; Bedford 2001), increasingly this is via digital means through the employment of emergent digital technology such as 3D modelling and printing, immersive experiences via Virtual and Augmented Reality, mobile applications and online explorations (Wong 2015).

21.2 CEEF1: 3D Replicas within the UCM

Working in conjunction with TS3D and the FM's 'Do Not Touch' Project, and considered the development of guidance to best practice for museums who are considering working with 3D prints. The potential for museum collections to use 3D printing has been considered both formally (Di Giuseppantonio Di Franco et al. 2015) and there is a wealth of informal (anecdotal) evidence as to its potential (including that developed by our creative industries partner, TS3D).

Tactile experiences and replicas (Cormier 2018), are not a new development to the museum or heritage sector: early vestiges of the museum in the seventeenth century incorporated touch and 'manual investigation' as an integral element to understanding objects (Classen 2005). However, modern museum practices sanitised the museum experience, not only limiting our understanding of collections to a uni-sensory visual experience (Candlin 2008), conditioning us into an understanding that touching in museums is expressly forbidden (Bacci and Pavani 2014).

The turn of the century saw a return to object handling as part of the engaging museum learning experience with the notion that tactility can allow us to understand the objects and collections in new ways and that it is these experiences that enchant and excite visitors (Levent and McRainey 2014).

The re-introduction of these experiences is not straightforward; curators and conservators have pertinent concerns about the impact these experiences will have on the objects in their care. The successful introduction of long-term, mediated and permanently located object handling desks within large museums, for example the British Museum (2008) has recently incorporated 3D prints in, e.g., the Sunken Cities exhibition (Dey 2018). These handling desks are often created and maintained via large museums with institutional privileges, which included the allocation of resources to facilitate engagements through their permanent and volunteer staff have propelled this type of intervention beyond the reach of smaller museums. This being seen as an extension of the digital divide.

This project therefore focused on the adoption of 3D prints as part of un-facilitated engagements, i.e., without a member of staff or volunteer actively engaged with the objects. The project's intention was to produce a guide to best practices, following observational analysis of two 3D prints of sections of objects installed in the Antiquities galleries of the FM in late 2019 as part of the 'Do Not Touch'. Data was gathered during two hourly sessions over four days, both during the week and weekend, and at different times of day in line with the project protocol.

The first 3D intervention is an extract from an ancient Egyptian shrine built by King Thutmosis III at El Kab (E.40.1902). Dedicated to the goddess Nekhbet, the outer walls of the shrine are inscribed, but the low levels of lighting in the gallery make the inscriptions harder to identify visually. The second 3D print is taken from a large marble slab carved with a Greek inscription of the Honours for Antiochus (Loaned from Trinity College, Cambridge: Loan Ant.21) hung facing away from the centre of the room, often overlooked by visitors.

These objects were not displayed under optimal conditions—minimal temporary signage was placed next to the 3D objects and demonstrated some of the traditional museological views that needed to be overcome to facilitate this work. There was a green glyph icon showing a finger pointing towards the print encouraging visitors to touch, but the curatorial/interpretation team made a deliberate decision to provide no explanation/interpretation about the 3D prints. An opportunity exists to test the effect when enhanced interpretation is provided.

A small-scale evaluation was undertaken with 115 individuals or groups (included in the data capture individuals or groups had to walk directly past the 3D print) were observed over several sessions in August/September 2019, out of which 73 individuals or groups did not notice the print. Of those who did observe the print a further 22 did not engage with the print—leaving only 20 visitors who did interact. The small sample size can therefore lead to suppositions and insights gained from these interventions to be seen as not having significant impact, compared to the research conducted by Di Franco (Di Giuseppantonio Di Franco et al. 2015) at the Museum of Archaeology and Anthropology.

Low level oral responses were elicited from the sample, and in four instances individuals initiated the rest of their group into engaging with the prints promoting extended discourse and therefore social interaction around the artefacts and print. Interactions like these are indicative of a positive visitor experience through collaboration and social engagement discussed by Katifori et al. (2016).

The print of the 'Honours for Antiochus' was placed away from any interpretation of the artefact below the object, out of the sightline of the majority of visitors, but ideal for children and those in a wheelchair. The print from the Egyptian shrine built by King Thutmosis III at El Kab, was placed much closer to the intended view of the artefact, but below the object, so a cursory glance could miss the intervention easily. The artefact itself is on a thoroughfare so many visitors do not stop to engage. In both instances, the prints were deliberately deployed by FM curatorial and interpretation staff without full explanation about what they are or why they were placed there. The process brought out the need for advocacy and the need to demonstrate the additional value of these interventions.

These limitations highlight the need for museum staff to work in consultation with the fabricator to ensure that the prints are produced and deployed in-gallery most effectively. Simple insights obtained from this observational analysis made obvious recommendations to the FM interpretation team with the key concept being the paramount importance of object placement (much in the same vein as the original piece of work).

Derived from this, the following guidance is suggested for museum staff to develop an effective/affective experience using 3D prints to facilitate interaction and understanding of objects on display without jeopardising the conservation and protection of the artefacts.

1.   **Selection**: From the initial consideration of introducing a 3D print into a gallery, it is vital to consult all relevant stakeholders and have a clear understanding why you are undertaking this work, e.g., is it in response to visitor feedback?

2. **Specification**: Once museum staff are in agreement on their selection, a discussion with the maker is important prior to commissioning. It is important to note that there is a wide variation between what a '3D print maker-artist' and '3D print maker' does: it is crucial to be clear if you are looking for a high-quality 3D print that a maker-artist would be more appropriate; if you are looking for lower-quality, higher-volume prints, a 3D print maker might be more appropriate.
3. **Installation**: The print needs to be installed in close association with the original, visible to all visitors and easily accessible.

These recommendations have since been deployed with the commissioning of a 3D print of a fossil at the Polar Museum and will be used in future at the FM.

Insights from working with TS3D and through their publications (Dey 2018) included: printing is not always the best option for creating 3D replicas, but It is often a more rapid means for replication of complex objects, it can remove the need for highly skilled crafts people, reduce costs and produce derived digital 3D model(s) which might be used for multiple purposes. Printing can often negate knowledge loss in the making process for replication of cultural artefacts whilst it can often be the starting point for more traditional craft work to occur. A print could be used to create moulds or for the production of casts.

21.3   CEEF2: The Pop-Up Egyptian Coffins Project

The FM's interdisciplinary ancient Egyptian coffins project has been running since 2014, with a team of Egyptologists, conservators, a pigment analyst, an expert in historical painting techniques, an ancient Egyptian woodworking specialist and a consultant radiologist. This research project harnessed the application of advanced imaging techniques such as Computed Tomography (CT) scanning and X-radiography, to reveal unprecedented insights into how coffins were made and decorated, the ancient Egyptian economy and attitudes to death and the afterlife.

In 2016, this research culminated in a major exhibition and publication, *Death on the Nile: Uncovering the Afterlife of Ancient Egypt*, which was visited by 91,782 people. Despite this impressive figure, audience demographics identified an alarming division; the proportion of gap in the exhibition's visitation among socially and economically diverse visitors. In a survey conducted with 334 exhibition visitors, 67% were educated to degree level or equivalent and predominantly resided in the local Cambridge area.

As part of an institution-wide effort to remedy statistics like this, the FM Egyptian coffins team developed a 'Pop-Up' Museum—a community outreach initiative where researchers bring real museum objects, craft replicas, hands-on activities and digital experiences into the heart of communities who might not otherwise have access to our research (Fig. 21.2).

Fig. 21.1 Left: 3D print of a section of the 'Honours for Antiochus' Right: 3D print of a section of the ancient Egyptian shrine built by King Thutmosis III at El Kab (E.40.1902). Produced by ThinkSee3D (D. Pett)

Fig. 21.2 The FM Egyptian Coffin Project's 'Pop-Up' in The Wheatsheaf Inn, Wisbech (M. Pitkin)

Fig. 21.3 The installation of Museum in a Box stations and the artist's prints (D. Pett)

Fig. 21.4 The wooden dig box with 3D prints, postcards and the MiAB (J. Wexler)

This is done through unexpected interventions—namely the appearance of 'Pop-Ups' in locations where people would not normally expect to have a cultural encounter, for example in a pub, supermarket, shopping centre and food bank. This concept has its origins in an outreach project initiated at the Museum of Applied Arts and Sciences (MAAS) in Sydney, Australia in 2012 as part of the exhibition *Faith, fashion, fusion: Muslim women's style in Australia.* Exhibition curators, Jones and Pitkin, travelled into the heart of Sydney's Muslim community (approximately 1 h from Sydney's Central Business District) with real objects from the collection, activities and giveaways in order to broaden their reach with their research and strengthen community relationships.

With the support of the Arts and Humanities Impact Fund (AHIF, UCAM) and the Global Challenges Research Fund (GCRF, UCAM), we were able to pilot this concept in two regions, the Fenland town of Wisbech in Cambridgeshire and in Cairo and Damietta, Egypt. Wisbech was selected owing to its location and status as one of the most deprived towns in the United Kingdom (National Conversation 2017); one-third of residents are from Eastern Europe; according to the 2011 census 35.1% of its population lack qualifications, 19.1% possess literacy skills at entry level or below (Cambridgeshire County Council 2016).

A key challenge presented by the 'Pop-Up' concept was how we would best engage diverse non-academic audiences in culturally underserved areas; how would we make the content accessible, relevant, multilayered, tactile and visually stimulating? How could we get people to invest their time in us? And, how could we encourage them to follow-up on their experience with further engagement in the subject of ancient Egypt and/or by visiting a museum? Given that our research angle was already heavily focused on industry and the handmade—something that many people, particularly those already involved in a trade, can relate to—we approached this via carpentry, pigments and painting and the concepts of ancient Egypt and museums.

The 'Pop-Up' offered the following experiences: the display of a genuine 3000-year-old fragment of a yellow coffin face and hand displayed in a secure, airtight showcase; a selection of craft replica tools from ancient Egypt displayed in a secure, airtight showcase; craft replica joints for handling; a painting activity where visitors can make their own replica ancient Egyptian paint brushes and paint with them using ancient-inspired pigments; iPads linked to the Fitzwilliam Egyptian coffins website; A3 colour photographic visual aids, to facilitate conversation with participants around the role of CT scanning and X-ray in coffin studies; and free giveaways such as the Museum's publication 'How to make an Egyptian coffin' (Dawson 2019), bookmarks and replica scarabs.

The opportunity to work with creative industry partner TS3D therefore opened up a new world of possibilities for our 'Pop-Up' project, particularly in terms of the ability to offer more tactile and visually arresting experiences. From the outset of the project, for example, we envisaged producing some type of interactive experience where visitors could actively assemble and disassemble a coffin, or parts of a coffin, in order to better understand wood construction and joinery. It would also serve as a visual aid to help illustrate the types of technical terms we might use when explaining how a coffin is made (for example, dowels and mortise and tenon joints) and help to give participants a sense of accomplishment through successfully putting it back together.

Since the element of portability was important for our project, we selected a small rectangular box coffin from the Museum's collection believed to have been made for a dog called *Heb*. Given that TS3D specialises in 3D printing, it seemed instinctive for us to first consider recreating the dog coffin in the form of a 3D print.

The production costs of a 1:1 scale 3D coffin print made in durable materials for repeat handling, such as gypsum, were too high for the project budget. A smaller version would raise questions around the importance of authenticity and the multi-sensory experience. According to a 2017 study (Wilson et al. 2017) on visitor attitudes to touchable 3D printed replicas in museum exhibitions 'many interviewees'' stated that, '…the more authentic and realistic looking that the 3D prints were, the better'.

By 3D printing a smaller version of the dog box coffin, therefore, authenticity would be significantly lacking—not only in terms of size, but also material, weight, texture and smell (the original coffin is made from the sweet smelling *Cedrus libani*, or Lebanese cedar tree). An integral facet of our research is experimentation through the use of ancient processes for recreation and reproduction.

We commissioned Dr Geoffrey Killen, a specialist in ancient Egyptian wood-working techniques, to produce a 1:1 scale craft replica of the dog box coffin using the same species of wood. His approach enabled us to gain a better understanding of the mindset of the ancient carpenter who constructed the coffin. Killen estimated it would have taken 4–5 days to produce, something not apparent from a 3D print. This replica offered participants a more multi-sensory experience, particularly via its materiality, weight and the strong, sweet smell that emanates from the freshly cut *Cedrus libani* tree—which often stimulated much discussion with participants around types of native and imported timbers used in ancient Egypt. The only feature Killen was unable to reproduce was the warped effect of the wood caused by thousands of years of ageing and changed environmental conditions, which a 3D print could have generated.

Although 'authenticity' and process were important for us, we wanted to know if this was the same for participants in our 'Pop-Up' Museum. We therefore conducted an evaluation where we asked visitors what they preferred, i.e., real objects, replicas or digital experiences. The majority of respondents indicated that they preferred to see real objects because it 'invoked a sense of awe', but in the unprompted responses many people specifically pointed out how much they enjoyed 'chatting with real subject specialists'. Due to lower literacy levels of respondents, the evaluation study took on three iterations. The first was a written survey completed by 20 respondents between March and April 2019. The second was a visual chart and verbal questionnaire completed by 12 respondents between May and June 2019 and the third was an observation-tracking study.

We conducted observations with 30 participants, tracking their engagement with the different components of the 'Pop-Up' to see where people spent the most time. Considering the role our facilitation played in this process, and the nature of the hands-on activities, it is perhaps not surprising that participants spent most time talking to subject specialists followed by the painting activity. Another later addition to our evaluation, was a wellbeing study where we invited people to share how they felt both before and after their encounter with the 'Pop-Up' Museum. In almost all cases, participants reported feeling an elevated sense of happiness and inspiration after engaging with us.

The main focus of our collaboration with TS3D was the production of a digital 3D animation (Dey et al. 2019) recreated from its CT scans of a 21st Dynasty coffin box belonging to a high official named Nespawershefyt. This takes people beyond the surface of the coffin's decoration to better understand what lies beneath using CT scan technology—for example, the number of pieces of wood used in its construction, how they are joined together and how we can identify reused pieces of wood from other objects, including other coffins. Visitors 'fly-through' the coffin to see how it was assembled with narrated commentary and subtitles (in English and Arabic—which were produced by our Arabic-speaking associates).

This digital resource has since been used within the Museum's GCRF funded work with the Egyptian Museum Cairo and its 'Pop-Up' work with the Wisbech Museum and beyond. The bilingualism and visual nature of this resource provides an ideal teaching aid, supplementing the other digital content (Pitkin et al. 2019) presented on the dedicated coffins website. This work pushed the boundaries for TS3D in terms of production time (a relatively new offering for TS3D), but also offered new ideas for the manufacture of their large-scale 3D prints (joints, segments).

While Nespawershefyt's inner coffin box is now in a ready state to be 3D printed, at least for this project it has been shown how craft replicas can offer alternative experiences to 3D prints, particularly in terms of their multi-sensory dimensions, authenticity and enhanced academic understanding of ancient processes of production. They also offer another way of preserving what is gradually becoming the endangered slow crafts movement of making things by hand. The experience of a craft replica can certainly be heightened using a digital 3D model by allowing visitors to compare and contrast the two examples when portably displaying the real object is not an option.

21.4 CEEF3:'The Fitz, but in Bit'

A rare cheese; compostable sanitary towels; tailored shirts; glittery nail polish; and gluten-free snacks for toddlers: just a few of the interests (or aspirations) catered to through subscription boxes. But if these boxes can cater to both the easily left-off-the-shopping list and to the connoisseur's prize, then why not try creating a version for museums? After all, the museum is a place for everyday access to the extraordinary.

To this end, we created and tested a prototype of a subscription box service for 3D printed replicas of objects in the FM, building on the technology created by MiaB. The test audience comprised eight adults and two children. All were based in Cambridgeshire or the London suburbs so that they could easily attend evaluation sessions at the Museum. By developing small, themed collections of low-cost 3D printed objects and paper materials for consumers to use with MiaB, we posited that we could increase the reach of the Museum's collections as well as attract new and more diverse audiences to the museum itself. The project involved collaborations with a local arts collective, voice actors and historians, with the prototype collection themed around the FM's major exhibition, *F&F* (original pre-Covid19 run—26th November 2019–26th April 2020).

The project was divided into two tasks: producing the physical boxes and their intellectual content. Developing a complete prototype box involved the design and/or procurement of postal packaging, branded mailer sleeves, printed 'menus' (displaying the copyright information for each museum object), and collections of 3D printed objects/postcards with NFC stickers attached. Developing the intellectual content of the boxes meant meeting with collections staff to identify suitable objects;

researching objects' background; writing copy for the recordings; acquiring voice actors, and recording appropriate material. Once this was acquired, each NFC sticker was encoded with the appropriate audio file, using the MiaB content management system.

In order to produce 3D models, each fellow was given training in photogrammetry and the basics of Agisoft's MetaShape. A long scanning session took place during the official preparatory FM exhibition photography for a mock-Baroque feast. Building the models in the software was the project of several months: the complicated nature of the subjects meant that we needed to fine-tune the models multiple times before they could be viable prints; for example, the lobster used in the feast had trailing tendrils, thin and translucent sections and hard to capture areas.

Outsourcing the design of the sleeves was important not only in aesthetic terms, but also to fulfil one of the AHRC's aims: to stimulate the local creative economy. Local artists Cambridge Art Makers designed and made custom linocut sleeves for the mailer boxes (each limited-edition print was then wrapped in vellum to protect it during transit), based on the FM's visual language and the Wisbech Swan Register.

To produce the box's content and to identify suitable models and research outputs to inform the design of our first collection, we worked closely with Dr. Victoria Avery, co-curator of the *F&F* exhibition. Once the boxes were complete, they were sent to each member of our test group through Royal Mail. Each member returned the enclosed feedback form, with questions designed to assess their experience of 'unboxing'. Because sending each member a MiaB would have been prohibitive both in cost and inventory terms, instead these individuals were invited to the FM for a recorded assessment of their reaction to using their collection on a MiaB.

The design of the mailer sleeves attracted widespread commendation, and each arrived at its destination more or less intact (some minor scuffs to the vellum notwithstanding). Positive feedback from the test subjects included 'beautiful, enticing, neat'; 'easy access, quality wrapped, pretty'; and 'elegant, trim'. All subjects confirmed that the mailers fit through their post box; 'a very good size of parcel'. One of the project's aims was to assess reaction to a number of different delivery styles for the copy: male/female voices, curatorial/ 'lay' delivery, educational/humorous. Thanks in large part to the skill of the voice actors recruited, these categories were represented in the final product.

The test study's participants had mixed reactions to being asked to assess the objects without any further context. Some found the initial engagement 'intriguing' and 'inviting'; others commented that they were disappointed, claiming that 'at the moment, it seems very detached'. There was also some confusion regarding the second stage of evaluation; some subjects felt that future recipients would need 'a little more briefing as to how they were supposed to use the objects'. This could be simply rectified by producing a simple document for inclusion in the box, explaining the process (or indeed streamlining the process altogether). To demonstrate the success of this project, the exhibition team installed 3 boxes within *F&F* for the duration of the exhibition (26 November 2019–26 April 2020) (Fig. 21.6). The 'Wisbech Swan' design caught the eye of the curators: and shop staff alike; their work was hung in the 'creative zone' of the exhibition space above the installation of the boxes. The artists were also commissioned to produce a limited run of art prints, cushions and scarves for sale in the museum shop during the exhibition. The project has thus increased their visibility, profit and platform within the Cambridge community and beyond (the exhibition was predicted to attract 80–90,000 visitors, but realised 61,254 over two segments interrupted by Covid19).

Through the installation of these commissioned pieces, the creative industry partners gained an unexpected larger shop window showcasing the outputs of digital humanities research projects within the museum and potentially reach many thousands of visitors.

The outcomes of this project were trialed within a clinical setting, using extra funding from University of Cambridge for a spin-off project entitled *Phish and ChYpPS*, at the Dialysis Unit, Addenbrookes' hospital and at a series of events on Parker's Piece. Surveys and interviews showed tools like this have potentially significant impact in terms of health, wellbeing and loneliness, all current national and international societal challenges. Boredom and isolation are known issues in clinical settings, and it is well-documented that intellectual stimulation and active entertainment (i.e., games, arts and crafts/creative play as opposed to passive entertainment like TV) improve the wellbeing and recovery time of many patients (APPG 2017; Uwajeh & Timothy 2016; Corrigan et al. 2017). MiaB would be an excellent contribution to these settings, allowing accessible but stimulating education and entertainment. Furthermore, the nature of the acrylic MiaB and 3D printed objects mean that they can also be sanitised easily to avoid cross-contamination.

The processes outlined above should provide ample opportunity for expansion. It is anticipated that we will be able to iron out a number of design and distribution flaws so that the creation of further collections would be significantly streamlined for future researchers.

This project has demonstrated that there may be viability for a museum subscription box. The materials here are cost-effective, and readily available online or through local producers. Content concepts are, indeed, almost limitless. Although somewhat time-consuming to design and assemble, such boxes could form part of any major exhibition's promotional materials. Aside from such pragmatic concerns, the outcomes of this small pilot study have also demonstrated the possibility of engaging wider audiences, in particular those who might be remote from the museum. The major sticking point in this process is the availability and cost of MiaB hardware; although they come at a reasonable price (£249), it is not a figure that many can afford.

21.5   CEEF4: Box of Travelling Objects/Ideas

This project, led by Jennifer Wexler, focused on the FM's Ancient Mediterranean collections in conjunction with the forthcoming major exhibition *(BAI)*. The aim of the BAI project is to provide a platform to debate cultural evolution in the Mediterranean islands, extending to the discussion of Britain's own (perceived or not) island identity, showcasing objects from the Aegean and Cypriot Collections of the FM. This project has been using BAI themes to look at different ways of how a MiaB can be used as a tool for storytelling and exploration, with a focus on developing new and exciting ways to tell stories around museum research and archaeological collections. This is aligned with MiaB's desired goals, which specify the importance of bringing a wealth of context and background to the museum experience and to help audiences to really explore an object's history and place in the world (Oates 2019).

By using these innovative tools for creating tactile explorations of museum collections, we can look at new ways of creating meaningful engagements and dialogues with audiences. As part of this project, we have been able to take part in the MiaB's 'Make Your Own' Pilot Scheme (Oates 2018). This has allowed us to access the MiaB's backend content management system in order to create/edit all box content in-house at the FM. The great strength of this, it has allowed us to be experimental in our approach to content management, opening up the project to multiple perspectives and interpretations of the featured historical objects.

The nature of this project allows audiences to be exploratory, like the ancient navigators of the Mediterranean, using mixed media as well as digital technology to discover different routes, places, objects and stories. The technology developed by MiaB allows us to incorporate different types of tactile and digital media to tell these stories around the early Mediterranean, utilising new 3D models of collection objects, 3D prints (in conjunction with TS3D) and additional postcards/prints from the collections.

Inspired not only by the Fellow's background in Mediterranean archaeology (Wexler 2016) and previous research (Bevan et al. 2014; Wexler et al. 2015; Galvin & Wexler in press; Pett in press) employing 3D technology for different types of engagement in a museum setting, but more significantly by the work of Winifred Lamb, former honorary Keeper of Greek Antiquities at the FM, 1920–1958. Lamb modernised and greatly enhanced the Classical collections at the Fitzwilliam, but was also an active field archaeologist who worked extensively across Greece and Turkey, discovering a previously unrecorded prehistoric link between the Aegean, Turkey and the Balkans in her ground-breaking work at Thermi, on the Island of Lesbos (Cooper 2012; Gill 2018).

This project culminated in the creation of an old wooden 'dig' box of 3D objects (scanned from the FM permanent collection and reduced in scale for cost and storage), postcards and papers collected and 'sent back' to the FM by Winifred Lamb (see Fig. 21.8), through which the fellow aimed to evoke wonder by creating opportunities for exploration and enchantment with the archaeological record via our box. The box and its materials are inspired by cabinets of curiosities, becoming metonyms and objects of resonance, representative of a larger world. In the modern context, these can be used for institutional critique—a way to replace museum rules with values that seem 'engaging, intriguing and appropriate for today's audience' (Lubar 2018: 12,16; Adamopoulou and Esther 2016).

The 'world' represented by this box (an old chest) is essentially that of Winifred Lamb's—an archaeologist's 'dig box' full of archives and objects for audiences to explore and curate. Her 'voice', employing the vocal talents of Dr. Hannah Platts, is used as a guide, but also to envision a past lived by her, offering snippets of her life and background in order to deliver archaeological data around the themes of the box. While the box does not follow a strict narrative structure per se, it has narrative signposts accessed via the audio on NFC chips—a sort of 'choose your own adventure' for which strands of research or information you might follow depending on the type of content you choose.

Within the chest, there are five scaled 3D prints printed in gypsum, of objects chosen from the themes associated with the box and chosen in conjunction with the exhibition curator (Fig. 21.9). They have a timespan ranging from prehistory to the classical period, looking at the connections between objects and the development of ancient technological revolutions, such as metalwork, language, and artwork, in connection to the broader themes of maritime connectivity, island identities and contested geographies.

We wanted the 3D prints to be as realistic as possible to enhance tactile engagement and understanding of the objects (Di Giuseppantonio Di Franco et al. 2015; Morris, Peatfield & O'Neill 2018), so emphasis was placed on using photo-realistic gypsum material for the prints rather than a less expensive yet less realistic material. Gypsum works extremely well for this set of objects as the majority (beyond one bronze axe) are ceramic artefacts; thus the 3D prints have a similar texture and colour to the originals, though some of the prints needed to be scaled down due to funding constraints and box size. Feedback from participants undertaking initial testing of the box at Mozfest and various FM/UCM events overall responded favourably to the 3D printed materials.

Participants can explore the different elements of the box, with both short and longer engagements possible based on the level of exploration. The intention is that by discovering different elements of content and narrative will encourage participants to engage for longer and in more meaningful ways. Although each object is described by Lamb via the recorded clip on the NFC tag, participants will be asked to help 'curate' the objects—mapping and recording using the box's tools and map, and writing their thoughts/feedback in the included notebook. At a later stage, this feedback could be further employed for co-curation of the objects via additional NFC tags.

The core of this project is to evoke wonder by creating opportunities for exploration and enchantment with the archaeological record via our box. By envisioning the past as 'remembered' by Lamb, we are hoping to create a type of 'suspension of belief' that will allow users to become 'enchanted', or emotionally involved, in the data presented. This emotional involvement could be further enhanced via co-curation and participation suggested above. This builds on the concepts of Perry (2019), Tringham (2019), and Stutz (2018) calling for a further collaborative and emotional approach to presenting and using archaeological data for engagement.

Unfortunately due to time constraints of the fellowship, and the onset of the Covid19 pandemic, user testing of this box was restricted so the validity of this model is still to be tested. We hope this will happen when the exhibition is finally opened and, in the meanwhile, the box's content can be explored via our website.

21.6 Conclusion

The CEEF project brought many benefits to the FM, with multiple analogue and digital outputs that should have a lasting legacy within the Museum's physical and digital estates. Many lessons were learnt from these interventions and outputs, with processes being challenged and sometimes stretched due to the disruptive technologies and methodologies we employed for this work.

These projects enabled us to make several new interventions within the Museum's estate, including providing material for a new display of replica objects within the Museum's antiquities galleries, provision of 3 instances of MiAB boxes and bespoke content within the 'creative zone' of the *Feast and Fast* exhibition. Crucially, these interventions have meant that they have introduced and embedded focused new digital knowledge and skills within the FM non-digital team members. This is essential given the *Culture is Digital* (DCMS 2018: 1.2) report describing how 'technology offers unprecedented opportunities for the UK cultural sector and chimes with the Mendoza report' (2017:10,62): *'museums are thinking about digital in increasingly targeted ways and using it where it makes a difference'.*

Many of the outputs described above went far beyond the original scope of work. The CEEF team organised a major conference—Do Not Touch? 3D in Museums, facilitated workshops and lectures for the public, workshops for UCAM academics and students, convened sessions at Mozilla's Festival of the Open Web (Mozfest), delivered short 'bitesize' talks for FM staff, presented for the UCAM's Enterprise team at their conference, and delivered training sessions for the Royal Academy of Art's executive MBA course. The team also introduced a 1.5 sized tactile print of a fossil leaves (glossopteris) for the Scott Polar Museum to introduce a tactile 3D print from TS3D into their recently opened exhibition **Walking on Thin Ice**, which will see similar evaluation as the work described by Cooper above, conducted in December 2019.

This project proved to be a catalyst for bringing the Creative Economy partner's work further into UCM programming—TS3D now has a strong relationship with the FM and Museum of Archaeology and Anthropology and will be producing interventions for future work within the former. However, there were severe limitations—the fellowships were not long enough to truly become fully fledged research projects with solid evidence-based outcomes, museum staff were not available as frequently as we hoped to work with the fellows and the loss of a fellow in such a short programme meant that their replacement was not an option.

Acknowledgements The CEEF 3D team would like to thank; Dr Joanne Vine, Clare Cambridge, Will Wilson, Colin Yaxley, Dom Hill, Julia Wilson, Tom O'Hanlon, James Andrews, Helena Rodwell, Julie Dawson, Kerry Wallis, Liz Irvine, Helen Strudwick, Vicky Avery, Anastasia Christophilopoulou, David Evans, Andrew Bowker, Georgina Doji, Cambridge Art Makers, the AHRC, UKRI GCRF, AHIF, CHRG, Sabah Abd el-Raziq and the Egyptian Museum Cairo, Sara Hany Abed, Geoffrey Killen, Gavin Toomey, Patricia Wheatley, Hannah Platts, Julianne Piggott, Richard Rex, Katharine Fry, Philo Van Kemenade, Steve Dey (TS3D), George Oates and Charles Killick (MiaB) and finally Eugene Ch'ng for his patience with us as we meandered towards finishing this article.

References

Adamopoulou A, Solomon E (2016) Artists-as-curators in museums: observations on contemporary wunderkammern Thema (4):35–49

Adler C, Johnsson E (2006) Telling tales: a guide to developing effective storytelling programmes for museums. http://www.crickcrackclub.com/MAIN/TELLINGTALES.PDF. Accessed 15 Dec 2019

AHRC (2018) AHRC's heritage strategic priority area: future directions. https://ahrc.ukri.org/doc uments/strategy/heritage-strategy/. Accessed 15 Dec 2019

APPG (2017) All-party parliamentary group on arts, health and wellbeing inquiry report creative health: the arts for health and wellbeing, 2nd ed. https://www.culturehealthandwellbeing.org. uk/appg-inquiry/Publications/Creative_Health_Inquiry_Report_2017_-_Second_Edition.pdf. Accessed 15 Dec 2019

Bacci F, Pavani F (2014) First Hand," Not "First Eye" knowledge: bodily experience in museums. In: Levent N, Pascual-Leone A (eds) The multisensory museum: cross-disciplinary perspectives on touch, sound, smell, memory, and space. Rowman and Littlefield, Plymouth, UK, pp 17–22

Bedford L (2001) Storytelling: the real work of museums. Curator: Museum J. 44(1):27–34. https:// doi.org/10.1111/j.2151-6952.2001.tb00027.x

Bevan A, Pett D, Bonacchi C, Keinan-Schoonbaert A, Lombraña González D, Sparks R, Wexler J, Wilkin N (2014) Citizen archaeologists. Online collaborative research about the human past. Human Comput. 1(2):183–197 (2014). https://doi.org/10.15346/hc.v1i2.9

British Museum (2008) Touching history: an evaluation of hands on desks at the British Museum. https://www.britishmuseum.org/pdf/Hands%20On%20Report%20online%2030-12-2010.pdf. Accessed 12 Aug 2019

Cambridgeshire County Council (2016) Wisbech 2020 baseline evidence profile. https://cambri dgeshireinsight.org.uk/wp-content/uploads/2017/12/Wisbech-2020-Baseline-Evidence-Profile-2016.pdf. Accessed 24 Oct 2019

Candlin F (2008) Museums, modernity and the class politics of touching objects. In: Chatterjee H (ed) Touch in museums: policy and practice in object handling. Berg, Oxford, UK, pp 9–20

Classen C (2005) Touch in the museum. In: Classen C (ed) The book of touch. Berg, Oxford, UK, pp 275–288

Coates C (2019) How are some of the world's best known museums doing amazing things with 3D printing? https://www.museumnext.com/article/how-museums-are-using-3D-printing/. Accessed 13 Aug 2019

Cooper CL (2012) The antiquities department takes shape. The fitzwilliam in the early twentieth century. J History Collect 24(3):347–367. https://doi.org/10.1093/jhc/fhr036

Cormier B (ed) (2018) Copy culture: sharing in the age of digital reproduction. V&A Publishing, London

Corrigan C et al (2017) The perception of art among patients and staff on a renal dialysis unit. Irish Med J 110(9):632. http://hdl.handle.net/10147/622629

Dawson J (2019) How to make an Egyptian coffin: the construction and decoration of Nespawer-shefyt's coffin set. Fitzwilliam Museum, Cambridge

DCMS (2018) Policy paper: culture is digital. https://www.gov.uk/government/publications/cul ture-is-digital. Accessed 15 Dec 2019

Dey S (2018) Potential and limitations of 3D digital methods applied to ancient cultural heritage: insights from a professional 3D practitioner. In: Wood R, Kelley K (eds) Digital imaging of artefacts: developments in methods and aims. ArchaeoPress, Oxford

Dey S, Dawson J, Pitkin M, Pett DEJ, Strudwick H (2019) Animation of a CT scan of the box coffin of Nespawershefyt https://vimeo.com/356279697. Accessed 15 Dec 2019

Di Giuseppantonio Di Franco P, Camporesi C, Galeazzi F, Kallmann M (2015) 3D printing and immersive visualization for improved perception of ancient artifacts. Presence: Teleoperators Virtual Environ 24(3):243–264. https://doi.org/10.1162/PRES_a_00229

Galvin E, Wexler J (In Press) Hacking the collections: making digital objects accessible and available to wide audiences. In: Goldstein L, Watrall E (eds) Digital heritage and archaeology in practice. University Press of Florida, Gainesville

Gill D (2018) Winifred lamb: aegean prehistorian and museum curator. Archaeopress, Oxford

Katifori A, Perry SE, Vayanou M, Pujol L, Kourtis V, Ioannidis Y (2016) Cultivating mobile-mediated social interaction in the museum: towards group-based digital storytelling experiences. MW2016: Museums and the Web 2016

Levent NS, Lynn McRainey D (2014) Touch and narrative in art and history museums. In: Levent N, Pascual-Leone A (eds) The multisensory museum: cross-disciplinary perspectives on touch, sound, smell, memory, and space. Rowman and Littlefield, Plymouth, UK, pp 61–82

Lubar S (2018) Cabinets of curiosity: what they were, why they disappeared, and why they're so popular now. https://medium.com/@lubar/cabinets-of-curiosity-a134f65c115a. Accessed 16 Dec 2019

Mendoza N (2017) The mendoza review: an independent review of museums in England. DCMS available at https://assets.publishing.service.gov.uk/government/uploads/system/uploads/attach ment_data/file/673935/The_Mendoza_Review_an_independent_review_of_museums_in_Engl and.pdf

Morris C, Peatfield A, O'Neill B (2018) 'Figures in 3D': digital perspectives on cretan bronze age figurines. Open Archaeol 4:50–61. https://doi.org/10.1515/opar-2018-0003

National Conversation (2017) National Conversation http://nationalconversation.uk/wp-content/upl oads/2017/08/March-Report.pdf. Accessed 24 Oct 2019

Oates G (2018) If the pilot was wildly successful, what might that look like for you? https://museum inabox.org/if-the-pilot-was-wildly-successful-what-might-that-look-like-for-you/. Accessed 4 Nov 2010

Oates G (2019) Technology is a tool, not our master. https://museuminabox.org/technology-is-a-tool-not-our-master/. Accessed 30 Aug 2019

Pitkin M, Pett D, Strudwick H (2019) Fitzwilliam Museum/egyptian coffins: The Fitzwilliam Museum Egyptian Coffins Website source code (Version 1.0). Zenodo. https://doi.org/10.5281/ zenodo.2598492.

Perry S (2019) The enchantment of the archaeological record. European J Archaeol 22(1). https:// doi.org/10.1017/eaa.2019.24

Pett D (In press) Digital humanities and the british museum: a short lived experiment? In: Goldstein L, Watrall E (eds) Digital heritage and archaeology in practice. University Press of Florida, Gainesville

Reilly P (2015) Additive archaeology: an alternative framework for recontextualising archaeological entities. Open Archaeol 1(1). https://doi.org/10.1515/opar-2015-0013

Stutz LN (2018) A future for archaeology. In: Defense of an intellectually engaged, collaborative and confident archaeology. Norwegian Archaeol Rev 51:1–2, 48–56. https://doi.org/10.1080/002 93652.2018.1544168

Tringham R (2019) Giving voices (without words) to prehistoric people: glimpses into an archaeologist's imagination. Eur J Archaeol 22(3):338–353. https://doi.org/10.1017/eaa.2019.20

Uwajeh P, Timothy I (2016) Visual art and arts therapy for healing in hospital environments. Int J Manag Appl Sci (IJMAS) 2(2):159–165. https://doi.org/10.1258/jrsm.2010.100256

Wexler J (2016) Ancestors in the rock: a new evaluation of the development and utilisation of rock-cut tombs in copper age sicily (4000–3000 Cal BC). In: Nash G, Townsend A (eds) Decoding Neolithic Atlantic and Mediterranean Island Ritual. Oxbow Books, Oxford, Philadelphia, pp 187–201. http://www.jstor.org/stable/j.ctvh1dwb7.17

Wexler J, Bevan A, Bonacchi C, Keinan-Schoonbaert A, Pett D, Wilkin N (2015) Collective re-excavation and lost media from the last century of british prehistoric studies. J Contemp Archaeol Media Archaeol Forum 2(1). https://doi.org/10.1558/jca.v2i1.27124

Wilson PF, Stott J, Warnett J, Attridge A, Smith M, Williams P (2017) Evaluation of touchable 3D-printed replicas in museums. Curator Museum J 60(4). https://onlinelibrary.wiley.com/doi/ epdf/10.1111/cura.12244

Wong A (2015) The whole story, and then some: 'digital storytelling' in evolving museum practice, https://mw2015.museumsandtheweb.com/paper/the-whole-story-and-then-some-digital-storytelling-in-evolving-museum-practice/. Accessed 16 Dec 2019

Chapter 22
The Face of Stonehenge: 3D Surface Scanning, 3D Printing and Facial Reconstruction of the Winterbourne Stoke Cranium

Oscar Nilsson, Tom Sparrow, Andrew D. Holland, and Andrew S. Wilson

Abstract Stonehenge is one of the world's most iconic archaeological sites and yet we know relatively little about the people that created this important prehistoric monument. This chapter contributes to this narrative by reconstructing the face of a high-status male who was recovered during nineteenth-century excavation of a Neolithic Long Barrow. Situated in the barrow cemetery at Winterbourne Stoke, this site is important to the contextual setting and contemporary development of Stonehenge as a ceremonial and ritual centre. The chapter reports on the combination of digital bioarchaeology and visual heritage methods, together with forensic reconstruction, that transformed the physical remains of the individual into digital data that was manipulated for 3D printing; and subsequent anatomical and visual art interpretation to yield physical life-like characteristics. His facial features have been rebuilt on the 3D printed skull, muscle by muscle, to create a highly realistic face from the era. The aim of this project was to provide a tangible connection to the archaeology of the Stonehenge landscape and to the people that developed its ceremonial and ritual significance—narrowing the temporal distance through the emotional experience it means to gaze into the eyes of a Neolithic individual.

Keywords Facial reconstruction · Forensics · Neolithic · Stonehenge

22.1 Introduction

In 2012 English Heritage commissioned work to create a facial reconstruction of a Neolithic man found in 1863 at Winterbourne Stoke Long Barrow near Stonehenge. This would form part of the planned new visitor centre at Stonehenge which opened

O. Nilsson
OD Nilsson, The Sculptors Studio, Stockholm, Sweden

T. Sparrow · A. D. Holland · A. S. Wilson (✉)
Visualising Heritage/Biological Anthropology Research Centre, School of Archaeological and Forensic Sciences, University of Bradford, Bradford, England
e-mail: A.S.Wilson2@bradford.ac.uk

© Springer Nature Switzerland AG 2022
E. Ch'ng et al. (eds.), *Visual Heritage: Digital Approaches in Heritage Science*,
Springer Series on Cultural Computing,
https://doi.org/10.1007/978-3-030-77028-0_22

in December 2013. The Visualising Heritage team at the University of Bradford was contacted by English Heritage because of our pioneering digital bioarchaeology 3D scanning work with the Jisc-funded project *Digitised Diseases* (Digitised Diseases 2013; Wilson 2014). Similarly, Oscar Nilsson had developed a portfolio of work, including the facial reconstruction of sailors from Henry VIII's flagship, the Mary Rose (Burton 2014). The project brief was to scan, and 3D print the cranium to facilitate the life-like facial reconstruction of this individual for display.

The choice of this particular individual was guided by the good state of preservation of his remains; and the fact that he was clearly an individual of great importance for his society and the Stonehenge environs, having been buried in a prominent Neolithic long barrow at Winterbourne Stoke (Bewley et al. 2005), some 500 years before the first stone circles were erected.

Both 3D scanning at the University of Bradford, and Oscar's initial contact with the skeleton from Winterbourne Stoke in Portsmouth, occurred in the spring of 2013. Lasting impressions of these first encounters included how striking and distinctive the skull appeared, with rather beautiful squarish features in the oblong facial skeleton, and also the variance in recording practice evidenced by the accession numbers, notes and other classifications written all over in black ink, in comparison with the ethical treatment of human remains today.

The skeleton was excavated in 1863 when archaeology was dominated by Anti-quarians, and the remains have had an interesting and varied history since—eventually being curated within the Duckworth Collection, at the Leverhulme Centre for Human Evolutionary Studies, University of Cambridge. Over the years, various labels and accession numbers had been added to the remains (Fig. 22.1) and any labelling today would be much more discrete to ensure that metric data is not compromised, and mindful of the ethical treatment of human remains. The remains have now been returned close to where they were originally buried and are on display (on long term loan) at the Stonehenge visitor centre along with the facial reconstruction discussed here.

Whilst your face is not much larger than your open hand its enormous psycho-logical importance cannot be overestimated. Your identity is strongly tied to it, your emotions are expressed through it, and every day you read reactions to it in the faces of the people around you. We have no reason to believe that these things worked differently in Neolithic times as they are fundamental human responses within any social group.

The work of a facial reconstructor for archaeology sometimes exposes one to human skeletal remains that could be described as objectified artefacts. It is easy to forget that these were a live individual, with thoughts and emotions. One of the main reasons why this work is important, is to bring some of the humanity and dignity back to the individual.

At the opening of the Stonehenge Visitor Centre in December 2013 it was noted that the glass of the large showcase was neatly polished, but that there were a few fingerprints on the glass surface here and there—evidence that visitors had tried to get as close as possible to view the skeletal remains on the other side of the glass, alongside the facial reconstruction of the individual from Winterbourne Stoke.

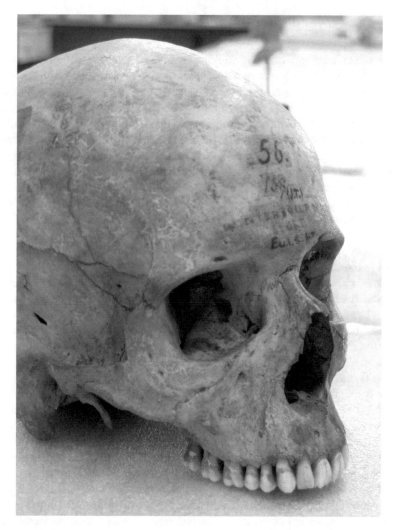

Fig. 22.1 Photograph showing the cranium of the individual from Winterbourne Stoke (A. Wilson)

A highly realistic, reconstructed face gives the audience an experience of meeting the person in life. This demands a very high degree of realism, but when it succeeds, it affords the viewer an emotional response. You cannot be neutral to a face you're allowed to study so closely. Who was he? What were his thoughts? His feelings? These questions probably arise in every visitor's mind, regardless of age, background or cultural belonging. We will never know who he was, and we will never know his thoughts or feelings, of course, but as this chapter will describe, it is possible to get a detailed image of, and come close to, his physical appearance.

22.2   Background/Literature Review

Digital bioarchaeology, bridging biological anthropology with digital or visual heritage methods, has emerged as a discipline within the last decade with the arrival of significant online resources, including work by the Visualising Heritage team at the University of Bradford (Wilson 2014; Wilson et al. 2017a,b; www.digitiseddis eases.org). This is also evidenced in a growing number of edited texts on the subject (Errickson and Thompson 2017; Seguchi and Dudzik 2019). Ethical considerations relating to the display of human remains have also explored digital bioarchaeological evidence (Hassett 2018) and devised a WAC resolution on best practice (Hassett et al 2018). In some situations, restrictions on 3D printing have been an important issue based upon the nature of the collection, or the wishes of the Trustees (Ulguim 2018), although the potential of such work is being explored in forensic applications (Walls and Errickson 2020). These constraints have, in part, meant that less attention has been paid to innovations that have responded to opportunity to provide high-fidelity data from bioarchaeological evidence.

A facial reconstruction rebuilds a face from a skull. The reconstructor, executing the reconstruction, must have anatomical knowledge, scientific data as well as artistic skills. It is an interdisciplinary field that mixes science and art. The technique has been used to bring archaeological remains to life. To literally give a human face to people from the past allows history to come to life, and is personalised as individuals become visible. Notable examples include the face of Philip II of Macedonia, Ötzi, Richard III and Tutankhamun all of which have been re-created by variants of this approach, ranging from fully analogue methods, to fully digital methods (Gerasimov 1971; Neave and Prag 1999; Taylor 2001; Wilkinson 2009). In 1895 the anatomist Wilhelm His claimed to have identified the remains of the composer Johann Sebastian Bach using measurements of tissue depth in the face, and then applying these on the presumed skull, (Wilkinson 2008; Zegers et al 2009). This was one of the first attempts to undertake such a task and has recently been revisited.

The technique, more than 100 years old, is also used by the police today and facial reconstruction of an unidentified victim can provide the police with vital tips that lead to a resolution of the case. The technique itself is based on facial tissue depth measurements taken on individuals at anatomical points of the head, and has been developed and refined by anatomists, scientists and artists working together (Gibson 2008; Gray 1974; Petrén 1972; Rauber-Kopsch 1916, 1955; Gerasimov 1971; Krogman 1939; Baleuva and Lebendiskaya 1991). More recently, the potential of whole genome sequencing offers scope to assess eye and hair colour and other traits which would otherwise be regarded as rather speculative (Rasmussen et al 2010). Collectively this work does, of course, increase the accuracy of reconstructions considerably.

22.3   Methods

Here we present an approach that draws from digital capture to create a 3D model
that provided the basis for a traditional facial reconstruction that combines accurate
data, with realism and aesthetics to evoke a response from the public within a high
profile museum display. The 3D surface morphology of the skull was captured using
an arm-based laser scanner—the FARO Quantum Arm with a V3 Laser Line Probe
(FARO) at the University of Bradford by the Visualising Heritage team. The surface
colour information ('texture' imagery) was collected separately using conventional
photography and then combined with the 3D models from the laser scanner to produce
a high-fidelity model of the skull.

The scans were recorded using the Polyworks software suite (InnovMetric) with
the IMAlign module with the FARO Laser Line Probe (Fig. 22.2). During each
'scan pass', the point cloud was meshed as it was being captured, to help with the
visualisation of the scan progress to the user. Scanning was optimised to the average
surface colour prior to scanning, using the exposure and noise filtering threshold level
functions within the FARO Laser Line Probe plugin, because the surface colour of
an object being scanned can have a strong influence on the quality of the laser return.
Multiple scan passes were made over the skull to ensure good capture of the full
surface. To minimise the alignment error between the point clouds of the individual
scan passes, a best fit alignment algorithm was applied using an iterative least squares
method and until a user selected convergence between each point cloud of 0.000001
was achieved.

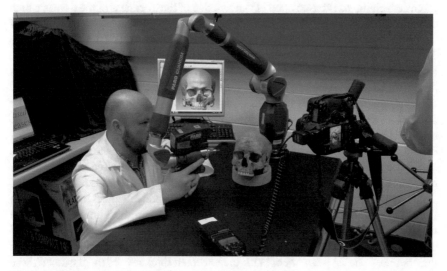

Fig. 22.2. 3D capture of the Winterbourne Stoke Cranium using the FARO Quantum Arm with
V3 laser (A. Wilson)

The resultant point cloud for the skull was rendered out to a 3D meshed surface model in the IMMerge module of the Polyworks software suite, using a 0.05 mm surface sampling step and a low smoothing pass. The IMMerge meshing algorithm sub-samples the combined point cloud, and averages the points within each 0.05 mm domain. The point clouds were then meshed using a Delaunay triangulation method to produce the 3D surface model in .OBJ format.

Since the FARO laser scanner utilises a red laser it was unable to capture the colour of the object's surface. To provide the surface colour information for the final 3D model, conventional photography was used. A Nikon D300s was used to provide multiple overlapping high-quality images and complete surface coverage of the skull. The lighting conditions were strictly controlled and diffused to reduce specular highlights and strong shadows that would otherwise appear on the surface of the final 3D object. All the photography was colour corrected using a colour card to provide accurate colour reproduction. These texture images then had to be applied to the 3D mesh to form the final 3D image of the original object. This is a highly skilled process, called UV mapping and texturing, UV mapping was carried out in Maya (Autodesk). The 3D data and each digital photograph were then manually aligned in Mudbox (Autodesk) and the colour information was transferred from the digital photograph to the 3D model's mapped texture file by 'painting' the photograph onto the 3D model's corresponding areas with a brush tool. Figure 22.3 shows the final model produced from the scanning and texturing process. The scanning process was not able to fully capture the surface of the skull, as can be seen in the detail shown within the eye sockets (Fig. 22.4).

In order to reconstruct a face from a cranium, the reconstruction of a face using forensic techniques is based upon (1) knowledge of the thickness of the tissues which consists of the muscles, fat and skin surrounding the skull, and (2) reconstruction of the facial muscles. Reconstructions are very seldom carried out on the original skulls. They are often fragile, and from a conservator's perspective it would be unacceptable to see the fragile skull surface covered with clay, risking potential damage. So, it is necessary to get a replica of the skull onto which the reconstruction can be carried out by generating a 3D prototype as described above. The biological profile of the remains is important—age, sex and ancestry are the sorts of questions that need to be answered before the process of reconstructing the face can begin. All these factors have a bearing on being able to estimate the facial tissue thickness. Assumptions have to be made as to the weight of the individual, based on possible evidence of, for instance, malnutrition as witnessed from the bones and studies of muscle attachments.

Over the past 100 years, standard measurements of skin thickness have been taken from 32 landmarks—representing very precise points on the human face. These measurements (accurate to within a quarter of a millimetre) are then transferred onto wooden or plastic pegs and placed on those precise spots on the prototype of the cranium. The 32 pegs, then, mark the expected thickness of the tissue on these crucial facial points. The next stage involves reconstructing the muscles, the face being built up muscle by muscle from the inside and working outwards. Simply put, the muscles and tissue of the face are sculpted, and the pegs are used as a basic guideline to determine how thick the sculpting clay should be applied. The shape of

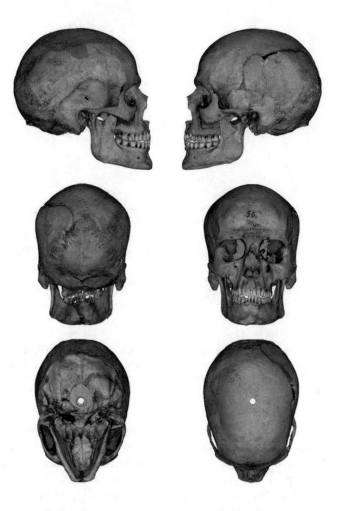

Fig. 22.3 Orthographic images of the scanned and textured model showing the old labels and accession numbers (T. Sparrow)

the nose can be decided by examining the size of the nasal cavity, its direction and bone structure. The lower third of the nasal bone, and the anterior nasal spine, are of great interest as they give a rough indication of the general shape of the nose. It is also possible to predict the shape of the mouth. The teeth are closely examined, as the design of the mouth relies heavily on the dental pattern. The front six teeth in both the upper and lower jaw are of great significance and are closely studied and measured. For example, the width of the mouth corresponds approximately to the width between the maxillary canine teeth.

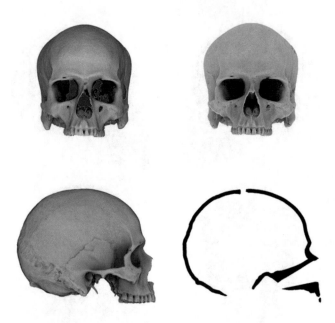

Fig. 22.4 Untextured orthographic images, top left shows the raw mesh from the scanning process, with the edges of the mesh highlight in red, top right shows the edited mesh, with the hole filled eye sockets. Bottom left shows the edited mesh, with a cross section on the right showing the internal structure which allow it to be 3D printed (T. Sparrow)

When the eyeballs (often prosthetic eyes) are placed in the sockets, the depth of the orbit as well as the character of the bones surrounding it should be studied. The protrusion of the eyes is determined by studying the bone above and below the orbit, as well as the depth of the orbit. Seen in profile, an eyeball of average protrusion should be placed so that the iris of the eye touches a tangent taken from the bone just above and just below the orbit. The ears are more speculative, as is the colour of the eyes and hair, though with whole genome sequencing even eye colour can be predicted.

22.4 Results and Discussion

22.4.1 Creating a High-Fidelity Printable 3D Model

The primary purpose of undertaking the scanning was to produce a 3D print to form the base of the 3D facial reconstruction. Whilst all the key areas were captured as part of the scanning process, the resultant model needed further processing and editing, in order for it to be able to be 3D printed. It is perhaps more commonplace to produce 3D models of crania from CT imagery, which captures the whole object and allows a model to be produced with both the internal and external surfaces. However, because this model was produced via laser scanning, only the external surfaces that are visible to the FARO Laser Line Probe are captured.

In order to be able to 3D print the 'skull' the model needed to be made watertight, i.e. without holes. Two options were considered for printing—the first would have been to fill all the holes in the model and print as a solid object, or the second option was to give the model a 'wall' thickness and produce a model with a cavity similar to a real skull. The second option was chosen as this was considered the most likely to achieve an aesthetically better looking and more stable print, and required less of the polyamide polymer as the skull was printed using laser sintering. During the printing process, powdered polyamide is fused using a laser layer by layer. If the print is solid or the wall thickness is too big, the thermal mass produced during printing can cause stresses within the model, which may lead to fractures forming, as the unfused polyamide powder that supports the subsequent layers act as an insulator.

The process of hole-filling and creating the interval structure of the skull was carried out using Mimics base/3-Matic (Materialise) and Magics (Materialise). When working with surface scan data, the resultant meshes may not necessarily produce valid 3D data that can be 3D printed, so some level of data clean-up and editing is always necessary, and depending on the object or materials being scanned, this can be relatively minor, or can require major editing. In this instance, the teeth needed some significant editing because of the enamel opacity, which does not produce good scan data. This is due to the sub-surface scattering of the laser within the tooth, which causes multiple layers in the resultant point cloud with interlinkages made during the meshing process. This could have been reduced at the point of capture, by applying a fine powder to the surface (although this would not have been seen as good conservation practice), or as in this case dealt with in post-processing of the data.

Hole-filling is the processing used to in-fill voids or lack of data within the triangulated mesh to create a complete closed surface. This was carried out by bridging the data and where possible following the surface contours of the surrounding data to produce a smooth surface within the Materialise software (Figs. 22.4 and 22.5). Where possible, and where appropriate, these were done so as not to affect the anatomically important areas used in facial reconstruction. However, there were some situations where for practical modelling and printing reasons the finish is not entirely anatomically correct, such as within the eye sockets where the fissures and optical canal were blanked off. Similarly, the internal nasal passages were simplified to help with 3D printing of the fine bone surfaces within the nose, which would have otherwise been too thin and weak to 3D print. The completed model was sent for 3D printing by CRDM in natural colour PA12 polyamide, with a C3 finish—consisting of all powder removed and a light grit blast finish (Fig. 22.6).

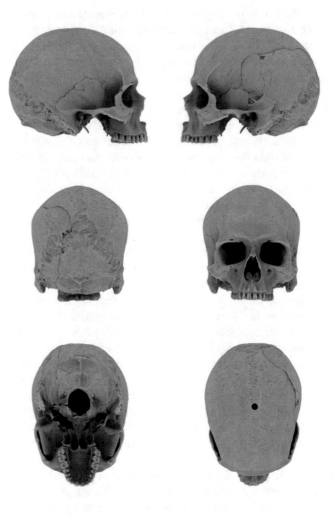

Fig. 22.5 Edited scan data ready for 3D printing (T. Sparrow)

22.4.2 Reconstructing the Face of Winterbourne Man

The high-fidelity approach developed by the Visualising Heritage team was fundamental to the success of this reconstruction. A skull offers many clues as to how
the face that once covered it was shaped. A cranium provides the framework for the
uniqueness of our facial appearance—offering clues to your age, sex, ethnicity and
health. In order to achieve individuality, a face itself can represent emotion and the
aim is to achieve the individuality of the face from the skull itself. When used by
the police in order to identify victims of crime, the rate of cases solved is usually

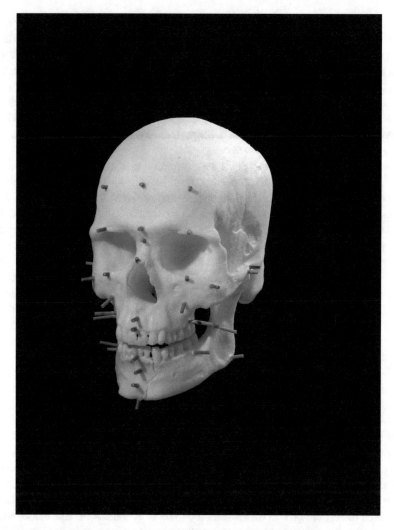

Fig. 22.6   Placement of wooden pegs on the 3D printed cranium (O. Nilsson)

around 60% upwards. The most authentic aspects, of course, are the proportions of the face, i.e. the relation for example between the mouth, eyes and nose. The shape of the face is evident within the skull, and the means by which the nose is predicted is also highly reliable.

Bioarchaeological evidence undertaken by Dr Simon Mays at English Heritage suggests that the man from Winterbourne Stoke was taller than average, reaching an adult height of 172 cm, and had a fairly slender build. His estimated age of death is not more than between 25 and 40 years. No cause of death could be established and there was no evidence of severe illness or other stress markers (Ceurstemont 2014).

His teeth showed much lighter wear than many other examples from this period and he seems to have consumed a much less coarse diet than was normal at the time. Isotope analysis also revealed that his diet consisted of a much higher percentage of meat and dairy produce than would normally be expected at the time (Ceurstemont 2014). Analysis of his teeth tells us that he probably grew up in the Wales area and also shows that as a two-year-old boy he moved to an area of chalk geology, probably the Wiltshire region. During his childhood, he seems to have moved back and forth between those two areas. Associated dating evidence was used to suggest that he was born roughly around 5,500 years ago.

On initial receipt of the 3D print it was important to spend time simply studying the replica of the skull in order to become familiar with his cranial individuality, or more simply put, what made his skull special and different from others. Each skull has its own characteristics, and it is often the most striking feature that stay in your mind after an initial examination. This individual's skull was clearly masculine, and the most striking aspect was the oblong shape of the facial skeleton. The orbits were square in shape, with the supraorbital ridge unusually straight and horizontal. The facial skeleton gave a profiled impression when seen from above, with the maxilla protruding and the chin being clearly marked and pointy. Once this procedure of getting acquainted was completed, it was necessary to choose a suitable table of tissue depth measurement for the Winterbourne man, corresponding to the assumptions of his sex, age, ancestry and weight and 3 mm thick wooden pegs were measured, cut and placed on the skull.

The hair and eye colour, where unknown, is of course the most speculative part of the work but essential to the appearance. It is not, however, a matter of producing a portrait that corresponds in every detail. But the likelihood is that the subject's family and friends would recognise the person in a reconstruction. The choice of eye colour is always a matter of some delicacy. When there is no genetic data available, one has to rely on qualified guesses. The decision was passed to researchers at English Heritage who considered that hazel brown was an appropriate tone to use. When prosthetic eyes are used in reconstructions, the orbits are studied closely to assess whether the orbital profile is of normal or abnormal form. In the case of the Winterbourne Stoke individual the orbital profile was considered to be of average form and shape, with a depth profile that would have seen a normal protrusion of the eyeballs (Fig. 22.7).

Following study, it was decided that his eyes were most probably slanting just slightly upwards, which is a quite common feature. The evidence for this was found in the lateral region of his orbits: the malar tubercle. This small lump, that together with the lacrimal fossa determines the slope of the eye fissure, was in a quite common location. The eyes were fixed in their sockets and eyelids sculpted around them. His horizontal and straight supraorbital rim gave indications on how the upper eyelid as well as the eyebrows would have been shaped, following the same direction and shape.

The human face is built up of many muscles, and plasticine clay was used to shape about twenty of the major muscle groups. After careful studies of the muscle attachments on his bone, the Winterbourne man's skull was slowly covered by one facial muscle after another. According to the osteological analysis he had fairly

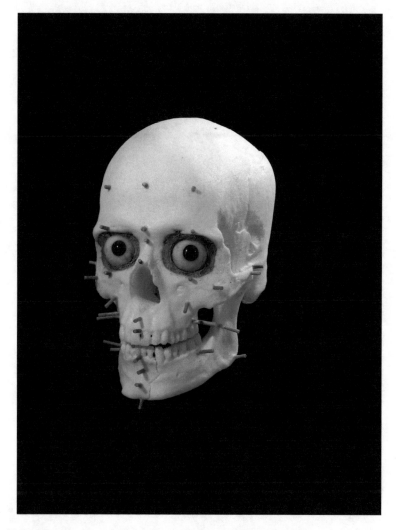

Fig. 22.7.   3D print with eyeballs in place within the orbits (O. Nilsson)

slender build, although his masseter muscles and temporalis muscles were probably quite well developed (Fig. 22.8).

It is not normally advisable to provide a reconstruction with dramatic facial mimicry or distinct expressions, because this can influence the way in which you might view and potentially describe the personality of an individual, instead of objectively reconstructing a face. It is important to stress that a reconstruction can only deal with the physical characteristics and the character and personal qualities of the subject can never be determined through this technique. The aim is to 'find' the face, rather than create it. The reconstruction technique and the skull should decide the

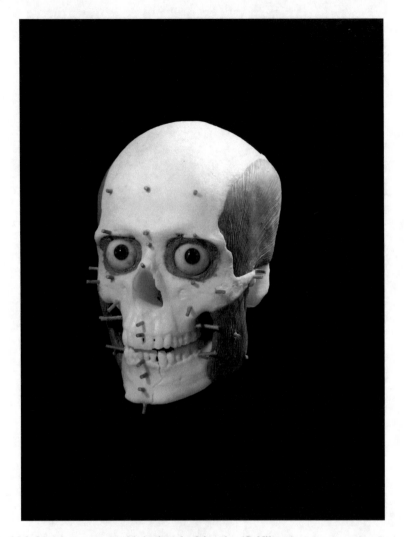

Fig. 22.8 Muscle groups are added using plasticine clay (O. Nilsson)

result. The Winterbourne man was provided with a focused expression, with peering eyes gazing into the landscape to convey a sense of presence.

Looking at an ancient skull, people are often fascinated by the condition of the teeth. They often seem unharmed despite the many thousands of years being buried in the ground. In this case, this impression was even more striking. The mouth looked strong, beautiful without any missing teeth.

The six front teeth in the upper jaw and the six front teeth in the lower jaw are the most important when reconstructing the mouth. In short, the dental pattern shapes the appearance of the mouth. From a profile view, his maxilla is a bit protrusive with a slight overbite. The rather large teeth together with a prominent dental profile indicated that this man had a quite prominent mouth, a bit broad with large lips (Fig. 22.9).

Having studied the nasal cavity and the bones surrounding it, it was possible to conclude that the Winterbourne man's nose would have been of normal size, with a quite straight profile. However, the angle of the nasal bone was quite prominent, and his profile in life would have been a normal sized nose distinctly projecting from the oblong face. The width of his nasal cavity indicated a normal- to large-sized width of nose. This harmonised with the size of his well-defined nasal spine, indicating a bit roundly shaped with a marked nose tip (Fig. 22.10).

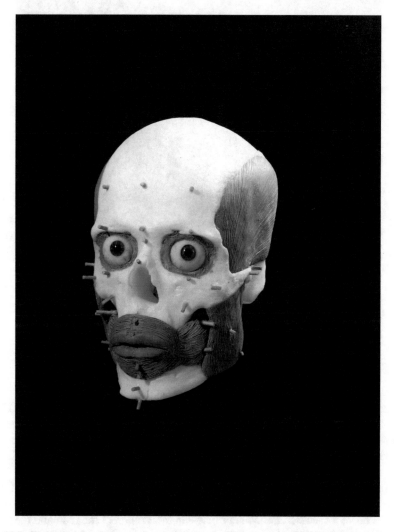

Fig. 22.9 Major facial muscle groups are added to the 3D printed cranium (O. Nilsson)

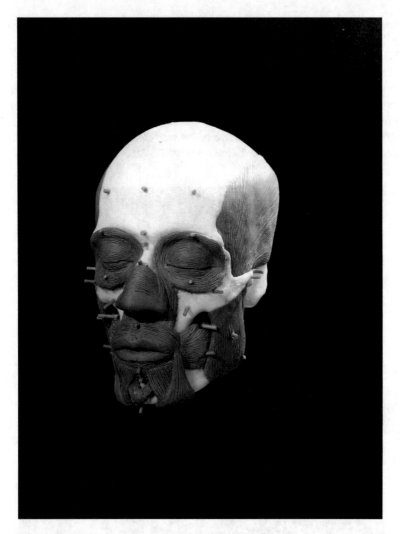

Fig. 22.10 Showing the shape of the face emerging (O. Nilsson)

Centred from his auditory canal, the ears were sculpted to harmonise with the rest of the face. Below and behind the auditory canal the cranium showed a quite prominent mastoid process. This indicated ears slightly larger than average, although it is necessary to keep in mind that ears are notoriously hard to predict with any accuracy in a reconstruction (Fig. 22.11).

After the facial muscles and subcutaneous fat were sculpted, a thin layer of clay representing the skin was laid upon the face (Fig. 22.12).

To achieve a successful encounter between the Winterbourne man and the audience, the creation of a highly realistic impression was needed. Using small needles, the skin was textured with small pores and wrinkles. A nerve-wracking job, but with a

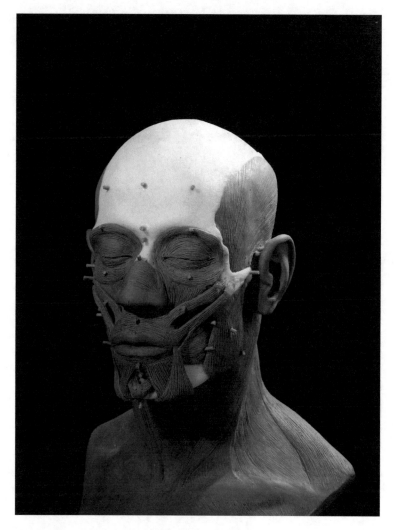

Fig. 22.11 The ears are added to the reconstruction (O. Nilsson)

rewarding result. Once the face was finished, plaster moulds were made, from which the head was cast using skin coloured silicon. Silicon is an ideal material for imitating skin: it is somewhat translucent, just like our skin, and hair can be punched into it. The illusion of hair growing out from the silicon can be made very convincing. The silicon was painted with a mixture of pigments and silicon. As we have good reason to believe that people in the Neolithic spent more time outdoors than we do today, the Winterbourne man's skin was pigmented to look a little weathered and tanned by the sun. The hair colour chosen was dark brown with some red tones although no DNA information on the colours of his hair, eyes and skin were available, so these decisions were best-guess approximations.

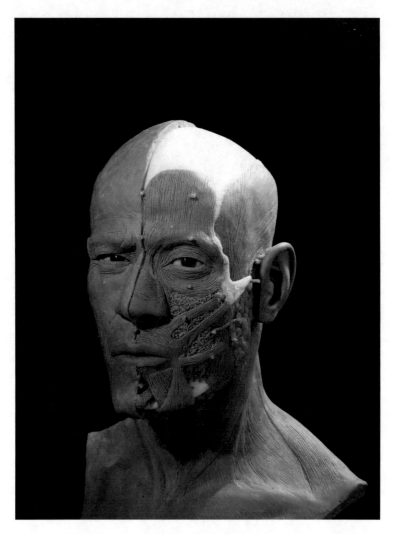

Fig. 22.12 Thin layer of clay representing the skin was laid upon the face (O. Nilsson)

Real human hair was punched into the silicon on the scalp. Seen in profile, the hairline should not encroach onto the vertical area of the forehead according to the reconstruction technique. This gave the Winterbourne man a quite low set hairline. This was however compensated by a slightly receding hairline (a pure speculation) and a beard of 20–30 mm was also punched into the silicon, hair by hair (Fig. 22.13).

The eyebrows and the eyelashes were glued onto the silicon, because it is easier to retain precision this way. His clothes were made from goat skin, gently coloured to match the rest of the reconstruction (Fig. 22.14).

Fig. 22.13   Hair was added to the silicon cast (O. Nilsson)

22.5   Conclusions

In order to make a faithful facial reconstruction a highly accurate 3D model is necessary. This chapter has outlined the steps taken using surface scanning methods, as opposed to CT scanning, in order to generate an accurate base model for significant public benefit.

Whilst a facial reconstruction is not supposed to be a portrait in the traditional sense, it can be considered to be a reflection of the face in a somewhat unpolished and blurred mirror. The technique is often referred to as facial approximation, and

Fig. 22.14 Final finishing and dressing of the completed facial reconstruction (Used with kind permission of Claire Kendall)

that is because whilst the details are not precisely established, the overall shape, the proportions and the individuality of the face can be re-created with high precision. With the use of new techniques including whole genome sequencing (Rasmussen et al. 2010), the quality of reconstructions is improving constantly, and the details are becoming more precise and accurate.

The most certain features and characteristics of this individual's face is the overall shape and the relationship between the features, as in any human face. What is clearly individual in this case, is the oblong face and its profiled contour, when observed from above. From a profile perspective his nose would have been a distinctive feature, projecting at a characteristic angle from the rest of the face. The horizontally directed eyebrows also would have been an individual features of some note. Less certain are the ears, as the technique to reconstruct those with accuracy is somewhat deficient. Purely speculative aspects include the colouring of his eyes, hair and skin, as well as his hairstyle, including his receding hairline and beard.

The most common question encountered is: 'How close did you get to the original face?' As the use of such reconstructions in criminal cases may result in the resolution of up to 60% or more of cases, then it seems reasonable so suggest that, in this case, there would have been enough individual features for his family and friends to recognise him. Whilst such a statement is hypothetical, as his family and friends are now long gone, it is true that approximately 1.6 million visitors to Stonehenge have come face to face with this man's iconic features during 2019 alone, and they have come to know and recognise him (Luty 2020).

References

Balueva TS, Lebedinskaya GV (1991) Anthropological reconstruction. Russian Academy of Sciences, Moscow

Bewley RH et al (2005) New light on an ancient landscape: lidar survey in the Stonehenge World Heritage Site. Antiquity 79(305):636–647

Burton A (2014) The mary rose museum: the story continues.... Pitkin Publishing, Stroud

Ceurstemont S (2014) Stonehenge Man: not just a pretty face. New Scientist 221(2951):49

Digitised Diseases (2013) www.digitiseddiseases.org. Accessed Dec 2013/Nov 2020

Errickson D, Thompson T (eds) (2017) Human remains: another dimension. The application of imaging to the study of human remains. Academic Press, Elsevier, London

Gerasimov M (1971) The face finder. Hutchinson & Co Ltd., London

Gibson L (2008) Forensic art essentials. Academic Press, Elsevier

Gray H (1974) Anatomy, descriptive and surgical. Running Press, Philadelphia, Pennsylvania

Hassett B (2018) Which bone to pick: creation, curation, and dissemination of online 3D digital Bioarchaeological data. Archaeologies 14:231–324

Hassett BR, Rando C, Bocaege E, Durruty MA, Hirst C, Smith S, Ulguim PF, White S, Wilson AS (2018) Transcript of WAC 8 digital Bioarchaeological ethics panel discussion, 29 August 2016 and resolution on ethical use of digital bioarchaeological data. Archaeologies 14(2):317–337

Krogman W (1939) Facing facts of face growth. Am J Orthod Oral Surg 25(8):724–731

Luty J (2020) Number of visitors to Stonehenge in England 2010–2019. https://www.statista.com/statistics/586843/stonehenge-visitor-numbers-united-kingdom-uk/. Accessed 25 Aug 2020

Neave R, Prag J (1999) Making faces—using forensic and archaeological evidence. British Museum Press, London

Petrén T (1972) Anatomi 1—Rörelseapparaten. Gummessons boktryckeri. Falköping

Rasmussen M, Li YR, Lindgreen S, Pedersen JS, Albrechtsen A, Moltke I, Metspalu M, Metspalu E, Kivisild T, Gupta R, Bertalan M, Nielsen K, Gilbert MTP, Wang Y, Raghavan M, Campos PF, Kamp HM, Wilson AS, Willerslev E et al (2010) Ancient human genome sequence of an extinct Palaeo-Eskimo. Nature 463(7282):757–762

Rauber-Kopsch (1916) Lehrbuch der Anatomie. Verlag von Georg Thieme, Leipzig

Rauber-Kopsch (1955) Lehrbuch und Atlas der Anatomie des Menschen. Georg Thieme Verlag, Stuttgart

Seguchi N, Dudzik B (eds) (2019) 3D data acquisition for bioarchaeology, forensic anthropology, and archaeology. Academic Press

Sobotta-Becher (1957) Atlas der deskriptiven Anatomie des Menschen. Urban & Schwarzenberg, München-Berlin

Spalteholz W (1903) Handatlas der Anatomie des Menschen. Verlag von S. Hirzel, Leipzig

Taylor KT (2001) Forensic art and illustration. CRC Press, Boca Raton

Ulguim P (2018) Models and metadata: the ethics of sharing bioarchaeological 3d models online. Archaeologies 14:189–22

Walls R, Errickson D (2020) An overview of 3D printing in forensic science: The tangible third dimension. J Forensic Sci. https://doi.org/10.1111/1556-4029.14442

Wilkinson C (2009) Forensic facial reconstruction. Cambridge University Press, Cambridge

Wilkinson C (2008) Building the face of Bach. http://app.dundee.ac.uk/pressreleases/2008/prfeb08/bach.html. Accessed 25 Aug 2008

Wilson AS (2014) *Digitised diseases*: preserving precious remains. Br Archaeol 136:36–41

Wilson AS, Holland AD, Sparrow T (2017a) Chapter 9—Laser scanning of skeletal pathological conditions. In T Thompson and D. Errickson (eds) Human remains: another dimension: the application of imaging to the study of human remains. Academic Press, Cambridge, pp 123–134. https://doi.org/10.1016/B978-0-12-804602-9.00010-2

Wilson AS, Manchester K, Buckberry J, Storm R, Croucher KT (2017b) Digitised diseases: seeing beyond the specimen to understand disease and disability in the past. In: Tilley L, Schrenk AA (eds) New developments in the bioarchaeology of care: further case studies and expanded theory. Springer Nature, Basel, pp 301–315

Zegers R, Maas M, Koopman AG, Maat G (2009) Are the alleged remains of Johann Sebastian Bach authentic? Med J Aust 190:213–216

Chapter 23
A Framework for Sharing Cultural Heritage Objects in Hybrid Virtual and Augmented Reality Environments

Yue Li and Eugene Ch'ng

Abstract The emulation of social environments within which ideas, knowledge and interpretation are exchanged is a challenge for Extended Reality (XR) technologies. One aspect of the challenge is the concept of Extended Reality itself, and this within the broad spectrum of the physical and virtual reality continuum. As users settle down into the spectrum via their preferred devices, so must we investigate the viability of communication between users adopting different modes of XR. In this chapter, we discuss three attributes of virtual objects and explore the concept of a Hybrid Virtual and Augmented Reality (HVAR) environment. We look at how users from different realities could interact, engage and communicate in a shared space via objects. We believe that the use of HVAR environments is the way forward for connecting worlds, and that it will facilitate future communications around virtual objects, developing and flourishing across time, space and devices, much like how social media has facilitated user-generated contents, empowering individual interpretations and the formation of collective meanings. The concept of a hybrid space aims to gather communities from disparate backgrounds and cultures, and to facilitate discussions around objects of interest.

Keywords Extended reality · Virtual reality · Augmented reality · Digital heritage · Virtual heritage

Y. Li (✉)
Department of Computing, School of Advanced Technology, Xi'an Jiaotong-Liverpool University, 111 Renai Road, Suzhou, China
e-mail: yue.li@xjtlu.edu.cn

E. Ch'ng
NVIDIA Joint-Lab On Mixed Reality, University of Nottingham Ningbo China, 199 Taikang East Road, Ningbo, China
e-mail: eugene.chng@nottingham.edu.cn

E. Ch'ng et al. (eds.), *Visual Heritage: Digital Approaches in Heritage Science*,
Springer Series on Cultural Computing,
https://doi.org/10.1007/978-3-030-77028-0_23

23.1 Introduction

Prior research in Digital Heritage has seen the use of both Virtual Reality (VR) and Augmented Reality (AR) in museums, for immersive visualisation and the augmentation of virtual objects in physical spaces. These reality technologies were primarily configured for use within museums, often as an enhancement to the relics as displays are not physically accessible to visitors. Recent advances in the usability and affordability of Extended Reality (XR) technologies are also providing new opportunities for cultural heritage to be accessed outside the walls of cultural institutions (Bekele et al. 2018). However, virtual and physical objects have significant differences and it remains a challenge for XR to emulate the physical, material and social aspects of an actual museum visit. In resolving the issues, the diversity of devices preferred by users should be a factor taken into the account of designing for large audiences, this being one of the central and core ideas of visitor centricity that we believe in, in the design of XR systems. In addressing such a need, we explore the ability for users to socialise between reality technologies, by constructing an environment that can facilitate the connection of people from different worlds—a Hybrid Virtual Augmented Reality (HVAR) environment (Fig. 23.1).

VR experience is 'any in which the user is effectively immersed in a responsive virtual world' (Brooks 1999). However, AR does not replace the real world with

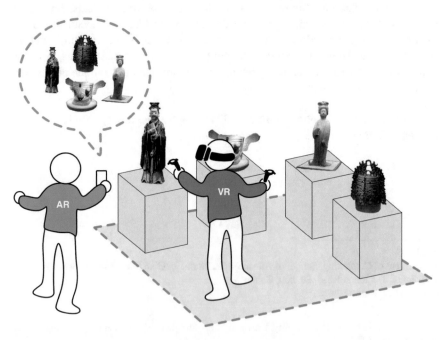

Fig. 23.1 A scenario of use in the hybrid virtual and augmented reality environment (Y. Li and E. Ch'ng)

an entirely simulated environment as VR does, but it instead combines the real and virtual to supplement the physical world with augmented objects (Azuma 1997). Both VR and AR register objects in 3D and support real-time interactions. We observed three significant trends in present VR and AR technologies. First, VR and AR have become increasingly accessible to individual users. Two decades ago, VR and AR were primarily used in institutions, organisations and research laboratories for specific visualisation research and training purposes. We have progressed to witness an increasing number of consumer-level VR and AR devices in the market that range from desktop VR Head-Mounted Displays (HMDs) to smartphones that support both VR and AR. Corporate investments and recent demands have brought VR and AR technologies to the general public and making them increasingly accessible to individual users for more general purposes, including entertainment, education, social networking, e-commerce and marketing (Cipresso et al. 2018).

Second, a growing variety of VR and AR devices will likely be supporting social interactions. When Facebook acquired Oculus in 2014, Facebook CEO Mark Zuckerberg (2014) envisioned that 'one day, this kind of immersive, augmented reality will become a part of daily life for billions of people'. VR and AR are expected to be used for social networking with mass-market adoption. Although we have yet to see such a prediction come true, industries are working towards it. Recent updates have demonstrated their potential use in the social context. For example, Oculus and Valve have both launched wireless standalone VR devices with 'inside-out tracking', such as the HTC Vive Focus (VIVE Enterprise 2018) and the Oculus Quest (Facebook 2019). This recent trend is enabling VR devices to be used in more practical scenarios and is very likely to become regularly used for sociality. Recent applications such as VRChat (VRChat Inc. 2017), AltspaceVR (Microsoft 2018) and Avatar Chat (Magic Leap 2018) have also demonstrated the potentials of VR and AR for enabling social interactions, such as personalised 3D avatars, selfies and multi-viewer 360-degree videos that replicates a cinema audience. As users adopt preferred devices between the XR spectrum, we think that it is essential to investigate social interactions that can be facilitated at the intersection of devices and across the XR spectrum.

Third, there is the merging of the real and virtual. We predict that hybridity in reality technologies will be a future trend. Speicher et al. (2019) interviewed domain experts in VR and AR as a part of their survey of XR research. Results from the interview suggest that the distinctions between AR, Mixed Reality (MR) and VR are diminishing and will continue in the trend in the coming 5–10 years. Users are likely to internalise the differences as they are exposed to more of such technologies. Researchers have also introduced ideas and frameworks of hybrid realities, such as the One Reality framework (Roo and Hachet 2017) presenting six levels of realities that incrementally bring the physical world into the virtual. VR and AR are essentially 3D interfaces that are capable of presenting information with common modalities— text, audio, video, 3D models and so on. Depending on the use case scenarios, situated environments, subjective preferences and available devices, users may opt for augmented visualisation, immersive VR experience, or a transition between the two. The line between the real and virtual is increasingly blurring and thus, hybridity in reality technologies will become a future trend.

VR and AR technologies have become accessible and affordable with a growing variety of XR devices in the consumer market. As users adopt preferred devices used for XR, the need to support open and connected social experiences become mandatory research with very practical future outcomes. In the following section, we demonstrate how virtual objects can be used as an interface between VR and AR for connecting hybrid environments. We present the Visualisation, Interaction and Presentation (VIP) Framework of Virtual Objects and the Contextual Experience Cycle of Virtual Exhibitions. We then present a design of HVAR system applying the VIP Framework of virtual objects, supported by a qualitative analysis that evaluates multiuser interactions using the Contextual Experience Cycle of Virtual Exhibitions. The theoretical contribution provides a practical foundation for the application of VR and AR both in contemporary thinking, and in the future of digital cultural heritage.

23.2 Virtual Objects—Connecting the Virtual and the Real Environments

Champion and Dave (2007) classified virtual heritage environments into three types: visualisation-based, activity-based and hermeneutic environment. The first and most common type concerns the visualisation of objects and environments in a static and immutable form, which is thus of limited use in designing environments that conserve and preserve history. The activity-based environments allow one or more users to alter some character or element in pursuit of a defined goal, with similar interactions used in computer games, such as navigation within an environment and social interaction with embodied avatars. The third type is hermeneutic environments, which emphasise on the cultural aspect and provide a depth of affordance to users' interpretation of a natively residing culture and social perspectives. Based on the classification, we further focused the attributes of virtual objects into a framework that will be used in our research. These are visualisation, interaction and presentation in the pyramid of the VIP Framework of Virtual Objects (Fig. 23.2).

Visualisation presents an authentic physical object as digital representations. This involves 3D scanning, 3D modelling and the processes involved in the reconstruction of cultural heritage objects. The processes that lead to visualisation consists of components that include 3D meshes, textures and materials, and all that determines the visual, authentic appearance of an object. Similar to physical museums, different lighting and layouts do affect an object's appearance. This process only displays objects in a static and immutable form, which is insufficient for users to understand, learn and experience cultural contents as pointed out by Caggianese et al. (2014). We felt that visualisation is merely a first step towards replicating the experience of cultural heritage.

Interaction is a major factor towards an engaging virtual heritage environment, for it provides the key affordances for virtual objects to be interactive that would otherwise be static. The intrusive handling of museum artefacts is often restricted to

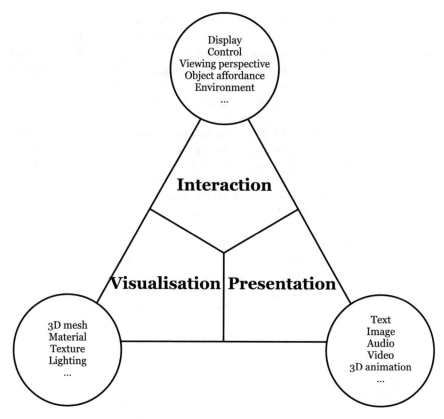

Fig. 23.2 Visualisation, interaction and presentation (VIP) framework of virtual objects (Y. Li and E. Ch'ng)

a few selected objects. Virtual objects, on the other hand, offer flexible and diverse interactions as afforded by the display and control methods of the enabling technologies. For example, Bruno et al. (2010) designed rotation and zoom-up interactions for a collection of virtual objects to allow users to observe them in 360 degrees and in detail. Ch'ng (2013) further provides affordances for objects on multi-touch tables that include simulated physical weight, gravity, physics on cloth and affordances such as the conceptual connection of objects that are not possible in the physical environment. Interactions with virtual objects support users' learning from exploratory activities (Ch'ng et al. 2020) as well as their accomplishments of goals and tasks in activity-based environments. The design of interactions is thus essential for an environment to be engaging.

Presentation is distinct from visualisation in that it provides additional data that complements the artefacts. In museums, text labels, audio guides and video clips are used to introduce an object which includes information such as its name, historical periods, measures, purpose of use, cultural influence and stories. The presentation of object information can be easily integrated into the virtual environments or embedded in virtual objects as digital technologies genuinely afford a rich array of media information. The presentation of virtual objects relates to hermeneutic richness (Champion and Dave 2007) in that it supports interpretation from users of different cultural and social perspectives. Presentation, in combination with interaction, can further facilitate meaning-making as a result of their interaction with it (Falk and Dierking 2000). The two attributes, interaction and presentation, can thus contribute to the hermeneutic virtual heritage environments.

Interactions with a virtual object are built on top of visualisation and presentation. The design of object interaction is informed by the visual appearance and physical affordances as indicated in the object's function, utilities and stories. For example, Gaitatzes et al. (2004) demonstrated the Ancient Olympic Games story with an interactive game—visitors were presented with an animation of an ancient Olympic contest once they put together the pieces of an ancient pottery vase. Such interactions can support the appreciation of an object's visual appearance (e.g., the vase) as well as the understanding of the associated information (the ancient Olympic contest). Interactions with virtual objects can support active engagement with objects within the environment. This satisfies the objective of virtual heritage research that provides educational experiences through manipulations of time and spaces (Ch'ng 2009; Stone and Ojika 2000). Therefore, we believe that it is through interaction design that we define the uniqueness and advantage of virtual objects. This should be different for each project.

23.3 Contextual Experience Cycle of Virtual Exhibitions

Interactions with objects and with other users are known to be closely linked to positive user experience within virtual exhibitions. Virtual exhibitions aim to convey meanings, significance and cultural values all within the scope of a visitor's learning experiences (Lester 2006). A useful method for understanding user-centred learning is Kolb's (1984) Experiential Learning Cycle. Kolb considers the continuum of perception and processing and identified four stages of learning: concrete experience (feeling), reflective observation (watching), abstract conceptualisation (thinking) and active experimentation (doing) (Fig. 23.3). The Experiential Learning Cycle emphasises the dominant role of an individual in the learning experience. Despite Kolb's theory being holistic and informative in understanding the cognitive learning process, it is less helpful in informing the design of interactions and the evaluation of experiences with objects and the situated environment, especially when XR becomes the focal technology. It is not clear how objects, the environments and other subjects may affect one's process of learning.

Dissimilar to the user-centred perspective that the Experiential Learning Cycle has taken, Falk and Dierking's (2000) Contextual Model of Learning highlighted the significant role that contexts play in the interactive experience with objects in museums (Fig. 23.4). They proposed that contextual considerations are significant, but often missing in traditional models of learning. Falk et al. (2006) advocated the

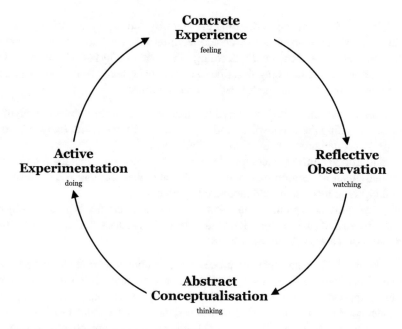

Fig. 23.3 Experiential learning cycle (Kolb 1984)

Fig. 23.4 Contextual model
of learning (Falk and
Dierking 2000)

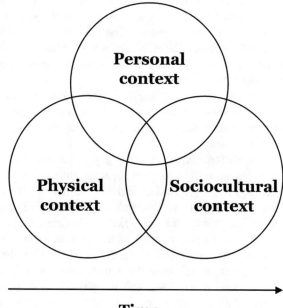

use of free-choice learning to describe the learning and experience of objects that might occur in the museum. Free-choice learning proposes nonlinear, personally motivated, and personal choices for deciding when, where, why and what to learn. The Contextual Model of Learning described learning experience as a process/product of the interactions between the following three contexts:

- **Personal context**, implying everything that the subject brings to the environment, including their motivation and expectations, interest, prior knowledge and experience, and preferences of choice and control.
- **Sociocultural context**, encompassing factors that recognise that learning is both an individual and group experience. It indicates that learning is influenced by within-group mediations and facilitated by others.
- **Physical context** explains the fact that the learning experience is rooted in objects and the situated environment. It includes the sights, sounds and smells, as well as the design features of the experience.

Dierking (2002) stated that the process of free-choice learning with objects is a situated dialogue between a subject and the environment. Over time, these three contexts support the construction of knowledge. Falk and Dierking's model supports the understanding of virtual exhibition experience as an overall process through the lens of contexts. However, it does not indicate users' subjective perception of activities during the process. Although relationships between objects, environments and other subjects were implied in the three contexts, an explicit analysis is needed to understand users' process of meaning-making. Therefore, we combined the two frameworks as the Contextual Experience Cycle of Virtual Exhibitions (Fig. 23.5).

The Contextual Experience Cycle of Virtual Exhibitions describes user experience of cultural heritage as an iterative process, segmented based on the relationship between subject, object and environment using a user-centred approach. The process involves a subject's interaction with the external environment, and the engagement with objects and environment that generates understanding. It includes communication with other subjects that invokes the expression of subjective interpretations.

Interaction refers to the direct physical actions between a subject and the external environment, such as the viewing and manipulation of objects. Virtual objects differ from physical objects in their technological affordances, such as the interaction possibilities and augmented information that are contextual to the object. Hein (1999) argued that interactions with objects allow for a constructivism approach that encourages the active participation of the visitors. Users' interactions with objects and environments are therefore a fundamental need for virtual exhibitions.

Engagement refers to the active, goal-directed, flexible, constructive, persistent, focused interactions with the physical and social environments (Furrer and Skinner 2003). While interaction concerns the physical actions of users, engagement relates their psychological states (O'Brien and Toms 2008). This means that internal thoughts and feelings are produced in the understanding of cultural heritage through engagement. Engagement primarily indicates the relationship between a subject and the objects/environments but may also involve other subjects if they are situated in

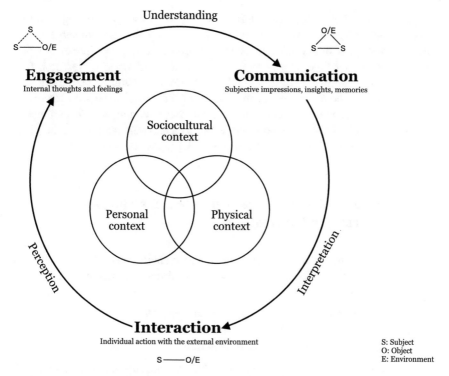

Fig. 23.5 Contextual experience cycle of virtual exhibitions (Y. Li and E. Ch'ng)

the same social environment. It refers to a quality of user experience that can reflect the subjective evaluation of a digital environment (O'Brien and Cairns 2015; O'Brien and Toms 2008). Engagement has been identified as a major factor of the success of virtual heritage, in terms of users' emotional and social connections, explorations and learning through realistic visualisations (Tost and Champion 2007).

Communication occurs when users interact with each other, and when they share thoughts and subjective interpretations. Communication plays a significant role in museum visitor experience as most visitors visit as a group in the west (Bitgood 2011) and also in the east (Ch'ng et al. 2019a). Similarly, the use of technologies should support group communication as it can form an essential part of the social environment for free-choice learning (Falk and Dierking 2000). Jacobson and Holden (2005) argued that the reconstruction and visualisation of cultural heritage should ultimately be used as an interface to develop interactive narratives and communication potentials. However, previous virtual exhibitions barely support sociality and group communication, which are nevertheless necessary for mass dissemination and use of virtual heritage (Tan and Rahaman 2009).

In Kolb's (1984) Experiential Learning Cycle, learning is the most effective when all stages are involved but that is not often the case. Similarly, the experience of virtual exhibitions is the most positive when communication and sharing are supported in parallel with object interaction, and when users can engage with the physical and social environment. In prior research, we observed that subjects may enter at any stage of the cycle and each stage is influenced by the three overlapping contexts throughout time. Our proposed framework is informed by research from two studies—a multiuser hybrid VR and AR environment with 52 paired users (Li et al. 2018), and the evaluation of the effects of VR environments on the acceptance, experience, and expectations of cultural heritage learning with 61 participants (Ch'ng et al. 2020). Further unpublished research on experimentation with hybridity contributed to the solidification of the framework proposed in this chapter.

23.4   Designing the HVAR Environments for Sharing Cultural Heritage Objects

There are three steps toward the designing of HVAR environments for the sharing of cultural heritage objects. The steps are based on the three attributes of virtual objects described in Sect. 23.2:

1. The reconstruction of virtual objects for **visualisation**
2. The preparation of virtual objects for **presentation**
3. The design of virtual objects for **interaction**.

In our particular research, we reconstructed six cultural heritage objects (Fig. 23.6) and created a multiuser environment that supports the hybrid use of VR and AR in a session that connects, in our case, two users.

We reconstructed six virtual objects using the digital close-range photogrammetry technique (Ch'ng et al. 2019b). Considering the different computing capacity of desktop VR and mobile AR, we used a simple retopology technique, a process of remeshing the geometry of a model in combination with texture-baking in a way that reduces polygon count but retains the qualitative appearance of the original model. This optimises the models for cross-platform, real-time usage in both VR and AR. The presentation information of these virtual object was collated from museums, websites and includes texts, images and audios. These processes lay a foundation for our interaction design. Table 23.1 summarises the interaction comparisons between desktop VR and mobile AR. These two types of technologies cover the two major platforms in general use, i.e., desktop and mobile, and are a good representation of the typical devices used for VR and AR. We have discussed control methods for mobile virtual exhibitions in Li et al. (2019b).

Social interaction is the key feature of our HVAR system. VR users are donned with a headset with the accompanying hand-held controllers. These provide users with full immersion and embodied interaction made possible by the tracking of movements via the headset and handheld controllers. Users interact by picking up and putting down virtual objects using the controllers within the VR environment (Fig. 23.7). On the other hand, AR users were provided with a cube consisting of six faces, each measuring 6 cm and containing an image pattern that a cultural heritage

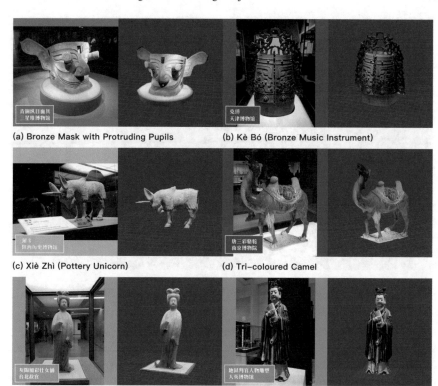

(a) Bronze Mask with Protruding Pupils (b) Kè Bó (Bronze Music Instrument)

(c) Xiè Zhì (Pottery Unicorn) (d) Tri–coloured Camel

(e) Pottery Figure of a Standing Lady (f) Figure of an Assistant to the Judge of Hell

Fig. 23.6 Cultural heritage objects side by side the physical original and the virtual copy (Y. Li and E. Ch'ng)

Table 23.1 Comparison of interaction design in desktop VR and mobile AR

	Desktop VR	Mobile AR
Display	Immersive Head-Mounted Display (HMD)	Flat-screen Hand-Held Display (HHD)
Control (Tracking)	External and built-in sensors	Camera-based tracking
Control (Inputs)	Hand-held controllers and HMD	Touchscreen
Viewing perspectives	6 DOF with tracked HMD and controller	6 DOF with tracked camera
Object affordances	Supported by body movements and navigation control	Limited support due to restricted display and control methods
Environments	Objects in simulated environments	Objects superimposed onto the real world

Fig. 23.7 VR control of virtual objects with hand-held controllers (Y. Li and E. Ch'ng)

object is augmented with (Fig. 23.8). Users view digital objects using a smartphone supporting interactions via touchscreen controls. Within the HVAR, virtual objects are used as an interface between VR and AR and the object itself becomes the connection between synchronised user interactions in HVAR. Virtual object rotations are synchronised in both environments, providing visual cues for each user on how the object is being manipulated by the other user. Aural cues are triggered when

Fig. 23.8 AR control of virtual object with the AR cube (Y. Li and E. Ch'ng)

objects are interacted with for both VR and AR. Users in both environments can converse with each other at any time during the experiment.

23.5 Evaluating the HVAR Environments for Sharing Cultural Heritage Objects

We conducted a user study on the HVAR system described in the previous section, with 52 participants at the NVIDIA Joint-Lab on Mixed Reality, at the University of Nottingham's China campus. Our user study involved paired users in each HVAR session, one in VR and the other using AR (Fig. 23.9). As part of the communication aspect of this study, participants were asked to discuss two topics during their experience of the virtual exhibition:

1. the object you like most
2. the historical chronological order of the six objects.

Our study provides an indication of how HVAR is acceptable for sharing cultural heritage objects. It demonstrates the significance of social influence on the behavioural intentions of users (see Li et al. 2018). This study also demonstrates how the social nature of museum visits can be transferred into HVAR, and how virtual objects can mediate interaction and communication. In this section, we present an in-depth qualitative analysis of the observation and interview data and evaluate user

Fig. 23.9 Paired users looking at a shared virtual object in HVAR, one in VR using the HTC Vive (right), and the other with the smartphone AR application in combination with the AR cube (Y. Li and E. Ch'ng)

interaction, engagement and communication using the Contextual Experience Cycle of Virtual Exhibitions.

We first applied the Contextual Experience Cycle of Virtual Exhibitions to understand the process of meaning-making in virtual exhibitions with a user-centred approach. We considered the personal, sociocultural and physical contexts of learning (Falk and Dierking 2000), we also analysed the relationships between objects, subjects and environments via their actions and dialogues. Finally, we mapped these data to the three stages of the framework: interaction, engagement and communication.

The snippet below describes an experience with the *Assistant to the Judge of Hell* object, where we observed communication and meaning-making between users. We begin with the AR user's interaction with the object, to the initiation of the conversation by the VR user, and through to the mutual engagement and interaction with the object. Brief personal experiences are observed.

[AR user triggered the augmentation of the Assistant to the Judge of Hell]	**I-Eo***
VR: *'Are you also looking at this one (the Assistant to the Judge of Hell)? [try to grab the object] It's heavy, I can't pick it up.'*	**I-Eo/Es-C**
AR: *[read the label] 'Yes. It is a she. So special.'*	**I-Eo/Es-C**
VR: *'What? [read the label] Oh I got it. Yeah, she even got earrings. It is special.'*	**C-I-Eo/Es-C**
AR: *'Yeah, it's rare to see ancient female statues, especially in hell.'*	**Eo/Es-C**
VR: *'British Museum. . . Why didn't I see this when I went there?'*	**Eo/Es-C**
AR: *'You won't remember everything even if you've seen it. British Museum is too big.'*	**Es-C**
[continue talking about the previous visit to the British Museum]	**Es-C**

*I: Interaction, **Eo**: Engagement with objects, **Es**: Engagement with subjects, **C**: Communication

Interaction—The AR user first triggered the augmentation of the *Assistant to the Judge of Hell* object on the cube, which resulted in the matched rotation of the same object in VR. The VR user then noticed the change in the situated environment (physical context) and proceeded to grab the object. Both users in AR and VR viewed the object (visualisation) and interacted with the information label (presentation) to understand the information of the object.

Engagement—Engagement proceeds from interaction with the virtual object, and learning occurs when individual users began to acquire knowledge on the object's properties such as its scale, weight, appearance and the host museum. The sharing of how they have understood the object is observed (sociocultural context).

Communication—Engagement between users and objects leads to personal interpretations, all of which were communicated verbally. For instance, the AR user found the object special due to the object's gender (i.e., female). The VR user then associated this observation with her previous visits to the British Museum (personal and sociocultural context).

The following example illustrates a process of meaning-making as a result of the mutual interaction of users with the *Pottery Unicorn* object. A shared understanding is created through the co-exploration of the object and its affordances. The mutual interaction with a feature of the *Pottery Unicorn* object, i.e., its horn reinforces understanding. Such a connected experience can contribute to the AR user's attempt at interpreting the object.

AR: *'Hey, go and check out the pig. It's so cute.'*	**I-Eo/Es-C**
VR: *'What pig? Xie Zhi? It's a unicorn!'*	**C-I-Eo/Es-C**
AR: *'Unicorn... I didn't know unicorn is in the Chinese culture.'*	**Eo/Es-C**
VR: *'It says that it's a beast that symbolises justice... the sinner will be killed by the horn... ' [grab and observe the horn, try to use the horn to attack the Figure of a Standing Lady]*	**I-Eo/Es-C-I**
AR: *'Be careful! Don't break it!'*	**Eo/Es-C**
VR: *'Ha-ha I just wanted to see what would happen. Clearly there is no interaction allowed here.'*	**Eo/Es-C**

Interaction—The AR user looked at the *Pottery Unicorn* object (visualisation) and proposed that the VR user move the object in the virtual environment (physical context). Both users then read the information label (presentation) to obtain information. The VR user explored affordances of the *Pottery Unicorn* object by interacting with the horn and the *Figure of a Standing Lady* object in the virtual environment. This observation suggests that there is an awareness of the physical context associated with the object.

Engagement—The AR user falsely perceived the object as a pig before the VR user, in reading the object label corrected the AR user that it is a unicorn. The AR user assumed an understanding of the object from prior knowledge about Chinese culture (personal context). The VR user, on the other hand, acquired knowledge from reading the object label (presentation), which led to the exploration of the object affordances (physical context).

Communication—Communication initiated by the AR user helped the VR user understand the object better, which contributed to further interaction within the object in the virtual environment. Furthermore, the AR user shared a personal thought, that the virtual object should not be broken and further expressed objection to the VR user's intended action (sociocultural context).

By applying the Contextual Experience Cycle of Virtual Exhibitions to the analysis of user experience in HVAR, we found that the three contexts do contribute to the collective understanding of the learning process. At the same time, the user-centred approach helps in identifying the stages of interaction, engagement and communication within the learning process, presenting the differences between VR and AR users. The experience described in the first example demonstrated how communication in the hybrid environment can contribute to learning. The second example showed how interaction and observing the partner's interaction with virtual objects influence the process of meaning-making.

Here, we summarise a list of themes and apply a theme-based content analysis (Neale and Nichols 2001) in our research to further understand the interaction, engagement and communication in the hybrid use of VR and AR. Table 23.2

Table 23.2 Interactions with objects in HVAR

Theme	User	Action and dialogue	Pair ID
Shape (5)	VR (2)	*This cow (unicorn) looks unique.*	P3
		I'm gonna use the cow (unicorn) horn to 'kill' you	P13
	AR (3)	*Hey, go and check on the pig (unicorn).*	P9
		Check on this pig (unicorn)!	P13
		The cow (unicorn) is adorable.	P16
Colour and texture (12)	VR (7)	Comment on the detailed looks of the objects (assistant and camel's colour, lady and music instrument's texture).	P1, P7, P9, P11, P18
		Try to feel the texture of the music instrument using controllers.	P14
		Why is this Tang artefact (lady) so pale? Shouldn't it be more colourful?	P22
	AR (5)	Comment on the detailed looks of the objects (mask's look, camel's colour, instrument's material).	P2, P10, P12, P19, P24
Affordance (14)	VR (13)	Put on / wear the mask.	P4, P11, P15, P20, P25
		Use the horn of the unicorn to 'attack' other objects.	P9, P11, P13, P15
		Try to put an object on the ground (camel and lady).	P18, P25
		Try to break an object and see what will happen.	P19, P20
	AR (1)	*I want to hear the sound (of the music instrument).*	P7
Size and weight (6)	VR (6)	*It (assistant) is heavy, I can't pick it up.*	P1
		It (camel) is huge.	P3
		I think this (lady) looks much smaller than the one I saw in the museum.	P9
		We should work together to lift it (assistant) up.	P25
		Feel scared when picking up the camel (because of the size).	P15, P19
Environment (8)	VR (8)	Walk around the pedestal.	P9, P21, P22
		Try to avoid bumping into an object.	P15, P19
		Try to put controllers on the virtual pedestal.	P9, P20
		Try to put multiple objects on one pedestal.	P22

sumarises the interactions in HVAR between subjects and objects, and Table 23.3 lists the engagement and communication in HVAR between subjects.

23.6 Discussion

23.6.1 Interactions with Objects

In our observation, we noted that AR user tended to interact with objects based on their shape, colour and texture. Both VR and AR users initiated conversations by describing the appearance and name of the object so that both users are matched with the right object. In addition to the visual modes embodied in the visualisation and presentation of virtual objects, VR users fare better at the perception of affordances attributed to the model, especially in the object's use, size and weight, as well as within the situated environment. For example, many VR users have attempted to 'wear' the *Bronze Mask with Protruding Pupils* object or explored affordance with features of an object, such as the horn of the *Pottery Unicorn* object. The size of an object translates to users as weighty, i.e., users have commented that some models such as the *Assistant to the Judge of Hell* object were too heavy to lift.

As compared to the mere object augmentations in AR, the spatial layout of objects in VR has supported the physical context in users' learning of cultural heritage objects. In addition, embodied interaction (Li et al. 2019a), whereby user head and torso movements tracked by controllers are mapped to the virtual environment, does contribute to engagement in VR. Users commented in the interview that the immersive display and action possibilities of VR have significantly contributed to their experience in their learning of cultural heritage objects.

23.6.2 Engagement and Communication Between Subjects

In terms of user engagement and communication, VR users tended to more frequently attract the attention of their AR partner than the other way around. This was due to a large screen display showing the full view of the VR user's virtual environment, while VR users were only able to sense interactions of the AR user from object rotations and sound effects. This limitation highlighted the need for better indicators for VR users.

Users in both VR and AR have prior knowledge of the objects on display, and both have shared personal experiences, which collectively contributed to their learning experience. Communication here is a key factor. The most prominent example was the use of the 'Tang Song Yuan Ming Qing' (a verse of Chinese dynasties) to justify their rankings of the historical chronological orders of objects (please see Sect. 5 for details). Users have also shared their subjective interpretations, mentioning the

Table 23.3 Engagement and communication between subjects in HVAR

Theme	User	Action and dialogue	Pair ID
Attract attention (17)	VR (13)	Check if the AR user sees him/her.	P1, P4, P5, P7
		Check if the AR user is looking at an object.	P2, P8, P9
		Ask the AR user to look at an object together.	P8, P14, P19, P26
		Ask the AR user to watch an interaction (wearing a mask, swapped th eobjects, using one object to interact with another, etc.)	P7, P21
	AR (4)	Ask the VR user to look at an object together.	P4, P19
		Check if the VR user can see the rotation.	P12, P18
Knowledge and personal experience (22)	VR (12)	Use the verse of Chinese dynasties to help rank the chronological order	P1, P3, P7, P13, P17, P19, P23
		Discuss why the assistant statue is at the British Museum.	P1, P8
		Ask their partner if a face looks like a friend of them (lady and assistant).	P14, P26
		Was this one (mask) on the National Treasure show?	P2
	AR (10)	Use the verse of Chinese dynasties to help rank the chronological order	P2, P8, P10, P14, P18, P20, P22, P26
		I've seen another one (mask) at the Jinsha Museum, but that one does not have the protruding eyes and such huge ears.	P12
		I remember I've watched a documentary about this (mask). These are really important for Chinese history.	P15
Feel related to an artefact story (5)	VR (2)	Discuss how rare and special the statue of the assistant is (for being a female official in the hell).	P5
		Discuss the plump figure of the lady and the ideal qualities of Tang feminine beauty.	P22

(continued)

Table 23.3 (continued)

Theme	User	Action and dialogue	Pair ID
	AR (3)	Discuss how rare and special the statue of the assistant is (for being a female official in the hell).	P1
		I wish I can have the magic sight and hearing (like the mask).	P1
		I guess I'll see her when I die. I'm a good guy. You see? It says she takes notes of people doing good things.	P4
Social norm and order (14)	VR (11)	Worried about 'breaking' the object.	P1, P6, P11, P14
		Ask the partner to stop messing around with objects.	P2, P13
		Swap the object positions and then put them back.	P3, P17, P18, P21, P25
	AR (3)	*I really want to take a picture of you.*	P2
		Oh it's falling! Put it back!	P19
		Be careful! Don't break it!	P23
Cooperation (8)	HVAR (8)	Ask the partner to help remember the historical period of an object.	P1, P3, P19
		AR user acts as a tour guide for VR user, reading the labels and explaining the stories.	P4
		AR user makes the assistant rotate so that the VR user can see the back of the assistant.	P24
		VR user asks the AR user to trigger rotation of an object (assistant and lady).	P8, P19, P26

relevant documentaries they have watched and experiences of past museum visits. They commented in the interview that the exchange of information and interpretations have contributed to their understanding of objects.

We have also observed users complying to social norms as they would in a museum. The most prominent was to 'not break' cultural heritage objects. We observed multiple cases where users have reminded others to 'not break the objects', or have expressed a fear of accidentally 'breaking' the objects. They reported in the interview that the realism of the objects has convinced them that they were real, and that cultural heritage objects should be treated with respect even in virtual reality. Many users have tried to swap the position of objects in VR. In the end, they were put back to their original location before the experiment is over. In the interview, they expressed aversion in confusing other visitors if the objects were wrongly placed. This care for other users is a sign that social norms can indeed be transferred into virtual environments.

We have observed spontaneous cooperation even though we have not designed for it. For example, we noted a series of similar cooperative action on the *Assistant to the Judge of Hell* object. The object is made to be immovable in VR due to its size. Its positioning means that the back of the model will not be visible. Interestingly, as AR users can rotate objects, several pair of users have discovered this cooperative technique to allow the VR users to view the obscured back of the model. This spontaneity in cooperation has illustrated that users can become creative in taking advantage of asymmetric interaction so as to explore possibilities in HVAR.

23.7 Conclusion

In this chapter, we presented the Visualisation, Interaction and Presentation (VIP) Framework of Virtual Objects that can be used to model user interaction in Hybrid Virtual and Augmented Reality (HVAR) environments. We presented cultural heritage objects within our HVAR environment using three attributes associated with the access of virtual objects and evaluated how user interaction, engagement and communication would sit in the VIP framework. The chapter continued by presenting the Contextual Experience Cycle of Virtual Exhibitions combining two learning theories (Kolb 1984; Falk and Dierking 2000). Hybrid Virtual and Augmented Reality environments are a relatively unexplored landscape, and the model framework presented here serves to lay a foundation for future research where hybrid environments and devices can be used for co-exploring and co-learning cultural heritage objects.

Acknowledgements This work was carried out at the NVIDIA Joint-Lab on Mixed Reality. The authors acknowledge the financial support from the Ningbo Science and Technology Bureau (2017D10035), the University of Nottingham and Xi'an Jiaotong-Liverpool University (RDF-20-02-47, TDF20/21-R22-142).

References

Azuma RT (1997) A survey of augmented reality. Presence Teleoperators Virtual Environ 6(4):355–385

Bekele MK, Town C, Pierdicca R, Frontoni E, Malinverni EVAS (2018) A survey of augmented, virtual, and mixed reality for cultural heritage. ACM J Comput Cult Herit 11(2):36

Bitgood S (2011) Social design in museums: the psychology of visitor studies

Brooks FP (1999) What's real about virtual reality? IEEE Comput Graphics Appl 19(6):16–27

Bruno F, Bruno S, De Sensi G, Luchi ML, Mancuso S, Muzzupappa M (2010) From 3D reconstruction to virtual reality: A complete methodology for digital archaeological exhibition. J Cult Herit 11(1):42–49

Caggianese G, Neroni, Gallo L (2014) Natural Interaction and Wearable Augmented Reality for the Enjoyment of the Cultural Heritage in Outdoor Conditions, vol 8853. pp 267–282

Ch'ng E, Cai S, Zhang TE, Leow FT (2019b) Crowdsourcing 3D cultural heritage: best practice for mass photogrammetry. J Cult Herit Manag Sustain Dev

Ch'ng E (2009) Experiential archaeology: is virtual time travel possible? J Cult Herit 20(2009):458–470

Ch'ng E (2013) The mirror between two worlds: 3d surface computing inter- action for digital objects and environments. Digital media and technologies for virtual artistic spaces. IGI Global, Hershey

Ch'ng E, Cai, Leow FT, Zhang TE (2019a) Adoption and use ofemerging cultural technologies in China's museums. J Cult Herit 37:170–180

Ch'ng E, Li Y, Cai S, Leow FT (2020). The effects of VR environments on the acceptance, experience, and expectations of cultural heritage learning. J Comput Cult Herit 13(1):1–20

Champion E, Dave B (2007) Dialing up the past. Theorizing digital cultural heritage

Cipresso P, Giglioli IAC, Raya A, Riva G (2018) The past, present, and future of virtual and augmented reality research: a network and cluster analysis of the literature. Front Psychol 9:1–20

Dierking LD (2002) The role of context in children's learning from objects and experiences. Perspectives on object centered learning in museums. pp 3–16

VIVE Enterprise (2018) HTC VIVE Focus

Facebook (2019) Oculus Quest

Falk JH, Dierking LD, Adams M (2006) Living in a learning society: Museums and free-choice learning. Compan Museum Stud 1:323–339

Falk JH, Dierking LD (2000) Learning from museums: Visitor experiences and the making of meaning

Furrer C, Skinner E (2003) Sense of relatedness as a factor in children's academic engagement and performance. J Educ Psychol

Gaitatzes A, Christopoulos D, Papaioannou G (2004) The ancient olympic games: being part of the experience. In: Proceedings of the 5th international symposium on virtual reality, archaeology and cultural heritage (VAST). Eurographics Association, VAST'04, Aire-la-Ville, Switzerland, Switzerland. pp 1–10

Hein GE (1999) The constructivist museum. The educational role of the museum

Jacobson J, Holden L (2005) The Virtual Egyptian Temple. Proceedings of EdMedia: World Conference on Educational Media and Technology 2005:4531–4536

Kolb DA (1984) Experiential learning: experience as the source of learning and development. J Org Behav

Magic Leap (2018) Avatar chat

Lester P (2006) Is the virtual exhibition the natural successor to the physical? J Soc Archiv 27(1):85–101

Li Y, Ch'ng E, Cai S, See S (2018) Multiuser interaction with hybrid VR and AR for cultural heritage objects. In: Digital heritage 2018, IEEE, San Francisco, USA

Li Y, Ma T, Ch'ng E (2019a) Enhancing VR experiential learning through the design of embodied interaction in a shared virtual environment. In: 23rd Pacific Asia conference on information systems (PACIS 2019)

Li Y, Tennent P, Cobb S (2019b) Appropriate control methods for mobile virtual exhibitions. In: Duguleană M, Carrozzino M, Gams M, Tanea I (eds) VR technologies in cultural heritage, vol 904. Communications in Computer and Information Science, Springer, Cham

Microsoft (2018) AltspaceVR

Neale H, Nichols S (2001) Theme-based content analysis: a flexible method for virtual environment evaluation. Int J Hum Comput Stud 55(2):167–189

O'Brien H, Cairns P (2015) An empirical evaluation of the user engagement Scale (UES) in online news environments. Inf Process Manage 51(4):413–427

O'Brien HL, Toms EG (2008) What is user engagement? a conceptual framework for defining user engagement with technology. J Am Soc Inform Sci Technol 59(6):938–955

Roo JS, Hachet M (2017) One reality: augmenting how the physical world is experienced by combining multiple mixed reality modalities. In: UIST 2017—Proceedings of the 30th annual ACM symposium on user interface software and technology. pp 787–795

Speicher M, Hall BD, Nebeling M (2019) What is mixed reality? In: Proceedings of the 2019 CHI Conference on Human Factors in Computing Systems—CHI' 19. ACM Press, New York, USA. pp 1–15

Stone R, Ojika T (2000) Virtual heritage: What next? MultiMedia, IEEE 7(2):73–74

Tan BK, Rahaman H (2009) Virtual heritage: reality and criticism. Joining languages, cultures and visions—CAADFutures 2009. Proceedings of the 13th international CAAD futures conference. pp 143–156

Tost LP, Champion EM (2007) A critical examination of presence applied to cultural heritage. In: PRESENCE 2009 the 12th annual international workshop on presence, Oct 2007. pp 245–256

VRChat Inc. (2017) VRChat

Zuckerberg M (2014) Mark Zuckerberg—I'm excited to announce that we've agreed to acquire Oculus VR, the leader in virtual reality technology

Part V
Intangible and Hidden Narratives

Chapter 24
'Britons: Your Crowdsourcing Commemorative Page Needs You': Imaging and Re-imagining the Digital Memory of the First World War

Ross Wilson

Abstract The use of crowdsourcing to democratise heritage and empower individuals and communities has become a prominent feature of academic and professional practice within the last decade. There has been a quiet revolution in how the wider public are involved in campaigns and curation through digital sources. These structures are frequently considered to be 'value-free' and have only recently been subject to critique as to how they frame conceptions of heritage (Ridge in Crowdsourcing our cultural heritage, Routledge, London and New York, 2014). This chapter will examine one of the most prominent examples of crowdsourcing and co-creation connected to the commemoration of the First World War during the centenary years of 2014–2018. Lives of the First World War was a platform created by the Imperial War Museum to serve as a public repository of images, as a memorial and as a future research tool. Using the approach of Critical Code Studies, the organisation, function and appearance of this website will be examined to assess the visual framing of knowledge and participation is encouraged. By extensively examining the platform as a mode of representation, composed of genres, discourses and styles, the structures of knowledge presented in this resource will be assessed as reinforcing the role of the institution and challenging the wider processes of social memory.

Keywords Critical code studies · Lives of the First World War · Co-creation · Visual data · Public engagement

24.1 Introduction—The First World War and Popular Memory

From August 2014 to November 2018, groups and individuals across the world participated in activities and initiatives to mark the outset, events and denouement

R. Wilson (✉)
School of Cultures, Languages and Area Studies, University of Nottingham, Nottingham, UK
e-mail: Ross.Wilson@nottingham.ac.uk

© Springer Nature Switzerland AG 2022
E. Ch'ng et al. (eds.), *Visual Heritage: Digital Approaches in Heritage Science*,
Springer Series on Cultural Computing,
https://doi.org/10.1007/978-3-030-77028-0_24

of the First World War. The scale and variety of this commemoration were unprecedented. From the grand public displays of nation states that spoke of peace and global cooperation, to small communities remembering the service and sacrifice of those from their local town or village, this was a complex interplay of memory, place and identity. However, this performance of remembrance was beset with complexities regarding the visual heritage of the war. These difficulties in the commemoration of the war derive from the particular ways in which this conflict has become part of national narratives in Australia, Britain, Canada and New Zealand. To mention the war, 'the trenches', Somme, Passchendaele, Ypres or Gallipoli is to immediately conjure images of death, destruction and pity (Wilson 2013) (Fig. 24.1). There is a distinct 'visual grammar' in this remembrance that emphasises the emotional connection that some individuals feel in response to the First World War. The war is seen as a tremendous loss of life which evokes questions regarding authority, responsibility and identity.

This social memory of the conflict has been forged through the events of the twentieth century as societies have experienced vast changes in politics, economics and culture (see Fussell 1975). Whereas during the war itself, the prevailing attitude was popular patriotism, by the end of the twentieth century, the memory of the conflict had become so loaded with sentimentality that some historians defined it as, 'rats,

Fig. 24.1 Official photographs taken on the British Western Front Battle of Menin Road. Wounded being carried off the battlefield. Shell Bursts too near to be healthy. France, 1918. February. Photograph. https://www.loc.gov/item/2017671891/

gas, mud and blood' (Corrigan 2003; McCartney 2014). It is this vision of the war in Australia, Britain, Canada and New Zealand that has become so important for class and national identity. Some 'revisionist' historians have been vocal critics of the way the war is remembered (Badsey 2001; Bond 2002; Sheffield 2002). They highlight how the representation of the conflict in film and television frequently reiterates this popular version rather than examining what is regarded as an 'accurate' historical portrayal of the war (see Hanna 2009). With the advent of the centenary, there was considerable political and media debate regarding how the war could be seen and remembered differently by communities across the world (see Williams 2009).

It was in Britain where this debate was hugely influential in the creation of commemorative schemes. Whilst the war could be said to have not been forgotten in this country, the British Government alongside prominent public institutes created a series of structures that framed the centenary events from 2012 (Pennell 2012). This included a sustained effort to create a different visual imagery of the war beyond the established image of the conflict of mud and trenches (Andrews 2015). To address what was regarded as the myopic memory of the war that focussed on the British experience, a global history was sought to re-vision 1914–1918 within social memory. This was achieved through the consultation of historians to create different narratives of the conflict beyond the established tropes. As the centenary of the outbreak of the war in August 2014 arrived, the framework of the war was set by institutions but what marked this process was the way in which the public was encouraged to volunteer. As contemporary British society addressed and negotiated their relationship to this past and considered its impact in the future, a great emphasis was placed upon 'public participation'.

24.2   Crowdsourcing the Centenary

To aid this programme of engagement, communities across Britain were asked to engage with this history. Whilst community history events and projects were initiated through the help of significance funds being made available by the Heritage Lottery Fund, it was online where the public were asked to volunteer and be ready for action (see Fell and Meyer 2015). Mirroring the campaign for volunteers to fight the war in August 1914, high-profile projects were formed that relied upon individuals and groups to upload personal photographs, images of objects or scans of documents to websites that sought to 'preserve' the memory of the conflict. These websites were formed by national or international consortium that sought to commemorate the war through crowdsourcing and digital co-creation (Wilson 2012). However, the form and function of this remembrance was a marked departure from the social memory that has been generated in former combatant countries. The process marked a movement from the personal to the institutional (after Arnold-de-Simine 2016).

The presence of digital projects which used co-creation tools and crowdsourcing for content to mark the centenary of the First World War was a means to ensure the democratisation of memory. In the context of national schemes of remembrance, projects which asked individuals and groups to share content and to help shape the reflection on the past were viewed as an alternative means of engagement. However, in the context of a war that was already well-remembered, embedded into local and national memory, the presence of these platforms was to transform the practice of memory from the affective to the effective. Whilst providing a means for public engagement and participation, these sites frequently serve to assert the vision of the expert and curtailment of meanings regarding visual heritage.

The use of co-creation and crowdsourcing initiatives within the heritage sector has proliferated since the realisation of Web 2.0 capacities for social engagement and interaction (Harrison 2009). Museums, galleries and archives have participated in small-scale and grand projects which utilise public engagement as a means of generating content. From basic user feedback to the formation of gifs and memes with objects and materials, institutions have harnessed these platforms for a range of purposes (Ridge 2013). Primarily, this use of technology is heralded as an equalising force and a means of democratising the structures of representation. Indeed, the deployment of these tools is often accompanied by a validation of the progressive social and political agenda they represent.

The extent to which this mode of public engagement of crowdsourcing and co-creation represents a sea-change in participation and democratic modes of representation has been critiqued by scholars. Whilst seemingly opening up the possibility of shared or collective endeavours, these schemes reiterate the structures of knowledge that exist within society rather than challenging or disrupting established or ingrained ideals (after Oomen and Aroyo 2011). The reason for this failure of crowdsourcing is within the frameworks that are created within the website coding and computing software which enables individuals to participate but ultimately renders their perspective inline with prevailing norms and ideals. Whilst seemingly value-free and neutral modes of communication, these systems organise and categorise knowledge and understanding in a designed and systematic way (see Ridge 2014). These designs are inevitably based upon the established patterns of organisation and management that exist in wider society.

24.3   Methods—Critical Code Studies and the Discourses of Crowdsourcing

To identify these modes of representation, the coding and organisation of websites can be assessed to reveal the relations of power that exist within these digital interactions. This can be undertaken through the application of Critical Code Studies. This analytical approach is less a set of identifiable methodologies but rather a commitment to assess the extra-functional significance of code (Marino 2006). This emphasises that coding, the language that is used to display websites or to enable the functionality of forms and forums, has purpose, symbolism, ideology and is a means of discipline and the exertion of power. Rather than being a mere scaffold for the presentation of data, code possesses the ability to shape perceptions as it represents information to wider society. Within the HTML, JavaScript, XML or YAML used to allow audiences to read data, browse archives and upload material, is the presence of control and the detailing of order. In these structures, information is regulated, processed and compartmentalised (see Fuller 2008).

The use of Critical Code Studies within this analysis is in the recognition it provides that online data is structured and organised as a distinct discourse. Therefore, websites can be critically read for their structure and content but also their relationship to other discourses in society within the political, media and public sphere. Following from the methods proposed by Fairclough (1993, 1995, 2001) of a 'critical discourse analysis', the way in which genres, discourses and styles are used to represent visual data within the crowdsourcing sites created to commemorate the First World War will be assessed. In this analysis, genres refer to a particular way of manipulating and framing discourse; examples of genres within a wider context are church sermons, interviews and political speeches. Genres are significant because they provide a framework for an audience to comprehend discourse, though evidently due to this quality, 'genres' can be the locus of power, domination and resistance. 'Discourses' are crucial in assessing the means by which apparently similar aspects of the world can be appreciated and understood from different perspectives or positions. Finally, 'styles' are the ways in which discourse is used to constitute a sense of being and identity, how identification is located through the application and manner of particular discourses (after Fairclough and Wodak 1997).

Therefore, whilst crowdsourcing may appear to offer a radical alternative to the archive or museum, it can serve as a digital reification of the abstract concepts of power that dictate and shape the form of the physical spaces where documents and objects are conserved and preserved. This can be witnessed in the creation of online public archives, where individuals and groups are encouraged to 'donate' or 'share' their photographs, documents or artefacts to be digitised for posterity. In the effort to ensure the 'realness' of social memory is maintained through crowdsourcing or digital co-curation, we observe the passing of the real into the institutional. The private memories of individuals become the detached remembrances of the collective. Essentially, moving from the 'milieux de mémoire' to the virtual 'lieux de mémoire' (after Nora 1989). As crowdsourcing activities ask for participation, it removes the object of interest from its context, frames it within a wider concept and renders it into a site of memory that can be bereft of the emotion and meaning of its original place. This is what is achieved through the discourses that create platforms that allow for public participation but not always public knowledge.

24.4   Results and Discussion—Creating Narratives of Memory and Engagement

During the centenary of the First World War in Britain the use of crowdsourcing programmes proliferated as a means of engaging the public in a democratic dialogue regarding the war and its legacy. Several major projects were created that formed a distinct visual heritage of the conflict through the structure of their coding and the discourses they represented. These include the Imperial War Museum's Lives of the First World War, The Great War Archive led by the University of Oxford, Europeana 1914–1918 which was organised by the European Union's digital platform for cultural heritage with support from the team at the University of Oxford and Operation War Diary, a partnership project between The National Archives, the Imperial War Museum and the citizen science web portal Zooniverse. These crowdsourcing projects created a high degree of public participation in the commemoration of the First World War in Britain. However, this was a war which was already remembered and mourned with society. In this context, the coding structures of crowdsourcing served to normalise and neutralise the memory of the war in Britain.

To demonstrate this process, the type of representation featured in the major crowdsourcing site of Lives of the First World War is analysed here for the structures of knowledge it creates and the visual heritage it generates. The discourses present within these sites will be examined for the way users are guided and information is processed. As part of this analysis, the way in which the architecture of these websites reflects established modes of power and reiterates knowledge will be examined in the context of the social and cultural memory of the First World War in Britain (after Wilson 2013). This interplay between narratives reveals the way in which the commemoration of the centenary was organised upon the function of disassociating the emotional connection to the war in favour of amassing catalogues and archives which neutralised this aspect of remembrance (after Fairclough 1993). As individuals became agents in this process, by participating in crowdsourcing activities that provided democratic engagement but detached contextual meaning, the digital memory and visual heritage altered. From a conflict that conjured up images of devastation and pity, to an image of archived knowledge, the online commemoration of the war has provided a challenge to the popular memory of the war.

Lives of the First World War was launched by the Imperial War Museum in May 2014 and came to an end in March 2019. The initiative was conceived as an 'innovative, interactive platform' which was designed to bring material from 'museums, libraries, archives and family collections from across the world together in one place'. The project was created to 'explore, reveal and share the life stories' of those who witnessed the First World War (IWM 2016a, b). Individuals and communities were encouraged to participate and volunteer for the scheme whether through uploading photographs from the period, documents or images of objects that related to the experience of those at the front or those at home. Volunteers were able to search records online, verify the information and then add to the 'life stories' of individuals who had experienced the war.

Fig. 24.2 Lives of the First World War Homepage (June 2020)

From the outset, the genre used to define the project was one that was loaded with the notion of discovery and significance. The website was presented as a vital means of preserving the past and as a necessary act of 'democratic remembrance' where the history of individuals would be lost to posterity if action was not taken. The home page of the project (Fig. 24.2) stated:

> We believe that each and every one of the 8 million who served during WW1 deserves to be remembered. Join Imperial War Museums and help tell these Life Stories by adding your images, sharing their stories, find their records and adding known facts (IWM 2016a, b).

The genre of meaning and significance that was presented within the website, that it served as a vehicle to ensure the protection of memory was highly important in the context of the centenary. In Britain, with the preparations for the anniversaries of the outbreak, battles and the denouement of the war, the disparity between the popular memory and academic history of the conflict became politicised with accusations of bias and ulterior agendas in how the hundredth anniversaries of the conflict should be marked (Andrews 2015). The issues at stake were highlighted by the comments in support of the revisionist perspective of the war made by the Conservative MP Michael Gove, then Secretary of State for Education, in January 2014:

> The war was, of course, an unspeakable tragedy, which robbed this nation of our bravest and best. But even as we recall that loss and commemorate the bravery of those who fought, it's important that we don't succumb to some of the myths which have grown up about the conflict. Our understanding of the war has been overlaid by misunderstandings, and misrepresentations which reflect an, at best, ambiguous attitude to this country and, at worst, an unhappy compulsion on the part of some to denigrate virtues such as patriotism, honour and courage (Gove 2014).

This assessment of the representation of the war as 'myths' perpetuated by the media was immediately countered by critics who stated in turn that such interpretations of the conflict as an exemplum of nobility and loyalty in British society were similarly coloured by political connotations (Hunt 2014). With debates within the political and media sphere on the meaning of the war leading up to August 2014, the website appeared to offer the opportunity of an objective engagement with the past that could be accessed by everyone. This was highly valuable and served as a means to visualise the war and its remembrance as a collective endeavour. Indeed, it was this sense of partnership and communion that was present in the formation of 'Communities' on the platform (IWM 2016a, b). This function allowed users to collaborate and connect individuals who would have known each other or were from the same area and served in the conflict. The process was defined by the website as, 'reconnect friends and family members by curating your own group of Life Stories' (IWM 2015a). As such, the website structured the engagement with the history and remembrance of the war as a significant endeavour which was based on collective service. This created a distinct visual heritage of the conflict as a shared experience. The photographs and documents that were uploaded and shared with others formed part of everyone's participation in the commemoration and thereby the war effort.

The genre of exploration and collaboration that framed the entire platform offered visual cues to users to commemorate and remember the experience of others in the past. Whereas the cultural memory of the war had been built on the reiteration of a key set of images of desolate battlefields, piteous soldiers suffering stoically in the trenches, the endless sea of headstones or 'name upon name' inscribed into memorials, this was a commemoration of the war based on networks of images that focussed on the variety of individual experiences. The visual heritage of the war is therefore altered by the networked arrangement of pictures and documents that constituted the 'Life Stories' created on the site (IWM 2016a, b). Whereas the war was known through specific imagined scenes, the exploration of the kaleidoscope of experiences enabled through Lives of the First World War provided a new framework to place the memory of the war. Whilst the notion of the shared experience expands the awareness of the war, it can also serve to dilute the impact of the private sphere as the image of the experiences of others relayed through the communities created by users, places memory into history.

This channelling of social memory into institutional commemoration is also achieved through the discourse present within the website. The crowdsourcing feature provides a distinct mode of engagement as volunteers are called upon to verify and prove the elements of their accounts before uploading their documents and images. As such, Lives of the First World War offers a very directed point of perceiving the documents and images used within the platform. Volunteers were encouraged to engage with the 'facts' that they could establish to verify personal or professional data. Users of the platform are encouraged to participate in a corrective procedure to 'uncover' the factual lives of those who were part of the First World War to reveal the real story for future generations by connecting evidence (IWM 2016a, 271b).

As such, the digital memory of the war could be established as a historicization of social memory. The guidelines offered to volunteers were:

> Evidence is anything that proves a fact - evidence might be an official record showing an enlistment date, a photo showing someone's regiment, a family letter mentioning an address:

- Upload your own evidence, such as photos and papers
- Find evidence elsewhere in other websites or publications
- Find evidence here in our official genealogy records (IWM 2015b).

In the context of the criticism of the public memory of the First World War lacking veracity, the focus on establishing evidence and facts rather than emotional, social or cultural connections is distinctive. There is scope within the platform to forward family stories but the discourse present in the site is one that inevitably leads to volunteers establishing the primary of institutional knowledge over a public commemoration that might not conform to the expectations of professional historians and museum curators (after Samuel 1994). As such, the discourse present within Lives of the First World War is in line with character of the institution of the Imperial War Museum. The museum was founded in 1917 with the purpose of instructing the peoples of Britain and the wider British Empire of the significance of the sacrifice of the war dead. Since its inception, the museum has functioned as a memorial to the conflict and its combatants, but it has also served to 'historicise' the conflict (Kavanagh 1988). In this manner, the creation of the crowdsourcing initiative provides a means of engagement, but the traditional structures of knowledge still remain.

The discourses present to remember the conflict through this website are therefore focussed on the notion of accuracy and process. Volunteers and visitors to the platform are reminded of this process through the display of data that emphasises the scale and success of the process. The site's homepage in April 2016 stated clearly:

- 7,688,306 Life Stories Added
- 416,195 Remembered
- 2,268,141 Facts Added
- 7,121 Communities (IWM 2016a, b).

The social memory of the war is thereby transplanted as accuracy is emphasised. The volunteer is asked to become part of the process that can establish an authentic account of the conflict for researchers. The discourse here funnels the wider public commemoration into a specific focus on evidence. Whilst this is entirely appropriate for the institution, it serves to question the place of memory. The visual heritage of the war is restructured from one of feeling and emotional connection to images to one of a series of processes which establishes memory as data (after Samuel 1994). Through a series of prompts, volunteers were asked to see the images of people and places as points of fact rather than points of reflection. The instructions for adding images to the site ask individuals to order these chronologically and to select on the basis of relevancy. This is undertaken to 'illustrate facts on the timeline' of the person being researched (IWM 2015b). The visual ordering of material through this crowdsourcing scheme thereby reinforces institutional schemes of knowledge.

The visual heritage of the First World War is reformed in this scheme as a hierarchy of data is created through the platform as photographs of individuals, service records, accompanying images and scans of artefacts are divided through the upload process. If the volunteer is able to share personal images the discourses presented within the site provide reassurance and purpose for their value but ultimately, they become part of a wider narrative:

> Keep your precious family mementoes safe at home, but take a photo or scan them and upload the image to Lives of the First World War. With a project of this scale, IWM is not able to collect and preserve millions more items in the museum. However, uploading an image ensures it can be shared with the world and saved for future generations (IWM 2017a).

This concept of duty that is present within the work of volunteers and users of the site is part of the style of the platform. A sense of being and identity is formed through the creation of timelines, uploading materials and connecting images with wider records which focuses on the work for the institution. To participate in the crowdsourcing scheme is to become a curator of the visual and digital heritage of the conflict. Each participant is given this framework of understanding which governs their interaction with the site. Indeed, the architecture of the website was structured to enable this identification:

> We are creating a Life Story for every man and woman who made a contribution during the First World War, whether they died during the war or survived the conflict. We are asking you to 'Remember' them. By using the 'Remember' button on each Life Story, you are paying your respects and showing that their story won't be forgotten (IWM 2018).

By conducting work for the institution, where volunteers with familial connections to those they research and those who had no personal link to the subjects they studied, the creation of institutional memory over personal memory was made clear. The insistence that the work is being 'saved for future generations' places volunteers' identities as a parallel to the individuals who fought in the war itself (IWM 2016a, b). This style of discourse is maintained within the website to reiterate the identity of the volunteers as providing an essential service in the face of what otherwise might be cultural amnesia. The potential threat to the loss of the records of those who served frames the identities of users of this crowdsourcing initiative:

> There are many projects across the globe that commemorate individuals who were involved in the First World War. However, unless you know where someone was born, lived or died, or who they served with, it can be difficult to find those that relate to the person you are interested in (IWM 2017b).

In that sense, the work to upload and identify the images on the site takes upon the mantle of the utmost significance. Volunteers are asked to work on a project to maintain the memory of the war as well as to provide a resource for later research. The ways of identifying with the site are well-directed as the images used within the crowdsourcing activity are treated as vital historical records that need to be verified before becoming accessible to the wider public. In this manner, the visual heritage of the war is given a platform where it can proliferate but also where it is viewed as 'at risk'. The translation from the public to the institutional could conversely place these images under greater threat as they lose the personal and social attachment and become placed within a wider historicising process. As such, the style of representation here is in keeping with a broader concern expressed at the outset of the centenary, that the war be brought back from popular memory and placed within the context of historical research. The visual heritage that once framed the social commemoration of the war has been reframed as historical evidence in need of protecting and preserving for research and a future memorial. Therefore, the democratisation offered through crowdsourcing creates equality in engagement, but can serve to challenge the modes of commemoration that maintain the place of events and experience within the national narrative.

24.5   Conclusion

By the time of its conclusion, Lives of the First World War had worked with over 130,000 individuals to represent the experience of those who witnessed the events of 1914 to 1918. Undoubtedly, the project marked a major achievement in public engagement and participation, providing a framework for future partnerships. The work undertaken by thousands of volunteers was immense, with significant details added to the understanding of the past through meticulous research. However, with the use of crowdsourcing as a means of acquiring engagement and visual material, the manner in which the site engages with the popular memory of the war raises issues regarding representation and participation. Crowdsourcing offers a form of direct engagement with the public as well as modes of participation that allows individuals to make a direct impact on the outcome of projects and assist in the way events are remembered and researched in the future. Nevertheless, in the context of the First World War in Britain, this was an event that was well-remembered and held a prominent place within national narratives. Indeed, the social memory of the war which had been formed through the twentieth century held an important part in the formation of class, political, regional and national identity in Britain.

Crowdsourcing to commemorate the First World War offered a means to engage with the public memory of the war. Indeed, in a co-created online exhibition organised by the Imperial War Museum on the social media platform Flickr, Faces of the First World War. Within this project, the process of democratisation was followed with communities and users able to create narratives and respond to the array of photographs of individuals uploaded onto the site by the museum. On this forum, users were not required to verify or provide evidence for their assessment. Rather, this was offered as an opportunity to engage with public memory. Whereas this format did not rely on crowdsourcing, it did utilise the visual heritage of the conflict to engage the wider public with their participation in commemorative activity. As crowdsourcing initiatives develop, the opportunity to expand public engagement and create democratic modes of representation has expanded. However, where this point of engagement is problematised is the way it provides structures of knowledge that reiterate established traditions. Where individuals and communities are asked to upload and share materials, visual heritage becomes a means of defining one institutional vision of the past rather than allowing for a plethora of stories and voices to emerge through the images we share.

References

Andrews M (2015) Poppies, Tommies and remembrance: commemoration is always contested. Sound: J Polit Cult 58:104–115

Arnold-de-Simine S (2016) Between memory and silence, between family and nation: remembering the First World War through digital media. In: Dessingué A, Winter J (eds) Beyond memory: silence and the aesthetics of memory. Routledge, London and New York, pp 143–161

Badsey S (2001) Blackadder goes forth and the "two Western Fronts" debate. In: Roberts G, Taylor PM (eds) The historian, television and television history. University of Luton Press, Luton, pp 113–125

Bond B (2002) The unquiet western front. Cambridge University Press, Cambridge

Corrigan G (2003) Mud, blood and poppycock: Britain and the Great War. Cassell, London

Fairclough N (1993) Discourse and social change. Polity Press, Cambridge

Fairclough N (1995) Critical discourse analysis: the critical study of language. Longman, London

Fairclough N (2001) Language and power. Longman, London

Fairclough N, Wodak R (1997) Critical discourse analysis. In: van Dijk T (ed) Discourse as social interaction. Sage, London, pp 258–284

Fell A, Meyer J (2015) Introduction: untold legacies of the First World War in Britain. War Soc 34(2):85–89

Fuller M (2008) Introduction. In: Fuller M (ed) Software studies: a lexicon. MIT Press, Cambridge, MA, pp 1–14

Fussell P (1975) The Great War and modern memory. Oxford University Press, Oxford

Gary S (2002) Forgotten victory, the First World War—myths and realities. Review, London

Gove M (2014) Why does the left insist on belittling true British heroes? Daily Mail, 2 January. http://www.dailymail.co.uk/debate/article-2532930/MICHAEL-GOVE-Why-does-Left-insist-belittling-true-British-heroes.html. Accessed 21 Jan 2010

Hanna E (2009) The Great War on the small screen: representing the First World War in Contemporary Britain. Edinburgh University Press, Edinburgh

Harrison TM (2009) Wielding new media in Web 2.0: exploring the history of engagement with the collaborative construction of media products. New Media Soc 11(1–2):155–178

Hunt T (2014) Michael Gove, using history for politicking is tawdry. The Guardian. https://www.theguardian.com/commentisfree/2014/jan/04/first-world-war-michael-gove-left-bashinghistory. Accessed 4 Jan 2014

IWM (2015a) What is a community. Lives of the First World War. http://support.livesofthefirstworldwar.org/knowledgebase/articles/354509-what-is-a-community. Accessed 1 Sept 2015

IWM (2015b) How do I add information to a life story. Lives of the First World War. http://support.livesofthefirstworldwar.org/knowledgebase/articles/316829-how-do-i-add-information-to-a-life-story. Accessed 20 April 2015

IWM (2016a) Lives of the First World War. https://livesofthefirstworldwar.org/. Accessed 5 March 2015

IWM (2016b) How will you use information or images I add? Lives of the First World War. http://support.livesofthefirstworldwar.org/knowledgebase/articles/322173-how-will-you-use-information-or-images-i-add. Accessed 4 March 2016

IWM (2017a) Can I send you my photos/memorabilia? Lives of the First World War. http://support.livesofthefirstworldwar.org/knowledgebase/articles/316836-can-i-send-you-my-photos-memorabilia. Accessed 14 Nov 2017

IWM (2017b) How is lives of the First World War different from other centenary projects? Lives of the First World War. http://support.livesofthefirstworldwar.org/knowledgebase/articles/321908-how-is-lives-of-the-first-world-war-different-from. Accessed 14 Nov 2017

IWM (2018) Help us to tell the stories of millions of men and women. Lives of the First World War. https://livesofthefirstworldwar.org/tour. Accessed 20 Dec 2018

Kavanagh G (1988) Museum as memorial: the origins of the Imperial War Museum. J Contemp Hist 23(1):77–97

Marino M (2006) Critical code studies. Electron Book Rev Electropoet. http://www.electronicbo okreview.com/thread/electropoetics/codology.

McCartney H (2014) The First World War soldier and his contemporary image in Britain. Int Aff 90(2):299–315

Nora P (1989) between memory and history: Les Lieux de Mémoire. Representations 26:7–25

Oomen J, Aroyo L (2011) Crowdsourcing in the cultural heritage domain: opportunities and challenges. In: Proceedings of the 5th international conference on communities and technologies, pp 138–149. https://dl.acm.org/citation.cfm?id=2103354. Accessed 14 June 2019

Pennell C (2012) Popular history and myth-making: the role and responsibility of First World War historians in the centenary commemorations, 2014–2018. Hist Speak 13(5):11–14

Ridge M (2013) From tagging to theorizing: deepening engagement with cultural heritage through crowdsourcing. Curator 56(4):435–450

Ridge M (2014) Crowdsourcing our cultural heritage. Routledge, London and New York

Samuel R (1994) Theatres of memory. Verso, London

Sheffield G (2002) Forgotten victory the First World War: Myths and Realities. Hodder, London

Todman D (2005) The Great War: myths and memories. Sutton, Stroud

Wilson R (2012) Volunteering for service: digital co-curation and the First World War. Int J Herit Digit Era 1(4):519–534

Wilson R (2013) The cultural heritage of the Great War in Britain. Ashgate, Farnham

Winter J (2006) Remembering war: the Great War between memory and history in the twentieth century. Yale University Press, New Haven, CT

Williams D (2009) Media, memory, and the First World War. McGill-Queen's University Press, Kingston, ON

Chapter 25
Telling Difficult Stories: VR, Storytelling and Active Audience Engagement in Heritage Sites and Museums

Gabriele Neher

Abstract The emergence of heritage science as an interdisciplinary field of studies over the past couple of decades coincided with a surge of research into audience engagement, politics of display, storytelling and co-creation. Arguably, what remains missing is a study that brings these two hitherto largely distinct fields of studies together. This article focuses on storytelling as a narrative device to increase audience engagement with displays and exhibits, and proposes that by using VR, museums in fact create an 'other space', a heterotopia which is especially suited to engaging viewers with difficult stories. The article explores one case study, that of 'The Eye as Witness: Recording the Holocaust' travelling exhibition, as a project that has been purposefully designed by a regional UK museum with access to limited resources that is rethinking its story-telling strategy. By drawing on a collaborative approach that brings together experts from museums and universities, and by harnessing the potential of interactive digital technologies, in particular VR, as an integral part of its design, 'The Eye as Witness' brings together traditional and innovative ways of audience engagement. The aim? To shift the focus of the museum experience away from being object-based and instead making it experience-focussed.

Keywords Digital museum · Digital heritage · Virtual reality · Storytelling · Audience engagement

25.1 Introduction

Storytelling, and in particular, storytelling that actively engages the viewer in immersing themselves in the narratives, especially if these narratives are challenging previously held conceptions, can be a powerful way of creating audience engagement. In its widest possible definition, 'audience engagement' has become an umbrella term that focusses on audience behaviour where, say, the visitor to a heritage site, spends time reading wall text, then they might stop and look at a particular exhibit or engage

G. Neher (✉)
University of Nottingham, Nottingham, UK
e-mail: gabriele.neher@nottingham.ac.uk

© Springer Nature Switzerland AG 2022
E. Ch'ng et al. (eds.), *Visual Heritage: Digital Approaches in Heritage Science*,
Springer Series on Cultural Computing,
https://doi.org/10.1007/978-3-030-77028-0_25

with an interactive kiosk. Outside the actual physical estate of the site, there might be engagement with the cultural site on social media channels. Audience engagement at its most inclusive level covers any activity where the visitor interacts with a display beyond just a walk through. It is understood that we need to spend more time reflecting on what is actually captured under the umbrella term 'audience engagement'. In particular, we need to be clearer on how to measure successful audience engagement in the first place, but the baseline of this article follows the assumption that increasing audience engagement is a desirable aim for any museum and cultural institution in the twenty-first century. In fact, 'the right of access to, and enjoyment of cultural heritage' is actively promoted by the United Nations Human Rights Commission as of particular significance for the identity and development processes for both individuals and communities (Shaheed 2011). Nina Simon coined the term of the 'participatory museum', and in her eponymous study, she highlighted a shift away from the museum as a static repository of expert-generated-content and as authoritative single voice of instruction, towards a site for audience-generated content with a very different social feel (Simon 2010). Simon's study, with its focus on methods of display, encouraged cultural heritage sites to reconsider how the space and design of museum buildings and the exhibits contained within become themselves sites for contestation of meaning, and crucially, their space for increased audience engagement. One very common response to this challenge has been to harness new technologies to update and replace existing interactive displays (where they were already used) or to introduce interactivity where this had been hitherto absent. One particular trend has been the introduction of Virtual Reality (VR) displays, where most commonly visitors wear a headset that allows them to enter into an immersive space.

This chapter examines the way in which 'The Eye as Witness-Recording the Holocaust' travelling exhibition developed by a project team at The National Holocaust Centre & Museum (NHCM) Newark (Nottinghamshire, UK), used VR not as an add-on but as an integral part of the conception and design of the exhibition, suggesting a new and sustainable approach to exhibition design. The VR element of the exhibition was an integral part of the exhibition planning from its conception and has been specifically used as a significant storytelling device. The VR element is integrated into the overall experience of the exhibition, aiming to challenge viewers to take a new look at seemingly familiar images of the Holocaust by entering into a hypothetical best guess (virtual) recreation of the historical time and place of the taking of the original photograph. The viewer is placed in the position of the witness of this moment, which means a necessarily more active role as viewer/participant than when faced with a traditional photograph on its own.

Some major museums and galleries, notably The Metropolitan Museum New York (The Met 360, 2017), The Tate (Modigliani *Atelier Ochre*, 2018) and The Louvre (Leonardo da Vinci, 2019) have long pioneered the use of VR projects as a means of enhancing and augmenting a visitor's experience of an exhibition. The Met, The Tate and The Louvre though are major institutions that invested heavily into these blockbuster showcase events but the resources required to do this, by outsourcing substantial projects, the cost and range of these projects, have until now put them beyond the reach of most museums and heritage sites (Mekele et al. 2018). What has changed though is that as the technology for integrating Augmented Reality, Virtual Reality and Mixed Reality has become more accessible to a wider range of institutions, the debate needs to shift and reflect on 'how' these technologies are being used for the greatest audience engagement impact. As a storytelling device has come within reach of a much wider range of cultural heritage sites, how can you have the greatest impact?

The NHCM's adoption of VR as an integral part of the storytelling of its travelling exhibition 'The Eye as Witness' shows a regional museum venturing into the VR arena, and arguably offers a case study for exploring the storytelling potential of VR. The exhibition also marks an attempt at bridging the gaps between heritage science and museum studies, potentially heralding a new phase of interdisciplinary collaboration between these two fields. Carefully designed and conceptually integrated VR, digital technology that stands at the beginning of the design of an exhibition and is not added as an afterthought, might in fact allow a much wider range of museums and cultural heritage sites to engage with 'difficult' and even controversial narratives. It also suggests the potential for rethinking the skills needed for a curatorial team, and suggests that we are a long way off yet from understanding and tapping into the role digital heritage can play in furthering audience engagement. Of course, the widespread adoption of VR for travelling exhibitions, for example, also suggests a tantalising glimpse of these exhibitions reaching into non-traditional sites, such as for example shopping malls, bringing audience engagement with cultural heritage into the very spaces where social interactions are increasingly taking place. VR has the potential for breaking down spatial and conceptual boundaries.

25.2   Background/Literature Review

Of course, VR has not come out of nowhere but its use follows in the footsteps of the many interactive displays which have long been used by museums as a way to increase audience engagement with their collections, especially in displays aimed at children. One of the best known examples in the UK remains the 1977 'An Exhibition of Ourselves', Human Biology Gallery at the Natural History Museum, London, which pioneered the introduction of levers to push, buttons to press, lights that flashed up to highlight specific parts of an exhibit. These displays may be limited in the options offered to the visitor, but are tactile, playful, accessible to a very wide cross-generational demographic and provide instant feedback to the user, in other words, draw on sound design principles. These displays allowed for repetitive and limited engagement only, and were often quite mechanical, but they remain popular with visitors because at the heart of the interactives is fun. Pushing levers and pressing buttons respond to the clearly recognised value of play and interaction as a means for entertaining visitors (Miles 1986). The next step in their evolution was a recognition that these displays were conceived and delivered as an add-on to wall texts and labels that carried the core information. In other words, the interactives were an add-on to a narrative told through different means, and arguably it is only now that the potential of the interactives to become a key part of the storytelling of a cultural heritage site is being recognised. Technology from VR to touch screen displays, to smart phones, QR codes, websites, apps and social media platforms extends far beyond the physical estate of the museum, effectively creating a digital estate for the sites. How to best look after and exploit this digital estate remains to be seen though, because no museum has yet demonstrated what a mature digital domain may look like.

Has the most significant transformative factor to impact on the experience of museum visitors over the past couple of decades then been the widespread and ongoing adoption of digital technology? This is explored by the #CultureIsDigital initiative (launched by the UK Department for Digital, Culture, Media & Sport in 2018), which states that 'digital experiences are transforming how audiences engage with culture and are driving new forms of cultural participation and practice [...] especially [with regards to] younger audiences. ... Audiences are creating, adapting and manipulating as well as appreciating art and culture'. What this statement captures is an aspiration towards achieving a mature, nuanced and developed practice of integrating technology into the workings of a museum and heritage site. Because, the paper concedes, 'cultural organisations are [only] beginning to harness the potential of digital technology to engage audiences through new formats and mediums and by diversifying their distribution channels' (DCMS 2018). In reality then, there is still comparatively little empirical data that tracks how impactful and transformative the introduction of these technologies to museums and heritage sites has been, given

(a) the short time for such technologies to mature and embed themselves (particularly considering this against the accelerating pace of change of the technological hardware and software) and
(b) the (as yet) scarcity of scholarly studies on the subject.

In other words, while the potential of technologies to transform audience engagement is clearly acknowledged, what is less clear is what digital maturity in museums might look like and how museums and cultural heritage sites are going to make these technologies work for them. The speed of the digital transformation is currently so rapid, that there is a disconnect between the comparative permanence and stability of a site's on-site, physical display, and the rapid change and seemingly endless permutations of narratives possible through digital means and in social media spaces. Storytelling that bridges the physical and digital estates of a cultural heritage site is therefore emerging as a key consideration for museums' development of their physical and digital presence; the Victoria & Albert Museum (V&A, London) commissioned research into the use of their collections which found that stories were of prime interest to its audience. Their visitors wanted to both 'understand the connections objects have with other objects, people and the cultural and societal contexts', at the same time as wanting to tell of their own stories and their own connections to the museum and its collection (Craig 2019). Which narrative is 'correct' and carries authenticity? What stories are being told where and how? How does the museum visitor become a co-creator for the narratives that are visible in the digital and/or physical estate of the museum? These are questions that still go looking for answers but they underline the dynamic nature of the debates in the field and the opportunities for digital technologies to play a major role in re-imagining the narrative landscapes of the modern museum.

25.3 Methodology

Of course, this raises questions about what the future digital landscape of museums and cultural heritage institutions might actually look like, and how best to get there, a process that may have been accelerated by the least expected of external factors, the onset of the 2020 COVID-19 pandemic. When governments adopted lockdown measures to curb the spread of the virus, many cultural heritage institutions responded by increasing their activities online. The reopening of museums varied depending on local context, from some institutions operating strict social distancing protocols and access only via pre-booked and timed entry slots, to others able to return to the practices in operation before the onset of the global pandemic. The COVID-19 virus may be transmitted by touch, so may have a long-lasting impact on how cultural heritage sites choose to use hands-on interactives going forward.

#CultureIsDigital espouses the ideal of audiences embracing technologies to co-generate content in digitally mature environments, which seems quite a leap from the status quo. It does emphasise though the timeliness of taking a snapshot of how digital technology has so far been utilised in cultural heritage sites to better understand where the opportunities for development lie and potentially, which platforms to invest in, for museums which enter the market with budgetary constraints and very little existing infrastructure to build on. Here, focussed user studies still remain scarce, but one recent survey which has looked at issues surrounding both the adoption of digital technology in museums, and has also observed audience interaction with these systems, offers a starting point for thinking about best practice with regards to digital technology. A team led by Professor Eugene Ch'ng from the University of Nottingham Ningbo (China) studied 22 sites over 15 cities in China and evaluated 800 samples of data, capturing a snapshot of how cultural technology has been embedded (Ch'ng et al. 2018). Maybe surprisingly, given current trends with regards to the adoption of digital technology to aid visitor engagement, Ch'ng's study reveals very low rates of satisfaction with the experience of digital technologies in museums and cultural heritage sites, suggesting that 'only 17.14% respondents felt satisfied with the current installation of multimedia systems' (Liu et al. 2012). The survey suggests that successful engagement with the digital technology in a museum or a cultural heritage site depends on a multitude of factors, both physical and conceptual. For example, it established that the most engaged audience with regards to digital exhibits are family groups—this is borne out elsewhere (Price 2018). Engaging digital exhibits therefore need to be accessible (including at the right height for children), permit space for groups to gather around the exhibit and be located in such a way that other groups of visitors can continue to circulate in the gallery around the digital exhibit. The noise generated by the group gathered around the digital exhibit must not compete with the auditory ambience of the remainder of the gallery; given that research into soundscapes is live and topical, there are competing agendas here for the shape of an impactful gallery environment, and all of these factors need to be combined and considered (Stafford and Mansell 2020). Maybe it is not yet common practice in museums and cultural heritage sites to carry out this type of Impact Assessment Exercise, either at all, or to repeat it regularly, in order to keep the spaces and displays fresh and up to date with developments? Clearly, one side effect of the rise of VR is that the physical and digital estates of museums are expected to work together much harder, and the work of scholars such as Ch'ng is starting to formulate a set of questions that could start to form the basis of developing protocols for institutions that measure digital impact on audience engagement, generating data for future reviews.

With regard to the content of good interactives, there needs to be enough and varied content available for a group made up of different ages, yet Ch'ng's study found that very few visitors engage with the content fully, and most spend a maximum of 4 min at a console. The study concluded that the type of experience and the length of the digital exhibit were important, as few visitors engaged with everything, often barely skimming the many (too many?) options available. All too often, there remains a disconnect between the intentions of the technology and how end users actually access it. In other words, museums which might have an internal structure that includes a curatorial team, are suddenly challenged to incorporate principles of good user experience design into the conception of their exhibitions, and need to develop 'experience strategies' for their visitors where before the storytelling, focus of the team may have been elsewhere (Price 2018). What this suggests is an emerging skills gap in the makeup of traditional museum and cultural heritage teams, and it is not always clear where the needed skills can be acquired. Often, these skills are more commonly found in areas previously external to the museums sector, and the acquisition of these new skills through, for example, bespoke CPD training programmes (such as the 'Telling Stories' workshops offered by the University of Nottingham (2015–19) in collaboration with external partners such as the V&A, The Met and Beijing's Natural History Museum) can stretch training budgets for the institutions, challenging the traditional makeup of museums' staff teams even further. The pertinent issue here is one of collaboration between different partners to pool expertise, which is something discussed below in Sect. 25.4.

Location and accessibility of the interactives in the gallery, agility and responsiveness of the technology, configuration of both the physical and the digital space, ergonomics and height of console(s), connectivity and access to free Wi-Fi, access to charging stations for mobiles—all of these factors go beyond the traditional emphasis on the curator(s) voice in shaping display and storytelling in the physical estate of the museums and cultural heritage sites. In fact, institutions are increasingly enabling digital interactions beyond the walls of the museum and are encouraging visitors to extend their visit and take to social media, creating a digital estate all of which again raises questions about the important role technology can play in the modern museum. Ch'ng's study shows that museums and cultural heritage sites may have been quick to adopt technology, but remain in a transitional phase with regard to exploiting the potential of new and emerging technologies for their collections. The very pace of technological change, and the high costs connected to acquiring and maintaining the hardware, as well as either purchasing software or developing bespoke programmes still remains a forbidding obstacle for many. It is also worth noting that different age demographics engage differently with the physical and digital estate of the museum; teenagers and young adults are keen users of social media initiatives and respond well to targeted events, particularly embracing game-based and experience-focussed technology (Lewis 2014a, b). All of this suggests the potential for museums and cultural heritage sites on attracting and retaining different audiences, and the value of rethinking the space of the museum is clearly recognised. But, how to get there?

Here then is where the crossover between technology and museums studies throws up some interesting shared questions about, for example, audience engagement, display, storytelling and co-creation which have been dominant themes for discussion in the (scholarly) discipline over the past couple of decades. What this article seeks to do, is bring some of these debates together by focussing on one case study, that of 'The Eye as Witness-Recording the Holocaust' travelling exhibition, as a project that has been purposefully designed by a regional museum that is rethinking its storytelling strategy. The National Holocaust Centre and Museum (NHCM), by drawing on interactive digital technologies, in particular VR, as an integral part of its design, has developed 'The Eye as Witness' as an innovative, experimental and experiential foray into engaged storytelling, and in order to do so, it brings together traditional and innovative ways of audience engagement. The aim? To shift the focus of the museum experience away from being object-based and instead making it experience-focussed.

25.4 Case Study: 'The Eye as Witness-Recording the Holocaust' (National Holocaust Centre and Museum, Newark, UK), 2020

For the National Holocaust Centre and Museum (NHCM) in Newark (UK), its focus has long been on enabling visitors to meet Holocaust survivors and to encounter their difficult stories first hand and face to face. Far from avoiding difficult encounters, the NHCM foregrounds its work with survivors as a key part of its mission to remembering the past and therefore protecting the future. With its main modus operandi inherently built on participation and audience engagement, the NHCM has long had to think of how to preserve the stories of the rapidly passing generation of the Holocaust survivors. For the NHCM, digital technology is at the heart of preserving and disseminating their stories in this transformational point in its institutional history. In other words, digital technology is rapidly becoming an essential storytelling device, and this explains their pioneering work which seeks to exploit and harness the technology's potential to enrich visitors' engagement with the physical and digital estate of the institution. The NHCM has its physical base in Laxton, Newark, in Notting-hamshire, and this location in the East Midlands necessarily restricts the number of visitors able to engage with the Centre. For the Centre, reaching out to a geographi-cally diverse audience far beyond its usual reach, makes perfect sense. Researching, designing and delivering 'The Eye as a Witness' has pushed the NHCM into new ways of operating, and key to achieving this has been a collaborative approach, bringing in key external expertise. Professor Maiken Umbach (University of Nottingham) has led a team of interdisciplinary researchers as part of an AHRC-funded project on 'Photography as Political Practice in National Socialism' (2018–2021), a project that, on top of the exhibition, will also result in a range of publications examining photo-graphic albums as sites of memories (Nora 1989; Umbach, forthcoming; Necker, forthcoming).

Umbach and her team worked with the NHCM on developing a travelling exhibi-tion whose key premise was to problematise photographs as 'records', and to consider photographs instead as complex and ideological artefacts. Photographs are infinitely more than objective documents, and in challenging the role of photographs in story-telling, the importance of the 'Eye as Witness' came to the fore, and hence the focus of the exhibition. The NHCM involved an interdisciplinary team of external experts right from the start of the conception of this exhibition, bringing together researchers from History, Education and Computer Science, and by leveraging expertise both internal to the institution but complemented and supplemented by the external experts, as well as working closely with visitor focus groups, the 'Eye as Witness' developed into a co-creation project. From the point of conception of the exhibition, the prin-ciples were less those of a carefully created, one-directional information exchange, but rather those of an experiential, co-curated engaged dialogue enabled by a focus on storytelling. The project, which marks the 75th Anniversary year of the liberation of the Nazi concentration camps, has been years in the making and was enabled by drawing on external funding, as the operating budget of the NHCM has no provi-sion for this kind of initiative (which is not unusual for the budgets of museums and cultural heritage sites). Drawing down external funding was only possible in the first place through collaboration with researchers, suggesting that heritage sites may need to be agile in their ways of working going forward, with the plus side of course that this significantly diversifies expertise and by implication, the scope for developing new projects. The exhibition asks visitors to engage with questions about the role of the witness, about the act of looking as a way of creating memories and the role of the witness in constructing stories and creating memories of events, particularly by challenging visitors to look again at Holocaust photography. The exhibition seeks to go behind those photographs, and in one case, uses VR to enable the visitor to step inside the frame of a photograph, where they bear witness to the moment the photographer chooses to take his shot and to create his image (Tennent 2020). They become witnesses to the photographer's choice on which 'decisive moment' he will seek to capture (Fig. 25.1).

The visitor literally steps through a projected curtain into the photographer's world, where they find themselves behind the camera—and where usually in a photo-graph, the people depicted are subjected to the gaze of the spectator, in this case, the

Fig. 25.1 Entry into the 'Eye as Witness' VR Experience through a projected curtain (Photo credit @David Parry. Image courtesy of Dr. Paul Tennent, Mixed Reality Laboratory, University of Nottingham)

subjects of the photograph can look at the spectator, creating quite a different kind of dialogue (Fig. 25.2).

The visitor, wearing their headset, 'walks through' from this starting point and is then presented in the headset with the view below (Fig. 25.3).

Inside the headset, the static scene of the original photograph has been animated and the visitor becomes a witness to the moment the photograph they have been looking at in the Gallery is being taken, as shown in the next scene (Fig. 25.4).

The photographer makes one choice of many alternative choices available, and the question is whether in the act of looking at a photograph, we as viewers ever consciously consider that what the photograph shows is not an objective record, but a subjective storytelling choice. And the VR experience of witnessing this through the headset, puts the viewer into the photographer's shoes. This also raises questions as to who that photographer is and what his intentions are. The social historian Michael Baxandall wrote in 1972 that 'paintings are the deposit of a social relationship' (Baxandall 1972). Photographs work the same way: somebody wants to record a specific moment which has arisen as a result of a sequence of events, and the act of recording that moment suggests a narrative intention of using this image as part of a story that is being told. 'The Eye as Witness' seeks to challenge the viewer to look afresh at Holocaust images and to engage with ideas about intention, purpose and construction of the image. What were the choices behind choosing the particular moment that has been captured? Who has made this choice? What other options

Fig. 25.2 Entry point into the VR experience (Photo credit @ Dr. Paul Tennent, Mixed Reality Laboratory, University of Nottingham)

Fig. 25.3 Inside the headset: the render of the photo from the Stroop report (4 K render from inside the headset) (Photo credit @ Dr. Paul Tennent, Mixed Reality Laboratory, University of Nottingham)

have been disregarded? Is the story told from the point of view of the ideologically motivated perpetrator or that of the victim? Who is behind the camera and what are they wanting us to see? After all, whatever story is being told, somebody has made a choice to privilege one version of events, and to disregard alternative views.

Fig. 25.4 Behind the photographer (4 k render from inside the headset) (Photo credits @ Dr. Paul Tennent, Mixed Reality Laboratory, University of Nottingham)

No photo is an objective record; Susan Sontag described this active process of viewing an image, engaging with it and deriving meaning from it as 'viewing ethics' (Sontag 1977); Umbach develops this idea further and suggests that photography becomes a site for ideological contestation in National Socialism (Harvey et al. 2019). In 'The Eye as Witness', the viewer's 'viewing ethics' are challenged and tested—but in the privacy of the VR experience. The safety of the VR space therefore becomes an enabling device for enabling disruptive interactions, allowing difficult and contested stories to be told. Much of the photographic record documenting the Holocaust, for example, the 1944 Stroop Report, consists of commissioned propaganda pieces, in effect perpetrator photography, which is carefully constructing an image for effect. The historian Stephen Greenblatt describes this carefully selective process of using images in the construction of a message for propaganda as a process of self-fashioning, of the ability of images to self-consciously, deliberately and artfully determine that which is seen by witnesses (Greenblatt 1980). That which is visible, is the 'truth', as the witness can see it with their own eyes—or is it? 'The Eye as Witness' uses VR to allow the visitor to step into the frame of the image and witness a 360-degree view of the scene captured in the photograph. They can experience alternative viewpoints and explore the context for the photograph, with the VR space providing the visitor with agency which the person(s) photographed may not have had. Propaganda imagery generates, or, using Greenblatt's term, fashions, specific views of events, and 'The Eye as Witness' deliberately sets out to disrupt that authoritative viewpoint by offering alternatives. In the case of the exhibition, delivering that challenge comes partially through the immersion of the visitor in the VR environment of a photograph, so the object (the photograph) becomes the gateway to an experience.

Fig. 25.5 Thresholds (Photo credit @ Dr. Paul Tennent, Mixed Reality Laboratory, University of Nottingham)

Paul Tennent (University of Nottingham) developed *PhotoRealiser VR* to deliver this spatial experience, first experimenting with this technology for the 2019 *Thresholds* project (Fig. 25.5).

Thresholds, by artist Mat Collishaw, recreated the Model Room of the King Edward's School in Birmingham in 1839, recreating an exhibition of 93 Henry Fox Talbot's 'photogenic drawings'. Tennent has discussed how the biggest challenge for *Thresholds* was the complexity of the spatial challenge, bringing together and overlaying the physical space of the museum with the virtual space of the VR installation (Tennent et al. 2020). For 'The Eye as Witness', he again worked on the principle of a VR experience that is overlaid on a physical space, which gives the visitor more scope for sensory experiences, which of course enriches their mnemonic engagement with the photograph at the heart of the VR installation. VR becomes an integral part of the experience of the exhibition from the moment of conception, and not an afterthought.

The initial VR immersion in one of the images from the Stroop Report (1944), taken to document the process of evacuating a ghetto, gives way to images from the Lodz Ghetto, drawing on the work of Henryk Ross, and Joanna Szydlowska's covertly taken images from Ravensbrück. The Stroop Report documents an orderly process of moving people, while Ross, as victim of this forcible relocation, tells of the human emotions of pain, loss and fear. Szydlowska records, at considerable personal risk, what happens to these dislocated people who have been transported to camps. Her images are particularly harrowing to look at and tell difficult stories, of the 74 so-called Ravensbrück Rabbits, the de-humanised female victims of horrendous and illegal medical experiments, that left the young female 'subjects' either dead or permanently disabled, disfigured and in pain. Deep wounds were inflicted on the women's legs (the youngest was only 15), and then the cuts were deliberately infected with tetanus, in a simulation of festering battle wounds. Many of the victims died of these horrific experiments, but some survived with the help of camp fellows. Szydlowska's covertly taken images show the women displaying their wounds hidden behind a shed, with the images, the visual record and evidence of the atrocities, preserved on a film that was carefully concealed and remained undeveloped until the camp was liberated in 1945. There was real danger associated with taking images of that which was to remain hidden and unseen, and the very act of taking these images bears witness to the victims' need to tell their story and to have witnesses to their ordeal. The images bear witness to the unspeakable; they demand courage from the witness and they ask for action. The act of witnessing precipitates the need to react; the women of Ravensbrück understood this, and looking at their images challenges the witness to question their 'viewing ethics' to use Sontag's term again. Szydlowska's images also raise questions which their victims were unable to articulate, about the perverse mutilation of young female victims, of sexualised and almost ritualised violence perpetrated on female bodies, of dehumanising treatment that goes beyond ideologically motivated racism. The experience of the Ravensbrück Rabbits is less that of an isolated group of the victims of one regime, and the images instead become part of an ongoing and alas all too topical debate about sexual violence in the context of genocidal conflicts. What happened in 1944 is not an isolated event but part of an ongoing story of dehumanisation in war, and violence against refugees—something the exhibition illustrates in its final section, an installation by the artist Lina Selander. Her installation shows fragments of Holocaust imagery that appear reflected in a mirror that lies underneath a table, evoking ideas about objects as sites for memory while challenging and frustrating the visitor in only seeing fragments and glimpses of the past. The focus is on enabling the visitor to become an active participant in co-creating their own version of the exhibition. For example, there is emphasis on survivors' testimonies, and these are at the heart of the NHCM's way of working. The 'Forever Project', which contributes the video testimonials to the exhibition, seeks to sensitise audiences for the deeper meaning of testimony as conscious 'act of witnessing' and it challenges the visitors to create their own meaning.

In a way, the visitors' act of witnessing becomes part of the storytelling but in a different phenomenological space. One possible model for considering the potential of VR in creating different spaces for engaging with difficult narratives and contested stories is Michel Foucault's concept of the heterotopia. In his essay 'Of other spaces', Foucault establishes the definitions that determine a heterotopia. He describes spaces as defined by 'a set of relationships that define positions', and in particular,

> there also exist, and this is probably true for all cultures and civilizations, real and effective spaces which are outlined in the very institution of society, but which constitute a sort of counter arrangement, of effectively realized utopia, in which all the real arrangements, all the other real arrangements that can be found within society are at one and the same time represented, challenged and overturned (Foucault 1968).

The space of the museum has long been recognised as functioning like a heterotopia, complying, often very constructively, with several of Foucault's 'principles'. For example, the second principle states that 'an existing heterotopia has a precise and determined function within a society and the same heterotopia can, according to the synchrony of the culture in which it occurs, have one function or another' (Foucault 1968). The site of the museum is set apart from 'normal' space as it requires the visitor to enter the space, and to engage with the relationships created by the various objects and experiences sited within it. The museum brings together carefully selected, curated, objects and it stages an encounter between these objects, their stories and associations and the visitor (third principle). The museum and cultural heritage site also plays with notions of temporality in juxtaposing a contemporary viewer with a historic object (fourth principle), enabling an engagement with what Foucault calls 'slices of time'. Now, arguably, what VR and experience-based storytelling in museums permit is for the visitor to enter the boundaried space of a heterotopia where, for example, in the case of 'The Eye as Witness', they experience the context that led a photographer to deciding on a particular composition for their shot. In Foucault's terms then, the VR facilitates the visitor entering into a 'slice of time' and occupying an individual and isolated space that is not freely accessible (fifth principle). Arguably, what VR creates is a new narrative space that enables new dimensions of affective storytelling because it creates a narrative and emotive landscape all of its own.

25.5   Conclusions

The National Holocaust Centre and Museum's ambitious 'The Eye as Witness' travelling exhibition demonstrates how a regional museum with limited resources embraces digital technology at a transformational point in its institutional history. For the NHCM, storytelling and first-hand exposure to Holocaust survivors' stories, has been at the core of their activities. 'The Eye as Witness' continues this approach and imaginatively and creatively draws on new technology to enable storytelling that reaches a wider and different audience. The NHCM has extended the reach of its physical estate by harnessing the opportunities afforded by a move into the digital estate of the museum without altering its core operating principles.

'The Eye as a Witness' has become one of a crop of new exhibition projects which exploits the heterotopic narrative space of the VR environment in an exhibition that has been purposefully designed by a collaborative team where the storytelling design has included a VR element from the point of conception. This approach has previously been pioneered by larger, national institutions such as Tate Modern which included 'Modigliani VR: The Ochre Atelier' as part of its blockbuster Modigliani exhibition (November 23, 2017–April 2, 2018). For the VR experience, a team made up of experts from the Audio-Visual, Digital, Conservation and Curatorial in-house teams of Tate combined to recreate Modigliani's studios, offering visitors to the main exhibition an extension that was experience-based and allowed visitors to a blockbuster show some private space (Tate, 2017). What has enabled the NHCM to enter this space is the rapid evolution of the technology which is bringing the cost of these projects down, allowing regional and local museums and heritage sites to start moving into these spaces. And it is this democratisation, and levelling of the playing field, that is slowly but surely leading to the establishment of storytelling practices which are impacting deeply on audience engagement.

While not yet common, the inclusion of VR elements for blockbuster experiences has certainly become more common, with two major museums (The Louvre, Paris and The National Gallery, London) augmenting their Leonardo Da Vinci Blockbuster exhibition through the addition of VR elements. For the 'Leonardo da Vinci' retrospective at the Louvre, marking the 500th anniversary of Da Vinci's death in Amboise in 2019, the Louvre deliberately decided not to include the actual painting of the *Mona Lisa* in the exhibition as the lure of this one painting is so powerful, it has its own one-way queuing system to keep the gallery it occupies visitable. Including the *Mona* Lisa in a blockbuster exhibition would have made the exhibition 'practically unvisitable' (Rea 2019), and would also impact the millions of visitors to the Louvre who come on a pilgrimage to Paris just to see this one painting. Rather than temporarily moving the actual painting of the *Mona Lisa* into the ticketed exhibition space, the curators behind the exhibition opted instead for the inclusion of a VR extension. Following in the footsteps of the Tate, and even employing the same company, HTC Vive, 'Mona Lisa: Beyond the Glass' is a specially commissioned 7-min experience that combines information and experience, confirming an emerging trend for museums and cultural heritage sites to outsource the development of VR. The reason is easy to see: traditional museum structures have not yet been expanded to include VR expertise in their in-house teams.

One notable exception is New York's Metropolitan Museum of Art which launched its acclaimed 'The Met 360° Project' in 2016, raking in Webby Awards in 2017 and setting a new benchmark for the cultural heritage sector (The Met, 2016). The Met is unusual in the size and depth of its in-house digital team, and this has long enabled The Met to be sector-leading in its use and development of the digital. Ultimately, it is the integrated nature of the design, digital and curatorial teams in The Met that have given this particular institution such dominance in its digital work, and watching The Met gives an exciting glimpse at what the #CultureIsDigital future for museums and cultural heritage sites might look like. The aim of achieving a culture in museums and digital heritage sites where 'digital experiences are transforming how audiences engage with culture and are driving new forms of cultural participation and practice […] especially '[with regards to] younger audiences. …' (DCMS 2018) is getting closer. While few museums have the depth and breadth of teams that support The Met, the NHCM's 'The Eye as Witness' exhibition has important lessons to teach. It has demonstrated above all that for museums and cultural heritage sites, collaboration and creativity across non-traditional boundaries brings about maximum effect, and the means to achieve this is through a renewed focus on storytelling as the key that unlocks memories and co-creates context.

Much work remains to be done with regards to understanding the new, emerging landscapes of the participatory museum. While evaluations with a focus on how the device, the technology works are comparatively easy, more work is needed on the 'end-user experience', that is how audiences are reacting to the new configurations of the physical and digital estates of the museum. Emerging digital technologies are a key factor for the sustainable preservation and communication of cultural heritage for audiences of the future, and Ch'ng even suggests that technology is enabling a 'paradigm shift in [that] the nature of museums transitioned from having 'object-centredness' to visitor experience' at its core (Ch'ng et al. 2018).

The nature of the debates around the meaning of 'engagement' has also changed, with engagement increasingly coming to mean contact with a museum or cultural heritage site beyond a visit to its physical estate; the term 'experience economy' has been used to describe a digital estate that needs to extend simultaneously across a range of different platforms. Of course, each different social media platform works like its own heterotopic and boundaried space with its own distinctive narrative conventions and storytelling modes, so for a mature digital estate, museums and cultural heritage sites need to start to respond to these spaces by creating diverse content. Or rather than generate that content themselves, they need to enter these spaces for the express purpose of collaborative and dialogic co-creation of content of/By/For All engaged visitors (Simon 2017).

Museums often rely on a visitor's ability to read image—but rarely provide visual descriptions. One experiment, at MCA, highlighted just how complex the task of describing an image is Bahram and Lavatelli (2018). The discussion above of 'The Eye as Witness' has surely demonstrated just how the act of looking is heavily loaded with interpretation. Different viewers 'see' different meaning, and describing visual meaning is nothing more or less than an act of cultural translation. Asking visitors for their translations unlocks content and creates value which becomes inclusive of the many voices of a community, and again, it is the digital space as an extension of the physical estate of the museum and cultural heritage site that allows for this process to take shape. That process unlocks stories that otherwise might have been lost and this is what makes museums and cultural heritage sites such important sites for memory (Nora 1989). Arguably, there is no sector that suits the embracing of the digital more than that of arts and heritage organisation because it is the digital in its broadest sense that offers 'an opportunity to shift our relationship with […] audiences and battle […] engrained organisational culture. We have what it takes to do this well: a wealth of content, an ability to generate new ideas and a desire to build relationships with audiences' (#CultureIsDigital, 2018).

References

Bahram S, Lavatelli AC (2018) Using Coyote to describe the world. https://mw18.mwconf.org/paper/using-coyote-to-describe-the-world/

Baxandall M (1972) Painting and experience in fifteenth-century Italy. Oxford University Press, Oxford

Ch'ng E, Cai Y, Thwaites H (eds) (2018) Special issue on VR for culture and heritage with virtual reality

Ch'ng E, Cai S, Leow FT, Zhang T (2019) Adoption and use of emerging cultural technology in China's Museums. J Cult Herit 37:170–180

Craig J (2019) How are the V&A's online collections used? https://www.vam.ac.uk/blog/digital/how-are-the-vas-online-collections-used

Culture is digital. Policy Paper, DCMS, published 7 March 2018. https://www.gov.uk/government/publications/culture-is-digital

Culture is Digital, DCMS, March 2018, p 9. https://assets.publishing.service.gov.uk/government/uploads/system/uploads/attachment_data/file/687519/TT_v4.pdf

Foucault M (1968) Of other spaces. Diacritics 16:22–27

Greenblatt S (1980) Renaissance self-fashioning: from more to Shakespeare. Chicago University Press, Chicago

Harvey E, Hürter J, Umbach M, Wirsching A (eds) (2019) Private life and privacy in Nazi Germany. Cambridge University Press, Cambridge

Lewis A (2014a) How to gather data to show how visitors really use your site-specific features. https://www.vam.ac.uk/blog/digital/capturing-user-behaviour-specific-to-your-services

Lewis A (2014b) What can we learn from watching groups of visitors using digital museum exhibits? https://www.vam.ac.uk/blog/digital/digital-exhibits-observational-research

Liu H, Zhu X, Gao Y (2012) Museum digitisation construction analysis—survey into the public perception and use of Museum (博物馆数字化建设探析—公众对博物馆的认 知和使用状况调查). In: China Research Institute for Science Popularization (ed) Proceedings of the 19th National Conference on Theory Study Science Population. International Forum on Communication. Popular Science Press, Beijing, pp 343–349

Mekele MK, Pierdicca R, Frontoni E, Malinverni ES, Gain J (2018) A survey of augmented, virtual, and mixed reality for cultural heritage. ACM J Comput Cult Herit 11. https://dl.acm.org/doi/10.1145/3145534

Miles RS (1986) Lessons in 'human biology': testing a theory of exhibition design. Int J Museum Manage Curatorship 5:227–240

Modigliani VR. The Ochre Atelier (2017) https://www.tate.org.uk/whats-on/tate-modern/exhibition/modigliani/modigliani-vr-ochre-atelier

Mona Lisa: beyond the glass (Musee du Louvre, Paris, October 24, 2019–February 24, 2020). https://arts.vive.com/us/articles/projects/art-photography/mona_lisa_beyond_the_glass/

Necker S (forthcoming) German-Jewish family albums and the narration of identities from imperial Germany to the post-war years. https://www.nottingham.ac.uk/humanities/departments/history/research/research-projects/current-projects/photography-as-political-practice/photography-as-political-practice-in-national-socialism.aspx

Nora P (1989) Between memory and history: Les Lieux de Mémoire. Representations 26:7–24

Price K (2018) Designing a new welcome experience at the V&A. https://www.vam.ac.uk/blog/digital/designing-a-new-welcome-experience-at-the-va

Rea N (2019) 'The 'Mona Lisa' experience: how the Louvre's first-ever VR project, a 7-minute immersive da Vinci Odyssey, works. https://news.artnet.com/exhibitions/louvre-embraced-virtual-reality-leonardo-blockbuster-1686169

Shaheed F (2011) Report of the independent expert in the field of cultural rights. A/HRC/17/38. https://www.right-docs.org/doc/a-hrc-17-38/

Simon N (2010) The participatory museum. Museum 2.0

Simon N (2017) One by one. Building Digitally Confident Museums. https://one-by-one.uk/

Sontag S (1977) On photography. Farrar, Straus and Giroux, New York

Stafford J, Mansell JG (2020) Sound and place: digital mapping and community listening practice. National Science and Media Museum

Tennent P (2018) Thresholds. https://paultennent.wordpress.com/2018/06/07/thresholds/

Tennent P (2020) The eye as witness. https://paultennent.wordpress.com/2020/01/27/the-eye-as-witness/

Tennent P, Martindale S, Benford S, Darzentas D, Brundell P, Collishaw M (2020) Thresholds: embedding virtual reality in the Museum. J Comput Cult Herit 12. https://doi.org/10.1145/336 9394

The Met 360° Project. https://www.metmuseum.org/art/online-features/met-360-project

Umbach M (forthcoming) German private photo albums between subjectivity and ideology under National Socialism

Chapter 26
Virtual Environments as Memory Anchors

Eugene Ch'ng

Abstract In the future, the past will be as accessible as the present. This statement is becoming as true with respect of the near past, as it is true for ancient history, following the previous two decades of digital transformation of archaeological research. Institutions have a tendency to favour recording large historical events over smaller, less significant happenstance. The same institutions endorse more distant material cultures over contemporary artefacts, trivialising that which is in abundance over rare historical objects. Yet, the memory of every individual has value, at least to that person and their family, whilst each individual has a moral responsibility to remember their own pasts. In this context, the chapter presented here discusses the notion of memory anchors and how immersive virtual environments can facilitate the process of remembering, reliving, sharing, and retention of individual memory. It examines what virtual reality can offer to remembrance, and the resilience of memory anchors within such environments. The chapter argues that physical objects and spaces associated with each individual must be captured as a moral obligation, and that the responsibility of such activities should rest at the level of family units where these memories reside.

Keywords Memory anchors · Virtual reality · Immersive virtual environments · Near heritage

26.1 Introduction

We live through the passage of time, and within the boundaries of our physical dwellings and environments, where our identities are shaped and where memories of social interactions reside. But much like physical matter embodying cultural identities and values, that which dwells in the mind is eroded by time and distractions, particularly in the digital age where short attention spans define the individual. Within

E. Ch'ng (✉)
NVIDIA Joint-Lab on Mixed Reality, University of Nottingham Ningbo China, 199 Taikang East Road, Ningbo, China
e-mail: eugene.chng@nottingham.edu.cn

© Springer Nature Switzerland AG 2022
E. Ch'ng et al. (eds.), *Visual Heritage: Digital Approaches in Heritage Science*,
Springer Series on Cultural Computing,
https://doi.org/10.1007/978-3-030-77028-0_26

527

cities, rapid economic development threatens the perpetuity of premises, the human need to improve and adapt transforms dwelling spaces, and as a consequence, the old is continually being replaced by the new. Memories of relationships sweet and bitter, embedded within objects distributed within such spaces, diminish and, in time, the spaces that are home to these memories are lost, together with those that used to dwell in them.

Cultural heritage evaluated at the national level holds cultural and symbolic values that are institutionally preserved and conserved, and heritage items that have an economic value may be exploited for heritage tourism. However, the majority of heritage objects and monuments that are considered worth preserving are from antiquity. Figure 26.1 shows a graph plotting the 2018 listing of UNESCO World Heritage Sites. The majority of sites are clustered around 100 to 5,000 years before the present, and with a mean of 700. The sparser plots are sites that are ancient and naturally rare, and sites that are below 100 years old, but in abundance, are rarely registered and thereby equally sparse.

The question is, when can objects and places which preserve and link memories from the near past, but have no significant contemporary value at the national level, warrant preservation? Perhaps after 50 years have passed, yet we must not forget that time can erode living memories. These objects, or the spaces they are associated with are usually discarded together with the memories embedded within them. The people who have used them are also gone, leaving behind no records of the life they once lived. In time, perhaps hundreds of years later, future archaeologists will excavate

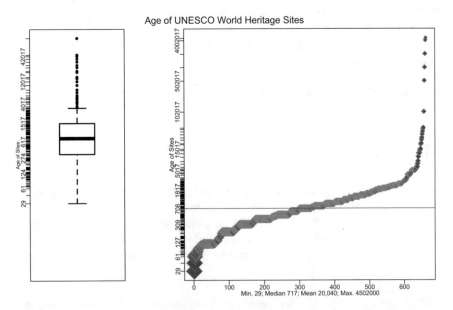

Fig. 26.1 A graph of UNESCO World Heritage Listing. The majority of sites are clustered between 100 and 5,000 years, sparse points are ancient and new sites (E. Ch'ng)

these sites, repeating the same cycle yet again, wondering what it was like living in the distant past.

Personal memories are important to individuals for a number of reasons. We do not merely live in the moment because we are differentiated from the animals. One 'clings relentlessly to the past: however far and fast he may run, this chain runs with him' (Nietzsche 1997). As human beings we remember, and there is the moral responsibility to remember (Blustein 2008), for 'our sense of ourselves depends crucially on the subjective experience of remembering our pasts' (Schacter 1995). Other reasons may exist to remember, as Ross stated, for others' amusements with stories fashioned from memories, for curiosity, for self-understanding, and as a means of learning about preferences and abilities (Ross 1989). Memory, therefore, is often called upon to provide a 'usable past' (Zamora 1997), an account of events and actors that can be harnessed for some purpose in the present. Literatures are saturated with common reasons for the invocation of a usable past in individual or collective claims for identity (e.g. Sacks 1985; Novick 2000).

Can we preserve our life and memory as bequests for our children, so that memories can be retained and that our future generations can relive our present? Can the elderly relive their childhood by being brought back to their pasts? Can we record, in essence, the image of a scene and include stories so as to trigger memories and reinforce identity? Are we able to continue from where we were, by virtually extending the past and also constructing new memories from it? Here, I am not referring to videos or any traditional media recordings but the increasingly pervasive nature of digital capture, and especially Virtual Reality as a medium, as spaces and place from which we may record and sustain memories, relive our past, and as a means of accessibility for our future generations. Like an artist recording objects, scenes, and people that are meaningful to them, we will soon be able to capture objects and spaces that are meaningful to us as a permanent record within virtual environments.

This chapter explores the significance of digital capture and the ubiquity of Virtual Reality in our lives, and the implications of such technologies when used for preserving our memories via memory anchors embedded within objects and spaces through virtual environments.

26.2 Background

History and memory are different but related terms, they involve distinct yet relative time periods between containers of memory. The difference is that which is being kept alive and the distant past we have no immediate personal memory of. According to Olick and Robbins 'History is the remembered past to which we no longer have an "organic" relation—the past that is no longer an important part of our lives—while collective memory is the active past that forms our identities' (Olick and Robbins 1998, p. 111). Olick and Robbins suggested that we could celebrate even that which we have not personally experienced by 'keeping the given past alive for us,' or that 'it can be alive in historical records.' The latter perhaps can be through curation in galleries, libraries, archives, and museums. Cultural festivals and traditions as heterotopias have kept the past alive for us, and museums in particular have done well in keeping histories alive via active curation and exhibitions. The question is for how long can memory persists, and by what means can we extend memories in ways which will keep them alive, at least for far longer than our ability to remember? Are there ways in which we could continue our past by extending memories from it? While there can be no 'real memory' (Nora 1989), only that which each one can remember and each person's interpretation of what has been retained in the carriers of memory, the means by which we encapsulate the details of memorial events within spaces therefore do matter.

While histories are constructed, memories can be contained or carried in physical objects (Keenan 1998; Stewart 1994), in environments (Smith 1988), in our bodies (Connerton 1989), and in new media (Garde-Hansen et al. 2009; Neiger et al. 2011). Carriers of memory require that one has made direct relationship with them, the stronger the relationship, the more impressionable they are. Thus, it is really individuals who retain memories from which static objects, environments, the body act as clues and from which memories are stored and recalled. The difference between new media, as compared to the aforementioned carriers of memory, is that it requires an active record and construction. But that which is recorded using new media is perhaps more a history than a memory. New media also allows more information to be recorded, i.e. thoughts to be recorded as texts, events as photos, and activities as videos. Social media acts as an asynchronous, interactive carrier from which exchanges occur, and from which captured traces of the past are recorded and recalled.

Physical objects such as souvenirs can act as traces of authentic experiences (Stewart 1994), surviving as a sign of events existing only as narratives, 'pertaining only to the possessor of the object (p. 137), and meaningless to those who have no relationships with the possessor, and the event from which the souvenir was acquired.' Photographs too, provide cues from which memories are recollected. We return to our collections of photographs in order to re-live the memory of an event (Keenan 1998), yet there is the possibility that the memorial function of the photograph is negated, and that it both supplements but also configures memory (p.60), becoming instead 'false memory' (Benjamin 1999; Kracauer and Levin 1993). There is the argument that photography is 'never, in essence, a memory ... but it actually blocks memory, quickly becomes a counter-memory' (Barthes 1981). Others argue that memory retains that which is significant to a person, and that photography captures everything, it 'grasps what is given as a spatial (or temporal) continuum' (Kracauer and Levin 1993). Yet, the notion that photography has the ability to capture everything is perhaps falsified by the nature of the medium itself. Photography can really only capture the moment of a scene, momentous or insignificant as it may be. It may be able to tell a story, but only to the capacity of a two-dimensional image. Videography, including clips of sequences of images are able to capture, due to their temporal nature, more details of activities but it has its limits. The act of making a photograph or a video implies an agency at work, that is, the person capturing the scene frames that scene, and therefore the memory. The angle of the capture, the time of day, the subject, and context all require an act of interpretation, and that which seems to be most important to the person at the moment of capture. A photograph or a video is necessarily framed and thereby, has the tendency to configure memory.

All that which is recorded is constructed, and all that is consumed and remembered of the constructed is personal and subjective. There can never be neutrality in the information that has been captured. I contend that spaces which have become places can store much more, and therefore, the scope of recollection of episodic events can be much more than a mere picture. Neutrality exists if entire spaces rather than a moment can be captured. Virtual environments can depict entire spaces rather than mere images of them, and places therefore can be reconstructed by each individual. There is no distinction between analogue and digital pictures, or videos, for they all project the same image, and that picture resolution is a minor factor in memory anchors. As such, any medium that is intended for use for capturing the context of memories must therefore capture entire spaces including the objects therein.

Spaces that have become places for people can become environments whereby memory of 'lost' experiences are retained. Smith's long-term 'reinstatement effects' (Smith 1979) explain 'the flood of memories one experiences when returning to a former residence after a long absence' (Smith 1988, p. 14). As a stronger memory site, in comparison to photographs, this can only be attributed to the 'rich integration in memory of experiences with environmental information' provided by dwelling in a place for a long period of time (ibid, p. 14). This points to episodic memory (Tulving 1972) contained within individuals. This particular form of memory involves 'the remembering of episodes of our lives and is contextually bound; that is, the time and place of occurrence are inextricable parts of memory for episodes. This type of memory enables the mental time travel in which we engage when we think back to an earlier occasion' (Roediger and Goff 1998, p. 250).

Memories are also recalled within social frameworks in contemporary thinking, as opposed to the Freudian approach to psychology. For example, Connerton questioned how the social memory of groups can be 'conveyed and retained' (Connerton 1989). Such collective memories are, according to him, organised and legitimated via 'embodied memory' within the context of social activities, such as commemorative ceremonies (inscribing) and bodily practices (incorporating). Inscribing relates to activities that facilitate the storing and retrieving of memory such as photography, writing, computers, etc., and incorporating refers to physical activities such as the repertoires of gestures, a handshake, for example, or orality, rituals, performances, etc. The former uses external media or devices as a means for storing and retrieving memory and the latter, the use of the body with its postures, gestures, and activities as a device for remembering. The notion of the body as a device for remembering, a carrier of memory in relation to bodily practices is more authentic, and occurs within a social context as they are direct memories which are embodied in a person, as opposed to that which has been inscribed, much like the use and abuse of new media.

Although memories are retained within the individual's body, they are often never constructed and recalled outside of social activities. We are not isolated beings and memories are constructed more strongly, and recalled externally, within social frameworks. Halbwachs recalled that '... if we examine a little more closely how we recollect things, we will surely realize that the greatest number of memories come back to us when our parents, our friends, or other persons recall them to us' (Halbwachs 1992). Halbwachs proposed that individual memory is formed and recollected in social contexts, within groups. '[I]t is in society that people normally acquire their memories. It is also in society that they recall, recognize and localize their memories...' (ibid. p. 38), and is therefore collective. It is important to make a distinction here. According to Halbwachs, it is the individuals who remember, even though they tend to remember within the social context, and as groups. This remembering has been augmented by the nature of the digital (Negroponte 1996), where social media posts are contributed to asynchronously, via comments by family members. I propose that, since the use of virtual reality is a bodily practice, it affords the phenomenology of embodiment as opposed to the passive viewing of photographs or videos, and that memories are formed and recollected within social contexts. A shared space that is virtually reconstructed from the past is a venue for sharing, and therefore a venue for memory recollection.

Digital media certainly plays a role in contemporary memory storage. Although there is no need to expound collective memory and mass media, social media has certainly become a repository of personal memory. The past decades of development and use of the social web have only exacerbated the human need to record everything from the triviality of junk food on the table, to personal opinions and collective sentiments regarding public events. Borrowing the term 'memory boom' (Huyssen 2003), this is marked by the mass affordability and the availability of recording and dissemination channels such as social media. Personal, generational, and public memory have found new platforms as carriers of memory from which memories are stored and also inscribed. This is where every race, gender, social class, and institutions can curate memories, both collectively and individually with influences from the likes and comments from their immediate social circle. Biographies are no longer only given to elites, social media has given rise to the construction of distributed biographies of the non-important, of selfies and foods, and of trivial moments, all democratised by digital technologies. The convenience and mobility of smart phones has loosened the need to construct proper sentences, and as a consequence the need to think carefully before posting to social media. Habitual posting to social media involves little cost and thereby the moment of posting is the moment where instantaneous thoughts are captured and, to an extent, more candid. Of course, for the majority, the awareness of the need to construct online personas biases memory but is nevertheless a personal memory in itself.

26.3 Memory Anchors

Memory anchors are psychological anchors attached to objects and spaces at a moment in time upon which their future exposure will mentally usher a person back to the moment when the anchor was placed. Memory anchors are not carriers, but they necessarily exist within carriers. Such memories can be extremely vivid, if they are personally significant and emotionally arousing. I wish to relate memories recalled via memory anchors to 'flashbulb memories' (Brown and Kulik 1977) although they differ from the extremity of hyperthymesia (Parker et al. 2006). They are anchors for that reason, for they function as a weight on a locale to which a person's memory is fastened. Often, the deeper the impression of a scene, the firmer the anchor is embedded on the site of memory. Memory anchors, as a concept, are much more specific than memory cues. They involve a specific scene, an image of a past experience that is attached to a physical object, a collection of objects, a place, and a moment in time where the anchor was placed. It involves no conscious effort, for the event itself is the anchor. A photograph from which a scene or an image is captured, or a video depicting the scenario may also act as cues from which the anchor is invoked. A memory cue is a broader term in comparison to that of a memory anchor, and may refer to signals upon which an action, or memories that are not specific to an experience are triggered. Rather, cues are more general to the triggering of information. Memory anchors are also differentiated from carriers of memory, which are containers of information associated with memories. Memory anchors are therefore not difficult to define, and the notion of memory anchors is intuitive for the fact that we have all experienced them.

An old photograph, or a tree leaf falling out of a book, can trigger the memory of the site where the leaf was collected, up to the point that it was placed onto the specific page, and perhaps even beyond that scene. An old photograph recalls in the person not only the scene of the insertion of it within the book, but also the memory of that photograph. Similarly, gifts of sentimental values may invoke an anchor attached to them. The gifts themselves are anchors upon which scenes of pleasant memories are recalled. Sensations that are not visual and tactile, such as olfactory and aural cues, can all act as anchors upon which we are brought back in time to the places where such memories are anchored. Spaces that are sites upon which objects exist, and where events occur, are better-conditioned surfaces on which memory anchors can be embedded. Other non-visual senses can only serve to augment the holding power of memory anchors. Digital photos and videos are no different than analogue and physical media, where memory anchors occur, although the physicality of a hardcopy and the tactility of an object do provide more senses from which memories stored within our bodies are summoned.

From these experiences of mental time travel, many stories can be recalled and told within social frameworks, and memories can be kept alive as a result. Memory anchors provide a means from which stories internal to oneself can be shared. The problem is that whilst these memories are real to the narrator, the audiences can only imagine as they have never experienced them. When shared, the memories become the imagined memory of close family and friends. This concept on the sharing of what is real to the sharer and the imagination of the audiences will be expounded later.

How resilient are memory anchors? Memory anchors persists as long as a person is alive, or the persons sharing the same memory can continue telling their stories.

Regardless, the demise of a person where actual memory resides does mean the death of that person's memory anchors. There is no possible means of retrieving them if the carrier of memory is deceased. Unless there is a transcription of memory in some medium, such as an autobiography, the memory is therefore dead. Memory anchors can eternalise the moment as long as the person is alive.

26.3.1 Virtual Environments as Memory Anchors

Whilst carriers of memories can all become memory anchors through which we mentally travel back to the past, some tended to provide weaker modes of travel than others. Of course, the capacity to recall is dependent on many factors, one of which is the mental faculty of the individual. However, and as argued, the strongest invocation of memory anchors are where there is are sites where anchors are cast, and within entire environments. As memory does not reappear but is actively recalled from traces from the past (Neisser 2014), richer contexts may provide stronger, multiple cues from which memories are richly recalled. Virtual environments, where entire physical spaces, including the objects, moods, and other sensual information, such as olfactory cues and aural information that are digitally captured and made accessible, will provide a stronger context from which memories can be recalled. The completeness of knowledge of an environment is therefore a core factor, for we will never know which aspect of the place is significant to the subject.

We rely on our mental capacity invoked by memory anchors to gain access to the past, but memories are often eroded with the passing of time, with only the essence of the event recalled, and without details of the surroundings. We get the substance of the scene without the minutiae. As we understand, memory recollections and reconstructions can be assisted via technology. To record, or to leave traces from which events may be reconstructed is a trait of nature, and this physical law has benefited curious intellectuals for centuries. From the record of climate trends in fossil pollens (Overpeck et al. 1990) and insect remains (Elias 1991), to the recording of natural events such as palaeo-tsunamis on sedimentary microfossil characteristics of deposits (Smith et al. 2004), nature leaves traces from which we may reconstruct the past. Homo sapiens have not departed from this trait of nature. We tend to embellish the moment an effective recording method is found, such as the invention of the cuneiform system of writing thousands of years ago (Walker 1987). Once a recording medium is discovered, the systematisation of recording events is made possible, and records are used for all sorts of benefits, for communication, for scientific knowledge, education, entertainment, and for advancing civilisation. Recording in other forms stretches far a back and includes the carving of a female mammoth ivory figurine 35,000 years ago (Conard 2009). The rise of social media serves only to satisfy the need to record everything through the convenience of a mobile device.

We often record through digital photographs events and objects which we deemed important. Whilst that which is important is relative to each individual, a sequence of composed snapshots can capture the story of the scene at the time of leisure, whilst larger sequences of images from multiple angles are recorded in more professional activities. The number of photographs within the sequence is probably directly proportional to the image of the event and therefore more photographs can translate to more complete details of the image of the scenario, which allows the reality at the time of capture to be mentally reconstructed later. The consequential development of close-range photogrammetry techniques and accessible methods for capturing objects and scenes (Ch'ng et al. 2019a; Hanan et al. 2015; Samaan et al. 2016) have coincided with the accessibility of higher resolution mobile imaging devices, in combination with the excessive, obsessive photo-taking habits of the generation (Macmillan 2016), makes perfect sense for recording sites of memory anchors. A combination of technologies with the ease of digital photography have made it possible to extend 2D photography into accessible 3D spaces. Environments and objects that are digitally captured via close-range photogrammetry, and subsequently processed into immersive virtual environments can embed more information than sequences of images or videos.

Immersive virtual environments can reduce the cognitive load. By reconstructing entire spaces within 3D, and providing cues as well as facilitating the invocation of memory anchors, we make possible a more accurate recollection of the image of the scene based on more complete reconstructions of the place.

26.4   How Can Immersive Virtual Environments Sustain Memory?

Can virtual environments eternalise memory anchors even when a person is deceased? Virtual environments can be where memories and imagination conjoin. The capturing of entire spaces provide stronger cues whereby memories can be recollected and shared, and where the listener need not invoke imagination, but rather be at the same place, looking at the same object at the moment of capture. We often do not think about this. When we share a story that is still vivid in our minds, to us the stories we tell are our reality. The stories are what we have personally experienced and we need only recall them, invoking the memory anchor which is so deeply embedded in the site. To our audiences however, as the events we have shared are not part of their memory, they can only experience the story based on our narrative (Fig. 26.2). If our narratives are emotionally arousing, and our audiences are attuned to our sentiments, they may at most be touched by the feelings we convey. They will not be able to share the same space where the events have occurred. By capturing the environment at the moment of the event, and sharing that virtual space with our audience, both the narrator and the audience can share the same space from the moment of capture from x number of years ago. Such spaces can provide a means of keeping memories alive. Such spaces are better than photographs and videos, they capture more information that can act as traces from the past (Schacter 1995), and that can be used for memory recollection. I contend that virtual environments can become sites from which the

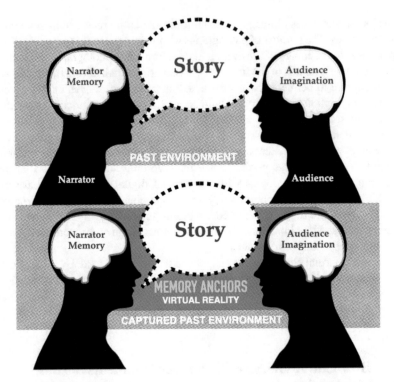

Fig. 26.2 Memory recall and the sharing of past reality remains outside of the experience of the audience and therefore can at best be an imagination. Virtual environments that capture spaces and permits the sharing of the same place and thereby the sharing and transfer of memory (E. Ch'ng)

transfer of living stories, and personal memory anchors, may be embedded in another person. This may be the meeting point of Nora's (Nora 1989) *lieux de memoir* and *melieux de memoir*. Here, Nora refers to *melieux de memoir* as the real environment of memory which may no longer exist, 'There are *lieux de mémoire*, sites of memory, because there are no longer *milieux de mémoire*, real environments of memory,' and *lieux de memoir* is 'any significant entity, whether material or non-material in nature, which by dint of human will or the work of time has become a symbolic element of the memorial heritage of any community,' spoken in the collective sense. Virtual environments can capture the real environment of memory. At once natural and artificial, simple and ambiguous, concrete and abstract, they are lieux—places, sites, causes—in three senses—material, symbolic and functional" (ibid.) and thus, the meeting point of *lieux de memoir* and *melieux de memoir*.

Virtual environments can be spaces for sharing memories, where memory anchors can be invoked. Furthermore, memory recollections can occur in relation to another individual or group, where 'they recall, recognize, and localize their memories' (Halbwachs 1992). This is where stories can be told and memories can be kept alive within our social framework in the individual, and also passed on to our kindreds and acquaintances.

We know that particular medium can provide cues from which memories are recalled, and that episodic memories can be recollected by revisiting spaces where past events have occurred. But can places from the past and reconstructed in virtual environments be used for virtual time travel (Ch'ng 2009)? I argue that it is entirely possible, at least visually and as long as virtual environments are perceived as real. Formal studies on the reaction of VR users using believability metrics, anecdotal evidences, and observations from reactions to VR experiences suggest that the believability of computer reconstructions of environments can be simulated via sight, mapped to positional and rotational tracking of the gaze and the physical body of the user. A body of literature accumulated over several decades investigating the sense of believability and psychological immersion indicates that virtual time travel can be made possible. Pioneers of the concept of spatial presence, defined as the sense of 'being there' (Biocca 1999; Lombard and Ditton 1997; Steuer 1992) have examined psychological transport within simulated environments. The sense of the virtual self of a person using VR experienced as an actual self, and the concept of 'social presence' or the 'sense of being with another' have also been explored (Biocca et al. 2003). Such works have led to applications within cultural heritage whereby behaviours of first-time users of VR were observed (Leow et al. 2017). The study (*ibid.*) reveals that observers were also affected by the realism of the virtual site. More formal, extended studies suggest that virtually reconstructed heritage sites that are believable can create meanings and form memories within users (Ch'ng et al. 2019b). Psychological phenomena directly affecting physiological behaviours, such as proprioception or the sense of self-movement and awareness of body position embodied in a virtual avatar can be simulated according to formal experiments (Sanchez-Vives and Slater 2005; Valori et al. 2020; Wyszecki et al. 1986; Yuan and Steed 2010).

A sense of nostalgia can also be invoked using Virtual Reality. Cai et al.'s pioneering research (Cai et al. 2018) comparing photographs, 360° immersive videos, and virtual reality reported that 360° videos can induce a stronger sense of nostalgia if compared to photographs, but VR provided the strongest sense of nostalgia in participants. The reason that true virtual environments can provide stronger invocations of nostalgia is that users can travel within the environment. Unlike 360° videos where users are confined to a passive viewer position in an immersive environment, true VR environments allow objects to be picked up and interacted with, together with navigation using full body movements. The use of VR involves embodied interactions within both the place itself and with the objects and therefore, has accords with a digital phenomenology of embodiment (Husserl 1950, 2012; Merleau-Ponty 1976). This is where an adopted virtual body becomes the lived centre of experience within the virtual reconstruction of a real site.

Within virtual environments, virtual objects captured from the original physical object, if processed properly, will have little visual qualitative differences. The visual appearance can be as real as the original. Virtual objects can be picked up and interacted with, and virtual environments can become much more than photographs

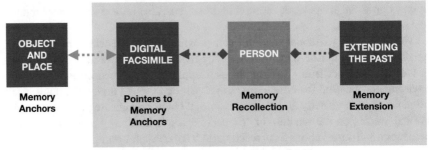

Fig. 26.3 Virtual environments hosting memory anchors can act as a bridge that connects the past to the present. Within the virtual environment, the reliving and extending of the past sustains and continues shared memories (E. Ch'ng)

and videos, in that they can be entered and embodied within familiar spaces. Although interactions in present VR have not advanced to a stage where haptic feedbacks and material tactility can be simulated, the visual quality of the objects themselves is sufficient for them to become sites of memory anchors. Having haptic feedbacks and material tactility could provide much more information from which memory anchors are invoked, but the visual provides the 'believability' of virtual objects. When considering the practicality of such a position, there are also the issues of digital storage and sustainability of access, as hardware, platforms, and operating systems change over time, but these are beyond the scope of this chapter.

True VR environments and the composition of objects within them can become extensions of past places. They can act as a bridge from which the past can be continued in the present. Virtual environments can become a means for virtual time travel, linking spaces from the past with present activities, and thereby continuing memory (Fig. 26.3).

26.4.1 Purpose and Responsibility

How can we make use of virtual environments for keeping memories alive, and what can be done to facilitate the continuation of memory within such spaces?

Memories are important to individuals, for they define the person's identity (i.e. the Lockean view) from which reflections are based. A personal memory is important for self-understanding, and is a useful resource from which stories are fashioned for others' benefits—for entertainment, for sharing moments, for learning, and for mentoring. The individual memory is therefore a 'usable past' for both the person and for his or her social circle. The individual memory is thus important for the person, and an immediate social circle. Places, which are sites upon which memories have been anchored, are important for capture. Such places may become attached to some experiences, and these have become meaningful to the extent that place attachment occurs (Florek 2011; Lewicka 2011). Such places have meanings, defined by Schroeder as 'the thoughts, feelings, memories and interpretations evoked by a landscape' (Schroeder 1991). Such places may also be preferred over others for personal reasons, such as a place of comfort, a place where one feels secure, or where emotional attachments have occurred. A sense of place can occur as a result of the cultivation of meaning, and artefacts may be associated with such places (Giuliani 2003). Virtual environments captured from such places can be used to augment the 'usable past.'

We have seen that memories are never recalled outside of social frameworks, and therefore shared memories between family and friends within spaces are important to capture. This is the move from the immediate level to the individual memory. The digital capture and curation of individual and shared memory is the responsibility of the respective individual and family units, from which memories can be kept alive, and transferred from generation to generation. At a broader level, collective memory at the community and societal level can be captured. Whilst individuals and family units share meaning in places, communities may derive meaning from religious, historical, or cultural events and activities (Scannell and Gifford 2010). It is proposed that virtual environments captured at this level should be curated by community museums. It has been argued that a site at which one has acquired place attachment to (Lewicka 2011, p. 207–230) must be recorded by the individual as a responsibility. However, there may be symbolic values attached to a given place even if the individual and the family unit have not lived there for a sufficient time to have developed a bond, to be rooted, or to acquire a sense of place for the particular site. Regardless, any environment that has become a place where there are memory anchors should be captured, for they are bound to disappear with the passage of time.

26.4.2 Risks and Responsibility

As Virtual Reality technology becomes a powerful tool, the risk of memory reconfiguration as a result of experiencing simulated reality must be mitigated. The negative consequences of misusing technology, particularly when such technology can transform perception and consequently behaviours (Slater et al. 2020) must be mitigated. As with photography, there is the risk of having memories reconfigured. Virtual environments carry a greater risk than photography as they are are highly editable, i.e., virtual objects, their properties and entire sites can be changed, and objects can be excluded and new items can be inserted. Whilst the mediatisation of memory makes the past more visible, accessible, and fluid (Garde-Hansen et al. 2009, p. 29), we should take note of the risk that '... any medium used to record and archive memory has a redemptive function and that any attempt to save memory always entails loss and forgetting as well as additions and supplements' (p. 19). Digital technology has indeed made the past more accessible, but the use of digital technology must be moderated so that its deliberate use for wrongful purposes is avoided.

Although the effects of virtual environments in reconstructing and reconfiguring memory have not been formally studied, persistent virtual worlds are known to influence the psychology of users (see for example, Partala 2011). Risks have to be mitigated in such practices, so as to prevent memory distortion in the experience and sharing of reconstructed sites.

26.5 Conclusion

This chapter examined the concept of memory anchors, and proposes virtual environments as sites for the sharing, reliving, and recollection of memory and thereby making the past accessible. Memory is transient and resides only within individuals. Memories that are alive, and carried within us, are linked and embedded within physical objects, through gestures and our bodily activities. Memory is also distributed in new media, all of which have a parallel lifespan of their own, as they are shared across the web. The temporality of each carrier of memory, in combination with our capacity to remember, thus decides the longevity of memory. Physical objects persist for as long as their materiality, spatial temporality, and mobility, for not all objects are in our possession forever. Our bodily practice and gestures are equally impermanent, they change according to our culture and are shaped by our lifestyle activities. The lifespan of new media is subject to the management of digital information in our personal devices. It is linked to and decided by the business models of the Cloud services of technological corporations. The digital media that carries traces of our memory are conditional upon the sustainability of these corporations. As a consequence, our trust in the corporate management of digital media, from which we recall memory, is as reliable as the hope that our personal memories may have some importance to memory institutions such as libraries and museums, and insofar as they might be interested in documenting them. Therefore, there is a responsibility to use whatever means possible to record our personal memory as best we can, so that they may persist for as long as is feasible or required.

This chapter argues that there are ways of keeping memories alive, and permit memory anchors to be invoked, before they become reconstructed history or, intellectual representations of the past. As opposed to the general belief that photos and videos can capture everything, they are, at best, glimpses of a scenario, as the act of framing a photo or video requires selectivity and interpretation. For all that is recorded is constructed, and all that is consumed and remembered of the constructed is personal and subjective. A counter argument may be given, as any act of capture is selective and a deliberate attempt to frame a subject. Selectivity is only true of the space and moment of capture of an event or site that is meaningful to us. It excludes all that is outside of the place. As close-range photogrammetry captures photographs of every visible surface, including light and shade, it captures the entirety of the visible environment into which one may enter. Thus, selectivity and framing is left to the person entering the space, for one can choose to navigate and view every aspect of the environment.

The argument provided in this chapter proposes that spaces which have become places can store much more information, and that the spaces captured as virtual environments will afford an unframed image from which the recollection of memory can be shared. Such a virtual environment is neutral and is complete as far as the visual materiality of the place is concerned, and can be a means of keeping memories alive through sharing. Often, memory tends to flood the mind of one who has returned to a place of significance after an extended period of time. While many details of the place may have been forgotten, the essence of the space and the familiarity of it can bring back fond memories. This is true even when furniture, fittings, and objects might have changed or have been removed. A virtual environment is different from a photograph in this sense, in that the entire space with both their essence and objects are captured at the moment of significance, perhaps by the same person that have found the moment to be meaningful and therefore, even if selectivity and framing is unavoidable, that capture is personal. Virtual environments are places where memories and imagination are conjoined, for the audience and the sharer can both be at the same space when stories are told.

Virtual Reality is a powerful medium, and virtual spaces of memory anchors once captured can be permanently owned by us. This is the digital means to capture and share memory that is neutral and unframed, and without the need to fill in physical details during recollection. This therefore, is a more neutral approach for re-enacting, recalling, sharing and extending memories. Finally, as the projection of memory affects the individual and their immediate social circle, the use of immersive virtual environments must acknowledge the ethics of use. The power to reconfigure memories with virtual environments will need to be evaluated given the mutability and increasing 'believability' of virtually recorded scenes. Finally, care should be taken as it remains a tragedy of technology that the tools that we use to preserve significant memory may also be used for distorting and reconfiguring them.

References

Barthes, R. (1981). Camera Ludda: Reflection on Photography, trans. *Richard Howard (New York: Hill & Wang, the Noonday Press, 1981)*. Benjamin, W. (2010). A small history of photography.

Benjamin W (1999) A short history of photography, selected writings. In: Michael WJ, Howard E, Gary S (eds) Cambridge, Massachusetts, and London, England: The Belknap Press of Harvard University Press, vol 2, 1927–1934

Biocca F (1999) The cyborg's dilemma: Progressive embodiment in virtual environments. Human Factors in Information Technology 13:113–144

Biocca F, Harms C, Burgoon JK (2003) Toward a more robust theory and measure of social presence: Review and suggested criteria. Presence 12(5):456–480

Blustein J (2008) The moral demands of memory. Cambridge University Press

Brown R, Kulik J (1977) Flashbulb memories. Cognition 5(1):73–99

Cai S, Ch'ng E, and Li Y (2018) A comparison of the capacities of VR and 360 degree video for coordinating memory in the experience of cultural heritage. In: Digital heritage 2018, San Francisco, USA. IEEE

Ch'ng, E. (2009) Experiential archaeology: is virtual time travel possible? J Cult Herit 20(2009):458–470

Ch'ng E, Cai S, Zhang TE, Leow F-T. (2019a) Crowdsourcing 3D cultural heritage: best practice for mass photogrammetry. J Sustain. Dev. 9(1):24–42.

Ch'ng E, Li Y, Cai S, Leow F-T (2019b) The effects of VR environments on the acceptance, experience and expectations of cultural heritage learning. J Comput Cult Herit

Conard NJ (2009) A female figurine from the basal Aurignacian of Hohle Fels Cave in southwestern Germany. Nature 459(7244):248

Connerton P (1989) How societies remember. Cambridge University Press

Elias SA (1991) Insects and climate change. Bioscience 41(8):552–559

Florek M (2011) No place like home: Perspectives on place attachment and impacts on city management. J City Manag 1(4):346–354

Garde-Hansen J, Hoskins A (2009) Reading A. Save as... digital memories. Springer

Giuliani MV (2003) Theory of attachment and place attachment. na.

Halbwachs M (1992) The social frameworks of memory. On collective memory, pp 35–189

Hanan H, Suwardhi D, Nurhasanah T, Santa Bukit E (2015) Batak Toba cultural heritage and close-range photogrammetry. Procedia Soc Behav Sci 184:187–195

Husserl E (1950) Ideen zu einer reinen Phänomenologie und phänomenologischen Philosophie

Husserl E (2012) Ideas pertaining to a pure phenomenology and to a phenomenological philosophy: first book: General introduction to a pure phenomenology, vol 2. Springer Science & Business Media

Huyssen A (2003) Present pasts: urban palimpsests and the politics of memory. Stanford University Press

Keenan C (1998) On the relationship between personal photographs and individual memory. Hist Photogr 22(1):60–64

Kracauer S, Levin TY (1993) Photography

Leow F-T, Ch'ng E, Zhang T, Cai S, See S (2017) "In-The-Wild" observation and evaluation of a Chinese heritage VR environment with the HTC VIVE. In: International conference on virtual systems and multimedia (VSMM), 31 Oct–2 Nov, Dublin, Ireland

Lewicka M (2011) Place attachment: how far have we come in the last 40 years? J Environ Psychol 31(3):207–230

Lombard M, Ditton T (1997) At the heart of it all: the concept of presence. J Comput Mediat Commun 3(2):0

Macmillan R (2016) What's lost when we photograph life instead of experiencing it? The Conversation. https://theconversation.com/whats-lost-when-we-photograph-life-instead-of-experiencing-it-58392 (Accessed July 28, 2019)

Merleau-Ponty M (1976) Phénoménologie de la perception (1945). Libraqire Gallimard, Paris

Negroponte N (1996) Being digital. Vintage

Neiger M, Meyers O, Zandberg E (2011) On media memory: collective memory in a new media age. Springer

Neisser U (2014) Cognitive psychology: classic edition. Psychology Press

Nietzsche F (1997) Nietzsche: untimely meditations. Cambridge University Press

Nora P (1989) Between memory and history: Les Liex de Mémoire. Representations 26:7–25

Novick P (2000) The Holocaust and collective memory: The American experience. Bloomsbury London

Olick JK, Robbins J (1998) Social memory studies: from "collective memory" to the historical sociology of mnemonic practices. Ann Rev Sociol 24(1):105–140

Overpeck JT, Rind D, Goldberg R (1990) Climate-induced changes in forest disturbance and vegetation. Nature 343(6253):51

Parker ES, Cahill L, McGaugh JL (2006) A case of unusual autobiographical remembering. Neurocase 12(1):35–49

Partala T (2011) Psychological needs and virtual worlds: case second life. Int J Hum Comput Stud 69(12):787–800

Roediger H, Goff L (1998) Memory. In: Bechtel W, Graham G, Balota DA (eds) A companion to cognitive science. Blackwell, Oxford, pp 250–264

Ross M (1989) Relation of implicit theories to the construction of personal histories. Psychol Rev 96(2):341

Sacks O (1985) The man who mistook his wife for a hat. Macat Library

Samaan M, Deseilligny MP, Heno R, Vaissière EDL, Roger J (2016) Close-range photogrammetric tools for epigraphic surveys. J Comput Cult Heritage (JOCCH) 9(3):16

Sanchez-Vives MV, Slater M (2005) From presence to consciousness through virtual reality. Nat Rev Neurosci 6(4):332

Scannell L, Gifford R (2010) Defining place attachment: a tripartite organizing framework. J Environ Psychol 30(1):1–10

Schacter DL (1995) Memory distortions: how minds, brains, and societies reconstruct the past. In: This book consists of papers presented at the 1st conference sponsored by the Harvard Ctr for the Study of Mind, Brain, and Behavior, Cambridge, MA, May 6–8, 1994. Harvard University Press

Schroeder HW (1991) Preference and meaning of arboretum landscapes: Combining quantitative and qualitative data. J Environ Psychol 11(3):231–248

Slater M, Gonzalez-Liencres C, Haggard P, Vinkers C, Gregory-Clarke R, Jelley S, Watson Z, Breen G, Schwarz R, Steptoe W (2020) The ethics of realism in virtual and augmented reality. Front Virtual Reality 1:1

Smith DE, Shi S, Cullingford RA, Dawson AG, Dawson S, Firth CR, Foster IDL, Fretwell PT, Haggart BA, Holloway LK (2004) The holocene storegga slide tsunami in the United Kingdom. Quatern Sci Rev 23(23–24):2291–2321

Smith SM (1979) Remembering in and out of context. J Exp Psychol Human Learn Memory 5(5):460

Smith SM (1988) Environmental context—dependent memory

Steuer J (1992) Defining virtual reality: dimensions determining telepresence. J Commun 42:72–92

Stewart S (1994) Objects of desire. Interpreting objects and collections, pp 254–257

Tulving E (1972) Episodic and semantic memory. Org Memory 1:381–403

Valori I, McKenna-Plumley PE, Bayramova R, Zandonella Callegher C, Altoè G, Farroni T (2020) Proprioceptive accuracy in immersive virtual reality: a developmental perspective. PloS One 15(1):e0222253

Wyszecki G, Boff KR, Kaufman L, Thomas JR (1986) Handbook of perception and human performance

Yuan Y, Steed A (2010) Is the rubber hand illusion induced by immersive virtual reality? In: 2010 IEEE virtual reality conference (VR). IEEE, pp 95–102

Zamora LP (1997) The usable past: the imagination of history in recent fiction of the Americas. Cambridge University Press

Chapter 27
Afterword

Eugene Ch'ng, Henry Chapman, Vincent Gaffney, and Andrew S. Wilson

Digital heritage approaches have developed at an accelerated pace, and with applications that increasingly extend across a greater range of heritage needs and opportunities and alongside other sectors that have been influenced by digital transformations. Hence, whilst receiving and collating the scholarly contributions that have led to the completion of this volume, we were fascinated by the wealth of the contents and the diverse heritage science approaches represented across the chapters by our global community of authors. The five themes that we have used to carefully partition the volume demonstrate the expanse and reach of a relatively young discipline that only emerged, perhaps, two decades ago when openness to collaborate and the imagination to transcend disciplines began to coalesce with collaborative groups adopting digital approaches for heritage. The themes that we agreed upon testify to the broad reach of heritage science, not only in the diverse application areas spanning archaeology, conservation, museology, memory studies, forensic science and heritage management, but also covering a timescale that spanned two million years of natural and cultural history.

The 27 chapters in this volume add significantly to the successful first volume 'Visual Heritage in the Digital Age', which was published in 2013 with 18 chapters.

E. Ch'ng (✉)
University of Nottingham Ningbo China, Ningbo, China
e-mail: eugene.chng@nottingham.edu.cn

H. Chapman
University of Birmingham, Birmingham, UK
e-mail: h.chapman@bham.ac.uk

V. Gaffney · A. S. Wilson
University of Bradford, Bradford, UK
e-mail: v.gaffney@bradford.ac.uk

A. S. Wilson
e-mail: a.s.wilson2@bradford.ac.uk

© Springer Nature Switzerland AG 2022
E. Ch'ng et al. (eds.), *Visual Heritage: Digital Approaches in Heritage Science*,
Springer Series on Cultural Computing,
https://doi.org/10.1007/978-3-030-77028-0_27

The diversity of contents that we received demonstrate the ubiquity of digital technology that has emerged across all areas of cultural heritage. The diverse range of digital approaches illustrated within the volume have revealed further the continuing, transformative nature of digital heritage applications. The range of contributions also tells us that digital technology has become mandatory within the many processes and activities that have come to define the field. Production of the volume coincided with the COVID-19 global pandemic. This necessitated that all physical activities were shifted online, affording us with new ways of working with technology. Whilst not ideal, and certainly lacking the human touch that we have become accustomed to, digital platforms have at least made it possible to connect as a group and work towards the completion of the volume across time zones and at other ends of the globe, and yet united within a shared practice.

Indeed, through the unfolding of the chapters within each theme, we have come to realise that there is much common ground and shared expertise across the discipline. Whilst the broad subject areas that are discussed in this volume encompass shared global issues that the heritage community faces, the use of digital technology still affords the opportunity to bring individual perspectives and considerations. *Global Perspectives in Heritage Science and Technology*, the opening theme of the volume elaborated the need to retain an open mind and a global dialogue. This, together with an ethical framework that governs the professional activity of digital recording and data handling are critical to sustainability given the present rate of technology penetration across the domain, within an increasingly digital technology-oriented society. This is especially important and will guide how we co-design our use of technology to sustain future heritage development and support capacity building across the sector and in line with the UN sustainable development goals. Important frameworks will develop that can support professional and community-led activities, protect threatened sites and sustain those marginalised groups that are vulnerable to exploitation, misrepresentation and misuse.

A key aspect of contemporary digital transformation is the ability to acquire new types of information that traditional approaches have not yet been able to achieve. New types of data facilitate and enhance our ability to interpret and will remain a fundamental component of any research within Heritage Science. The capacity to process and visualise information in new ways marks the distinctiveness of the research presented within the volume. Research within the second and third themes within this volume—*Modelling, Interpreting and Reconstructing the Past*, and *Digital and Virtual Heritage Research and Applications* consolidate and exemplify the methods and technologies that have made it possible to achieve these goals. *Cultural Connections and the Creative Industry* propels digitisation into the public domain, at the same time as the UN recognised 2021 as the Year of the Creative Economy for Sustainable Development. By engaging with audiences in-the-wild we create awareness of heritage activity which otherwise would have been concealed within the academic sphere. Public engagement and outreach now offer scope to interweave physical and virtual assets. The web and social media spaces make use of the products of digital technologies that are also made tangible through processes such as 3D printing, whilst immersive technologies usher audiences into heritage information spaces that transcends our physical boundaries. Collectively these drive novel insights into how heritage is perceived and consumed in the public sphere, and the trends of dissemination via social media. The final theme provides insight into the importance of *Intangible and Hidden Narratives*, and how digital technology can unveil stories within media and how such resources can perpetuate the remembering of the past.

Together, the chapters presented within the book reveal a vision to transform the many processes and activities that have been traditionally situated within the heritage domain. The foreword by Professor Carl Heron contextualises this—emphasising the history and genesis of this book and the legacy of the preceding volume, and the parallel development of a series of dedicated digital research centres associated with the editors. This is significant, not simply for what has happened but for what will happen into the future. It is clear that the VISTA Centre at Birmingham represented a change from the spatial and GIS research centres that preceded it. VISTA was created to represent the world as an image and to disseminate this through the web. Its successor, the Birmingham Digital Humanities Hub developed alongside the digital native and the raised expectations surrounding mobile and touch screen devices, the change in the knowledge economy alongside the creative industries and cultural learning as a discipline.

The aspirations of these early research centres have been exceeded and we now face a new set of aspirational challenges; challenges that were brought about by key technologies that have evolved our digital culture—processing power through horizontal scaling, technological connectivity, the capacity to store and access data at scale, and consequently a digital appetite that can only be sated via technology-driven media contents. The concept of the digital collection is becoming as important as physical collections, with a move from dispersed or singular repositories, towards connectivity and resilience with the widespread adoption of the FAIR principles of 'Findability, Accessibility, Interoperability and Reuse' (Wilkinson et al. 2016).

As the chapters in this volume demonstrate, we can now anticipate a post-digitalisation world where digital existence is further compounded via a copy culture, at a rate that is exponential. The sum total of the connectivity of the internet, and its capacity for disseminating information, affords the social spaces that we now inhabit. Much as the world has become unrecognisable since the inception of the first mobile phone and subsequently the introduction of the first touchscreen-based smartphone. Seeking to address our hunger for ever-more information, and a society living in hyperreality, becomes the black hole of our digital universe in which we spiral uncontrollably into dimensions that we may not recognise. The age of 'digital clones' has arrived and with it the opportunity for not simply increased connectivity or even better immersive capacity, but a world where value can be created and stored through digital means and where creativity, intellectual property rights and the nature of ownership are being re-assessed. When musician Grimes sold digital artwork for $6 million using NFT (non-fungible tokens) technology, the new 'owners' did not own the work in the manner of a private collector during the Renaissance—only the token provides value in any specific sense (BBC 2021). These new avenues for redefining original artwork are literally also making waves in the music industry.

Former Scottish postman Nathan Evans' rendition of nineteenth-century sea shanty 'The Wellerman' went viral on TikTok, spawning remixes that have been released as a series of limited edition NFTs (Richards 2021).

In a separate development in our technological culture, in October of 2018, an AI-generated artwork titled *Edmond de Belamy, from La Famille de Belamy* was auctioned and sold for 45 times its high estimate at the price of US$432,500 in a Christies' bid that lasted only 7 min (CHRISTIES 2018). This is a rare example of auctioned artworks that are solely generated by machines. The future is yet untold with regards to the role of machines in all aspects of our heritage. Whilst the value of NFTs and cryptocurrencies may be maintained via distributed ledgers facilitated by machines, for creativity and art as part of our culture, is machine art really acceptable in the artworld? Who owns the IP and can machines be creative remain a question (Ch'ng 2019a).

In some sense this emerging culture is truly digital heritage in the making and, excitingly, this may resolve the issues of intangible heritage as the capacity of digital worlds to represent the real world is enhanced and improved beyond the scope of the physical universe. UNESCO's concept of digital heritage has been enhanced to incorporate cultural information that can emanate 'from different communities, industries, sectors and regions', which includes individuals, organisations and communities that 'express what they value and what they want to pass on to future generations' (UNESCO 2021).

Those tokens provide meaning in a world which needs no other presence (Fig. 27.1)—they also provide new ways of commodification which can also have an egalitarian aspect in respect of ownership of tangible and intangible heritage— designs, sounds or images, and even social media posts such as tweets (Kolodny 2021). All of these may now be commodified through blockchain technology—the original copy of indigenous labours is with us and may be purchased now (Ch'ng 2019b).

The disengagement of value from nation states, and through cryptocurrency, is merely another stage in our development. How the global political class reacts to these emergent and distributed value systems remains to be seen. Aside from the environmental impact and ensuring ethical debate linked to these value tokens, the threat of such currencies may be to the polity rather than the global economy. If blockchain technology survives the body politic, that is not the end of our story. Our engagement with these worlds and their emerging digital heritage has yet to be imagined. Simulations, virtual worlds, augmented and mixed reality, embodied experience, intelligent and creative agents that collaborate rather than facilitate will compete within these future digital domains and, again the nature and relationship of culture, society and heritage will be questioned. The chapters in this volume can only partially represent these dramatic changes. They are, however, offered as a provocation of future heritage debates.

It is clear that digital heritage is just one element of an increasingly digitally enabled and digitally aware world. But it is also clear from the chapters presented in this volume and its predecessor that heritage is a driving force for innovation and change within technology and society. From novel approaches to data capture, including crowd sourcing and re-tasking of existing imagery, to innovative

Fig. 27.1 In late 2021 LaCollection began a partnership with the British Museum to trade in NFTs based upon a debut theme of the timeless works of Katsushika Hokusai sold across three scarcity levels, including Ultra Rare, Super Rare and Open Edition

approaches to engaging audiences; arguably there has never been such an exciting time to study or engage with heritage.

References

BBC (2021) NFT blockchain drives surge in digital art auctions. Available via BBC. https://www.bbc.co.uk/news/technology-56252738. Accessed 16 June 2021.

CHRISTIES (2018) Is artificial intelligence set to become art's next medium? Available via CHRISTIES. https://www.christies.com/features/A-collaboration-between-two-artists-one-human-one-a-machine-9332-1.aspx. Accessed 28 May 2021

Ch'ng E (2019a) Art by computing machinery: Is machine art acceptable in the artworld? ACM Trans Multimed Comput Commun Appl 15(2s). https://doi.org/10.1145/3326338

Ch'ng E (2019b) The first original copy and the role of blockchain in the reproduction of cultural heritage. Presence: Teleoperators Virtual Environ 27(1). https://doi.org/10.1162/PRES_a_00313

Kolodny L (2021) Elon Musk turns down $1 million offer to buy his tweet as an NFT Available via CNBC. https://www.cnbc.com/2021/03/17/elon-musk-turns-down-1-million-offer-to-buy-his-tweet-as-an-nft.html. Accessed 16 June 2021

Richards W (2021) Viral sea shanty hit 'The Wellerman' to be sold as NFTs. Available via NME. https://www.nme.com/news/music/viral-sea-shanty-hit-the-wellerman-to-be-sold-as-nfts-2925664. Accessed 10 June 2021

UNESCO (2021) Concept of Digital Heritage. Available via UNESCO. https://en.unesco.org/the mes/information-preservation/digital-heritage/concept-digital-heritage. Accessed 10 June 2021

Wilkinson MD, Dumontier M, Aalbersberg IJ, Appleton G, Axton M, Baak A, Mons B (2016) The FAIR guiding Principles for scientific data management and stewardship. Sci Data 3(1):1–9

Correction to: Applications of 3D Modelling of Rock Art Sites Using Ground-Based Photogrammetry: A Case Study from the Greater Red Lily Lagoon Area, Western Arnhem Land, Northern Australia

Jarrad Kowlessar, Ian Moffat, Daryl Wesley, Tristen Jones, Maxime Aubert, Mark Willis, Alfred Nayinggul, and the Njanjma Aboriginal Corporation

Correction to:
Chapter 6 in: E. Ch'ng et al. (eds.), *Visual Heritage: Digital Approaches in Heritage Science*, Springer Series on Cultural Computing, https://doi.org/10.1007/978-3-030-77028-0_6

In the original version of the book, the following belated corrections have been incorporated in chapter Applications of 3D Modelling of Rock Art Sites Using Ground-Based Photogrammetry: A Case Study from the Greater Red Lily Lagoon Area, Western Arnhem Land, Northern Australia.

The co-author's name "Max Aubert" has been corrected to "Maxime Aubert"
The chapter and book have been updated with the changes.

The updated version of this chapter can be found at
https://doi.org/10.1007/978-3-030-77028-0_6